# RESEARCH HANDBOOK ON ECONOMIC, SOCIAL AND CULTURAL RIGHTS AS HUMAN RIGHTS

RESEARCH HANDBOOKS IN HUMAN RIGHTS

*Elgar Research Handbooks* are original reference works designed to provide a broad overview of research in a given field whilst at the same time creating a forum for more challenging, critical examination of complex and often under-explored issues within that field.

Chapters by international teams of contributors are specially commissioned by editors who carefully balance breadth and depth. Often widely cited, individual chapters present expert scholarly analysis and offer a vital reference point for advanced research. Taken as a whole they achieve a wide-ranging picture of the state-of-the-art.

This highly original series offers a unique appraisal of the state-of-the-art of research and thinking in human rights law. Each volume, edited by a prominent expert, either covers a specific aspect of human rights law or looks at how human rights impacts upon, or intersects with, other areas of law. Combining positivist approaches to international and human rights law, with more critical approaches, the volumes also draw, where appropriate, on research from adjacent disciplines. Addressing current and sometimes controversial legal issues, as well as affording a clear substantive analysis of the law, these *Research Handbooks* are designed to inform as well as to contribute to current debates.

Equally useful as reference tools or introductions to specific topics or issues, the *Research Handbooks* will be used by academic researchers, post-graduate students, practicing lawyers and lawyers in policy circles.

Titles in the series include:

Research Handbook on Human Rights and Humanitarian Law
*Edited by Robert Kolb and Gloria Gaggioli*

Research Handbook on Human Rights and the Environment
*Edited by Anna Grear and Louis J. Kotzé*

Research Handbook on Human Rights and Digital Technology
Global Politics, Law and International Relations
*Edited by Ben Wagner, Matthias C. Kettemann and Kilian Vieth*

Research Handbook on Labour, Business and Human Rights Law
*Edited by Janice R. Bellace and Beryl ter Haar*

Research Handbook on Human Rights and Business
*Edited by Surya Deva and David Birchall*

Research Handbook on Economic, Social and Cultural Rights as Human Rights
*Edited by Jackie Dugard, Bruce Porter, Daniela Ikawa and Lilian Chenwi*

# Research Handbook on Economic, Social and Cultural Rights as Human Rights

*Edited by*

Jackie Dugard

*Associate Professor, School of Law, University of the Witwatersrand, South Africa*

Bruce Porter

*Executive Director, The Social Rights Advocacy Centre, Canada*

Daniela Ikawa

*Legal Officer, Open Society Justice Initiative and Adjunct Professor, Columbia University, USA*

Lilian Chenwi

*Professor, School of Law, University of the Witwatersrand, South Africa*

RESEARCH HANDBOOKS IN HUMAN RIGHTS

 Edward Elgar
PUBLISHING

Cheltenham, UK • Northampton, MA, USA

Published by
Edward Elgar Publishing Limited
The Lypiatts
15 Lansdown Road
Cheltenham
Glos GL50 2JA
UK

Edward Elgar Publishing, Inc.
William Pratt House
9 Dewey Court
Northampton
Massachusetts 01060
USA

A catalogue record for this book
is available from the British Library

Library of Congress Control Number: 2020944213

This book is available electronically in the **Elgar**online
Law subject collection
http://dx.doi.org/10.4337/9781788974172

Printed on elemental chlorine free (ECF)
recycled paper containing 30% Post-Consumer Waste

ISBN 978 1 78897 416 5 (cased)
ISBN 978 1 78897 417 2 (eBook)

Printed and bound in the USA

# Contents

# Contributors

**Radhika Balakrishnan** is Faculty Director at the Center for Women's Global Leadership and Professor in Women's Gender and Sexuality Studies at Rutgers University. Her research and advocacy work has sought to change the lens through which macroeconomic policy is interpreted and critiqued by applying international human rights norms to assess macroeconomic policy.

**Joanna Bourke-Martignoni** is Senior Researcher at the Geneva Academy of International Humanitarian Law and Human Rights and an Affiliate of the Gender Centre at the Graduate Institute for International and Development Studies. She is the coordinator of the Swiss government-supported DEMETER (gender, land and the right to food) longitudinal research for development project, which examines the impact of agricultural and land commercialization on gender equality and the right to food in Cambodia and Ghana. She has also worked on a number of action-research studies related to the right to education, climate change and disaster risk reduction, children's rights, political participation, trade and labor standards, intersectional discrimination and gender-based violence.

**Virginia Brás Gomes** was a Member of the UN Committee on Economic, Social and Cultural Rights for 14 years and served as Vice-Chair, Rapporteur and Chair of the Committee. She is Senior Social Policy Adviser in the Ministry of Employment, Solidarity and Social Security of Portugal, Chair of the Board of UNICEF Portugal and a Member of the International Advisory Council of the Equal Rights Trust, of the Advisory Boards of the Centre for Civil and Political Rights and of the Geneva Human Rights Platform, as well as of the International Board of the Programme for Women's Economic, Social and Cultural Rights and of the Portuguese National Commission for Human Rights. She has conducted training on human rights, gender equality and treaty body reporting in Africa, Asia and Europe.

**Lilian Chenwi** is Professor at the School of Law, University of the Witwatersrand. She was previously Head of the Socio-Economic Rights Project at the Dullah Omar Institute for Constitutional Law, Governance and Human Rights (formerly Community Law Centre), University of the Western Cape, South Africa. Lilian participated in the discussions and drafting processes of two key international documents: the Optional Protocol to the International Covenant on Economic, Social and Cultural Rights and the Maastricht Principles on Extraterritorial Obligations of States in the Area of Economic, Social and Cultural Rights.

**Joie Chowdhury** is Program Coordinator for Networkwide Projects at the International Network for Economic, Social and Cultural Rights (ESCR-Net). For more than 15 years she has worked in human rights litigation, advocacy and research in several countries, including India, Kosovo, the United States and Switzerland. Joie has taught courses on the role of strategic litigation in the realization of economic, social and cultural rights.

**Allison Corkery** is Director of Strategy and Learning at the Centre for Economic and Social Rights. A central focus of her work is how to strengthen interdisciplinary human rights research so as to support more strategic and evidence-based advocacy. Based in South Africa, she has written extensively about the need to expand human rights research methods in both academic and non-academic publications.

**Catarina de Albuquerque** is Chief Executive Officer of Sanitation and Water for All, a global multi-stakeholder partnership promoting the political prioritization of rights to water and sanitation at a global level, helping build consensus and establishing strategic partnerships. She was the first UN Special Rapporteur on the right to safe drinking water and sanitation and presided over the negotiations of the Optional Protocol to the International Covenant on Economic, Social and Cultural Rights from 2004 to 2008. She is an invited Professor at the Law Faculties of the Universities of Braga and Coimbra (Portugal) and Senior Legal Adviser at the Office for Documentation and Comparative Law under the Portuguese Prosecutor General's Office. In 2009 Ms. Albuquerque was awarded the Human Rights Golden Medal by the Portuguese Parliament and the Order of Merit by the Portuguese President of the Republic.

**Kate Donald** is Director of Program at the Center for Economic and Social Rights in New York, where she focuses in particular on inequalities and economic policy. She has been involved in research and advocacy focused on the 2030 Agenda and its intersection with human rights for several years. Her previous positions include Adviser to the United Nations Special Rapporteur on extreme poverty and human rights, and Research Fellow at the International Council on Human Rights Policy.

**Jackie Dugard** is Associate Professor at the School of Law, University of the Witwatersrand, where she teaches Property Law and Bill of Rights. With a background in law and social sciences, Jackie works on the role of law in social change and justice, with a focus on socio-economic rights and gender. She was the co-founder and first director of the Socio-Economic Rights Institute of South Africa (SERI), and is an Associated Senior Researcher at the Chr. Michelsen Institute (CMI, Norway) and an Advisory Board member of the Southern Centre for Inequality Studies (SCIS, South Africa).

**Siri Gloppen** is Professor of Comparative Politics at the University of Bergen (UiB), Norway, Senior Researcher at the Chr. Michelsen Institute and Director of *LawTransform* the CMI-UiB Centre on Law & Social Transformation. Her research focuses on *lawfare* – the use of rights, law and courts as tools for social change – and the effects of lawfare strategies in different fields and across contexts, particularly in Africa, Latin America and India. She has led a number of international research projects investigating lawfare in areas such as health, sexual and reproductive rights and democratic development, in addition to research on the role of law and litigation in relation to climate policy.

**Mario Gomez** is Executive Director at the International Centre for Ethnic Studies, an independent think-tank based in Sri Lanka. He was a onetime lecturer in the Faculty of Law at the University of Colombo and teaches occasionally at the University of Colombo. Recent publications have addressed political and legal developments in Sri Lanka, including responses by the courts to executive abuse of power, human rights in the context of reconciliation, prosecuting religious violence, the right to information and constitutionalizing ESCR.

**James Heintz** is Andrew Glyn Professor of Economics at the University of Massachusetts, Amherst. His work has focused on the intersections of economic theory, policy and human rights; macroeconomics and finance; employment and informal labor markets; and feminist economics.

**Daniela Ikawa** leads the Project on Climate Justice at the Open Society Justice Initiative (OSJI), and teaches human rights at Columbia University. Before joining OSJI, she coordinated the Working Group on Strategic Litigation at the International Network for Economic, Social and Cultural Rights, supporting ESCR litigation before the CESCR, the Inter-American System and national jurisdictions. She is author of numerous publications on human rights law.

**Viviana Krsticevic** is Executive Director of the Center for Justice and International Law (CEJIL), a civil society organization that works throughout the Americas to promote human rights through the use of international law and the Inter-American System for the Protection of Human Rights. She is also a founding Member of the Gqual Campaign, an initiative to promote gender parity in international representation. Viviana has litigated numerous leading cases on behalf of victims of human rights violations before both the Inter-American Commission and Court of Human Rights. She regularly teaches at American University Washington School of Law and Saint Thomas University.

**Colm O'Cinneide** is Professor of Constitutional and Human Rights Law at University College London. He has published extensively in the field of comparative constitutional, human rights and anti-discrimination law. He has acted as specialist legal adviser to the Joint Committee on Human Rights and the Women & Equalities Committee of the UK Parliament, and advised a range of international organizations including the UN, ILO and the European Commission. From 2006 to 2016 he was a member of the European Committee on Social Rights of the Council of Europe, serving as Vice-President of the Committee from 2010 to 2014.

**Kate Paterson** is an Associate in the Public Law and Regulatory Practice at Bowmans in Johannesburg. She specializes in education and health law and policy, with further experience in environmental and land law. From 2017 to 2018, Kate clerked for Justice Edwin Cameron at the Constitutional Court of South Africa.

**Bruce Porter** is Executive Director of the Social Rights Advocacy Centre and a Maytree Fellow and was Chief Advisor to the UN Special Rapporteur on the right to adequate housing from 2014 to 2019. He co-directed a major ten-year research project in social rights in Canada involving multiple NGOs and universities and was active in promoting and negotiating the adoption of the Optional Protocol to the ICESCR. He is the author of numerous publications focused on access to justice for ESC rights and the right to housing internationally and in Canada.

**Virginia Roaf** is an independent consultant focusing predominantly on water, sanitation and the practical applications of human rights to improve access to services. She is currently involved with various programs that promote the human rights to water and sanitation globally and locally, including with the global multi-stakeholder partnership Sanitation and Water for All. From 2010 to 2015 she was Senior Advisor to the UN Special Rapporteur on the human rights to water and sanitation.

**Ignacio Saiz** is Executive Director of the Center for Economic and Social Rights, based in New York. He previously served as Director of Policy at the International Secretariat of Amnesty International, where he oversaw the organization's first program of work on economic, social and cultural rights, and as Deputy Director of Amnesty's Americas Program, responsible for its work in Mexico, Central America, Venezuela and the Caribbean.

**Magdalena Sepúlveda** is Executive Director of the Global Initiative for Economic, Social and Cultural Rights. From 2008 to 2014 she was the United Nations Special Rapporteur on extreme poverty and human rights. From 2013 to 2017 she was a member of the High-Level Panel of Expert on Food Security and Nutrition of the United Nations Committee on World Food Security. Ms. Sepúlveda has worked as a researcher at the Netherlands Institute for Human Rights, as a staff attorney at the Inter-American Court of Human Rights, as Co-Director of the Department of International Law and Human Rights of the United Nations-mandated University for Peace in Costa Rica and as Research Director at the International Council on Human Rights Policy, in Geneva. She has published widely on human rights, social protection, fiscal policies and poverty and has taught university courses in Latin America and the United Kingdom.

**Catalina Vallejo** is Postdoc Fellow at the Faculty of Law of the University of Bergen, where she studies the polycentric governance of climate change in the Amazon, as a member of the interdisciplinary research project 'Causes and Consequences of the Legal Architecture of Climate Politics' (LEG-ARCH). She is a lawyer from Colombia and holds an MA in Peace Studies and a PhD in Law. Her doctoral dissertation studied climate change litigation against governments of the world and the emerging climate jurisprudence. She is affiliated as a researcher to the Universidad Autónoma Latinoamericana-UNAULA in Colombia and to *LawTransform* in Norway.

**Faranaaz Veriava** is Head of the Education Rights Programme at the public interest organization, SECTION27. She is also Extraordinary Professor within the Faculty of Law at the University of Pretoria, where she teaches a course on Education and the Law. Faranaaz's doctoral research focused on the contribution of the courts and civil society to the normative development of the right to basic education in the South African Constitution. She has published on the right to education and on socio-economic rights more generally.

**Stuart Wilson** is an advocate practicing at the Johannesburg Bar. He has appeared in most of the leading housing rights cases to have come before the South African courts. He has published widely on the right to housing, and the relationship between law and social change. He co-founded, with Jackie Dugard, the Socio-Economic Rights Institute of South Africa (SERI), which is internationally recognized for its work in advancing the rights to housing and basic services. Stuart teaches property law at the University of the Witwatersrand, Johannesburg.

**Alicia Ely Yamin** is Senior Fellow at the Petrie-Flom Center for Health Law Policy, Biotechnology and Bioethics (PFC) at Harvard Law School, and Adjunct Faculty Member of the Harvard TH Chan School of Public Health. Yamin's career at the intersection of global health and human rights has bridged academia and activism, as well as law and global health/ development.

# Abbreviations

| | |
|---|---|
| AAAQ | Availability, Accessibility, Acceptability, Quality |
| Aarhus Convention | Convention on Access to Information, Public Participation in Decision-Making and Access to Justice in Environmental Matters |
| ACERWC | African Committee of Experts on the Rights and Welfare of the Child |
| ACHPR or African Commission | African Commission on Human and Peoples' Rights |
| ACHR or American Convention | American Convention on Human Rights |
| ACRWC | African Charter on the Rights and Welfare of the Child |
| ACtHPR or African Court | African Court on Human and Peoples' Rights |
| ADP | Protocol to the African Charter on Human and Peoples' Rights on the Rights of Persons with Disabilities in Africa |
| African Charter | African Charter on Human and Peoples' Rights |
| AHRS | African Human Rights System |
| AIDS | Acquired Immunodeficiency Syndrome |
| American Declaration | American Declaration of the Rights and Duties of Man |
| AOPP | Protocol to the African Charter on Human and Peoples' Rights on the Rights of Older Persons |
| APRM | African Peer Review Mechanism |
| ASEAN | Association of Southeast Asian Networks |
| AU | African Union |
| AUCA | Constitutive Act of the African Union |
| AWP | Protocol to the African Charter on Human and Peoples' Rights on the Rights of Women in Africa |
| BPC | *Benefício de Prestação Continuada da Assistência Social* (Continuous Cash Benefit Programme) |
| CADE | UNESCO Convention Against Discrimination in Education |
| Canadian Charter | Canadian Charter of Rights and Freedoms |
| CAT | Convention against Torture and Other Cruel, Inhuman or Degrading Treatment or Punishment |
| CAT Committee | Committee against Torture |
| CBDR | Common But Differentiated Responsibilities |

| | |
|---|---|
| CCL | Centre for Child Law |
| CCPR | Human Rights Committee |
| CDM | Clean Development Mechanism |
| CED | Committee on Enforced Disappearances |
| CEDAW | Convention on the Elimination of All Forms of Discrimination against Women |
| CEDAW Committee | Committee on the Elimination of Discrimination against Women |
| CERD | Committee for the Elimination of Racial Discrimination |
| CESCR | Committee on Economic, Social and Cultural Rights |
| CESR | Center for Economic and Social Rights |
| CFS | Committee on World Food Security |
| CJEU | Court of Justice of the EU |
| CMW | Committee on Migrant Workers |
| Convention of Belém do Pará | Inter-American Convention on the Prevention, Punishment and Eradication of Violence Against Women |
| COP | Conference of the Parties |
| COVID or Covid (19) | 2019 Novel Corona Virus |
| CPR | Civil and Political Rights |
| CRC | Convention on the Rights of the Child |
| CRC Committee | Committee on the Rights of the Child |
| CRPD | Convention on the Rights of Persons with Disabilities |
| CRPD Committee | Committee on the Rights of Persons with Disabilities |
| CSW | Civil Society Mechanism of the UN Committee on World Food Security |
| ECHR | European Convention on Human Rights |
| ECLAC | Economic Commission for Latin America and the Caribbean |
| ECOSOC | United Nations Economic and Social Council |
| ECOSOCC | Economic, Social and Cultural Council |
| ECSR | European Committee on Social Rights |
| ECtHR or ECrtHR or European Court | European Court of Human Rights |
| EE | Equal Education |
| EHRC | Equality and Human Rights Commission (England, Scotland and Wales) |

| EITI | Extractive Industries Transparency Initiative |
|---|---|
| ESC | European Social Charter |
| Escazú Agreement | Regional Agreement on Access to Information, Public Participation and Justice in Environmental Matters in Latin America and the Caribbean |
| ESCER | Economic, Social, Cultural and Environmental Rights |
| ESCR | Economic, Social and Cultural Rights |
| ESCRP&G | Principles and Guidelines on the Implementation of Economic, Social and Cultural Rights in the African Charter on Human and Peoples' Rights |
| ESPI | Egypt Social Progress Indicators |
| ESR | Economic and Social Rights |
| ETO(s) | Extraterritorial Obligation(s) |
| EU | European Union |
| EU Charter | European Union Charter of Fundamental Rights and Freedoms |
| EWCA | England and Wales Court of Appeal |
| FAO | Food and Agricultural Organization of the United Nations |
| FCTC | Framework Convention on Tobacco Control |
| FDI | Foreign Direct Investment |
| FIAN | Foodfirst Information and Action Network |
| G77 | Group of 77 |
| GANHRI | Global Alliance of National Human Rights Institutions |
| GHG | Greenhouse gas |
| GNI | Gross National Income |
| GNP | Gross Domestic Product |
| HIV | Human Immunodeficiency Virus |
| HLPF | High-Level Political Forum on Sustainable Development |
| HRBA | Human Rights-Based Approach/es |
| HRC | Human Rights Council |
| HRL | Human Rights Law |
| HRMI | Human Rights Measurement Initiative |
| IACHR or Inter-American Commission | Inter-American Commission on Human Rights |
| IACtHR or Inter-American Court | Inter-American Court of Human Rights |

| | |
|---|---|
| IASHR | Inter-American System of Human Rights |
| IBAHRI | International Bar Association Human Rights Institute |
| IBP | International Budget Partnership |
| ICCPR | International Covenant on Civil and Political Rights |
| ICEPD | International Convention for the Protection of All Persons from Enforced Disappearance |
| ICERD | International Convention on the Elimination of All Forms of Racial Discrimination |
| ICESCR | International Covenant on Economic, Social and Cultural Rights |
| ICMW | International Convention on the Protection of the Rights of All Migrant Workers and Members of Their Families |
| IFFs | Illicit Financial Flows |
| IHR | International Health Regulations |
| ILO | International Labour Organization |
| IPCC | Intergovernmental Panel on Climate Change |
| LGBTQ | Lesbian, Gay, Bisexual, Transgender and Queer |
| LGERA | Local Government and Environmental Reports of Australia |
| LRC | Legal Resources Centre |
| MAR | Maximum Available Resources |
| MDGs | Millennium Development Goals |
| MESECVI | Follow-up Mechanism to the Belém do Pará |
| NDC | Nationally Determined Contributions |
| NEPAD | New Partnership for Africa's Development |
| NGO | Non-Governmental Organization |
| NHRI | National Human Rights Institution |
| OAS | Organization of American States |
| OAS Charter | Charter of the Organization of American States |
| OAU | Organisation of African Unity |
| ODA | Official Development Assistance |
| OECD | Organisation for Economic Co-operation and Development |
| OHCHR | Office of the United Nations High Commissioner for Human Rights |
| OP | Optional Protocol |

| | |
|---|---|
| OP1-ICCPR or OP-ICCPR | Optional Protocol to the International Covenant on Civil and Political Rights |
| OP2-ICCPR | Second Optional Protocol to the International Covenant on Civil and Political Rights |
| OP-CAT | Optional Protocol to the Convention against Torture and Other Cruel, Inhuman or Degrading Treatment or Punishment |
| OP-CEDAW | Optional Protocol to the Convention on the Elimination of All Forms of Discrimination against Women |
| OP-CRC-AC | Optional Protocol to the Convention on the Rights of the Child on the involvement of children in armed conflict |
| OP-CRC-IC | Optional Protocol to the Convention on the Rights of the Child on a communications procedure |
| OP-CRC-SC | Optional Protocol to the Convention on the Rights of the Child on the sale of children, child prostitution and child pornography |
| OP-CRPD | Optional Protocol to the Convention on the Rights of Persons with Disabilities |
| OPERA Framework | Outcomes, Policy Efforts, Resources and Assessment Framework |
| OP-ICESCR or ICESCR-OP | Optional Protocol to the International Covenant on Economic, Social and Cultural Rights |
| PLHIV | People Living with HIV |
| PSS or Protocol of San Salvador | Additional Protocol to the American Convention on Human Rights in the Area of Economic, Social and Cultural Rights |
| PWD | Persons with Disabilities |
| REDD+ | Reducing Emissions from Deforestation and Forest Degradation |
| RPF | Respect, Protect, Fulfill |
| RTE Act | Right of Children to Free and Compulsory Education Act |
| RTI | Right to information |
| SADC | Southern African Development Community |
| SAHRC | South African Human Rights Commission |
| SARS | Severe Acute Respiratory Syndrome |
| SASSA | South African Social Security Agency |
| SCA of GANHRI | Sub-Committee on Accreditation (of GANHRI) |
| SDG(s) | Sustainable Development Goal(s) |

| | |
|---|---|
| SERF Index | Social and Economic Rights Fulfilment Index |
| SERs | Socio-Economic Rights |
| SLAPP | Strategic Lawsuits Against Public Participation |
| SPF(s) | Social Protection Floor(s) |
| SPT | Subcommittee on Prevention of Torture and Other Cruel, Inhuman or Degrading Treatment or Punishment under OP-CAT |
| SRHR | Sexual and Reproductive Health Rights |
| TEU | Treaty of European Union |
| TMB | Treaty Monitoring Body |
| TRIPS | Trade-Related Aspects of Intellectual Property |
| UDHR | Universal Declaration of Human Rights |
| UK | United Kingdom |
| UN | United Nations |
| UNDRIP | United Nations Declaration on the Rights of Indigenous Peoples |
| UNESCO | United Nations Educational, Scientific and Cultural Organization |
| UNFCCC | United Nations Framework Convention for Climate Change |
| UNGA | United Nations General Assembly |
| UNICEF | United Nations Children's Fund |
| UNTS | United Nations Treaty Series |
| UPR | Universal Periodic Review |
| US or USA | United States of America |
| VGGT | FAO Voluntary Guidelines on the Governance of Land Tenure |
| Vienna Convention | Vienna Convention on the Law of Treaties |
| Vienna Declaration | Vienna Declaration and Programme of Action |
| VNR | Voluntary National Reviews |
| WFS | World Food Summit |
| WHO | World Health Organization |
| XR | Extinction Rebellion |

# Introduction to the *Research Handbook on Economic, Social and Cultural Rights as Human Rights*

*Bruce Porter, Jackie Dugard, Daniela Ikawa and Lilian Chenwi*

The publication of a handbook on economic, social and cultural rights (ESCR) at the commencement of the 2020s is timely. Human rights movements are confronted with unprecedented challenges that lie squarely in the socio-economic realm. The dramatic rise in socio-economic inequality, privatization of public services, financialization of land, housing and food systems, economic displacement and migration, widespread homelessness and hunger in even the most affluent countries, the global climate crisis and the COVID-19 pandemic have highlighted the failure of dominant human rights paradigms to address the most pressing human rights issues or to create a framework for multilateral responses to global threats. Some have even suggested that the inability of human rights movements to respond effectively to these new challenges signals 'the endtimes of human rights'.[1]

Failures of dominant human rights paradigms that have largely excluded ESCR should not, however, be mistaken for failures of human rights at large. The failures of dominant human rights paradigms to challenge emerging patterns of socio-economic inequality and exclusion and the incapacity of governments to ensure fundamental human rights to health, housing, food, water, sanitation or social security may instead be considered as an urgent call to reclaim human rights that include ESCR, which were central to the post-World War II commitment to human rights and recognized in the Universal Declaration of Human Rights (UDHR) as essential to human dignity and the development of the human person. It is the subsequent treatment of ESCR as 'second-generation' rights, still conceived in some quarters of the global north as merely aspirational and to be left to governments to implement as they choose, that should be questioned in light of contemporary challenges.

Indeed, the 2020 COVID-19 pandemic has starkly 'illuminated the critical role of socio-economic rights in securing a dignified life for all and in countering social and economic inequalities'.[2] While there are certainly civil and political rights challenges raised in the responses to the pandemic, the central human rights challenges have been to ensure right to health, food, a safe home, social security, access to work and the ESCR protection of the most vulnerable. The pandemic has fundamentally exposed the limits of governance regimes that neglect these core human rights obligations and fail to establish and maintain public institutions necessary for effective, collective responses. The hazards of the neoliberal deconstruction of governmental capacity have become dangerously apparent and there is now an almost desperate demand by people across the world for governments to reclaim their role in organizing economies, supporting those in need and ensuring fundamental ESCR. As noted in the context of the COVID-19 pandemic: 'This crisis may provide an opportunity to see the value of truth and trust in democracy and multilateralism, and the starkly dystopian reality we

---

[1]    Stephen Hopgood, *The Endtimes of Human Rights* (Cornell University Press 2013); Samual Moyn, *Human Rights and the Uses of History* (Verso 2014).

[2]    Sandra Liebenberg, 'Covid-19 and the Critical Importance of Achieving Socio-Economic Rights' (20 March 2020) <www.dailymaverick.co.za/article/2020-03-20-covid-19-and-the-critical-importance -of-achieving-socio-economic-rights/>.

face without them.'[3] The work undertaken to develop models of governance based on ESCR in previous decades, often drowned out by the clamor of neoliberalism, must be urgently revived. We are hopeful that this Handbook will provide a resource for pursuing a more inclusive and effective human rights practice and a new architecture of progressive rights-based governance through which the international community, as well as all levels of government, can meet the challenges of the new decade and ground a legitimate hope for a more equal, sustainable and secure world.

If human rights movements in the 2020s are destined to face unprecedented challenges in the socio-economic domain, they should also draw from commitments made by states in that realm. States have pledged, in the 2015 Sustainable Development Goals (SDGs), to eliminate poverty, homelessness and hunger, to ensure access to health care, water and sanitation, decent work and quality education and to take urgent action to address climate change by the end of the decade.[4] Admittedly, governments have demonstrated a propensity to sign on to commitments such as these without any real intention of meeting them, and the economic consequences of the COVID-19 pandemic makes these goals harder to achieve. The COVID-19 crisis also reminds us, however, of the capacity of governments to act when action is seen as necessary and of the critical importance of multilateralism and shared commitments to a sustainable world. The adoption of the SDGs reflect a new consensus that the neoliberal model of development, based on reliance on unregulated markets and characterized by growing inequality in income and assets, widespread socio-economic deprivation, environmental degradation and abandonment of public institutions, is unsustainable. The rise of new social movements and a nascent politics in opposition to exclusionary socio-economic paradigms, and the wake-up call of the COVID-19 pandemic, suggest that it will be difficult for states to simply abandon the SDG commitments. The commitment 'to leave no one behind', the central pledge of the SDG commitments, cannot be fulfilled by governments on their own. Those who have been left behind, whether in the global south or north, must be empowered to claim SDG goals, targets and timelines as human rights entitlements and insist on meaningful engagement in the realization of their rights. The SDG commitments must be articulated and claimed as fundamental rights.

This Handbook responds to both the challenges and the promises of the new decade by surveying a domain of human rights law and practice that has been marginalized within dominant human rights discourse and under-resourced by governments and human rights funders. The diverse set of authors includes human rights advocates, practitioners and scholars from all regions of the world and across disciplines. Their chapters explain how rights to food, housing, water and sanitation, health, work and social security have been defined and elaborated by human rights bodies and increasingly claimed and adjudicated under domestic, regional and international law. They describe an evolving understanding of state obligations to which all levels and branches of government can and should be held accountable, as well as responsibilities and legal obligations of businesses, transnational corporations, international financial institutions and development agencies. As such, they suggest the possibility of a revitalized

---

[3]     Alicia Ely Yamin and Roojin Habibi, 'Human Rights and Coronavirus: What's at Stake for Truth, Trust, and Democracy?' (1 March 2020) <www.hhrjournal.org/2020/03/human-rights-and-coronavirus -whats-at-stake-for-truth-trust-and-democracy/>.

[4]     UN General Assembly Resolution 70/1, 'Transforming our World: The 2030 Agenda for Sustainable Development' (21 October 2015) A/RES/71/1. See Chapter 18.

form of human rights advocacy in which ESCR and those who claim them must assume a more central place; a field of human rights practice capable of challenging deprivations of equal dignity and rights in the socio-economic realm; and a field of human rights practice capable of laying claims to sustainable development as a human rights entitlement and forming the basis of a new, more inclusionary politics and world order.

The authors do not, however, speak with one voice, and the book does not seek to articulate a unified or universally applicable framework for ESCR. ESCR practice is as diverse as those who claim rights and the circumstances in which they live. The growing awareness that prevailing paradigms of universal rights have been rooted in political dominance and colonization demands a more nuanced understanding of universality that recognizes diverse experiences and constantly changing forms of socio-economic exclusion and oppression. To be effective, the human rights project must commit to shared norms and values to which states can be held accountable, and on which basis rights claims can be advanced and adjudicated. Human rights norms and values must be derived from the UDHR premise that everyone is 'equal in dignity and rights'. They must be nurtured by claims from those whose rights have been denied or silenced and continually evolve in response to these claims. ESCR described in the Handbook are central to this dynamic of evolving human rights norms because they advance claims by those whose human rights have been previously ignored or denied access to justice. They redefine the scope of human rights protections in order to engage the social and economic realities in which rights claimants live. While the authors of the Handbook write from a range of perspectives and disciplines, covering diverse rights and human rights systems, a common theme running throughout is the drive towards a more inclusive human rights paradigm, engaging the lived realities of rights claimants. It is a quest, therefore, to pursue a more nuanced and transformative understanding of universal rights.

While the Handbook might seem to be premised on a conceptualization of ESCR as a separate category of rights, a more nuanced reflection understands ESCR practice as a different iteration of rights, derived from the inclusion of those whose rights are violated by socio-economic deprivation or by government neglect. ESCR practice fundamentally rejects the restrictions and exclusions implicit in 'negative rights' paradigms, according to which human rights claims are conceived primarily as limits and restraints on governments rather than as claims to positive measures required to realize rights. 'Negative rights' paradigms have, predictably, proven to be inadequate as a basis to challenge human rights violations resulting from the retreat under neoliberalism from social programs and regulatory measures and the systemic neglect of the needs of marginalized groups. The neoliberal agenda has in fact been supported by a negative rights paradigm that privileges legal challenges to governmental interference while denying access to justice for violations resulting from government neglect, inaction or failure to regulate private actors.

Although it is generally acknowledged that civil and political rights also require positive measures and resource allocation, ESCR law and practice has engaged positive obligations more directly and elaborated standards on the basis of which compliance may be assessed. Article 2(1) of the International Covenant on Economic, Social and Cultural Rights (ICESCR) articulates the obligation to achieve progressively the full realization of rights 'by all appropriate means, including particularly the adoption of legislative measures' and applying the 'maximum of available resources'. Compliance with this obligation is now assessed in individual cases under the Optional Protocol to the ICESCR (OP-ICESCR) as well as in the growing number of ESCR cases being adjudicated before domestic and regional courts and human rights bodies. The ESCR focus on positive obligations serves as a model for a more effective and transformative application of civil and political rights. As noted in several chapters in this Handbook, the UN Human Rights Committee, as well as the African and Inter-American Commissions and domestic courts, have recognized that the right to life, previously understood primarily as a negative right, must now be understood to impose positive obligations on governments to address threats to life linked to socio-economic deprivation. The recognition of positive as well as negative obligations in both categories of rights further merges those two categories, focusing on the interest to be protected and the most effective remedy, rather than on whether a violation was caused by state action or state inaction. Thus, ESCR practice is pivotal in ensuring access to justice for those whose human rights have been violated by inaction, neglect and exclusion and has been instrumental in establishing a more inclusive human rights practice and iterating a more egalitarian and accountable vision of rights-based social and economic orders.

As radical and potentially transformative as the implications of the ESCR law and practice described in the Handbook are, it must also be recognized that ESCR is still an emerging field of knowledge and practice. Complaints of violations of ESCR under the OP-ICESCR have only been possible since 2013. As at the time of writing, only 24 states have ratified the OP-ICESCR. By comparison, individual cases have been adjudicated under the Optional Protocol to the International Covenant on Civil and Political Rights (OP-ICCPR) for more than 40 years and 116 states have ratified the OP-ICCPR. Access to justice for ESCR in domestic and regional systems continues to be extremely limited, if not by the absence of explicit ESCR protections in law, then by other barriers to access facing those living in poverty, including cost, literacy, language barriers and absence of legal representation or knowledge of rights. Victims of violations of ESCR are more likely to experience courts as agents of the state in criminalizing poverty and homelessness than as venues in which to claim their rights.[5] In many countries, even progressive members of the legal profession fail to support access to justice for claimants of ESCR, expressing paternalistic concerns that this may encourage reliance on elitist institutions and detract from political action. Many human rights funders are similarly disinclined to allocate resources to ESCR advocacy.

ESCR law and practice is still at an 'experimental' stage in which various strategies and approaches are being developed, tried and refined. Many challenges remain. Assessing compliance with the standard of 'maximum of available resources', addressing extraterritorial violations, linking individual to systemic claims and remedies, overseeing the implementation of structural remedies over time, responding to the mushrooming of reactionary politics (in countries such as Brazil, Hungary, India and the United States of America) and the extraordinary threat posed by climate change are among key challenges that are the subject of ongoing experiment and innovation.

While these and other aspects of ESCR adjudication and remedy may be considered 'experimental', the importance of advancing ESCR claims ought not to be in question. Any assessment of the benefits of ESCR litigation at these early stages of development must consider outcomes not only in relation to demands for effective remedies for particular ESCR

---

[5] Human Rights Council, Guidelines for the Implementation of the Right to Adequate Housing: Report of the Special Rapporteur on Adequate Housing as a Component of the Right to an Adequate Standard of Living, and on the Right to Non-discrimination in this Context (26 December 2019) A/HRC/43/43 para 4.

violations but also in relation to the need for transformations in the administration of justice and the understanding of rights more broadly. It is too early to assess outcomes in an instrumentalist manner. Any negative effect of losses in particular cases must be balanced against the damage done to human rights protections by the denial of access to justice to ESCR claimants. Indeed, unsuccessful ESCR claims may be necessary to challenge and ultimately disrupt unjust systems, as, even if unsuccessful, they may provide voice to or amplify the claims of marginalized groups.

ESCR in and of themselves, or the courts and human rights bodies charged with adjudicating claims and enforcing remedies, do not provide a complete solution to current socio-economic human rights challenges. They are, however, an essential ingredient. It will be difficult, if not impossible, to meet the human rights challenges of the 2020s without a robust, reinforced ESCR practice. The contemporary turn to ESCR is not simply a response to the need for human rights accountability in the socio-economic domain, or even in the dominant human rights paradigm. It is also a response to contradictions and exclusions in the prevailing socio-political and economic order that can no longer be accepted. This is because, beyond important material achievements from cases and campaigns, the power of rights lies in their ability to catalyze and support agents of change. The paradox of rights is that by drawing attention to the inequality, discrimination and exclusion of the current status quo, human rights affirm the untenability of injustice in the present and articulate the conditions and contours of justice in the future.[6] The emancipatory potential of socio-economic rights as pursued in this Handbook is thus not so much to act as ends, or even instruments, but in articulating what equality, inclusion and freedom might look like and, through their instantiation, providing the space to organize and mobilize for progressive change.

## STRUCTURE OF THE BOOK AND OVERVIEW OF CHAPTERS

The book proceeds in three Parts. Part I chapters (Chapters 1–5) are the framing chapters, which cover the relevant ESCR-related structures and mechanisms in the international, regional and domestic spheres.

Against the backdrop of the indivisibility and interdependence of all human rights, as well as the interplay of the various human rights systems outlined in Part I of the book, Chapter 1 provides an overview of the international human rights system that includes an analysis of the layers, applicability and universality of the system in its entirety. The chapter first traces the development – largely as a response to the atrocities of World War II – of the Charter-based system plus the two cornerstone international human rights treaties, the International Covenant on Civil and Political Rights (ICCPR) and the ICESCR. Thereafter, the chapter provides a brief overview of each of the international treaties in the treaty-based system, with a focus on ESCR.

Chapter 2 discusses the main UN treaty focused on the protection of economic, social and cultural rights: the ICESCR, as well as its optional complaints procedure, the OP-ICESCR. It covers four aspects: (a) the historical and contextual framework for the adoption of both treaties; (b) the main rights, principles, and state obligations recognized by the ICESCR; (c) the

---

[6]  Wendy Brown, 'Suffering the Paradoxes of Rights' (2000) 7 Constellations 208, stating this from a feminist perspective.

specific mechanisms of protection, including the jurisprudence of the Committee on Economic, Social and Cultural Rights (CESCR); and (d) CESCR's nascent implementation procedure for remedies in individual communications. While the entry into force of the Optional Protocol in 2013 strengthened the view that ESCR matter as much as civil and political rights, the recent establishment of a participatory follow-up process could enhance the levels of implementation at the UN Treaty Body System. In the coming years, the joint work of a strong CESCR and innovative civil society organizations might lead the system to have greater visibility not only in the protection of ESCR but also in the protection of human rights more broadly.

Chapter 3 provides an overview of the normative frameworks on ESCR and the mechanisms relevant to their enforcement in the African human rights system. The chapter begins with the evolution of ESCR at the African regional level. Thereafter, the chapter provides an overview of the specific ESCR recognized in key African regional human rights treaties and the correlating state obligations, as well as the key regional mechanisms relevant to their enforcement.

Beginning with an overview of Europe's national welfare and social citizenship history, Chapter 4 highlights that all European states have ratified the ICESCR and the eight core International Labour Organization (ILO) conventions, and 43 of the 47 Council of Europe member states have also ratified the European Social Charter (ESC). Traversing the complex European arrangements for human rights generally and ESCR rights specifically, the chapter examines the content and trajectory of relevant rights under the ESC, European Convention on Human Rights (ECHR) and European Union (EU) law. It highlights the unique 'collective complaint' mechanism that allows categories of collective organizations to complain to the European Committee on Social Rights and explains the jurisdiction of the European Court of Human Rights, the European Committee on Social Rights, and the Court of Justice of the EU.

Chapter 5 sets out the legal framework for the protection of economic, social, cultural and environmental rights (ESCER) in the Inter-American System of Human Rights (IASHR), followed by a description of the monitoring and protection mechanisms. It tackles the IASHR's most salient jurisprudential and doctrinal developments and highlights the system's commitment to human rights defenders and the community engaged in the defense of ESCER. Despite its various limitations, the IASHR has made significant contributions to the development of ESCER in the Americas. The Inter-American Commission on Human Rights (IACHR) and the Inter-American Court of Human Rights (IACtHR) have conscientiously developed the tools available to them through their doctrine, jurisprudence, interim measures, rapporteurships, and reparations to extend the protection of ESCER. As highlighted in the chapter, the IASHR's remarkable interpretations of the social rights aspects of fundamental rights, as well as the recognition and enforcement of ESCER under the American Convention, provide a solid foundation for the further advances necessary to meet current and ongoing challenges.

Part II chapters (Chapters 6–12) provide the details, contours, debates, interpretation and current developments of each thematic right, incorporating the relevant scholarship and jurisprudence from the different systems.

Chapter 6 reviews the scope and content of the right to social security and describes how courts and quasi-judicial bodies have ensured it in both international and domestic contexts. Despite its early recognition as a right in the Universal Declaration of Human Rights, in the ICESCR, within the ILO and in regional systems, it was several decades before social security gained political support and acceptance as a critical tool for development and poverty reduction. Today there is renewed emphasis on the right to social security and it has been placed at the center of the 2030 Agenda for Sustainable Development. Despite increased attention to and remarkable progress in the coverage, however, the right to social security is not yet a reality for most of the world's population. This chapter argues that the dramatic coverage gap in the enjoyment of the right to social security derives in part from a lack of understanding about the meaning of a rights-based approach to social protection.

Chapter 7 highlights education as a multi-dimensional empowerment right, which is a critical component of achieving many other ESCRs. Using relevant cases and commentary, the authors pursue a 'four A' scheme – availability (the obligation to establish a system of schools and to provide a conducive environment for teaching and learning), accessibility (physical and economic accessibility, as well as non-discrimination), acceptability (religious convictions and private education) and adaptability (inclusivity and discipline) – to explore the contours of the right and the progress made in terms of achieving the right. Noting a relatively high level of recognition of the right to education internationally, regionally and domestically, the authors nonetheless flag some important fault line issues including the role of private education, the need for greater clarity and compliance regarding minimum standards and the need to ensure adequate education for vulnerable groups such as migrants.

As traversed in Chapter 8, the human right to adequate food is something of a paradox. Since its recognition in 1948 as a component of an 'adequate standard of living' in Article 25 (1) of the Universal Declaration of Human Rights, there has been significant attention paid to the development of norms, policies and implementing frameworks for the right to food at the national, regional and international levels, and there has been significant social movement mobilization related to the right to food particularly in the wake of the global food price and financial crises in 2008. At the same time, hunger and malnutrition are increasing in many parts of the world and there remains sustained opposition from certain state and non-state actors to the very existence of a legally enforceable right to food. Chapter 8 provides a contextual analysis of this paradoxical situation, starting with an overview of the historical development and content of international, regional and a selection of national frameworks on the human right to adequate food and inter-related rights such as the rights to land, water and other natural resources, work, health and social security. The chapter also focuses on several of the emerging issues connected to the promotion and protection of the right to food in the context of feminist critiques of food systems, food sovereignty movements and the rights of indigenous and smallholder farmers, the creation of corporate accountability frameworks and the challenges that climate change poses for the realization of the right to food.

Chapter 9 begins by contextualizing the right to health as closely related to the right to dignity and deeply impacted by power structures including class, gender and race. Canvassing the social and political determinants of health and medical care, the chapter pursues a human rights-based approach to health in its analysis of contested contours of the right to health within the international human rights system, including transboundary issues and regimes such as Trade-Related Aspects of Intellectual Property (TRIPS) and Extra-Territorial Obligations (ETOs).

Chapter 10 surveys the international, regional and domestic entrenchment of the right to adequate housing, together with the ways in which textual formulations of the right have been deployed in concrete contexts. The chapter argues that assertions of housing rights often mean the limitation of property rights and the disruption of economic hierarchies that are based on them. This claim is illustrated by an analysis of housing rights jurisprudence from around the world, with a focus on the South African national jurisprudence that is arguably the most coherent housing rights-related corpus of litigation, and dealing thematically with the rights of informal settlers, unlawful occupiers, residential tenants and women with precarious land tenure.

Chapter 11 considers two human rights that were not explicitly recognized in the UDHR or the ICESCR – the rights to water and sanitation. These rights were affirmed by the UN General Assembly and the UN Human Rights Council only in 2010. Though dramatic inequality in access to safe drinking water and sanitation persists, the decade since the rights to water and sanitation were finally recognized has seen significant progress in understanding their content, principles and obligations as well as in developing laws, policies and practices for the realization of these rights. After laying out the legal foundations and content of the rights to water and sanitation under international human rights law, this chapter explores how key human rights principles of equality, transparency, accountability and participation apply and describes State obligations to implement rights-based planning, adequate financing and effective monitoring. The challenges of ensuring services for informal settlements and rural areas are explored, as well as the regulatory frameworks that must be applied to the range of service providers, both public and private, formal and informal. Finally, the chapter describes important advances in ensuring access to justice for the rights to water and sanitation, whereby effective remedies have been ensured for violations of States' obligations not only to respect, but also to protect and fulfil the rights to water and sanitation.

Chapter 12 tackles three main issues: (a) legal provisions and cross-cutting principles regarding the right to work and rights at work, such as the minimum wage, equal pay for equal work, health and safety at work, freedom from harassment, paid leave, trade union affiliation and the right to strike, under the ICESCR, drawing on the normative interpretation of the UN Committee on Economic, Social and Cultural Rights and the technical guidance of the ILO; (b) the jurisprudence under the Optional Protocol to the ICESCR and the Collective Complaints Procedure of the European Committee of Social Rights; and (c) human rights indicators. The concept of work and workers has evolved from the time of drafting the Covenant in line with economic and social changes across the world to include new categories of workers and raise the accountability bar on the part of public authorities and employers regarding working conditions that not only contribute to the well-being of workers and the success of enterprises, but ultimately reinforce the fabric of our societies. The understanding of work will continue to evolve but it will not cease to be an element of our individual and collective identity.

Chapter 13 examines the concepts of minimum core and reasonableness as standards of review that courts or international bodies may use in assessing state compliance with their socio-economic rights obligations and how the standards might contribute to the effective enjoyment of ESCR. The chapter considers the conceptual foundations of the standards; key related normative developments and practice at the international, regional and domestic levels; critical fault lines in the context of the standards; and strategies to sharpen their potential to realize the transformative power of human rights. The chapter argues that for the transformative potential of socio-economic rights to be truly realized, in addition to these standards, other factors – such as respect for the rule of law, political will, independence of the judiciary and the momentum of involved civil society organizations and social movements – are essential. In the end, as the chapter avers, whatever approach is adopted in terms of standards, the aim should always be to interpret ESCR in a way that addresses not only individual needs but also systemic concerns, and foregrounds the needs of the most vulnerable.

Chapter 14 examines challenges in holding governments accountable to the obligation to progressively realize economic, social and cultural rights to the maximum of available resources. The chapter explains the key normative components of the obligation, accentuating challenges of its interpretation addressed by human rights monitoring bodies as well as considering the means and methods that can be used to assess compliance with the norms in practice. The chapter argues for 'more comprehensive, context-sensitive analytical frameworks that assess progress in rights realization in light of a state's fiscal and other policy efforts' and for full and effective use of the 'redistributive and egalitarian potential of the concept of progressive realization'. It concludes by highlighting some strategic opportunities and entry points for deploying these tools in the human rights, development and economic policy arenas, in ways that can advance meaningful accountability and transformative policy change.

Chapter 15 considers the concept of the interdependence of human rights in relation to the historical struggle of ESCR claimants for equality in dignity and rights. It traces the evolution of the idea of interdependence from an earlier notion premised on the unequal status of ESCR to a modern conception premised on equal voice, equal access to justice and 'human rights made whole'. The author argues that both civil and political rights and ESCR have been damaged by their separation into two categories and that a failure to adequately engage with the principle of interdependence allows many of the most egregious systemic violations of human rights, lying in the interstices between categories of rights, to go unchallenged. It argues for a new form of unified human rights practice grounded in the lives of rights holders, recognizing the complexity and multidimensionality of struggles for equal dignity and rights, and rejecting the differential treatment of 'positive' and 'negative' rights claims by courts and human rights bodies. It calls for a more inclusive and transformational paradigm of human rights based on a modernized understanding of the interdependence of human rights, recognizing the critical role that governments and international institutions must play, and insisting on the full inclusion of those whose claims have been marginalized or silenced.

Chapter 16 discusses the important roles that national human rights institutions (NHRIs) can play in advancing economic and social rights. It describes the emergence of NHRIs, considers some of the applicable international standards and examines specific features of NHRIs, including their institutional flexibility, their mandate and their location within the scheme of governance. The chapter analyzes how NHRIs have used public inquiries, monitoring budgets and policy, and litigation to advance economic and social rights, with illustrations from specific countries. It argues that NHRIs should see themselves as part of a larger institutional landscape that seeks social transformation through a broad range of actions. NHRIs, because of their ability to initiate a variety of interventions, their constitutional or statutory mandate, and their location between state and civil society, from which they are able to equally engage with both, are uniquely placed to intervene to advance ESR. The chapter considers the factors that will drive their transformative impact, including a vision and a plan of action that encompasses strategic engagement, principled decision-making and creative interventions.

In view of the intimate connection between economics and human rights, Chapter 17 examines how a human rights framework that gives due regard to ESCR can be applied to assess and evaluate economic policies. The chapter explains the normative framework for economics and illustrates how various human rights obligations and principles could be applied to economic policy. To illustrate the connections between human rights and economic policy, the chapter examines a number of interventions: government spending, taxation, deficit spending and debt, and monetary policy. As globalization increasingly affects both economic policy formulation and the ability of governments to meet their human rights obligations, the chapter also specifically engages with the human rights concept of ETOs and explores their implications for policy. The chapter argues for government accountability for human rights violations resulting from the conduct of its economic policies and the need to promote 'a vibrant and participatory democracy where the government can discipline the actions of finance and trans-national corporations and correct power imbalances in the economy'.

Chapter 18 highlights the significance of the 2030 Agenda for sustainable development for ESCR. It asserts that, much like the Millennium Development Goals, the SDGs are already altering and conditioning the development landscape, especially in terms of funding flows and data availability. The chapter analyzes how far the 2030 Agenda and ESCR are complementary and argues that, based on a nuanced understanding of the content, scope, strengths and weaknesses of the Agenda, ESCR advocates can use the SDGs as a lever for improvements in ESCR enjoyment.

The Handbook ends with a chapter on mobilization and litigation action to confront the systemic challenge posed by the contemporary global climate crisis, which poses severe threats to ESCR. As canvassed in Chapter 19, mitigation failure (inability to contain emissions) threatens ecosystems and constitutes a risk or violation of the ESCR of current and future humans. Adaptation failure (lack of action to protect those already at risk) is a breach of their ESCR. But climate mitigation and adaptation measures may themselves also threaten ESCR: closing of high-emission industries may cause job and livelihood loss; new, green energy sources (hydroelectric dams, windmills, soybean farms) and deforestation-prevention programs may cause displacement and culture loss. Highlighting that litigation is increasingly important as a strategy to force action to address the climate crisis, Chapter 19 outlines the emergency of climate litigation and the role of ESCR within it, surveying the cases being lodged before domestic and international courts and tribunals across the globe to force climate mitigation policies; compliance with existing rules; and more equitable policies for climate adaptation.

# PART I

# THE HUMAN RIGHTS FRAMEWORK FOR ESCR

# 1.   The international human rights system

*Jackie Dugard*

## 1.   HISTORICAL AND CONTEXTUAL OVERVIEW

This book focuses on economic, social and cultural rights (ESCR), and the respective chapters explore the specificities of ESCR globally, regionally and domestically. Due to the indivisibility and interdependence of all human rights (see in particular Chapter 15), as well as the interplay of various regional human rights systems (covered in Chapters 3, 4 and 5), it is useful to locate the book's analysis within an overview of the international human rights system as a whole, with specific focus on the United Nations (UN) system. This chapter therefore outlines the UN framework within which the human rights work covered in the subsequent chapters takes place. The chapter first provides an overview of the historical emergence of the international human rights system and then outlines the key issues of layers, applicability and universality, before analyzing the charter-based system and the treaty-based system, including eight of the nine core international human rights treaties, from an ESCR perspective.

### 1.1   Emergence of the International Human Rights Law System

The contemporary international human rights system was developed largely in response to the atrocities of World War II, as a means to assert universally applicable human rights norms and standards, and to establish binding mechanisms to hold states accountable for human rights failures and violations. There were, however, some pre-World War II precursors to the contemporary system. For example, humanitarian law, which focuses on trying to reduce wartime casualties and suffering, has its origins in the Geneva Convention for the Amelioration of the Condition of the Wounded in Armies in the Field of 1864 (First Geneva Convention), and the International Labour Organization (ILO), which seeks to improve working conditions, was created in 1919.[1] The international movement away from slavery, which gained momentum in the course of the struggles against colonialism in the late nineteenth and early twentieth centuries, can also be regarded as an instance (however reluctant) of the international recognition of inalienable human rights. However, notwithstanding these aspects of international law that focused on the welfare and liberty of individuals, until 1945, international law was largely concerned with relationships between states. The guiding principle, as articulated in Article 15(8) of the Covenant of the League of Nations of 1920, was a prohibition on intervention in the domestic affairs of states, which 'ensured that states failed to intervene in Germany before 1939 despite awareness of the atrocities committed by the Nazis against their own nationals'.[2]

---

[1]   On the formation of the ILO see for example Rhona Smith, *International Human Rights Law* 8th edition (Oxford University Press 2018) 22–23.

[2]   John Dugard and Jackie Dugard, 'Human Rights', *Dugard's International Law: A South African Perspective* 5th edition (Juta 2019) 455.

The failures of the League of Nations and its Covenant to prevent the horror of World War II provided the backdrop for a new system of international law that recognized human rights. The new system was originally outlined in the Charter of the United Nations of 1945 (UN Charter), under which the UN was established on 24 October 1945.

Shortly after the end of World War II, in 1946, the Economic and Social Council of the UN (ECOSOC) formed a Commission on Human Rights (subsequently replaced by the Human Rights Council), which was tasked with drafting an overarching declaration, as well as various multilateral treaties, on international human rights. As part of this process, the Universal Declaration of Human Rights (UDHR) was adopted by UN member states on 10 December 1948, setting out a global agreement on common human rights standards, including ESCR – for instance, social security (Article 22); work (Article 23); an adequate standard of living, health and well-being, including food, clothing, housing (Article 25); education (Article 26); and cultural life (Article 27). Although articulated in aspirational language and not a binding treaty, the UDHR serves as a morally persuasive document that no state has ever explicitly denounced.[3] It is generally accepted that the UDHR, or some of its principles – such as non-discrimination, the right to a fair trial and the prohibition against torture – have attained the status of customary international law,[4] and the UDHR certainly served as the inspiration for many of the subsequent international human rights treaties. The idea, following the adoption of the UDHR, was to draft a binding human rights treaty. Unfortunately, the realities of the Cold War divide between socialist and capitalist blocs meant that it took until 1966 and the formulation of two separate treaties – the International Covenant on Civil and Political Rights (ICCPR) and the International Covenant on Economic, Social and Cultural Rights (ICESCR) – for there to be a degree of consensus regarding how to concretize the spirit of the UDHR.[5] Adopted by the UN General Assembly (UNGA) in 1966, the ICCPR and ICESCR came into force in 1976. Along with these three cornerstone human rights documents (sometimes referred to as the international bill of rights), seven additional international human rights treaties, together with their associated Optional Protocols, have been adopted.

## 1.2   Layers, Applicability and Universality

The supra-national human rights system operates at two main levels: the international level and the regional level. This chapter provides an overview of the international level system under the UN Office of the High Commissioner for Human Rights (OHCHR), which was established on 20 December 1993 from the mandate set out, inter alia, in Articles 1, 13 and 55 of the UN Charter. The OHCHR sits in Geneva and oversees multiple mechanisms and procedures under two sets of bodies: the Charter-based system, which is based on states' membership of the UN; and the treaty-based system (discussed in section 3 of this chapter), which

---

[3]   When the UDHR was adopted by the UN, 48 states approved it and no states voted against it. However, eight states abstained (the Byelorussian Soviet Socialist Republic, Czechoslovakia, Poland, Saudi Arabia, the Union of South Africa, the Ukrainian Soviet Socialist Republic, the Union of Soviet Socialist Republics and Yugoslavia).

[4]   Dugard and Dugard (n 2) 461.

[5]   Frans Viljoen, 'International Protection of Human Rights' in Hennie Strydom (ed) *International Law* (Oxford University Press 2016) 331.

is based on states' voluntary acceptance (through signature and ratification)[6] of international human rights treaties.

There are currently three internationally recognized regional human rights systems: the African system (covered in Chapter 3), the European system (covered in Chapter 4) and the Inter-American system (covered in Chapter 5). These three systems are governed by conventions that bind states parties, and each system has institutional structures and mechanisms that oversee monitoring and reporting and complaints within that system. Although there are not yet consolidated regional systems for the rest of the world, there are fledgling systems emerging for South East Asia and for Arab and Muslim countries.[7] Beyond the international and regional human rights systems, the main human rights work occurs at the domestic level within nation states, the majority of which recognize human rights in national constitutions and laws, and many of which in addition are bound to global and regional human rights machinery.

While human rights systems should ideally complement and reinforce each other, the coexistence of overlapping human rights institutions and procedures raises the question of which route or approach affected persons should take when their human rights have been compromised and there has been a failure of enforcement at the national level.[8] This is a relevant question especially for the millions of people who live in states with weak domestic, and limited or absent regional, enforcement of human rights including ESCR. In general, recourse to an international human rights mechanism will depend on which treaties are binding on the specific state, which of these binding treaties provide for the substantive right at stake, and, the circumstances (including time and place) of the violation. It is worth noting that, as long as a claim falls within the jurisdiction of an international body even when international enforcement is not guaranteed, there could be significant symbolic and systemic gains made for claimants and affiliated organizations through using the international system.

One of the enduring criticisms of the international human rights system is that – in contrast to aspirational claims that human rights are universal – human rights law (as consolidated in the UN mechanisms) exerts a specific, 'Western' worldview.[9] Certainly, much of the world's population was not represented in the UN when the UDHR was drafted, as the majority of African and Asian countries were still under colonial rule and the defeated Axis powers (Japan, Germany, Italy and their allies) were excluded from the deliberations. Nonetheless, prominent experts from some of these countries played an active and influential role as independent members of the Human Rights Commission, prompting Brazil's Belarmino de Athayde to conclude on 10 December 1948 that, as a result of the substantive collaboration and cooperation among delegates, the UDHR did not reflect the view of any one people or group of peoples or any particular political or philosophical system.[10] Regardless of the genesis,

---

[6]   International treaties are first adopted by the UNGA, and enter into force through attaining the requisite number of ratifications (or accessions) by member states according to the requirements of the particular treaty. In this chapter, ratification refers inclusively to accession.

[7]   See Viljoen (n 5) 341–43.

[8]   It is a principle of international and regional human rights systems that domestic systems must first be exhausted before seeking redress through regional or global systems.

[9]   See for example Makau Mutua, 'The Complexity of Universalism in Human Rights', in András Sajó (ed), *Human Rights with Modesty* (Springer 2004) 51.

[10]   Mary Anne Glendon, *A World Made New* (2001) 221 cited in Philip Alston and Ryan Goodman, *International Human Rights: The Successor to International Human Rights in Context, Law, Politics and Morals* (Oxford University Press 2013) 147. See also Miloon Kothari, 'India's Contribution to the

it is clear that in the contemporary world order, for many individuals and groups of people around the world, the international human rights system represents an important – and in some cases the only – mechanism for asserting their rights (often in the wake of their government attempting to justify any violation by asserting its right to national sovereignty). Furthermore, whatever the arguments about civil and political rights, in relation to ESCR, arguments about Western domination clearly do not hold. Indeed, the development and pursuit of ESCR domestically, regionally and internationally has been led by countries of the global south, notably India, Kenya and South Africa, along with Latin American countries such as Argentina, Brazil, Colombia and Costa Rica.

## 2.    CHARTER-BASED SYSTEM

Unlike the treaty-based system discussed below, which applies only to those member states that are a party to the particular treaty ('states parties'), all UN member states fall under the Charter-based system. The Charter-based system comprises the Security Council,[11] the General Assembly,[12] the International Court of Justice,[13] the Economic and Social Council,[14] and the Human Rights Council (previously the Commission on Human Rights), which is the main human rights institution of the UN Charter-based system.

The Commission on Human Rights, which was established in 1946, was a sub-committee of ECOSOC comprising state representatives. Over the years, it came to be regarded as being over-politicized and as applying double standards.[15] In 2006, following a report by then UN Secretary-General Kofi Annan,[16] the Commission on Human Rights was replaced

Universal Declaration on Human Rights' (2018) 17 Journal of the National Human Rights Commission 65. Here, Kothari highlights that most sources on the UDHR overlook the significant contributions of the representatives of countries such as Chile, China, India, Lebanon, Mexico and Philippines.

[11]    The Security Council, which has its permanent office at the UN headquarters in New York City, has primary responsibility for ensuring international peace and security, and because international disputes are often precipitated by human rights violations, the Security Council is sometimes drawn into human rights matters (see Rhona Smith, *International Human Rights Law* (Oxford University Press 2018) 55–57).

[12]    The General Assembly, which meets under its president or secretary-general in annual sessions at the UN headquarters in New York City, has specific human rights mandates that include receiving and monitoring all reports by treaty-monitoring bodies and through the Economic and Social Council and the Human Rights Council. In addition, it is charged with increasing state ratifications of human rights treaties and takes resolutions on human rights-related issues.

[13]    Although it does not hear individual human rights complaints, the International Court of Justice (which succeeded the Permanent Court of International Justice, and is located at The Hague) hears inter-state complaints and issues judgments and advisory opinions that sometimes have a human rights component (see Walter Kälin and Jörg Künzli, *The Law of International Human Rights Protection* (Oxford University Press 2011) 264–67).

[14]    The Economic and Social Council, which has its offices at the UN headquarters in New York City, has a broad remit to initiate human rights-related studies and reports, and it receives all UN Human Rights Committee and Commission reports. A sub-committee, the Commission for the Status of Women, is tasked with preparing recommendations and reports on the advancement of women's civil and political as well as ESCR rights.

[15]    Ibid 331–32.

[16]    UN, 'In Larger Freedom: Report of the Secretary-General of the United Nations for decision by the Heads of State and Government in September 2005' <http://www.un.org/en/events/pastevents/in_larger_freedom.shtml>.

by the Human Rights Council, which, like the Commission, has its headquarters in Geneva. A subsidiary organ of the UNGA, the Human Rights Council comprises 47 member states elected for three-year terms by the UNGA on the basis of equitable geographic distribution of the UN's five regions (13 seats for African states; 13 seats for Asia-Pacific states; 8 seats for Latin American states; 7 seats for Western European and Other states; and 6 seats for Eastern European states).[17] The Human Rights Council is charged with 'the promotion and protection of all human rights across the globe'.[18]

Although elected member states may be suspended from the Human Rights Council if they commit 'gross and systematic violations of human rights',[19] to date this has only occurred once, in the case of Libya in 2011.[20] Moreover, the Human Rights Council has not escaped being politicized, which has arguably impacted its ability to act as an impartial international arbiter. For example, under President Donald Trump, the United States of America (USA) withdrew its membership of the Human Rights Council on 20 June 2018, claiming that it was 'hypocritical' and chronically biased against Israel.[21] The reason the USA considers the Human Rights Council to be biased against Israel is that, unlike most other international institutions, the Human Rights Council is dominated by developing countries, which often support the Palestinian struggle 'as a litmus test for human rights'.[22]

Two of the main ways that the Human Rights Council undertakes its work is through the Universal Periodic Review (UPR) and Special Procedures mechanisms.[23] Regarding the UPR, since 2008, all UN member states have been required to undertake a periodic review of their human rights compliance, which is overseen by the Human Rights Council.[24] The fact that all UN member states (even those that have not ratified the ICESCR) are reviewed for compliance on all human rights (including ESCR) is an important accountability tool. The reviews occur in four-year cycles, with the first cycle from 2008 to 2011, the second cycle from 2012 to 2016, and the third UPR cycle having started in 2017 (2017–2021).[25] Countries are assigned to specific cycles and must report on their human rights record (for UN member states that have ratified international treaties, there is often some overlap with the reporting requirements

---

[17]   See 'Membership of the Human Rights Council' <www.ohchr.org/EN/HRBodies/HRC/Pages/Membership.aspx> (in July 2018, following the withdrawal from the Human Rights Council by the United States of America, Iceland was elected to take its place from 13 July 2018 to 31 December 2019).

[18]   Website of the UN Human Rights Council <www.ohchr.org/en/hrbodies/hrc/pages/home.aspx>.

[19]   UN General Assembly Resolution 60/251 (15 March 2006) para 8.

[20]   See United Nations, 'General Assembly Suspends Libya from Human Rights Council' <www.un.org/press/en/2011/ga11050.doc.htm>.

[21]   See BBC News, 'US Quits "Biased" UN Human Rights Council' (20 June 2018): <www.bbc.co.uk/news/44537372>.

[22]   Dugard and Dugard (n 2) 486. See also John Dugard, 'The Future of International Law: A Human Rights Perspective' (2007) Leiden Journal of International Law 81.

[23]   The Human Rights Council also has a Complaint Procedure, which focuses on identifying, investigating and reporting on gross human rights violations; and a Human Rights Council Advisory Committee, which is an expert think-tank that provides expertise to the Council (see Kälin and Künzli (n 13) 252).

[24]   See United Nations Human Rights Council, 'Basic Facts about the UPR' <www.ohchr.org/EN/HRBodies/UPR/Pages/BasicFacts.aspx>.

[25]   See United Nations Human Rights Council, 'Cycles of the Universal Periodic Review' <www.ohchr.org/EN/HRBodies/UPR/Pages/CyclesUPR.aspx>.

for states parties under each treaty they have ratified).[26] The Human Rights Council appoints a Working Group to review each state's report, which is considered alongside a report by the UN Office of the High Commissioner for Human Rights and a summary report of issues raised by 'other stakeholders', which are often international and national non-governmental organizations. The stakeholder reports, posted online, and the summary report provide an important opportunity for ESCR advocates to raise relevant issues to be considered as part of the UPR process, as well as to make recommendations.[27] The review itself comprises a three-hour interactive dialogue between the state under review and Council members, facilitated by three rapporteurs from different regional groups (selected through members of the Council drawing lots).[28]

Special Procedures mechanisms of the Human Rights Council are central to the UN's human rights machinery, comprising special rapporteurs, independent experts and working groups made up of independent experts appointed in their personal capacity to deal with specific human rights issues. Special Procedures mandates can be thematic – including a number of ESCR issues such as the Special Rapporteur on the right to education; the Special Rapporteur on the right to food; the Special Rapporteur on the rights to safe drinking water and sanitation; the Special Rapporteur on adequate housing as a component of the right to an adequate standard of living, and on the right to non-discrimination in this context; and the Special Rapporteur on the right of everyone to the enjoyment of the highest attainable standard of health – or country-specific, currently: Belarus, Cambodia, Central African Republic, Democratic People's Republic of Korea, Eritrea, Islamic Republic of Iran, Mali, Myanmar, Palestinian territories occupied since 1967, Somalia, Sudan and Syrian Arab Republic.[29] Special Procedures mandate-holders undertake country visits, act on individual cases, send communications to states, conduct thematic studies, convene expert consultations, engage in advocacy and report annually to the Human Rights Council (and in many instances also to the UNGA).[30] They provide an important accountability and compliance mechanism including regarding ESCR issues, which is dealt with in further detail, where relevant, in the chapters in Part B of this book.

---

[26] To assist states to undertake periodic reviews, the OHCHR has prepared the following guidelines, which clarify how to report and particularly which aspects of human rights to report on: <www.ohchr.org/Documents/HRBodies/UPR/TechnicalGuideEN.pdf>.

[27] There are several ways in which ESCR advocates can participate in their country's UPR. As it is often difficult to get to Geneva, it is helpful to meet with ambassadors in one's own country to explain particular issues that should be raised. One embassy may agree to host a meeting and invite staff from other embassies to make this process more efficient. Where ESCR advocates can get to Geneva, the organization UPRinfo.org organizes professional panels and dialogues at which issues can be explained and recommendations suggested to state delegates. Direct meetings or correspondence with staff of permanent missions in Geneva can also be helpful. While the UPR process, as well as the uptake of the recommendations by the particular state, is voluntary, most governments accord it considerable attention and the recommendations emerging from it can be used in an ongoing way in ESCR advocacy.

[28] Kälin and Künzli (n 13) 246.

[29] See United Nations Office of the High Commissioner, 'Country Mandates' <https://spinternet.ohchr.org/_layouts/15/SpecialProceduresInternet/ViewAllCountryMandates.aspx>.

[30] See United Nations Office of the High Commissioner, 'Special Procedures of the Human Rights Council' <www.ohchr.org/en/hrbodies/sp/pages/welcomepage.aspx>.

## 3.    TREATY-BASED SYSTEM

The nine core international human rights treaties are, in chronological order (on the basis of entry into force): the International Convention on the Elimination of All Forms of Racial Discrimination (ICERD), which is overseen by the Committee on the Elimination of Racial Discrimination (CERD); the ICCPR, which is overseen by the Human Rights Committee (CCPR), and the ICESCR, which is overseen by the Committee on Economic, Social and Cultural Rights (CESCR); the Convention on the Elimination of All forms of Discrimination against Women (CEDAW), which is overseen by the CEDAW Committee; the Convention against Torture and Other Cruel, Inhuman or Degrading Treatment or Punishment (CAT), which is overseen by the CAT Committee; the Convention on the Rights of the Child (CRC), which is overseen by the CRC Committee; the International Convention on the Protection of the Rights of All Migrant Workers and Members of Their Families (ICMW), which is overseen by the Committee on Migrant Workers (CMW); the Convention on the Rights of Persons with Disabilities (CRPD), which is overseen by the CRPD Committee; and the International Convention for the Protection of All Persons from Enforced Disappearance (ICEPD), which is overseen by the Committee on Enforced Disappearances (CED). Each of these treaties – apart from the ICESCR and its Optional Protocol (which are analyzed in depth in Chapter 2) – along with its committee and, where relevant, its Optional Protocol (OP), is discussed here.

One of the main functions of the treaty-based system is to enable individuals to complain about violations of their human rights under the various treaties. This occurs in three main ways: individual communications; inter-state complaints; and inquiries. All nine international human rights treaties provide for individual communications procedures in terms of which an individual can lodge a complaint against her own state (often via the relevant optional protocol), as long as the state has ratified the relevant treaty or its optional protocol (the individual complaints procedure for the ICMW has not yet come into force), and following exhaustion of domestic remedies.[31] Regarding the ICESCR, during the long period between entering into force on 23 March 1976 and having an individual complaints mechanism through the entry into force of the Optional Protocol to the ICESCR (OP-ICESCR) on 5 May 2013, individuals who wanted to use the international human rights system to complain about state violations

---

[31]    There are two different ways in which the individual communications procedures become binding on states parties – either through the relevant optional protocol or through making the necessary declaration under the treaty. Regarding the optional protocol route, the CCPR may consider individual communications alleging violations of the ICCPR by states parties to OP1-ICCPR; the CESCR may consider individual communications alleging violations of the ICESCR by states parties to the OP-ICESCR; the CEDAW Committee may consider individual communications alleging violations of CEDAW by states parties to the OP-CEDAW; the CRC Committee may consider individual communications alleging violations of the CRC, OP-CRC-AC or OP-CRC-SC by states parties to the OP-CRC-IC; and the CRPD Committee may consider individual communications alleging violations of the CRPD by states parties to the OP-CRPD. Regarding the declaration route, the CERD may consider individual petitions alleging violations of ICERD by states parties that have made the necessary declaration under Article 14 of ICERD; the CAT Committee may consider individual complaints alleging violations of CAT by states parties that have made the necessary declaration under Article 22 of CAT; and the CED may consider individual communications alleging violations of the ICED by states parties that have made the necessary declaration under Article 31 of ICED. The individual complaint mechanism for ICMW has not yet entered into force and will only do so when ten states parties make the necessary declaration under Article 77 of the ICMW.

of ESCR had to use the other treaties and committee processes outlined below. For citizens of states that have not ratified the ICESCR and/or OP-ICESCR, the individual complaints procedures under the various other international treaties remain a critical mechanism for addressing ESCR-related concerns. Subsequent chapters detail the relevant communications under other treaties, including: *Nell Toussaint v Canada*, in which in 2018 the CCPR found Canada to have violated its healthcare-related obligations on the basis of the irregular migration status of the complainant;[32] *E.S. and S.C. v Tanzania*, in which in 2015 the CEDAW Committee found that the United Republic of Tanzania's customary laws of inheritance discriminated against girl children;[33] *Gröninger v Germany*, in which in 2014 the CRPD Committee found Germany to have failed to promote the right to work by failing to facilitate the inclusion of a person with disabilities into the labor market;[34] and *Da Silva Pimentel v Brazil*, in which in 2011 the CEDAW Committee found Brazil to have violated the health-care-related rights of a national who died following inadequate obstetrical care.[35]

In addition to the individual communications (complaints) procedure, all the treaties and/or their optional protocols (apart from the CRPD) provide for inter-state complaints mechanisms of one kind or another, under varying arrangements,[36] allowing a state party to complain to the relevant treaty body about another state party's failure to realize the obligations, and/or to refer a state party to arbitration over the contested interpretation, of the relevant treaty. During 2018, three inter-state communications were submitted under Article 11 of ICERD – the first time in history, at the UN level, that the inter-state mechanism has been used for any of the treaties.[37] Finally, all the treaties, apart from the ICCPR, ICERD and ICMW, provide for inquiry procedures to deal with systemic violations by states, but these are not often engaged. In all these treaties, except ICEPD, states can opt out of the inquiry procedure. The inquiry procedure can be used as an effective mechanism for ESCR, such as the 2016 inquiry into the impact of the United Kingdom's austerity measures on persons with disabilities' rights that was undertaken by the CRPD Committee.[38]

Each of the nine treaties is overseen by a committee of elected independent experts (usually elected for renewable terms of four years), which performs the following key roles: hearing individual complaints (described above); providing clarity on the meaning and scope of the relevant rights through formulating general comments (sometimes referred to as general recommendations); and receiving and commenting on initial and periodic state reports. General comments are a means for the various committees to provide information on internal procedures and to clarify the scope and content of the various rights under the relevant treaty.

---

[32]   CCPR, *Toussaint v Canada* (24 July 2018) CCPR/C/123/D/2348/2014.

[33]   CEDAW Committee, *E.S. and S.C. v Tanzania* (2 March 2015) CEDAW/C/60/D/48/2013.

[34]   CRPD Committee, *Gröninger v Germany* (4 April 2014) CRPD/C/D2/2010.

[35]   CEDAW Committee, *Da Silva Pimental v Brazil* (25 July 2011) CEDAW/C/49/D/2008.

[36]   See United Nations Office of the High Commissioner for Human Rights, 'Human Rights Bodies – Complaints Procedures' <www.ohchr.org/en/hrbodies/tbpetitions/pages/hrtbpetitions.aspx>.

[37]   *State of Qatar vs. Kingdom of Saudi Arabia; State of Qatar vs United Arab Emirates; and State of Palestine vs State of Israel* – see UN Human Rights Bodies, Committee on the Elimination of Racial Discrimination, 'Inter-state Communications' <www.ohchr.org/EN/HRBodies/CERD/Pages/InterstateCommunications.aspx>. None of these inter-state complaints is directly about ESCR.

[38]   See CRPD Inquiry concerning the United Kingdom of Great Britain and Northern Ireland carried out by the Committee under Article 6 of the Optional Protocol to the Convention Report of the Committee (6 October 2016) <www.ohchr.org/Documents/HRBodies/CRPD/CRPD.C.15.R.2.Rev.1 -ENG.doc>.

Although not binding per se, general comments are regarded as soft law that can assist states to better understand the UN system and its human rights obligations. General comments dealing with ESCR are dealt with in Chapter 2 and subsequent chapters of the book, but some of the general comments from the other committees are relevant to ESCR. For example, the following are relevant general comments from the CCPR: General Comment No. 31: Nature of the General Legal Obligation Imposed on States Parties to the Covenant (26 May 2004) CCPR/C/21/Rev.1/Add.13;[39] and General Comment No. 36: Article 6 (the right to life) (2 November 2018) CCPR/C/GC/36[40] which is a right that has been used by ESCR advocates as a way to pursue health-related issues such as in the *Nell Toussaint v Canada* complaint.[41] Regarding the state report function, which is the main way through which the human rights compliance of states parties is monitored, contracting parties have to submit initial and periodic reports to the relevant committees on the measures they have pursued to give effect to the relevant treaty. These reports are reviewed by the relevant committee, which subjects such reports to a critical expert review in the presence of a delegation from the same country.[42]

### 3.1   ICERD (Racial Discrimination)

ICERD was adopted by the UNGA on 21 December 1965 and entered into force on 4 January 1969, making it the oldest international human rights treaty. ICERD has been ratified by 179 states, including the world's two largest economies – the USA and China. Article 2 condemns racial discrimination and compels states parties to eliminate it by all appropriate means. Expanding on Article 2's ambit, Article 5 specifies various ESCR-related dimensions of the prohibition on racial discrimination, including work, housing, health, social security, education and cultural life. ICERD is overseen by the CERD, which comprises 18 members.

### 3.2   ICCPR (Civil and Political Rights)

The ICCPR was adopted by the UNGA on 16 December 1966 and entered into force on 23 March 1976. It has been ratified by 172 states, including the world's largest economy, the USA (the world's second largest economy, China, is a signatory but has not ratified the ICCPR). The (First) Optional Protocol to the ICCPR (OP1-ICCPR), which establishes an individual complaints mechanism, was adopted by the UNGA on 16 December 1966 and entered into force on 23 March 1976, at the same time as the ICCPR was adopted and came into force. The OP1-ICCPR has been ratified by 116 states, excluding China and the USA.

Like the ICESCR, the ICCPR begins by recognizing the right to self-determination (Article 1), with its ESCR dimensions as related to economic, social and cultural development. Article 6 of the ICCPR sets out the right to life, which, as described in Chapter 15, has been interpreted by the Human Rights Committee to include the right to 'enjoy a life with dignity' and to require that states address 'the general conditions in society that may give rise to direct threats

---

[39]   See UN Treaty Body Database <https://tbinternet.ohchr.org/_layouts/15/treatybodyexternal/Download.aspx?symbolno=CCPR%2fC%2f21%2fRev.1%2fAdd.13&Lang=en>.

[40]   See UN Treaty Body Database <https://tbinternet.ohchr.org/_layouts/15/treatybodyexternal/Download.aspx?symbolno=CCPR%2fC%2fGC%2f36&Lang=en>.

[41]   *Toussaint v Canada* (n 32).

[42]   Kälin and Künzli (n 13) 206.

to life or prevent individuals from enjoying their right to life with dignity'.[43] Article 6 has been used by ESCR advocates as a way to pursue health-related rights. The death penalty is not prohibited except in respect of people under 18 years old and pregnant women. However, the Second Optional Protocol to the ICCPR, on the abolition of the death penalty (OP2-ICCPR), was adopted by the UNGA on 15 December 1989 and entered into force on 11 July 1991. The OP2-ICCPR, which has been ratified by 86 states, comprehensively outlaws the death penalty for ratifying states (neither the USA nor China, both of which still have the death penalty, has ratified the OP2-ICCPR). Other key provisions are the prohibition of torture; cruel, inhuman or degrading treatment (Article 7); and slavery (Article 8). Another key provision is dignity (Article 10), which sometimes has ESCR-related applicability. Article 26 prohibits discrimination based on 'race, colour, sex, language, religion, political or other opinion, national or social origin, property, birth or other status' – the non-discrimination guarantees can be used by ESCR advocates to address ESCR-related discrimination.[44] The ICCPR and its Optional Protocols are overseen by the CCPR, which comprises 18 members.

### 3.3    CEDAW (Women)

CEDAW was adopted by the UNGA on 18 December 1979 and entered into force on 3 September 1981. CEDAW has been ratified by 189 states, including China but excluding the USA (which is a signatory). The Optional Protocol to CEDAW (OP-CEDAW), which establishes complaint and inquiry processes for CEDAW, was adopted by the UNGA on 6 October 1999 and entered into force on 22 December 2000. The OP-CEDAW has been ratified by 109 states, excluding the USA and China.

CEDAW condemns discrimination based on sex that 'has the effect or purpose of impairing or nullifying the recognition, enjoyment or exercise by women, irrespective of their marital status, on a basis of equality of men and women, of human rights' in any field, and obliges states to pursue measures to guarantee equal rights to women in all spheres of life (Article 1). As with the non-discrimination provisions of ICERD and ICCPR (and CRC, ICMW and CRPD discussed below), CEDAW's non-discrimination provisions extend to ESCR, which explicitly include education (Article 10), work (Article 11), health (Article 12) and, specifically in relation to rural women, equal access to housing, sanitation, electricity and water supply (Article 14). Affirmative action measures are explicitly recognized in Article 4(1). CEDAW and OP-CEDAW are overseen by the 23-member CEDAW Committee.

### 3.4    CAT (Torture)

CAT was adopted by the UNGA on 10 December 1984 and entered into effect on 26 June 1987. CAT has been ratified by 165 states, including China and the USA. CAT prohibits torture, and other cruel, inhuman or degrading treatment or punishment, and is possibly the least ESCR-relevant international treaty, apart from in the intersection between forms of torture and health.

---

[43]    CCPR, General Comment No. 36: Article 6 (the right to life) (2 November 2018) CCPR/C/GC/36. See Chapter 15.

[44]    See Chapter 15 for references and discussion of cases in which Article 26 has been used to advance ESCR.

The Optional Protocol to the Convention against Torture and Other Cruel, Inhuman or Degrading Treatment or Punishment (OP-CAT), which establishes an international inspection system for prisons, was adopted by the UNGA on 18 December 2002 and entered into effect on 22 June 2006. It has been ratified by 88 states, excluding the USA and China. OP-CAT is overseen by the 25-member Sub-Committee on Prevention of Torture and Other Cruel, Inhuman or Degrading Treatment or Punishment under OP-CAT (SPT), while CAT itself is overseen by the CAT Committee, comprising ten members.

### 3.5   CRC (Children)

The CRC was adopted by the UNGA on 20 November 1989 and entered into force on 2 September 1990. It has been ratified by 196 states, meaning that the USA (which is a signatory) is the only UN member state not to have ratified the CRC.[45] The CRC seeks to protect children from discrimination and it asserts their civil and political, as well as ESCR-related, rights, including: the right to enjoy the highest attainable standard of health, specifically through the provision of adequate nutritious foods and clean drinking water and environmental sanitation (Article 24); the right to social security (Article 26); the right to an adequate standard of living, particularly regarding clothing and housing (Article 27); and the right to education (Article 28).

The Optional Protocol to the Convention on the Rights of the Child on the sale of children, child prostitution and child pornography (OP-CRC-SC) was adopted by the UNGA on 25 May 2000 and entered into force on 18 January 2002. The OP-CRC-SC has been ratified by 175 states, including the USA and China. The Optional Protocol to the Convention on the Rights of the Child on the involvement of children in armed conflict (OP-CRC-AC) was adopted by the UNGA on 25 May 2000 and entered into force on 12 February 2002. It has been ratified by 168 states, including China and the USA. The Optional Protocol to the Convention on the Rights of the Child on a communications procedure (OP-CRC-IC) was adopted by the UNGA on 19 December 2011 and entered into force on 14 April 2014. It has been ratified by 40 states, which do not include China or the USA. The CRC and its Optional Protocols are overseen by the 18-member CRC Committee.

### 3.6   ICMW (Migrant Workers)

The ICMW was adopted by the UNGA on 18 December 1990 and entered into force on 1 July 2003. It has been ratified by 54 states, excluding the USA and China. ICMW proclaims the rights of migrant workers and seeks to protect them against all forms of civil and political, as well as ESCR-related, discrimination among member states as relating to work (Article 25), social security (Article 27), emergency medical care (Article 28) and education (Article 30). ICMW is overseen by the 14-member CMW.

---

[45]   Somalia, the second last state not to ratify, ratified the CRC in October 2015.

### 3.7 CRPD (Disability)

The CRPD was adopted by the UNGA on 13 December 2006 and entered into force on 3 May 2008. It has been ratified by 177 states, including China but excluding the USA (which is a signatory). CRPD aims to tackle discrimination against persons with disabilities and to ensure that persons with disabilities are treated with dignity. Specific ESCR provisions include the right to education (Article 24), health (Article 25), work (Article 27), adequate standard of living and social protection (Article 28) and participation in cultural life (Article 30). At the same time as the CRPD was adopted, the Optional Protocol to the CRPD (OP-CRPD) was adopted by the UNGA, on 13 December 2006, and entered into force on 3 May 2008. The OP-CRPD has been ratified by 92 states, which exclude the USA and China. The CRPD and the OP-CRPD are overseen by the CRPD Committee, which comprises 18 members.

### 3.8 ICEPD (Enforced Disappearance)

ICEPD was adopted on 20 December 2006 and entered into force on 23 December 2010. It has been ratified by 59 states, excluding the USA and China. ICEPD, which is modelled on CAT, aims to eradicate enforced disappearances and compels states parties to investigate and provide appropriate criminal justice systems to prosecute offenders and assist victims of enforced disappearances. Along with CAT, ICEPD has fewer ESCR-related intersections than the other international treaties but there are, potentially at least, health-related implications of its provisions. ICEPD is overseen by the ten-member CED.

## 4.    CONCLUSION

Recently described by the Supreme Court of Canada as 'the phoenix that rose from the ashes of World War II and declared global war on human rights abuses',[46] the contemporary international human rights system has developed a series of mechanisms to hold states accountable to human rights obligations and to provide remedies to individuals. These mechanisms are aimed at ensuring that human rights norms act as 'moral imperatives and legal necessities' rather than 'theoretical aspirations or legal luxuries'.[47] Key mechanisms outlined in this chapter were the UPR and special procedures under the Charter-based system; and the general comments, individual complaints and state reporting under the treaty-based system. Highlighting how the international system provides important ESCR protections, even for states that have not ratified the more directly relevant ESCR instruments, this chapter has introduced and contextualized the ESCR provisions pursued in the rest of the book.

---

[46]   *Nevsun Resources Ltd. v Araya* 2020 SCC 5 (Supreme Court of Canada) at para 1.
[47]   Ibid.

# 2. The International Covenant on Economic, Social and Cultural Rights and the Optional Protocol

*Daniela Ikawa*

## 1. HISTORICAL AND CONTEXTUAL OVERVIEW

This chapter discusses the main UN treaty focused on the protection of economic, social and cultural rights – the International Covenant on Economic, Social and Cultural Rights (ICESCR) – as well as its optional complaints procedure, the Optional Protocol to the ICESCR (OP-ICESCR). Section 1 covers the historical and contextual framework for the adoption of both treaties. Section 2 enumerates the main rights, principles, and State obligations recognized by the ICESCR, and Section 3 tackles specific mechanisms of protection and existing jurisprudence of the Committee on Economic, Social and Cultural Rights (CESCR). Finally, Section 4 addresses the CESCR's nascent implementation procedure for remedies in individual communications.

### 1.1 Adoption of the International Covenant on Economic, Social and Cultural Rights and Indivisibility

As described in Chapter 1, the Universal Declaration on Human Rights (UDHR) recognized both civil and political rights (Articles 1 to 21), on the one hand, and economic, social, and cultural rights (Articles 22 to 27), on the other. The Cold War, however, led to the adoption of two separate legally binding documents: the International Covenant on Civil and Political Rights (ICCPR) and the ICESCR.

The ICESCR entered into force on 3 January 1976 and, as of July 2020, it had 171 State parties.[1] Since its adoption, the Economic and Social Council of the UN (ECOSOC) has consecutively assigned three different bodies the responsibility for supervising the Covenant's implementation by states parties: the Sessional Working Group on the Implementation of the ICESCR; the Sessional Working Group of Governmental Experts on the Implementation of the International Covenant; and, from 1985, the CESCR, consisting of 18 members 'who shall be experts with recognized competence in the field of human rights, serving in their personal capacity, due consideration being given to equitable geographical distribution and to the representation of different forms of social and legal systems'.[2] Initially, the CESCR relied on only two mechanisms to clarify State obligations and to hold States accountable to these. First, the

---

[1]    OHCHR, 'Status of Ratification Interactive Dashboard, ICESCR' <http://indicators.ohchr.org>.
[2]    ECOSOC Res. 1985/2017, Review of the composition, organization and administrative arrangements of the Seasonal Group of Governmental Experts on the Implementation of the ICESCR (28 May 1985) E/RES/1985/17.

Committee conducts periodic reviews of State reports on the implementation of the Covenant, to be submitted every five years, followed by dialogue with the State party's representatives at a scheduled session of the Committee and the adoption of concluding observations identifying positive measures, concerns, and recommendations.[3] Second, the Committee develops and adopts General Comments that provide authoritative interpretations of the Covenant and provide direction to States and others regarding what is required for compliance, both with respect to particular rights and with cross-cutting principles.

In the absence of individual communications between the entry into force of the ICESCR and the OP-ICESCR, General Comments primarily drew on the Committee's experience of interpreting and applying the Covenant in the context of periodic reviews of States,[4] as well as on the normative standards developed by treaty bodies and regional systems, academic commentaries and other normative documents. With the entry into force of the OP-ICESCR in 2013, mechanisms of protection were expanded, as will be discussed in Section 3 of this chapter. Nevertheless, there was a long gap between the adoption of the ICESCR and that of the OP-ICESCR, and there are still very few States which have ratified the OP-ICESCR.

## 1.2   Adoption of the Optional Protocol to the ICESCR and Justiciability

The OP-ICESCR was adopted by the UN General Assembly on 10 December 2008. This adoption followed many years of advocacy by civil society organizations and work by the CESCR. The Committee submitted a statement on the effectiveness of the UN Treaty Body System to the 1993 Vienna World Conference on Human Rights,[5] and proposed a preliminary draft for an Optional Protocol to the UN Commission on Human Rights in 1997.[6] An Open Ended Working Group was appointed by the UN Commission on Human Rights in 2002, with an expanded mandate from the newly formed UN Human Rights Council in 2006 to proceed to develop a draft of the Optional Protocol. The main issues raised in the final discussions for its adoption by the Open Ended Working Group focused on whether the OP-ICESCR should adopt a comprehensive or an à la carte approach to the protection of economic, social, and cultural rights; whether there could be collective complaints;[7] and whether the standard of review should be margin of appreciation or reasonableness.[8] In the preliminary debates within the Working Group, a comprehensive approach was supported by one group of countries

---

[3]   ICESCR and ECOSOC Resolution 1985/15 (28 May 1985) Articles 16–19.

[4]   Ben Saul, David Kinley and Jacqueline Mowbray, 'Introduction in the ICESCR: Commentary, Cases and Materials', Legal Studies Research Paper No. 14/05 (January 2014) 4–5.

[5]   UN General Assembly, Contribution of the CESCR to the World Conference on Human Rights (23 March 1993) A/CONF.157/PC/62/Add.5.

[6]   ECOSOC, Note by the Secretary-General on the draft optional protocol to the International Covenant on Economic, Social and Cultural Rights (18 December 1996) E/CN.4/1997/105.

[7]   Tara Melish, 'Introductory Note to the OP-ICESCR' (2009) 48 ILM 262.

[8]   Bruce Porter, 'Reasonableness and Article 8(4)', in Malcolm Langford, Bruce Porter, Rebecca Brown and Julieta Rossi (eds), *The Optional Protocol to the International Covenant on Economic, Social and Cultural Rights: A Commentary* (PULP 2016) 8–11.

and interest groups;[9] however,[10] another group supported an à la carte approach.[11] And while countries including Egypt, Norway, Poland, Sweden, Switzerland, and the United States defended the idea that States should have a broad margin of appreciation,[12] 'Mexico, Amnesty International, the ICJ and the NGO Coalition expressed concern about referring to the broad margin of appreciation'.[13] In contrast, Bangladesh, Ecuador, Greece, India, and Liechtenstein supported reasonableness as the standard of review.[14] Ultimately, a consensus position was reached such that the OP-ICESCR covered all rights recognized by the ICESCR (comprehensive approach). It did not allow for collective complaints as such, but permitted the submission of complaints by groups of individual victims; and it adopted a standard of reasonableness, strengthening the international protection of ESCR.

The OP-ICESCR entered into force on 5 May 2013, establishing three new mechanisms of protection: an individual complaints procedure, an inter-State complaints procedure, and an inquiry procedure. Although ESCR had been protected internationally through individual complaints before other UN Committees, such as CEDAW, CERD, CRPD Committee, CRC Committee, and HRC, the entry into force of the OP-ICESCR marked a symbolic change. It more explicitly recognized the justiciability of ESCR in the international sphere, stressing the fact that ESCR should be taken as seriously as CPR. It also established a practical change, allowing a specialized body to apply specific principles to ESCR cases, such as the principles of the maximum of available resources and progressive realization.

By July 2020, 24 States had ratified the OP-ICESCR: Argentina, Belgium, Bolivia, Bosnia and Herzegovina, Cape Verde, Central African Republic, Costa Rica, Ecuador, El Salvador, Finland, France, Gabon, Honduras, Italy, Luxembourg, Mongolia, Montenegro, Niger, Portugal, San Marino, Slovakia, Spain, Uruguay, and Venezuela.[15]

---

[9]    Belgium, Bolivia, Brazil, Burkina Faso, Chile, Ecuador, Egypt (on behalf of the African Group), Ethiopia, Finland, France, Guatemala, Italy, Liechtenstein, Mexico, Nigeria, Norway, Peru, Portugal, Senegal, Slovenia, South Africa, Spain, Sweden, Uruguay, Venezuela (Bolivarian Republic of), Amnesty International, CETIM, FIAN, the ICJ, the NGO Coalition and International Women's Rights Action Watch (IWRAW) Asia-Pacific Human Rights Council, Report of the Open-ended Working Group on an Optional Protocol to the International Covenant on Economic, Social and Cultural Rights, Report of the Fourth Session (30 August 2007) A/HRC/6/8 paras 19 and 33.

[10]    ECOSOC, Elements for an optional protocol to the International Covenant on Economic, Social and Cultural Rights (30 November 2005) E/CN.4/2006/WG.23/2 para 5.

[11]    Australia, China, Denmark, Germany, Greece, Japan, the Netherlands, New Zealand, Poland, the Republic of Korea, Russia, Switzerland, Turkey, the United Kingdom and the United States. Human Rights Council, Report of the Open-ended Working Group on an Optional Protocol to the International Covenant on Economic, Social and Cultural Rights, Report of the Fourth Session (30 August 2007) A/HRC/6/8 para 37.

[12]    Human Rights Council, Report of the Open-ended Working Group on an Optional Protocol to the International Covenant on Economic, Social and Cultural Rights, Report of the Fourth Session (30 August 2007) A/HRC/6/8 paras 95–96 and 98.

[13]    Human Rights Council, Report of the Open-ended Working Group on an Optional Protocol to the International Covenant on Economic, Social and Cultural Rights, Report of the Fourth Session (30 August 2007) A/HRC/6/8 para 100.

[14]    Human Rights Council, Report of the Open-ended Working Group on an Optional Protocol to the International Covenant on Economic, Social and Cultural Rights, Report of the Fourth Session (30 August 2007) A/HRC/6/8 paras 101, 153.

[15]    OHCHR (n 1).

The relatively recent adoption of the OP-ICESCR and the low number of ratifications to date means that in many States, claimants and civil society continue to rely on the Periodic Review and have no access to adjudication and remedy at the international level. The time gap between the ratification of the OP-ICPR and the ratification of OP-ICESCR means that international jurisprudence continues to be heavily weighted in favor of civil and political rights. Nevertheless, the adoption of the OP-ICESCR by the General Assembly and the important jurisprudence that has already emerged under the Optional Protocol has clarified the obligations to ensure access to justice for ESCR that apply to all states parties, whether or not they have ratified the OP-ICESCR. In periodic reviews, the Committee has emphasized that all States must ensure access to effective remedies for ESCR, consistent with the obligations laid out in General Comment No. 9.

## 2. RIGHTS AND STATE OBLIGATIONS

### 2.1 Rights

The ICESCR covers a number of social, economic, and cultural rights and the content of most of the rights is further developed by General Comments (GC): the right to work (Article 6 and GC No. 18/2006[16]); the right to just and favorable conditions of work (Article 7 and GC No. 23/2016[17]); the right to form and join trade unions and the right to strike (Article 8); the right to social security (Article 9 and GC No. 19/2008[18]); the right to protection and assistance for the family and the prohibition of child labor (Article 10); the right to an adequate standard of living for oneself and one's family, including adequate food, clothing and housing and to the continuous improvement of living conditions (Article 11, GC No. 4/1991,[19] and GC No. 7/1997 on the right to housing,[20] GC No. 12/1999 on the right to food,[21] and GC No. 15/2002 on the right to water[22]); the right to the highest attainable standard of physical and mental health (Article 12, GC No. 14/2000,[23] and GC No. 22/2016[24]); the right to education (Articles 13 and 14, GC No. 13/1999,[25] and GC No. 11/1999[26]); the right to take part in cultural life

---

[16]  CESCR, General Comment No. 18: The right to work (Article 6) (6 February 2006) E/C.12/GC/18.

[17]  CESCR, General Comment No. 23: The right to just and favourable conditions of work (27 April 2016) E/C.12/GC/23.

[18]  CESCR, General Comment No. 19: the right to social security (04 February 2008) E/C.12/GC/19.

[19]  CESCR, General Comment No. 4: the right to adequate housing (13 December 1991) E/1992/23.

[20]  CESCR, General Comment No. 7: the right to adequate housing (20 May 1997) E/1998/22.

[21]  CESCR, General Comment No. 12: the right to adequate food (12 May 1999) E/C.12/1999/5.

[22]  CESCR, General Comment No. 15: the right to water (20 January 2003) E/C.12/2002/11.

[23]  CESCR, General Comment No. 14: the right to the highest attainable standard of health (11 August 2000) E/C.12/2000/4.

[24]  CESCR, General Comment No. 22: the right to sexual and reproductive health (02 May 2016) E/C.12/GC/22.

[25]  CESCR, General Comment No. 13: the right to education (08 December 1999) E/C.12/1999/10.

[26]  CESCR, General Comment No. 14: the right to the highest attainable standard of health (10 May 1999) E/C.12/1999/4.

and to benefit from scientific progress (Article 15 and GC No. 21/2009[27]), and the right of everyone to benefit from the protection of the moral and material interests resulting from any scientific, literary or artistic production of which he or she is the author (Article 15 and GC No. 17/2005[28]). Part B of this book focuses on the contours and development of each of these rights.

## 2.2   State Obligations

States have general and specific obligations under the ICESCR. General obligations established in the ICESCR include the obligation of the State to progressively realize Covenant rights 'to the maximum of its available resources' and to do so 'by all appropriate means, including particularly the adoption of legislative measures'[29] on non-discrimination,[30] including equal rights of women and men to the enjoyment of Covenant rights.[31] Other general obligations that have been developed by the CESCR in General Comments and concluding observations include the concept of minimum core obligations, and non-retrogression. Specific State obligations encompass the obligations to respect, protect, and fulfill.

### 2.2.1   General obligations

#### 2.2.1.1   *Maximum availability*
States must use the maximum of their available resources 'towards fully realizing the provisions of the Covenant'.[32] The CESCR is 'called upon to scrutinize very carefully the extent to which the State concerned has taken steps to the maximum of its available resources to provide the greatest possible protection for the economic, social and cultural rights of each individual living within its jurisdiction'.[33]

By available resources, the ICESCR refers to 'both the resources existing within a State as well as those available from the international community through international cooperation'.[34] Available resources also include possible taxation measures or measures to address corruption and tax evasion.[35] This is a complex and relatively undeveloped area that is analyzed more fully in Chapter 17.

---

[27]   CESCR, General Comment No. 21: the right of everyone to take part in cultural life (21 December 2009) E/C.12/GC/21.
[28]   CESCR, General Comment No. 17: the right of everyone to benefit from the protection of the moral and material interests resulting from any scientific, literary or artistic production of which he or . she is the author (12 January 2006) E/C.12/GC/17.
[29]   ICESCR Article 2(1).
[30]   ICESCR Article 2(2).
[31]   ICESCR Article 3.
[32]   ECOSOC, An Evaluation of the Obligation to Take Steps to the 'Maximum of Available Resources' Under an Optional Protocol to the Covenant (10 May 2007) E/C.12/2007/1 para 5.
[33]   CESCR, General Comment No. 8: The relationship between economic sanctions and respect for economic, social and cultural rights (12 December 1997) E/C.12/1997/8 para 10.
[34]   Ibid 32.
[35]   CESCR, General Comment No. 24: State Obligations under the International Covenant on Economic, Social and Cultural Rights in the Context of Business Activities (23 June 2017) E/C.12/ CG/24 paras. 15, 23, 37.

*2.2.1.2    Minimum core*

As described in more detail in Chapter 13, CESCR has stated that States also have 'a minimum core obligation to ensure the satisfaction of, at the very least, minimum essential levels of each of the rights [...]'.[36]

> Thus, for example, a State party in which any significant number of individuals is deprived of essential foodstuffs, of essential primary health care, of basic shelter and housing, or of the most basic forms of education is, prima facie, failing to discharge its obligations under the Covenant. [...] [I]t must be noted that any assessment as to whether a State has discharged its minimum core obligation must also take account of resource constraints applying within the country concerned.[37]

This minimum core obligation is closely connected to the maximum availability obligation:

> In order for a State party to be able to attribute its failure to meet at least its minimum core obligations to a lack of available resources, it must demonstrate that every effort has been made to use all resources that are at its disposition in an effort to satisfy, as a matter of priority, those minimum obligations.[38]

As it is clarified in Chapter 13, the obligation of progressive realization based on available resources and subject to a standard of reasonableness remains the central obligation of States, of which minimum core is a component. States' obligations should never be reduced to minimum core obligations alone. When States fail to meet even a minimum core obligation with respect to a particular right, however, this is a *prima facie* violation that can only be justified based on extraordinary circumstances.

*2.2.1.3    Progressive realization and non-retrogression*

Article 2 (1) of the ICESCR establishes the State obligation to take steps 'with a view to achieving progressively the full realization of the rights recognized' in the Covenant. According to the CESCR, the idea of progressive realization constitutes

> on the one hand, a necessary flexibility device, reflecting the realities of the real world and the difficulties involved for any country in ensuring full realization of economic, social and cultural rights. On the other hand, the phrase must be read in the light of the overall objective, indeed the raison d'être, of the Covenant which is to establish clear obligations for states parties in respect of the full realization of the rights in question. It thus imposes an obligation to move as expeditiously and effectively as possible towards that goal.[39]

Non-retrogression is therefore the rule that: 'any deliberately retrogressive measures [...] would require the most careful consideration and would need to be fully justified by reference to the totality of the rights provided for in the Covenant and in the context of the full use of the maximum available resources.'[40]

---

[36]    CESCR, General Comment No. 3: The nature of States parties obligations (14 December 1990) E/1991/23 para 10.
[37]    Ibid para 10.
[38]    Ibid para 10.
[39]    Ibid para 9.
[40]    Ibid para 9.

Although the CESCR has recognized that the obligations of progressive realization and maximum of available resources should be analyzed with some flexibility, such State obligations should also be interpreted in light of the standard of reasonableness, as described in Chapters 13 and 14. The CESCR has stated that the following criteria should be considered:

> (a) the extent to which the measures taken [by the State party] were deliberate, concrete and targeted towards the fulfilment of economic, social and cultural rights; (b) whether the State party exercised its discretion in a non-discriminatory and non-arbitrary manner; (c) whether the State party's decision (not) to allocate available resources is in accordance with international human rights standards; (d) where several policy options are available, whether the State party adopts the option that least restricts Covenant rights; (e) the time frame in which the steps were taken; (f) whether the steps had taken into account the precarious situation of disadvantaged and marginalized individuals or groups and, whether they were non-discriminatory, and whether they prioritized grave situations or situations of risk.[41]

### *2.2.1.4    Non-discrimination*

The State obligation of non-discrimination is described broadly by Article 2.2 of the ICESCR and General Comments no. 5,[42] 6,[43] 16,[44] and 20,[45] covering discrimination based on 'race, color, sex, language, religion, political or other opinion, national or social origin, property, birth or other status'.[46] By other status, the CESCR has understood disability, age, marital and family status, sexual orientation and gender identity, health status, place of residence, and economic situation.[47] The State obligation not to discriminate encompasses formal and substantive forms of discrimination as well as direct and indirect discrimination.[48] 'Eliminating formal discrimination requires a State ensuring that its constitution, laws and policy documents do not discriminate on prohibited grounds', while eliminating substantive discrimination requires 'eliminating discrimination in practice'.[49] States should pay

> sufficient attention to groups of individuals which suffer historical or persistent prejudice instead of merely comparing the formal treatment of individuals in similar situations. States parties must therefore immediately adopt the necessary measures to prevent, diminish and eliminate the conditions and attitudes, which cause or perpetuate substantive or de facto discrimination. For example, ensuring that all individuals have equal access to adequate housing, water and sanitation will help to overcome

---

[41]    Ibid 32 para 8.

[42]    CESCR, General Comment No. 5: Persons with Disabilities (09 December 1994) E/1995/22.

[43]    CESCR, General Comment No. 6: The economic, social and cultural rights of older persons (24 November 1995).

[44]    CESCR, General Comment No. 16: The equal right of men and women to the enjoyment of all economic, social and cultural rights (11 August 2005) E/C.12/2005/4.

[45]    CESCR, General Comment No. 20: Non-discrimination in economic, social and cultural rights (2 July 2009) E/C.12/GC/20 paras. 28-35.

[46]    Ibid paras 28–35.

[47]    Ibid paras 28–35

[48]    CESCR, General Comment No. 16: The equal right of men and women to the enjoyment of all economic, social and cultural rights (2 July 2009) E/C.12/2005/4.

[49]    CESCR, General Comment No. 20: Non-discrimination in economic, social and cultural rights (2 July 2009) E/C.12/GC/20 paras. 8-10.

discrimination against women and girl children and persons living in informal settlements and rural areas.[50]

States also have the obligation to eliminate direct discrimination, which 'occurs when an individual is treated less favourably than another person in a similar situation for a reason related to a prohibited ground; e.g. where employment in educational or cultural institutions or membership of a trade union is based on the political opinions of applicants or employees', and indirect discrimination, which occurs when apparently neutral laws, policies or practices 'have a disproportionate impact on the exercise of Covenant rights as distinguished by prohibited grounds of discrimination. For instance, requiring a birth registration certificate for school enrolment may discriminate against ethnic minorities or non-nationals who do not possess, or have been denied, such certificates.'[51]

Finally, States have the obligation not only to eliminate discrimination but also to promote equality. 'Temporary special measures may sometimes be needed in order to bring disadvantaged or marginalized persons or groups of persons to the same substantive level as others'.[52]

### 2.2.2 Specific obligations to respect, protect, and fulfill

States have also specific obligations to respect, protect, and fulfill rights. According to the CESCR, the

> obligation to respect requires states parties to avoid measures that hinder or prevent the enjoyment of [a right]. The obligation to protect requires states parties to take measures that prevent third parties from interfering with the enjoyment of [a right]. The obligation to fulfil (facilitate) requires States to take positive measures that enable and assist individuals and communities to enjoy the right [...]. Finally, states parties have an obligation to fulfil (provide) [...] a specific right in the Covenant when an individual or group is unable, for reasons beyond their control, to realize the right themselves by the means at their disposal.[53]

The obligations to respect, protect and fulfill the equal right of men and women to the enjoyment of all economic, social and cultural rights includes, respectively, the obligation 'to refrain from discriminatory actions that directly or indirectly result in the denial of the equal right of men and women to their enjoyment of economic, social and cultural rights',[54] the obligation 'to take steps aimed directly at the elimination of prejudices, customary and all other practices that perpetuate the notion of inferiority or superiority of either of the sexes, and stereotyped roles for men and women',[55] and the obligation 'to promote equal representation of men and women in public office and decision-making bodies'.[56] The obligation to fulfill the right of

---

[50]  Ibid paras 8–10.

[51]  Ibid paras 8–10.

[52]  CESCR, General Comment No. 16: The equal right of men and women to the enjoyment of all economic, social and cultural rights (2 July 2009) E/C.12/2005/4 para 15.

[53]  CESCR, General Comment No. 13: The right to education (8 December 1999) E/C.12/1999/10. See also CESCR, General Comment No. 16: The equal right of men and women to the enjoyment of all economic, social and cultural rights (2 July 2009) E/C.12/2005/4 para 17.

[54]  CESCR, General Comment No. 16: The equal right of men and women to the enjoyment of all economic, social and cultural rights (2 July 2009) E/C.12/2005/4 para 18.

[55]  Ibid para 19.

[56]  Ibid para 21.

everyone to take part in cultural life requires States to include, for instance, 'cultural education at every level in school curricula'.[57] The State obligation to fulfill the right of everyone to benefit from the protection of the moral and material interests resulting from any scientific, literary or artistic production of which he or she is the author requires States to take 'financial and other positive measures which facilitate the formation of professional and other associations representing the moral and material interests of authors, including disadvantaged and marginalized authors'.[58]

Considering the right to education (further discussed in Chapter 7), the obligations to respect, protect, and fulfill the right to education includes the obligation to do so in regard to

> each of [its] essential features (availability, accessibility, acceptability, adaptability) […] [A] State must respect the availability of education by not closing private schools; protect the accessibility of education by ensuring that third parties, including parents and employers, do not stop girls from going to school; fulfil (facilitate) the acceptability of education by taking positive measures to ensure that education is culturally appropriate for minorities and indigenous peoples, and of good quality for all; fulfil (provide) the adaptability of education by designing and providing resources for curricula which reflect the contemporary needs of students in a changing world; and fulfil (provide) the availability of education by actively developing a system of schools, including building classrooms, delivering programmes, providing teaching materials, training teachers and paying them domestically competitive salaries.[59]

## 3.    MECHANISMS OF PROTECTION

Beyond the protection of ESCR by a number of UN Treaty Bodies, as mentioned in Chapter 1, and beyond the CESCR's review of State reports and issuing of General Comments, noted above under Section 1 of this chapter, the OP-ICESCR has adopted three additional mechanisms of protection: inter-State communications, individual communications, and an inquiry procedure.

A State party to the OP-ICESCR may initiate inter-State communications, if it understands that another State party to the OP-ICESCR is not fulfilling its obligations under the ICESCR. Inter-State communications are an opt-in clause, which is applicable upon a declaration of a State party, recognizing the competence of the CESCR to analyze such communications.[60] Inter-State complaints are not often utilized. In 2018, three inter-State communications were submitted for the first time in history under another international Covenant, ICERD.[61] By 30

---

[57]    CESCR, General Comment No. 21: Right of everyone to take part in cultural life (21 December 2009) E/C.12/CG/2.

[58]    CESCR, General Comment No. 17: The right of everyone to benefit from the protection of the moral and material interests resulting from any scientific, literary or artistic production of which he or she is the author (12 January 2006) E/C.12/CG/17.

[59]    CESCR, General Comment No. 13: The right to education (8 December 1999) E/C.12/1999/10 para 50.

[60]    Article 10, OP-ICESCR.

[61]    OHCHR, 'Human Rights Bodies – Complaints Procedures' <www.ohchr.org/en/hrbodies/tbpetitions/pages/hrtbpetitions.aspx>.

July 2020, five States had made the declaration that they accepted inter-State communications under the OP-ICESCR: Belgium, El Salvador, Finland, San Marino, and Portugal.[62]

The CESCR can also start an inquiry procedure, which could include an onsite visit to a State party, if the Committee receives reliable information indicating grave or systematic violations concerning any rights under the ICESCR. This, too, is an opt-in clause, requiring not only ratification of the OP-ICESCR but also explicit declaration by the State party recognizing the competence of the CESCR to initiate inquiry procedures.[63] By 19 July 2020, the same five States mentioned in the previous paragraph had also recognized the competence of the CESCR to conduct inquiry procedures under Article 11 of the OP-ICESCR.[64] According to Article 11 of the OP-ICESCR and the OP-ICESCR's Rules of Procedure, all documents and proceedings regarding inquiry procedures are confidential.[65]

In addition to inter-State communications, and to the reporting and inquiry procedures, the CESCR can also consider communications brought by individuals claiming violations of any rights under the ICESCR.[66] Individual communications are the strongest mechanism of protection available under the CESCR. Both individuals and groups of individuals may submit communications, claiming violations of rights recognized by the ICESCR. Following a general rule in international human rights law, claimants must exhaust domestic remedies before applying to the CESCR, unless such remedies are unreasonably prolonged. Communications should be submitted within one year of exhaustion and only in regard to facts occurring after ratification of the OP-ICESCR by the challenged State party, unless the facts pertain to a continuing violation. Communications will not be considered admissible if the same matter has already been examined by the CESCR or by another international human rights body; if the communication is incompatible with the ICESCR, manifestly ill-founded, or exclusively based on the media; if there is an abuse of the right to submit a communication; or if it is anonymous or not in writing.[67] Approximately two thirds of individual communications considered by the CESCR between the OP-ICESCR's entry into force in 2013 and October 2018 have been declared inadmissible.[68]

Individual communications are subject to the CESCR's assessment of a clear disadvantage.[69] Such criterion should not be perceived as an admissibility requirement, as it is subject to the discretion of the CESCR in case there is an excessive caseload.[70]

---

[62] United Nations Treaty Collection, OP-ICESCR, Declarations made under Articles 10 and 11, <https://treaties.un.org/pages/ViewDetails.aspx?src=TREATY&mtdsg_no=IV-3-a&chapter=4>.

[63] Article 11, OP-ICESCR.

[64] United Nations Treaty Collection, 'OP-ICESCR, Declarations Made under Articles 10 and 11', <https://treaties.un.org/pages/ViewDetails.aspx?src=TREATY&mtdsg_no=IV-3-a&chapter=4>.

[65] CESCR, Provisional rules of procedure under the Optional Protocol to the International Covenant on Economic, Social and Cultural Rights, adopted by the Committee at its forty-ninth session (15 January 2013) E/C.12/49/3 Rule 25.

[66] OP-ICESCR Article 2.

[67] OP-ICESCR Article 3.

[68] OHCHR, 'Recent Jurisprudence' <http://juris.ohchr.org/en/search/results/1?sortOrder=Date&typeOfDecisionFilter=0&countryFilter=0&treatyFilter=0>.

[69] OP-ICESCR Article 4.

[70] Christian Courtis and Juliana Rossi, 'Individual Complaints Procedure', in Malcolm Langford, Bruce Porter et al (eds), *The Optional Protocol to the International Covenant on Economic, Social and Cultural Rights* (PULP 2016) 59.

Individual communications are addressed in light of the 'reasonableness of the steps taken by State parties' to implement the ICESCR without merely conceding States a margin of appreciation. The adoption of reasonableness as standard of review gives States the flexibility to adopt 'a range of possible policy measures of implementation',[71] while establishing benchmarks to assess progress. The CESCR issued a statement in 2007 on maximum availability of resources that enunciated such benchmarks. As mentioned before, the CESCR should assess, under the standard of reasonableness, whether a State party has taken non-discriminatory, timely, deliberate, and concrete measures, which least restrict Covenant rights and which take into consideration the risks for disadvantaged and marginalized individuals or groups.[72]

Requests for interim measures may be presented at any time between the receipt of an individual communication and before the determination of merits to avoid irreparable damage to the victims. The CESCR has the discretion to decide whether or not to grant interim measures.[73] Between 2017 and mid-2018, the CESCR issued 18 interim measures against evictions in Spain, in situations where plaintiffs established a lack of adequate alternative housing. The practice brings the UN Committee closer to the protection of ESCR on the ground, increasing levels of effectiveness. Under close monitoring of local movements, organizations and activists, the decisions of the CESCR have, moreover, raised visibility of the problem of evictions in Spain.[74]

In March 2019 there were 46 cases already communicated to State parties pending before the CESCR: 44 against Spain, one against Luxembourg, and one against Belgium. Of those cases, 45 related to the right to housing (44 specifically to evictions), and one to union rights.[75] Between May 2013 and January 2018, the CESCR analyzed 23 cases.[76]

By July 2020, the CESCR had adopted Views on seven cases: five of them against Spain, one against Ecuador, and one against Italy, regarding the rights to housing, social security, and health.[77] In all cases where the CESCR found a violation, it issued not only individual recommendations but also general recommendations, in order to guarantee non-repetition. In its first housing rights cases, the CESCR recognized the connection between ESCR and due process guarantees, to protect individuals from abusive evictions (*I.D.G. v Spain*, 2015),[78] and

---

[71]   Melish (n 7).
[72]   ECOSOC (n 32).
[73]   OP-ICESCR Article 5.
[74]   Diego Sanz Paratcha, 'La lluvia fina de las órdenes de la ONU contra los desahucios en España', *El Salto* (18 July 2018) <www.elsaltodiario.com/vivienda/desahucios-medidas-cautelares-onu-espa%C3%B1a>.
[75]   CESCR, 'Table of Pending Cases Before the Committee on Economic, Social and Cultural Rights, considered under the Optional Protocol to the International Covenant on Economic, Social and Cultural Rights' <www.ohchr.org/en/hrbodies/cescr/pages/pendingcases.aspx>. See also OHCHR, 'Italy: Forced Pregnancy Violated a Woman's Human Right to Health, Say UN Experts', Geneva (27 March 2019) <www.ohchr.org/EN/NewsEvents/Pages/DisplayNews.aspx?NewsID=24411&LangID=E>.
[76]   CESCR, 'Statistical Survey of Individual Complaints Dealt with by the Committee on Economic, Social and Cultural Rights under the Optional Protocol to the International Covenant on Economic, Social and Cultural Rights' (January 2018) <www.ohchr.org/en/hrbodies/cescr/pages/cescrindex.aspx>.
[77]   OHCHR, Jurisprudence <http://juris.ohchr.org/Search/Results>.
[78]   CESCR, *I.D.G. v Spain* (17 June 2015) E/C.12/55/D/2/2014. See also Daniela Ikawa and Chris Grove, 'Historic Step towards Access to Justice for ESCR Violations at the UN', Open Global Rights (1 December 2015), <www.opendemocracy.net/en/openglobalrights-openpage/historic-step-towards -access-to-justice-for-escr-violatio/>.

it applied the principles of reasonableness and maximum availability of resources in order to assure alternative housing, especially to vulnerable groups (*Ben Djazia et al v Spain*, 2017).[79] In 2019 and 2020, the CESCR again issued Views on the right to adequate housing. In the 2019 case, the CESCR established that authorities should 'assess the proportionality of the aim pursued by the measure relative to the consequences for the persons evicted, and its compatibility with the Covenant in all cases, including when the properties are occupied, without legal title'.[80] In the 2020 case, the CESCR considered relevant issues of gender and disability, while assessing the plaintiff's right to adequate housing.[81] The Committee also consolidated the possibility of third party interventions, increasing not only civil society participation but also the overall contextual knowledge around each individual communication.[82] In its first case on pension rights, the CESCR analyzed the connection between ESCR and gender-based discrimination, concluding that 'States must review restrictions on access to social security schemes to ensure that they do not discriminate against women in law or in fact (General Comment n. 19 para 30)', recognizing that 'the persistence of stereotypes and other structural causes, women spend much more time than men in unpaid work' (*Trujillo Calero v Ecuador*, 2018).[83] Finally, in its first case on health rights, the CESCR addressed the issue of reproductive care, ruling that Italy had 'violated a woman's human right to health after laws around fertility treatment led her to undergo a forced pregnancy'.[84] The CESCR established that the State parties have the obligation to assure 'the appropriate conditions to enable [one's] right to access in vitro fertilization treatments', including with respect to the 'right to withdraw [one's] consent', and to ensure protection 'from any unwanted medical intervention' (*S.C. and G.P. v. Italy*, 2019).[85] Cases on social security, health, and housing rights are further discussed in Chapters 6, 9, and 10, respectively.

## 4.   IMPLEMENTATION PROCEDURE FOR COMMUNICATIONS

Aside from addressing initial cases at a relatively fast pace, the CESCR has also envisioned a participatory implementation procedure that could lead to greater efficiency of the UN Treaty Body System. The implementation procedure, or the 'follow up process for individual communications', is regulated by Article 9 of the OP-ICESCR, which establishes that State parties 'shall submit to the Committee, within six months, a written response, including information on any action taken in the light of the views and recommendations of the Committee'.

In June 2017, this follow up process was further detailed by the CESCR in its 'Working methods concerning the Committee's follow-up to Views under the Optional Protocol to the International Covenant on Economic, Social and Cultural Rights'.[86] The CESCR strengthened implementation by establishing a non-confidential procedure and by allowing for the partici-

---

[79]   CESCR, *Ben Djazia et al v Spain* (20 June 2017) E/C.12/61/D/5/2015 paras 20–21.
[80]   CESCR, *López Alban v. Spain* (11 October 2019) E/C.12/66/D/37/2018 para 17.
[81]   CESCR, *Gómez-Limón Pardo v. Spain* (5 March 2020).
[82]   See, for instance, Ikawa and Grove (n 78).
[83]   CESCR, *Trujillo Calero v Ecuador* (26 March 2018) E/C.12/63/D/10/2015 para 13.4.
[84]   OHCHR (n 75).
[85]   CESCR, *S.C. and G. v Italy* (28 March 2019) E/C.12/65/D/22/2017 paras 13–14.
[86]   CESCR, 'Working Methods Concerning the Committee's Follow-up to Views under the Optional Protocol to the International Covenant on Economic, Social and Cultural Rights, Adopted by the CESCR

pation in the process not only of plaintiffs but also of third party interveners, such as national human rights institutions and NGOs. The CESCR's decision to make the follow up process public and participatory goes hand in hand with the standard of reasonableness adopted by the CESCR in its analysis of merits, and with the principle of non-repetition adopted in a number of Views by the Human Rights Committee.[87]

This participatory process of implementation has already been applied to CESCR's Views on *Ben Djazia et al v Spain*,[88] regarding the protection of the right to housing in Spain. A number of NGOs that had already intervened as amicus briefs in the case joined housing movements in Spain in order to guarantee implementation. The monitoring group, which includes Observatori DESC (Spain), Centro de Asesoría y Estudios Sociales, CAES (Spain), Amnesty International, Plataforma de los Afectados por Hipotecas (Spain), and SRAC (Canada), among others, has covered an ample number of activities, from making the CESCR Views available to the general public to fostering a dialogue between the CESCR and the Spanish Public Defenders' Office.[89]

## 5.    CONCLUSION

While the entry into force of the Optional Protocol in 2013 strengthened the view that ESCR matter as much as civil and political rights, the recent establishment of a participatory follow up process could enhance the levels of implementation at the UN Treaty Body System. In the coming years, joint work between a strong CESCR and innovative NGOs might increase the System's visibility not only in the protection of ESCR but also in the protection of human rights more broadly.

In the same timeframe, the adjudication of ESCR in international, regional, and domestic courts might further develop the connection between rights and public policies, towards a rights-oriented social reform which will be more effective in the protection of rights for the most vulnerable groups. The strengthening of ESCR protection for the most vulnerable groups have been shown to be extremely urgent, in light of the 2020 pandemic and in light of the pandemic's disproportionate effects on those living in poverty, women, persons with disabilities, immigrants, and racial minorities.

---

at its 61th session (29 May–23 June 2017) <www.ohchr.org/Documents/HRBodies/CESCR/Follow -upViews.docx>.

[87]    See, for instance, ESCR-Net, Key Proposals regarding the Follow-up on Views Issued by UN Human Rights Treaty Bodies, Discussion Paper, 2016 <www.escr-net.org/sites/default/files/ attachments/key_proposals_regarding_the_follow-up_on_views_issued_by_un_human_rights_treaty _bodies_0.pdf>.

[88]    See n 79.

[89]    See, for instance, the website: ESCR-Net, 'Implementing UN CESCR Decisions on Housing Issues in Spain', <https://www.escr-net.org/group/2562/area/2980>; and ESCR-Net, 'The Right to Housing in Spain: MBD v Spain [Ben Djazia et al v. Spain]' (June 2018).

# 3. The African system

## Lilian Chenwi

## 1. INTRODUCTION

The African human rights system (AHRS) is the 'least-resourced' and youngest of the three most well established current regional human rights systems;[1] yet it 'may be singled out as holding the most promise for the realization of justiciable economic, social and cultural rights' (ESCR).[2] It initially functioned under the auspices of the Organization of African Unity (OAU), and later (up to the present day) the African Union (AU).[3] Its establishment was a response to, inter alia, Africa's slave trade and colonial history, during which the oppression of African people and denial of various violations of human rights, including health, livelihood, and culture, was evident.[4] For instance, there was land grabbing from African people, and the imposition upon them of foreign cultures at the cost of African cultures and traditions.[5]

The AHRS was unveiled with the adoption of the African Charter on Human and Peoples' Rights (African Charter),[6] which has as one of its unique features the recognition of ESCR alongside civil and political rights (CPR) and peoples' rights, and both use the same enforcement mechanisms.[7] This chapter considers the normative frameworks on ESCR and the mechanisms relevant to their enforcement in the AHRS. As the focus is at the regional level, sub-regional ESCR frameworks are not considered.[8] Following this introduction, Section 2 of the chapter discusses the evolution of ESCR at the African regional level. Section 3 sets out the specific ESCR recognized in key regional human rights treaties and correlating 'general' state

---

[1]   Rhona K.M. Smith, *International Human Rights Law* (9th edn, OUP 2020) 126 and 142; Philip Alston and Ryan Goodman, *International Human Rights* (OUP 2013) 1025.

[2]   Frans Viljoen, 'Regional Institutional and Remedial Arrangements for the Judicial Enforcement of Economic, Social and Cultural Rights in Africa' in Danwood M. Chirwa and Lilian Chenwi (eds), *The Protection of Economic, Social and Cultural Rights in Africa: International, Regional and National Perspectives* (CUP 2016) 245.

[3]   On the transition from OAU to AU, see Lee Stone, 'A Court Not Found?' (2007) 7(2) African Human Rights Law Journal 522, 524–25.

[4]   Danwood M. Chirwa and Lilian Chenwi, 'The Protection of Economic, Social and Cultural Rights in Africa' in Chirwa and Chenwi (n 2) 3; Bience Gawanas, 'The African Union: Concepts and Implementation Mechanisms relating to Human Rights' in Anton Bösl and Joseph Diescho (eds), *Human Rights in Africa: Legal Perspectives on Their Protection and Promotion* (Konrad Adenauer Stiftung 2009) 136.

[5]   Chirwa and Chenwi (n 4) 4.

[6]   Adopted 27 June 1981, entered into force 21 October 1986, CAB/LEG/67/3 rev. 5, 1520 UNTS 217. African Charter preamble.

[7]   Danwood Mzikenge Chirwa, 'African Regional Human Rights System: The Promise of Recent Jurisprudence on Social Rights' in Malcolm Langford (ed), *Social Rights Jurisprudence: Emerging Trends in International and Comparative Law* (CUP 2008) 323.

[8]   On ESCR at African sub-regional level, see generally, Solomon T. Ebobrah, 'Sub-regional Judicial Enforcement of Economic, Social and Cultural Rights' in Chirwa and Chenwi (n 2) 274–301.

obligations. Section 4 considers key African regional mechanisms relevant to the enforcement of ESCR. Section 5 concludes the chapter.

## 2.    EVOLUTION OF ESCR WITHIN OAU/AU

The development of ESCR within the OAU/AU should be understood against the background of the development of African regional human rights law (HRL), as it establishes the extent to which ESCR or related principles featured in the various stages of African regional HRL's evolution.

A disenchanting state of regional human rights *law* existed in pre-1979 Africa. The first call (in 1961, contained in the Law of Lagos) for the adoption of 'an African Convention on Human Rights'[9] was not taken seriously by African governments, with no immediate response to the call. Subsequent instruments – the Charter of the Organization of African Unity (OAU Charter)[10] and the Convention Governing the Specific Aspects of Refugee Problems in Africa (African Refugee Convention)[11] – bear testimony to the resistance to and non-prioritization of human rights at the time. The resistance could be attributed to the fact that newly independent African states viewed human rights as 'an imposition of the departing colonial masters on the newly established independent states'.[12]

The OAU's focus on territorial sovereignty, independence, and non-interference in the internal affairs of states resulted in inadequate attention to human rights.[13] Though recognizing the need to guarantee 'the welfare and wellbeing of [African] peoples',[14] the OAU Charter only reiterated member states' adherence to the principles of the Charter of the United Nations (UN Charter)[15] and the Universal Declaration of Human Rights (UDHR)[16] and required member states to give 'due regard' to these treaties in the context of international cooperation,[17] as well as to 'coordinate and harmonize their general policies' on, inter alia, '[e]conomic cooperation', '[e]ducational and cultural cooperation', and '[h]ealth, sanitation, and nutritional cooperation'.[18]

The African Refugee Convention that followed failed to include explicit human rights provisions, beyond prohibiting member states from rejecting, returning, or expelling persons

---

[9]    Centre for Human Rights, University of Pretoria (in collaboration with the African Commission on Human and Peoples' Rights), *A Guide to the African Human Rights System: Celebrating 30 Years Since the Inauguration of the African Commission on Human and Peoples' Rights 1987–2017* (PULP 2017) 1.

[10]    Adopted 25 May 1963, entered into force 13 September 1963, 479 UNTS 39.

[11]    Adopted 10 September 1969, entered into force 20 January 1974, 1001 UNTS 45.

[12]    Chirwa and Chenwi (n 4) 4–5.

[13]    B. Obinna Okere, 'The Protection of Human Rights in Africa and the African Charter on Human and Peoples' Rights: A Comparative Analysis with the European and American Systems' (1984) 6(2) Human Rights Quarterly 141, 142; Chidi Anselm Odinkalu, 'Implementation of Economic, Social and Cultural Rights under the African Charter on Human and Peoples' Rights' in Malcolm Evans and Rachel Murray (eds), *The African Charter on Human and Peoples' Rights: The System in Practice, 1986–2000* (CUP 2002) 178–218, 180.

[14]    OAU Charter preamble.

[15]    Adopted 26 June 1945, entered into force 24 October 1945, 1 UNTS XVI.

[16]    Adopted 10 December 1948, A/810 at 71.

[17]    OAU Charter preamble and Article 2(1)(e).

[18]    Ibid Article II(2)(b)(c) and (d), respectively.

in the context where their 'life, physical integrity or liberty would be threatened'.[19] However, it expanded the definition of refugees, from one that is subjective and restrictive to one that includes objective circumstantial (socio-political) factors, with implications for ESCR. The definition goes beyond that provided by the UN,[20] by also including persons who flee their country of residence 'owing to external aggression, occupation, foreign domination or events seriously disturbing public order in either part or the whole of his country of origin or nationality'.[21] Factors that can be considered under the broadened definition include 'serious natural disasters', such as famine,[22] which implicates ESCR with regard to matters such as food and other rights relating to socio-economic livelihood. In addition, 'entitlements' or 'indirect rights' are implicit in obligations such as the obligation to grant asylum to refugees (which is 'a peaceful and humanitarian act').[23] This would give rise to human rights/ESCR entitlements.[24]

The 1980s saw the adoption of the first regional human rights instrument: the African Charter, in 1981.[25] It guarantees ESCR and CPR equally[26] – a ground-breaking stance, considering that it was adopted at a time when the justiciability of ESCR at the international level was still highly contested. Its recognition of ESCR was a response to the 'dire poverty', and other pressing socio-economic needs relating to, for example, water, housing, and food, that Africa was experiencing at the time, and was 'an acknowledgement that accountability through the law was part of the solution'.[27] However, there was a fear of burdening the newly independent states with many obligations;[28] as a result, a limited number of ESCR were explicitly recognized.

The 1990s saw the intensification of democratic change in Africa and the associated adoption of new constitutions at the national level,[29] resulting in renewed attention and progressive steps relevant to human rights at the regional level. Two key regional treaties were adopted. First was the African Charter on the Rights and Welfare of the Child (African Children's Charter or ACRWC),[30] which recognizes children's CPR and ESCR.[31] The reasons for its

---

[19]   African Refugee Convention Article 2(3).
[20]   See Article 1 of the Convention Relating to the Status of Refugees, adopted 28 July 1951, entered into force 22 April 1954, 189 UNTS 137.
[21]   African Refugee Convention Article 1(1) and (2).
[22]   Frans Viljoen, *International Human Rights Law in Africa* (2nd edn, OUP 2012) 243.
[23]   African Refugee Convention Article 2(2).
[24]   Viljoen (n 22) 242.
[25]   See Section 3.1 below.
[26]   African Charter preamble. See also, African Commission on Human and Peoples' Rights (African Commission), Principles and Guidelines on the Implementation of Economic, Social and Cultural Rights in the African Charter on Human and Peoples' Rights (24 October 2011), preamble and para 21 (ESCRP&G). The principle of indivisibility has been relevant in the enforcement of the recognized ESCR in the Charter and has also facilitated the use of recognized ESCR and other rights such as life, equality and dignity in the Charter as tools to recognize new ESCR (see Lilian Chenwi, 'Permeability of Rights in the Jurisprudence of the African Commission' (2014) 39(Supp) South African Yearbook of International Law 93, 98–106).
[27]   Viljoen (n 22) 215.
[28]   Ibid; Manisula Ssenyonjo, 'The Protection of Economic, Social and Cultural Rights under the African Charter' in Chirwa and Chenwi (n 2) 91–120, 92–93.
[29]   Chirwa and Chenwi (n 4) 5; Viljoen (n 22) 161.
[30]   Adopted 1 July 1990, entered into force 29 November 1999, CAB/LEG/24.9/49 (1990).
[31]   See Section 3.2 below.

adoption were both political and legal: a response to the perceived marginalization of African states in the drafting of the Convention on the Rights of the Child (CRC),[32] and the need for legal protection that addresses, inter alia, the 'socio-economic, cultural, traditional and developmental circumstances, natural disasters, armed conflicts, exploitation and hunger' that rendered the situation of most African children critical.[33] However, there was still some resistance to binding human rights instruments at the time, and it took a decade for the African Children's Charter to come into force.[34]

The second treaty was the Protocol to the African Charter on Human and People's Rights on the Establishment of the African Court on Human and Peoples' Rights (ACtHPR Protocol),[35] which established the African Court on Human and Peoples' Rights (ACtHPR or African Human Rights Court) to adjudicate cases of violations of human rights in the African Charter and other treaties ratified by the relevant African state.[36]

The year 2000 ushered in the AU, established through the adoption of the Constitutive Act of the African Union (AUCA),[37] with subsequent expansion of the scope of recognized human rights – including ESCR – through the adoption of additional regional human rights treaties. The AU, unlike the OAU, has an explicit human rights mandate: to promote and protect human and peoples' rights in the African Charter and other relevant human rights instruments.[38] The AUCA also requires that 'due regard' be given to the UN Charter and UDHR in the context of international cooperation.[39] The AU's objectives include cooperating with international partners in the 'eradication of preventable diseases and the promotion of good health on the continent'.[40] The AU's principles include respect for human rights and '[p]romotion of social justice to ensure balanced economic development'.[41] The AU Executive Council is required to coordinate and take policy decisions in the areas of, inter alia, '[f]ood, agricultural and animal resources, livestock production and forestry', '[w]ater resources and irrigation', 'environmental protection, humanitarian action and disaster response relief', '[e]ducation, culture, health', and '[s]ocial security, including the formulation of mother and child care policies, as well as policies relating to [persons with disabilities (PWD)]'.[42] The possibility for civil society organizations (CSOs) to have a voice within AU institutions and decision making processes relating to ESCR, for example, is made possible through the establishment of the Economic, Social and Cultural Council as an advisory organ of the AU.[43] However, observance of human rights is not explicitly stated as a requirement for admission to the AU.[44]

---

[32]   Adopted 20 November 1989, entered into force 2 September 1990, 1577 UNTS 3 (1989).

[33]   ACRWC preamble; Viljoen (n 22) 391–92.

[34]   Viljoen (n 22) 162.

[35]   Adopted 10 June 1998, entered into force 25 January 2004, OAU/LEG/EXP/AFCHPR/PROT (III).

[36]   See Section 4.3 below.

[37]   Adopted 11 July 2000, entered into force 26 May 2001, CAB/LEG/23.15.

[38]   AUCA preamble & Article 3(h).

[39]   Ibid Article 3(e).

[40]   Ibid Article 3(n).

[41]   Ibid Article 4(l)–(p). Emphasis added.

[42]   Ibid Article 13(1)(c)–(e), (h) and (k).

[43]   Ibid Article 22. See also African Union, 'The Economic, Social and Cultural Council (ECOSOCC)' <https://au.int/en/organs/ecosocc>.

[44]   For criticisms of the AUCA from a human rights perspective, see Viljoen (n 22) 165–66.

The period from 2001 to the present has seen further recognition and advancement of ESCR, through the AU's adoption of policy initiatives and treaties and, as seen in Sections 3 and 4 of this chapter, through regional mechanisms' development, interpretation, and enforcement of ESCR. One such policy initiative is the New Partnership for Africa's Development (NEPAD), a program of action for the redevelopment of the African continent, which advances ESCR through its focus on, inter alia: improving access to water and sanitation, education and health; poverty reduction; achieving food security through improving agricultural performance; protection and nurturing of culture; and socio-economic development.[45] As regards key human rights treaties adopted by the AU, the following are worth noting. First is the Protocol to the African Charter on Human and Peoples' Rights on the Rights of Women in Africa (African Women's Protocol or AWP),[46] which recognizes women's CPR, ESCR, and collective rights.[47] Its significance is threefold: it remedies the inadequacy of the African Charter in relation to women's issues/rights and includes rights that are not explicitly recognized in the African Charter; the scope of ESCR is stated in much more detail in the Protocol than in the Convention on the Elimination of All Forms of Discrimination against Women;[48] and it 'is the first treaty to place "medical abortion" [and] HIV/AIDS ... in a binding human rights framework'.[49] Second is the Protocol to the African Charter on Human and Peoples' Rights on the Rights of Older Persons (African Older Persons Protocol or AOPP),[50] which recognizes older persons' CPR and ESCR.[51] Its adoption was based on, inter alia, the need 'to institute urgent measures aimed at addressing' the needs of older persons such as access to resources, employment, health services, basic social services (food, shelter, water and clothing, among others), and recognition of the fundamental role of older persons in society.[52] Third is the Protocol to the African Charter on Human and Peoples' Rights on the Rights of Persons with Disabilities in Africa (African Disability Protocol or ADP),[53] which recognizes PWD's CPR and ESCR.[54] Its adoption was based on, inter alia, concerns regarding, for example, 'human rights violations, systematic discrimination, social exclusion, prejudice within political, economic and social spheres', and 'high levels of poverty' experienced by PWD; hence the need for a legal framework to address the concerns.[55]

The AU has thus deepened Africa's human rights/ESCR commitments. It has given more prominence to the socio-economic well-being of African people, which can be achieved through, inter alia, the recognition and enforcement of ESCR.

---

[45]  See generally, New Partnership for Africa's Development Framework Document, October 2001 <www.nepad.org/publication/new-partnership-africas-development>.

[46]  Adopted 13 September 2000, entered into force 25 November 2005, CAB/LEG/66.6 (2001) 1 African Human Rights Law Journal 40, Annex A.

[47]  See Section 3.3 below.

[48]  Adopted 18 December 1979, entered into force 3 September 1981, 1249 UNTS 13; 19 ILM 33 (1980).

[49]  Viljoen (n 22) 254.

[50]  Adopted 31 January 2016, not yet in force.

[51]  See Section 3.4 below.

[52]  AOPP preamble.

[53]  Adopted 29 January 2018, not yet in force.

[54]  See Section 3.5 below.

[55]  ADP preamble.

# 3.    SPECIFIC ESCR AND STATE OBLIGATIONS

This section focuses on examining key African regional human rights instruments, with a view to highlighting the ESCR rights explicitly or implicitly recognized, other rights with ESCR dimensions, and the correlating obligations of states and non-state actors. In relation to obligations, due to the limited scope of the chapter, the focus is states parties' general obligations and those relating to special measures of protection, as well as the obligations on non-states parties. Of note is the fact that specific provisions within the treaties contain specific obligations to be read together with the general obligations.

## 3.1    African Charter

### 3.1.1    Specific ESCR
The ESCR guaranteed by the African Charter can be classified under 'explicit' and 'implicit' ESCR. In addition to the explicit ESCR ('individual ESCR'), there are group (peoples') rights that, at least in part, have ESCR dimensions or implicate ESCR ('collective ESCR').[56] Explicitly recognized individual ESCR in the African Charter are property,[57] work (under equitable and satisfactory conditions),[58] health,[59] education,[60] and culture.[61] Collective ESCR in the African Charter include: self-determination (which includes the right of people to pursue socio-economic development);[62] free disposal of wealth and natural resources;[63] economic, social and cultural development;[64] and general satisfactory environment favorable to development.[65] In addition, the African Commission, the supervisory body of the African Charter,[66] has, based on a joint reading of explicitly recognized CPR and/or ESCR in the Charter, established that certain ESCR are implicitly recognized in the Charter. These are the rights to: housing (which includes a prohibition against unjust evictions), implicit in rights to property, health, and protection of the family, read together;[67] food, implicit in the rights to life, health,

---

[56]    For further reading on African Charter group rights in the context of ESCR, see Danwood M. Chirwa, 'Group Rights and the Protection of Economic, Social and Cultural Rights' in Chirwa and Chenwi (n 2) 212–42.

[57]    African Charter Article 14; ESCRP&G (n 26) paras 51–55.

[58]    African Charter Article 15; ESCRP&G (n 26) paras 56–59.

[59]    African Charter Article 16; ESCRP&G (n 26) paras 60–67.

[60]    African Charter Article 17; ESCRP&G (n 26) paras 68–71.

[61]    African Charter Articles 17(2) and (3), 18(1) and (2); ESCRP&G (n 26) paras 72–76.

[62]    African Charter Article 20; ESCRP&G (n 26) paras 41–47.

[63]    African Charter Article 21. On the importance of the freedom to dispose of wealth and natural resources, see *Social and Economic Rights Action Centre and the Centre for Economic and Social Rights v Nigeria*, Communication No. 155/96 (2001) AHRLR 60 (ACHPR 2001) para 56 (*SERAC*).

[64]    African Charter Article 22. See also *Centre for Minority Rights Development (Kenya) and Minority Rights Group International on behalf of Endorois Welfare Council v Kenya*, Communication No. 276/2003, (2009) AHRLR 75 (ACHPR 2009) paras 277–98 (*Endorois*).

[65]    African Charter Article 24.

[66]    See Section 4.1 below.

[67]    *SERAC* (n 63) para 60; ESCRP&G (n 26) para 77 (see also paras 78–79). See further, *Sudan Human Rights Organisation and Centre on Housing Rights and Evictions v Sudan*, Communication Nos 279/03 and 296/05 (2009) AHRLR 153 (ACHPR 2009) (*Sudan*) paras 186 and 189 (right not to be forcibly evicted or displaced derived from the right to freedom of movement and residence).

and economic, social and cultural development, read together;[68] social security, implicit in 'but not limited to' the rights to life, dignity, liberty, work, food, health, protection of the family, and protection of the 'aged' and 'disabled', read together;[69] and water and sanitation, implicit in 'but not limited' to the rights to life, dignity, work, food, health, economic, social and cultural development, and a satisfactory environment.[70] The ESCR have to be enjoyed without discrimination, in law or practice.[71]

### 3.1.2 General obligations

The general obligation of African Charter states parties is to 'recognize the rights, duties and freedoms enshrined in [Chapter I of the Charter]' and 'adopt legislative or other measures to give effect to them'.[72] Three points are worth noting in relation to the formulation of the general obligation. First, it does not contain any territorial limitation; hence, it is capable of extraterritorial reach.[73] Second, the provision is not formulated with internal limitations of 'progressive realisation' and 'within available resources'; however, these have been found to be implicit in the Charter.[74] Despite the recognition of obligations of progressive character, the African Charter also imposes immediate obligations on states parties, which 'include but are not limited to the obligation to take steps, the prohibition of retrogressive steps, minimum core obligations and the obligation to prevent discrimination in the enjoyment of economic, social and cultural rights'.[75] Third, despite the use of 'or' in the provision, the African Commission and ACtHPR are of the view that both legislative *and* other measures are required. Considering the 'overarching applicability' of the provision, the violation or non-achievement of any of the rights, duties, and freedoms would result in consequential violation of the relevant state's general obligation.[76] The general obligation encompasses an obligation to ensure key elements of ESCR: availability, adequacy, physical and economic accessibility (affordability), and acceptability.[77] The African Charter also requires states to adopt special measures of protection

---

[68] *SERAC* (n 63) para 60; ESCRP&G (n 26) para 83 (see also paras 84–86).
[69] ESCRP&G (n 26) para 81 (see also paras 81–82).
[70] ESCRP&G (n 26) para 87 (see also paras 88–93). See further, *Sudan* (n 67) paras 209–10 and 212 (interdependency of the right to water and the right to health), and *Free Legal Assistance Group v Zaire*, Communication Nos. 25/89, 47/90, 56/91 and 100/93, 2000 AHRLR 74 (ACHPR 1995) para 211 (*Free Legal Assistance*) (interdependency of the right to water and the right to health).
[71] African Charter Articles 2 and 3 (see also Article 19); *Purohit and Moore v The Gambia*, Communication No. 241/2001, (2003) AHRLR 96 (ACHPR 2003) para 49 (*Purohit*).
[72] African Charter Article 1; ESCRP&G (n 26) para 2.
[73] On extraterritorial reach of the African Charter, see Lilian Chenwi and Takele Soboka Bulto, 'Extraterritoriality in the African Regional Human Rights System from a Comparative Perspective' in Lilian Chenwi and Takele Sboka Bulto (eds), *Extraterritorial Human Rights Obligations from an African Perspective* (Intersentia 2018) 13, 19–22 (see also 22–35 on extraterritorial dimensions of other African Charter obligations and some Charter rights, and 36–41 on the African Commission's jurisprudence on the extraterritorial reach of the African Charter).
[74] ESCRP&G (n 26) para 13.
[75] Ibid para 16 (see also paras 17–20 elaborating on each of these immediate obligations; immediate obligations are also outlined under the respective ESCR).
[76] See, for example, *African Commission on Human and Peoples' Rights v Kenya*, Application No. 006/2012, Judgment (ACtHPR 2017) paras 214–17 (*Ogiek*).
[77] ESCRP&G (n 26) para 3.

in relation to the family, women and children (as guaranteed in international instruments), and older persons and persons with disability ('in keeping with their physical or moral needs').[78]

In addition to states' duties, the African Charter provides for individual duties towards other individuals, the family, society, state, other legally recognized communities, and the international community.[79] Individuals have to exercise their ESCR 'with due regard to the rights of others, collective security, morality and common interest'.[80]

## 3.2     African Children's Charter

### 3.2.1     Specific ESCR

The ACRWC guarantees a limited number of ESCR for children:[81] education,[82] culture,[83] health,[84] nutrition,[85] and housing.[86] In addition, the right to survival and development has ESCR dimensions,[87] relating to, for example, access to nutrition, early childhood development services, and primary health care.[88] The right to name and nationality is also crucial to the enjoyment of ESCR,[89] based on its interdependence with the rights to health, education, and social welfare, and the right to inherit property.[90] The ESCRs have to be enjoyed 'irrespective of the child's or his/her parents' or legal guardians' race, ethnic group, colour, sex, language, religion, political or other opinion, national and social origin, fortune, birth or other status'.[91] Other key principles relevant to ESCR of children include the 'best interests of the child' principle (requiring that '[i]n all actions concerning the child undertaken by any person or authority the best interests of the child shall be the primary consideration')[92] and the right to free participation ('either directly or through an impartial representative').[93]

### 3.2.2     Duties

The general obligation on ACRWC states parties is to 'recognize the rights, freedoms and duties enshrined in [the African Children's] Charter' and take 'the necessary steps, in accord-

---

[78]   African Charter Article 18. For further elaboration on the nature and context of the right to protection of the family in the context of ESCR, see ESCRP&G (n 26) paras 93–95.

[79]   African Charter Articles 27–29.

[80]   Ibid Article 27(2).

[81]   A child is defined in the ACRWC Article 2, as 'every human being below the age of 18 years'.

[82]   Ibid Article 11.

[83]   Ibid Article 12.

[84]   Ibid Article 14.

[85]   Ibid Article 20.

[86]   Ibid.

[87]   Ibid Article 5.

[88]   ACERWC, General Comment No. 5: State Party Obligations under the African Charter on the Rights and Welfare of the Child (Article 1) and Systems Strengthening for Child Protection (2018) 12 (link between socio-economic rights (SER) and right to survival and development). See also Julia Sloth-Nielsen, 'The Protection of Children's Economic, Social and Cultural Rights under the African Children's Charter in Chirwa and Chenwi (n 2) 155–79, 163 and 165–66.

[89]   ACRWC Article 6.

[90]   ACERWC, General Comment No. 2: Right to Birth Registration, Name and Nationality (16 April 2014) ACERWC/GC/02 paras 31–32 and 35–36.

[91]   ACRWC Article 3; ACERWC, General Comment No. 5 (n 88) 9–11.

[92]   ACRWC Article 4(1); ACERWC, General Comment No. 5 (n 88) 11–12.

[93]   ACRWC Articles 4(2) and 7; ACERWC, General Comment No. 5 (n 88) 13–14.

ance with their Constitutional processes and with the provisions of the present Charter, to adopt such legislative or other measures as may be necessary to give effect to the provisions of this Charter'.[94] Thus, as in the African Charter, no reference is made to progressive realization or resources. However, these are implicit in the African Children's Charter in relation to both CPR and ESCR, and progressive realization 'must be understood in the context of the urgency required to fulfil children's rights'.[95] The African Children's Charter also makes provision for 'special' measures of protection, with correlating state obligations, for children with disabilities, or special needs and for children in identified vulnerable situations.[96] The use of the word 'special', as interpreted by the ACERWC, 'implies a much higher level of obligation for states parties than that required in ordinary circumstances'.[97]

In addition to states' obligations, the African Children's Charter places 'responsibilities' on parents (or other persons responsible for a child) and on children. Parents 'have the primary responsibility of the upbringing and development of the child' and 'the duty' to, inter alia, 'secure, *within their abilities and financial capacities,* conditions of living necessary to the child's development'.[98] Children, subject to 'age', 'ability', and 'limitations' in the African Children's Charter, 'have responsibilities towards [their] family and society, the State and other legally recognized communities and the international community'.[99]

### 3.3 African Women's Protocol

#### 3.3.1 Specific ESCR

The AWP guarantees the following women's ESCR: education and training;[100] economic and social welfare rights ('equal opportunities in work and career advancement and other economic opportunities');[101] health, including sexual and reproductive health;[102] food security (including access to clean drinking water);[103] adequate housing;[104] positive cultural context;[105] and property rights.[106] Other rights in the AWP that have ESCR dimensions are the right to a healthy and sustainable environment,[107] and the right to sustainable development (which

---

[94]  ACRWC Article 1.
[95]  ACERWC, General Comment No. 5 (n 88) 6–8.
[96]  Ibid Articles 13, 17, 25, 26 and 30.
[97]  ACERWC, General Comment No. 1: Children of Incarcerated and Imprisoned Parents and Primary Caregivers (8 November 2013) para 34.
[98]  ACRWC Article 20(1). Emphasis added.
[99]  Ibid Article 31. For elaboration on children's duties, see generally, ACERWC General Comment No. 3: Article 31 of the African Charter on the Rights and Welfare of the Child on the Responsibilities of the Child (2017).
[100]  AWP Article 12.
[101]  Ibid Article 13.
[102]  Ibid Article 14. See also: African Commission, General Comment No. 1: Article 14 (1) (d) and (e) of the Protocol to the African Charter on Human and Peoples' Rights on the Rights of Women in Africa (6 November 2012); African Commission, General Comment No. 2: Article 14 (1) (a), (b), (c) and (f) and Article 14 (2) (a) and (c) of the Protocol to the African Charter on Human and Peoples' Rights on the Rights of Women in Africa (28 November 2014).
[103]  AWP Article 15.
[104]  Ibid Article 16.
[105]  Ibid Article 17.
[106]  Ibid Article 21.
[107]  Ibid Article 18.

includes, inter alia, 'women's access to and control over productive resources such as land and their right to property').[108] The ESCR rights are to be enjoyed without discrimination.[109] The right to participation recognized in the AWP is also relevant in ensuring that women participate in decision making processes relating to ESCR policies and programs.[110]

### 3.3.2   Duties

The general obligation of AWP states parties is 'to adopt all necessary measures and in particular ... provide budgetary and other resources for the full and effective implementation of the rights' therein.[111] Prioritization of resources for the realization of ESCR relevant to social development and promotion of women (including their rights), is evidenced in the obligation on states to 'take the necessary measures to reduce military expenditure significantly in favour of spending on social development in general, and the promotion of women in particular'.[112] States are further required to ensure 'special protection' for elderly women,[113] women with disabilities,[114] and women in distress,[115] in line with their 'physical, economic and social needs', and to take 'appropriate' measures to realize the rights of rural women,[116] and of widows.[117] The AWP further acknowledges that violence against women can be addressed through, inter alia, realization of ESCR where socio-economic deprivations are the cause of such violence.[118]

Unlike the African Charter and ACRWC, the African Women's Protocol does not include a provision on the general duties of women towards, for instance, society or the state. However, in the context of social welfare rights, the Protocol recognizes that 'parents bear the primary responsibility for the upbringing and development of children' and that 'the State and the private sector have secondary responsibility' in this regard.[119]

### 3.4   African Older Persons Protocol

### 3.4.1   Specific ESCR

The ESCR of older persons guaranteed in the AOPP relate to:[120] employment (non-discrimination in employment and appropriate work opportunities);[121] adequate social protection;[122]

---

[108]   Ibid Article 19.
[109]   Ibid preamble and Article 2. See also Article 12(1)(a) and (b).
[110]   See for example, ibid preamble and Articles 9, 17, 18(2)(a), 19(b), 23(a).
[111]   Ibid Article 26(2). See also Article 4(2)(i) (states to 'provide adequate budgetary and other resources' in the prevention and eradication of violence against women, which as highlighted in the Protocol has a socio-economic dimension).
[112]   AWP Article 10(3).
[113]   Ibid Article 22.
[114]   Ibid Article 23.
[115]   Ibid Article 24.
[116]   Ibid Articles 14(2)(a) and 19(d).
[117]   Ibid Article 20.
[118]   Ibid Articles 4(2)(b) and 5. See also preamble and Articles 2(1)(b), 2(2).
[119]   Ibid Article 13(l).
[120]   AOPP Article 1, defines older persons as 'those persons aged sixty (60) years and above'.
[121]   Ibid Article 6.
[122]   Ibid Article 7.

'access to health services that meet their specific needs';[123] access to education;[124] land and property rights of older women;[125] and culture.[126] In addition, the provisions on care and support,[127] as well as those on residential care,[128] have an ESCR dimension, as they facilitate provision of ESCR such as housing to older persons. Despite acknowledging in its preamble that water and food are among the basic social services to which older persons should have access, the Protocol fails to include specific provisions on these rights. However, based on the principle of interdependence of rights, states are not freed from duties relating to these rights. The ESCR have to be enjoyed without discrimination, including equal protection before the law.[129] Recognition of the right to make decisions and to actively participate in socio-economic development ensures that the voice of older persons will be heard in relation to the development and implementation of ESCR policies and programs affecting them or their well-being.[130]

### 3.4.2   Duties

The general obligation of AOPP states parties is two-fold: to 'recognize the rights and freedoms enshrined in [the] Protocol', which includes the adoption of 'legislative or other measures to give effect to them', and to include in their national laws, as legally binding principles, the United Nations Principles of Independence, Dignity and Self-fulfilment, Participation and Care of Older Persons of 1991.[131] In addition, states have specific obligations in relation to older women,[132] older persons with disabilities,[133] and older persons living in situations of conflict and disaster.[134] States are further required to provide 'financial, material and other support' to older persons taking care of vulnerable children.[135]

The AOPP also places duties on older persons 'towards their families, their communities, the wider society, the state and international community'.[136] The duties are however more limited than individuals' duties in the African Charter, focusing on knowledge and experience transfer, mentorship, conflict mediation and resolution, and fostering and facilitating inter-generational dialogue and solidarity.

---

[123]   Ibid Article 15.
[124]   Ibid Article 16
[125]   Ibid Article 9.
[126]   Ibid Article 17.
[127]   Ibid Article 10.
[128]   Ibid Article 11.
[129]   Ibid Articles 3 and 4. See also Article 5(1).
[130]   Ibid Articles 5 and 17.
[131]   Ibid Article 2.
[132]   Ibid Article 9.
[133]   Ibid Article 13.
[134]   Ibid Article 14.
[135]   Ibid Article 12.
[136]   Ibid Article 20.

### 3.5     African Disability Protocol

#### 3.5.1     Specific ESCR
The ESCR of persons with disabilities guaranteed in the ADP are:[137] education (which includes 'inclusive quality education');[138] health (which includes sexual and reproductive health and right of women and girls with disabilities 'to retain and control their fertility');[139] work;[140] adequate standard of living ('for themselves and their families, which includes adequate food, access to safe drinking water, housing, sanitation and clothing, continuous improvement of living conditions and social protection');[141] and culture.[142] In addition, the right to live in the community has an ESCR dimension, as it relates to, inter alia, housing/shelter.[143] These ESCR have to be enjoyed without discrimination, in law and practice.[144] Other general principles that underpin the realization of ESCR of persons with disabilities include full and effective participation, reasonable accommodation,[145] accessibility, and best interests of the child.[146]

#### 3.5.2     Duties
The general duty on ADP states parties is to 'take appropriate and effective measures, including policy, legislative, administrative, institutional and budgetary steps, to ensure, respect, promote, protect and fulfil the rights and dignity of persons with disabilities, without discrimination on the basis of disability'.[147] This obligation includes ensuring that 'adequate resources, including through budgetary allocations' are put in place for the 'full implementation' of rights.[148] The steps to be taken by states, in the context of ensuring accessibility, have to be 'reasonable and progressive'.[149] In addition, there are specific ESCR obligations in relation to women and girls with disabilities,[150] children with disabilities,[151] youth with disabilities,[152] and older persons with disabilities.[153]

---

[137]   ADP Article 1, defines persons with disabilities to 'include those who have physical, mental, psycho-social, intellectual, neurological, developmental or other sensory impairments which in interaction with environmental, attitudinal or other barriers hinder their full and effective participation in society on an equal basis with others'.
[138]   Ibid Articles 16 and 28(i).
[139]   Ibid Articles 17, 27(k), 29(h) and 30(f).
[140]   Ibid Article 18.
[141]   Ibid Article 20.
[142]   Ibid Articles 25 and 27(i).
[143]   Ibid Article 14.
[144]   Ibid Articles 5–7.
[145]   Reasonable accommodation is defined as 'necessary and appropriate modifications and adjustments where needed in a particular, to ensure to persons with disabilities the enjoyment or exercise on an equal basis with others of all human and peoples' rights' (ibid Article 1).
[146]   Ibid Article 3.
[147]   Ibid Article 4.
[148]   Ibid Article 4(i).
[149]   Ibid Article 15(2).
[150]   Ibid Article 27.
[151]   Ibid Article 28.
[152]   Ibid Article 29.
[153]   Ibid Article 30.

The ADP also places duties on persons with disabilities 'on an equal basis with other persons as elaborated in the African Charter'.[154] The provision however goes further than the African Charter, by placing an obligation on states to assist and support persons with disabilities through, inter alia, 'reasonable accommodations', as required in the fulfillment of their duties.[155]

# 4. ENFORCEMENT MECHANISMS

This section focuses on the institutional arrangements under the treaties considered in Section 3 of this chapter. These are the African Commission, ACERWC, and ACtHPR. It also considers, briefly, the African Peer Review Mechanism (APRM) under NEPAD. As specific ESCR cases are considered in the chapters on rights in this book, the section does not discuss specific decisions of the bodies considered.

## 4.1 African Commission

The African Commission is a quasi-judicial body established under the African Charter.[156] It consists of 11 members (commissioners) which are nominated by states parties to the African Charter and elected by the AU Assembly, but serve in their personal capacity. The Commission has both promotional and protective mandates with regard to the African Charter, AWP, AOPP, and ADP. It is also mandated to '[p]erform any other tasks which may be entrusted to it by the [AU Assembly]'.[157]

The African Commission's promotional mandate includes promoting human and peoples' rights through research, dissemination of information and cooperation with other human rights institutions, formulating and adopting human rights principles and rules, and reviewing states' implementation through examination of state reports on realization of human and peoples' rights.[158] Accordingly, the African Commission has adopted general comments, resolutions, and principles, including in the area of ESCR. Examples include the African Commission's ESCR Principles and Guidelines, which elaborate on ESCR in the African Charter and correlating state obligations;[159] Pretoria ESCR Declaration, which highlights, among others, state obligations and constraints to be tackled in relation to ESCR;[160] General Comment No. 2 on reproductive health rights;[161] and General Comment No. 3 on the right to life, which establishes the link between the right to life and ESCR, stating, inter alia, that 'progressive realisation of various economic, social and cultural rights will contribute to securing a full and dignified

---

[154] Ibid Article 31(1).

[155] Ibid Article 31(2).

[156] See African Charter Articles 30–44.

[157] Ibid Article 45(4).

[158] Ibid Articles 45(1) and 62; AWP Article 26(1); AOPP Article 22(1); ADP Article 34(1).

[159] ESCRP&G (n 26).

[160] Pretoria Declaration on Economic, Social and Cultural Rights in Africa (2004) <www.achpr.org/sessions/36th/resolutions/73/>.

[161] African Commission, General Comment No. 2 (n 102).

life'.[162] Through its promotional mandate, the African Commission has also established special mechanisms, some of which have an ESCR-specific mandate. Sections 4.1.1 and 4.1.2 below further elaborate on state reporting and special mechanisms.

The protective mandate of the African Commission includes interpreting the provisions of the African Charter, AWP, AOPP, and ADP, which it can do through its communications procedure (elaborated on in Section 4.1.3 below); alternatively, it can refer the matter of interpretation and enforcement to the ACtHPR.[163] The Commission's protective mandate also includes onsite or fact finding investigative missions.[164]

### 4.1.1   State Reporting Procedure

State parties to the African Charter, AWP, AOPP, and ADP are required to submit periodic reports ('every two years') to the African Commission 'on the legislative or other measures taken' towards realization of the rights and freedoms guaranteed by these treaties.[165] The Commission has developed guidelines for state reports, including ESCR-specific reporting guidelines. These are: the 1989 Reporting Guidelines;[166] the 1998 Simplified Reporting Guidelines;[167] the AWP Reporting Guidelines;[168] the ESCR Reporting Guidelines;[169] and the African Charter Articles 21 and 24 Reporting Guidelines.[170] NGOs participate in the process through submission of shadow or alternative reports, but lack of access to state reports has diminished the impact of their participation.[171] An ESCR Section is included in the African Commission's concluding observations under Sections on both positive aspects and areas of concern (this structure is evident in more recent concluding observations).[172] Other Sections

---

[162]   African Commission, General Comment No. 3: The Right to Life (Article 4) (12 December 2015) para 34 (see also paras 41–42).

[163]   African Charter Article 45(3) (see also Article 45(2)); AWP Article 32 (though the ACtHPR is currently tasked with interpretation (AWP Article 27), the Court can transfer cases to the Commission and, in dealing with admissibility, it can seek the Commission's opinion); AOPP Article 22(2) (see also Article 22(3)); ADP Article 34(3) (see also Article 34(4)).

[164]   This is undertaken by virtue of African Charter Article 46.

[165]   African Charter Article 62; AWP Article 26(1); AOPP Article 22(1); ADP Article 34(1).

[166]   Guidelines for National Periodic Reports (1989) <www.achpr.org/files/instruments/guidelines _national_periodic_reports/achpr_guide_periodic_reporting_1989_eng.pdf>.

[167]   Guidelines for National Periodic Reports under the African Charter (1998), reprinted in Christof Heyns and Magnus Killander, *Compendium of Key Human Rights Documents of the African Union* (6th edn, PULP 2016) 199.

[168]   Guidelines for State Reporting under the Protocol to the African Charter on Human and Peoples' Rights on the Rights of Women in Africa (2010), reprinted in Heyns and Killander (n 167) 200–02.

[169]   State Party Reporting Guidelines for Economic, Social and Cultural Rights in the African Charter on Human and Peoples' Rights (2011) <www.achpr.org/files/instruments/economic-social -cultural-guidelines/achpr_instr_tunis_reporting_guidelines_esc_rights_2012_eng.pdf> (also referred to as 'Tunis Reporting Guidelines').

[170]   State Reporting Guidelines and Principles on Articles 21 And 24 of the African Charter relating to Extractive Industries, Human Rights and the Environment (2017) <www.achpr.org/files/instruments/ state-reporting-guidelines/state_reporting_guidelines_and_principles_on_articles_21_and_24_eng .pdf>.

[171]   Christof Heyns and Magnus Killander, 'Africa' in Daniel Moeckli, Sangeeta Shah and Sandesh Sivakumaran (eds), *International Human Rights Law* (OUP 2018) 474.

[172]   See, for example, Concluding Observations and Recommendations on Sixth Periodic Reports of the Republic of Namibia on the Implementation of the African Charter on Human and Peoples' Rights (2011–2013) (20th Extra-Ordinary Session 2016) para 12 and 32; Concluding Observations and

on, for example, women's rights, refugees, and indigenous peoples' rights, as well as on other rights, also deal with some ESCR aspects. The state reporting procedure's effectiveness is, however, hampered by many challenges, including tardiness in reporting and non-compliance with recommendations.

### 4.1.2 Special mechanisms

The special mechanisms established by the African Commission comprise special rapporteurs, working groups, and committees. Of particular relevance to ESCR is the Working Group on Economic, Social and Cultural Rights, established in 2004, with a mandate to 'develop and propose' ESCR principles and guidelines, 'elaborate' on ESCR state reporting guidelines, 'undertake studies and research on specific [ESCR]', and report regularly on its work.[173] Its mandate was subsequently expanded, requiring it to further define 'State obligations related to access to medicines and to develop model monitoring and assessment guidelines'[174] and to perform any other tasks relating to the principles and guidelines developed.[175] Members of the Working Group are Commissioners of the African Commission and experts (from, for example, academia or NGOs). Other special mechanisms such as the Committee on the Protection of the Rights of People Living with HIV (PLHIV) and Those at Risk, Vulnerable to and Affected by HIV,[176] the Working Group on the Rights of Older Persons and Persons with Disabilities, and the respective special rapporteurs on women, refugees, and prison conditions – among others – are also relevant in enforcing ESCR as applicable within their respective mandates.

### 4.1.3 Complaints procedure

The African Commission's protective mandate in relation to rights violations is fulfilled in cooperation with the ACtHPR, since the Commission, as stated above, can refer cases to the Court. The Commission's complaints procedure consists of individual complaints ('other communications')[177] and inter-state complaints ('communications from states').[178]

As regards individual complaints, the African Charter is silent on who can bring a complaint, but the African Commission's practice establishes that complaints can be brought by individuals and NGOs. The applicants have to comply with several admissibility requirements.[179] The African Commission has addressed ESCR violations in a number of cases, finding violations

---

Recommendations on the Combined Second Periodic Report under the African Charter on Human and Peoples' Rights and the Initial Report under the Protocol to the African Charter on the Rights of Women in Africa of the Republic of South Africa (20th Extra-Ordinary Session 2016) para 11 and 31.

[173] African Commission, Resolution 73: Resolution on Economic, Social and Cultural Rights in Africa (36th Ordinary Session 2004).

[174] African Commission, Resolution 141: Resolution on Access to Health and Needed Medicines in Africa; The African Commission on Human and Peoples' Rights (44th Ordinary Session 2008).

[175] African Commission, Resolution 193: Resolution on the Renewal of the Mandate of the Working Group on Economic Social and Cultural Rights in Africa (50th Ordinary Session 2011).

[176] African Commission, Resolution 163: Resolution on the Establishment of a Committee on the Protection of the Rights of People Living with HIV (PLHIV) and Those at Risk, Vulnerable to and Affected by HIV, The African Commission on Human and Peoples' Rights (47th Ordinary Session 2010).

[177] African Charter Articles 55–59.

[178] Ibid Articles 47–54.

[179] Ibid Article 56.

of, for example, the rights to food, to housing, to health, to property, to a general satisfactory environment, to freely dispose of wealth and natural resources, to economic, social and cultural development, and to cultural rights.[180]

The inter-state complaints procedure relates to complaints brought by a state party that 'has good reasons to believe that' another state party has violated African Charter obligations. Two avenues can be pursued: a conciliatory route (the complainant state writes to the violating state with the aim of bringing to its attention the violation so that it can address it);[181] and/ or a non-conciliatory route (direct referral of the case by the complainant state to the African Commission).[182] For the second, admissibility requirements of exhaustion of all existing local remedies has to be fulfilled ('unless it is obvious to the Commission that the procedure for achieving these remedies would be unduly prolonged').[183] The African Commission has addressed violations of ESCR in the single inter-state communication decided thus far (*Democratic Republic of the Congo v Burundi, Rwanda and Uganda*), finding a violation of the rights to, inter alia, cultural development, property, health, and education, and to freely dispose of wealth and natural resources.[184]

The African Commission's jurisprudence does not provide much clarity as to the standard of reviewing states' compliance with ESCR obligations. It has referred to reasonableness of measures and minimum core, and engaged in proportionality analysis and an interdependence approach. Though the Commission has issued significant ESCR decisions, their impact is limited by, inter alia, states' partial compliance with, or tardiness in implementing, the decisions.[185]

It should be noted that the African Commission, prior to deciding a case, may issue provisional measures to prevent irreparable harm.[186] At the time of writing, it has done so mainly in CPR cases, and in the case involving the Ogiek community relating to ESCR,[187] but the order was met with non-compliance.

## 4.2    African Children's Committee

The African Committee of Experts on the Rights and Welfare of the Child (African Children's Committee, or ACERWC) is a quasi-judicial body established under the ACRWC, with both promotional and protective mandates with regard to the ACRWC.[188] It consists of 11 members

---

[180] See generally, for example, *SERAC* (n 63), *Purohit* (n 71) and *Endorois* (n 64). For a discussion of the ESCR cases decided by the Commission, see Ssenyonjo (n 28) 99–117.

[181] African Charter Article 47.

[182] Ibid Articles 48–49.

[183] Ibid Article 50.

[184] Communication No. 227/99, (2004) AHRLR 19 (ACHPR 2003) paras 87–88 and 94–95.

[185] The *Endorois* decision, for instance, was followed by long delays in implementation as well as non-representation and non-consultation of the community in the implementation stages (see Committee on Economic, Social and Cultural Rights, Concluding Observations on the Combined Second to Fifth Periodic Reports of Kenya (6 April 2016) E/C.12/KEN/CO/2-5 paras 15 and 16).

[186] Rules of Procedure of the African Commission on Human and Peoples' Rights (47th Ordinary Session 2010) rule 98.

[187] See *Ogiek* (n 76) paras 4–5. The Commission referred the case to the ACtHPR after the state failed to respond to the Commission's provisional measures request.

[188] ACRWC Articles 32 and 42.

elected by the AU Assembly from a list of persons nominated by states parties to the ACRWC, who serve in their personal capacity.[189]

The ACERWC's promotional mandate includes promoting children's rights in the ACRWC through research and information dissemination, formulation and adoption of rules and principles on the rights and welfare of African children and monitoring implementation through, for example, examining state reports.[190] As part of its promotional mandate, it has adopted general comments such as General Comment No. 5, which as stated above establishes the link between SER and the right to survival and development.[191] It has also established special mechanisms. Sections 4.2.1 and 4.2.2 elaborate on ACERWC state reporting and special mechanisms.

The Committee's protective mandate includes interpreting the provisions of the ACRWC and investigative missions.[192] Unlike the African Commission, the ACERWC is not able to refer contentious cases to the ACtHPR but can bring requests for advisory opinions before the Court.[193] The Committee is further mandated to '[p]erform such other task as may be entrusted to it by the Assembly of Heads of State and Government, Secretary-General of the [AU] and any other organs of the [AU] or the United Nations'.[194] The complaints procedure of the ACERWC is further elaborated on in Section 4.2.3 below.

### 4.2.1 State reporting procedure

States parties to the ACRWC are required to submit periodic reports on measures adopted and progress made in the implementation of the African Children's Charter.[195] Initial reports are to be submitted after two years following the entry into force of the treaty for the state concerned, and periodic reports are to be submitted every three years.[196] Guidelines on reporting are contained in the ACRWC,[197] as well as in the Initial Reports Guidelines,[198] and there are plans to develop guidelines for periodic reports. The reporting procedure has been harmonized with the CRC, as states can re-submit reports already submitted under the CRC together with a supplementary report addressing provisions not dealt with in the CRC report.[199] NGOs can participate in the process through submission of shadow or alternative state reports. Unlike recent concluding observations of the African Commission, there is no main section titled ESCR in the concluding observations of the ACERWC. These rights are dealt with under specific rights, principles, or special protection measures. The reporting procedure under the

---

[189]  Ibid Articles 33–36.

[190]  Ibid Article 42(a) and (b).

[191]  ACERWC, General Comment No. 5 (n 88) 12.

[192]  ACRWC Articles 42(b)(c) and 45.

[193]  The ACERWC's standing before the African Human Rights Court was confirmed in *African Committee of Experts on the Rights and Welfare of the Child on the Standing of the African Committee of Experts on the Rights and Welfare of the Child before the African Court on Human and Peoples' Rights* Request No. 002/2013, Advisory Opinion (ACtHPR 2014).

[194]  ACRWC Article 42(d).

[195]  Ibid Article 43(1).

[196]  Ibid.

[197]  Ibid Articles 43(2) and (3).

[198]  Guidelines for Initial Reports of State Parties to the African Charter on the Rights and Welfare of the Child (2003), Cmttee/ACRWC/2 II Rev 2, reprinted in (2003) 3(2) *African Human Rights Law Journal* 347–53.

[199]  Ibid para 24.

ACRWC also suffers from challenges of lack of political will or tardiness in reporting and complying with recommendations made.

### 4.2.2   Special mechanisms

Like the African Commission, the ACERWC has appointed special rapporteurs under various thematic areas, including health, welfare and development, and child participation, among others. Their mandate includes standard setting and development of strategies to better promote and protect children's rights within the thematic focus, undertaking studies, conducting missions, engaging with states and non-state actors to enhance the thematic area, and bringing cases of grave violations to the attention of the ACERWC, among others.[200] Specific mandates for each special rapporteur are contained in the respective resolutions establishing the mandates.[201]

### 4.2.3   Complaints procedure

The ACRWC provides that the ACERWC 'may receive communication' from individuals, groups, or NGOs 'relating to any matter covered by this Charter'.[202] Communications can also be submitted by a state party, an intergovernmental organization, or a specialized organ or agency of the AU and the UN.[203] Guidelines on submission of complaints are contained in the African Children's Charter,[204] as well as in the Guidelines on Communications of the Committee.[205] The Guidelines on Communications also provide admissibility requirements that have to be complied with.[206] Like the African Commission, the ACERWC has powers to grant provisional measures to prevent grave or irreparable harm.[207] The ACERWC has addressed children's ESCR in its jurisprudence, finding a violation of the rights to, inter alia, health and education in *Institute for Human Rights and Development in Africa (IHRDA) and Open Society Justice Initiative (on behalf of Children of Nubian Descent in Kenya) v Kenya*,[208] and non-violation of both in *Michelo Hansungule and Others (on behalf of the Children of Northern Uganda) v Uganda*.[209] In *Centre for Human Rights (University of Pretoria) and La Rencontre Africaine pour la Defense des Droits de l'Homme (Senegal) v Senegal*, it found a violation of the rights to, inter alia, survival and development, education, health, and protection against harmful social and cultural practices.[210] The Committee's standard of reviewing states' compliance with its ESCR obligations includes applying reasonableness, due diligence and margin of discretion standards, interdependence approach and a proportionality analysis.

---

[200]   See ACERWC, 'About Special Rapporteurs' <https://acerwc.africa/about/>.
[201]   The respective resolutions are available at ACERWC, 'Special Rapporteurs' <www.acerwc.africa/special-rapporeurs/>.
[202]   ACRWC Article 44(1).
[203]   ACERWC, Revised Guidelines for the Consideration of Communications (1st Extra-Ordinary Session 2014) 3 <https://acerwc.africa/wp-content/uploads/2018/07/Revised_Communications _Guidelines_Final-1.pdf>.
[204]   ACRWC Article 44(2).
[205]   ACERWC, Revised Guidelines (n 203) 3–5.
[206]   Ibid 10.
[207]   Ibid 7–9.
[208]   Decision No. 002/Com/002/2009 (ACERWC 2011) paras 59–68.
[209]   Decision No. 001/Com/001/2005 (ACERWC 2013) paras 61–75.
[210]   Decision No. 003/Com/001/2012 (ACERWC 2014) paras 40–56 and 69–73.

**4.3      African Human Rights Court**

The ACtHPR is a judicial body with a protective mandate with regard to the African Charter and other international human rights treaties ratified by the state concerned in a case before it. The adoption of the African Court Protocol in 1998 paved the way for its establishment.[211] It consists of 11 judges from AU member states, nominated by states parties to the Protocol and elected by the AU Assembly. They act in an individual capacity.[212] The Court addresses deficiencies in the African Commission's protective mandate, as it is vested with more concrete and binding judicial powers, including remedial powers.[213] Its mandate includes contentious, advisory, and conciliatory ('amicable settlement') jurisdiction.[214]

The Court's advisory jurisdiction extends to 'any legal matter relating to the [African] Charter or any other relevant human rights instruments, provided that the subject matter of the opinion is not related to a matter being examined by the [African] Commission'.[215] It is therefore not restricted to giving its opinion on treaties ratified by the concerned states, due to the lack of such qualification in the provision. Requests for advisory opinions can be brought by a Member State of the AU, the AU, any AU organs, or any African organization recognized by the AU.[216] Individuals cannot bring such requests. NGOs that have African Commission accreditation but not AU accreditation cannot bring such requests.[217] The Court has not yet issued an advisory opinion relating to ESCR, with the only two opinions issued on the request so far relating to interpretation of standing rules.

For contentious matters, direct access to submit cases is granted to the African Commission, a state party that has lodged a complaint to the Commission, a state party against which the complaint has been lodged at the Commission, a state party whose citizen is a victim of a human rights violation, and African intergovernmental organizations.[218] Hence, as stated above, ACERWC does not have standing before the Court to bring contentious cases. For NGOs and individuals to bring cases, they have to be permitted, through an Article 34(6) declaration, by the state; NGOs must also have observer status with the African Commission.[219] This restrictive standing is problematic, limiting the ability of individuals and NGOs to bring rights claims before the Court, as states parties have been hesitant to make the relevant decla-

---

[211]   The ACtHPR is currently functioning as a separate court. But subsequent structural changes aimed at transforming it into a three chambered African Court of Justice and Human Rights, with an expanded structure and mandate, are to occur in the future. See Protocol on the Statute of the African Court of Justice and Human Rights, 2008 (merging the African Court with the AU Court of Justice; not yet in force) and Protocol on Amendments to the Protocol on the Statute of the African Court of Justice and Human Rights 2014 (creating a criminal section within the joint court; not in force).

[212]   ACtHPR Protocol Articles 11–14.

[213]   Ibid Articles 27 and 30.

[214]   Ibid Articles 3, 4, 9 and 28(3)–(4).

[215]   Ibid Article 4.

[216]   Ibid.

[217]   See, for example, *Socio Economic Rights and Accountability Project (SERAP)*, Request No. 001/2013, Advisory Opinion (ACtHPR 2017).

[218]   ACtHPR Protocol Article 5(1).

[219]   Ibid Article 5(3) read with Article 34(6).

ration.[220] The Court can also issue provisional measures to prevent irreparable harm;[221] it has done so in several cases mainly implicating CPR, but also in *Ogiek* implicating ESCR.[222] The order in *Ogiek* was met with non-compliance.[223] The jurisprudence of the Court in contentious matters has mainly dealt with CPR. However, in *African Commission on Human and Peoples' Rights v Kenya* it found a violation of the right to land, and consequential violations of rights to, inter alia, culture, free disposal of wealth and natural resources, and economic, social and cultural development.[224] The decision was met with non-compliance.[225] The Court has also, in *Association pour le Progrès et la Défense des Droits des Femmes Maliennes (APDF) and Institute for Human Rights and Development in Africa (IHRDA) v Mali*, found a violation of the right to equitable share in inheritance of property, among others.[226] In *Anudo v Tanzania*, following a violation of right to nationality, it found consequential violation of the rights to, inter alia, health and work.[227]

## 4.4    African Peer Review Mechanism

The APRM is a self-monitoring and control mechanism established by the AU to ensure compliance with principles of NEPAD.[228] The APRM process deals with a range of governance activities, of which human rights is one component. AU member states voluntarily accede to the APRM by undertaking to submit periodic peer reviews as well as facilitate such reviews. The first country review ('base review') is done within 18 months of a country becoming a member of the APRM. Periodic reviews are then undertaken every two to four years. States can also request that they be reviewed, or, where there are early signs of imminent political or economic crisis in a country, a review could also be instituted.[229] NGOs can make submissions during the review process. As with the UN Human Rights Council's Universal Periodic Review and state reporting procedure,[230] the APRM aims to facilitate dialogue between the state and society. Remedies for deficiencies are implemented through a National Programme of Action. As 'human rights' are a core component of APRM, the mechanism is relevant to

---

[220]    Only ten of the states parties to the Protocol – Benin, Burkina Faso, Cote d'Ivoire, Gambia, Ghana, Malawi, Mali, Rwanda, Tanzania, and Tunisia – had made the declaration, but Rwanda, Tanzania, Benin and Cote d'Ivoire subsequently withdrew their declaration.

[221]    ACtHPR Protocol Article 27(2).

[222]    *African Commission on Human and Peoples' Rights v Kenya*, Application No. 006/2012, Order for Provisional Measures (ACtHPR 2013).

[223]    Report on the Activities of the African Court on Human and Peoples Rights: 1 January–31 December 2016 (Executive Council 30th Ordinary Session 2017, EX.CL/999(XXX)) para 21(ii).

[224]    See generally *Ogiek* (n 76). See also *Ajavon v Benin*, Application No. 013/2017, Judgment (Merits) (ACtHPR 2019), in which the the Court reiterated its position in *Ogiek* on what the right to property comprises.

[225]    Activity Report of the African Court on Human and Peoples' Rights: 1 January–31 December 2018 (Executive Council 34 Ordinary Session 2019, EX.CL/1126(XXXIV)) paras 18(i) and 49.

[226]    Application No. 046/2016, Judgment (ACtHPR 2018) paras 111–15 and 135(vii)(ix).

[227]    Application No. 012/2015, Judgment (ACtHPR 2018) paras 118–21.

[228]    See NEPAD (n 45).

[229]    See New Partnership for Africa's Development, 'The African Peer Review Mechanism' (2003) 4 <www.dfa.gov.za/au.nepad/nepad49.pdf>.

[230]    See Chapter 1 of this book, where this mechanism is explained.

monitoring implementation of ESCR and making recommendations to remedy deficiencies hindering its realization.

## 5.   CONCLUSION

The AHRS has guaranteed a broad range of human rights – CPR, ESCR, and group rights – in binding as well as non-binding instruments. The African Charter broke ranks from the UN and other regional human rights systems in its recognition of ESCR alongside CPR and group rights, on equal footing, and as justiciable rights, at a time when the justiciability of ESCR was questionable at the international level. However, poverty, underdevelopment, pandemics in the face of defective health systems, ongoing conflicts, and inadequate implementation of human rights commitments, among other challenges, limit the ability of people to enjoy the protected ESCR. Institutional and other mechanisms exist for the enforcement of ESCR, including in cases of violations, but also have some challenges, such as restrictive access for some, and limited ability to bring ESCR claims. Lack of political will from states also affects implementation and compliance with reporting obligations and recommendations or decisions (some of which are groundbreaking) aimed at addressing deficiencies in the realization of ESCR or violations of ESCR.

# 4.   The European system
## *Colm O'Cinneide*

## 1.   INTRODUCTION

Social rights protection at national level has a long history in Europe, with the development in the twentieth century of comprehensive national welfare states built around the concept of 'social citizenship'. However, it is relatively rare for national law to provide much in the way of substantive *legal* protection for social rights, which tend, as elsewhere, to be viewed as matters best left to the political system. In contrast, greater legal protection is provided by the European regional human rights frameworks established under the auspices of the Council of Europe or the European Union (EU), which complement and at times go beyond that available under the UN system (discussed elsewhere in this book).

In particular, the vast majority of European states have agreed to be bound by the European Social Charter (ESC), a Council of Europe treaty instrument.[1] This sets out a range of binding socio-economic rights commitments and establishes two enforcement mechanisms – a state reporting system and a ground-breaking collective complaints procedure – to help ensure state parties comply with their commitments. The continent's best developed and most effective human rights mechanism, the European Convention on Human Rights (ECHR, another Council of Europe treaty instrument), also provides an indirect degree of protection for social rights. For states that are members of the EU, social rights also receive legal protection through specific elements of EU law, in particular through the provisions of the EU Charter of Fundamental Rights. However, these layers of charters and conventions are not always easy to disentangle – and the protection they offer tends to be limited in important ways.

This chapter will focus primarily on the ESC, on the basis that it is the primary regional mechanism concerned with vindicating social rights. However, the relevant aspects of ECHR and EU law will also be discussed. The first section of this chapter will focus on the evolution of social rights protection across Europe, at the national level and (principally) at the level of the ESC, ECHR and EU. The second section will set out the substance of the social rights protection provided within each of these legal frameworks. The third section will examine the challenges involved in enforcing these standards, with particular reference to the ESC.

---

[1]   The Council of Europe is a pan-European regional organization established to promote respect for human rights, democracy and rule of law: with the exception of Belarus, all European states are members, including Russia and Turkey. It should be distinguished from the European Union (EU), which was established to promote economic and political integration among its member states. The Council of Europe has 47 member states; the EU now has 27, after the UK left in January 2020.

## 2. EVOLUTION OF SOCIAL RIGHTS PROTECTION WITHIN EUROPE

To provide an overview of the social rights obligations that bind European states, it is necessary to trace the evolution of social rights thinking within the European context before turning to the three specific legal mechanisms that play the most important roles in protecting social rights at the regional level – namely the European Social Charter, the 'social dimension' of EU law, and the spill-over of civil and political rights protection under the ECHR into the domain of social rights.

### 2.1 European Concepts of Social Citizenship and the 'Social State' Principle

Social rights are sometimes viewed as a recent conceptual innovation, born out of the post-1945 expansion of international human rights law and discourse. However, within Europe, social rights have a much older history.[2] As early as 1793, the French National Convention adopted a constitutional text which acknowledged the rights to work and to receive social assistance as fundamental rights. Similar provisions were also included in some of the short-lived radical constitutions of the nineteenth century.[3] As Katrougalos has argued, they gave initial expression to the then radical idea that individuals were entitled as of right to receive protection from the state against hunger, poverty and want.[4] With the emergence of the organized trade union movement of the late nineteenth century, and the growing political strength of social democratic parties, this idea grew in strength. Beginning with Bismarck's social insurance reforms of the 1870s, and later gaining momentum in the aftermath of two devastating world wars and the Great Depression of the early 1930s, it ultimately led to the establishment after 1945 of the European welfare states.[5]

Designed to protect citizens against the more extreme consequences of capitalist commodification and inequalities in the distribution of wealth, these post-war welfare states were far from perfect.[6] However, they gave expression to the concept of 'social citizenship' as famously outlined by T.H. Marshall, whereby the state assumed responsibility for ensuring that its citizens enjoyed the 'right to a modicum of economic welfare and security' and 'to share to the full in the social heritage and to live the life of a civilized being according to the standards prevailing in the society [in question]'.[7]

At national level, a European legal concept of social rights evolved in tandem with the construction of the welfare state. By virtue of this 'social state principle', the legislative and executive arms of the state were expected, as part of their constitutional obligations, to

---

[2]  George S. Katrougalos, 'The (Dim) Perspectives of the European Social Citizenship', *Jean Monnet Working Paper 05/07* .

[3]  See e.g. Title VIII of the Portuguese Constitutional Charter of 1826, and Article 13 of the short-lived French Constitution of 1848.

[4]  Katrougalos (n 2).

[5]  See generally T. Judt, *Postwar: A History of Europe Since 1945* (Penguin 2005) 777 et seq.

[6]  See generally C. Offe, *Contradictions of the Welfare State* (Hutchinson 1984); G. Esping-Andersen, *The Three Worlds of Welfare Capitalism* (Polity 1990).

[7]  T.H. Marshall, *Citizenship and Social Class* (Pluto 1992) (reprinted from his 1949 Cambridge Lectures) at 8. See also U. Preuss, 'The Concept of Rights in the Welfare State' in G. Teubner (ed.), *Dilemmas of Law in the Welfare State* (W. de Gruyter 1986) 151–72.

establish and maintain an adequate welfare state framework in place – while courts could take this obligation into account in interpreting and applying legislation and other relevant legal standards.[8] Many European constitutional texts now contain express affirmations that they are 'social states',[9] and/or set out a list of protected social rights.[10] However, for the most part, such social rights provisions are not directly enforceable in law: they are primarily viewed as directive principles addressed to the legislative and executive branches of government, with courts being slow to intervene in the socio-economic realm.[11] As such, much of the legal protection afforded to social rights within Europe arises from attempts to embed the 'social state' principle within Council of Europe and EU supranational frameworks.

## 2.2    The Protection of Social Rights in European Regional Human Rights Framework

Furthermore, all European states remain committed to respecting social rights as part of their international human rights obligations. All European states have ratified the International Covenant on Economic, Social and Cultural Rights (ICESCR), with eight also signing up to the individual complaints procedure.[12] All European states have also ratified the eight core International Labour Organization (ILO) conventions.

### 2.2.1    The European Social Charter (ESC)
More specifically to Europe, 43 of the 47 Council of Europe member states have also ratified the European Social Charter. This is a treaty instrument established under the auspices of the Council of Europe and opened for signature in 1961. The ESC was a ground-breaking instrument, being one of the first international human rights treaties to set out a comprehensive list of social rights.[13] State parties were required to respect and give effect to these rights by virtue of the legally binding provisions of Part II of the Charter, whose detailed provisions covering a range of labor, social welfare and migrant rights were partly inspired by existing ILO standards. (See Section 3.1 below for further detail as to the substance of these commitments.)

The ESC also established a monitoring mechanism, whereby state parties were required to report periodically on how they were giving effect to their commitments under the Charter.[14] These national reports were submitted to a Committee of Independent Experts (subsequently renamed the European Committee on Social Rights). Elected by the Committee of Ministers of

---

[8]    Katrougalos (n 2) at 4.

[9]    See e.g. German Basic Law Article 20; Constitution of Spain Article 1(1); Constitution of Portugal Article 2; Constitution of Slovenia Article 2.

[10]    See e.g. Constitution of Belgium Article 23; Constitution of the Netherlands Articles 19, 20, 22; Constitution of Greece Articles 21, 22; Constitution of Portugal Articles 56, 59, 63–72, 108–09, 167, 216. See in general C. Fabre, 'Social Rights in European Constitutions' in G. De Búrca and B. De Witte (eds) *Social Rights in Europe* (Oxford University Press 2005) 15–28.

[11]    C. O'Cinneide, 'Austerity and the Faded Dream of a Social Europe' in A. Nolan (ed.) *Economic and Social Rights after the Global Financial Crisis* (Cambridge University Press 2014) 169–201.

[12]    Portugal, Spain, France, Belgium, Montenegro, Bosnia and Herzegovina, Finland and Slovakia.

[13]    It predated the UN International Covenant on Economic, Social and Cultural Rights (ICESCR) by five years.

[14]    For a general overview of the ESC monitoring system, see R. Brillat, 'The Supervisory Machinery of the European Social Charter: Recent Developments and Their Impact' in G. De Búrca and B. De Witte (eds) *Social Rights in Europe* (Oxford University Press 2005) 31.

the Council of Europe, its guiding political organ, the role of the Committee of Experts was to provide an authoritative legal interpretation of the text of the Charter and to determine whether the law and policy of state parties adhered to its requirements.[15] Its conclusions in respect of national reports were subsequently discussed by a Governmental Committee (GC) composed of officials from each of the contracting states, before being referred to the Committee of Ministers – who were given the authority to issue recommendations to states to take remedial action to bring their national law and policy into conformity with the Charter.[16]

The ESC came into force in February 1965 after having been ratified by five states, with the Committee of Independent Experts issuing its first conclusions in 1969. By 1989, this original Charter had been ratified by the great majority of Council of Europe member states.[17] By that stage, its provisions had become widely recognized as significant reference points in the development of domestic legal standards across Europe, especially in the field of labor law.[18] Furthermore, the Committee's conclusions in respect of national reports had built up a detailed interpretative framework of standards, which helped to put flesh on the bones of the Charter's requirements as they applied to specific national situations. However, the Charter also often lacked exposure, being overshadowed by the ECHR and subsequently by the gradual development of the social dimension to EU law (discussed further below). Furthermore, states often dragged their feet in responding to Committee conclusions of non-conformity, or simply disregarded them – contributing further to the uncertain profile of the Charter.

As a consequence, a formal process of 'revitalization' of the Charter was launched by the Council of Europe Ministerial Conference on Human Rights held in Rome in November 1990.[19] This aimed to update and reboot the ESC system of rights protection, increase its profile and widen its scope beyond its original primary focus on labor rights. Subsequently, a revised version of the Social Charter was opened for signature in 1996, containing an extended and modernized list of socio-economic rights. Most European states have ratified the revised ESC. Of the 47 Council of Europe member states, 33 are now bound by the updated version, with only ten still bound by the provisions of the original 1960 instrument. The extended scope of the revised Charter has helped to raise the profile of the ESC mechanism in general, especially in areas such as non-discrimination, housing, disability rights and anti-poverty policy, which had formerly only been addressed indirectly by the provisions of the original Charter. The modernized provisions of the revised Charter even give it additional 'bite' when it comes

---

[15] State parties are not under a formal legal obligation to give effect to decisions of the Committee. However, the Committee's conclusions in respect of national reports constitute formal legal findings within the ESC process: no other body is authorized to provide a legal interpretation of Charter rights, with the result that its views should be regarded as authoritative interpretations of its requirements. As a result, the Committee was in essence established to perform a similar role to the already existing ILO Committee of Experts – which in turn resembles the role subsequently assigned to the UN Committee on Economic, Social and Cultural Rights within the ICESCR system, and the other UN expert treaty bodies within the UN human rights frameworks more generally.

[16] For a general overview of the ESC monitoring system, see R. Brillat, 'The Supervisory Machinery of the European Social Charter: Recent Developments and Their Impact' in G. De Búrca and B. De Witte (eds) *Social Rights in Europe* (Oxford University Press 2005) 31.

[17] For a comprehensive overview of signatures and ratifications relating to both the original and revised ESC along with its various protocols, see <www.coe.int/en/web/european-social-charter>.

[18] C. O'Cinneide, 'The European Social Charter and EU Labour Law' in A. Bogg, C. Costello and A. Davies (eds) *Research Handbook on EU Labour Law* (Edward Elgar Publishing 2016) 191–213.

[19] See D. Harris, 'A Fresh Impetus for the European Social Charter' (1992) 41 ICLQ 659.

to areas, such as collective association rights, which had been well protected by the original instrument.

In addition, 15 states – a combination of states bound by the original and revised ESCs – have signed up to the ground-breaking 'collective complaint' mechanism set out in the Additional Collective Complaints Protocol of 1995. This is a unique feature of the ESC system, without parallel elsewhere. The Protocol provides for international NGOs with consultative status with the Council of Europe (and national NGOs, if the state party consents to this),[20] as well as national employer and employee associations, to bring complaints to the European Committee on Social Rights (ECSR) alleging the existence of a situation of non-conformity that has a 'collective' dimension, that is, which is not confined to individual cases. Such collective complaints are handled via a quasi-judicial procedure, with both the complaint organization and the state party submitting extensive written arguments in an adversarial process before the ECSR reaches a decision on the merits of the claim.[21] The Committee's decision is referred to the Committee of Ministers, which in the case of upheld complaints considers what the relevant state party is doing to ensure Charter conformity.

As Cullen has noted, this procedure was the first quasi-judicial process in international human rights law to have been established specifically to deal with socio-economic rights claims.[22] It has allowed the Committee to develop a wide-ranging case-law, which has put flesh on the provisions of the ESC and evolved into perhaps the most developed framework of social rights norms that exists at the international level.[23] In particular, it has clarified the scope of state obligations under the ESC in relation to a wide range of issues, including the right to strike, the right of access to adequate public housing, the right to social welfare, the right to access adequate health care and the extent to which states can justify reducing social rights while pursuing austerity measures.[24] Strikingly, the collective complaints procedure has proved to be popular with civil society and trade union organizations: at the time of writing, 185 complaints in total had been submitted to the Committee, with 130 complaints having been submitted since 2009 from a wide range of different states and organizations. Many of the Committee's collective complaints decisions have been high-profile, with some generating significant changes to national law and policy.

Having highlighted the successful elements of the Charter revitalization program, it should be noted that the ESC is still overshadowed by EU law and the ECHR. National governments still do not recognize ECSR decisions as having binding force, and regularly do not give effect to the Committee's determinations. Compliance with the national reporting process, which remains the primary monitoring mechanism for both the original and revised Social Charters, can be patchy. Furthermore, the Committee of Ministers has taken a political decision not to monitor actively how states respond to ECSR conclusions of non-conformity. However, the

---

[20]   Thus far, only Finland has consented to this.

[21]   The ECSR has the ability, if it wishes, both to ask the parties follow-up questions and to stage a public hearing on the matter at issue. It determines the admissibility of complaints initially, before proceeding to rule on the merits.

[22]   See H. Cullen, 'The Collective Complaints System of the European Social Charter: Interpretative Methods of the European Committee on Social Rights' (2009) 9(1) Human Rights Law Review 61–93, 61.

[23]   See Brillat (n 16) 31–44. At the time of writing, the Committee has received 185 collective complaints.

[24]   Ibid. See also Cullen (n 22).

ESC's profile at national level has increased substantially, and NGOs and trade unions are increasingly invoking the collective complaints procedure as a way of putting pressure on national governments to ensure better protection of social rights. (See Section 4.1 below for more detail on this.)

In general, the ESC in its original and revised forms remains the primary legal instrument directly concerned with ESCR in Europe at present, while the case-law generated by the collective complaints procedure is the most developed set of ESCR norms generated within the European legal context. However, the ESC's status is still often obscured by other elements of the pan-European legal architecture. Presenting a full picture of the scope of ESCR protection in Europe thus also requires some discussion of the two most significant elements of this architecture – namely the most prominent Council of Europe human rights treaty instrument, the ECHR, and EU law, which enjoys supremacy over conflicting norms of the national law of EU member states.

### 2.2.2    The 'spill-over' of civil and political rights protection under the European Convention on Human Rights (ECHR) into the domain of ESCR

All 47 Council of Europe member states are the provisions of the ECHR. Opened for signature in 1950 in the immediate post-1945 period, the Convention only protects civil and political rights. However, unlike its sister Council of Europe treaty instrument the ESC, the provisions of the ECHR (i) are acknowledged to give rise to strong legal obligations upon state parties to bring national law into conformity with their requirement, and (ii) have been incorporated and made judicially enforceable within the domestic law of all state parties. Furthermore, in interpreting and applying the rights set out in the ECHR, the European Court of Human Rights (ECrtHR) has recognized the undesirability of attempting to draw a clear demarcation line between socio-economic and civil and political rights.[25] As the ECrtHR commented in *Airey v Ireland*,

> the mere fact that an interpretation of the [civil and political rights protected by the ECHR] may extend into the sphere of social and economic rights should not be a decisive factor against such an interpretation; there is no water-tight division separating that sphere from the field covered by the Convention.[26]

As a result, the ECrtHR has for example held that states may in certain specific circumstances be required to take positive steps to provide particular categories of individuals in need with access to adequate emergency medical care, safe living conditions and legal aid, as an aspect of state obligations under the Convention to respect core civil and political rights such as freedom from inhuman and degrading treatment, the right to life and the right to a fair trial, respectively.[27] The non-discrimination guarantee set out in Article 14 of the ECHR, which guarantees equal treatment in the enjoyment of Convention rights, can also have a significant

---

[25]    Note Judge Pinto De Albuquerque's strong endorsement of this 'integrated' approach in his partly dissenting opinion in *Konstantin Markin v Russia,* no. 30078/06, Judgment of 22 March 2012.

[26]    (1980) 2 EHRR 305 (26).

[27]    See e.g. *Airey v Ireland* (1980) 2 EHRR 305; *MSS v Greece and Belgium,* Application No. 30696/09, Judgment of 21 January 2011; *Tarakhel v Switzerland,* Application No. 29217/12, Judgment of 4 November 2014; *Asiye Genç v Turkey,* Application No. 24109/07, Judgment of 27 January 2015; *Béláné Nagy v Hungary,* Application No. 53080/13, Judgment of 10 February 2015.

indirect impact on individual enjoyment of ESCR – with, for example, the ECrtHR being pre-pared to strike down social welfare cuts which have a disproportionate impact on vulnerable women and which cannot be shown to be objectively justified.[28] The same impact can be had by the right to private life as protected by Article 8 ECHR[29] – and even, in some limited con-texts, the right to property protected by Article 1 of the First Protocol to the Convention.[30] The right to freedom of association set out in Article 11 ECHR has also been interpreted to protect trade union association rights, and even in certain circumstances the right to organize and to engage in collective bargaining.[31]

Thus, over time, the Convention has become an indirect source of limited social rights protection.[32] Furthermore, as discussed in Section 4.2 below, there are times when the ECrtHR cross-refers to ESC standards and the case-law of the ECSR – meaning, in the limited range of situations where thus occurs, that Social Charter norms can exercise some influence over the development of the ECHR case-law.

### 2.2.3   The 'social dimension' of EU law

At the time of writing, and following the UK's exit from the EU on 31 January 2020, 27 European states are members of the EU. EU membership brings with it some potentially important legal obligations relating to ESCR – which, as an aspect of EU law, take direct effect within the law of member states and enjoy supremacy over clashing rules of national law.

The scope and extent of ESCR protection under EU law has been a source of controversy. Initially, EU law was primarily focused on market integration, and lacked much in the way of a social dimension.[33] However, from an early stage in the development of its jurisprudence, the Court of Justice of the EU (CJEU) has acknowledged that EU legislation needs to be interpreted and applied with reference to the 'social objectives' of the Union.[34] A non-binding Community Charter of the Fundamental Social Rights of Workers was also adopted in 1989, with a view to guiding the development of EU social policy. This was followed by the adop-tion of a range of directives and treaty amendments in the 1990s that expanded workers', family and environmental rights.[35] More generally, since the coming into force of the Treaty of Lisbon in 2009, the Preamble to the Treaty of European Union (TEU) now confirms the attachment of the EU member states to 'fundamental social rights' rights as defined in the European Social Charter.[36]

---

[28]   *JD v UK and A v UK*, Application No. 32949/17 and 34614/17, Judgment of 24 October 2019.
[29]   See e.g. *Connors v UK* [2004] 40 EHRR 189.
[30]   See e.g. Application No. 53080//13, *Béláné Nagy v Hungary*, Judgment of 10 February 2015.
[31]   See e.g. *Demir and Baykara v Turkey* (2009) 48 EHRR 54.
[32]   I. Leitjen, 'Defining the Scope of Economic and Social Guarantees in the Case Law of the ECrtHR' in E. Brems and J. Gerards (eds) *Shaping Rights in the ECHR: The Role of the European Court of Human Rights in Determining the Scope of Human Rights* (Cambridge University Press 2014) 109–36.
[33]   A significant exception was Article 119 of the original Treaty of Rome, which required member states to give effect to the principle of equal pay for work of equal value as between men and women.
[34]   See e.g. Case C-43/75, *Defrenne v Sabena (No. 2)* [1976] ECR 455 para 10.
[35]   For a useful overview of the activity of the EU in this regard, see the overview and associated links accessible at the 'Social Protection' webpage hosted on the European Commission's Europe site <http://ec.europa.eu/social/main.jsp?langId=en&catId=1063>.
[36]   Article 3(3) of the TEU proclaims that the EU shall work towards the establishment of a 'highly competitive social market economy … aiming at full employment and social progress', while also pro-moting 'social justice and protection'.

Furthermore, the EU Charter of Fundamental Rights, which since December 2009 has the same binding legal status as the EU treaties, contains an extensive list of social rights – which both the EU institutions and member states are bound to respect in implementing EU law.[37] Some of these social rights set out in the EU Charter, such as the rights of the elderly recognized in Article 25, do not appear to create directly enforceable subjective rights. Instead, they set out objective norms which – like the 'social state' principle in national constitutional law – do not generate subjective rights but must be respected by the EU legislator and member states in giving effect to EU law.[38] Furthermore, the scope of the Charter is confined to situations where EU law or national legislation implementing EU law is at issue.[39] However, these provisions make it possible for acts of the EU institutions, or member states implementing EU law, to be reviewed for compliance with the social rights requirements of the Charter – and for EU legislation to be interpreted by reference to their substance.

## 3.   THE GENERAL ESCR OBLIGATIONS OF STATES UNDER EUROPEAN REGIONAL HUMAN RIGHTS FRAMEWORKS

Having outlined the evolution of social rights protection in Europe, it is necessary to set out the specific nature of the obligations that arise under the different European human rights frameworks.

### 3.1   Obligations under the European Social Charter

Part One of the 1961 Charter requires contracting states to take steps to ensure the effective realization of a number of listed social rights and principles. This vague commitment is essentially declaratory in nature.[40] In essence, it only serves as a backdrop to the substantive provisions of Part Two – the heart of the Charter – whereby state parties undertake to be bound by a number of specific legal obligations set out in Articles 1–19 of the ESC. Each of these Articles protects a specific social right. These rights include the right to work (Article 1); to enjoy just conditions of work, safe and healthy working conditions and fair remuneration (Articles 2–4); to organize and engage in collective bargaining (Articles 5 and 6); to have access to vocational guidance and training (Articles 9–10), health care (Article 10), social security (Article 12) and social and medical assistance (Article 13); and to benefit from social welfare services (Article 14). The ESC also protects the right of certain vulnerable groups to social protection, including children and young persons (Article 7), female employees who were pregnant or had given birth (Article 8), persons with disabilities (Article 15), families in need of social, economic and legal protection (Article 16) and mothers and children in a similar situation (Article 17). The right of nationals of a contracting state to engage in gainful

---

[37]   See in general K. Lenaerts and J. Antonio Gutierrez-Fons, 'The Place of the Charter in the EU Constitutional Edifice' in S. Peers et al. (eds) *The EU Charter of Fundamental Rights: A Commentary* (Hart 2014) 1559–95.

[38]   See Explanations Relating to the Charter of Fundamental Rights [2007] OJ C303/02 (prepared by the Praesidium of the drafting Convention).

[39]   See Charter of Fundamental Rights [2000] OJ C364/01 Article 51(1).

[40]   Article 20.1 of the original 1961 Charter provides that Part I is a 'declaration of the aims' which contracting states are to pursue 'by all appropriate means'.

occupation in the territory of other contracting parties is guaranteed by Article 18, while the right of migrant workers and their families to social protection is guaranteed by the provisions of Article 19.

These provisions of the original ESC have now been supplemented by the extended obligations set out in the Revised European Social Charter (which, as noted above, now bind all but ten of the Council of Europe member states). The revised Charter retains the basic structure of the original Charter, but includes an updated and extended list of protected social rights and associated obligations.[41] In particular, the revised Charter reflects a more developed understanding of equality and non-discrimination rights, and also recognizes a wider range of employment and social welfare rights than did the original 1961 ESC.

Specifically, the revised Charter extended protection to the right to equal opportunities and equal treatment in matters of employment and occupation, covering gender equality (Article 20); the right of workers to information and consultation (Article 21) and to take part in the determination and improvement of their working conditions and working environment (Article 22); the right of elderly persons to social protection (Article 23); the right to protection in cases of termination of employment (Article 24); the right of workers to the protection of their claims in the event of insolvency of their employer (Article 25); the right to dignity at work, covering both sexual and 'moral' harassment (Article 26); the right of workers with family responsibilities to equal opportunities and equal treatment (Article 27); the right of workers' representatives to protection and facilities (Article 28); the right to information and consultation in collective redundancy procedures (Article 29); the right to protection against poverty and social exclusion (Article 30); and housing rights (Article 31).[42] The revised Charter also extends the provisions of Article 19 to confer additional rights protection on migrant workers, and updates the wording of various other provisions of the original Charter.

Exceptionally, when contracting states ratify either the original ESC or the revised version, they can elect to be bound by some of the binding legal obligations set out in Part Two of the Charter but not others.[43] This *à la carte* ratification mechanism was intended to give some states some flexibility in determining what legal commitments they would be bound by under the Charter. However, this flexibility is not absolute. All states must agree to be bound by a minimum number of the substantive legal obligations set out in Part Two, including at least two-thirds of what are defined to be the 'core' provisions of the Charter: namely, the right to work; the right to organize; the right to collective bargaining; the right to social security; the right to social and medical assistance; the right to social, legal and economic protection for the family; and the right to social protection for migrant workers. Furthermore, the Council of Europe encourages contracting states to consider accepting additional provisions of the Charter: while states are generally slow to do this, it is not an unknown occurrence.[44]

---

[41]    CETS No. 163, opened for signature in Strasbourg on 3 May 1996. The Revised European Social Charter entered into force on 1 July 1999.

[42]    Each of the Articles in both the original and revised Charters protecting a particular social right also contains a number of sub-paragraphs which set out specific obligations relating to the effective enjoyment of the right in question.

[43]    As Khaliq has noted, the ESC is 'unique among human rights treaties in permitting its parties not to accept all the rights it contains'. U. Khaliq, 'The EU and the European Social Charter: Never the Twain Shall Meet?' (2014) 15 Cambridge Yearbook of European Legal Studies 169, 174.

[44]    See for example the acceptance by Belgium in June 2015 of Articles 26–28 of the revised ESC.

Contracting states to the ESC are therefore bound to respect and give effect to a wide range of specific social rights obligations, which extend across the spheres of employment, vocational training, social welfare, health care and migrant rights. Some of these obligations are 'progressive' in nature, in that they require states to take reasonable steps to give effect to the right at issue: for example, Article 2§1 of both the original and revised ESC requires that, 'to provide for reasonable daily and weekly working hours, the working week [be] progressively reduced to the extent that the increase of productivity and other relevant factors permit'. Other obligations are more immediate in effect, requiring that national law and/or policy provide concrete guarantees relating to the enjoyment of the right in question: for example, Article 2§3 of the original and revised Charters requires contracting states 'to provide for a minimum of two weeks annual holiday with pay'.

Restrictions on the enjoyment of these rights must, under Article 31 of the original Charter and Article G of the revised version, be 'prescribed by law and ... necessary in a democratic society', that is, must satisfy the standard European test of proportionality. Thus, in Complaint No 59/2009, *European Trade Union Confédération (ETUC) et al v Belgium*,[45] the Committee concluded that the broad powers enjoyed by Belgian courts to injunct strike action on the basis of a unilateral application by an employer constituted a disproportionate restriction on the right to collective bargaining protected by Article 6 ESC.

Furthermore, all states parties are also required to comply with certain general, cross-cutting principles in how they give effect to Charter rights, in particular with the principle of non-discrimination set out in the Preamble to the original Charter and Article E of the revised Charter.[46] Article E is worded in similar terms as Article 14 of the ECHR: it provides that the enjoyment of Charter rights 'shall be secured without discrimination on any ground such as race, colour, sex, language, religion, political or other opinion, national extraction or social origin, health, association with a national minority, birth or other status'. The ECSR has therefore adopted a similar approach as the ECrtHR does to Article 14 ECHR. Thus, the Committee has taken the view that additional 'status' grounds, such as disability, are protected under Article E even if they are not explicitly listed in its text.[47]

Furthermore, again following the general case-law approach of the ECrtHR, the Committee has concluded that any unequal treatment based on personal 'status' must be shown to be objectively justified – with discrimination on the basis of 'suspect' grounds such as race, gender, sexual orientation or social origin attracting more intensive scrutiny. In line with the ECrtHR's judgment in *Thlimmenos v Greece*,[48] the ECSR has also recognized that a failure to take the particular needs of a vulnerable group into account may also qualify as discrimination. Thus, in Complaint 27/2004, *ERRC v Italy*,[49] the Committee concluded that the inadequate supply of housing for Roma communities in Italy, the failure to take into account their specific accommodation needs and a failure by local authorities to implement administrative degrees requiring the provision of adequate shelter and support for these communities constituted

---

[45] Decision on the merits of 16 September 2011.

[46] C. O'Cinneide, 'Equality and Non-Discrimination Rights within the Framework of the European Social Charter' [2015] 1 European Discrimination Law Review 1.

[47] See e.g. Collective Complaint 13/2000, *Association internationale Autisme-Europe (AIAE) v France*, decision on the merits of 4 November 2003, §51.

[48] (2001) 31 EHRR 15.

[49] Decision on the merits of 7 December 2005.

a violation of Article 31 of the revised ESC taken together with Article E.[50] Similarly, in Collective Complaint 45/2007, *INTERIGHTS v Croatia*, the ECSR concluded that the use of homophobic and stereotyping educational materials in the curriculum of Croatian schools was not in conformity with Croatia's obligations under Article 16 of the ESC taken together with the equality clause.[51]

The Appendix to the original and revised ESC contains various provisions clarifying its scope of application and the interpretation of specific rights guarantees set out in its text. In particular, it provides that ESC rights apply to non-nationals 'only in so far as they are nationals of other Parties lawfully resident or working regularly within the territory of the Party concerned', subject to the understanding that these Articles should be interpreted 'by reference to' the migrant rights provisions set out in Articles 18 and 19 of the two Charters and refugee rights under the Geneva Convention.

This ambiguous provision has caused serious problems of interpretation. On its face, it appears to limit the ESC's scope of aplication to migrants 'lawfully resident' or working regularly' in the state concerned. The ECSR has nevertheless concluded that this restrictive provision in the Appendix had to be read subject to the wider principled orientation of the ESC taken as a whole, as set out in Part One of the Charter, with its overriding emphasis on securing human dignity. Thus, in Complaint No. 90/2013, *Conference of European Churches (CEC) v the Netherlands*, the Committee concluded that a Dutch law precluding irregular migrants from accessing emergency housing breached the requirements of the ESC.[52]

In general, in interpreting Charter rights, the Committee gives particular regard to (i) the need to ensure that Charter rights are effectively enjoyed, (ii) the need for changing socio-economic circumstances to be taken into account in interpreting the text of the Charter, and (iii) the pan-European context in which the Charter is embedded.[53] In relation to this latter point, the Committee will take into account the existence of any emerging or established European consensus as to how ESC rights should be interpreted and applied. It also cross-refers to ICESCR, ILO and EU standards in developing its case-law, although the Committee emphasizes that it adopts its own independent interpretation of the Charter – and has made it clear that it will not defer to EU standards which in its view do not adequately protect social rights.[54]

---

[50]   See also Complaint 51/2008, *ERRC v France*, Decision on the merits of 19 October 2009.

[51]   Decision on the merits of 30 March 2009.

[52]   Decision on the merits of 1 July 2017. See also Collective Complaint 86/2012, *FEANTSA v The Netherlands*, Decision on the merits of 9 July 2014. Both decisions are accessible at <https://hudoc.esc.coe.int/>.

[53]   See J.-F. Akandij-Kombé, 'The Material Impact of the Jurisprudence of the European Committee of Social Rights' in G. De Búrca and B. de Witte, *Social Rights in Europe* (Oxford University Press 2005) 89–108.

[54]   See e.g. Complaint No. 66/2011, *General Federation of Employees of the National Electric Power Corporation (GENOP-DEI) and Confederation of Greek Civil Servants' Trade Unions (ADEDY) v Greece*, Decision on the merits of 18 June 2012; Complaint No. 85/2012, *Swedish Trade Union Confederation (LO) and Swedish Confederation of Professional Employees (TCO) v Sweden*, Decision on the merits of 19 July 2013.

## 3.2 Obligations under the ECHR

Discussion of the ESCR obligations under the ECHR will be briefer. After all, as the ECrtHR has put it itself, the Convention 'does not guarantee, as such, socio-economic rights'.[55] However, as already noted, certain obligations arise by virtue of the protection afforded by the Convention to civil and political rights, which spill over in the realm of social rights.[56] These 'spill-over' obligations are linked to specific elements of the ECrtHR's approach to interpreting the Convention.

First of all, the ECrtHR adopts a purposive approach to the interpretation of the Convention, interpreting its provisions so as to ensure effective protection for the rights set out in its text. As part of that approach, the Court recognizes that states are subject to certain positive obligations to take proactive action to protect rights. The Court further recognizes that such positive obligations may require states (i) to provide certain basic levels of social protection to individuals at particular risk of harm, or (ii) to adjust national law regulating education, social welfare or labor relations so as to ensure effective enjoyment of the Convention right at issue.

Thus, for example, in relation to the absolute right to freedom from inhuman and degrading treatment (Article 3 ECHR), the Court has accepted that, in situations of 'serious deprivation or want incompatible with human dignity' which clearly engage state responsibility, a state party may be subject to a positive obligation to provide basic social and medical support to vulnerable individuals. In *MSS v Greece and Belgium*, the Court ruled that reception conditions for asylum seekers in Greece did not satisfy this threshold.[57] In *Asiye Genç v Turkey*,[58] the Court concluded that Turkey had violated Article 2 ECHR (right to life) by failing to provide adequate emergency medical care to a baby born prematurely.

Similarly, in relation to the right to non-discrimination on the enjoyment of Convention rights protected by Article 14 ECHR, the Court in *JD and A v UK* concluded that a failure to exempt victims of domestic violence accommodated in special housing from cuts to housing benefit constituted unjustified sex discrimination.[59] In relation to the right to freedom of association protected by Article 11 ECHR, the Court in *Demir and Baykara v Turkey* concluded that national law which restricted the rights of civil servants to form trade unions and engage in collective bargaining constituted a breach of Turkey's obligations under the Convention,[60] and ruled that collective bargaining constituted an integral element of freedom of association.[61]

However, the Court has also been at pains to emphasize that the Convention remains 'essentially directed at the protection of civil and political rights', as asserted by the majority of the Grand Chamber of the Court in *N v UK*,[62] and that the Convention could not be invoked to

---

[55] *Bulgakova v Russia*, Judgment of 18 January 2007, no. 69524/01.

[56] For a comprehensive overview of the relevant case-law see I. Leitjen, *Core Socio-Economic Rights and the European Court of Human Rights* (Cambridge University Press 2018).

[57] Application No. 30696/09, Judgment of 21 January 2011.

[58] Application No. 24109/07, Judgment of 27 January 2015.

[59] Application Nos 32949/17 and 34614/17, Judgment of 24 October 2019. See also e.g. Article 8 ECHR (right to private, home and family life) cases of Application No. 66746/01 *Connors v the United Kingdom*, Judgment of 27 May 2004; Application No. 25446/06, *Yordanova and Others v Bulgaria*, Judgment of 24 April 2012.

[60] (2009) 48 EHRR 54.

[61] Ibid para 154.

[62] Application No. 26565/05, *N v the United Kingdom*, Judgment of 27 May 2005.

plug every gap in national health care or social security systems.[63] It also grants states a wide margin of appreciation in the area of social and economic policy, in particular where resource allocation is at issue.[64]

As a result, the 'spill-over' of ECHR rights protection into the domain of social rights will usually only arise in situations where an individual's socio-economic situation is eroding her enjoyment of a Convention right, and state responsibility for generating those conditions or preventing their occurrence is clearly engaged.[65] Consequently, the scope of protection indirectly afforded to social rights under the Convention is often not very clear: as Ingrid Leijten notes, 'when the Court is confronted with economic or social interests that demand positive action, this [evokes] some hesitation'.[66]

### 3.3    Obligations under EU Law

The evolving 'social dimension' of EU law is generally set out in the provisions of various directives adopted by the EU institutions, which must be implemented in national law by member states. For example, EU directives have laid down minimum standards in areas such as worker health and safety, non-discrimination in employment, and family-friendly policies – with the Race Equality Directive 2000/43/EC (prohibiting race discrimination in employment and access to goods and services), the Framework Equality Directive 2000/78/EC (prohibiting discrimination on grounds of age, disability, sexual orientation and religion or belief in employment and occupation), the Framework Occupational Health and Safety Directive 1989/391/EEC, the Pregnant Workers' Directive 1992/85/EEC and the Part-time Work Directive 97/81/EC all being prominent examples of such directives.

However, as noted above, the most direct form of social rights protection is provided for by the provisions of the EU Charter on Fundamental Rights. The EU Charter was initially drawn up in 2000, with a view to providing guidance to the Court of Justice of the EU (CJEU) and other EU institutions as to what fundamental rights should be regarded as forming part of the 'general principles' of EU law. With the Lisbon Treaty in 2009, the EU Charter was given the same status as the EU treaties – meaning that all EU law, and national legislation touching upon or implementing matters regulated by EU law, must respect the rights set out in its text.[67] Among its wide-ranging rights provisions are a set of social rights. These include the right to choose an occupation and engage in work (Article 15), the rights of the elderly to social protection (Article 25), the right of persons with disabilities to social integration (Article 26), the right to social security and social assistance (Article 34), the right to health care (Article 35) and a series of employment rights set out in Articles 27–32 which include the rights to information and consultation, to engage in collective bargaining, to just and fair working conditions and to protection in the event of unjustified dismissal.[68]

---

[63]    See e.g. *Botta v Italy*, Judgment of 24 February 1998, Reports of Judgments and Decisions 1998-I.

[64]    See e.g. Application No. 36448/97, *Marzari v Italy*, Judgment of 4 May 1999.

[65]    See C. O'Cinneide, 'A Modest Proposal: Destitution, State Responsibility and the European Convention on Human Rights' (2008) 5 European Human Rights Law Review 583–605.

[66]    I. Leijten, 'The German Right to an *Existenzminimum*, Human Dignity, and the Possibility of Minimum Core Socioeconomic Rights Protection' (2015) 16(1) German Law Journal 171–96, 174.

[67]    See Articles 51 (field of application) and 52 (scope of guaranteed rights) of the EU Charter.

[68]    See D. Ashiagbor, 'Economic and Social Rights in the European Charter of Fundamental Rights' (2004) 9 European Human Rights Law Review 63–72.

The text of these social rights provisions draws heavily upon the equivalent provisions of the ESC, as well as ICESCR and various ILO instruments. Their effect is to impose legal obligations on the EU institutions, and national authorities implementing EU law or related national legislation, to respect a range of core socio-economic rights – with national courts having the power to review compliance with this requirement, and to refer related legal interpretation questions as required to the CJEU for final determination.[69] Given that EU Charter rights must be given direct effect, and take precedence over conflicting national legislation, these social rights provisions thus open up the possibility of litigants being able to challenge state action which infringes such rights before the CJEU, insofar as it relates to areas that come within the scope of EU competency.

However, the status and substantive content of the social rights set out in the Charter remains uncertain. In particular, it remains to be seen which Charter rights will be classified as giving rise to subjective individual entitlements, and how the Court will interpret the vague language of the Charter's social provisions.

In drafting the Charter, a distinction was drawn between (i) rights which should be interpreted as giving rise to subjective individual entitlements which could be directly enforced through the courts, and (ii) rights which should be read as setting out 'principles' rather than subjective rights as such. According to the explanations relating to the content of the Charter agreed by the Praesidium of the Convention which drafted the Charter in 2000, such principles 'may be implemented through legislative or executive acts' of the EU institutions and member states, but 'become significant for the [c]ourts only when such acts are interpreted or reviewed' and do not 'give rise to direct claims for positive action by the Union's institutions or Member States authorities'.[70] This does not mean that they lack all legal effect. A failure to respect principles of EU law may result in EU legislation or national implementing measures being overturned by the courts, while these principles may also be invoked by the CJEU and national courts in interpreting EU and national legislation. However, as at the national level, individuals cannot directly rely on these rights to show that their subjective entitlements have been denied.[71]

Thus, in the case of *AMS*, the CJEU concluded that Article 27 of the Charter, which guarantees the right of workers to information and consultation, could not be invoked in a horizontal dispute between private entities, on the basis that it constituted a 'principle' rather than a subjective right capable of being applied directly in law.[72] Some of the social rights set out in the EU Charter, such as the rights of the elderly recognized in Article 25 and the right to social security and social assistance set out in Article 34, would appear to fall within this category of 'principles'. However, in the cases of *Bauer* and *Max-Planck*, the Court concluded that the right to a period of paid annual leave set out in Article 31(2) of the EU Charter was sufficiently

---

[69] For detailed commentary on these provisions, and the impact of the Charter in general, see Peers et al (eds) (n 37).

[70] See Explanations Relating to the Charter of Fundamental Rights [2007] OJ C303/02 (prepared by the Praesidium of the drafting Convention). Article 52(7) of the Charter provides that 'due regard' should be given to the 'explanations drawn up as a way of providing guidance' on the appropriate interpretation of the Charter.

[71] J. Krommendijk, 'After *AMS*: Remaining Uncertainty about the Role of the EU Charter's Principles', *EUtopia Law Blog*, 29 January 2014 <https://eutopialaw.com/2014/01/29/after-ams-remaining-uncertainty-about-the-role-of-the-eu-charters-principles/>.

[72] C-176/12, *Association de médiation sociale*, Judgment of 15 January 2014.

precise to generate subjective individual rights, and to be applied directly in the context of the horizontal relationship between an employer and his employees.[73]

The scope of application of the Charter itself is also uncertain. As previously noted, Article 52 of the Charter provides that it only applies to EU law and measures taken by national authorities to implement to the requirements of EU law. Thus far, the CJEU has taken the view that salary cuts and other austerity measures introduced by national governments within the eurozone to give effect to their general obligations to ensure monetary stability under the relevant provisions of EU law 'clearly' fall outside the scope of EU law.[74] Furthermore, the CJEU confirmed in the *Pringle* case that the European Stability Mechanism, an inter-governmental vehicle for providing indebted eurozone states with financial assistance subject to strict budget conditionality, also falls outside the framework of EU law.[75] It would thus appear that the social provisions of the Charter may only apply to state action which relates directly to the implementation of specific provisions of EU legislation or the EU treaties – thus limiting their impact in substantial ways.

Thus far, few cases concerning the social rights provisions of the EU Charter have reached the CJEU. This probably reflects both uncertainty as to the status and substance of the social rights set out in the EU Charter, and the limited scope of the instrument in general. However, the CJEU has taken account of these provisions in interpreting the requirements of EU legislation, even when they are interpreted as not giving rise to directly enforceable subjective norms.[76] Furthermore, the *Bauer* and *Max-Planck* judgments cited above show that the CJEU is prepared to give direct effect to the social rights provisions of the EU Charter in the context of horizontal relationships, if they are deemed to be sufficiently specific and concrete as so to constitute subjective rights. It remains to be seen how this jurisprudence will develop in the future.

## 4.   THE ENFORCEMENT AND IMPLEMENTATION OF SER WITHIN THE EUROPEAN HUMAN RIGHTS FRAMEWORK

Having outlined the scope and substance of the social rights protection provided by the ESC, the ECHR and EU law, it is necessary to outline its effectiveness – and the barriers that exist to its implementation.

### 4.1   Enforcement of the European Social Charter

As previously discussed, the ECSR performs an analogous role with respect to the ESC as the UN Committee on Economic, Social and Cultural Rights does with respect to the ICESCR. It also suffers from some of the inherent weaknesses of such bodies. State parties are not under a formal legal obligation to give effect its determinations. Furthermore, as previously noted,

---

[73]   C-569/16 and C-570/16, *Bauer*, Judgment of 6 November 2018; C-684/16, *Max-Planck*, Judgment of 6 November 2018.

[74]   See e.g. Case C-128/12, *Sindicato dos Bancários do Norte and Others v BPN - Banco Português de Negócios, SA* [2013] OJ C129/04.

[75]   Case C-370/12, *Pringle v Government of Ireland*, Judgment of 27 November 2012.

[76]   Case C-282/10, *Dominguez*, Judgment of 24 January 2012.

state parties to the ESC face little if any diplomatic pressure to conform to their Charter commitments. The Committee of Ministers can issue recommendations to states to take remedial action to bring their national law and policy into conformity with the Charter – but rarely if ever does so, in contrast to the situation with respect to the ECHR.

Furthermore, the national reporting mechanism, which is still the primary route for monitoring states' compliance with their ESC commitments, suffers from some inherent defects. The national reports prepared by state parties often lack detail. Furthermore, they are often submitted late, or contain incomplete information. This means that the Committee often must base its conclusions on an assessment of existing state law and official policy, rather than on the actual situation on the ground.[77]

In addition, the ESC monitoring mechanism is procedurally complex. States submit their national reports in accordance with a fixed reporting cycle.[78] Each year, states report on how they are complying with a particular group of Charter rights linked by a common theme – with the cycle being repeated every four years. Such constant reporting allows for regular Committee scrutiny – but it also makes it difficult for NGOs and other interested groups to keep up with this relentless cycle.

The collective complaint procedure does not suffer from these defects. The civil society and trade union/employer organizations with standing to bring an action under the Collective Complaints Protocol 1996 do not need to have exhausted domestic remedies before initiating a complaint. Furthermore, there is no time limit within which a complaint must be started. The adjudicative procedure the ECSR uses to resolve such complaints is flexible, and the Committee generally produces final decisions on the merits within a year or so of complaints being submitted (despite the serious resource constraints under which the Committee operates). Furthermore, the process allows the Committee to delve deeper into the specifics of a specific national situation than is usually possible in the context of the national reporting system – which helps to generate more detailed and concrete reasoning from the Committee in arriving at its final decision.

But, despite all these positive aspects, the effectiveness of the collective complaints procedure remains limited by the lack of diplomatic pressure on states to comply with Committee decisions. Furthermore, as noted above, the majority of state parties to the ESC have not agreed to participate in this process.

However, none of the above should be read as suggesting that ESC rights are unenforceable, or lack any substance. The ECSR's determinations in respect of both national reports and collective complaints can still exert influence at state level, depending on the specific national context at issue.[79] An ECSR finding of a Charter breach may result in national governments coming under pressure to rectify the situation, especially if domestic NGOs, trade union/employer organizations, media or opposition politicians take up the issue. Furthermore,

---

[77]  See P. Alston, 'Assessing the Strengths and Weaknesses of the European Social Charter's Supervisory System', in G. De Búrca and B. De Witte, *Social Rights in Europe* (Oxford University Press 2005) 45–67.

[78]  State reports are prepared by reference to a standard template, which is approved and periodically revised by the Committee of Ministers of the Council of Europe: see <www.coe.int/t/dghl/monitoring/socialcharter/ReportForms/FormIndex_en.asp>.

[79]  C. Salcedo Beltrán, 'The Social Constitution of Europe (*European Social Charter*): Reality and Effect of Rights' <www.housingrightswatch.org/content/social-constitution-europe-european-social-charter-reality-and-effect-rights>.

national courts may take account of the ECSR's determination, as may the ECrtHR in interpreting ECHR rights that overlap with ESC rights. In all these different situations, the ECSR's case-law may end up having 'bite', despite their ambiguous status at the international law level.

Whether such factors kick in to enhance the weight of the ECSR's conclusions will often vary from state to state, and from legal issue to legal issue. However, the growing profile of the ESC across Europe, and its potential as a mechanism for protecting social rights, is reflected in the remarkable growth in the number of collective complaints over the last decade. NGOs and trade union organizations in particular often view the collective complaint mechanism as a way of generating a concrete determination of the scope and substance of social rights guarantees set out in the ESC, which can then be invoked in subsequent campaigning work.

Selected examples of the ECSR's collective complaints case-law generating law reform and/or substantial debate within state parties include the following: Complaint No. 48/2008, *European Roma Rights Centre v Bulgaria*, where the Bulgarian government repealed legislation which barred individuals unemployed for more than six months from receiving unemployment relief after the Committee ruled it was not in conformity with the right to social assistance set out in Article 13§1 ESC;[80] the above-mentioned ECSR decision in Complaint No. 90/2013, *Conference of European Churches (CEC) v the Netherlands*,[81] which ultimately after much controversy resulted in the Dutch government watering down a statutory ban on irregular migrants from accessing emergency housing; the 'Greek austerity' cases of Complaint 66/2011, *General Federation of Employees of the National Electric Power Corporation (GENOP-DEI) v Greece*,[82] and Complaint 76/2012, *Federation of Employed Pensioners of Greece (IKA-ETAM) v Greece*,[83] where the Committee ruled that emergency cuts to social welfare support that infringed upon the core of the right to social security and social assistance could not be justified even by the particular conditions of the Greek economic crisis; and the Committee's findings in Complaint No. 33/2006, *International Movement ATD Fourth World v France*,[84] and Complaint 39/2006, *Feantsa v France*,[85] that French housing law breached Article 30 (right to protection against poverty and social exclusion), and Article 31 (right to housing) of the Revised Social Charter on the basis that it failed to give 'due priority for the provision of social housing for the most socially deprived', which influenced subsequent reform of the relevant legislation.

## 4.2    Enforcement of the 'Social Dimension' of EU and ECHR Law

Few issues of enforcement and effectiveness arise in relation to the social rights dimension of EU and ECHR law. As a result, they can be dealt with together, notwithstanding the significant differences between both systems.

---

[80]    Decision on the merits of 18 February 2009.
[81]    Decision on the merits of 1 July 2017. See also Collective Complaint 86/2012, *FEANTSA v The Netherlands*, Decision on the merits of 9 July 2014.
[82]    Decision on the merits of 23 May 2011.
[83]    Decision on the merits of 7 December 2012.
[84]    Decision of 4 February 2008.
[85]    Decision of 4 February 2008.

As already discussed, EU law must be given direct effect in national legal systems, and enjoys supremacy over conflicting norms of national law. Therefore, any judgment of the CJEU in relation to the contents of EU directives affecting the enjoyment of social rights, or the social rights provisions of the EU Charter itself, must be implemented at national level. National courts have at times resisted giving full implementation to CJEU judgments.[86] But this remains rare. As a consequence, the enforcement and implementation of CJEU judgments as they affect social rights is not generally an issue. What is an issue is the uncertain and highly tentative state of the existing CJEU case-law in this area. This may be discouraging litigants from raising EU law points relating to social rights before national courts, who are the 'gatekeepers' of the CJEU system of adjudication. Another problem is the limited scope of application of the EU Charter as a whole, which inevitably constrains its impact.[87]

In contrast, ECrtHR judgments are not generally given full direct effect within national legal systems, and are not 'supreme' as a matter of national law. However, strong diplomatic pressure exists for state parties to comply with ECrtHR judgments. Furthermore, the Convention has been incorporated into the national law of all Council of Europe member states, with the effect that ECrtHR judgments are often highly influential within national legal systems. There are compliance issues: states often drag their feet before complying, or only implement judgments to a partial degree, while national courts can at times be slow to embrace Strasbourg jurisprudence.[88] But none of these issues are specific to the elements of the ECrtHR's jurisprudence that has a social dimension.

Instead, the issue in this regard are the wider legitimacy issues that surround the Court, which inevitably make it cautious in developing new jurisprudence – which by extension may contribute to the ECrtHR's reluctance to stretch the definition of the civil and political rights set out in the Convention to include a substantial social rights dimension.[89] Even when it interprets such rights by reference to ESC/ECSR standards, as it did with freedom of association in *Demir and Baykara* (as discussed above), the Court tends to be reluctant to extend this jurisprudence into controversial terrain.[90]

## 5. CONCLUSION

The three main institutional mechanisms for protecting social rights in Europe have different strengths and weaknesses. The ESC guarantees a comprehensive and detailed list of socio-economic rights, with its reporting and (in particular) the collective complaints mechanism providing a means for the ECSR to develop a detailed set of standards. However, its enforcement mechanisms remain weak, limiting the impact of the Social Charter – which remains widely viewed as a distinctly inferior and less important mechanism than either the ECHR or EU law. The ECHR provides spill-over protection for a small sub-set of social rights,

---

[86] See e.g. Case 15/2014, *Dansk Industri, acting for Ajos A/S v Estate of A*, Judgment of the Danish Supreme Court, 6 December 2016, UfR 2017.824H.

[87] O'Cinneide, 'Austerity and the Faded Dream of a Social Europe' (n 11).

[88] F. de Londras and K. Dzehtsiarou, 'Mission Impossible? Addressing Non-execution through Infringement Proceedings in the European Court of Human Rights' (2017) 66(2) International and Comparative Law Quarterly 467–90.

[89] O'Cinneide, 'Austerity and the Faded Dream of a Social Europe' (n 11).

[90] See e.g. Application No. 31045, *RMT v UK*, Judgment of 8 April 2014.

but remains a civil and political rights mechanism. The social rights provisions of the EU Charter have the advantage of forming part of EU law, with its qualities of direct effect and supremacy over domestic law – but their scope is restricted, and their substance is uncertain.

Taken together, this means that social rights protection within Europe remains in an underdeveloped state – despite the potential of, in particular, the ESC and its enforcement mechanisms, and the persisting European attachment at national level to the idea of 'social citizenship' and the concept of the 'social state'. However, there are also some grounds for optimism. The austerity crisis of the early 2010s shook up much of the complacency that used to exist about Europe's record on social rights. The collective complaints process has breathed new life into the ESC, the CJEU has tentatively begun to engage with the social rights provisions of the EU Charter in cases such as *Bauer* (discussed above), and the ECrtHR has shown more readiness in recent years to recognize the spill-over impact of Convention rights in the social sphere. It remains to be seen how far this 'social turn' will extend.

# 5.   The Inter-American System

*Viviana Krsticevic[1]*

## 1.   INTRODUCTION

The protection of the Inter-American System of Human Rights ('IASHR') is rooted in a region with a long tradition of constitutional recognition of social rights, and, at the same time, alarming levels of inequality and backsliding democracies. The history of the IASHR features some groundbreaking international treaties that protect not only civil and political rights, but also economic, social, cultural, and environmental rights ('ESCER'). These treaties have established multiple protection mechanisms and built up an innovative jurisprudence.

During the past 60 years, the IASHR has been a critical space for the protection of human rights and the struggle for a continent free of injustice, dictatorships, and misery. The Inter-American Commission on Human Rights ('IACHR') and the Inter-American Court of Human Rights ('IACtHR' or 'Court'), both monitoring organs of the IASHR, have helped promote and protect ESCER and the communities linked to their defense, including indigenous peoples, labor activists, environmental and land defenders, women's rights organizations, and student movements, among others.

The contributions of the IASHR to the protection of ESCER make it an important system to study, particularly in the context of the present historical juncture, both regionally and globally. The Americas region is faced with pressing responsibilities to address climate change, high levels of deforestation, an unprecedented migration crisis, persistent inequality, and disquieting levels of violence, particularly for those defending ESCER. Furthermore, social policies have regressed due to regional and world economic cycles, democratic commitments have waned, and spaces for protest and civic engagement have shrunk in many States globally.

Those major challenges make regional and global spaces important loci for concerted action in order to address problems that are regional or global in nature, and to create additional leverage under more restrictive domestic conditions. ESCER are, moreover, critical for the consolidation of democracies, since they amount to some of the expected democratic outcomes.[2] Hence, it is a timely moment to consider how the mechanisms and structures of the IASHR can impact the guarantee of ESCER.

This chapter lays out the legal framework for the protection of economic, social, cultural, and environmental rights in the IASHR, followed by a description of the monitoring and pro-

---

[1]   I would like to acknowledge the research and editing support of Xinia Bermúdez in the elaboration of this article, as well as the comments provided by Gisela de Leon and Alejandra Vicente.

[2]   'The promotion and observance of economic, social, and cultural rights are inherently linked to integral development, equitable economic growth, and to the consolidation of democracy in the states of the Hemisphere.' 'Inter-American Democratic Charter' (adopted 11 September 2001) Article 13 <www.oas.org/charter/docs/resolution1_en_p4.htm>. 'The exercise of democracy promotes the preservation and good stewardship of the environment. It is essential that the states of the Hemisphere implement policies and strategies to protect the environment, including application of various treaties and conventions, to achieve sustainable development for the benefit of future generations.' Ibid Article 15.

tection mechanisms. It then summarizes some of the IASHR's most salient jurisprudential and doctrinal developments and highlights the system's commitment to human rights defenders and the community engaged in the defense of ESCER. The chapter concludes with an outlook for the protection of ESCER in the region.

## 2.   THE LEGAL FRAMEWORK FOR ESCER IN THE INTER-AMERICAN SYSTEM

The IASHR is based on a set of treaties and declarations that provide a robust, if uneven, framework for the protection of ESCER in the region. Many countries have ratified most Inter-American human rights treaties, but the levels of commitment to a broad set of rights, and specific protections to groups in situations of vulnerability vary enormously from north to south, leaving citizens and scholars puzzled at the differentiated levels of accountability agreed to by different States. Most countries in North America and the Caribbean have assumed lower levels of treaty ratifications, in contrast to those in continental Latin America, which have ratified a cluster of key human rights treaties.

The Charter of the Organization of American States ('OAS Charter') is the OAS's foundational treaty, and binds all Member States of the international organization. The OAS Charter recognizes several economic, social, and cultural rights, including the rights to culture, education, and the principle of equality.[3] It also includes democratic principles that are critical to the enjoyment of these rights.[4]

Among the first declarations and treaties that recognized human rights at the international level, including some critical for the recognition and enjoyment of economic, social, and cultural rights, are the American Declaration of the Rights and Duties of Man ('American Declaration'), the American Charter of Social Guarantees, the Inter-American Convention on the Granting of Political Rights to Women, and the Inter-American Convention on the Granting of Civil Rights to Women, all adopted in 1948.[5]

The American Declaration represents a valuable contribution of the Americas to international human rights law. It is the first document of its kind that recognized a broad set of human rights in a supra-national forum.[6] Its text is permeated by the thinking of several traditions, including key Latin American jurists of the first half of the past century, constitutional

---

[3]   Charter of the Organization of American States (adopted 30 April 1948, entered into force 13 December 1951) 119 UNTS 3.

[4]   Ibid.

[5]   American Declaration of the Rights and Duties of Man, OAS Res XXX adopted by the Ninth International Conference of American States (1948) reprinted in Basic Documents Pertaining to Human Rights in the Inter-American System OEA/Ser L V/II.82 Doc 6 Rev 1 at 17 (1992); American Charter of Social Guarantees, OAS Res XXIX, adopted by the Ninth International Conference of American States (1948) reprinted in Basic Documents Pertaining to Human Rights in the Inter-American System OEA/Ser L V/II.82 Doc 6 Rev 1 at 17 (1992); Inter-American Convention on the Granting of Political Rights of Women (adopted 5 February 1948, entered into force 29 December 1954) 1438 UNTS 63; and Inter-American Convention on the Granting of Civil Rights to Women (adopted 2 May 1948, entered into force 17 March 1949) 1438 UNTS 51.

[6]   Kathryn Sikkink, 'Latin America's Protagonist Role in Human Rights' [2015] Sur Intl J on HR 207, 208.

frameworks from the region, the Catholic Church's social doctrine, and liberal ideas.[7] At the time of its adoption by the Ninth International Conference of American States in 1948, the Declaration protected a number of economic, social, and cultural rights, including the rights to health,[8] education,[9] work,[10] social security,[11] culture,[12] and property.[13]

The American Charter of Social Guarantees, which focused on workers' rights, was adopted at the same time as the Declaration.[14] Social and economic equality was catalyzed at the same International Conference of American States with the adoption of two additional treaties that promoted equal rights for women: the Inter-American Convention on the Granting of Political Rights to Women,[15] and the Inter-American Convention on the Granting of Civil Rights to Women.[16] Understanding that access to political power is a key element to ensure that all rights are protected, the first treaty aimed to guarantee access to political rights to women in a context where women's political participation was still restricted (in Central and South America).[17] The second treaty granted women the same civil rights that men enjoyed.[18]

In 1969, the American States adopted the American Convention on Human Rights ('ACHR'), which included vast protection of civil and political rights.[19] In contrast, the Convention's chapter on economic, social, and cultural rights contained a single Article on the right to progressive development of those rights.[20] (Chapter 14 of this book addresses issues of progressive realization.)

Almost two decades later, the Organization of American States ('OAS') adopted the Additional Protocol to the American Convention on Human Rights in the Area of Economic, Social and Cultural Rights ('Protocol of San Salvador' or 'PSS' or San Salvador Protocol), which timidly embraced the protection of economic, social, cultural, and environmental

---

[7]    Mary Ann Glendon, 'The Influence of Catholic Social Doctrine on Human Rights' [2013] 10 J Cath. Soc. Thought 69, 71; Kathryn Sikkink, 'Latin America's Protagonist Role in Human Rights' [2015] Sur Intl J on HR 207, 208.

[8]    American Declaration of the Rights and Duties of Man, OAS Res XXX adopted by the Ninth International Conference of American States (1948) reprinted in Basic Documents Pertaining to Human Rights in the Inter-American System OEA/Ser L V/II.82 Doc 6 Rev 1 at 17 (1992) Article XI.

[9]    Ibid Article XII.

[10]    Ibid Article XIV.

[11]    Ibid Article XVI.

[12]    Ibid Article XIII.

[13]    Ibid Article XXIII.

[14]    American Charter of Social Guarantees, OAS Res XXIX, adopted by the Ninth International Conference of American States (1948) reprinted in Basic Documents Pertaining to Human Rights in the Inter-American System OEA/Ser L V/II.82 Doc 6 Rev 1 at 17 (1992).

[15]    Inter-American Convention on the Granting of Political Rights of Women (adopted 5 February 1948, entered into force 29 December 1954) 1438 UNTS 63.

[16]    Inter-American Convention on the Granting of Civil Rights to Women (adopted 2 May 1948, entered into force 17 March 1949) 1438 UNTS 51.

[17]    Inter-American Convention on the Granting of Political Rights of Women (adopted 5 February 1948, entered into force 29 December 1954) 1438 UNTS 63.

[18]    Inter-American Convention on the Granting of Civil Rights to Women (adopted 2 May 1948, entered into force 17 March 1949) 1438 UNTS 51 Article 1.

[19]    American Convention on Human Rights (adopted 22 November 1969, entered into force 18 July 1978) 1144 UNTS 123.

[20]    Ibid Article 26.

rights,[21] including the rights to a healthy environment, food, education, the family, culture, and work, among others. (Part B of this book focuses on the contours and development of most of these rights.) However, the PSS was seen as a limited instrument that reinforced the Cold War view of a strong division between civil and political rights and ESCER. As such, despite including language that reinforced the principle of indivisibility, it drastically curtailed monitoring and protection mechanisms. The PSS only attributed jurisdiction to the IACHR and the Court to interpret violations of the rights to education and to organize trade unions,[22] and added a reporting mechanism on progressive measures to ensure that rights are being fulfilled.[23] This treaty did not enter into force until ten years after its adoption.

Since the 1990s, the OAS has adopted seven specialized conventions that expand guarantees against certain types of violations or recognize rights of special groups.[24] They range from the Protocol to the American Convention on Human Rights to Abolish the Death Penalty, in 1990, to the Inter-American Convention on the Prevention, Punishment and Eradication of Violence Against Women, or 'Convention of Belém do Pará', in 1994 – this was the first treaty on the eradication of violence against women. The latest Inter-American Convention, on Protecting the Human Rights of Older Persons, was adopted in 2015. Many of these conventions include a broad range of protections for ESCER and a series of supplementary mechanisms to protect those rights.

Some of the earlier specialized conventions, such as the Convention of Belém do Pará, have been widely ratified. In fact, the Convention of Belém do Pará is the most widely ratified regional human rights treaty in the Americas, with 32 out of 35 OAS Member States having ratified it.[25] It is a pioneering convention that advances the rights of women through the

---

[21]   Additional Protocol to the American Convention on Human Rights in the Area of Economic, Social and Cultural Rights (adopted 17 November 1988, adopted 16 November 1999) 28 ILM 156 (Protocol of San Salvador).

[22]   Ibid Article 18.

[23]   Ibid Article 19.

[24]   Protocol to the American Convention on Human Rights to Abolish the Death Penalty (adopted 8 June 1990) OASTS No 73; Inter-American Convention on Forced Disappearance of Persons (adopted 9 June 1994, entered into force 28 March 1996) 33 ILM 1429; Inter-American Convention on the Prevention, Punishment and Eradication of Violence Against Women 'Convention of Belem do Para' (adopted 9 June 1994, entered into force 5 March 1995) 33 ILM 1534; Inter-American Convention on International Traffic in Minors (adopted 18 March 1994, entered into force 15 August 1997) 33 ILM 72; Inter-American Convention on the Elimination of all Forms of Discrimination Against Persons with Disabilities (adopted 14 September 2001) AG/RES. 1608 (XXIX-O/99); Inter-American Convention against Racism, Racial Discrimination and Related Forms of Intolerance (adopted 5 June 2013, entered into force 11 November 2017) OASTS No 68; Inter-American Convention against All Forms of Discrimination and Intolerance (adopted 5 June 2013) OASTS No 69; and Inter-American Convention on Protecting the Human Rights of Older Persons (adopted 15 June 2015, entered into force 11 January 2017) 55 ILM 98.

[25]   'Inter-American Convention on the Prevention, Punishment and Eradication of Violence Against Women "Convention of Belem do Para" Signatories and Ratifications', *Organization of American States* <www.oas.org/juridico/english/sigs/a-61.html>. Cuba has not participated at the OAS since its suspension was lifted in 2009, putting the number of active Member States at 34. 'OAS Revokes Resolution Suspending Membership of Cuba in the Inter-American System', *Organization of American States* (3 June 2009) <www.oas.org/en/media_center/press_release.asp?sCodigo=GA-12-09>. The Bolivarian Republic of Venezuela has denounced the OAS Charter and is in the process of disengaging itself from the OAS. Multimedio VTV, 'Delcy Rodríguez: Venezuela inicia retiro de la OEA y procedimiento durará 24 meses' (26 April 2017) <www.youtube.com/watch?v=unQVyr5m3D4>.

eradication of violence against them, and has led to important developments in the protection of women's rights to health and physical integrity.[26] The later Inter-American conventions, including the 'twin conventions' to eliminate discrimination and racism,[27] and the Convention on the Rights of Older Persons,[28] have very few ratifications.[29] The twin conventions include protections against discrimination in the enjoyment and exercise of all fundamental rights and in areas of employment, education, housing, health, and social protection, among others.[30] The Inter-American Convention on Protecting the Human Rights of Older Persons includes important developments of ESCER of older persons such as the rights to work, health, education, culture, housing, a healthy environment, accessibility, and personal mobility, and information necessary for the exercise of these rights, among others.[31]

The Inter-American Democratic Charter, a widely acclaimed declaration adopted in 2001, has recognized the importance of the mutually reinforcing role of ESCER and democracy. More specifically, it calls for the protection of ESCER, economic development, and the fight against inequality and poverty, among others, in order to strengthen democratic institutions.[32]

Another interesting development for the protection of ESCER in the Americas is the 2018 adoption of the Regional Agreement on Access to Information, Public Participation and Justice in Environmental Matters in Latin America and the Caribbean, also known as the Escazú Agreement.[33] In a process spearheaded by the Economic Commission for Latin America and the Caribbean ('ECLAC'), the treaty was adopted in March 2018 in Costa Rica and deposited at the United Nations in September 2018.[34] The document is considered a sister treaty to the Convention on Access to Information, Public Participation in Decision-Making and Access to Justice in Environmental Matters ('Aarhus Convention') in Europe and includes

---

[26] Inter-American Convention on the Prevention, Punishment and Eradication of Violence Against Women 'Convention of Belem do Para' (adopted 9 June 1994, entered into force 5 March 1995) 33 ILM 1534.

[27] Inter-American Convention against Racism (n 24); Inter-American Convention against All Forms of Discrimination and Intolerance (adopted 5 June 2013) OASTS No 69.

[28] Inter-American Convention on Protecting the Human Rights of Older Persons (adopted 15 June 2015, entered into force 11 January 2017) 55 ILM 98.

[29] See 'Inter-American Convention against Racism, Racial Discrimination and Related Forms of Intolerance Signatories and Ratifications', *Organization of American States* <www.oas.org/en/sla/dil/inter_american_treaties_A-68_racism_signatories.asp>; 'Inter-American Convention against All Forms of Discrimination and Intolerance Signatories and Ratifications', *Organization of American States* <www.oas.org/en/sla/dil/inter_american_treaties_A-69_discrimination_intolerance_signatories.asp>; 'Inter-American Convention on Protecting the Human Rights of Older Persons Signatories and Ratifications', *Organization of American States* <www.oas.org/en/sla/dil/inter_american_treaties_A-70_human_rights_older_persons_signatories.asp>.

[30] Convention against Racism (n 24) Articles 2 & 7; Convention against All Forms of Discrimination and Intolerance (n 27) Articles 2 & 7.

[31] Convention on Protecting the Human Rights of Older Persons (n 28) Articles 18–21, 24–26.

[32] 'Inter-American Democratic Charter' (adopted 11 September 2001) Article 13 <www.oas.org/charter/docs/resolution1_en_p4.htm>.

[33] Regional Agreement on Access to Information, Public Participation and Justice in Environmental Matters in Latin America and the Caribbean (adopted 4 March 2018) LC/PUB.2018/8 (Escazú Agreement).

[34] 'Fourteen Countries Sign New Generation Agreement at UN Headquarters on Access to Information, Public Participation and Justice in Environmental Matters', *Economic Commission for Latin America and the Caribbean* (27 September 2018) <www.cepal.org/en/pressreleases/fourteen-countries-sign-new-generation-agreement-un-headquarters-access-information>.

important protections of the rights to access to information, public participation, and justice.[35] Such rights are considered as pillars to secure the rights of every person and of future generations to a healthy environment and sustainable development.[36] The Convention also adds a foundation to the architecture of rights, recognizing the importance of guaranteeing a safe and enabling environment for persons, groups, and organizations that promote and defend human rights in environmental matters and the need to prevent, investigate, and punish attacks against environmental defenders.[37]

Despite the multiplicity of Inter-American treaties dealing with ESCER, these rights have been primarily protected through the ACHR, at the expense of other treaties. This trend might be partially explained by the generous interpretation of the ACHR by the IACHR and IACtHR, as well as the lack of widespread ratification of the other treaties.[38] The available legal framework has impacted the paths followed by the IASHR for the protection of ESCER, as is more fully explained in the section on jurisprudential and doctrinal developments.

## 3.    MONITORING AND PROTECTION MECHANISMS

### 3.1    The Inter-American Commission and Court on Human Rights

The IASHR's monitoring bodies are primarily the Inter-American Commission and Court of Human Rights. Through the OAS Charter, the IACHR is competent to monitor and promote human rights in the region.[39] It was created during the Fifth Meeting of Consultation of the Ministers of Foreign Affairs of the Organization of American States of 1959,[40] and the OAS Charter later established the IACHR as one of its principal organs in 1967.[41] The IACHR has jurisdiction over all OAS Member States and it promotes and protects fundamental rights through a vast range of monitoring tools, as well as through the processing of individual cases.[42]

The American Convention on Human Rights provides the legal basis for the establishment of the IACtHR, which functions as a complementary jurisdictional body for the protection of human rights in the Americas.[43] States can opt in for the Court's contentious jurisdiction by making a declaration after ratifying the ACHR.[44]

---

[35]    See generally Escazú Agreement (n 33).
[36]    Ibid.
[37]    Ibid Article 9.
[38]    Both factors might have reinforced each other.
[39]    OAS Charter (n 3) Article 106.
[40]    Declaration of Santiago, Chile, adopted on occasion of the Fifth Meeting of Consultation of Ministers of Foreign Affairs, Santiago, Chile, August 12–18, 1959, Final Act, Doc. OEA/Ser.C/II.5, 4–6 <www.oas.org/consejo/MEETINGS%20OF%20CONSULTATION/minutes.asp>.
[41]    Protocol of Amendment to the Charter of the Organization of American States 'Protocol of Buenos Aires' (adopted 27 February 1967, entered into force 12 March 1970) 721 UNTS 324 Article XV.
[42]    'Statute of the Inter-American Commission on Human Rights', *Organization of American States* (1 November 1979) OEA/Ser.P/IX.0.2/80, Vol 1, 88.
[43]    American Convention on Human Rights (n 19) ch VIII.
[44]    American Convention on Human Rights (n 19) Article 62.

The IACtHR started its activities in 1979, a year after the ACHR entered into force.[45] The Court protects fundamental rights through two main tools: the issuance of Advisory Opinions and the processing of individual cases.[46] This tribunal is considered the last jurisdictional recourse to establish State responsibility for human rights violations[47] – as opposed to criminal liability or the civil responsibility of private entities or individuals – for persons in States that have ratified the American Convention, the Convention of Belém do Pará, and other Inter-American treaties.[48]

Most Inter-American human rights treaties also include norms of attribution of responsibility that enable the IACHR and the IACtHR to engage in the monitoring of human rights compliance and to establish State responsibility for violations of the protected rights through individual petitions and other tools, such as reports and press releases.[49] However, some of the latest regional treaties have also created additional bodies for the promotion of rights or have limited the scope of the competence of the IASHR derived from the specific conventions – as will be explored later in this chapter.

### 3.1.1 Individual petitions and interim measures

Individual petitions are a key instrument for the protection of rights under the IASHR. These petitions can determine State responsibility for violations of rights protected under the American Declaration, the American Convention, or one of the other Inter-American treaties that bind the State through ratification.[50]

There are few requirements to file a petition before the Inter-American Commission on Human Rights. Any person, group of persons, or nongovernmental organizations recognized in one of the OAS Member States can submit a petition to the IACHR.[51] The submission of complaints can be done on behalf of persons or a group of persons, such as indigenous peoples; however, the rights of corporations or other similar legal entities are not protected under the regional system.[52] In addition, the subject of the petition should not be pending in another

---

[45]   Jo M. Pasqualucci, *The Practice and Procedure of the Inter-American Court of Human Rights* (Cambridge University Press 2013) 6.

[46]   American Convention on Human Rights (n 19) Articles 62 & 64.

[47]   American Convention on Human Rights (n 19) Article 61.

[48]   In all, 23 countries have ratified the American Convention on Human Rights. See 'American Convention on Human Rights "Pact of San Jose" Signatories and Ratifications', *Organization of American States* <www.oas.org/dil/treaties_B-32_American_Convention_on_Human_Rights_sign .htm>; 'Inter-American Convention on the Prevention, Punishment and Eradication of Violence Against Women "Convention of Belem do Para" Signatories and Ratifications', *Organization of American States* <www.oas.org/juridico/english/sigs/a-61.html>.

[49]   'Rules of Procedure of the Inter-American Commission on Human Rights', *Inter-American Commission on Human Rights* Article 23 <www.oas.org/en/iachr/mandate/basics/rulesiachr.asp>.

[50]   Ibid.

[51]   Ibid. The submission of complaints can be done on behalf of persons or groups of persons, or indigenous or tribal peoples, or unions. See *The Standing of Legal Entities in the Inter-American Human Rights System*, Advisory Opinion OC-22/16. Inter-American Court of Human Rights Series A No 22 (26 February 2016).

[52]   Ibid. See also *The Standing of Legal Entities in the Inter-American Human Rights System*, Advisory Opinion OC-22/16, Inter-American Court of Human Rights Series A No 22 (26 February 2016).

international settlement procedure.[53] There are several exceptions to this rule, however. If the petitioner in the other procedure is a third party or a nongovernmental entity, the Commission may consider the petition.[54] The Commission may also consider the petition if the other procedure is limited to a general investigation and there has been no decision regarding the specific facts in the petition before the Commission, or it will not lead to an effective settlement.[55]

The IACHR requires the exhaustion of domestic judicial remedies before it can consider a petition.[56] There are several exceptions to this rule too, which are foreseen in the ACHR, the Commission's Rules of Procedure, and jurisprudence. They include, but are not limited to, unwarranted delay in the rendering of justice, denial of access to justice, lack of due process, and monetary barriers to accessing justice.[57] Initial petitions must be submitted within six months of the party's notification of the final judgment (if there is one), or within a reasonable time if an exception to the rule of exhaustion of domestic remedies applies.[58]

For a Member State to lodge a petition against another Member State before the Commission, both States must have ratified the American Convention, as well as having filed a separate declaration recognizing the competence of the Commission.[59]

The individual process is based on a set of key principles including good faith, pro personae, equality of arms, and publicity, among others. The aggrieved party has the burden of proof of the allegations submitted in the complaint. The standard of proof is that of reasonability and it takes patterns of violations and custody into account among the circumstances that may revert the burden of proof. Evidentiary rules are very flexible in admitting different sorts of evidence. These rules are of special importance in the IASHR, since most States contest many of the facts alleged in the initial complaint, making the process not only one where legal standards and admissibility requirements are relevant, but one where evidentiary standards are critical for the international process.[60]

---

[53]    American Convention on Human Rights (n 19) Article 47. 'Rules of Procedure of the Inter-American Commission on Human Rights', *Inter-American Commission on Human Rights* Article 23 <www.oas.org/en/iachr/mandate/basics/rulesiachr.asp>. For the Court's jurisprudence on the matter, see *Ricardo Baena et al. v Panama*, Merits, Reparations, and Costs, Judgment, Inter-American Court of Human Rights Series C No. 72 (2 February 2001).

[54]    American Convention on Human Rights (n 19) Article 47; 'Rules of Procedure of the Inter-American Commission on Human Rights', *Inter-American Commission on Human Rights* Article 23 <www.oas.org/en/iachr/mandate/basics/rulesiachr.asp>.

[55]    American Convention on Human Rights (n 19) Article 47; 'Rules of Procedure of the Inter-American Commission on Human Rights' (*Inter-American Commission on Human Rights*) Article 23 <www.oas.org/en/iachr/mandate/basics/rulesiachr.asp>.

[56]    American Convention on Human Rights (n 19) Article 46; Commission Rules of Procedure (n 54) Article 31.

[57]    American Convention on Human Rights (n 19) Article 46.2; Commission Rules of Procedure (n 54) Article 31; *Exceptions to the Exhaustion of Domestic Remedies (Articles 46(1), 46(2)(a) and 46 (2) (b) of the American Convention on Human Rights)*, Advisory Opinion OC-11/90, Inter-American Court of Human Rights, Series A No 11 (10 August 1990).

[58]    American Convention on Human Rights (n 19) Article 46.1(b); Commission Rules of Procedure (n 54) Article 32. See also e.g. *Osmín Ricardo Tobar Ramírez, Jeffrey Rainiery Arias Ramírez et al. v Guatemala*, Case 12.896, Inter-American Commission on Human Rights, Report No 8/13, Admissibility paras 49–50 (2013).

[59]    American Convention on Human Rights (n 19) Article 45.

[60]    This is different from the European system of regional protection of human rights, in which generally the applicant must prove that there was an interference with one of his or her rights enshrined in

Once the Commission receives a petition, it preliminarily evaluates the petition, and makes a decision as to the petition's admissibility.[61] The Commission then engages in fact-finding procedures, receives pleadings of fact and law by both parties, and attempts to bring about a friendly settlement between the parties.[62] If the Commission attributes any violations of human rights to the State, it issues a report on the merits, as explained below.[63]

If a State does not comply with the Commission's recommendations, or if a State wishes to challenge the Commission's attribution of responsibility, the case may be referred to the IACtHR, as long as the State has ratified the ACHR and accepted the compulsory jurisdiction of the Court.[64] As such, if the Court finds the State accountable for human rights violations, the State is legally bound to comply with the judgment of the Court.[65]

For cases that cannot be submitted to the Court due to lack of competence or jurisdictional reasons, individual petitions end with a final report by the Commission, which states its findings of facts, law, and recommendations.[66] Those recommendations must be considered in good faith by Member States; a number of scholars consider them binding.[67] Both the Commission and Court have follow-up procedures to ensure compliance,[68] and they retain their competence until their decisions and judgments have been fully implemented.[69]

---

the European Convention. If the interference is proven, the respondent State must prove that it can be justified (if such a justification is permitted by the applicable provision). Mónika Ambrus, 'The European Court of Human Rights and Standards of Proof' in Wouter Werner and Lukasz Gruszczynski (eds) *Deference in International Courts and Tribunals: Standard of Review and Margin of Appreciation* (OUP 2014) (see Chapter 4 of this book).

[61] American Convention on Human Rights (n 19) Article 47. 'Rules of Procedure of the Inter-American Commission on Human Rights' (*Inter-American Commission on Human Rights*) Articles 35–36 <www.oas.org/en/iachr/mandate/basics/rulesiachr.asp>.

[62] American Convention on Human Rights (n 19) Articles 48–51.

[63] Commission Rules of Procedure (n 54) Article 44.

[64] American Convention on Human Rights (n 19) Article 62; Commission Rules of Procedure (n 54) Article 45. The State could also accept the Court's jurisdiction for a specific case. The Commission submits a case to the Court after hearing the victims, and assessing if justice has been done taking into account, *inter alia*, the petitioner's view, the nature and seriousness of the violation, the need to develop the jurisprudence, and the effect of the judgment at the domestic level.

[65] American Convention on Human Rights (n 19) Article 62. This two-tiered system was inspired by the European system, which was originally composed of a Commission and a Court. In 1998, the European System abolished the Commission in Protocol no 11, replacing the European Commission of Human Rights and the original ECHR with a new permanent, full time court with sole compulsory jurisdiction over determinations of admissibility, fact-finding and issues of law. Protocol No 11 to the Convention for the Protection of Human Rights and Fundamental Freedoms, ETS 155 (see Chapter 4 of this book).

[66] Commission Rules of Procedure (n 54) Articles 43–44.

[67] See ESCR-Net's Strategic Litigation Working Group, 'Implementation of Decisions of the Inter-American Commission on Human Rights Discussion Paper' 5 <www.escr-net.org/sites/default/files/201802-discussion-paper-of-escr-nets-strategic-litigation-working-group.pdf>.

[68] Commission Rules of Procedure (n 54) Article 48; 'Rules of Procedure of the Inter-American Court of Human Rights', *Inter-American Court of Human Rights* Article 69 <www.cidh.oas.org/Basicos/English/Basic20.Rules%20of%20Procedure%20of%20the%20Court.htm>.

[69] American Convention on Human Rights (n 19) Articles 33, 61(1), 62(3) & 65; Court Rules of Procedure (n 68) Article 69; 'Statute of the Inter-American Court of Human Rights', *Inter-American Court of Human Rights* Article 30 <www.oas.org/en/iachr/mandate/basics/statutecourt.asp>. The process before the Court includes the victims and the State as parties, and only procedurally, the Commission. The Commission's role at the Court is still very relevant but it consists primarily in ensuring the pres-

Interim measures can secure the rights protected under the Inter-American treaties or the integrity of access to the IASHR under exceptional circumstances. Precautionary measures and provisional measures may be issued by the IACHR and the IACtHR respectively when there is an imminent danger of irreparable harm to a right protected under the ACHR or relevant Inter-American treaty to a person or group of persons.[70] A petitioner or his/her representative can request interim measures for cases pending before the Commission or the Court. The Commission can grant interim measures even if there is not a case pending before the IASHR in order to prevent the infliction of irreparable harm. Moreover, a petitioner can request that the IACHR submit a request for provisional measures even before a case is referred to the IACtHR. Additionally, both monitoring bodies can act on their own initiative and issue interim measures without a request from the petitioner.[71]

In practice, interim measures are in high demand but are not granted in the majority of cases.[72] They have been applied less to secure goods in dispute or the execution of the judgment, and more to ensure the protection of victims, lawyers, indigenous peoples, defenders, and journalists at risk.[73]

Precautionary measures are not subject to a requirement of exhaustion of domestic remedies, though there is a need to explain what measures were taken to secure the right domestically.[74] Moreover, the facts that support precautionary measures are not subject to the same standard of proof as a complaint. They must be credible and consistent *prima facie* and their conclusions do not influence the case on the merits later on.[75] Some interesting features of the Commission's precautionary measures are: (1) its mandate includes consultation with those whose rights are at risk in order to determine the necessary measures of protection; (2) its orders oftentimes include a recommendation to take into account culturally appropriate

---

ervation of public interest. In contrast to the process at the Commission, the Court's process generally includes an oral phase where issues of admissibility, merit, and reparations are debated.

[70]   Commission Rules of Procedure (n 54) Articles 25 & 76; American Convention on Human Rights (n 19) Article 63(2). For more detailed background on precautionary measures, see Brian Griffey and Viviana Krsticevic, 'Interim Measures' in Malcolm Langford, Bruce Porter, Rebecca Brown and Julieta Rossi (eds) *The Optional Protocol to the International Covenant on Economic, Social and Cultural Rights: A Commentary* (PULP 2016).

[71]   Commission Rules of Procedure (n 54) Article 25.1; Court Rules of Procedure (n 68) Article 27. The IACHR can issue precautionary measures in situations that are not linked to petitions. See Commission Rules of Procedure (n 54) Article 25.1. The IACtHR can issue provisional measures on pending cases or while supervising the execution of its judgments. *See* Court Rules of Procedure (n 68) Article 27 ('*At any stage* of proceedings involving cases of extreme gravity and urgency, and when necessary to avoid irreparable damage to persons, the Court may, on its own motion, order such provisional measures as it deems appropriate…') (emphasis added); see also e.g. *Bámaca Velázquez v Guatemala*, Provisional Measures, Order of the Court, Inter-American Court Human Rights Series E No 4, at 1, 'Decides' para 2 (5 September 2001) (the IA Court ordered urgent measures of protection, upon request of the representative of the victims after the case has already been decided as to the merits). The Court can also order provisional measures in cases being processed by the Commission at its request. *See* Court Rules of Procedure (n 68) Article 25.2.

[72]   Only 4.3 per cent of requested precautionary measures were granted in 2017. See 'Annual Report 2017', *Inter-American Commission on Human Rights* (2018) 71–73 <www.oas.org/en/iachr/docs/annual/2017/TOC.asp>.

[73]   See Griffey and Krsticevic (n 70) at 313–16.

[74]   Commission Rules of Procedure (n 54) Article 25.

[75]   See e.g. Matter of Fred Smith and others regarding the Bahamas, Inter-American Commission on Human Rights, MC 706/16, 4 November 2016.

measures; (3) precautionary measures are adopted on behalf of groups of persons that are sometimes identified but not personally named; and (4) they generally include an order to investigate the sources of threats or attacks under the logic that deactivation of the risks is the ultimate measure of protection.[76]

Many precautionary measures have been issued to protect environmental defenders and others involved in the protection of ESCER in their rights to physical integrity, life, and residence.[77] A few precautionary measures have been granted for the direct protection of ESCER, primarily for the protection of the rights to health, territory, cultural rights, and education.[78] These include measures focused on the right to health based on access to treatments or medicines;[79] measures linked to potential health consequences of pollution and non-refoulement based on lack of access to treatment;[80] right to secure a people's territory;[81] and measures that involve access to education of children with disabilities.[82]

The Court has a long tradition of issuing provisional measures as well; many provisional measures are related to cases pending in or decided by the Court. According to its jurisprudence, provisional measures can have a protective or precautionary purpose.[83] The vast majority of measures have been granted to protect the rights to physical integrity and/or life, and only in exceptional circumstances have been coupled with other rights, such as freedom of expression.[84]

---

[76] See generally 'Precautionary Measures', *Inter-American Commission on Human Rights* <www.oas.org/en/iachr/decisions/precautionary.asp>.

[77] Some of those measures include: Berta Caceres, Honduras, Inter-American Commission on Human Rights, MC 196/09; Members of the community Cerrito Lindo, Honduras, Inter-American Commission on Human Rights, MC 935/04; Juana Calfunao and others, Chile, Inter-American Commission on Human Rights, MC 46/14; Erlendy Cuero Bravo and others, Colombia, Inter-American Commission on Human Rights, MC 204/17; Fred Smith and others, Bahamas, Inter-American Commission on Human Rights, MC 706/16, MC 658/16; Jani Silva, Hugo Miramar, and Saúl Luna (Leaders of the Perla Amazónica Reserve Zone), Colombia, Inter-American Commission on Human Rights, MC 204/17; Sergio López Cantera, Mexico, Inter-American Commission on Human Rights, MC 1165/18; Mónica López Baltodano and family, Nicaragua, Inter-American Commission on Human Rights, MC 1130/18; and Mônica Tereza Azeredo Benício, Brazil, Inter-American Commission on Human Rights, MC 767/18.

[78] For an in-depth discussion of several of these cases, see Griffey and Krsticevic (n 70) at 314–16.

[79] Luis, Colombia, Inter-American Commission on Human Rights, MC 747/16; TSGT, Colombia, Inter-American Commission on Human Rights, MC 283/18; CL and others, Venezuela, Inter-American Commission on Human Rights, MC 145/18.

[80] Community of La Oroya, Peru, Inter-American Commission on Human Rights, MC 1473/06; MBBP, Panama, Inter-American Commission on Human Rights, MC 490/18.

[81] Members of the Siona People, Colombia, Inter-American Commission on Human Rights, MC 395/18.

[82] Irene, Argentina, Inter-American Commission on Human Rights, MC 38/16. The resolution on the measures only indirectly mentions access to education through the protection of her right to life and physical integrity.

[83] See *Four Ngöbe Indigenous Communities and their Members v Panama*, Provisional Measures, Order of the Court, Inter-American Court on Human Rights Series E 'Considering That' para 3 (28 May 2010).

[84] Since 2014, the Inter-American Court on Human Rights has systemized the decisions it has issued on provisional measures. The latest version was updated in December 2017. See 'Sistematización de las resoluciones sobre medidas provisionales emitidas por la Corte Interamericana de Derechos Humanos', *Inter-American Court of Human Rights* <www.corteidh.or.cr/sitios/libros/todos/docs/Sistematizacion.pdf>.

Nevertheless, in the last few years provisional measures have been granted for an increasingly narrow range of issues, and they have been required to meet a higher standard of proof.[85] Furthermore, the Court has stated that it would not take contextual elements into account when evaluating risks, basing this limitation on prior Court decisions.[86] It has also taken a restrictive position on the types of provisional measures that it can issue, asserting that orders to investigate attacks and threats do not fall in the realm of provisional measures.[87] Over the past decade, the number of new requests for provisional measures that the Commission has submitted to the Court has declined.[88]

Interestingly for the development of ESCER, in a recent provisional measure, the IACtHR granted and maintained a number of measures in favor of communities belonging to the Miskito indigenous people, including measures to study the underlying causes of conflict and violence in the Atlantic Coast of Nicaragua, and proposed steps to overcome the displacement and violence that plagued the ancestral lands of the Miskito.[89]

### 3.1.2    Advisory opinions and reports

The development of doctrine by the IACHR and IACtHR has also been an important way to expand the guarantee of rights. Two of the main tools used have been the adoption of Advisory Opinions (issued by the Court) and Reports or Recommendations (issued by the Commission).

Advisory Opinions are authoritative statements on different human rights issues adopted by the IACtHR in response to questions posed by OAS Member States and a limited set of OAS organs.[90] The Court has no authority to issue Opinions without a formal request by an authorized party.[91] To address compatibility of domestic laws with the human rights framework, the Court must receive a formal request by the Member State that issued the laws in question.[92]

Advisory Opinions permit the IACtHR to interpret States' obligations concerning the protection of human rights that derive from the ACHR or other applicable treaties.[93] The Court's Opinions have included not only human rights treaties, but also obligations under general

---

[85]    See e.g. *La Rochela Massacre v Colombia,* Provisional Measures, Order of the Court, Inter-American Court on Human Rights Series E No 3 (16 February 2017) 'Considering That' para 38.

[86]    See e.g. *Rosenda Cantú v Mexico,* Provisional Measures, Order of the Court, Inter-American Court on Human Rights Series E No 4 (23 February 2016) 'Considering That' para 19.

[87]    *Bámaca Velázquez v Guatemala,* Provisional Measures, Order of the Court, Inter-American Court Human Rights Series E No 12 (22 September 2018).

[88]    Compare 'Annual Report of the Inter-American Court on Human Rights 2010', *Inter-American Court of Human Rights* (2011) 76–81 <www.corteidh.or.cr/sitios/informes/docs/ENG/eng_2010.pdf> with 'Annual Report of the Inter-American Court on Human Rights 2017', *Inter-American Court of Human Rights* (2018) 101–103 <www.corteidh.or.cr/tablas/informe2017/ingles.pdf>.

[89]    *Members of the Miskitu Indigenous People of the North Caribbean Coast v Nicaragua,* Provisional Measures, Order of the Court, Inter-American Court on Human Rights Series E (1 September 2016) 'Decides'.

[90]    American Convention on Human Rights (n 19) Article 64(1).

[91]    American Convention on Human Rights (n 19) Article 64.

[92]    American Convention on Human Rights (n 19) Article 64(1).

[93]    American Convention on Human Rights (n 19) Article 64.

international law, refugee law, gender, and others.[94] A recent landmark Opinion develops some of the standards for the protection of the right to a healthy environment.[95]

The IACHR has done extensive monitoring of the human rights situation in the region through country and thematic reports. While most of these reports have dealt with violations of civil and political rights, incrementally, the Commission has included analysis of the interlinkages between violations of civil rights and violations of ESCER.[96] Moreover, the Commission has recently issued a report on poverty,[97] and another on the impact of extractive industries on indigenous peoples, Afro-descendants, and natural resources in the region.[98]

### 3.1.3 Thematic or general hearings

The IACHR has used thematic or general hearings as a tool to obtain relevant information of the situation of human rights in the region, including ESCER.[99] This tool can focus on a country, the whole region, or a sub-region, and can tackle one or several topics.[100]

---

[94] See *Entitlement of legal entities to hold rights under the Inter-American Human Rights System (Interpretation and scope of Article 1(2), in relation to Articles 1(2), 8, 11(2), 13, 16, 21, 24, 25, 29, 30, 44, 46 and 62(3) of the American Convention on Human Rights, as well as of Article 8(1)(A) and (B) of the Protocol of San Salvador)*, Advisory Opinion OC-22/16, Inter-American Court on Human Rights Series A No 22 (26 February 2016); *The institution of asylum, and its recognition as a human right under the Inter-American System of Protection (interpretation and scope of Articles 5, 22(7) and 22(8) in relation to Article 1(1) of the American Convention on Human Rights)*, Advisory Opinion OC-25/18, Inter-American Court on Human Rights Series A No 25 (30 May 2018); *Gender identity, and equality and non-discrimination with regard to same-sex couples. State obligations in relation to change of name, gender identity, and rights deriving from a relationship between same-sex couples (interpretation and scope of Articles 1(1), 3, 7, 11(2), 13, 17, 18 and 24, in relation to Article 1, of the American Convention on Human Rights)*, Advisory Opinion OC-24/17, Inter-American Court on Human Rights Series A No. 24 (24 November 2017).

[95] *The Environment and Human Rights (State obligations in relation to the environment in the context of the protection and guarantee of the rights to life and to personal integrity – interpretation and scope of Articles 4(1) and 5(1) of the American Convention on Human Rights)*, Advisory Opinion OC-23/17, Inter-American Court on Human Rights Series A No. 23 (15 November 2017).

[96] See Inter-American Commission on Human Rights, *Report on the Situation of Human Rights in Guatemala: Diversity, Inequality and Exclusion*, OEA/Ser.L/V/II., Doc.43/15 (2015); Inter-American Commission on Human Rights, *Indigenous women and their human rights in the Americas*, OEA/Ser.L/V/II. Doc.44/17 (2017 Inter-American Commission on Human Rights, *Missing and Murdered Indigenous Women in British Columbia*, Canada, OEA/Ser.L/V/II. Doc.30/14 (2014); and Inter-American Commission on Human Rights, *Towards the Effective Fulfillment of Children's Rights: National Protection Systems*, OEA/Ser.L/V/II. Doc.206/17 (2017) paras 384–87.

[97] Inter-American Commission on Human Rights, *Report on poverty and human rights in the Americas*, OEA/Ser.L/V/II.164 Doc. 147 (2017).

[98] Inter-American Commission on Human Rights, *Indigenous peoples, Afro-descendent communities, and natural resources: Human rights protection in the context of extraction, exploitation, and development activities*, OEA/Ser.L/V/II.Doc. 47/15 (2015).

[99] Commission Rules of Procedure (n 54) Article 66. In the handling of individual cases, the IACHR can also call for hearings to debate issues of admissibility, merits, friendly settlements, precautionary measures, and so on. However, most of the actual process before the IACHR is generally exclusively written. Parties generally engage in conversations, friendly settlement processes and other actions to secure the implementation of precautionary measures or the decisions of the IACHR with limited engagement by the Commission or the Secretariat.

[100] Commission Rules of Procedure (n 54) Article 66.

Generally, the IACHR has three to six periods of sessions where Commissioners and Rapporteurs host hearings on a wide variety of topics, reaching more than 200 thematic hearings a year.[101] The Commission can receive proposals for hearings or call them on its own initiative.[102]

Most hearings include civil society organizations or individuals and State representatives who present factual information or legal arguments. Some of the information collected at general hearings permeates country or thematic reports, as well as precautionary measures.[103]

Hearings are generally public, unless they might entail risks to those participating in them, in which case they may be closed.[104] Most hearings are available in real time, through livestreaming, and are archived in the Commission's website for future reference.[105]

In the past decade, many hearings have dealt with key aspects of ESCER in the region, ranging from the protection of environmental defenders, afro-descendant communities, and indigenous peoples,[106] to the right to water;[107] the right to health;[108] State and corporate responsibility of extractive industries;[109] reproductive health and maternal mortality;[110] and the right to education of persons with disabilities.[111]

### 3.1.4    Rapporteurships and the Special Rapporteur on ESCER

The IACHR has also organized its monitoring and protection work through rapporteurships based on specific topics, specific protected groups, or countries. The rapporteurships include a focus on indigenous peoples, women, children, migrants, human rights defenders, persons

---

[101]   In 2017, the Commission held four sessions, which included 117 hearings. See 'IACHR Sessions', *Inter-American Commission on Human Rights* <www.oas.org/en/iachr/activities/sessions.asp>.

[102]   Commission Rules of Procedure (n 54) Article 61.

[103]   See e.g. *Reports of Human Rights Violations and Criminalization of Defenders in the Context of Extractive Industries in Nicaragua* (168 Session of Inter-American Commission of Human Rights, 7 May 2018); *PM-112-16: Berta Cáceres – Honduras* (170 Session of Inter-American Commission of Human Rights, 6 December 2018); *Repression and Violations of Human Rights in Nicaragua* (170 Session of Inter-American Commission of Human Rights, 6 December 2018).

[104]   Commission Rules of Procedure (n 54) Article 69.

[105]   Commission Rules of Procedure (n 54) Article 70. See also 'IACHR Sessions', *Inter-American Commission on Human Rights* <www.oas.org/en/iachr/activities/sessions.asp>.

[106]   *Reports of Killings, Threats, and Forced Displacement of Defenders of Land Rights of Indigenous Peoples and Afro-descendants in Colombia* (169 Session of Inter-American Commission on Human Rights, 3 October 2018).

[107]   *Human Rights and Water in America* (156 Session of Inter-American Commission on Human Rights, 23 October 2015).

[108]   See e.g. *Right to Health and Lack of Medicine in the Americas* (159 Session of Inter-American Commission on Human Rights, 6 December 2016); *Situation of the Right to Health in Guatemala* (159 Session of Inter-American Commission on Human Rights, 6 December 2016); *Right to Health and Access to Medicine in Venezuela* (158 Session of Inter-American Commission on Human Rights, 7 June 2016).

[109]   *Serious Health Problems Experienced by Peruvian Miners and State and Corporate Responsibility* (169 Session of Inter-American Commission on Human Rights, 1 October 2018).

[110]   See e.g. *Maternal Mortality in the Americas* (137 Session of Inter-American Commission on Human Rights, 6 November 2009); *Right to Reproductive Health of Women who Live with HIV/AIDS in the Americas* (140 Session of Inter-American Commission on Human Rights, 26 October 2010).

[111]   *Right to Education of Persons with Disabilities in the Americas* (137 Session of Inter-American Commission on Human Rights, 6 November 2009).

deprived of their freedom, LGTBI, freedom of expression, and, since 2017, ESCER.[112] The rapporteurships on freedom of expression and ESCER are special rapporteurships, staffed with an independent expert.[113]

For the past ten years, IACHR rapporteurs have issued reports dealing with different aspects of ESCER, including indigenous peoples' access to land, discrimination in accessing ESCER, maternal mortality, access to health information, environmental issues, and poverty.[114]

The appointment of a Special Rapporteur on ESCER has significantly increased the capacity of the IACHR to pursue, deepen, and highlight the interdependence of ESCER with many of the issues currently on the agenda of the IASHR,[115] as well as to protect ESCER. Since its establishment, the rapporteurship has focused primarily on the development of standards on business and human rights, promoting hearings on the topic, and participating in IACHR visits and activities with the purpose of strengthening its mandate.[116]

## 3.2 Supplementary Mechanisms

A number of Inter-American conventions contain monitoring frameworks which supplement the role of the IACHR and increase the possibility of accessing the Court, while also establishing 'follow-up' mechanisms. Most of these follow-up mechanisms are composed of a Committee of Experts, with each State Party appointing one expert to a Convention's Committee.[117]

These follow-up mechanisms monitor and assess State Parties' compliance with the various conventions focused on specific rights or groups, allowing States to hold each other accountable on a number of issues.[118] In formulating the objectives and principles of the follow-up mechanisms, Member States have followed the models provided by the follow-up

---

[112] 'Thematic Rapporteurships and Units', *Inter-American Commission on Human Rights* <www .oas.org/en/iachr/mandate/rapporteurships.asp>. Soledad Garcia Munoz was named as first ESCER Rapporteur of the IACHR for a period of three years. See 'IACHR Chooses Soledad García Muñoz as Special Rapporteur on Economic, Social, Cultural, and Environmental Rights (ESCER)' (*Inter-American Commission on Human Rights*, 5 July 2017) <www.oas.org/en/iachr/media_center/PReleases/2017/090 .asp>.

[113] Commission Rules of Procedure (n 54) Article 15(4).

[114] See 'Thematic Reports', *Inter-American Commission on Human Rights* <www.oas.org/en/iachr/ reports/thematic.asp>.

[115] Chapter 15 of this book addresses the issue of interdependence further.

[116] See 'Unit on Economic, Social and Cultural Rights', *Inter-American Commission on Human Rights* <www.oas.org/en/iachr/desc/>.

[117] See Committee of Experts, 'Rules of Procedure of the Committee of Experts of the Mechanism to Follow Up on the Implementation of the Inter-American Convention on the Prevention, Punishment, and Eradication of Violence against Women, "Convention of Belém do Pará"' (*Follow-up Mechanism to the Belém do Pará*, 24–25 Aug. 2005) Article 2 <www.oas.org/en/mesecvi/docs/MESECVI -BasicDocuments-EN.doc>; Convention on Persons with Disabilities (n 24) Article VI; Convention against Racism (n 24) Article IV; Convention against All Forms of Discrimination (n 27) Article IV; and Convention on Protecting the Human Rights of Older Persons (n 28) Article 35. Since the Convention of Belém do Pará is the only one of these conventions in force, its follow-up mechanism will be discussed in the following paragraph.

[118] 'Follow-Up Mechanisms', *Organization of American States* <www.oas.org/en/about/mechanisms .asp>.

mechanisms of the Inter-American Convention against Corruption,[119] and of the multilateral evaluation mechanism, the latter of which was established to implement antidrug strategies in the region.[120] The adaptation of models that were originally intended as follow-up mechanisms for non-human rights obligations to Inter-American human rights conventions has been widely criticized,[121] particularly as they require peer review rather than judicial review for alleged violations.

Under a mandate of the OAS General Assembly,[122] the Inter-American Commission of Women, the first inter-governmental body established to ensure recognition of women's human rights,[123] established the Follow-up Mechanism to the Belém do Pará ('MESECVI'), which 'analyzes progress in the implementation of the Convention by the states party, as well as persistent challenges to an effective State response to violence against women'.[124] In addition to a Committee of Experts,[125] as mentioned earlier, MESECVI also consists of the Conference of states parties,[126] the Technical Secretariat,[127] and civil society.[128] States inform the Committee of Experts on their compliance with selected indicators and the Committee then prepares national reports for each of the States that has submitted information, and consolidates these results into a broad Follow-up Report.[129] To date, there have been three Hemispheric Reports on the Implementation of the Belém do Pará Convention.[130] It is worth

---

[119]   Mechanism for Follow-Up on the Implementation of the Inter-American Convention against Corruption, OEA/Ser.P AG/RES. 1784 (XXXIO/01) 5 June 2001.

[120]   Inter-American Drug Abuse Control Commission (CICAD), Multilateral Evaluation Mechanism (MEM), Resolution 1/99 (XXVI-O/99) 5–7 October 1999.

[121]   See 'Evaluation of the Statute of the Mechanism to Follow-Up on the Implementation of the Convention of Belém do Pará', *Center for Justice and International Law* (2006) <www.cejil.org/sites/default/files/legacy_files/position_paper_2.pdf>; Ariel Dulitzky, 'The Inter-American Human Rights System Fifty Years Later: Time for Changes' [2011] Quebec J Int'l L 127, 148; and Susana Chiarotti Boero, 'Women's Citizen Security' [2011] 65 U Miami L Rev 797.

[122]   Third Biennial Report on Fulfillment of Resolution, AG/RES. 1456 (XXVII-O/97) 'Promotion of the Inter-American Convention on the Prevention, Punishment, and Eradication of Violence against Women, "Convention of Belém do Pará"', AG/RES. 1942 (XXXIII-O/03) 10 June 2003.

[123]   'CIM Mission and Mandate', *Organization of American States* <www.oas.org/en/CIM/about.asp>.

[124]   'What is MESECVI?' *Organization of American States* <www.oas.org/en/mesecvi/about.asp>.

[125]   The MESCEVI Committee of Experts developed a matrix of indicators to be distributed to states parties on the implementation of the Convention, to review their responses and to elaborate recommendations in the national and hemispheric reports. *See* 'Committee of Experts', *Organization of American States* <www.oas.org/en/mesecvi/experts.asp>.

[126]   The Conference of States Parties is a political body of states party representatives (Competent National Authorities) who discuss national reports and adopt hemispheric reports produced by the Committee of Experts. 'States Party to the Belém do Pará Convention', *Organization of American States* <www.oas.org/en/mesecvi/states.asp>.

[127]   The Technical Secretariat is responsible for the strategic and administrative operation of MESECVI. 'MESECVI Secretariat', *Organization of American States* <www.oas.org/en/mesecvi/secretariat.asp>.

[128]   Civil society present shadow reports to the Committee of Experts of the MESECVI on State Parties' implementation of the Convention of Belém do Pará. 'Civil Society Organizations', *Organization of American States* <www.oas.org/en/mesecvi/civilsociety.asp>.

[129]   For a detailed overview of the process, see 'The MESECVI Process', *Organization of American States* <www.oas.org/en/mesecvi/process.asp> and 'Indicators [sic] of the Exercise of Women's Right to Live Free of Violence', *Organization of American States* <www.oas.org/en/mesecvi/indicators.asp>.

[130]   'Library', *Organization of American States* <www.oas.org/en/mesecvi/library.asp>.

noting that the region maintains the highest rate of gender-based sexual violence against women in the world.[131]

The Working Group on the Protocol of San Salvador ('Working Group') is the monitoring body of the Protocol of San Salvador, composed of four government experts, two independent experts, and two Commissioners from IACHR, representing a total of seven countries in the region.[132] The Working Group was established to examine the progress reports of the State Parties to the Protocol.[133] State Parties to the Protocol are required to submit periodic reports on the progressive measures they have taken to ensure due respect for the rights set forth in the Protocol.[134] To measure State Parties' progress, the Working Group proposed progress indicators, which OAS General Assembly approved in 2012.[135] The reports are prepared through a participatory dialogue with different sectors of civil society in a complementary way that does not replicate the reports drafted for other international human rights protection mechanisms. Unlike the other follow-up mechanisms in the Inter-American system, the Working Group does not promote comparison between States; nor does it aspire to rank their compliance, instead evaluating each national process separately.

The Escazú Agreement has a significantly different implementation and follow-up mechanism, primarily because it was adopted under the auspices of ECLAC, not the OAS.[136] For example, it does not have a complaint mechanism composed by independent or governmental experts, nor does it have a norm of attribution of responsibility that grants competence to the IASHR. The agreement calls for State Parties to report the measures that they have adopted to implement the Agreement to a Conference of Parties.[137] When the Agreement enters into force, the Conference will also prepare protocols and establish the subsidiary bodies necessary to implement the Agreement.[138] These subsidiary bodies will draft reports and recommendations for the Conference's consideration.[139] The expectation is that Aarhus, and its monitoring tools and practices, might serve to inspire the Escazú process.

---

[131] 'From Commitment to Action: Policies to End Violence Against Women in Latin America and the Caribbean', *UNDP* and *UN Women* (2017) 6, <www.latinamerica.undp.org/content/dam/rblac/docs/Research%20and%20Publications/Empoderamiento%20de%20la%20Mujer/UNDP-RBLAC-ReportVCMEnglish.pdf>.

[132] 'Protocol of San Salvador: Working Group', *Organization of American States* <www.oas.org/en/sare/social-inclusion/protocol-ssv/working-group.asp>.

[133] Organization of American States, *Protocol of San Salvador: Composition and Functioning of the Working Group to Examine the Periodic Reports of the States Parties*, AG/RES. 2262 (XXXVII-O/07) 5 June 2007.

[134] Protocol of San Salvador (n 21) Article19.

[135] Laura Pautassi, *Monitoring Access to Information from the Perspective of Human Rights Indicators* (2013) 18 Sur Intl J on HR 55, 58.

[136] See n 34.

[137] Escazú Agreement (n 33) Article 15.5(c).

[138] Escazú Agreement (n 33) Article 15.5(a)–(e).

[139] Escazú Agreement (n 33) Article 15.5(b).

4.      JURISPRUDENTIAL AND DOCTRINAL DEVELOPMENTS
        OF THE IASHR ON ECONOMIC, SOCIAL, CULTURAL, AND
        ENVIRONMENTAL RIGHTS

Over the past two decades, the IASHR has developed an interesting jurisprudence on ESCER, primarily through a comprehensive interpretation of the scope of the rights recognized in the ACHR and other treaties. Through its development of the right to property, the system has protected the right to survival, land, and culture of indigenous peoples.[140] Through the rights to life and physical integrity, it has developed the protection of a dignified life and has considered positive State obligations.[141] Through the right to due process, the system has protected the right to strike and the right to free legal assistance to persons in poverty when necessary for a fair hearing.[142] Through the right to movement and residence, it has protected the right not to be forcibly displaced.[143]

These developments have been criticized by some for widening the scope of rights. However, through its jurisprudence, the IASHR has developed a truly interdependent analysis of rights that considered the economic and social aspects of several rights that were traditionally analyzed through a narrower lens. As an example, in a case where 49 individuals in Guatemala were diagnosed with HIV, the IACtHR found that Guatemala had violated the right of non-discrimination by failing to guarantee the victims the medical care that they required.[144] The Court also found that the State did not comply with its positive duty to guarantee the rights to health, integrity, and life by not providing the victims with any public medical care from the time that they were diagnosed with HIV/AIDS (between the years of 1992 and 2004) until 2006 and 2007, when the State began providing minimal assistance to some people living with HIV.[145]

The IACtHR had long recognized its competence to adjudicate violations of Article 26 of the American Convention on Human Rights through the 'existing interdependence and indivisibility between civil and political rights and economic, social and cultural rights', stating 'that they must be understood comprehensively and as a whole without the existence of hier-

---

[140] *Sawhoyamaxa Indigenous Community v Paraguay*, Merits Reparations, and Costs, Judgment, Inter-American Court of Human Rights Series C No 146 (29 March 2006) paras 118; Inter-American Commission on Human Rights, *Annual Report of the Inter-American Commission on Human Rights 1994*, 175–76, OEA/Ser.L/V/II.88, Doc. 9 rev. (1995) (noting that land transfer is the program that has suffered 'the most delays' under the Peace Agreement, that the program was '*virtually paralyzed*' for significant periods and that the government has failed to meet even the previous year's targets).

[141] *See Gonzales Lluy et al. v Ecuador*, Merits, Reparations, and Costs, Judgment, Inter-American Court of Human Rights Series C No 298 (1 September 2015); *Loren Laroye Riebe Star et al. v Mexico*, Case 11.610, Inter-American Commission on Human Rights, Report No 49/99 (1999); *Villagrán Morales et al. v Guatemala*, Merits, Reparations, and Costs, Judgment, Inter-American Court of Human Rights Series C No 63 (19 November 1999) paras 79, 167.

[142] *Ricardo Baena et al. v Panama*, Merits Reparations, and Costs, Judgment, Inter-American Court of Human Rights Series C No 72 (3 February 2001) para 134; *Exceptions to the Exhaustion of Domestic Remedies (Article 46(1), 46(2)(a) and 46(2)(b) of the American Convention of Human Rights)*, Advisory Opinion OC-11/90, Inter-American Court of Human Rights Series A No 11 (10 August 1990) para 28.

[143] *María Mejía v Guatemala*, Case 10.553, Inter-American Commission on Human Rights, Report No 32/96 (1996) paras 64–65.

[144] *Cuscul Pivaral et al. v Guatemala*, Merits, Reparations, and Costs, Judgment, Inter-American Court of Human Rights Series C No 359 (23 August 2018) Puntos Resolutivos paras 1–9.

[145] *Cuscul Pivaral et al. v Guatemala*, Merits, Reparations, and Costs, Judgment, Inter-American Court of Human Rights Series C No 359 (23 August 2018) Puntos Resolutivos paras 1–9.

archy'.[146] Nevertheless, it was not until the Court's decision in *Lagos del Campo* that it found a violation of Article 26.[147]

The broader impact of the case law coming out of the Commission and Court is also associated with its generous reparations system that tackles some of the causes and consequences of gross violations. As a result, these decisions have impacted groups or classes beyond those individuals that have litigated the case. An example is the implementation of legal measures to protect the right of pregnant teens to be in school. Pursuant to the friendly settlement agreement in the Carabantes case before the Commission, Chile's National Congress approved the General Law for Education, which incorporated international human rights standards relating to access to education, thereby increasing the number of pregnant women able to attend high school.[148]

Lastly, the IASHR has developed groundbreaking standards regarding State responsibility for private actors which are relevant for the protection of ESCER. Standards have been established through IASHR case law, Advisory Opinions, and thematic reports that attribute responsibility to States for the actions of non-State actors, such as private providers of public services for issues including slave labor and trafficking with the purpose of labor exploitation, for the right to a clean environment, and for the right to health, among others.[149]

## 5. A COMMITMENT TO STRENGTHENING THE HR COMMUNITY ENGAGED IN THE PROTECTION OF ESCER

The protection of rights requires the functioning of the rule of law, democracy, and the ability of those affected by rights violations, their communities, and others to organize, protest, mobilize, speak out, and use the justice system, including the international system, without fear of reprisal.

The Escazú Agreement recognizes the State's obligation 'to guarantee a safe and enabling environment for persons, groups and organizations that promote and defend human rights in environmental matters, so that they are able to act free from threat, restriction and insecuri-

---

[146] *Lagos del Campo v Perú*, Preliminary Objections, Merits, Reparations and Costs, Judgment, Inter-American Court of Human Rights Series C No 340 (31 August 2017) para 141. Chapter 12 of this book addresses the right to work in depth. Nevertheless, it was not until the Court's decision in *Lago de Campo* that it found a direct violation of a social right (right to job security) based on a violation of Article 26 of the ACHR. See n 147.

[147] *Lagos del Campo v Perú*, Preliminary Objections, Merits, Reparations and Costs, Judgment, Inter-American Court of Human Rights Series C No 340 (31 August 2017) para 154.

[148] 'Mónica Carabantes', *Center for Justice and International Law* <www.cejil.org/en/monica-carabantes>.

[149] *See Suárez-Rosero v Ecuador*, Merits, Judgment, Inter-American Court of Human Rights Series C No 35 (12 November 1997); *Hacienda Brasil Verde Workers v Brazil*, Preliminary Objections, Merits, Reparations and Costs, Judgment, Inter-American Court of Human Rights Series C No 318 (20 October 2016); *The Environment and Human Rights (State obligations in relation to the environment in the context of the protection and guarantee of the rights to life and to personal integrity – interpretation and scope of Articles 4(1) and 5(1) of the American Convention on Human Rights)*, Advisory Opinion OC-23/17, Inter-American Court of Human Rights Series A No 23 (15 November 2017).

ty'.[150] Simply put, there cannot be a robust protection of rights without strong protections of those that put their lives on the line for the defense of ESCER.

Unfortunately, the Americas have accounted for a disproportionate share of attacks and killings of human rights defenders.[151] Globally, almost 80 per cent of the human rights defenders killed worked on environmental, land, or indigenous peoples' rights.[152] Many of those killed were indigenous peoples, afro-descendants, and 'campesinos'.[153] Some other pervasive attacks – including killings, rapes, and defamation – are linked to cultural and political battles around the role of women and women activists, and include the vilification of women human rights defenders, especially those working in the areas of reproductive rights or gender identity.[154] Another critical tool to silence activists in the region is the criminalization of journalists and human rights defenders through overly broad laws or trumped up charges; this last trend has particularly impacted indigenous peoples, journalists, and activists.[155]

Taking into account the context of violence in the Americas, the use of IASHR tools for the protection of human rights defenders is critical to the protection of ESCER. Consequently, it is critical that those who use the Inter-American system to protect ESCER understand the mechanisms that are relevant to protect human rights defenders and indigenous peoples engaged in this area. These include the Rapporteurship on Human Rights Defenders of the IACHR,[156] the use of precautionary measures, and voicing concerns through reports, hearings, and press releases. The Rapporteurship on Human Rights Defenders has released several reports on the situation of human rights defenders in the region, a report on public policies, numerous press releases and advocacy strategies to pursue an enabling space for civil society, and accountability for those defending rights.

Moreover, the Americas has numerous networks and organizations that facilitate the exchange of experiences, learning processes, advocacy strategies, analyses, and litigation on behalf of a broad range of ESCER defenders, social movements, unions, and indigenous peoples, which are also important social loci for the domestic, regional, and international protection of rights. In pursuing strong protection of rights in the region, the human rights community has focused not only on domestic and international institutional mechanisms,

---

[150] Escazú Agreement (n 33) Article 9.1.

[151] Approximately 75 per cent of the killings of defenders in 2018 occurred in the Americas region. 'Front Line Defenders Global Analysis 2018', *Front Line Defenders* (2019) 4 <www.frontlinedefenders .org/sites/default/files/global_analysis_2018.pdf>.

[152] 'Front Line Defenders Global Analysis 2018', *Front Line Defenders* (2019) 4 <www .frontlinedefenders.org/sites/default/files/global_analysis_2018.pdf>.

[153] 'IACHR Condemns Murders of Human Rights Defenders in the Region', *Inter-American Commission on Human Rights* (7 February 2017) <www.oas.org/en/iachr/media_center/preleases/2017/ 011.asp>.

[154] 'Front Line Defenders Global Analysis 2018', *Front Line Defenders* (2019) 8–9 <www .frontlinedefenders.org/sites/default/files/global_analysis_2018.pdf>.

[155] 'Front Line Defenders Global Analysis 2018', *Front Line Defenders* (2019) 11–12 <www .frontlinedefenders.org/sites/default/files/global_analysis_2018.pdf>.

[156] Other thematic rapporteurships, such as those working on the rights of Indigenous Peoples, Freedom of Expression, and Afro-descendants, have also been key actors in the protection of the rights of defenders working on ESCER.

based on the IASHR and the United Nations, but also on social processes, experiences, and organizations that have provided support for the work of defenders in the region.[157]

## 6.    CONCLUSION

Important challenges remain for the protection of ESCER in the Americas. The region is still plagued by inequality, exclusion, and violence that is explained and replicated by insufficient guarantees of ESCER. In turn, social rights are critical for the legitimacy of human rights, democracies, sustainable development, and lasting peace and for the protection of other fundamental rights. Buttressing the protection of ESCER should be a priority shared by all for the protection of rights of the future generations.

To pursue these goals, the IASHR must strengthen its substantive and instrumental agenda by developing its jurisprudence, empowering its thematic rapporteurship, tracking progressive implementation, implementing measures to stop the erosion of rights in the current economic and political context, and safeguarding spaces in which the right to defend human rights, including ESCER, is guaranteed. The tools for the protection of these rights must be expanded by increasing the number of ratifications of the ESCER treaties, so as to allow their complementary monitoring bodies to function effectively.

Despite its various limitations, the Inter-American System on Human Rights has made significant contributions to the development of ESCER in the Americas. The IACHR and the IACtHR have conscientiously developed the tools available to them through their doctrine, jurisprudence, interim measures, rapporteurships, and reparations to extend the protection of ESCER. The IASHR's remarkable interpretations of the social rights aspects of fundamental rights, as well as the recognition and enforcement of ESCER under the American Convention, provide a solid foundation for the further advances necessary to meet current and ongoing challenges.

---

[157] 'The Time is Now', *Center for Justice and International Law* and *Protection International* (2018) <www.cejil.org/sites/default/files/es_tiempoya_interactivo.pdf>.

# PART II

# CONTENT OF THE RIGHTS

# 6. The right to social security

*Magdalena Sepúlveda*

## 1. INTRODUCTION

The right to social security or social protection was one of the few economic, social and cultural rights (ESCR)[1] included in the Universal Declaration of Human Rights of 1948 (UDHR).[2] While the right was already included in the Declaration of Philadelphia of 1944,[3] its inclusion in the UDHR was a progressive step. It has meant that, for more than 70 years, social security has been recognized as a *right* that every member of society should enjoy—by virtue of being human, and derived from his/her dignity.

After its inclusion in the UDHR, the right to social security was included in various United Nations (UN) human rights treaties, including: the International Covenant on Economic, Social and Cultural Rights (ICESCR, 1966) (Articles 9 and 10);[4] the International Convention on the Elimination of All Forms of Racial Discrimination (1979) (Article 5(e)(iv));[5] the Convention on the Elimination of All Forms of Discrimination against Women (1979) (Article 11(1)(e));[6] the Convention on the Rights of the Child (1989) (Article 26);[7] the International Convention on the Protection of the Rights of All Migrant Workers and Members of Their Families (1990) (Article 27);[8] and the Convention on the Rights of Persons with Disabilities (CRPD, 2006) (Article 28).[9]

The right to social security is also enshrined in several regional human rights treaties, such as the Additional Protocol to the American Convention on Human Rights in the Area of Economic, Social and Cultural Rights (Article 9),[10] the European Social Charter (Article 12),[11]

---

[1]  Following the position of ILO and human rights treaty bodies, this chapter uses the terms 'right to social protection' or 'right to social security' interchangeably to refer to the right of all people, without discrimination, to enjoy a set of policies and programs designed to reduce and prevent poverty, vulnerability and social exclusion throughout their life cycle. See, for example, CESCR, General Comment No. 19: The Right to Social Security (4 February 2008) E/C.12/GC/19 (hereafter, CESCR, General Comment No. 19) para 4; and ILO, *World Social Protection Report 2017–2019: Universal Social Protection to Achieve the Sustainable Development Goals* (ILO 2017).

[2]  Adopted 10 December 1948, A/810 at 71.

[3]  Adopted at the 26th Session of the International Labour Conference held in Philadelphia (10 May 1944).

[4]  Adopted by the UN General Assembly on 16 December 1966 through GA Resolution 2200A (XXI).

[5]  Adopted by the UN General Assembly Resolution 2106 (XX) (21 December 1965).

[6]  Adopted by the UN General Assembly (19 December 1979).

[7]  Adopted by the UN General Assembly (20 November 1989).

[8]  Adopted by the UN General Assembly Resolution 45/158 (18 December 1990).

[9]  Adopted by the UN General Assembly Resolution 61/106 (13 December 2006).

[10]  Adopted at the Eighteenth Regular Session of the General Assembly of the Organization of American States, San Salvador, El Salvador (17 November 1988).

[11]  ETS No. 163, Adopted in Strasbourg (3 May 1996).

the African Charter on Human and Peoples' Rights[12] (Articles 4, 5, 6, 15; 16; 18(1), (2) and (4)),[13] and the Arab Charter on Human Rights (Article 36).[14] At the domestic level, the right to social security is enshrined in many constitutions as well as national laws.[15]

Additionally, this right is enshrined in several conventions adopted within the framework of the International Labour Organization (ILO), such as Convention 102 (1952), Convention 118 (1962), Convention 157 (1982), Convention 168 (1988) and Convention 183 (2000).

Despite its early recognition as a right, decades passed before social security (social protection) gained political support and acceptance as a critical tool for development and poverty reduction. For some authors, social security expansion in the past two decades is viewed as 'a quiet revolution' in development.[16]

Today, there is renewed emphasis on the right to social security. World leaders have put it at the center of the 2030 Agenda for Sustainable Development. While the Millennium Development Goals were silent about social protection, the 2030 Agenda gives it unique prominence by including it in several targets (for example, targets 1.3, 3.8, 5.4 and 10.4). Under Sustainable Development Goal (SDG) 1, for example, States commit to 'implement nationally appropriate social protection systems for all, including floors' for reducing and preventing poverty (SDG 1.3). This is an extraordinary recognition of the universal character of the right to social security. Considering that, according to the Declaration,[17] the Agenda should be implemented in line with human rights standards, the inclusion of social protection in the SDGs is also a recognition of an obligation to implement social protection programs from a rights perspective. The impact of social protection is expected to significantly increase in the coming years, as the 2030 Agenda for Sustainable Development exerts maximum impact.

Moreover, ILO and other UN agencies are putting the universal expansion of this right at the core of their work, and UN human rights monitoring bodies are lending unprecedented attention to it. Various national constitutions and legal frameworks around the world include a right to social security that is enforced by courts and quasi-judicial bodies. We are seeing more and more legal rulings on the right to social protection.

Despite the increased attention to and the remarkable progress in the coverage of social protection programs, the right to social security is not yet a reality for most of the world's

---

[12]    Adopted in Nairobi (27 June 1981).

[13]    Although the right to social security is not explicitly protected in the African Charter, according to the African Commission on Human and Peoples' Rights, it can be derived from a joint reading of a number of rights guaranteed under the Charter. See African Commission on Human and Peoples' Rights, 'Principles and Guidelines on the Implementation of Economic, Social and Cultural Rights in the African Charter on Human and Peoples' Rights' <www.achpr.org/files/instruments/economic-social-cultural/achpr_instr_guide_draft_esc_rights_eng.pdf>.

[14]    Adopted by the Council of the League of Arab States (22 May 2004).

[15]    For a detailed analysis of the constitutional provisions from around the world containing the right to social security, see the legal depository of the Social Protection and Human Rights Platform <http://socialprotection-humanrights.org/category/legal-depository/legal-instruments/domestic-legislation/>. For a focus on Europe, see ILO, *The Protection of the Right to Social Security in European Constitutions* (ILO Online edition 2012) <www.ilo.org/normes>.

[16]    Armando Barrientos and David Hulme, 'Social Protection for the Poor and Poorest in Developing Countries: Reflections on a Quiet Revolution' [2008] Brooks World Poverty Institute (BWPI) Working Paper 30.

[17]    'Transforming Our World: The 2030 Agenda for Sustainable Development', Resolution 70/1 adopted by the UN General Assembly (25 September 2015).

population. According to ILO, only 45 per cent of the global population is effectively covered by at least one social protection benefit, while the remaining 55 per cent—as many as four billion people—have been left unprotected.[18]

This dramatic coverage gap in the enjoyment of the right to social security derives in part from a lack of understanding about the meaning of a rights-based approach to social protection. A better understanding of the implications of human rights obligations regarding social security should contribute to reaching those still excluded. A rights-based approach would not only assist in identifying the obstacles that prevent the most disadvantaged from accessing programs on an equal basis with the rest of the population, but also provide guidance on how to improve program design to make them more inclusive. It should also help to give political prominence to this right at the domestic level.

A rights-based approach to social security or social protection does not seek to replace other approaches, nor does it claim to provide every answer to difficult choices regarding resource allocation. Rather, it emphasizes human rights obligations regarding how States establish social protection systems (process-related obligations) and the intended results of such systems (outcome-related obligations). It also provides accountability framework elements.

This chapter briefly reviews the scope and content of the right to social security, as well as how courts and quasi-judicial bodies have ensured it in both international and domestic contexts. It ends with an assessment of the existing case law.

## 2.    SCOPE AND CONTENT OF THE RIGHT

Over the years, the right to social security, as included in several UN human rights instruments, has been clarified by the work of UN treaty bodies,[19] by Special Procedures,[20] and through recommendations of the Universal Periodic Review (UPR) process.[21] Academia has also contributed greatly to developing a more systemic analysis of the right to social protec-

---

[18]    ILO, *World Social Protection Report* (n 1) XXIX.

[19]    Concluding Observations of the CESCR (December 2013) E/C.12/BIH/CO/2; CRPD, Concluding Observations Tunesia CRPD/C/TUN/CO/1 (13 May 2011) and CRPD, Concluding Observations Spain (19 October 2011) CRPD/C/ESP/CO/1; Committee on the Rights of the Child (CRC), Concluding Observations Uzbekistan (16 December 2013) CRC/C/UZB/CO/3-4 and CRC, Concluding Observations on Bolivia (16 October 2009) CRC/C/BOL/CO/4; Committee on the Elimination of All Forms of Discrimination Against Women, Concluding Observations Mozambique (11 June 2007) CEDAW/C/MOZ/CO/2; and Committee on the Protection of the Rights of All Migrant Workers and Members of Their Families, Concluding Observations Albania (10 December 2010) CMW/C/ALB/CO/1.

[20]    See e.g. reports of the former and current Special Rapporteurs on extreme poverty and human rights (until 2011, the mandate was called Independent Expert on the question of human rights and extreme poverty), including on cash transfer programs (27 March 2009) A/HRC/11/9; the role of social protection in the face of the global financial crisis (11 August 2009) A/64/279; non-contributory pensions (31 March 2010) A/HRC/14/31; the role of social protection in the achieving of the MDGs (31 March 2010) A/65/259; social protection in times of crisis and recovery (17 March 2011) A/HRC/17/34; on social protection floors (11 August 2014) A/69/297; on universal basic income (22 March 2017) A/HRC/38/33; and on the impact of the International Monetary Fund on social protection (8 May 2018) A/HRC/38/33. See also reports of the Special Rapporteur on the rights of persons with disabilities, on social protection (7 August 2015) A/70/297 and on the right to health (16 July 2018) A/73/161.

[21]    See e.g. UN Human Rights Council, 'Report on the Working Group on the "Universal Periodic Review of Bolivia"' (15 March 2010) A/HRC/14/7 para 98; and UN Human Rights Council, 'Report of

tion.[22] Thanks to this collective effort, there is now an enhanced understanding of the scope and content of the right to social security, as well as of the implications of a rights-based approach to social protection.

While the terms 'social security' and 'social protection' are used in institutions around the world with a variety of meanings, these two terms are synonymous from a human rights point of view.[23] This interpretation is in line with the definition given by ILO. According to ILO, 'social protection, or social security, is a human right and is defined as the set of policies and programs designed to reduce and prevent poverty and vulnerability throughout the life cycle'.[24]

Social protection includes benefits for children and families, maternity, unemployment, employment injury, sickness, old age, disability and survivors, as well as health protection.[25] Social protection systems address all these policy areas by a mix of contributory schemes (social insurance) and non-contributory benefits, financed mainly through taxes (social assistance).[26]

## 3.   OBLIGATIONS OF PROGRESSIVE REALIZATION AND MINIMUM ESSENTIAL LEVELS OF SOCIAL SECURITY: THE CONCEPT OF SOCIAL PROTECTION FLOORS

In 2012, at the 101st session of the International Labour Conference, governments, employers and workers from 185 countries unanimously adopted the Social Protection Floors Recommendation No. 202 (hereafter, ILO Recommendation No. 202).[27] This landmark Recommendation not only reaffirmed social security as a human right for all persons but was critical in providing guidance to States on how to progressively achieve universal protection of the right to social security,[28] and in clearly establishing the minimum core content of this right.[29]

Considering the recognized expertise of ILO (established in 1946 before the UN human rights instruments and monitoring bodies), its 'primary responsibility' for the realization of

---

the Working Group on the "Universal Periodic Review of Bangladesh"' (9 June 2009) A/HRC/11/18/Add.1 para 30.

[22]   See e.g. E. Riedel (ed.), *Social Security as a Human Right: Drafting a General Comment on Article 9 ICESCR. Some Challenges* (Springer 2007); Magdalena Sepúlveda and Carly Nyst, *The Human Rights Approach to Social Protection* (Ministry of Foreign Affairs of Finland 2012); Markus Kaltenborn, 'The Human Rights-based Approach to Social Protection' in Katja Bender, Markus Kaltenborn and Christian Pfleiderer (eds) *Social Protection in Developing Countries: Reforming Systems* (Routledge 2013); and Beth Goldblatt and Lucie Lamarche (eds), *Women's Rights to Social Security and Social Protection* (Hart Publishing 2014).

[23]   See n 1.

[24]   ILO, World Social Protection Report 2017–19 (n 1).

[25]   CESCR, General Comment No. 19 (n 1) para 2. The contingencies that have been traditionally covered by social security are reflected in ILO standards, in particular ILO Convention No. 102. They are: medical care; sickness; maternity benefits; unemployment benefits; family benefits; employment injury benefits; invalidity benefits; old age benefits; survivor benefits.

[26]   CESCR, General Comment No. 19 (n 1) para 4.

[27]   Recommendation concerning National Floors of Social Protection, adopted in Geneva on 14 June 2012.

[28]   See Chapter 14 of this book.

[29]   See Chapter 13 of this book.

the right to social security and the broad support from States and other stakeholders, ILO Recommendation No. 202 should be considered as an authoritative interpretation of the scope and content of the right to social security.[30] Thus, it complements General Comment No. 19 on the right to social security adopted by CESCR in 2018.[31]

According to General Comment No. 19, as States progressively advance in ensuring the right to social protection, they have a minimum 'core' obligation to ensure a *minimum essential level of benefits to all* individuals and families. Such benefits must enable them to acquire at least essential healthcare, basic shelter and housing, water and sanitation, foodstuffs and the most basic forms of education.[32] If a State party cannot provide this minimum level for all risks and contingencies within its maximum available resources, CESCR recommends that the State party, after a wide process of consultation, select a core group of social risks and contingencies.[33]

Moreover, the Committee clarifies that whatever the level of protection provided, States have an immediate obligation to ensure that there is no discrimination in accessing social protection programs. This means that no person or group of persons are unfairly excluded from accessing existing schemes. As examined below, the obligation to ensure that the right to social security is exercised without discrimination has been consistently applied by domestic courts in various jurisdictions.

These obligations of progressive realization and minimum essential levels are further developed through the concept of social protection floors (SPFs).[34] According to ILO,

> social protection floors are nationally defined sets of basic social security guarantees that should ensure, as a minimum that, over the life cycle, all in need have access to essential health care and to basic income security, which together secure effective access to goods and services defined as necessary at the national level.[35]

According to ILO Recommendation No. 202, the establishment of SPFs should include at least four basic social security guarantees: (1) access to essential healthcare, including maternity care; (2) basic income security for children, providing access to nutrition, education, care and any other necessary goods and services; (3) basic income security for persons in active age who are unable to earn a sufficient income, in particular in case of illness, unemployment, maternity and disability; and (4) basic income security for older persons.[36]

The establishment of SPFs is the starting point. SPFs constitute the minimum core content of the right to social security. From this minimum, States should move to progressively ensure higher levels of protection of social security according to their maximum available

---

[30]    Vienna Convention on the Law of Treaties (Article 31, 9 June 2009).

[31]    During the drafting process of the ICESCR, there is evidence of the drafters' intention for ILO standards to operate as the special law (*lex specialis*) in respect of the content of the right to social security enshrined in Article 9. See Ben Saul, David Kinley and Jaqueline Mowbray, *The International Covenant on Economic, Social and Cultural Rights. Commentary, cases and materials* (Oxford University Press 2014).

[32]    CESCR, General Comment No. 19 (n 1) para 59.

[33]    Ibid.

[34]    See Tineke Dijkhoff and George Letlhokwa Mpedi, *Recommendation on Social Protection Floors: Basic Principles for Innovative Solutions* (Kluwer Law International BV 2018).

[35]    Ibid.

[36]    ILO Recommendation No. 202 (n 27) para 5.

resources. SPFs are flexible in their implementation. According to ILO, SPFs are part of a two-dimensional strategy for extending social security, calling for a basic set of social guarantees for all (the 'horizontal dimension') as well as the gradual implementation of higher standards (the 'vertical dimension').[37] This two-dimensional social protection strategy is conceived as a 'social security staircase', where the floor represents a set of basic guarantees for all. For those who can pay taxes or otherwise contribute to programs, a second benefits level can be introduced. Finally, a 'top floor' of voluntary private insurance arrangements can be established for those who need or desire higher protection levels. States should pursue both the horizontal and vertical dimensions of social security in parallel, in line with their national circumstances.[38]

## 4.    HUMAN RIGHTS-BASED FRAMEWORK

Over the years, a better understanding of the rights-based framework for social protection has arisen. It has become evident that human rights obligations must guide social protection system design, implementation, and evaluation. These obligations refer to both outcomes and processes used. Thus, social protection programs' outcomes must all be in line with human rights standards (for example, they must ensure minimum essential levels of ESCR in a non-discriminatory manner while progressively extending coverage and levels of protection to achieve universality) and their implementation processes must conform to key human rights principles (such as transparency, participation, and accountability) as well as with certain procedural obligations (such as the duty to give priority to the most disadvantaged and vulnerable groups over other societal segments).

Influential UN agencies—for example, ILO,[39] UNICEF,[40] and FAO[41]—explicitly embrace a rights-based approach to social protection. Some countries have formally adopted a rights-based approach to social protection design and implementation. In Latin America, for example, there is formal recognition of the rights-based approach to social protection.[42] In Africa, social development, labor, and employment ministers have requested the African Commission on Human and Peoples' Rights of the African Union to prepare an additional protocol for the African Charter on Human and Peoples' Rights on the 'Rights of Citizens to Social Protection and Social Security' that would be binding for all Member States.[43]

---

[37]    See ILO, *Social Security for All: Building Social Protection Floors and Comprehensive Social Security Systems. The Strategy of the International Labour Organization* (ILO 2012) 3–7.

[38]    Ibid.

[39]    ILO, *World Social Protection Report 2017–19* (n 1).

[40]    United Nations Children's Fund (UNICEF), *Social Protection Strategic Framework* (UNICEF 2012).

[41]    See e.g. Food and Agriculture Organization of the United Nations (FAO), *The Rights to Social Protection and Adequate Food: Human Rights-based Frameworks for Social Protection in the Context of Realizing the Right to Food and the Need for Legal Underpinnings* (FAO 2016).

[42]    Simone Cecchini, Fernando Filgueira and Claudia Robles, *Social Protection Systems in Latin America and the Caribbean: A Comparative View* (Economic Commission for Latin America and the Caribbean (ECLAC) November 2014).

[43]    Christina Behrendt and others, 'Implementing the Principles of Social Protection Floors: Recommendation, 2012 (No. 202)' in Dijkhoff and Letlhokwa (n 34) 34, 65.

A human rights approach to social protection will not necessarily prescribe precise policy measures. States have the discretion to formulate the public policies which are most appropriate for their circumstances. However, it limits the policy options that States have. When confronted with alternative policy options, State authorities must choose those which do not violate human rights and are best aligned with their human rights obligations.

Social protection measures may assist States to comply with other human rights obligations, including the obligations to ensure the right to the highest attainable standard of physical and mental health, the right to food, and the right to education, among others. These beneficial impacts of social protection measures on the enjoyment of a range of human rights add further weight to the claim that there is a strong relationship between human rights and social protection.

Human rights create legal obligations to implement social protection systems and establish standards for designing, implementing, and evaluating such systems. In turn, the implementation of social protection facilitates complying with several other human rights obligations, most importantly those related to the enjoyment of minimum essential levels of economic, social, and cultural rights. Nonetheless, the success or failure of social protection systems in realizing human rights rests heavily on whether such systems are established and operated according to the standards that human rights require.

It is not the intention of this chapter to explain the human rights-based framework for social protection systems, which is well established in detail elsewhere.[44] This section will briefly focus on key elements of this framework.

## 4.1    Participation

Several human rights monitoring bodies have emphasized the idea that governments do not present a social protection system's 'finished products', but rather allow and enable active civil society engagement in social protection programs' design, implementation and monitoring.[45] ILO Recommendation No. 202 also specifies that national social security strategies should be designed and implemented based on national buy-in via effective social dialogue and public participation.[46] Other ILO instruments stress the importance of participation in social protection.[47] Special procedures have also further determined specific requirements with which participatory mechanisms must comply to be considered rights-based.[48]

There are numerous social protection programs featuring participatory mechanisms that have enjoyed varying degrees of success. For example, Thailand's successful implementation

---

[44]   See Sepúlveda and Nyst (n 22). See also the Human Rights and Social Protection electronic platform available at <http://socialprotection-humanrights.org/>.

[45]   See e.g. CESCR, General Comment No. 19 (n 1) paras. 26 and 69; and 'Report of the Special Rapporteur on Extreme Poverty and Human Rights', Magdalena Sepúlveda Carmona on the right to participation (11 March 2013) A/HRC/23/36.

[46]   ILO Recommendation No. 202 (n 27) para 13.

[47]   Articles 71 and 72 of ILO Convention 102 (1952) on Social Security (Minimum Standards) set out similar requirements.

[48]   See Reports of the Special Rapporteurs on extreme poverty and human rights, Magdalena Sepúlveda Carmona, on the right to participation of people living in poverty, and on the human right to safe drinking water and sanitation, Catarina de Albuquerque on common violations of the human rights to water and sanitation, A/HRC/23/36 (n 45) and (30 June 2014) A/HRC/27/55 respectively.

of its Universal Health Coverage Scheme has been attributed, among other reasons, to the critical role which civil society and social movements played in the program's formulation and design.[49] Brazil's Bolsa Familia program requires municipal governments to establish supervisory bodies composed of both local government and civil society representatives, who jointly make decisions on how best to implement the program within their community.[50]

## 4.2    Transparency and Access to Information

Social protection programs channel large amounts of public resources, providing opportunities and incentives for corruption, clientelism, and fraudulent practices.[51] Accurate information about social protection programs might prevent or mitigate those practices occurring, by limiting discretionary powers from program implementers.[52] When comprehensive information about a program is not publicly available, neither the beneficiaries nor the general public are able to understand how the program works. Thus, transparency and access to information are also critical elements for ensuring participation and accountability in social protection programs. When beneficiaries have limited access to information, their ability to participate, claim their rights, and hold program authorities accountable is impeded. Additionally, more transparent and effective programs strengthen the legitimacy of social assistance authorities in the eyes of the public, and their confidence in them. They might also attract greater public support and resource allocation from governments and donors.

Lack of information about social protection programs is particularly problematic for women, who have consistently lower literacy and education levels than men in the same socioeconomic group due to structural discrimination.[53] Moreover, because of social norms that confine women's responsibilities to domestic duties, their level of information might be lowered because of limited interaction with public officials.[54] An evaluation of the cash transfer program Juntos in Peru showed a correlation between lack of information about the program and its potential impact on women's economic empowerment. Researchers found that the lack of clarity about the program's objectives and the roles and responsibilities of the families led to inappropriate demands on beneficiaries. Organizations and individuals related to the program—such as health center representatives, community mayors, and program managers—were found to have demanded that beneficiaries participate in activities that were not part of the program, further limiting women's decisions and their empowerment.[55]

---

[49]    ILO, 'Fiscal Space and the Extension of Social Protection' [2012] ILO Working Paper No. 33, 154.

[50]    Report of the independent expert on the question of human rights and extreme poverty, Magdalena Sepúlveda, A/65/259 (n 20) para 89.

[51]    Transparency International, *Global Corruption Report 2003* (Transparency International, November 2002).

[52]    Christian van Stolk and Emil D. Tesliuc, 'Toolkit on Tackling Error, Fraud and Corruption in Social Protection Programs' [2010] World Bank Discussion Paper No. 1002.

[53]    World Bank, *World Development Report 2012: Gender Inequality and Development* (World Bank 2011).

[54]    Rebecca Holmes and Nicola Jones, *Beyond Mothers and Safety Nets: Why Social Protection Needs a Gender Lens* (Zed Books 2013) and Naila Kabeer, 'Women's Economic Empowerment and Inclusive Growth: Labour Markets and Enterprise Development' [2012] CDPR Discussion Paper 29/12.

[55]    Lorena Alcázar, Maria Balarin and Karen Espinoza, 'Impacts of the Peruvian Conditional Cash Transfer Program on Women Empowerment: A Quantitative and Qualitative Approach' [2016] Partnership for Economic Policy Working Paper, 19.

In General Comment No. 19, CESCR recommends that transparency be integral to social protection programs and plans of action.[56] Some UN Special Procedures have further developed these principles' practical implications.[57] For example, they have identified the various elements of social protection programs that should be made public, including selection methods, eligibility criteria, and benefit levels, as well as mechanisms for complaints and redress.[58] UN human rights monitoring bodies have also stated that social security systems must ensure that individuals and organizations can exercise their right to seek, receive, and impart information on all social security entitlements in clear and transparent ways.[59]

## 4.3 Privacy and Data Protection

Social protection programs require processing of significant amounts of data, often including sensitive information, such as household assets, health status, and physical or intellectual disabilities. Increasingly, social protection programs use unique, intimate biometric-technology data such as fingerprints, iris structure, and face topologies. Inextricably linked to the individual body, such data is more sensitive than other types of personal information.

The use of information technology and reliance on large databases as well as complex management information systems means that the personal data that social protection programs collect can be easily shared, domestically and internationally, with a variety of public and private actors. While collecting and sharing personal information can increase efficiency in social protection program management and monitoring, it can also threaten the rights, freedoms, and personal security of those whose data is processed (applicants and beneficiaries), and indeed of society at large.

Rights to privacy and data protection are well recognized in domestic and international law. Numerous legal instruments impose obligations on States regarding the protections of these rights. Social protection program beneficiaries do not renounce their rights to privacy and data security in exchange for the programs' benefits. From a human rights perspective, it is evident that social protection authorities must ensure that all programs comply with specific national and international rules that protect privacy and govern how information is processed.[60] Yet, privacy and data protection are not absolute rights. In some cases, there might be a trade-off between compliance with transparency standards and the protection of privacy and data protection. While sensitive data held by social protection authorities should never be published or exhibited,[61] a critical question is whether or not publishing recipients' names and the amount

---

[56]   CESCR, General Comment No. 19 (n 1) paras 26 and 69.

[57]   See e.g. Reports of the independent expert on the question of human rights and extreme poverty, Magdalena Sepúlveda Carmona (27 March 2009) A/HRC/11/9 paras 21–65; (11 August 2009) A/64/279 of 11 August 2009, pp. 14–18; (31 March 2010) A/HRC/14/31 paras 51–97 and (17 March 2011) A/HRC/17/34 paras 11–28.

[58]   See e.g. A/65/259 (n 20) paras 88–93. See also CESCR, General Comment No. 19 (n 1) para 70.

[59]   CESCR, General Comment No. 19 (n 1) para 26. See also A/HRC/11/9 (n 57) paras 44–50; and A/HRC/14/31 (n 57) paras 76–78.

[60]   For more information, see Magdalena Sepúlveda, 'Is Biometric Technology in Social Protection Programme Illegal or Arbitrary? An Analysis of Privacy and Data Protection' [2018] ILO Social Protection Department, Extension of Social Security, Working Paper No 59.

[61]   Sensitive data refers to a special category of personal data that by its nature poses a risk to the data subjects when processed. This includes information-revealing personal characteristics such as racial or

of benefits they receive would be in breach of privacy and data protection standards. In many flagship social protection programs, such as Bolsa Familia in Brazil, the list of beneficiaries and the amount received by them are publicly available. The argument in favor of making this information available is the need to ensure transparency in the use of public resources to help diminish opportunities for fraud and corruption. When the names of beneficiaries of social protection programs are displayed, one legitimate question is whether the disclosure of information could cause any harm to any beneficiary, including stigmatization or reputational harm.

Human rights standards require that, when collecting and processing social protection program beneficiary information, States must ensure they observe internally accepted privacy and confidentiality standards.[62] ILO Recommendation No. 202 is in line with these requirements, noting that States 'should establish a legal framework to secure and protect private individual information contained in their social security data systems'.[63]

### 4.4   Accountability Mechanisms and Effective Remedies

Holding responsible parties accountable is an essential component of the rights-based approach to social security. It means establishing mechanisms which ensure that policymakers, program administrators, and others whose actions have an impact on social security rights can be held accountable for their actions. Social protection programs should establish mechanisms to receive and process complaints, in particular to review program eligibility, report instances of error or abuse, and supervise benefit distribution.[64]

According to ILO Recommendation No. 202, complaint and appeal procedure mechanisms should be 'impartial, transparent, effective, simple, rapid, accessible and inexpensive'. The Recommendation stresses such procedures should be offered free of charge to applicants.[65] UN Special Procedures have also stressed that complaint procedures should guarantee confidentiality and allow for individual and collective complaints, must enjoy adequate operational resources, and must exist free from political interference. At the same time, they must be culturally appropriate and gender-sensitive.[66]

Some promising examples of programs appear to comply with these principles in several parts of the world. For example, cash transfer programs often feature mechanisms for addressing complaints (as with India's Mahatma Gandhi National Rural Employment Guarantee Scheme and the Bono de Desarrollo Humano in Ecuador).

Social protection programs, and the broader State apparatus that administers them, should also provide access to effective remedies before competent administrative or judicial authorities in cases where rights have been violated. CESCR recommends that all victims of viola-

---

ethnic origin, health status and financial standing. Existing legal frameworks prescribe more stringent rules of protection for sensitive data.

[62]   See e.g. Article 17 ICCPR; Article 8 European Convention on Human Rights (1950, ECHR); Article 23 European Social Charter and General Assembly resolution 68/167 (adopted on 18 December 2013). See also Report of the Office of the United Nations High Commissioner for Human Rights, 'The Right to Privacy in the Digital Age' (30 June 2014) A/HRC/27/37 and A/HRC/11/9 (n 57) para 40.

[63]   ILO Recommendation No 202 (n 27) para 23.

[64]   See e.g. A/HRC/11/9 (n 57) paras 44–50; A/HRC/14/31 (n 57) paras 79–82 and A/65/259 (n 20) paras 88-93.

[65]   ILO Recommendation No 202 (n 27) para 7.

[66]   See e.g. A/65/259 (n 20) para 91; and A/HRC/14/31 (n 57) paras 79–82.

tions of the right to social security be entitled to adequate reparation, including restitution, compensation, satisfaction, or non-repetition guarantees. National ombudspersons, human rights commissions, and similar national human rights institutions should be permitted to address social security rights violations.[67]

## 5.   JUSTICIABILITY OF THE RIGHT TO SOCIAL SECURITY

Often, decisions regarding the design and implementation of social protection programs do not include comprehensive assessments of the compatibility of the program design or implementation features with human rights norms and standards, which are included in diverse legal frameworks. Non-compliance with these legal standards not only violates rights but can also impact the effectiveness of social protection programs and may open a possibility for legal challenges at the domestic level or before an international human rights monitoring body.

Increasingly, when social protection practitioners ignore these legal principles, national courts, regional human rights tribunals, and UN treaty monitoring bodies request corrective measures. At the national level, there is an increased number of cases where courts directly protect the right to social security, in particular when the right is protected under the constitution and domestic laws. In Colombia, for example, the Constitutional Court, which regularly provides judicial protection to the right to social security, has emphasized that social security benefits aim to economically compensate those who are in circumstances of manifest weakness and protect the minimum conditions for a dignified life (*mínimo vital*) of the person and his/her nuclear family. Thus, it considers the right to social security an immediately enforceable constitutional right.[68]

This section includes diverse examples of case law related to the right to social security. The most prominent cases relate to the obligation to ensure that everyone enjoys the right to social security free from discrimination. It also includes cases where the substantive protection of social security benefits has been achieved through the protection of civil and political rights, as well as cases where the design and implementation of social protection programs have been challenged through procedural guarantees.

### 5.1   Right to Social Security and the Principle of Equality and Non-discrimination

States are obliged to guarantee the enjoyment of the right to social security without discrimination of any kind. CESCR has emphasized that any discrimination, whether in law or in fact, whether direct or indirect, on the grounds of race, color, sex, age, language, religion, political or other opinion, national or social origin, property, birth, physical or mental disability, health status (including HIV/AIDS), sexual orientation, and civil, political, social, or other status, which has the intention or effect of nullifying or impairing the equal enjoyment or exercise of the right to social security, is prohibited.[69]

---

[67]   CESCR, General Comment No. 19 (n 1) paras 77–81.
[68]   See Magdalena Sepúlveda, 'Colombia' in Malcolm Langford (ed.) *Social Rights Jurisprudence: Emerging Trends in International and Comparative Law* (Cambridge University Press 2008) 144–62. See also Colombian Constitutional Court, T-495/18 of 18 December 2018.
[69]   CESCR, General Comment No. 19 (n 1) para 29.

Since the late 1980s, the Human Rights Committee has enforced the prohibition of discrimination in the enjoyment of the right to social security through Article 26 International Covenant on Civil and Political Rights, 1966 (ICCPR)[70] (for example, in *Broeks v the Netherlands*).[71] These early cases clearly established that while the right to social security should be progressively realized, this must be done in compliance with the principles of equality and non-discrimination. Any differentiation in the right to social security (that is, any distinction, exclusion, restriction, or preference) must be reasonable and objective, must possess a legitimate aim (a legitimate purpose under international human rights law) and must bear a reasonable relationship of proportionality between the means employed and the aim sought to be realized.[72]

If these criteria are not complied with, there is a violation of the principles of equality and non-discrimination. Over the years, the prohibited grounds for discrimination in the enjoyment of the right to social security have been further developed at the international and domestic levels.

### 5.1.1    Discrimination based on gender and sexual orientation

States must ensure that men and women enjoy the right to social security on an equal basis. They must review and remove any de jure or de facto restrictions on equal access to social security programs. These obligations have been enforced by several courts.

For example, in *Taylor v United Kingdom*,[73] the European Court of Justice found that a difference in the age of eligibility between men and women for receiving social assistance (non-contributory social protection) was discriminatory. In the United Kingdom (UK), the age of eligibility for receiving a winter allowance was 60 years old for women and 65 years old for men. The British government responded to the verdict by announcing it would offer winter fuel subsidies to men aged 60 and above. Retrospective payments from 1998, when the new regulations came into force, were also announced.[74]

In 2015, CESCR found in *Trujillo Calero v Ecuador* that social security systems whose design does not take into account prejudices and stereotypes according to which women should undertake the bulk of unpaid caregiving and domestic work may entail indirect discrimination against them. In this case, the plaintiff was a woman who had made abundant contributions to the pension system but was disaffiliated for an inability to pay six consecutive

---

[70]    Adopted 16 December 1966, entered into force 23 March 1976, 999 UNTS 171.

[71]    Human Rights Committee, Communication No 172/1984, *S. W. M. Broeks v. The Netherlands*, Communication No. 172/1984 (9 April 1987) CCPR/C/OP/2 at 196 (1990).

[72]    These requirements have been developed by some of the major human rights supervisory bodies. See e.g. *Marckx v Belgium*, App. No. 6833/74 (ECtHR, 13 June 1979) para 33; I/A Court HR Advisory Opinion No. 4 'Proposed amendments to the naturalization provisions of the Constitution of Costa Rica', OC-4/84 of January 19, 1984 para 57; Human Rights Committee, General Comment No. 18: Non-discrimination (10 November 1989) HRI/GEN/1/Rev. 1 at 26 (1994) para 13; and CESCR, General Comment No. 20: Non-discrimination in Economic, Social and Cultural Rights (2 July 2009) E/C.12/GC/20.

[73]    European Court of Justice, *Taylor v United Kingdom*, Application No. 382/98, judgment of 16 December 1999.

[74]    At a domestic level, a prohibition of age-gender discrimination has been found by the South African High Court in the case *Christian Roberts v Minister of Social Development* (Case 32838/05, 1 August 2007).

monthly contributions.[75] CESCR also noted the gendered impact of voluntary contribution system requirements. Ultimately, the Committee declared a violation of Article 9 (right to social security) as well as Article 2(2) (prohibition of discrimination) and Article 3 (gender equality).

Still, case law should continue to evolve to ensure that laws, policies, and programs do not discriminate among different types of families, nor are based on the stereotypes of a male 'breadwinner' and a female 'housewife' to the detriment of other types of family structure, such as female-headed households, same-sex couples, or single-parent families. At the European level, in the case of *Karner v Austria*, the European Court of Human Rights (ECtHR) found a violation of the prohibition of discrimination (Article 14 of the European Convention on Human Rights (ECHR)) in conjunction with the protection of family life (Article 8 ECHR) because the applicant was denied the status of 'life companion', preventing him from succeeding in the tenancy of his former same-sex partner.[76] Over the years, a rapid evolution of social attitudes and laws addressing same-sex couples has occurred in many countries, so their equal rights to social security benefits should also be fully recognized.

### 5.1.2   Discrimination based on nationality

In some countries, landmark judicial decisions have extended social security guarantees to non-nationals. This has been the position of both the South African Constitutional Court and the Swiss Federal Court for more than 15 years.

In *Khosa et al. v Minister of Social Development*,[77] the applicants were Mozambican citizens who had acquired permanent residence in South Africa. They challenged the constitutionality of the Social Assistance Act, which reserved cash transfers (or 'social grants') for South African citizens only. Although the applicants met all other requirements established by law (except nationality), they were denied social assistance benefits because they were not South African citizens. The government argued that the State has an obligation toward its own citizens first, and that granting cash transfers only to citizens creates an incentive for permanent residents to naturalize. However, the Constitutional Court considered that the exclusion of permanent residents from social assistance cash transfers was a discriminatory and unreasonable restriction of the right to social security.

In this same ruling, it was accepted that, based on the principle of non-discrimination enshrined in the South African Constitution, children who are South African citizens should also have access to transfers, even if their parents or primary caregivers are not citizens (given that their cash transfers are delivered through their parents or caregivers). The Court emphasized that denying these South African children access to benefits because of their parents' nationality would be unconstitutional.[78] Since 2010, all South African non-contributory social

---

[75]   CESCR, *Trujillo Calero v Ecuador*, Communication No. 10/2015 (26 March 2018) E/C.12/63/D/10/2015.

[76]   App. No. 40016/98 (ECtHR, 24 July 2003).

[77]   *Khosa and Others v Minister of Social Development and Others, Mahlaule and Another v Minister of Social Development* (CCT 13/03, CCT 12/03) [2004] ZACC 11; 2004 (6) SA 505 (CC); 2004 (6) BCLR 569 (CC) (4 March 2004), judgment of 14 March 2004.

[78]   2004 (6) SA 505 (CC) para 33.

protection benefits, such as grants for children, disabled persons, and older people, are not limited to citizens; permanent residents and refugees can benefit from them as well.[79]

The Swiss case involved three brothers originally from the former Czechoslovakia (now the Czech Republic) who were denied access to social welfare benefits in Switzerland because of their undocumented status.[80] The brothers had been living in Switzerland since 1980 but were deported to Czechoslovakia in 1987 on criminal charges. They re-entered Switzerland in 1991. Though Switzerland categorized them as illegal, the Czech Republic had rescinded their citizenship, barring their return. The federal court stated that denying welfare benefits to the brothers violated the basic minimum subsistence levels that the constitution implicitly guaranteed. It went on to declare this right was required for full enjoyment of other rights such as the rights to life, human dignity, and equality. Citizens and non-citizens, the court stated, can claim minimum subsistence levels. The ruling led to changes in the Swiss Constitution that see emergency assistance as indispensable to a dignified life.

In Brazil, foreign nationals have gone to courts several times to demand that they be given the same protection as nationals in the enjoyment of social assistance. In a landmark case, a foreigner requested access to the non-contributory cash transfer program Benefício de Prestação Continuada da Assistência Social (BPC) (Continuous Cash Benefit Program), which had been denied precisely because he was not a Brazilian national.[81] According to the Brazilian Constitution (Article 203 paragraph V), the BPC must be granted to any person with a disability or to older persons who can demonstrate that they have no means to provide for their own maintenance and do not receive support from their family. The court concluded that, according to the Constitution, social assistance should be provided to any person who needs it, regardless of nationality. The ruling refers to the *mínimo vital* (vital minimum) doctrine according to which 'human beings must receive a series of essential benefits to simply have the ability to survive, and access to such goods constitutes a subjective right of a public nature'.[82] The ruling expressly rejects the argument that giving benefits to foreigners would deprive nationals of their access to them.

At the regional level, the ECtHR has also unanimously concluded that the denial of social security benefits solely on the basis of a different nationality constitutes a violation of the ECHR. In the case of *Gaygusuz v Austria*, the Court considered that the difference in treatment between Austrians and non-Austrians regarding the right to receive emergency assistance was not based on any 'objective and reasonable justification'.[83] Similarly, in *Koua Poirrez v*

[79]   See Reg. 6(1)(g) of Regulations Relating to the Application for and Payment of Social Assistance and the Requirements or Conditions in respect of the eligibility for Social Assistance (Social Assistance Act 2004).

[80]   *V. v Einwohnergemeinde X. und Regierungsrat des Kantons Bern*, Case No BGE/ATF 121 I 367, Judgment of 1997.

[81]   Extraordinary Writ 587.970. The Specialized Federal Court of the 3rd Region sentenced the National Institute of Social Security (*Instituto Nacional do Seguro Social*, INSS) to grant foreign residents the benefit enshrined in Article 203 para V of the Constitution.

[82]   Ibid para 11 (free translation).

[83]   *Gaygusuz v Austria*, App. No. 177371/9 (ECtHR, 16 September 1996). The Court considered a violation of Article 14 of the European Convention on Human Rights in conjunction with Article 1 of Protocol 1.

*France*,[84] the Court found that refusing a disability allowance on the ground of nationality was also discriminatory.

Despite some European governments' resistance to recognizing the right to social assistance for refugees and migrants, in 2018 the Court of Justice of the European Union ruled in *Ahmad Shah Ayubi v Bezirkshauptmannschaft Linz-Land* that all refugees, including those with only temporary residence permits, are entitled to the same treatment as citizens.[85]

Applying the European Social Charter, the European Committee on Social Rights consistently finds that national practices that exclude non-nationals—in particular, residency and qualifying-period requirements—violate rights to social security and social assistance.[86]

### 5.1.3   Other grounds of discrimination
Withholding pensions from prison inmates has also been considered discriminatory. In Azerbaijan, the Constitutional Court found that Article 109 of a 'Citizens' Pension-Maintenance Act' that allowed an 80 per cent reduction to entitled but incarcerated pensioners violated constitutional rights to social security, as well as the constitution's equality and non-discrimination policies.[87] The Court acknowledged that, in line with international standards, an individual's imprisonment was not legitimate grounds for denying social security rights. The Court's ruling cited the right to social security enshrined in both the UDHR (Article 22) and the ICESCR (Article 9).

In 2018, the Northern Ireland Supreme Court determined that the requirement that only parents who were married or in a civil partnership could claim the Widowed Parent's Allowance (a contributory, non-means-tested, social security benefit) discriminated against children on the basis of the marital status of their parents. The Court held that the promotion of marriage and civil partnership is a legitimate aim, but that denying the benefit to children whose parents were not married to each other was not a proportionate means of achieving this legitimate aim.[88]

### 5.2   Protection of the Right to Social Security through the Right to Life and the Prohibition of Ill Treatment

The case law of human rights monitoring bodies has been slowly evolving so as to recognize the links between the right to social security and the protection of the right to life and the prohibition of ill treatment.

### 5.2.1   Right to life
In the early 2000s, ECtHR noted that 'an issue may arise under Article 2' (right to life) of the ECHR 'where it is shown that the authorities of a Contracting State put an individual's

---

[84]   *Koua Poirrez v France*, App. No. 40892/98 (ECtHR, 30 September 2003).
[85]   Case C-713/17 (Court of Justice of the European Union, 21 November 2018).
[86]   See e.g. Complaint No. 14/2003 *International Federation of Human Rights Leagues (FIDH) v France* [2004] ECSR.
[87]   Judgment of 29 December 1999. English translation of official judgment available at <http://codices.coe.int/NXT/gateway.dll/CODICES/full/eur/aze/eng/aze-1999-3-010?f=templates$fn=document-frame.htm$3.0>.
[88]   In the matter of an application by Siobhan McLaughlin for Judicial Review (Northern Ireland) [2018] UKSC 48.

life at risk through the denial of health care which they have undertaken to make available to the population generally'.[89] In another case, it further recognized that 'it cannot be excluded that the acts and omissions of the authorities in the field of health-care policy may in certain circumstances engage their responsibility under Article 2 [the right to life]'.[90]

At the Inter-American level, the case for positive obligations of States regarding the provision of basic needs to sustain life has often been made. In 1999, in the landmark 'street children' case, which refers to the murder of five children 'who lived on the streets in a risk situation'[91] by agents of the State, the Inter-American Court of Human Rights (IACtHR) held:

> the right to life is a fundamental human right, and the exercise of this right is essential for the exercise of all other human rights. If it is not respected, all rights lack meaning. Owing to the fundamental nature of the right to life, restrictive approaches to it are inadmissible. In essence, the right to life includes, not only the right of every human being not to be deprived of his life arbitrarily, but also the right that he will not be prevented from having access to the conditions that guarantee a dignified existence.[92]

Over the years, the IACtHR has consistently maintained a broad interpretation of the right to life, which includes the duty to satisfy the basic needs necessary for sustaining the lives of those persons who cannot do so themselves because they are in a vulnerable and disadvantaged position in society (for example, indigenous peoples). In this regard, access to health as well as social assistance as a minimum floor for sustaining a dignified life is also included.

At the global level, the Human Rights Committee has taken longer to recognize the links between the right to life and the conditions necessary to live a life in dignity. A major step was taken in July 2018, with the Committee's decision in the case of *Toussaint v Canada*.[93] Ms Toussaint, the petitioner, claimed that the State party had failed to fulfill its positive obligation to protect her right to life by denying her the emergency and essential healthcare she needed. The petitioner challenged Canada's denial of healthcare coverage to undocumented immigrants under the federal government's program of healthcare to immigrants, called the Interim Federal Health Benefit Program. In its decision, the Human Rights Committee affirmed the positive obligation of States to ensure that everyone has access to essential healthcare services that are reasonably available and accessible when necessary to prevent foreseeable risks to life. Moreover, the Committee considered that denying health coverage on the basis of her 'immigration status' was not an objective, proportionate, or reasonable means of deterring illegal immigration, in particular as her life-threatening health conditions were not taken into account. The Committee requested Canada to provide adequate compensation to Ms Toussaint for the harm she had suffered. It also requested that the authorities review national legislation to ensure that irregular migrants have access to essential healthcare. In light of this decision, it is possible to conclude that states parties to ICCPR have the obligation to provide access to existing healthcare services that are reasonably available and accessible, when lack of access to healthcare would expose a person to a reasonably foreseeable risk that could result in loss

---

[89]    *Cyprus v Turkey*, App. No. 25781/94 (ECtHR, 10 May 2001) para 219.
[90]    *Nitecki v Poland*, App. No. 65653/01 (ECtHR, 21 March 2002).
[91]    IACtHR, *Villagrán Morales et al. v Guatemala*, Judgment of 19 November 1999, Series C No 77 para 188.
[92]    Ibid para 188.
[93]    (24 July 2018) Communication No. 2348/2014, CCPR/C/123/D/2348/2014.

of life. This decision is also critical to ensure access to health and other public services for undocumented migrants.

This obligation was further explained by the Human Rights Committee in its landmark General Comment No. 36 on the right to life (2018).[94] This General Comment clarifies that the states parties' duty to protect life also implies that they should take appropriate measures 'to address the general conditions in society that may give rise to direct threats to life or prevent individuals from enjoying their right to life with dignity', such as extreme poverty and homelessness.[95] The Committee expressly notes that the measures necessary for protecting the right to life include, 'where necessary, measures designed to ensure access without delay by individuals to essential goods and services such as food, water, shelter, health care, electricity and sanitation, and other measures designed to promote and facilitate adequate general conditions'.[96]

### 5.2.2   Prohibition of ill treatment and the right to social security

Since the 1990s, the ECtHR has discussed the lack of financial assistance by the State and the provision of certain commodities necessary for survival in the light of the prohibition of torture and inhuman treatment.[97] In this regard, it is worth noting that the ECtHR has suggested that, in circumstances where an 'abrupt withdrawal of facilities will entail the most dramatic consequences for an individual', such action would amount to inhumane treatment. In the case of *D v the United Kingdom*,[98] the applicant, a national of Saint Kitts and Nevis who was in an advanced stage of AIDS, was threatened with deportation from the UK. The applicant was in prison and was receiving medical assistance for his disease. The applicant argued that his removal to Saint Kitts and Nevis would entail a violation of the right to life by the UK (Article 2, ECHR), because he was terminally ill and medical evidence confirmed that his reduced life expectancy would be further shortened if we were to be suddenly deprived of the medical treatment that he was receiving in the UK. It was established in the case that the applicant would not receive adequate treatment for his disease in the receiving country. The Court found that the British government could not be considered responsible for the individual's limited life expectancy, which was the result of his fatal illness and the lack of medical treatment in his own country, and that Article 2 was therefore not applicable under the circumstances. However, the Court made clear that the complaint of the applicant under Article 2 (right to life) was 'indissociable from the substance of his complaint under Article 3 (prohibition of torture and ill treatment) in respect of the consequences of the impugned decision for his life, health and welfare'.[99] Finally, the Court concluded that the removal of the applicant to his own country where there were no facilities to treat his illness 'would amount to inhuman treatment by the respondent State in violation of Article 3'.[100] It is remarkable that the Court made clear that the UK had assumed responsibility for treating the applicant's condition and that he had

---

[94]   Human Rights Committee, General Comment No. 36: Right to Life (3 September 2019), CCPR/C/GC/36.

[95]   Ibid para 26.

[96]   Ibid.

[97]   For further analysis see Antonio Cassese, 'Can the Notion of Inhuman and Degrading Treatment Be Applied to Socio-economic Conditions?' [1991] 2 EJIL 141–45.

[98]   *D v the United Kingdom*, App. No. 146/1996 (ECtHR, 2 May 1997).

[99]   Ibid para 59.

[100]   Ibid para 54.

become reliant on the medical treatment he was receiving. Thus, his removal would expose him 'to a real risk of dying under most distressing circumstances and would thus amount to inhuman treatment'.[101]

At the domestic level, the UK House of Lords has found that the removal of substance support from asylum seekers exposed them to destitution and thus violated the prohibition of inhumane or degrading treatment under ECHR.[102]

Today, there is increased understanding of the critical role played by social security in determining health outcomes and protecting life, developing human capital, and guaranteeing the enjoyment of several other human rights. As human rights instruments must be interpreted in light of present day conditions, one might expect domestic courts and human rights monitoring bodies to more consistently raise issues under the right to life and the prohibition of inhumane and degrading treatment when the act or omission of a State results in the denial of minimum essential levels of social protection.

### 5.3    Procedural Guarantees

Several international and domestic courts have recognized certain procedural guarantees in decisions involving social security rights. For example, the ECtHR has extensively discussed the application of the procedural guarantees afforded under the right to a fair trial (Article 6, ECHR) to cases related to social security benefits.[103] Substantively, the ECtHR and the IACtHR have also protected social security benefits through the right to property (Article 1, First Protocol to ECHR and Article 21, American Convention on Human Rights).[104]

At the domestic level, several procedural aspects related to the right to social security have been protected. For example, the Colombian Constitutional Court has stressed that the State must ensure an effective enjoyment of social security benefits. Thus, the imposition of excessive administrative procedures will constitute an unjustified and unacceptable obstacle to the effective enjoyment of the right to social security.[105] In this regard, the Court has held, for example, that requesting that a person with a mental disability be declared interdicted as a necessary condition for the payment of invalidity benefits is discriminatory. Such a demand was considered 'unreasonable' (since there are other less invasive means to protect people with disabilities) and in violation of the CRPD.[106]

Other domestic jurisdictions have also expanded the protection of procedural dimensions related to the right to social security. For example, Argentina's Supreme Court has upheld the principles of transparency and access to information regarding social protection programs.

---

[101]  Ibid para 53.

[102]  *R v Secretary of State for the Home Department, ex parte Adam* [2005] UKHL 66.

[103]  See e.g. ECtHR cases of *Feldbrugge v the Netherlands*, App. No. 8562/79, (ECtHR, 29 May 1986); *Deumeland v the Federal Republic of Germany*, App. No. 9384/81 (ECtHR, 29 May 1986); *Salesi v Italy*, App. No. 13023/87 (ECtHR, 26 February 1993) and *Schuler-Zgraggen v Switzerland*, App. No. 14518/89 (ECtHR, 24 June 1993). See also Ana Gómez Heredero, *Social Security as a Human Right: The Protection Afforded by the European Convention on Human Rights* (Council of Europe, 2007).

[104]  See e.g. *Gaygusuz v Austria* (ECtHR, 16 September 1996); *Wessels-Bergervoet v the Netherlands* (ECtHR, 4 June 2002). See IACtHR, case of the *Five Pensioners v Peru*, judgment of 28 February 2003.

[105]  See e.g. Colombian Constitutional Court, judgments T-524 of 18 August 2015, T-698 of 15 September 2014, T-801 of 25 September 2006 and T-577 of 11 August 1999.

[106]  See e.g. Colombian Constitutional Court, T-495/18 of 18 December 2018.

In a 2014 ruling, the Court established a direct public interest in accessing social assistance program beneficiary names. The Court found that ensuring access to information from social protection programs ensures transparency and is critical to guaranteeing accountability as well as compliance with principles of rationality, effectiveness, and efficiency. The case was submitted by an NGO that was denied access to information concerning the beneficiaries of social assistance. According to the Supreme Court, far from stigmatizing beneficiaries, the government is helping to ensure equity by providing access to such information.[107]

A similar decision was reached in Chile. In 2014, the Ministry of Social Development received a request for information related to all the social benefits received by a citizen in the preceding seven years. The Ministry denied the request, arguing the need to protect the citizen's right to privacy. The requester appealed the decision to the national Transparency Council (*Consejo para la Transparencia*). The Transparency Council—an independent body, established by law to supervise compliance with the Chilean Access to Information Law—ordered the Ministry of Social Development to provide the information requested by the petitioner. The Council argued that by receiving a benefit from the State, the beneficiaries' scope of the right to privacy is reduced, to enable adequate social control of who is being granted such benefits.[108]

While the above decisions seek to ensure transparency in relation to the programs' beneficiaries (the restriction of the right to privacy of beneficiaries was considered acceptable due to the public benefits that it brings), the right to privacy of the beneficiaries has prevailed in other cases. In South Africa, the Constitutional Court has protected social protection beneficiaries' rights to privacy and data against abuses by private companies. In 2012, the South African Social Security Agency (SASSA) hired a company to undertake the payments of social grants. The company then partnered with other financial institutions to exploit the biometric database of grants beneficiaries and market financial services to them. In 2017, Black Sash, a non-profit organization, submitted a motion to the Constitutional Court seeking to protect several SASSA beneficiary rights (*Black Sash Trust v Minister of Social Development and Others*[109]). Among other issues, the motion sought to protect beneficiaries' privacy and data protection rights. Consequently, the Constitutional Court ordered SASSA to contractually require of private partners that personal data obtained in the payment process remain private and not be used for any purpose other than grant payments. The order also precluded inviting beneficiaries to 'opt-in' to sharing confidential information for goods-and-services marketing.[110]

Domestic courts have also challenged some design features of social protection programs, which are often considered purely technical. For decades, under pressure from donors and the World Bank, developing countries have used targeting methodologies in social protection programs with the aim of reaching a small percentage of the population living in poverty. However, the evidence has showed that fine targeting in social protection fails to reach the poorest segments of the population. Using data for nine African countries, a study has shown that, despite being a popular method of poverty targeting, proxy means testing methods

---

[107]   Supreme Court of Argentina, Case No. 1172/03, Judgment of 26 March 2014.

[108]   Transparency Council, *Waldo Florit Otero v Ministerio de Desarrollo Social*, Case No. C1008-14, decision of 23 September 2014.

[109]   CCT 48/17, 15 June 2017.

[110]   Constitutional Court of South Africa, *Black Sash Trust v Minister of Social Development and Others (Freedom Under Law NPC Intervening)*, CCT 48/17, 15 June 2017.

are particularly deficient in reaching the poorest.[111] Data from conditional cash transfers in Latin America show that the largest programs in the region (that is, in Brazil, Colombia, and Mexico) only cover an estimate of 50–55 per cent of the poor population.[112]

In theory, targeted programs might be considered an appropriate way of giving priority to the most excluded and disadvantaged in the context of resource scarcity. However, when evidence shows that targeted programs are in fact not reaching the poorest segments of society,[113] serious concerns about the compliance with the principle of equality and non-discrimination are raised. Whereas everyone has the right to social security, States must give special attention under this principle to those individuals and groups who traditionally face difficulties in exercising this right.[114]

In recent years, scholars and practitioners have strongly criticized the use of some targeting methodologies in social protection programs, particularly the use of proxy means testing. The proxy means test methodology has been proven to lack accuracy, objectivity, and transparency, and to be costly in implementation.[115]

An additional concern regarding targeted programs is that they require costly periodic retargeting to assess the ongoing eligibility of beneficiaries. However, in countries with low administrative capacity, retargeting may take several years. From a human rights perspective, this leads to a discriminatory result, as some eligible beneficiaries, who are entitled to the program, will be excluded simply because retargeting has not yet taken place.

In Argentina, a court found the lack of retargeting in a social protection program discriminatory to the extent that there is no objective, reasonable, and proportional distinction between those who comply with the requirements during the registration window and those who comply with the requirement after the registration has closed. In 2002, the government of Argentina launched a cash transfer program, Plan Jefes y Jefas de Hogar Desocupados (for unemployed male and female heads of households). The program targeted all unemployed heads of households aged 60 or older, or those with dependent children below 18 years old or with disabilities. However, applicants had to register before 17 May 2002 to become a beneficiary of the program.[116] No one could join the program after that date and no institutional

---

[111]  Caitlin Brown, Martin Ravallion and Dominique van de Walle, 'A Poor Means Test? Econometric Targeting in Africa' (2018) 134 Journal of Development Economics 109.

[112]  Marco Stampini and Leopoldo Tornarolli, 'The Growth of Conditional Cash Transfers in Latin America and the Caribbean: Did They Go Too Far?' [2012] Inter-American Development Bank, Policy Brief No. 185.

[113]  See e.g. Marcos Robles, Marcela Rubio and Marco Stampini, 'Have Cash Transfers Succeeded in Reaching the Poor in Latin America and the Caribbean?' [2015] Inter-American Development Bank (IDB) Policy Brief No. 246; Fabio Veras Soares, Rafael Perez Ribas and Rafael Guerreiro Osorio, 'Evaluating the Impact of Brazil's Bolsa Família: Cash Transfer Programmes in Comparative Perspective' [2007] International Policy Centre for Inclusive Growth (IPC) Evaluation Note, No. 1.

[114]  CESCR, General Comment No. 19 (n 1) para 31.

[115]  See e.g. Stephen Kidd and Emily Wylde, *Targeting the Poorest: An Assessment of the Proxy Means Test Methodology* (Australian Agency for International Development 2011); Stephen Kidd, Bjorn Gelders and Diloá Bailey-Athias, 'Exclusion by Design: An Assessment of the Effectiveness of the Proxy Means Test Poverty Targeting Mechanism' [2017] ILO, Extension of Social Security, Working Paper No. 56; Brown et al (n 111); and Stephen Kidd and Diloá Bailey-Athias, 'Hit and Miss: An Assessment of Targeting Effectiveness in Social Protection' [2019] Church of Sweden and Development Pathways.

[116]  This requirement was not included in the legal framework of the program, but it came from an ordinance from the Ministry of Labour, which oversaw the implementation of the program.

mechanisms were foreseen to ensure the inclusion of other eligible beneficiaries once registration had closed.

In practical terms, the time-bound registration implied that those who missed the registration window as well as those who became unemployed after registration had closed were excluded from the program. An NGO initiated strategic litigation representing two eligible beneficiaries who had been prevented from accessing the program.[117] Both cases—*case Molina*,[118] and *case Sales*[119]—challenged the legality of the imposition of a deadline for registration. The plaintiffs argued that all those who meet the requirements should be admitted to the program without discrimination and that excluding eligible beneficiaries simply because they did not register on time was discriminatory. In both cases, the courts agreed with the plaintiffs and ordered their admission into the program. The courts held that the program was part of the State's obligation to ensure the right to social security and found that the decision to deny coverage to those who had not registered before the deadline was arbitrary. While the rulings recognized that the decision to close the registration significantly reduced the overall costs of the program, the judgments did not find these arguments compelling. On the contrary, the Court noted that accepting the State's arguments regarding budget constraints and administrative problems would have threatened the victims' rights to life, health, and food, and would give priority to material aspects of implementation over human rights enshrined in the Constitution.

Administrative requirements of social protection programs have also been challenged by courts. In the United Kingdom, universal credit, which is a means tested single welfare payment comprising a basic personal amount and amounts to reflect the cost of caring for children, housing, and other prescribed needs, has been challenged in domestic courts several times since its implementation in 2013. In *TP and AR, R (On the Application of) v Secretary of State for Work and Pensions*,[120] the High Court of Justice found that the absence of 'top-up' payments for two severely disabled persons after they moved on to universal credit amounted to discrimination contrary to the ECHR.

In *Johnson & Ors v Secretary of State for Work and Pensions*,[121] four working single mothers challenged the method of calculating the amount of universal credit payable to each of them under the universal credit regulations. They argued that the Department for Work and Pensions was wrongly interpreting universal credit regulations, leaving them struggling financially. As the claimants succeeded in establishing that the relevant regulations had been wrongly interpreted in their cases, the High Court found it unnecessary to examine whether the interpretation entailed unlawful discrimination contrary to the ECHR (Article 14, read with Article 1 of the First Protocol).

Other programs' administrative requirements, such as automated application processes, mandatory waits for receiving a grant, or sanctions for not complying with behavioral requirements might also be challenged from a human rights perspective. For example, evidence

---

[117] Centro de Estudios Legales y Sociales (CELS), *La lucha por el derecho* (Siglo XXI Editores 2008).

[118] *Case Molina María Elvira Silvana c/Estado Nacional – Ministerio de Trabajo s/ amparo*, Case No 22.268/03, Juzgado Federal de Primera Instancia de la Seguridad Social N. 8.

[119] *Case Sales, Andrés Julio y otros v Estado Nacional – Ministerio de Trabajo s/amparos y sumarísimos*, Case No 8992/04, Judgment of 17 June 2004, Juzgado Federal de Primera Instancia de la Seguridad Social N. 9.

[120] [2018] EWHC 1474 (Admin) (14 June 2018).

[121] [2019] EWHC 23 (Admin) (11 January 2019).

shows that the mandatory five-week wait before receiving the initial payment and the difficulties encountered in the processing of universal credit in the UK have had adverse impacts on the enjoyment of rights. Such requirements have pushed families into debt, rent arrears, and food insecurity and have negatively impacted the physical and mental health of claimants and their families.[122] The Equality and Human Rights Commission, the UK national human rights institution, also questioned the negative impact of the two-child limit for tax credits imposed by the Child Tax Credit (Amendment) Regulations 2017 on the enjoyment of several rights, including non-discrimination and private life.[123]

## 6.    CONCLUSION

By virtue of the multitude of international human rights treaties, ILO treaties, and domestic legal frameworks, States have extensive human rights obligations regarding the right to social security. These obligations relate to the outcome (for example, providing a minimum core content of the right), and to the process in which it is implemented (for example, guiding States in the way social protection programs should be established).

Often, decisions regarding the design and implementation of social protection programs do not include comprehensive assessments of the compatibility of the program design or implementation features with human rights norms and standards. This is understandable. The team of practitioners and policymakers working on social protection tends not to include those familiar with these standards. These teams are often composed of economists or development practitioners who are not well versed in national or international human rights law. This is a major shortcoming. While human rights obligations do not provide precise policy recommendations, they do limit the discretion of policymakers. Not complying with these legal standards not only violates rights but also means that the programs might be challenged at the domestic and international levels. In fact, national courts, regional human rights tribunals, United Nations treaty monitoring bodies, and national human rights institutions increasingly request corrective measures. Such challenges have extensive social and economic costs. They also negatively impact political support for and social trust in such programs.

Through the contribution of human rights monitoring bodies, practitioners, and scholars, there is, nowadays, a more coherent and systematic understanding of the scope and content of the right to social protection and the implications of a rights-based approach. These developments have facilitated an increasing amount of persuasive case law related to the right to social security.

This chapter has reviewed some of the emerging jurisprudence on the right to social security. By doing so, it has shown that the judicial protection of the right to social security is not only legally possible but also a reality in many jurisdictions. This is particularly the case in countries with constitutional protection of the right to equality or the right to social security.

---

[122]    See e.g. the oral evidence presented to the Work and Pensions Committee of the House of Commons on 10 October 2018 <http://data.parliament.uk/writtenevidence/committeeevidence.svc/evidencedocument/work-and-pensions-committee/benefit-cap/oral/91648.html>.

[123]    Equality and Human Rights Commission, letter to the Department of Work and Pensions, dated 21 April 2017 <www.equalityhumanrights.com/sites/default/files/letter-to-damian-hinds-child-tax-credits-rape-clause-21-april-2017.pdf>.

A critical factor behind most of the cases reviewed here has been the presence of human rights organizations familiar with applying rights-based approaches to social protection. In recent years, there has been an increase in the number of non-governmental organizations actively monitoring the implementation of social protection programs on the ground, such as Black Sash in South Africa,[124] the Program on Women's Economic, Social and Cultural Rights in India,[125] the Southern African Social Protection Experts Network in the Southern African Development Community (SADC) region,[126] the African Platform for Social Protection, based in Kenya and working regionally,[127] and the Centro de Estudios Legales y Sociales in Argentina.[128] Moreover, there is also an international Global Coalition for Social Protection Floors, with more than 80 member organizations from around the world.[129] These organizations are also working directly with communities and local and national authorities to strengthen people's capacity to access benefits from social protection programs. Overall, these organizations are playing a critical role in strengthening the accountability of social protection programs and expanding the enjoyment of the right to social security.

Increased coverage of social protection programs has come with increased litigation and monitoring from civil society organizations. If this trend continues, one might expect to find more organizations such as NGOs, law clinics, and legal practitioners initiating legal cases (strategic litigation), representing the petitioners/victims of cases, or submitting *amicus curiae* briefs to assist the courts or human rights monitoring bodies in reaching their decisions on issues related to the right to social security. The capacity of these organizations to support victims and to initiate proceedings on their behalf can help increase the number of cases by reducing the economic and personal burdens for plaintiffs in bringing legal actions. Litigation is not a silver bullet,[130] but, when adequate conditions are in place, it can be a powerful tool to influence social protection policies. It should therefore never be neglected.

However, in many jurisdictions, the effect of judgments is limited to those who litigate or bring a claim, even when the cases related to social protection programs have a much wider significance. Thus, it is essential to continue deepening the understanding of the rights-based approach to social protection and disseminating its implications, with the aim to mobilize citizens to demand the universal enjoyment of the right to social security as well as rights-based social protection systems. In 2007, Lauchlan T. Munro stated: 'Advocates of the rights-based approach to social protection need to leave the ivory tower, roll up their sleeves, and contribute ideas on a rights-based design of social protection schemes.'[131] While this admonition may have had validity at the time, human rights scholars, monitoring bodies, and practitioners have met the challenge. They have actively provided strong and concrete guidelines on how to use the human rights framework to expand coverage and ensure that the design, implementation, and evaluation of social protection systems upholds rights. Now what is lacking is an increased

---

[124]   See <www.blacksash.org.za>.

[125]   See <www.pwescr.org/>.

[126]   See <www.saspen.org/>.

[127]   See <http://africapsp.org/>.

[128]   See <www.cels.org.ar/>.

[129]   For further information: <www.socialprotectionfloorscoalition.org>.

[130]   Malcolm Langford, 'The Justiciability of Social Rights: From Practice to Theory' in Langford (n 68) 3–45.

[131]   Lauchlan T. Munro, 'Risks, Rights and Needs: Compatible or Contradictory Bases for Social Protection?' International Development Research Centre, BWPI, Working Paper No. 7 (2007) 13.

commitment from States, inter-governmental organizations, and donors to effectively integrate human rights standards into their social protection work.

# 7. The right to education

*Faranaaz Veriava and Kate Paterson[1]*

## 1. INTRODUCTION

The right to education is entrenched as a fundamental human right at international, regional and national levels. It has become increasingly central to the broader human rights framework as a widely recognized 'empowerment' right. General Comment No. 13 of the Committee on Economic, Social and Cultural Rights (CESCR) describes education as:

> both a human right in itself and an indispensable means of realizing other human rights. As an empowerment right, education is the primary vehicle by which economically and socially marginalized adults and children can lift themselves out of poverty and obtain the means to participate fully in their communities ... Increasingly, education is recognized as one of the best financial investments States can make. But the importance of education is not just practical: a well-educated, enlightened and active mind, able to wander freely and widely, is one of the joys and rewards of human existence.[2]

In human rights academic parlance, the right to education has also been described as 'multi-dimensional'. Depending on how it is crafted, the right contains a socio-economic, equality and/or freedom dimension.[3] As we will explore in this chapter, these multiple dimensions of the right are met by a range of international, regional and national obligations, on states and private individuals, to act both negatively and positively.

Internationally, the right to education is recognized in Article 26 of the Universal Declaration of Human Rights (1948)[4] and Articles 13 and 14 of the International Covenant on Economic, Social and Cultural Rights (ICESCR).[5] The CESCR has issued a number of General Comments in which the rights enumerated in ICESCR are given content. The most relevant within the context of this chapter is General Comment No. 13, which sets out the 'four A' scheme. This framework provides one of the most useful foundations from which to begin to interpret and give substantive content to the right to education.[6] It states that, while the exact standard secured by the right to education may vary according to conditions within individual countries, education must exhibit the following features: availability, accessibility,

---

[1]   The authors would like to thank Vuyisile Malinga, Christy Chitengu and Motheo Brodie for research assistance.

[2]   UN Committee on Economic, Social and Cultural Rights, General Comment No. 13: The Right to Education (8 December 1999) E/C.12/1999/10 (General Comment No. 13).

[3]   Sandra Fredman, *Comparative Human Rights Law* (OUP 2018) 356.

[4]   Universal Declaration of Human Rights (UDHR).

[5]   As of September 2018, 169 State Parties had ratified the ICESCR.

[6]   The 'four A' scheme was developed by the late Katarina Tomaševski, who served as the first UN Special Rapporteur on the right to education. It was subsequently adopted by CESCR to provide guidance on Article 13 of the ICESCR. Tomaševski has written extensively on the 'four A' scheme and the content of the right to education. See, for example, Katarina Tomaševski, *Human Rights Obligations in Education: The 4-A Scheme* (WLP 2006).

acceptability and adaptability. When considering the appropriate application of these often interrelated and overlapping features, the best interests of the student are always a primary consideration.[7] The 'four A' scheme is therefore utilized in this chapter as an analytical framework from which to discuss the content of the right to education.

The right to education is also located in several international instruments protecting the rights of marginalized groups.[8] The inclusion of the right to education in these instruments acknowledges the interdependence of this right with other rights.

There is also significant protection of the right at regional level.[9] Elements of the Inter-American, African and European frameworks and jurisprudence will be discussed in the relevant sections below. The Arab states and South East Asian Network have newly developed regional human rights frameworks, each of which has specific provisions dealing with the right to education, but neither of which has yet produced relevant caselaw.[10]

At a national level, there is wide recognition of the right in varying degrees, ranging from general aspirational clauses to justiciable commitments, encompassing some or all of the dimensions of the right.[11]

Arguably, the predominant education rights issue over the past few decades has been the extension of access to education and universal enrollment, in particular, in pursuit of the millennium development goal (MDG) of universal primary enrollment by 2015. Education rights advocacy has focused on promoting access to schools for specific groups such as girl children. But the major barrier to universal enrollment remains the prohibitive cost of public education. Advocates for free primary education and equitable access to free secondary education have employed the human rights framework in several cases to challenge the cost of schooling. We discuss some of the relevant litigation in the section on accessibility.

More recently, however, the focus of education rights advocacy appears to have widened to include demands for quality public education and the regulation of private education. This new wave of advocacy occurs within a context in which many developing countries have initiated

---

[7]   General Comment No. 13 7.

[8]   See CEDAW, Convention on the Elimination of All Forms of Discrimination against Women (18 December 1979) 1249 UNTS 13 Article 10; Convention on the Rights of the Child (20 November 1989) 1577 UNTS 3 (CRC) Article 28; Convention on the Rights of Persons with Disabilities (13 December 2006) 2515 UNTS 3 (CRPD) Article 24; International Convention on the Elimination of All Forms of Racial Discrimination (7 March 1966) 660 UNTS 195 (CERD) Article 5(e)(v); and Convention against Discrimination in Education (14 December 1960) 429 UNTS 93.

[9]   Developing regions tend to offer more comprehensive protection to the right to education than the European Union, despite its strong early role in the United Nations' conventions and its relative wealth. It is also noteworthy that the United States of America (US) is not party to any regional treaty, and has not ratified the ICESCR or the CRC.

[10]   The right to education is entrenched in Article 43 of the Arab Charter on Human Rights, 22 May 2004, 12 Int'l Hum. Rts Rep. 893. The Charter has been ratified by all Arab states. In 2012, the Association of Southeast Asian Networks (ASEAN) issued the non-justiciable ASEAN Human Rights Declaration, but the Declaration is internally qualified in numerous respects and allows significant leeway to ASEAN states.

[11]   As of 2014, 160 states mention the right to education explicitly in their constitutions (82 per cent). Of those, 107 states provide a formally justiciable right to education while 53 states recognize the right as an aspirational goal. See Right to Education Initiative, *Accountability from a Human Rights Perspective: The Incorporation and Enforcement of the Right to Education in the Domestic Legal Order* (2017) 33–34 <www.right-to-education.org/sites/right-to-education.org/files/resource-attachments/RTE _Accountability_from_a_human_rights_perspective_2017_en.pdf>.

significant cuts under structural adjustments to their public services, leading to an increase of private actors in the education space. The impact of this has been a decline in quality in public education and the concomitant explosion of for-profit private education in developing countries.[12] Current developments regarding educational quality in public schools are discussed in the section on availability, while developments regarding private education are discussed in the section on acceptability.

Another major concern, despite improvement in enrollment rates globally,[13] is the persistent barriers to education for marginalized groups. For example, it is estimated that 93 million children worldwide experience some form of disability. These children are ten times less likely to attend school, or, if they do attend school, will do so in a segregated setting.[14] Undocumented migrant children also experience administrative barriers to accessing an education, resulting in expulsion from schools because of the absence of documentation or the denial of registration at the outset. The issue of discrimination, in education, against various marginalized groups is discussed in the section on accessibility. Within this context, each element of the 'four A' scheme is discussed in turn below.

## 2.    AVAILABILITY

The 'four A' scheme entails an education that is freely available to all children in primary school, and made progressively available for secondary and further education. Availability is conceptualized with a dual purpose. First, it highlights a state's obligation to establish a public school system with sufficient space to place every child.[15] Second, it requires base-line adequacy for schools: that the necessary educational inputs be provided for teaching and learning to occur.[16] Thus, schools must have safe and functional infrastructure and be staffed with properly trained and remunerated teachers,[17] who are given the tools they require to teach. Both state and private schools must comply with 'basic quality standards'.[18]

Certain educational inputs are necessary conditions for teaching and learning and, it follows, availability of education. Further, each input must itself be of a quality that meets a sufficient standard for adequacy. What constitutes a sufficient standard is by no means settled. General Comment No. 13 characterizes the adequacy requirement in terms of 'functionality'.[19] In other

[12]    Kishore Singh, 'Report of the Special Rapporteur on the Right to Education' (10 June 2015) A/HRC/29/30.
[13]    According to the MDG monitor, net enrollment at a primary level increased from 83 per cent in 2000 to 91 per cent in 2015: <www.mdgmonitor.org/mdg-2-achieve-universal-primary-education/>.
[14]    See <www.right-to-education.org/node/110>.
[15]    Katarina Tomaševski, 'Human Rights Obligations: Making Education Available, Accessible, Acceptable and Adaptable' (18 January 2001) 13 <www.right-to-education.org/sites/right-to-education.org/files/resource-attachments/Tomasevski_Primer%203.pdf>. See also General Comment No. 13 para 50.
[16]    Note that where we refer to 'schools' generally, this includes primary and secondary schools.
[17]    General Comment No. 13 para 6(a).
[18]    See Tomaševski (n 15). See also Sital Kalantry et al, 'Enhancing Enforcement of Economic, Social, and Cultural Rights Using Indicators: A Focus on the Right to Education in the ICESCR' (2010) 32 HRW 253, 276.
[19]    General Comment No. 13 [6(a)].

words, where the quality of a school is so poor that it can no longer be considered functional, it fails to meet the standard required for availability.

In this section, we analyze states' obligations to make education available, and consider certain instances where legal frameworks may be developed pursuant to these education guarantees. After a general overview of states' obligations, we look to two interrelated areas affecting availability: education systems and education provisioning.

## 2.1    States' Obligations to Make Education Available

Article 13(2)(a)–(e) of the ICESCR describes states' obligations differently for primary, secondary and tertiary education. States parties are under an immediate obligation to provide primary education. At a minimum, states must make primary education freely available within two years.[20] The inclusion of an explicit time period singles out free, compulsory primary education as a prioritized right where states demonstrate resource constraints.[21] Additionally, states are required immediately to adopt a plan for providing secondary and further education and continuously to monitor and evaluate the implementation of that plan.[22]

While the ICESCR remains the strongest statement on states parties' obligations to make education available, it is notable that most regional instruments include a similar framework divided between primary (or elementary), secondary and further education. The availability requirement is included in binding treaties, some of which are justiciable. Where regional instruments do not explicitly entail justiciable rights to education, the right may nonetheless be located in alternative provisions. For example, the Inter-American Court on Human Rights in *Xákmok Kásek* interpreted the right to life in Article 4(1) of the American Convention on Human Rights, 1969 (American Convention)[23] as including a right to education.[24] The Court in *Xákmok Kásek* was not asked to adjudicate obligations under the Protocol of San Salvador, 1988,[25] despite the Protocol including a right to education which is directly justiciable against its 16 states parties.[26] Nonetheless, the Court took account of the Protocol as setting an international standard for states' obligations to guarantee free, sustainable basic education.[27] The Court further imbued the right with a required level of adequacy that includes infrastructure, educational materials and access to food and water.

The African Charter on Human and People's Rights (ACHPR)[28] provides that '[e]very individual shall have the right to education' as part of a collection of cultural and community

---

[20]    Article 14.

[21]    Kalantry (n 18) 269.

[22]    Ibid 51–52.

[23]    American Convention on Human Rights (22 November 1969) 1144 UNTS 123.

[24]    *Xákmok Kásek Indigenous Community v Paraguay* IACtHR Series C No. 214 (24 August 2010) (*Xákmok Kásek*). See also *Girls Yean and Bosico v Dominican Republic* Series C No. 130 (8 September 2005) [185] where the Inter-American Court interpreted Article 19 of the American Convention as including the right to education.

[25]    Additional Protocol to the American Convention on Human Rights in the Area of Economic, Social and Cultural Rights (17 November 1988) OEA/Ser.L.V/II.82 doc.6 rev.1, 67 (Protocol of San Salvador) Article 13.

[26]    Article 19(6).

[27]    *Xákmok Kásek* (n 24) [211].

[28]    African Charter on Human and Peoples' Rights (27 June 1981) 21 ILM 58.

rights in Article 17. The ACHPR thus fills the right to education with a sense of a different purpose from other regional instruments.

Certain countries, such as South Africa, India and Brazil, have interpreted the education guarantees in their respective constitutions to include an availability component with a level of functionality and specific educational inputs.[29] The right to a basic education is an unqualified right entrenched in the Constitution of the Republic of South Africa, 1996 (South African Constitution).[30] The right has been interpreted to include significant educational inputs which are discussed below. In contrast with the framework right in the South African Constitution, the right to education in the Constitution of the Federative Republic of Brazil, 1988 (Brazilian Constitution)[31] details elements of the right with even greater specificity than the ICESCR. First, similarly to the ICESCR, it spells out differing obligations for different levels of education, but it also specifies 'educational assistance in all stages of basic education' to include 'supplemental programs of school books, teaching materials, transportation, nutrition and health care'.[32]

In 2002, the Indian Constitution was amended to include a justiciable right to education.[33] The amendment reads: 'The State shall provide free and compulsory education to all children of the age of six to fourteen years in such manner as the State may, by law, determine.'[34] Following the amendment, the Indian Parliament passed the Right of Children to Free and Compulsory Education Act, 2009 (RTE Act), which provides substantive markers and input requirements for the right.

### 2.1.1 Obligation to establish a system of schools

The right to education as currently understood entails, at a minimum, the right to attend a school. If education is to be compulsory, as primary education is under international law, the state must make available sufficient schools in appropriate locations for caregivers to be able to send children to schools. It follows that the right necessarily establishes a positive obligation on states.

Nonetheless, the right was traditionally characterized as protective, giving rise to only negative obligations. Its codification in early regional instruments, such as Protocol 1 to the European Convention on Human Rights (ECHR), is illustrative.[35] Article 2 of Protocol 1 is distinguished by its negative framing: 'No person shall be denied the right to an education.'[36]

---

[29]   See Faranaaz Veriava and Ann Skelton, 'The Right to Basic Education: A Comparative Study of the United States, India and Brazil' (2019) 35 SAJHR 1.

[30]   See Section 29(1)(a) of the South African Constitution: 'Everyone has the right to a basic education' as interpreted in *Governing Body of the Juma Musjid Primary School v Ahmed Asruff Essay N.O.* [2011] ZACC 13; 2011(8) BCLR 761 (CC) at para 37.

[31]   See Flavia Piovesan, 'Brazil: Impact and Challenges of Social Rights in the Courts' in Malcolm Langford (ed), *Social Rights Jurisprudence: Emerging Trends in International and Comparative Law* (CUP 2008) 182.

[32]   Brazilian Constitution Article 208(VII).

[33]   Vijayashri Sripati and Arun Thiruvengadam, 'Constitutional Amendment Making the Right to Education a Fundamental Right' [2004] International Journal of Constitutional Law 149.

[34]   Indian Constitution Article 21A.

[35]   Protocol to the Convention for the Protection of Human Rights and Fundamental Freedoms (18 May 1954) 213 UNTS 262.

[36]   See too the European Social Charter (1961) ETS No. 35. Article 14 locates the right to education within vocational rights and parental freedoms, rather than as a self-standing right. Article 17(2) further

In the *Belgian Linguistic Case*,[37] the European Court of Human Rights (ECtHR) held this negative formulation to indicate that states parties are not obliged to establish at their own expense, or to subsidize, education of a particular type or at any particular level; the right guarantees only access to existing institutions.

### 2.1.2    Obligation to provide what is necessary for teaching and learning

The obligation to develop a system of schools requires more than availability of schools. Schools must have safe and decent infrastructure, sufficient numbers of suitably qualified teachers, learning and teaching materials and support services effectively to operate as educational facilities.

The Inter-American Court adopted this approach, for example, in *Xákmok Kásek*, when finding that the right to life established obligations on the state to provide education. In *Xákmok Kásek*, the Indigenous Community argued that they were being systematically isolated and driven from their land by the state's failure to supply, among other things, adequate schools. The local school building had no walls,[38] a leaky roof, and no desks, chairs or educational materials.[39] The Court also noted that many students could not attend school because they did not have access to food or water.[40] This, the Court held, violated the Community's right to life, because 'the state [had] not provided the basic services to protect the right to a decent life of a specific group of individuals'.[41] It ordered the state to take measures 'immediately, periodically, or permanently' to provide 'materials and human resources for the school to guarantee the Community's children access to basic education'.

The case-studies of South Africa, India and Brazil illustrate that, in recent years, national courts have also actively sought to improve the quality of education in their respective countries by defining particular entitlements that make up the right to education and requiring the provisioning of those entitlements.

---

requires state parties to provide to children and young persons a free primary and secondary education as well as to encourage regular attendance at schools. The Charter is however not justiciable. At the time of writing, the Additional Protocol to the European Social Charter Providing for a System of Collective Complaints was ratified by only 15 members.

[37]    *Case relating to certain aspects of laws on the use of languages in education in Belgium* ECHR 1968-VI 22, 31 (*Belgian Linguistic Case*). The case dealt with a challenge to legislation specifying the language of learning in different regions of Belgium. The applicants asserted that the law in the Dutch speaking regions did not make adequate provision for French-language speakers. They further alleged that the Belgian state withheld grants from schools that did not comply with the language provisions. Further, the state did not allow the applicants' children to attend French schools in certain places, forcing them to attend school far from home, with attendant hardships. While the ECtHR found that the principle of non-discrimination had been violated in this case, it found there was no violation of the education guarantee. See also European Court of Human Rights 'Guide on Article 2 of Protocol No. 1 to the European Convention on Human Rights' (31 December 2018) (ECHR Guide) [5] <www.echr.coe.int/ Documents/Guide_Art_2_Protocol_1_ENG.pdf>. In contrast, see the African Commission's approach in *Kevin Mgwanga Gunme v Cameroon* (2009) 266/03 IHRL 3261 (*Gunme*). See also *Legal Assistance Group v Zaire* (1995) ACHPR Comm. No. 25/89, 47/90, 56/91, 100/93 [11] where the Commission noted the failure to provide access to institutions of learning violates the right to education in the African Charter.

[38]    *Xákmok Kásek* [213].

[39]    Ibid 209.

[40]    Ibid.

[41]    Ibid 217.

In South Africa, education provisioning cases have been spearheaded by underresourced schools, teachers and students represented by public interest organizations. These cases have incrementally begun to define the normative content of the unqualified right to basic education in the South African Constitution as including textbooks, suitably trained teachers and non-teaching staff, furniture and safe and decent school infrastructure.

The so-called textbooks cases were concluded in the Supreme Court of Appeal in 2015.[42] This litigation followed the introduction of a new curriculum in South African schools which relied heavily on textbooks in the teaching program to compensate for poor teacher content knowledge in many schools. However, schools reported not receiving textbooks on time for the beginning of the school year, particularly in the northern, rural province of Limpopo. The public interest organization, Section27, took the case to the High Court on behalf of schools in the province. The High Court and then, on appeal, the Supreme Court of Appeal confirmed that textbooks constitute one of the entitlements that makes up the right to basic education.[43]

In respect of suitably qualified teachers and other non-teaching staff, the Centre for Child Law (CCL) and Legal Resources Centre (LRC) pursued cases on post provisioning, the process by which the Department of Education annually declares the number of government-paid teaching posts to be allocated to a public school.[44] CCL sought to compel the Department to implement and declare the post establishments for teaching and non-teaching staff in the Eastern Cape, which they had not done for the upcoming school year. The Department ultimately acceded to and settled on all aspects of the claim except for non-teaching posts. The High Court ordered the Department to provide information on posts for non-teaching establishments, finding that '[i]f the administration and support functions of a school . . . cannot perform properly because of staff shortages, not only does this have a knock-on effect on the right to basic education but it also has the potential to threaten other fundamental rights.'[45]

Later, LRC represented schools with unfilled teaching posts and successfully applied for a class action to be certified to allow schools to opt into the litigation.[46] The Court held that the 'ongoing failure' to appoint teachers to vacant posts at public schools throughout the province was a violation of the right to basic education.

In *Madzodzo*,[47] also brought by LRC in the Eastern Cape, the High Court found that the state's failure to provide desks and chairs to schools breached their obligations under the right to basic education. Its often-quoted statement on the meaning of the obligation is worth repeating: '[the obligation] is not confined to making places available at schools. It necessarily

---

[42]   *Minister of Basic Education v Basic Education for All* [2015] ZASCA 198; [2016] 1 All SA 369 (SCA) (*BEFA* SCA). High Court decisions at *Section27 v Minister of Basic Education* [2012] ZAGPPHC 114; 2013 (2) SA 40 (GNP) and *Basic Education for All v Minister of Basic Education* [2014] ZAGPPHC 251; 2014 (4) SA 274 (GP) (*BEFA*). See Faranaaz Veriava, 'The Limpopo Textbooks Litigation – A Case Study into the Possibilities of a Transformative Constitutionalism' (2016) 32 SAJHR 321. See too Kate Paterson, 'Constitutional Adjudication on the Right to Basic Education: Are We Asking the State to Do the Impossible?' (2018) 34 SAJHR 112.

[43]   *BEFA* ibid 41 and *BEFA* SCA ibid 50.

[44]   *Centre for Child Law v Minister of Basic Education* [2012] ZAECGHC 60; 2013 (3) SA 183 (ECG).

[45]   Ibid 21.

[46]   *Linkside v Minister of Basic Education* [2014] ZAECGHC 111; and *Linkside v Minister of Basic Education* [2015] ZAECGHC 36.

[47]   *Madzodzo v Minister of Basic Education* [2014] ZAECMHC 5; 2014 (3) SA 441 (ECM) (*Madzodzo*).

requires the provision of a range of educational resources: schools, classrooms, teachers, teaching materials and appropriate facilities for learners.'[48]

In respect of safe and decent infrastructure, the South African government published the norms and standards regulations for school infrastructure in South Africa. The publication of these norms was precipitated by the persistent campaigning of a voluntary organization of school-going children, Equal Education (EE).[49]

Following the promulgation of the norms, EE launched litigation challenging the constitutionality of various of their provisions.[50] Primarily, EE objected to a provision making compliance with the minimum benchmarks 'subject to the resources and co-operation of other government agencies'. It argued that this created a legal loophole for government indefinitely to avoid its obligations to provide safe and adequate school infrastructure. The Court agreed that the provision limited the efficacy of the norms and was unconstitutional. It further held that infrastructure is 'indisputably [an] integral component of the right to basic education'.[51]

The Indian Supreme Court has considered a few cases on school infrastructure under the newly justiciable right to education. In the tragic case of *Mehrota*,[52] 93 children were killed in a fire at an ill-equipped, overcrowded school. The applicants petitioned the Court for improved school infrastructure on the basis of the rights to education and life. The Court's order established a new set of minimum standards for schools. It held that 'educating a child requires more than a teacher and a blackboard, or a classroom and a book. The right to education requires that a child study in a quality school, and a quality school certainly should pose no threat to a child's safety.'[53]

Another example of litigation under the new education guarantee under the RTE Act is the *Environmental and Consumer Protection Foundation* case.[54] Here, the applicants sought broad relief to improve conditions in schools across India. Their demands included the provision of toilet facilities and potable drinking water. The Court noted that the failure to provide toilet facilities may prevent parents from sending their children to schools and 'clearly violates the right to free and compulsory education'.[55]

The court ordered each state in India to provide toilet facilities at schools, including temporary toilets while permanent toilets were being constructed.

In Brazil, the Sao Paulo Court of Appeal extended the obligation to establish a system of schools beyond primary education. The compulsory school-going age was expanded to include four-year-olds in 2009, without any growth in early childhood development (ECD) infrastructure to support the new intake.[56] The absence of ECD infrastructure led to a slew of

---

[48]   Ibid 20.

[49]   *Equal Education v Minister of Basic Education* Case No. 81/2012, Eastern Cape High Court, Bhisho.

[50]   *Equal Education v Minister of Basic Education* [2018] ZAECBHC 6; 2019 (1) SA 421 (ECB).

[51]   Ibid 182.

[52]   *Mehrota v Union of India* (2009) 6 SCC 398 (*Mehrota*).

[53]   Ibid 30.

[54]   *Environmental and Consumer Protection Foundation v Delhi Administration* AIR 2013 SC 1111 (*Environmental and Consumer Protection Foundation*).

[55]   Ibid 4.

[56]   Open Society Justice Initiative, 'Strategic Litigation Impacts' (2017) 32 https://www.justiceinitiative.org/uploads/abbb6aa9-ece2-4b73-a962-6188619ff0db/strategic-litigation-impacts-education-20170322.pdf.

litigation culminating in *Movimento Creche para Todos*,[57] where the Court of Appeal ordered the municipality to provide at least 150,000 new places in childcare facilities and elementary schools by 2016 for children aged five and under. It required the municipality to present a plan for expansion of infrastructure, including the building of new schools, within 60 days.[58]

These cases demonstrate that, while courts' interventions in education provisioning and infrastructure may have far-reaching consequences for government programs and spending, courts may act as protectors of legal rights and remedies – for a right to education is meaningless without the tools required to exercise it.

## 3.    ACCESSIBILITY

Once a system of functioning schools is established, states must ensure that schools are generally, and individually, accessible.[59] The CESCR has described the feature of accessibility as having three overlapping dimensions: non-discrimination, physical accessibility and economic accessibility.[60] The corresponding obligations to ensure that education is accessible may be both negative and positive, and may differ depending on the level of schooling at issue.[61] We consider each of these dimensions of accessibility in turn.

### 3.1    Non-discrimination

The non-discrimination dimension of accessibility is perhaps the most readily accepted by states, because it is usually perceived as having a primarily negative obligation. As highlighted earlier, a plethora of international law instruments directly address non-discrimination in education. Most of these conventions are very well subscribed and provide a strong legal foundation for the principle of non-discrimination. In fact, state practice seems sufficiently broad to qualify this aspect of the right as customary international law.[62] We will briefly discuss the issue of non-discrimination below, in particular in respect of the equal treatment of children with disabilities and migrant children.

All rights in the ICESCR, including the right to education, are subject to the equality clauses spelled out in Articles 2(2) and 3. These read in part:

> The States Parties to the present Covenant undertake to guarantee that the rights enunciated in the present Covenant will be exercised without discrimination of any kind … [and] to ensure the equal right of men and women to the enjoyment of all economic, social and cultural rights set forth in the present Covenant.

---

[57]    *Movimento Creche para Todos vs Municipality of Sao Paulo* (2013) Tribunal de Justica do Estado de Sao Paulo, *Apelacao* no. 0150735-64.2008.8.26.0002 (*Movimento Creche para Todos*).

[58]    Open Society Justice Initiative (n 56) 36.

[59]    Klaus Beiter, *The Protection of the Right to Education by International Law, including a Systematic Analysis of Article 13 of the International Covenant on Economic, Social, and Cultural Rights* (Martinus Nijhoff Publishers 2006) 96.

[60]    General Comment No. 13 6(b).

[61]    Tomaševski (n 15) 13.

[62]    Beiter (n 59) 35.

This formulation of equality as a guarantee for how rights may be exercised indicates that non-discrimination is exercisable immediately and not subject to progressive realization. The Committee takes this position in General Comment No. 13 by listing access to education on a non-discriminatory basis as a core obligation to the right.[63] For the negative obligations attaching to the right, this will sit easily. But there are also clear positive steps required to ensure equality, some of which are codified in other equality conventions.[64]

The Convention on the Rights of the Child (CRC) mandates both a prohibition on discrimination and for states to take 'positive steps to ensure formal and substantive equality in the enjoyment of the right to education'.[65] In this sense, it is broader than the ICESCR. Broader still is the UNESCO Convention against Discrimination in Education, 1960, which defines education as including all levels of schooling and requires equality in access, quality and conditions under which education is given.[66]

Under the International Convention on the Elimination of All Forms of Racial Discrimination (CERD), states must ensure that no racial bar exists to admissions into public and private schools and that no discriminatory or segregatory practices are allowed within schools. The Committee for CERD has interpreted this as applying equally to higher education and vocational training.[67]

CERD also requires states to promote racial tolerance through 'the fields of teaching, education, culture and transformation, with a view to combating prejudices which lead to racial discrimination and to promoting understanding, tolerance and friendship among nations and racial or ethnic groups'.[68]

The ECtHR has interpreted Article 2 of Protocol 1 to the ECHR as having a close link to the prohibition of discrimination under Article 14 of the ECHR.[69] Any difference in treatment must pursue a legitimate aim,[70] and must be proportional to the desired outcome. However, the ECtHR has iterated that difference in treatment based on ethnic origin could never be

---

[63]   General Comment No. 13 57.

[64]   See Sandra Fredman, 'Providing Equality: Substantive Equality and the Positive Duty to Provide' (2005) 21 SAJHR 163, 167: 'To achieve genuine equality of opportunity requires positive measures to ensure that persons from all sections of society have a genuinely equal chance of satisfying the criteria for access to a particular social good.'

[65]   Article 2(1).

[66]   UNESCO joint expert group, *UNESCO Convention against Discrimination in Education (1960) and Articles 13 and 14 (Right to Education) of the International Covenant on Economic, Social and Cultural Rights: A Comparative Analysis* (United Nations 2006) 22–23.

[67]   In *Murat Er v Denmark* (2007), CERD/C/71/D/40/2007, a training college acceded to employers' requests to not place students of certain origins with them, in particular Pakistani students. The applicant was of Pakistani ethnicity but, the state argued, would not have been accepted into training placements in any case because of poor results. The Committee found that it was sufficient that the applicant was part of a group of people discriminated against, regardless of whether this discrimination or another element was the ultimate cause of his exclusion.

[68]   Article 7.

[69]   ECHR Guide (n 37) 11.

[70]   Ibid 39, referring to the *Belgian Linguistic Case* (n 37) 32. Put differently, discrimination has 'no objective or reasonable justification' (*Cam v Turkey* [2016] ECHR 206 (*Cam*) [54]).

objectively justifiable.[71] It is also impossible to waive the right not to be subjected to racial discrimination.[72]

The United States of America (US) offers a rich jurisprudence of dismantling racially segregated schools and attempting to provide children with equal access to education through litigation. Beginning with the seminal case of *Brown*,[73] the Supreme Court found that segregated schools violated the equal protection guarantees in the Constitution, even if all other elements of an education were provided to segregated schools equally. Although the US Constitution does not include a right to education, the Court held that states that had undertaken to provide an education had to make the right 'available to all on equal terms'.[74] The finding was premised on an understanding of the importance of education for public responsibilities, good citizenship and opportunities to succeed in life. The Court described education as 'perhaps the most important function of state and local governments'.[75]

Noteworthy too is that *Brown* precipitated a wave of equal opportunity litigation aimed at reforming the funding of state schools to improve the quality of education in many schools. Despite systematic segregation being unlawful, de facto segregation continued because of where schools were situated. Schools in areas with low property wealth, typically serving black and migrant children, continued to be poorly resourced.[76] However, the equal opportunity approach (extending the principles in *Brown*) was rejected by the Supreme Court in *Rodriguez*.[77] Here, the Court held that any proven discrimination had not resulted in 'absolute deprivation' and that the equality provisions did not require 'absolute equality or precisely equal advantages'.[78] The Court also held that education is neither explicitly nor implicitly protected by the federal Constitution.

This defeat, together with other setbacks, sparked a shift of strategy, resulting in litigation under the education clauses of various state-based constitutions. Under this approach, state courts were asked to determine the standard of adequacy implicit in the various state education guarantees, and to ensure the sufficiency of provisioning to meet this standard of adequacy. This state-based litigation is often referred to as standards-based or adequacy litigation, highlighting the intertwined dimensions of accessibility and availability under the 'four A' scheme.[79]

---

[71] *Sampanis v Greece* [2011] ECHR 1637 (*Sampanis*) [68]; *Timishev v Russia* [2005] ECHR 858; *DH v Czech Republic* [2007] ECHR 922 (*DH*) [176].

[72] *DH* (ibid) 204.

[73] *Brown v Board of Education* (1954) 347 US 483 (*Brown*). The judgment did not end segregation in schools, but instead spurred further litigation, mobilization and activism for the implementation of the court order throughout the US, eventually culminating in the passing of civil rights legislation.

[74] Ibid 493.

[75] Ibid.

[76] Ibid.

[77] In *San Antonio School District v Rodriguez* (1973) 411 US 1 (*Rodriguez*).

[78] Ibid 24.

[79] For a discussion of this litigation see: Cathy Albisa and Amanda Shanor, 'United States: Education Rights and the Parameters of the Possible' in Malcolm Langford, Cesar Rodriguez-Garavito and Julieta Rossi (eds), *Social Rights Judgments and the Politics of Compliance: Making It Stick* (CUP 2017); and Michael Rebel, 'Educational Adequacy, Democracy and the Courts' in Timothy Ready, Christopher Edley and Catherine Snow (eds), *Achieving High Educational Standards for All: Conference Summary* (National Academy Press 2002).

CEDAW similarly imposes both positive and negative obligations on states to make education equally accessible. It couples non-discrimination with substantive equality provisions, such as the reduction of female student dropout rates and programs to reduce any existing gap in education between adult women and men.[80] This may involve, for example, the introduction of incentives for parents.[81]

The Convention on the Rights of Persons with Disabilities (CRPD) is a relatively new treaty, coming unusually long after the Declaration on the Rights of Disabled Persons in 1975.[82] Article 24 endorses an inclusive approach to education, using reasonable accommodation and individualized support measures.[83] The right includes equal access to tertiary education and vocational training.[84] However, the broader right under the ICESCR overrides any limitation in the CRPD for those who have ratified both instruments.[85] To comply with the equality provisions of the ICESCR, students with disabilities must at the very least have access to the core right of free primary education,[86] with immediate effect under Article 2(2).[87]

In *Cam*,[88] the ECtHR considered the exclusion of a visually impaired student from admission to the Turkish National Music Academy, despite passing an entrance examination.[89] The conditions for enrollment in the Academy included providing a medical certificate of physical fitness. In determining whether there was a violation of Article 2 of Protocol 1, the ECtHR considered the right to education in other international treaties ratified by Turkey, including the European Social Charter and the CRPD.[90] It noted the importance of the principles of universality and non-discrimination in education in these and other texts and the progression towards inclusive education.[91] The applicant, it held, was entitled to be reasonably accommodated to correct factual inequalities that prejudiced her.[92] It did not define what reasonable accommodation would be in all circumstances, but noted that it might include 'physical or non-physical, educational or organizational [accommodation], in terms of the architectural accessibility of school buildings, teacher training, curricular adaptation or appropriate facilities'.[93]

States' obligations to educate migrant children are frequently misconstrued. Consider Article 2(3) of the ICESCR: 'Developing countries, with due regard to human rights and their national economy, may determine to what extent they would guarantee the economic rights recognized in the present Covenant to non-nationals.' Also consider that the International Convention on the Protection of the Rights of All Migrant Workers and Members of their

---

[80]    Article 10. See also General Comment No. 13 50.

[81]    Kalantry (n 18) 276.

[82]    The CRPD was adopted in 2007, almost 30 years after the Declaration was signed.

[83]    See 5.1 below.

[84]    Article 24(5).

[85]    See CRPD Article 4(4) and CRC Article 41.

[86]    See the *Standard Rules on the Equalisation of Opportunities for Persons with Disabilities* (1993) UNGA Resolution 48/96 of 20 December 1993, rule 6. See also Beiter (n 59) 133–34.

[87]    General Comment No. 13 31. See also Kalantry (n 18) 268.

[88]    *Cam* (n 70).

[89]    Ibid 62.

[90]    Ibid 53.

[91]    Ibid 64.

[92]    Ibid 65.

[93]    Ibid 66.

Families (2003) (ICMW)[94] has been ratified by only 54 states parties. This suggests relatively weak protection for migrant children in international law.

However, the UN Office of the High Commissioner considers Article 2(3) to be a narrow construction.[95] The qualification in the Article refers only to economic rights and not to social or cultural rights. It certainly does not impose any limits on education for migrant children. This is consistent with the UNESCO Convention, which enjoins states parties to undertake '[t]o give foreign residents within their territory the same access to education as that given to their own nationals'.[96]

The CRC also offers broad protection for migrant children, obliging states parties to take measures for refugee children to enjoy the rights in the CRC, including the right to basic education.[97] For states parties who have ratified the ICMW, the obligation includes registration of all children at birth, with specified nationalities, regardless of the immigration status of their parents.[98] The Committee on Migrant Workers has also interpreted the right to compulsory education for migrant children as including secondary school.[99]

At a regional level, the Inter-American Court in *Girls Yean* interpreted the Convention's development rights in Article 26 together with the right to equality.[100] Here, the applicant children were born in the Dominican Republic but had not been issued birth certificates due to their parents' status. The children had severe difficulties obtaining the documentation required to enroll in schools and one child missed a full year of schooling as a result. The Court held that the state had an obligation to guarantee access to primary education for all children, regardless of their origin or their parents' origin.[101]

---

[94]   International Convention on the Protection of the Rights of All Migrant Workers and Members of their Families (18 December 1990) A/RES/45/158.

[95]   Office of the High Commissioner on Human Rights, *The Economic, Social and Cultural Rights of Migrants in an Irregular Situation* (United Nations 2014) (ESCR of Migrants) 31.

[96]   Article 3(e). See also CESCR, General Comment No. 20: Non-discrimination in Economic, Social and Cultural Rights (2 July 2009) E/C.12/GC/20 (General Comment No. 20) [30]: 'All' means 'everyone including non-nationals, such as refugees, asylum-seekers, stateless persons, migrant workers and victims of international trafficking, regardless of legal status and documentation'.

[97]   See Beiter (n 59) 124. See also the Committee on the Rights of the Child, General Comment No. 6: Treatment of Unaccompanied and Separated Children outside of their Country of Origin (1 September 2005) CRC/GC/2005/56 [12], which states that the enjoyment of rights in the Convention must be available to all children, irrespective of their nationality, immigration status or statelessness. See further the Committee on the Elimination of Racial Discrimination, *General Recommendation XXX on Discrimination against Non-citizens*, 1 October 2002, which states that laws prohibiting racial discrimination should cover non-nationals, regardless of their immigration status.

[98]   Article 29. See also ESCR of Migrants (n 95) 25.

[99]   Committee on Migrant Workers, General Comment No. 1: Migrant Domestic Workers (23 February 2011) CMW/C/GC/1. This was also the position taken by the Constitutional Court of Spain in *Rights, Freedoms and Social Inclusion of Foreigners in Spain* STC 236/2007. Here, the statute governing the rights and freedoms of aliens excluded migrants from secondary education. Secondary education is part of the right to education in the Spanish Constitution and the Court found that the exclusion unconstitutionally excluded non-resident minors from accessing that portion of their right. Similarly, in *Timishev v Russia* (n 71), the ECtHR applied Russian law to a case excluding children of a Chechen migrant living in Russia. The ECtHR held that Russian law did not allow the exercise of the right to education to be made conditional on their parents' status or registration of residence.

[100]   *Girls Yean* (n 24).

[101]   Ibid 244.

The Committee on the ACRWC considered equal access to education in *IHRDA*.[102] The application was brought on behalf of children of Nubian descent, taken to Kenya from Sudan by British colonizers. The Nubians were treated as aliens because of their lack of an ancestral homeland in Kenya, and were systematically not registered at birth. The Committee found that Nubian children had less access to educational facilities than comparable communities of different descent based on the state's failure to provide them with birth certificates. It held that 'the de facto discriminatory system of distribution in education has resulted in their educational needs being systematically overlooked over an extended period of time'.[103]

The right of access requires substantive, thorough consideration of the meaning of equal treatment. This may at times demand active interventions to bring students onto an equal footing. For example, in *Sampanis*,[104] the ECtHR noted that the failure to correct an inequality may itself lead to a violation of the right.[105] *Sampanis*, as well as *DH*,[106] both dealt with a practice of segregating Roma children into special schools based on perceived social difficulties in their mainstream schooling. The ECtHR found this significantly to disadvantage students without reasonable justification. In *DH* the ECtHR found that admissions tests should have been and were not analyzed in the light of the special characteristics and needs of Roma children.[107] Similarly, in *Sampanis*, the ECtHR held that special considerations were needed for assessing the administrative documentation usually required to enroll children into school, given the need to correct historical inequalities.[108]

The ECtHR considered recognition of minority rights as part of an emerging 'international consensus' favoring protection of minorities not only for their development, but also in the interests of cultural plurality to the benefit of society generally.[109]

It is significant that in both *DH* and *Sampanis*, the parents of Roma children in special schools either consented to or specifically requested their admission. Nonetheless, the ECtHR found that the parents had not explicitly waived their children's rights to be treated equally (and it is not clear whether they would have been competent to do so). The same reasoning may apply to other traditionally excluded groups, in particular girls in some regions.

Therefore, the legal framework suggests that, despite state reservations or political rhetoric, the right of access to free primary education is protected under customary international law. If this is correct, then all states are obliged under international law to provide access to, at the minimum, free primary education to migrant children, regardless of whether they have ratified any of the applicable international instruments.

---

[102]   *Institute for Human Rights and Development in Africa and Open Society Justice Initiatie (on behalf of Children of Numbian Descent in Kenya) v Government of Kenya (IHRDA)* (2009) ACERWC Comm. No. 002/2009.

[103]   Ibid 65.

[104]   *Sampanis* (n 71).

[105]   Ibid 67.

[106]   *DH* (n 71).

[107]   Ibid 201.

[108]   *Sampanis* (n 71) 71.

[109]   Ibid 72.

## 3.2 Physical Accessibility

Physical accessibility refers to the ability of students to get to the schools that the state has made available for them, taking into account any relevant special needs the students may have. Practically, this amounts to schools being situated physically close to communities or the state providing transport to students to access them.[110] Students must be able to arrive safely at school or, if necessary, to access suitable distance-learning facilities.[111] The issue of where schools are situated in many instances overlaps with spatial planning benefiting the wealthy, for which equality of education is also relevant. Further, transport to school manifests as a hidden cost, which constitutes an economic barrier to education.

There is no explicit international or regional law protecting the right to transport to schools, nor is there any international precedent directly dealing with this.[112]

The right to state-sponsored transport to and from school was recognized by the High Court in South Africa in *Tripartite Steering Committee*.[113] The right is available to all children living a determined distance from school who cannot afford the cost of transport. In coming to its decision, the High Court held the following:

> The right to education is meaningless without … transport to and from school at State expense in appropriate cases. Put differently, in instances where scholars' access to schools is hindered by distance and an inability to afford the costs of transport, Government is obliged to provide transport to them.[114]

The state was directed to provide scholar transport to certain schools and to report to court by a specified date on progress made in adopting a new provincial policy on scholar transport.

## 3.3 Economic Accessibility

Education must be affordable to be truly accessible.[115] While most international and national instruments require that education be free at primary level and made progressively free at secondary level, these instruments recognize that the cost of further education is at times prohibitively expensive to be fully state-funded. Thus, the right to free primary education is firmly entrenched, in recognition of the importance of education and the state's responsibility towards and interest in protecting children. As Klaus Beiter puts it, '[e]ducation can only be compulsory if it is also made free'.[116] Interestingly, at the time of writing his textbook in 2002, Beiter observed:

---

[110] See Kalantry (n 18) 277.

[111] UNESCO joint expert group (n 66) 12. Distance learning is not specifically dealt with in most international instruments, however the African Youth Charter Article 4(f) requires states parties to undertake to '[m]ake higher education equally accessible to all including establishing distance learning centres of excellence'.

[112] See, however, the applicant's argument in *Kosa v Hungary* App. no. 53461/15 (ECHR, 17 June 2016).

[113] *Tripartite Steering Committee v Minister of Basic Education* [2015] ZAECGHC 67; 2015 (5) SA 107 (ECG) (*Tripartite Steering Committee*).

[114] Ibid [18]–[19].

[115] General Comment No. 13 [6(b)(iii)].

[116] Beiter (n 59) 96–97.

[I]n most countries most money goes to higher education, whose students are the most expensive to school, the fewest in number and the most likely to belong to the country's elite. The reason for this is that whereas university students are politically vocal, primary school children are not, which often means that the latter are neglected in the allocation of resources.[117]

As noted above, the ICESCR is clear that primary education must be made freely available.[118] Secondary and tertiary education must be made accessible 'by every appropriate means' with the progressive introduction of free education.[119] Thus, there is a core immediately realizable and justiciable component together with a progressive plan for realization of the remainder of the right. Tomaševski viewed the obligations to children of compulsory school-going age as 'all-encompassing'.[120] Further, she did not consider exemptions from school fees a viable alternative to free primary education because exemptions are 'often too cumbersome to comply with or too expensive to administer'.[121] Notably, however, the ECHR does not guarantee free primary education. The revised Social Charter includes an obligation on states parties to provide free primary and secondary education, but this is not currently justiciable.[122]

Nonetheless, the ECtHR has interpreted state laws regulating payments for education as being subject to a general obligation of equal treatment. In *Ponomaryovi*,[123] the ECtHR considered an allegation of discrimination against a school charging fees for non-nationals only. Here, two Russian nationals residing in Bulgaria were required to pay school fees for secondary education once they turned 18, when they could no longer legally reside on their parents' permits. Once they obtained residence permits they were able to attend school freely, but still owed large amounts for school fees incurred while staying in Bulgaria irregularly. The court a quo did not consider their right to education to be breached because they were still able to attend school continuously, despite owing money. However, the ECtHR found that any state with a free or subsidized education system had an obligation to afford effective access to it,[124] and that this extended to secondary education in some circumstances. In its Guide on Article 2 of Protocol 1, the ECtHR interpreted this to mean that any restrictions on access must not have a discriminatory effect in breach of Article 14.[125] ·

The constitutionality of charging school fees has been litigated in certain countries. In 2010, a case was initiated by the Colombian Coalition for the Right to Education in the Colombian Constitutional Court.[126] The Coalition challenged a national provision permitting school fees.

---

[117]   Ibid. 492.
[118]   Article 13(2)(a). See also UNDHR Article 26(1): 'Education shall be free, at least in the elementary and fundamental stages.'
[119]   Article 13(2)(b) and (c); Kalantry (n 18) 277.
[120]   Tomaševski (n 15) 14.
[121]   Commission on Human Rights, 'Preliminary report of the Special Rapporteur on the right to education, Ms. Katarina Tomaševski, submitted in accordance with Commission on Human Rights resolution 1998/33' (13 January 1999) E/CN.4/1999/49 para 35.
[122]   See n 36 above.
[123]   Resolution 1509 (2006) of the Council of Europe as interpreted by the ECHR in *Ponomaryovi v Bulgaria*, App. no. 5335/05 (ECHR, 26 June 2011) (*Ponomaryovi*).
[124]   Ibid [49].
[125]   ECHR Guide (n 37) 28.
[126]   Demanda de incons tucionalidad contra el ar culo 183 de la Ley 115 de 1994 'Por la cual se expide la ley general de educación'; Sentencia C-376/10; expediente D-7933. The case is in Spanish; a summary is available at <www.right-to-education.org/sites/right-to-education.org/files/resource-attachments/

They argued that the provision violated Article 67 of the Colombian Constitution that protected free and compulsory education. The Court upheld the challenge. It held that the national legal framework could not be interpreted as authorizing the government to charge fees, as this was contrary to Colombia's international and regional treaty obligations, including Article 16 of the Protocol of San Salvador.

The connection between charging fees and immigration status has also been litigated in national jurisdictions. In the US, in 1982 the Supreme Court had to consider a Texas statute that withheld funding for undocumented migrants from schools.[127] The Court did not consider immigration status to constitute a rational basis for denying students equal protection.[128] While acknowledging that the right to education is not protected in the US Constitution, the Court characterized the deprivation of public education as different from any other governmental benefit. It noted that '[p]ublic education has a pivotal role in maintaining the fabric of our society and in sustaining our political and cultural heritage; the deprivation of education takes an inestimable toll on the social, economic, intellectual, and psychological wellbeing of the individual, and poses an obstacle to individual achievement'.[129]

The Court, therefore, held that the obligation to pay fees deprived the children of their constitutional right to equal protection.

US case law also suggests that exemptions or 'fee-waiver schemes' do not comply with the free education guarantee, where such guarantee exists in a particular state. In the case of *Connell*,[130] while parents were not required to pay school fees for general tuition, they were required to pay for their children's extra-curricular activities at school. A fee-waiver policy was instituted by the District School Board to ensure that fees would not prevent children from participating in extra-curricular programs at the schools in the district. A parent challenged the fee-waiver scheme on the basis that it violated the state's constitutional guarantee of free education. The Court had to consider whether extra-curricular activities formed part of the free education guarantee and held that the imposition of fees for these activities violated the free education guarantee.

In India, economic access to private education has been subject to constitutional scrutiny. Section 12 of the RTE Act requires all schools, including private schools, to reserve 25 per cent of places for children from disadvantaged groups. In *Society for Un-aided Private Schools of Rajasthan*,[131] an association of private schools challenged the provision on the basis that it violated their constitutional rights to practice any occupation free from government interference, and of minority groups to establish and administer schools.

The Supreme Court upheld the provision,[132] reiterating that the state's primary obligation is to provide free and compulsory education to all children, particularly those who cannot afford primary education. However, the Court went on to make a distinction between all private schools and private minority schools. It therefore exempted minority schools from Section 12

---

Colombia%20Constitutional%20Court%2C%20Unconstitutionality%20of%20the%20General %20Education%20Law%2C%202010%20v3_0.pdf>.

[127] *Plyler v Doe* 457 US 202 (1982).

[128] Ibid 224–26.

[129] Ibid 202–03.

[130] *Hartzell v Connell* 679 P 2d 35 (Cal. 1984) (*Connell*).

[131] *Society for Un-aided Private Schools of Rajasthan v Union of India* AIR 2012 SC 3445 (*Society for Un-aided Private Schools of Rajasthan*).

[132] Ibid [5].

on the basis that to impose the 25 per cent quota on such schools would violate the right of minority groups to establish private schools.[133]

Regarding the progressively realizable aspect of the right, including for secondary education, the CESCR has taken the position that states are precluded from taking retrogressive measures. Thus, the introduction of fees where there were previously none, or the increase in fees, would be a violation of the ICESCR right.[134] It is notable that fees include '[i]ndirect costs, such as compulsory levies on parents … or the obligation to wear a relatively expensive school uniform'.[135]

Further, the CRC Committee expressed that it does not consider the lack of available resources as a reasonable justification for difference in treatment 'unless every effort has been made to use all resources that are at the State party's disposition in an effort to address and eliminate the discrimination, as a matter of priority'.[136]

## 4.    ACCEPTABILITY

Acceptability in education relates to education's suitability and quality in 'form and substance'.[137] Issues in acceptability have most often manifested in disputes between parents and states as to what should be taught in public schools, given parents' explicitly protected roles in their children's education, particularly in respect of religious and moral education.

In recent years, with the diminishing quality of education in many public education systems and the accompanying proliferation of private for-profit education institutions, there is also a renewed impetus for engagement with normative frameworks to clarify states' obligations with regard to the public and private provision of education.

Issues of religion in education and private education are discussed in turn below.

### 4.1    Religious Convictions

Article 13(3) of the ICESCR requires states to respect parents' rights to establish schools 'to ensure the religious and moral education of their children in conformity with their own convictions'. The CESCR interpreted this as including freedom of public school instruction in history

---

[133]  See too *Pramati Educational and Cultural Trust v Union of India* (2014) 8 SCC. Jayna Kothari has criticized the Supreme Court's decision to grant the exemptions to minority schools, particularly since it resulted in private schools 'clamoring' for minority status. See Jayna Kothari, 'Calling the Farce on Minority Schools' in Sandra Fredman et al. (eds) *Human Rights and Equality in Education* (Policy Press 2018).

[134]  See Concluding Observations of the CESCR, Netherlands (Netherlands Antilles) (second periodic report) (18th Session, 1999), E/1999/22 on the introduction of fees for secondary education and Concluding Observations of the CESCR, Canada (third periodic report) (19th Session, 1999), E/1999/22 expressing concern on the increase in graduate debt and recommending the state addresses it. See also Beiter (n 59) 572 and 594.

[135]  CESCR, General Comment No. 11: Plans of Action for Primary Education (10 May 1999) E/C.12/1999/4 (General Comment No. 11) para 7.

[136]  General Comment No. 20.

[137]  General Comment No. 13 6(c). See also Kalantry (n 18) 278.

of religions or even instruction in a particular religion if non-discriminatory exemptions or alternatives are provided.[138]

Article 2 of Protocol 1 to the ECHR requires states to 'respect the right of parents to ensure such education and teaching is in conformity with their own religious and philosophical convictions'.[139]

In *Kjeldsen*,[140] in 1976, the ECtHR considered an application from Danish parents objecting to compulsory sex education introduced under Denmark's State Schools Act, 1970. The ECtHR found that setting and planning the curriculum fell in the competence of the state and Article 2 of Protocol 1 did not permit parents to object to teaching with religious or philosophical implications.[141] While the state had an overall duty to ensure that any information of a religious or philosophical nature was conveyed in 'an objective, critical and pluralistic manner',[142] the ECtHR found incorporating sex education classes in the curriculum did not violate this obligation. Further, the ECtHR noted that parents in Denmark who considered sex education unconscionable could home school their children or send them to private schools.

More recently, the ECtHR considered a complaint against Norway by parents requesting exemptions from Christian and moral education classes.[143] The Norwegian Constitution, 1953 provides that Evangelical Lutheran Religion is the state's official religion and residents who subscribe to it must 'educate their children likewise'.[144] However, the ECtHR noted that the state must in all respects ensure that the curriculum is conveyed in an 'objective, critical and pluralistic manner'.[145] In coming to its conclusion that Norway violated Article 2 of Protocol 1 by failing to give full exemptions from religious education classes, the ECtHR highlighted the importance of minority interests and noted that 'democracy does not simply mean that the views of a majority must always prevail'.[146] This could not be remedied by availability of private schooling or even provision of large subsidies to attend private schools, because the state cannot dispense itself from its obligation to safeguard pluralism in state schools.[147]

More controversial perhaps is the decision of the ECtHR upholding the headscarf ban in *Sahin*.[148] The applicant, a Muslim Turkish national and medical student, was prohibited from taking her examination under a regulation barring the Islamic headscarf for women and beards for men. The applicant asserted that this amounted to a violation of Article 9 of the ECHR, which protects the freedom of thought, conscience and religion, and of Article 2 of Protocol 1. The Grand Chamber of the ECtHR upheld a Turkish Constitutional Court judgment enforcing

---

[138]   Ibid [28].

[139]   Similar provisions exist in other regional frameworks. Interestingly, ACRWC Article 11(4) requires 'religious and moral education of the child in a manner consistent with the evolving capacities of the child'. The Inter-American Convention Article 12(4) goes further, specifying that '[p]arents or guardians … have the right to provide for the religious and moral education of their children or wards that is in accord with their own convictions.'

[140]   *Kjeldsen, Busk Madsen and Pedersen v Denmark* [1976] ECHR 6.

[141]   Ibid [53].

[142]   Ibid.

[143]   *Folgerø v Norway* [2007] ECHR 546 (*Folgerø*).

[144]   Article 2.

[145]   *Folgerø* (n 143) B1(h).

[146]   Ibid B1(f).

[147]   Ibid 98.

[148]   *Sahin v Turkey* App. no. 44774/98 (ECHR, 10 November 2005) (*Sahin*).

the headscarf ban on the basis that it fulfilled a legitimate government aim of promoting secularity, which is considered a central tenet of Turkish democracy.[149]

## 4.2   Private Education

There are two significant aspects of private education. First, the right to establish private institutions is firmly entrenched in international, regional and some national jurisdictions.[150] This is premised on parents' rights to choose their children's religious and moral education.[151] However, courts have been clear that this right does not extend to the obligation on states to fund such institutions. In the *Belgian Linguistics* case discussed above, the ECtHR noted that, while the state may not prohibit the establishment of French schools, it was not under an obligation to subsidize the establishment of such schools.

Second, there is growing concern that private institutions are bypassing relevant human rights frameworks and national standards.[152] In *O'Keefe*,[153] the ECtHR held the state had an obligation to implement a child protection framework in private schools. The primary school system in Ireland is largely owned and managed by religious groups. The applicant in this case was a child subjected to repeated sexual abuse by a principal of a private Catholic school. As an adult, she instituted proceedings in the Irish courts against the principal and obtained default judgment against him, as well as against the state for vicarious liability. The Irish courts held that the state had no obligation towards students in private institutions. The applicants argued that Article 3 of the ECHR prohibits torture and inhuman and degrading punishment. Moreover, Article 1 imposes an obligation on the state to secure the rights in the

---

[149]   This decision is viewed as having paved the way for similar headscarf bans across Europe, which bans have been upheld by the ECtHR for both France and Belgium. See *SAS v France* [2014] ECHR 695; *Dakir v Belgium* App. no. 4619/12 (ECHR, 11 July 2017) and *Belcacemi and Oussar v Belgium* App. no. 37798/13 (ECHR, 11 July 2017). Noteworthy too is that in *Sahin*, one of the arguments of the respondent state was that wearing a headscarf was contrary to the principle of gender equality. The irony of this argument is not lost in the context of the particular facts of this case, since the applicant was barred from completing her medical degree in Turkey as a result of her choice to wear a headscarf. A final point is that the trend towards banning the headscarf across Europe may be contrasted with the approach of the South African Constitutional Court. In the case of *MEC for Education: KwaZulu-Natal v Pillay I* [2007] ZACC 21; 2008 (1) SA 474 (CC), a student sought an exemption from her school's code of conduct which prohibited the wearing of nose-rings on the basis that wearing a nose-ring was part of practicing her religion and culture as a Hindu girl. The Constitutional Court found that the prohibition unfairly discriminated against the learner on religious and cultural grounds. This judgment was premised on the recognition of diversity and plurality in South African society.

[150]   In one of the earliest South African Constitutional Court cases dealing with education, *Gauteng Provincial Legislature In re: Gauteng School Education Bill of 1995* [1996] ZACC 4; 1996 4 BCLR 537 (CC), the main issue was whether s. 32(c) of the interim Constitution, which guaranteed every person the right 'to establish where practicable, educational institutions based on a common culture, language or religion, provided that there shall be no discrimination on the ground of race', entailed a positive obligation on the state to establish educational institutions based on a common culture, language or religion as long as there is no discrimination on the ground of race. The Court held that no such positive obligation under s. 32(c) existed.

[151]   See ICESCR Article 13(3) and (4), UNESCO, Convention against Discrimination in Education Article 2(c), CRC Article 29(2) and UNDHR Article 26(3).

[152]   See Sylvain Aubry and Delphine Dorsi, 'Towards a Human Rights Framework to Advance the Debate on the Role of Private Actors in Education' (2016) 42 Oxford Review of Education 612.

[153]   *O'Keefe v Ireland* App. no. 35810/09 (ECHR, 28 January 2014) (*O'Keefe*).

ECHR. The ECtHR accepted this argument and found that there was an 'inherent positive obligation' on the state to protect children from ill treatment and that the state had failed to fulfill this obligation.[154]

In the context of the growing trend towards the privatization of education in many countries, education rights groups have increasingly advocated developing a normative framework to ensure that states do not abdicate their legal obligations. This includes regulation of private schools through minimum standards for, among other issues, safety, labor rights and, in particular in the context of this chapter, protecting the rights of students. In February 2019, the 'Guiding principles on the human rights obligations of States to provide public education and to regulate private involvement in education' (the Abidjan Principles) were adopted.[155] The Principles seek to provide a comprehensive compilation of states' obligations in respect of both public and private education and to provide more detailed commentary on these obligations.

## 5.   ADAPTABILITY

This last feature of the 'four A' scheme recognizes that education should be child-centric and cater to each individual child differently.[156] This propounds a broadly inclusive approach to education: a system must recognize that each child has different educational needs and it must be sufficiently flexible to cater for them.

The need for adaptability is derived from Article 3(1) of the CRC: 'In all actions concerning children, whether by public or private social welfare institutions, courts of law, administrative authorities or legislative bodies, the best interests of the child shall be a primary consideration.'[157] General Comment No. 13 describes this as obliging states to design and provide resources for schools 'which reflect the contemporary needs of students in a changing world'.[158] Thus, the Committee has recognized that children cannot be expected to adapt to educational programs and that programs should rather adapt to learners.[159] In doing so, the state, schools, and those who work in them need to consider children's backgrounds – whether they are from minority or indigenous populations – and their differing levels of ability. In this way, education serves both the children in the system and each school's broader community.[160] Tomaševski considers that this element also calls for a new approach to school discipline and, in particular, corporal punishment.[161] Within adaptability, we will first briefly consider the

---

[154]   Ibid 168. See too the case of *Christian Education South Africa v Minister of Education* [2000] ZACC 11; 2000 (4) SA 757 (CC) (*Christian Education*) discussed below where the South African Consititutional Court held that private schools could not be exempted from the corporal punishment ban.

[155]   Available at <https://www.abidjanprinciples.org>.

[156]   See Tomaševski (n 15) 31.

[157]   See too ACRWC Article 4(1): 'In all actions concerning the child undertaken by any person or authority the best interests of the child shall be the primary consideration.'

[158]   General Comment No. 13 50.

[159]   Klaus Beiter, 'Is the Age of Human Rights Really Over – The Right to Education in Africa – Domestication, Human Rights-Based Development, and Extraterritorial State Obligations' (2017) 49 Geo. J. Int'l L. 9, 14.

[160]   Kalantry (n 18) 279.

[161]   Tomaševski (n 15) 31.

theme of inclusivity, which should be read with section 3.1 above, and then turn to considerations of corporal punishment.

### 5.1    Inclusivity

Inclusivity conceives of disability as a systems failure rather than a difficulty inherent to a child. An adaptable education is one that as a rule molds to each child differently, as opposed to one that expects a child to integrate into a hostile system.[162]

The CRPD entrenches the right to an inclusive education system that must be fulfilled without discrimination and on the basis of equal opportunity.[163] It provides explicitly for reasonable accommodation, which may include infrastructure, devices and teaching support.

Prior to the adoption of the CRPD, the European Commission was asked to consider a complaint that a failure to accommodate a deaf child into mainstream schools was a breach of Article 2 of Protocol 1. The Commission observed that 'wherever possible, disabled children should be brought up with normal [sic] children of their own age' but did not consider this to oblige placing a child with a serious hearing impairment into a mainstream school at an additional expense 'or to the detriment of the other pupils' when education could be provided in a special school.[164] The adoption of the CRPD, however, and the decision in *Cam* discussed above in Section 3.1,[165] evinces a new way of thinking about disability in the ECtHR.

### 5.2    Discipline

The Committee on the ICESCR views corporal punishment as inconsistent with international law's recognition of each person's inherent dignity.[166] It requires states parties to intervene in all schools using corporal punishment and endorses 'positive', non-violent approaches to school discipline.[167]

It should also be noted that the Committee on the Rights of the Child has interpreted corporal punishment as including any use of force, 'however light', and characterizes it as 'inherently degrading'.[168] Corporal punishment includes hitting, kicking, throwing something, scratching, boxing ears, washing a child's mouth out with soap and forcing them to stay in uncomfortable positions.

The CRC protects children from corporal punishment through the dual provisions of Article 19(1), a general obligation on states to protect children from all forms of violence, and Article 28(2), which requires school discipline to be administered in a manner consistent with respect for human dignity.[169] Article 37(a) offers further protection against cruel, inhuman and degrading punishment.

---

[162]    Tomaševski (n 15) 32.

[163]    Article 24.

[164]    *Martin Klerks v The Netherlands* App. no. 25212/94 (4 July 1995).

[165]    *Cam* (n 70).

[166]    General Comment No. 13 41.

[167]    Ibid.

[168]    Committee on the Rights of the Child, General Comment No. 8: The Right of the Child to Protection from Corporal Punishment and Other Cruel or Degrading Forms of Punishment (2 March 2007) CRC/C/GC/8 para 11.

[169]    Article 37(a) offers further protection against cruel, inhumane and degrading punishment.

The prohibition of cruel and degrading punishment and its relationship to the right to education was considered in the context of the ECtHR in *Campbell*.[170] The applicants were two mothers who, it was accepted, were only able to send their children to state schools in Scotland. However, they objected to the institutionalized use of corporal punishment in state schools. Ms Campbell requested and was refused a guarantee that her son would never be given corporal punishment. The second applicant, Ms Cosan, contested her son's suspension after he refused corporal punishment. The ECtHR found a violation of Article 2 of Protocol 1 because there was no system of exemptions for individual pupils whose parents objected to corporal punishment. As a result, the parents' rights to educate their children according to their convictions was violated.[171]

In the South African Constitutional Court case of *Christian Education*,[172] the Court had to balance the rights of children at Christian private schools against the religious rights of their parents. In this case the parents argued that 'corporal correction' was an important part of their Christian faith and that a legislative ban on corporal punishment in schools violated their rights to freely practice their religion. The Court looked at the state's constitutional and international obligations and affirmed that it bears a duty to take all appropriate measures to protect children from violence, injury or abuse. The Court accordingly upheld the ban on corporal punishment.

## 6.     CONCLUSION

An analysis of current education campaigns and recent education jurisprudence suggests that there is a more nuanced approach globally to the challenges facing the realization of the right to education, which extends beyond issues of access to schools and universal enrollment to include ensuring that the necessary conditions for teaching and learning exist.

This is evident in the willingness of regional and national courts to engage with and develop the substantive content of education provisions to include a quality component and to establish minimum benchmarks for compliance with obligations. However, more must be done at a national level to ensure the establishment of and compliance with minimum standards. Noteworthy in this context is a report of previous UN Special Rapporteur on the right to education, Kishore Singh. The report emphasizes the need for the development of norms and standards at a national level by means of which to ensure a quality education that is consistent with 'relevant' international legal human rights frameworks.[173]

Another development to be welcomed is the recent publication of the Abidjan Principles. The Principles seek to refocus state commitments to public education while simultaneously providing a much needed normative framework for private education. Global education

---

[170]   *Campbell and Cosans v United Kingdom* App. no. 7511/76, A/48, [1982] ECHR 1, (1982) 4 EHRR 293, IHRL 33.

[171]   Article 19(1) of the ACRWC confers an obligation on states to 'take all appropriate measures to ensure that a child who is subjected to school or parental discipline shall be treated with humanity and with respect for the inherent dignity of the child' but does not explicitly prohibit corporal punishment. See also Articles 11(5) and 20(1)(c).

[172]   *Christian Education* (n 154).

[173]   Kishore Singh, 'Report of the Special Rapporteur on the right to education: Normative action for quality education' (2 May 2012) A/HRC/20/21.

campaigns appear to be focusing efforts on ensuring these principles are embraced in national frameworks.

The persistence of barriers to access to education for marginalized groups such as children with disabilities and migrant children remains a key area of concern. It is important that international, regional and domestic frameworks aiming to protect these children are strengthened and implemented. For example, in South Africa, despite the existence of a policy framework for inclusive education of children with disabilities, that framework has never been implemented, more than two decades after its publication.[174]

Finally, the wide entrenchment of the right to education in international, regional and national law, as noted, is premised first on the realization of individual potential, but also on its connection to the enjoyment of other rights and freedoms. To the extent, therefore, that state action or inaction continues to fail to facilitate the full enjoyment of the right to education, within its multiple manifestations, this must be challenged under the relevant human rights frameworks. As may be gleaned from many of the cases discussed in this chapter, civil society can play an integral role in initiating campaigns and legal challenges grounded in these human rights frameworks.

---

[174]   Human Rights Watch, 'Complicit in Exclusion: South Africa's Failure to Guarantee an Inclusive Education for Children with Disabilities' (2015) <www.hrw.org/report/2015/08/18/complicit-exclusion/south-africas-failure-guarantee-inclusive-education-children>.

# 8.   The right to food

*Joanna Bourke-Martignoni*

## 1.   INTRODUCTION

The human right to adequate food was recognized in 1948 as a component of an 'adequate standard of living', in Article 25 (1) of the Universal Declaration of Human Rights. Since that time, significant attention has been paid to the development of norms, policies and implementing frameworks for the right to food at the national, regional and international levels. The number of transnational social movements campaigning around issues related to the rights to food, land and natural resources, food sovereignty and the rights of peasants and other rural populations has also dramatically expanded over the past few decades. This right to food activism was given renewed impetus and institutional support following the global financial and food price crises in 2008. Although there appears to be widespread agreement that the right to food, as an essential element of the right to a dignified life, is a crucial pre-condition for the realization of a host of other civil, political, economic, social and cultural rights, there are a number of factors that continue to limit the development of measures for its effective implementation. It has been noted that the right to food is characterized by a form of ambivalence within domestic, regional and international institutions and policies that promote equal access to food and nutrition, while simultaneously supporting the liberalization of trade and agricultural investment, cuts in public spending and the privatization of public services.[1] Data from sources such as the Food and Agriculture Organization of the United Nations (FAO) highlight the persistence of, and even increases in, hunger and malnutrition among particular groups of people in many regions, and there remains sustained opposition from certain state and non-state actors to the very existence of a legally enforceable right to food.[2] Socio-economic inequalities, climate change, armed conflict and the increasing power of agribusinesses within food systems are all issues that pose considerable challenges to the realization of rights-based approaches to food.

The concept of food security is closely related to the right to adequate food and the fulfillment of the right to food is often viewed as a precondition for food security.[3] In 1996, the World Food Summit defined food security as being achieved 'at the individual, household, national, regional and global levels when all people, at all times, have physical and economic access to sufficient, safe and nutritious food to meet their dietary needs and food preferences

---

[1]   Jean Ziegler, Christophe Golay, Claire Mahon and Sally-Anne Way, *The Fight for the Right to Food: Lessons Learned* (Palgrave Macmillan 2011).

[2]   FAO, IFAD, UNICEF, WFP and WHO, *The State of Food Security and Nutrition in the World 2019: Safeguarding against Economic Slowdowns and Downturns* (FAO 2019); US Mission to International Organizations in Geneva, Explanation of Vote on the Right to Food (21 March 2017) A/HRC/34/L.21: 'we do not treat the right to food as an enforceable obligation.'

[3]   FAO, *Voluntary Guidelines to Support the Progressive Realization of the Right to Adequate Food in the Context of National Food Security* (FAO 2004).

for an active and healthy life'.[4] Although food security – with its four pillars of availability, accessibility, utilization and stability – and the right to food are often used interchangeably in policies and discourses, there are some important differences between the two frameworks.[5] Commentators have drawn attention to the fact that, unlike the right to food, food security paradigms are generally policy-based and not focused on individual and collective right-holders, binding legal obligations for duty bearers or public accountability mechanisms.[6] These critics have also argued that with the notable exception of the Civil Society Mechanism (CSM) established in 2009 within the UN Committee on World Food Security (CFS), many multi-stakeholder food security policy processes are contributing to the 'de-politicization' of global food governance and the subsequent 'lock in of neo-liberal norms and values'.[7]

More recently, international, regional and national social movements and a small but growing number of governmental actors have begun promoting the notion of food sovereignty. The term food sovereignty emerged from discussions in the mid-1990s led by La Vía Campesina, a transnational social movement of peasant and indigenous organizations.[8] The idea of food sovereignty was developed largely to act as a counterweight to the dominant discourse of food security, which, as mentioned above, many civil society actors argue fails to adequately consider the political economy of food systems and the power relations that govern them.[9] Food sovereignty is defined in the 2007 Declaration of Nyéléni as 'the right of peoples to healthy and culturally appropriate food produced through ecologically sound and sustainable methods, and their right to define their own food and agriculture systems'.[10] Unlike food security, food sovereignty is regarded as being more strongly grounded within a human rights framework that includes the right to food and the right to produce food, as well as a number of other associated rights, including those to land and natural resources.[11] These linkages between the right to food and the food sovereignty frameworks are recognized in the UN Declaration on the Rights of Peasants and Other People Working in Rural Areas, which was adopted by the Human Rights Council and by the General Assembly in 2018.[12]

This chapter discusses the historical development and content of international, regional and a selection of national frameworks on the human right to adequate food and inter-related rights such as the rights to land, water and other natural resources, work, education and social security. The final part of the discussion focuses on several of the emerging issues connected

---

[4]    Rome Declaration on World Food Security and World Food Summit Plan of Action (FAO 1996).

[5]    Adriana Bessa, *The Normative Dimension of Food Sustainability: A Human Rights-Based Approach to Food Systems Governance. Towards Food Sustainability* Working Paper No. 8 (CDE 2019).

[6]    Kerstin Mechlem, 'Food Security and the Right to Food in the Discourse of the United Nations' (2004) 10 EJL 631.

[7]    Jessica Duncan and Priscilla Claeys, 'Politicizing Food Security Governance through Participation: Opportunities and Opposition' (2018) 10 Food Sec. 1411, 1421.

[8]    Annette Aurélie Desmarais, *La Via Campesina: Globalization and the Power of Peasants* (Pluto Press 2007).

[9]    Marc Edelman, Tony Weis, Amita Baviskar, Saturnino M. Borras Jr, Eric Holt-Giménez, Deniz Kandiyoti and Wendy Wolford, 'Introduction: Critical Perspectives on Food Sovereignty' (2014) 41(6) The Journal of Peasant Studies 911.

[10]    Nyéleni Declaration 2007.

[11]    Priscilla Claeys, *Human Rights and the Food Sovereignty Movement: Reclaiming Control* (Routledge 2015).

[12]    United Nations Declaration on the Rights of Peasants and Other People Working in Rural Areas (28 September 2018) A/HRC/RES/39/12.

to the promotion and protection of the right to food in the context of feminist critiques of food systems, food sovereignty movements and the promotion and protection of the rights of indigenous peoples and peasants, the creation of corporate accountability frameworks and the challenges that climate change poses for the realization of the right to food.

## 2.     THE RIGHT TO FOOD IN INTERNATIONAL, REGIONAL AND NATIONAL LAWS AND POLICIES

> The right to food is the right to have regular, permanent and unrestricted access, either directly or by means of financial purchases, to quantitatively and qualitatively adequate and sufficient food corresponding to the cultural traditions of the people to which the consumer belongs, and which ensures a physical and mental, individual and collective, fulfilling and dignified life free of fear.[13]

Since the end of the Second World War, the urgent need to combat hunger through improved methods of agricultural production and more equitable systems of food distribution has been highlighted as a matter of international concern in human rights instruments.[14] The right to adequate food is now routinely invoked in national, regional and international policies and laws as a fundamental component of the right to a dignified life. This means that the right to food straddles the perceived divide between economic, social and cultural rights and civil and political rights.[15] As outlined in the following section, there are numerous laws and policies that provide protections for the right to food and inter-related rights, such as those to land and natural resources like water, health, decent work, education and social security.

Alongside the human rights mechanisms at the international and regional levels, the FAO is the institutional actor that has been the most directly concerned with the development of normative instruments, policies and monitoring mechanisms related to food security, agriculture and the governance of land and natural resources. It has been noted that the constitutive instrument creating the FAO in 1945 made no mention of the right to food, and instead 'the question of food and hunger was to be understood exclusively within the paradigm of modernization, technological development, trade, and nutritional adequacy'.[16] It was not until the World Food Summit in 1996 that the FAO first began to consider the development of an institutional approach to support the right to food.[17]

A large number of global cooperation frameworks, including those established in the context of the 2030 Sustainable Development Agenda (covered in Chapter 18), acknowledge the crucial role that equal access to food and nutrition plays in human development. At the national level, it is estimated that more than 30 countries currently have explicit constitutional recognition or framework legislation for the implementation of the right to adequate

---

[13]   Jean Ziegler, Christophe Golay, Claire Mahon and Sally-Anne Way, *The Fight for the Right to Food: Lessons Learned* (Palgrave Macmillan 2011) 15.

[14]   Ben Saul, David Kinley and Jacqueline Mowbray, *The International Covenant on Economic, Social and Cultural Rights: Commentary, Cases and Materials* (OUP 2014).

[15]   CCPR, General Comment No. 36: Article 6 (The Right to Life) (2 November 2018) CCPR/C/GC/36 para 26.

[16]   José Julian Lopez, 'The Human Right to Food as Political Imaginary' (2017) 30 Journal of Historical Sociology 239, 256.

[17]   Michael Windfuhr, 'The Code of Conduct: A Strategy to Strengthen the Right to Adequate Food', Hungry For What is Right: FIAN Newsletter (1998) 4.

food, while many others have adopted provisions in their constitutions that implicitly protect the right to food through the rights to life, an adequate standard of living, development and well-being.[18]

The following section provides an overview of a selection of key legal and policy instruments and institutions involved in the development, implementation and monitoring of food security and the right to food that have been created at various scales – national, regional and international – since the 1950s. The presentation of the right to food as contained in international agreements should not, however, be understood in a linear way, 'but as the contingent sometimes-stable concatenation of representations and organizational forms, and social technologies, subjectivities and modulated political action' that are open to change and constant renegotiation as 'political imaginaries'.[19]

## 2.1    International Legal Provisions

While the right to food was initially captured in international human rights law as one among several different elements of the right to an adequate standard of living, including clothing, housing, medical care and social security, it has since been singled out and expanded upon. The first international instrument to recognize the right to food was the Universal Declaration of Human Rights (UDHR), which provides in its Article 25 (1):

> Everyone has the right to a standard of living adequate for the health and well-being of himself and of his family, including food, clothing, housing and medical care and necessary social services, and the right to security in the event of unemployment, sickness, disability, widowhood, old age or other lack of livelihood in circumstances beyond his control.

Although there are ongoing disagreements concerning the customary law status of the rights contained in the UDHR, it is 'impossible to ignore its political as well as its moral influence on the conduct of international relations'.[20] There is also growing support for the view that the right to food, as one aspect of the right to life, should be regarded as a norm protected under customary international law.[21]

The most holistic expression of the right to food in international law has been developed within the framework of the International Covenant on Economic, Social and Cultural Rights (ICESCR). During the drafting of the Covenant in the 1960s it was asserted by a number

---

[18]   FAO, Database on the right to food around the globe <www.fao.org/right-to-food-around-the -globe/en/>; Lidija Knuth and Margret Vidar, *Constitutional and Legal Protection of the Right to Food around the World* (FAO 2011).

[19]   José Julian Lopez, 'The Human Right to Food as Political Imaginary' (2017) 30 Journal of Historical Sociology 239, 256.

[20]   Hurst Hannum, 'The Status of the Universal Declaration of Human Rights in National and International Law' (1995–6) 25 G.A. J Int'l & Comp. L 287, 350. On p. 348, Hannum argues in relation to Article 25 that 'Despite the fact that the United States, in particular, has often denied the status of "rights" to these norms, they may enjoy wider international support than some of the civil and political rights traditionally emphasized in U.S. jurisprudence'.

[21]   Smita Narula, 'The Right to Food: Holding Global Actors Accountable under International Law' (2006) 44 Columbia Journal of Transnational Law 791; A.P. Kearns, 'The Right to Food Exists via Customary International Law' (1998) 22 Suffolk Transnational Law Review 223; Lance Cotula and Margret Vidar, *The Right to Adequate Food in Emergencies* (FAO 2003).

of delegations that the right to food was the most important right in the whole treaty, as 'no human right (is) worth anything to a starving man'.[22] The right to food is elaborated along with the right to housing as part of an adequate standard of living in Article 11 of the ICESCR, and it has been argued that the abstract framing and wide scope of the provision reveal the 'tensions between the existential concern of sustaining life and the prosaic matter of how to express it in the form of a legal right capable of implementation and enforcement'.[23]

Article 11 reads:

1. The states parties to the present Covenant recognize the right of everyone to an adequate standard of living for himself and his family, including adequate food, clothing and housing, and to the continuous improvement of living conditions. The states parties will take appropriate steps to ensure the realization of this right, recognizing to this effect the essential importance of international co-operation based on free consent.
2. The states parties to the present Covenant, recognizing the fundamental right of everyone to be free from hunger, shall take, individually and through international co-operation, the measures, including specific programs, which are needed:

   (a) To improve methods of production, conservation and distribution of food by making full use of technical and scientific knowledge, by disseminating knowledge of the principles of nutrition and by developing or reforming agrarian systems in such a way as to achieve the most efficient development and utilization of natural resources;
   (b) Taking into account the problems of both food-importing and food-exporting countries, to ensure an equitable distribution of world food supplies in relation to need.

The structure of Article 11 (1) is somewhat unconvincing in that the right to adequate food is not forcefully enunciated and can be viewed as a 'relative right', whereas the right to be free from hunger in paragraph 2 is considered to be 'absolute'.[24] The *travaux préparatoires* for the second paragraph of Article 11 document the deep preoccupation of many members of the drafting group within the Third Committee with the high levels of hunger and malnutrition being experienced by people in Asia, Africa and South America during the 1950s.[25] It was the Director-General of the Food and Agriculture Organization (FAO) of the United Nations who proposed the structure of the paragraph, which addresses the negative right to freedom from hunger along with a series of process and outcome goals in line with the prevailing policy priorities of the FAO's Freedom from Hunger campaign, which was being launched at that time.[26] The wording of Article 11 (2) is striking in that it does not explicitly define the right to food but instead focuses on the mechanisms through which it might be achieved.

Following sustained advocacy on the right to food by a growing number of transnational civil society movements, the World Food Summit (WFS) held in Rome in 1996 drafted a Plan

[22] Ben Saul, David Kinley and Jacqueline Mowbray, *The International Covenant on Economic, Social and Cultural Rights: Commentary, Cases and Materials* (OUP 2014).
[23] Ibid.
[24] Katarina Tomaševski, *The Right to Food: Guide through Applicable International Law* (Martinus Nijhoff 1987).
[25] Ben Saul, David Kinley and Jacqueline Mowbray, *The International Covenant on Economic, Social and Cultural Rights: Commentary, Cases and Materials* (OUP 2014).
[26] Ibid.

of Action which, inter alia, called for the UN human rights system to 'better define the rights to food' contained in Article 11 of the ICESCR.[27] In response to this demand, the Committee on Economic, Social and Cultural Rights (CESCR) adopted its interpretive General Comment No. 12: The Right to Adequate Food. The General Comment outlines the core content of the right as well as the measures that must be taken by states and other duty bearers to ensure its full realization.[28] Along with the mandate provided by the WFS and concerns expressed by civil society on the need for greater clarity with respect to the content and scope of the right to food, the rationale given by the Committee for the adoption of its interpretive guidance was that the periodic reports it had received from states since 1979 were not providing it with enough detail in relation to the right to food to enable it to identify obstacles to its realization.[29]

The linkages between the right to food and a host of other human rights are recognized in General Comment No. 12, in particular the idea that the right to food is 'inseparable from social justice', along with an insistence that the right to food applies to 'everyone'.[30] The Committee provides the following definition of the right to adequate food, which, while clearly more expansive than the notion of the right to be free from hunger contained in the text of Article 11 (2), still raises a number of questions about what the obligations attached to guaranteeing the adequacy of food might entail in a given context:

> The right to adequate food is realized when every man, woman and child, alone or in community with others, has physical and economic access at all times to adequate food or means for its procurement. The right to adequate food shall therefore not be interpreted in a narrow or restrictive sense which equates it with a minimum package of calories, proteins and other specific nutrients. The right to adequate food will have to be realized progressively. However, States have a core obligation to take the necessary action to mitigate and alleviate hunger.[31]

General Comment No. 12 emphasizes the indivisibility of all human rights while positioning the right to food as 'indispensable for the fulfilment of other human rights enshrined in the International Bill of Human Rights'.[32] The Comment sets out the Committee's interpretation of the content of the right to food and states that food security can only be achieved when there is sustainable and adequate food that is available and accessible in sufficient quantity and quality, and that food must also be culturally acceptable.[33] Although the CESCR notes that the right to food is to be realized progressively, it underlines that there are immediate obligations for states to take necessary action to mitigate and alleviate hunger and malnutrition

---

[27]   WFS, Rome Declaration on World Food Security (1996), Plan of Action Objective 7.4 (e); Marc J. Cohen and Maary Ashby Brown, 'The Right to Adequate Food, Justiciability and Food Security' in Marco Borghi and Letizia Postiglione Blommestein (eds) *The Right to Adequate Food and Access to Justice* (Bruylant/Schulthess 2006) 219.

[28]   CESCR, General Comment No. 12: The Right to Adequate Food (12 May 1999) E/C.12/1999/5.

[29]   Christian Courtis, 'The Right to Food as a Justiciable Right: Challenges and Strategies' [2007] Max Planck Yearbook of United Nations Law.

[30]   Jean Ziegler, Christophe Golay, Claire Mahon and Sally-Anne Way, *The Fight for the Right to Food: Lessons Learned* (Palgrave Macmillan 2011) 16. The authors note that this means that the words 'for himself and his family' in Article 11 (1) should therefore not be construed as a limitation on the applicability of the right 'in the case of individuals or in the case of households headed by a woman'.

[31]   CESCR, General Comment No. 12: The Right to Adequate Food (12 May 1999) E/C.12/1999/5.

[32]   Ibid para 4.

[33]   Ibid para 8.

through respect for, protection of and fulfillment of the right to adequate food.[34] Identifying and redressing discrimination in access to food as well as to means and entitlements for its procurement form part of the minimum core obligations that must be given immediate effect.[35] States must use the maximum of their available resources to satisfy 'at the very least, the minimum essential level required to be free from hunger'.[36]

The respect, protect, fulfill (facilitate and provide) typology of obligations which is used in General Comment No. 12 helps to dispel the common misconception that the right to adequate food simply requires states to provide food, by instead drawing attention to the multiple actions that it will be necessary for all duty bearers to take in order to realize the right to food.[37] General Comment No. 12 further highlights the justiciability of the right to food at both the national and international levels and encourages states to incorporate the provisions of the ICESCR into their domestic legal orders to 'enhance the scope and effectiveness of remedial measures'.[38]

The Optional Protocol to the International Covenant on Economic, Social and Cultural Rights (OP-ICESCR), which entered into force in 2013, provides an additional layer of accountability for the realization of the right to food.[39] The OP-ICESCR allows the CESCR to receive and consider individual complaints alleging violations of the right to food once domestic remedies have been exhausted. To date, the Committee has adopted views on social security contributions that tangentially concern the right to food, but it has not issued any jurisprudence that directly addresses obligations to respect, protect and fulfill the right to food.[40]

While the content of the right to adequate food is articulated most extensively at the international level in Article 11 of the ICESCR as well as through the CESCR's General Comment No. 12 discussed above, it is also recognized as an element of the right to the highest attainable standard of physical and mental health in Article 12 of the ICESCR (as elaborated on in Chapter 9).[41]

In addition, the right to food has been interpreted by the Human Rights Committee as falling within the scope of the protection accorded by the right to life contained in Article 6 of the International Covenant on Civil and Political Rights (ICCPR). In its General Comment No. 36, the Committee noted that measures necessary to protect life may also include the provision of access without delay to 'essential services such as food' as well as the restitution of land for indigenous peoples.[42] The Human Rights Committee has also interpreted the traditional

[34] Ibid para 14.
[35] Ibid paras 17–18.
[36] Ibid para 17.
[37] Asbjorn Eide, Report Updating the Study on the Right to Food (1998) E/CN.4/Sub.2/1998/9; Sandra Raponi, 'A Defense of the Human Right to Adequate Food' (2017) 23 Res Publica 99.
[38] CESCR, General Comment No. 12: The Right to Adequate Food (12 May 1999) E/C.12/1999/5 para 32.
[39] UN General Assembly, Optional Protocol to the International Covenant on Economic, Social and Cultural Rights.
[40] See OHCHR jurisprudence database <https://juris.ohchr.org>.
[41] CESCR, General Comment No. 14: The Right to the Highest Attainable Standard of Health (11 August 2000) E/C.12/2004/4. Paras 4, 11 and 43 (b) of the General Comment include adequate food and nutrition as 'underlying determinants' of the right to health that states and other duty bearers are under an obligation to guarantee to all right holders.
[42] CCPR, General Comment No. 36: Article 6 (The Rght to Life) (2 November 2018) CCPR/C/GC/36/ para 26. The Committee goes on to cite its Concluding Observations on the Democratic People's Republic of Korea, CCPR/CO/72/PRK para 12.

hunting and fishing practices of indigenous and minority groups as cultural rights that are protected under Article 27 of the ICCPR.[43] The Committee further found in *Womah Mukong v Cameroon* (1994) that depriving a detainee of food was one element that constituted cruel, inhuman and degrading treatment in violation of Article 7 of the ICCPR.[44]

The right to adequate food is reiterated in international treaties that promote and protect the rights of specific groups, such as Articles 24 (2) (c) and 27 (3) of the Convention on the Rights of the Child, the Convention on the Elimination of All Forms of Discrimination against Women (Articles 12(2) and 14), the Convention on the Rights of Persons with Disabilities (Articles 25(f) and 28(1)) and Article 20 of the 1951 Convention on the Status of Refugees.

Various international humanitarian law instruments, including the Rome Statute of the International Criminal Court, provide for protections against the deprivation of food and the means for its production, as well as prohibitions on and sanctions for impeding relief supplies and the use of starvation as a method of warfare.[45] The Geneva Conventions and their Additional Protocols stipulate that relief supplies, including food, must be accessible to civilian populations, with specific measures being taken to ensure that interned or detained persons are not denied access to food.[46]

## 2.2    UN Special Rapporteur on the Right to Food

The development of international law, policies and monitoring of the right to food has also been heavily influenced by the work of the Special Procedures of the Human Rights Council and its predecessor, the Commission on Human Rights.[47] The first Special Rapporteur on the right to food was appointed by the Sub Commission on the Promotion and Protection of Human Rights in 1983. Following a number of years of reporting on different aspects of the right to food by the Sub Commission mechanisms, the Commission on Human Rights adopted resolution 2000/10, which created the role of Special Rapporteur on the right to food 'in order to respond fully to the necessity for an integrated and coordinated approach in the promotion and protection of the right to food'.[48] In March 2006, the Human Rights Council replaced the Commission and endorsed and extended the right to food mandate, which has subsequently been renewed by the Council every three years.[49]

The means used by the Special Rapporteur to implement the mandate include the preparation of annual thematic studies that are adopted by the Human Rights Council and the UN General Assembly, country visits, responding to individual communications alleging violations of the right to food and participation in dialogue with relevant actors working in the areas of food and

---

[43]    CCPR, General Comment No. 23: Article 27 (Rights of Minorities) (8 April 1994) CCPR/C/GC/23.

[44]    *Womah Mukong v Cameroon*, Communication No. 458/1991 (1994) CCPR/C/51/D/458/1991.

[45]    Rome Statute of the International Criminal Court (1998) UNTS vol. 2187 Article 8 (2) b (xxv); Jelena Pejic, 'The Right to Food in Situations of Armed Conflict: The Legal Framework' (2001) 83 (844) IRRC 1097; Lance Cotula and Margret Vidar, *The Right to Adequate Food in Emergencies* (FAO 2003).

[46]    Gilles Giacca, *Economic, Social and Cultural Rights in Armed Conflict* (OUP 2014).

[47]    Irene Biglino, Christophe Golay and Ivona Truscan, 'The Contribution of the UN Special Procedures to the Human Rights and Development Dialogue' (2012) 9 Sur International Journal of Human Rights 15.

[48]    Human Rights Commission, Resolution 2000/10 (17 April 2000) E/CN.4/RES/2000/10.

[49]    Human Rights Council, Resolution 6/2 (27 September 2007) A/HRC/RES/6/2.

nutrition. Some of the themes that have been addressed by the three mandate-holders to date include the right to water, the private sector and its role in large-scale land acquisitions and contract farming arrangements, gender equality and women's rights, the rights of agricultural workers, children's rights to food, intellectual property rights over seeds, the right to land, justiciability of the right to food, conflict, natural disasters and climate change.[50]

Despite the fact that states and other actors are not required to report to the Special Procedures and that these mechanisms do not act in a quasi-judicial capacity, the flexibility, responsiveness and relevance of the actions taken by successive Special Rapporteurs on the right to food have had a significant impact on international norms and practice.[51] In several cases, the Special Rapporteur has been the subject of vigorous political attack from governments and this may be taken as a sign that the mandate-holders are influencing global discussions on the scope and content of the right to food.[52]

## 2.3    International Guidelines, Policies and Soft Law

The Universal Declaration on the Eradication of Hunger and Malnutrition was adopted by governments at the World Food Conference in 1974. The Conference was convened as a response to the famines that had been experienced in Africa, Asia and South America in the early 1970s. The Declaration reiterated 'the right to be free from hunger and malnutrition' and proposed the establishment of the International Fund for Agricultural Development (IFAD), a UN financial institution focused on the needs of rural populations.[53]

Efforts led by civil society organizations to entrench the right to food within the international policy landscape continued throughout the 1980s and finally proved successful in 1996 at the WFS. The Rome Declaration on World Food Security, adopted by the WFS, stressed the importance of human rights – in particular the right of equal participation in food policy-making – for the achievement of sustainable food security for all.[54] The Plan of Action that emerged from the Summit called for the treaty bodies and other elements of the UN system to undertake efforts to more clearly define the rights related to food in Article 11 of the ICESCR and to propose pathways for their implementation, including the possibility of formulating 'voluntary guidelines for food security for all'.[55] The CESCR's General Comment No. 12 described above was one of the documents that was developed in response to the WFS request for greater clarity on the content and scope of the right to food, and the Voluntary

---

[50]    OHCHR, Special Rapporteur on the right to food <www.ohchr.org/EN/Issues/Food/Pages/FoodIndex.aspx>.

[51]    Ilias Bantekas and Lutz Oette, *International Human Rights Law and Practice* (CUP 2013).

[52]    See for example the objections raised by Israel in E/CN.4/2004/G/9; US Mission to International Organizations in Geneva, Explanation of Vote on the Right to Food (21 March 2017) A/HRC/34/L.21. The government's position was that the Special Rapporteur had 'inappropriately' introduced a discussion on pesticides.

[53]    Pierre Spitz, 'Investing in the Right to Food' in FAO, *The Right to Food in Theory and Practice* (FAO 1998).

[54]    WFS, Rome Declaration on World Food Security (1996).

[55]    WFS, Rome Declaration on World Food Security (1996), Plan of Action Objective 7.4 (e); Héctor Faundez Ledesma, 'An International Code of Conduct to Implement the Right to Food' in Marco Borghi and Letizia Postiglione Blommestein (eds) *For an Effective Right to Adequate Food* (Fribourg University Press 2002) 187.

Guidelines supporting the progressive realization of the right to adequate food in the context of national food security (Right to Food Guidelines) was the other.[56]

The Right to Food Guidelines were elaborated in 2004 by an Intergovernmental Working Group under the auspices of the FAO Council. The process of development of the Right to Food Guidelines was significant not only for the fact that they finally brought a human rights-based approach into the mainstream of the FAO's work on food security and agriculture, but also because the negotiations opened the door for increased civil society involvement in international food policy-making.[57] The Right to Food Guidelines were supplemented in 2012 by the Voluntary Guidelines on the Responsible Governance of Tenure of Land, Fisheries and Forests in the Context of National Food Security (VGGT); the Principles for Responsible Investment in Agriculture and Food Systems (RAI), which were endorsed by the Committee on World Food Security in 2014; and the Voluntary Guidelines for Securing Sustainable Small-Scale Fisheries in the Context of Food Security and Poverty Alleviation (2015).[58] These normative documents are voluntary in nature; however, the fact that they were developed through inter-governmental negotiations with the active participation of a range of civil society actors accords them a certain degree of legitimacy and a potential for effectiveness that may be absent from other food security instruments.

## 2.4 Regional Human Rights Laws and Jurisprudence

Several regional human rights instruments contain guarantees of the right to food. These include the Additional Protocol to the American Convention on Human Rights in the Area of Economic, Social and Cultural Rights (Protocol of San Salvador) (1988), the African Charter on the Rights and Welfare of the Child (1990) and the Protocol to the African Charter on Human and Peoples' Rights on the Rights of Women in Africa (2003). In South East Asia, Article 28 (a) of the ASEAN Human Rights Declaration (2013) recognizes 'the right to adequate and affordable food, freedom from hunger and access to safe and nutritious food'.

The African Charter on Human and Peoples' Rights (1981) does not contain a direct guarantee of the right to food; however, the African Commission on Human and Peoples' Rights has held that the right to food is implicitly protected through the rights to life, health and development that are acknowledged in the Charter.[59] The Inter-American Court of Human Rights has recognized claims from several indigenous and traditional local communities related to denials of access to land and traditional means of subsistence as violations of the right to life under

---

[56] Eibe Reidel, 'Economic, Social and Cultural Rights' in Catarina Krause and Martin Scheinin, *International Protection of Human Rights* (Abo Akademi University 2009) 129.

[57] Isabella Rae, Julian Thomas and Margret Vidar, 'History and Implications for FAO of the Guidelines on the Right to Adequate Food' in Wench Barth Eide and Uwe Kracht (eds) *Food and Human Rights in Development* (Intersentia 2007) 457.

[58] FAO, Voluntary Guidelines on the Responsible Governance of Tenure of Land, Fisheries and Forests in the Context of National Food Security (FAO 2012); CFS, Principles for Responsible Investment in Agriculture and Food Systems (FAO 2014); Voluntary Guidelines for Securing Sustainable Small-Scale Fisheries in the Context of Food Security and Poverty Alleviation (FAO 2015).

[59] *African Commission on Human and Peoples' Rights, Social and Economic Rights Action Centre and Another v Nigeria* (2001) ACHPR 60; *Centre for Minority Rights Development (Kenya) and Minority Rights Group International on behalf of Endorois Welfare Council v Kenya* (2010) 276/2003.

Article 4 of the American Convention on Human Rights.[60] The Inter-American Commission on Human Rights has also issued a number of reports which support its conclusion that

> the whole range of environmental impacts in the Amazon region are to a large extent undermining the indigenous peoples' enjoyment of the rights to water and food ... the pollution of water resources prompts a food crisis, given that fish are a vital part of their traditional diet for many communities in the Amazon region. The IACHR likewise notes that, since dietary habits are tied in with the cosmo-vision of indigenous peoples, some of the food supply measures taken by States have been culturally inappropriate ... In addition to the above, there are also impacts related to deforestation and the loss of biodiversity, which have reportedly impaired traditional hunting and gathering practices.[61]

Both the European Convention on Human Rights (1950) and the European Social Charter (1961) pre-date the adoption of the ICESCR, and neither of these instruments mentions the right to food.[62] In one of the few cases decided in connection with the right to food in Europe, the European Court of Human Rights has held that the failure to provide adequate, safe and nutritious food to persons in detention may amount to inhuman and degrading treatment and punishment.[63]

## 2.5    National Constitutions, Legislation and Jurisprudence on the Right to Food

A number of states have adopted specific Articles on the right to food in their national constitutions.[64] For example, the Constitutions of Bolivia, Ecuador, Kenya and South Africa all protect the right to have access to sufficient food and water and some of these documents contain further provisions on food sovereignty and land rights. Many more governments have developed constitutional protection for the right to food for particular groups within the population, such as children, the elderly or detainees.[65] Other countries have enacted constitutional provisions that mention the right to food within broader principles such as the right to an adequate standard of living, the right to life or the right to minimum subsistence.[66] In some federal states, constitutions have been adopted at the sub-national level that contain guarantees of the right to food and other related rights such as the rights to work and social protection.[67]

---

[60] *Inter-American Court of Human Rights, Sawhoyamaxa Indigenous Community v Paraguay* (2006) IACHR Series C No 146, IHRL 1530 (IACHR 2006).

[61] IACHR, *Situation of Human Rights of the Indigenous and Tribal Peoples of the Pan-Amazon Region* (IACHR 2019) 134.

[62] European Parliament, *The Role of Regional Human Rights Mechanisms* (European Parliament 2010); Cristina Grieco and Federica Musso, 'An International and European Perspective on the Right to Food and to Adequate Food for Elderly People and Its Justiciability' (2017) 3 Ordine Internazionale e Diritti Umani (2017) 373.

[63] *European Court of Human Rights, Ilaşcu and Others v Moldova and Russia* (2005) 40 EHRR 1030.

[64] Lidija Knuth and Margret Vidar, *Constitutional and Legal Protection of the Right to Food Around the World* (FAO 2011).

[65] Margret Vidar, Yoon Jee Kim and Luisa Cruz, *Legal Developments in the Progressive Realization of the Right to Adequate Food* (FAO 2014).

[66] Lidija Knuth and Margret Vidar, *Constitutional and Legal Protection of the Right to Food Around the World* (FAO 2011).

[67] Sandra Raponi, 'A Defense of the Human Right to Adequate Food' (2017) 23 Res Publica 99.

Finally, since the Right to Food Guidelines were agreed upon in 2004, many countries have enacted national framework laws on the right to food.[68]

Jurisprudence emerging from domestic jurisdictions – in particular the seminal right to food cases decided in India and the housing and health rights cases from South Africa – has had a strong influence on the development of international and regional human rights law and policies as well as in other national contexts.[69]

The Indian right to food campaign has been pivotal in drawing attention to the fact that hunger and malnutrition are not the products of a lack of food availability but are, instead, caused by structural forms of inequality that shape food distribution systems.[70] In *People's Union for Civil Liberties (PUCL) v Union of India*, the Indian Supreme Court used the right to life in Article 21 of the Constitution to develop a series of orders that directed the government to expand its programs on school meals, integrated child feeding, subsidized cereals, maternity protection, old age pensions, family benefits and rural employment so that a basic nutritional floor was guaranteed for the whole population.[71] In taking these measures and by mandating the appointment of two Commissioners to monitor their implementation, the Court converted social protection programs into 'entitlements or rights'.[72] The *PUCL* case is consistent with a long line of case law in which various Indian courts reaffirm the protection of the right to food as a component of the right to life.[73] This Indian jurisprudence, along with sustained advocacy from civil society, led to the adoption of the national Food Security Act in 2013.[74] Some critics have argued, however, that these promising measures have been less effective than they might have been in entrenching the right to food in India due to the fact that the prevailing economic model privileges a growth-based, neo-liberal form of development over the construction of a welfare state.[75]

---

[68]    Margret Vidar, Yoon Jee Kim and Luisa Cruz, *Legal Developments in the Progressive Realization of the Right to Adequate Food* (FAO 2014) 5. These countries include Brazil (2010), Ecuador (2009), Guatemala (2005), Indonesia (2012) and Zanzibar (2011).

[69]    Jean Ziegler, Christophe Golay, Claire Mahon and Sally-Anne Way, *The Fight for the Right to Food: Lessons Learned* (Palgrave Macmillan 2011); Marco Borghi and Letizia Postiglione Blommestein (eds) *The Right to Adequate Food and Access to Justice* (Bruylant/Schulthess 2006); Christian Courtis, 'The Right to Food as a Justiciable Right: Challenges and Strategies' [2007] Max Planck Yearbook of United Nations Law; IDLO and Irish Aid, *Realizing the Right to Food: Legal Strategies and Approaches* (IDLO 2014).

[70]    Marco Borghi and Letizia Postiglione Blommestein (eds), *The Right to Adequate Food and Access to Justice* (Bruylant/Schulthess 2006).

[71]    *PUCL v Union of India and Others*, Writ Petition [Civil] 196 (2001).

[72]    Harsh Mander, 'Food from the Courts: The Indian Experience' (2012) 43 IDS- Bull. 15.

[73]    *Francis Coralie v Administrator*, Union Territory of Delhi and Others (1981) 1 SCC 608; *Shantistar Builders v Narayan Khimalal Totame* (1990) 1 SCC 520; *Chameli Singh v State of U.P.* (1996) 2 SCC 549; *Ekta Shakti Foundation v Government of NCT of Delhi*, Writ Petition (Civil) 232 (2006); *Amit Kumar Jain v State of Rajasthan*, D.B. Civil Writ (PIL) Petition No. 4777 of 2005 (High Court of Rajasthan); *Pradeep Pradhan v State of Orissa and Others*, CRLMC No. 597 of 2008 in G.R. Case No. 168 of 2005 (High Court of Orissa); *Sri Kaheka Pralo v The State of Arunachal Pradesh*, Writ Petition (Civil) Appeal No. 376 of 2012 (High Court of Gauhati).

[74]    Ragav Puri, 'India's National Food Security Act (NFSA): Early Experiences' 14 LANSA Working Paper Series (2017); Ebenezer Durojaye and Enoch MacDonnell Chilemba, *Accountability and the Right to Food: A Comparative Study of India and South Africa* (DST-NRF Centre of Excellence in Food Security 2018).

[75]    Anupam Pandey, 'Hunger and the State: A Comparative Case Study of Cuba and India' (2019) 100 Studies in Political Economy 180.

South Africa is a jurisdiction in which the Constitution explicitly guarantees the rights to adequate food and nutrition.[76] In comparison to India, however, relatively few cases specifically alleging violations of the right to food have been the subject of litigation.[77] In *Kenneth George and Others v Minister of Environmental Affairs & Tourism*, the South African High Court ordered a revision of the Marine Living Resources Act, requiring the development of a new framework taking into account 'international and national legal obligations and policy directives to accommodate the socio-economic rights of [small-scale] fishers and to ensure equitable access to marine resources for those fishers'.[78] *Wary Holdings v Stwalo* (2008) dealt with the legality of buying and selling agricultural land and while the Constitutional Court recognized that the government was under an obligation not to violate the right to food, it did not discuss which forms of agricultural land tenure were more conducive to the implementation of the right to food.[79] In contrast, the Constitutional Court decided in a different case that agricultural lands had to be restituted to a Popela community who had been dispossessed as a result of apartheid-era practices.[80] It has been suggested that while the South African Constitution provides a solid foundation for the promotion and protection of the right to food, in practice the absence of strong civil society right to food campaigns, as well as the failure of courts to make specific, time-bound orders or to create monitoring mechanisms, has meant that strategic litigation has yet to have a meaningful impact on hunger and malnutrition.[81]

## 2.6    The Minimum Core of the Right to Food

The legal and policy landscape within which the right to adequate food is being implemented at different spatial scales – local, national, regional – is dynamic and complex. Even though local, national and regional contexts vary and different measures will be necessary to implement the right to food in these diverse settings, a certain number of minimum core characteristics of the right to food have been identified through the laws, policies, jurisprudence and practice outlined above.

In its General Comment No. 12, the CESCR develops an understanding of the contours of the right to adequate food and provides indications concerning the way in which the right should be applied domestically. The Committee's interpretation of the core content of the right to food, which is reiterated by the Special Rapporteur and in the Right to Food Guidelines, is grounded in the 'three As': adequacy, availability and accessibility.[82] Adequate food requires ensuring 'the availability of food in a quantity and quality sufficient to satisfy the dietary

---

[76]   Constitution of the Republic of South Africa (1996). Section 27 (1) (b) 'everyone has a right of access to sufficient food'; Section 28 (1) (c) 'every child has a right to basic nutrition'; Section 35 (2) (e) 'every detained person and prisoner has a right to adequate nutrition'.

[77]   Ebenezer Durojaye and Enoch MacDonnell Chilemba, *Accountability and the Right to Food: A Comparative Study of India and South Africa* (DST-NRF Centre of Excellence in Food Security 2018).

[78]   IDLO and Irish Aid, *Realizing the Right to Food: Legal Strategies and Approaches* (IDLO 2014).

[79]   *Wary Holdings v Stwalo*, CCT78/07 [2008] ZACC 12.

[80]   *Department of Land Affairs v Goedgelegen Tropical Fruits (Pty) Ltd* CCT69/06 (unreported).

[81]   Bright Nkrumah, 'Opening Pandora's Box: A Legal Analysis of the Right to Food in South Africa' [2019] De Jure Law Journal 47.

[82]   Sven Söllner, 'The "Breakthrough" of the Right to Food: The Meaning of General Comment no. 12 and the Voluntary Guidelines for the Interpretation of the Human Right to Food' (2007) 11 Max Planck Yearbook of United Nations Law 391.

needs of individuals, free from adverse substances, and acceptable within a given culture' and 'the accessibility of such food in ways that are sustainable and that do not interfere with the enjoyment of other human rights'.[83] The concept of adequacy refers to the quality, safety, and nutritional and cultural value of food. Availability and accessibility concern the means through which food is produced or acquired and the need for duty bearers to identify and eliminate structural barriers that may prevent specific groups from realizing their rights to food immediately and in the future.

Alongside the substantive content of the right to food that is to be guaranteed by states and other actors are a number of procedural requirements, such as the development of mechanisms to ensure the full and active participation by right-holders in food policy-making and the creation of transparent and accessible monitoring and remedy processes for violations of the right to food.[84]

## 3.    INTERDEPENDENT AND INTER-RELATED RIGHTS: LAND, WORK, SOCIAL SECURITY

The rights to land and natural resources, decent work and social security are indispensable to the realization of the right to adequate food.[85] It is largely through advocacy around the right to food that land and resource rights have been placed on the international human rights agenda.[86] The CESCR includes the obligation to respect access to productive agricultural land and resources under Article 11 of the ICESCR. The Committee also interprets the obligation to fulfill the right to food as requiring states to adopt measures aimed at improving right-holders' access to and utilization of resources and means to ensure their livelihoods, such as land reform.[87] Rights to own, use, develop and control land and resources and subsistence rights form a central component of the UN Declaration on the Rights of Indigenous Peoples (2007).[88] The UN Declaration on the Rights of Peasants and Other People Working in Rural Areas (UNDROP), adopted by the Human Rights Council and the UN General Assembly in 2018, places rights over land and natural resources at the front and center of its right to food and food sovereignty agenda.[89]

UN Special Procedures and international civil society movements have issued repeated calls for the recognition of a stand-alone right to land and territory in international human rights

---

[83]   CESCR, General Comment No. 12: The Right to Adequate Food (12 May 1999) E/C.12/1999/5.

[84]   FAO, *Right to Food: Human Rights Principles: PANTHER* (FAO Right to Food Team 2013).

[85]   Joanna Bourke Martignoni, 'Engendering the Right to Food? International Human Rights Law, Food Security and the Rural Woman' (2019) 9 Transnational Legal Theory 400.

[86]   Jeremie Gilbert, 'Land Rights as Human Rights: The Case for a Specific Right to Land' (2013) 18 SUR International Journal on Human Rights 115.

[87]   CESCR, General Comment No. 12: The Right to Adequate Food (12 May 1999) E/C.12/1999/5. In 2019, the CESCR commenced the process of drafting a General Comment on land and the governance of tenure.

[88]   United Nations Declaration on the Rights of Indigenous Peoples (13 September 2007) A/61/L.67 and Add.1. Articles 20, 25–28 and 32.

[89]   United Nations Declaration on the Rights of Peasants and Other People Working in Rural Areas (28 September 2018) A/HRC/RES/39/12.

law.[90] In his 2007 report to the Human Rights Council, the Special Rapporteur on the right to housing recommended that the right to land be recognized in international law.[91] In 2010, the Special Rapporteur on the right to food called on international human rights bodies to clarify 'the issue of land as a human right' and implement land redistribution programs in contexts where there is a high degree of land ownership concentration.[92]

Civil society organizations participating in the CFS CSM have included land tenure rights as a crucial element of their advocacy efforts and these groups view the adoption of the Voluntary Guidelines on the Governance of Land Tenure (VGGT), which recognize the 'legitimate tenure rights' upon which rural communities depend for their livelihoods, as an important achievement in this area.[93] The VGGT provide that states must protect and respect land tenure rights, including informal and customary rights, and protect land rights holders in the context of land transfers and large-scale land investments. They also highlight states' obligations to develop programs designed to adapt to and mitigate the impacts of climate change and to take steps to limit land speculation, concentration and forced evictions. States are encouraged to facilitate land reform processes where this is necessary to guarantee food security and sustainable livelihoods.[94]

## 4.    THE FUTURE OF THE RIGHT TO FOOD

This section briefly highlights several key themes that will play a decisive role in shaping the way in which the right to food is developed in the next few decades. These topics are inter-related and are already reflected within documents issued by UN human rights mechanisms and civil society organizations, and in many national laws and policies.

### 4.1    Feminist and Intersectional Approaches to Food Systems

> Gender relations shape food systems. They significantly influence how and what we produce, work and eat. Gender oppression has often had a negative effect on women and gender non-conforming people across all stages of food systems ... From growing and harvesting produce, to processing, transporting and consuming food, women play a pivotal role in food systems and economies.[95]

---

[90]    Priscilla Claeys, 'The Right to Land and Territory: New Human Right and Collective Action Frame' (2016) 75 Revue Interdisciplinaire d'Études Juridiques 115.

[91]    Miloon Kothari, 'Report of the Special Rapporteur on the right to adequate housing' (5 February 2007) A/HRC/4/18/2007.

[92]    Olivier De Schutter, 'Report of the Special Rapporteur on the right to food' (11 August 2010) A/65/281.

[93]    Lorenza Paoloni and Antonio Onorati, 'Regulation of Large-Scale Acquisitions of Land: The Case of the Voluntary Guidelines on the Responsible Governance of Land, Fisheries and Forests' (2014) 7 Law and Development Review 1.

[94]    FAO, Voluntary Guidelines on the Responsible Governance of Tenure of Land, Fisheries and Forests in the Context of National Food Security (FAO 2012).

[95]    FIAN and Brot für die Welt, *Right to Food and Nutrition Watch 2019: Women's Power in Food Struggles* (Global Network for the Right to Food and Nutrition 2019) Supplement.

Civil society, the human rights mechanisms and many states have emphasized that gender equality is a key factor in the realization of the right to food for everyone.[96] The accessibility element of the right to food includes duties for governments and non-state actors to adopt targeted measures to ensure that all right-holders have equal access to food, resources for food production, social security entitlements and income from decent work in order to procure food. The CESCR in its interpretive General Comment No. 12 on the Right to Adequate Food, notes that states have obligations to guarantee 'full and equal access to economic resources, particularly for women, including the right to inheritance and the ownership of land and other property, credit, natural resources and appropriate technology'.[97]

The text of the Convention on the Elimination of All Forms of Discrimination Against Women (CEDAW) refers to food and nutrition in its preamble in connection with women living in poverty, in Article 12 (2) on the right to health and the obligation to ensure adequate nutrition during pregnancy and lactation and in Article 14 as one component of an 'adequate standard of living' for rural women. The CEDAW Committee has issued several interpretive General Recommendations that address the need to implement the right to food on the basis of gender equality.[98] In particular, the Committee's General Recommendation No. 34 on the rights of rural women lays out the obligations contained in Article 14 of the Convention as they relate to women's rights to food and nutrition, as well as equal rights to access, use and control agricultural land and natural resources.[99] The General Recommendation also brings in the concept of food sovereignty and the idea that in this connection, rural women should have the 'authority to manage and control their natural resources'.[100]

Other international human rights mechanisms, including the Human Rights Council and its Special Procedures have reiterated that gender equality is a pre-condition for the realization of the right to adequate food and that states have binding legal obligations to enact laws and policies aimed at preventing and eliminating sex and gender-based discrimination in food systems.[101]

The FAO Right to Food Guidelines and the VGGT provide for concrete measures to be taken to guarantee that women and men are equally able to enjoy the right to food and the means for its production through rights over land and natural resources, or purchase by way of adequate income from decent work and from universal social security entitlements.[102]

---

[96]    Joanna Bourke Martignoni, 'Engendering the Right to Food? International Human Rights Law, Food Security and the Rural Woman' (2019) 9 Transnational Legal Theory 400; World Bank, *Gender in Agriculture Sourcebook* (World Bank 2009); FAO, 'Women in Agriculture Closing the Gender Gap for Development' in FAO, *The State of Food and Agriculture 2010–2011* (FAO 2011); IDLO, *Women, Food, Land: Exploring Rule of Law Linkages* (IDLO 2016); Resource Equity and Landesa, *Gender and Collectively Held Land* (Resource Equity and Landesa, 2016).

[97]    CESCR, General Comment No. 12: The Right to Adequate Food (12 May 1999) E/C.12/1999/5 para 26.

[98]    See also CEDAW Committee, General Recommendation No. 37: Gender-related Dimensions of Disaster Risk Reduction in the Context of Climate Change (2018) CEDAW/C/GC/37 Section E.

[99]    CEDAW Committee, General Recommendation No. 34: The Rights of Rural Women (2016) CEDAW/C/GC/34.

[100]    Ibid para 64.

[101]    Hilal Elver, 'Report of the Special Rapporteur on the Right to Food' (14 December 2015) A/HRC/31/51 para 17.

[102]    FAO, Voluntary Guidelines on the Responsible Governance of Tenure of Land, Fisheries and Forests in the Context of National Food Security (FAO 2012) part 3B para 4.

Sustainable Development Goals 2 and 5 contain further injunctions to ensure that women and girls have access to adequate food and nutrition and that they are supported in their roles as farmers and food producers through targeted agricultural development programs, land tenure reform and women's empowerment initiatives.[103] In 2018, the United Nations Commission on the Status of Women (UN CSW 62) 'reaffirm[ed] the right to food and recogniz[ed] the crucial contributions of rural women to local and national economies and to food production and to achieve food security and improved nutrition, in particular in poor and vulnerable households'.[104]

Gender equality demands have the potential to make visible and disrupt unequal power relations at different levels and provide a variety of mechanisms through which structural injustices in access to food, land and other natural resources might be observed and redressed. To date, however, the primary engagement of UN human rights mechanisms has been with those forms of discrimination and inequality that women face in accessing food in the 'private' and 'local' spheres of the family and community without convincingly connecting these to global inequalities in food systems.[105] The prevailing approach to gender equality being promoted through inter-governmental initiatives in connection with food and land rights is relatively apolitical, with most of the suggested solutions to gender and sex discrimination in food systems focused on increasing women's productivity in agriculture rather than examining the forms of power and domination that create and reproduce these unequal gender relations.[106] The other problematic aspect of many mainstream food security discourses around gender in food, nutrition and agriculture is that they unquestionably reproduce a binary approach to women and men and fail to consider intersectional power relations.[107]

In contrast, feminist constituencies within social movements have consistently made linkages between gender-based discrimination within the family and community and the broader macro-economic trends that influence food, agriculture, labor and land.[108] The food sovereignty agendas envisioned by feminist members of La Vía Campesina and other social movements encompass 'personal' sovereignty, including bodily and sexual autonomy, and freedom from violence in all of its manifestations, drawing attention to the continuum of violence from that experienced in the home, to corporate economic and environmental violence.[109]

---

[103]  FAO, *Food and Agriculture: Key to Achieving the 2030 Agenda for Sustainable Development* (FAO 2016).

[104]  ECOSOC, Report of the Commission of the Status of Women (2018) E/2018/27-E/CN.6/2018/20.

[105]  Bina Agarwal, 'Gender and Land Rights Revisited: Exploring New Prospects via the State, Family and Market' (2003) 3 Journal of Agrarian Change 184.

[106]  UNGA, 'Report by the Special Rapporteur on the Right to Food' (11 August 2010) A/65/281; Saturnino M. Borras, Ruth Hall, Ian Scoones, Ben White and Wendy Wolford, 'Towards a Better Understanding of Global Land Grabbing: An Editorial Introduction' (2011) 38 (2) The Journal of Peasant Studies 209; World Bank, 'Module 4: Gender Issues in Land Policy and Administration' in World Bank, *Gender in Agriculture Sourcebook* (World Bank 2009) 137.

[107]  Joanna Bourke Martignoni, 'Engendering the Right to Food? International Human Rights Law, Food Security and the Rural Woman' (2019) 9 Transnational Legal Theory 400.

[108]  CSM, Women's Vision Statement (2018) <www.csm4cfs.org/csm-womens-vision/>; La Via Campesina, VII International Conference: Women's Assembly Declaration (2017) <www.cadtm.org/VII-International-Conference-Women>; FIAN and Brot für die Welt, *Right to Food and Nutrition Watch 2019: Women's Power in Food Struggles* (Global Network for the Right to Food and Nutrition 2019).

[109]  La Via Campesina, *Women's Manifesto of the IV Women's Assembly of la Via Campesina, Jakarta* (2013).

These feminist constituencies within the food sovereignty movement have also consistently underlined the need for an intersectional approach to the right to food that acknowledges that experiences of gendered inequalities in food systems will also be conditioned by factors such as socio-economic class, geographic location, ethnic identity, age, gender identity and sexual orientation.[110]

Despite this strong articulation of a feminist agenda by rural social movements, there is an awareness within the groups advancing these demands that feminism is regarded by many peasant organizations as a radical and foreign concept.[111] A lot of these fears are related to the idea that feminist claims might destabilize the traditional smallholder family unit, which forms an integral part of the peasant identity that has been constructed in opposition to the large-scale, neo-liberal model of agriculture that agrarian social movements are contesting. In this regard, a number of peasants' rights activists have emphasized that the relatively timid references to gender equality and the rights of rural women that were retained in the final version of the UN Declaration on the Rights of Peasants will need to be interpreted using an explicitly feminist framework in order to ensure that it fulfills its emancipatory promise.[112]

### 4.2    Food Sovereignty Movements: Recognizing the Rights of Peasant Farmers

As outlined above, transnational social movements have made such an important contribution to the creation, development and monitoring of norms connected to the rights to food, land and natural resources that they may now be considered 'law makers' in this field.[113] Networks including La Vía Campesina and FIAN have focused on issues of food sovereignty, the governance of land tenure, the right to seeds, protection of biodiversity, decent working conditions for rural laborers and fair prices for agricultural commodities.[114] Their advocacy efforts were largely responsible for the adoption of the VGGT.[115]

More recently, the UN Declaration on the Rights of Peasants (UNDROP) was adopted following 17 years of advocacy by a number of agrarian social movements and human rights advocates working on issues of food sovereignty, land grabbing and trade liberalization.[116]

> UNDROP recognises the dignity of the world's rural populations, their contributions to global food production, and the 'special relationship' they have to land, water and nature, as well as their vulner-

---

[110]    CSM, Women's Vision Statement (2018) <www.csm4cfs.org/csm-womens-vision>.

[111]    La Via Campesina, *Report of the IV Women's Assembly of la Via Campesina, Jakarta* (la Via Campesina 2013).

[112]    Sandra Moreno Cadena, 'The Declaration and the Struggles of Peasant Women: Gender as an Unachieved Question' cited in Priscilla Claeys and Marc Edelman, 'The United Nations Declaration on the Rights of Peasants and Other People Working in Rural Areas' (2020) 47 The Journal of Peasant Studies 61.

[113]    Priscilla Claeys, 'The Rise of New Rights for Peasants: From Reliance on NGO Intermediaries to Direct Representation' (2019) 9 Transnational Legal Theory 386.

[114]    Annette Aurélie Desmarais, *La Via Campesina: Globalization and the Power of Peasants* (Pluto Press 2007); Priscilla Claeys, *Human Rights and the Food Sovereignty Movement: Reclaiming Control* (Routledge 2015).

[115]    Sofia Monsalve Suárez, 'The Human Rights Framework in Contemporary Agrarian Struggles' (2013) 40 (1) The Journal of Peasant Studies 239.

[116]    Priscilla Claeys and Marc Edelman, 'The United Nations Declaration on the Rights of Peasants and Other People Working in Rural Areas' (2020) 47 The Journal of Peasant Studies 1.

abilities to eviction, hazardous working conditions and political repression. It reiterates human rights protected in other instruments and sets new standards for individual and collective rights to land and natural resources, seeds, biodiversity and food sovereignty.[117]

The UNDROP was welcomed by food sovereignty and peasants' rights movements as a landmark in the international recognition of the peasantry as political and legal subjects with the agency to define the future shape of agricultural, food and environmental systems around the world.[118] This engagement of peasants' rights movements with international law is not unproblematic and it has been noted that it comes at the risk of potentially reinforcing and legitimizing the same systems of global capital and property that they seek to dismantle.[119] Nevertheless, the negotiating process provides an example of the way in which knowledge may be 'co-constructed' by agrarian social movements, human rights advocates and academics and alliances built across a wide range of different constituencies in order to create new human rights 'from below'.[120]

The focus since the adoption of the Declaration in 2018 has been on the implementation of the rights it contains through activities such as awareness-raising, the creation of participatory international monitoring mechanisms and lobbying for the enactment of domestic legislation on peasants' rights.[121] It remains to be seen whether the human rights framework on food that is recognized in the UNDROP will prevail over the dominant industrial food paradigm.[122]

## 4.3 Business Actors and the Right to Food

The involvement of businesses within food and agricultural governance institutions is not a new phenomenon and the creation of multi-stakeholder partnerships, such as the Committee on World Food Security, that include governmental, private sector and civil society members is a trend that has been promoted and encouraged under the 2030 Sustainable Development Agenda.[123] The expansion of private sector influence over food systems through agricultural and land commercialization, as well as by way of public–private partnerships in nutrition and food, has been a central concern for civil society organizations working on the right to food and has also been a topic of discussion in different human rights fora.[124]

---

[117] Ibid 1.

[118] Ibid.

[119] PCFS, 'UNDROP's Implementation Depends on Strength of Local Rural People's Movement' (2019) <www.counterview.org>; Margot Salomon, 'Nihilists, Pragmatists and Peasants: A Dispatch on Contradiction in International Human Rights Law' 2018/5 IILJ Working Paper 2018/5 (2018).

[120] Priscilla Claeys and Marc Edelman, 'The United Nations Declaration on the Rights of Peasants and Other People Working in Rural Areas' (2020) 47 The Journal of Peasant Studies 1.

[121] Christophe Golay, *The Implementation of the United Nations Declaration on the Rights of Peasants and Other People Working in Rural Areas* (Geneva Academy Research Brief 2019).

[122] Priscilla Claeys and Marc Edelman, 'The United Nations Declaration on the Rights of Peasants and Other People Working in Rural Areas' (2020) 47 The Journal of Peasant Studies 1.

[123] Jessica Duncan and Priscilla Claeys, 'Politicizing Food Security Governance through Participation: Opportunities and Opposition' (2018) 10 Food Sec. 1411; Herman Brouwer, *Are Multi-stakeholder Partnerships Effective to Reach SDG Goals?* (CFS 2019).

[124] Philip McMichael, 'New Directions in the Sociology of Global Development' (2005) 11 Research in Rural Sociology and Development 269; Nienke Busscher, Eva Lia Colombo, Lidewij van der Ploeg, Julia Inés Gabella and Amalia Leguizamón, 'Civil Society Challenges the Global Food System: The International Monsanto Tribunal' (2020) 17 Globalizations 16; Christopher Kaan and Andrea Liese,

Human rights advocates have highlighted the need for greater efforts to be made to hold states and corporations accountable for violations of the right to food arising from business practices including land grabbing, the privatization of common pool resources such as seeds, pastures, fisheries, forests and water, unfair contract farming and market pricing systems, as well as the exploitation of agricultural and food workers.[125] There are a number of initiatives being taken at various levels that seek to fill the accountability gap in relation to the impact of business activities on human rights, including the right to food. General Comment No. 12 adopted by the CESCR in 1999 expressly recognizes the obligations of states to regulate the private sector 'within the framework of a code of conduct conducive to respect of the right to adequate food, agreed upon jointly with the Government and civil society'.[126] In 2017, the Committee adopted General Comment No. 24 on Business and Human Rights which seeks to clarify the obligations that parties to the ICESCR have to prevent and redress the adverse impacts of business activities on human rights.[127] Paragraph 8 of the General Comment states: 'Among the groups that are often disproportionately affected by the adverse impact of business activities are women, children, indigenous peoples, particularly in relation to the development, utilization or exploitation of lands and natural resources, peasants, fisherfolk and other people working in rural areas.'[128]

In connection with its discussion on the obligation of states and business actors to fulfill Covenant rights, the General Comment notes the need for intellectual property laws to be designed in a manner that is consistent with the rights of farmers and others to access productive resources such as seeds that are 'crucial to the right to food'.[129]

A number of civil society organizations have highlighted the weaknesses of existing voluntary monitoring and grievance mechanisms within the fields of agriculture and food and are actively lending their support to the development of a binding treaty on business and human rights.[130]

## 4.4    The Right to Food and the Challenge of Climate Change

Climate change has negative impacts on agriculture while current agricultural practices and food systems are responsible for harming the environment, affecting social and environmental determinants of health and accelerating human-induced climate change. Moreover, climate change is under-

'Public Private Partnerships in Global Food Governance: Business Engagement and Legitimacy in the Global Fight against Hunger and Malnutrition' (2011) 28 Agric Hum Values 385.

[125]    Olivier De Schutter, 'Agribusiness and the Right to Food' (22 December 2009) A/HRC/13/33 and (29 December 2009) A/HRC/13/33/Add.1; Isabel Alvarez, 'Building New Agrifood Systems: Struggles and Challenges' (2017) 10 Right to Food and Nutrition Watch 42.

[126]    CESCR, General Comment No. 12 on the Right to Adequate Food (12 May 1999) E/C.12/1999/5 para 20.

[127]    CESCR, General Comment No. 24: State Obligations Under the International Covenant on Economic, Social and Cultural Rights in the Context of Business Activities (10 August 2017) E/C.12/GC/24.

[128]    Ibid 8.

[129]    Ibid 24.

[130]    FIAN, 'Negotiations over Treaty Wording Kick Off' (2019) <www.fian.org/en/press-release/article/negotiations-over-treaty-wording-kick-off-2219>; Carolijn Terwindt and Christian Schliemann, 'Why a Binding Treaty Is Necessary: The UN Complaint Mechanism's Lack of Teeth on Pesticides Management', Business and Human Rights Resource Centre <www.business-humanrights.org/en/why-a-binding-treaty-is-necessary-the-un-complaint-mechanisms-lack-of-teeth-on-pesticides-management>.

mining the right to food, with disproportionate impacts on those who have contributed least to global warming and are most vulnerable to its harmful effects.[131]

The 2018 edition of 'The State of Food Security and Nutrition in the World' (SOFI) cites the changing climate as the main cause of the dramatic growth in the number of people facing hunger and malnutrition worldwide.[132] The preamble to the Paris Agreement on Climate Change recognizes 'the fundamental priority of safeguarding food security and ending hunger, and the particular vulnerabilities of food production systems to the adverse impacts of climate change'.[133] As the international community becomes increasingly aware of the urgent need to address the impact of climate change, there have been repeated calls for the development and implementation of human rights-based responses.

In 2018, the CEDAW Committee adopted its General Recommendation No. 37 on the gender dimensions of disaster risk reduction in the context of climate change.[134] The General Recommendation underlines the need for coherent policy and legislative frameworks on climate change mitigation and adaptation that reflect the experiences of diverse groups of women, including those in rural and urban settings, indigenous women, women with disabilities, girls and older women.[135]

Successive UN Special Rapporteurs on the right to food have also drawn attention to the specific impacts of climate change on the rights to food for rural women, smallholder farmers, people living in poverty and indigenous communities.[136] The Rapporteurs have highlighted the importance of the role that agroecology and indigenous and traditional knowledge about climate change adaptation might play in guaranteeing the right to food. Both of the mandate-holders have also stressed the need to assert the primacy of human rights-based frameworks in the areas of food and agriculture over the technology and food production-based responses that climate change and food security institutions have tended to privilege.[137]

## 5.   CONCLUSION

The presence of facilitative human rights laws, jurisprudence, policies and institutions is not, on its own, sufficient to ensure the right to food globally. While notable advances have been made over the past few decades in reducing the levels of hunger and malnutrition experienced

---

[131]   Hilal Elver, 'The Adverse Impact of Climate Change on the Right to Food' (2015) A/70/287 para 3.

[132]   FAO, *FAO's Work on Climate Change: United Nations Climate Change Conference 2018* (FAO 2018).

[133]   Paris Agreement (2015) FCCC/CP/2015/L.9/Rev.1.

[134]   CEDAW Committee, General Recommendation No. 37: Gender-related Dimensions of Disaster Risk Reduction in the Context of Climate Change (2018) CEDAW/C/GC/37 Section E.

[135]   Joanna Bourke Martignoni, 'Intersectionalities, Human Rights, and Climate Change' in Sebastien Dyck, Sébastien Jodoin and Alyssa Johl (eds) *Routledge Handbook of Human Rights and Climate Governance* (Routledge 2018) 397.

[136]   Olivier De Schutter, 'Report Submitted by the Special Rapporteur on the Right to Food: Agroecology and the Right to Food' (17 December 2010) A/HRC/16/49; Hilal Elver, 'Report Submitted by the Special Rapporteur on the Right to Food: The Adverse Impact of Climate Change on the Right to Food (5 August 2015) A/70/287.

[137]   Anne Saab, 'An International Law Approach to Food Régime Theory' (2018) 31 (2) LJIL 251.

by right-holders around the world, these gains appear to be precarious and, in certain regions, short-lived.[138] The expansion of protection of the right to adequate food as a result of the struggles of civil society movements and a small number of activist national governments and courts, as well as through the work of international and regional human rights institutions, has occurred against the backdrop of trade and investment policies focused on the intensification of industrial food systems that are characterized by unsustainable resource extraction and exploitative labor relations.[139] These dominant forms of food production, distribution and consumption have been shown to increase socio-economic inequalities as well as food insecurity for both present and future generations.[140] Crucially, despite more than half a century of advocacy on the right to food, the continued focus on increasing food production within international, regional and many national food security policies tends to obscure the structural inequalities and barriers to democratic participation within food systems that lie at the heart of hunger and malnutrition.[141]

For human rights-based approaches to food security to prevail within situations of growing socio-economic inequality, trade liberalization, agricultural commercialization and climate change, a plurality of legal and non-legal strategies and methods will have to be deployed.[142] One of the crucial conclusions that emerges from critical reflections on the relationship between human rights in the books and human rights in practice is the need to go beyond formal legislative or technocratic measures to develop the multiple pathways through which equal rights to food and other natural resources might be realized in a given context at a particular moment in time. To reassert the disruptive power of rights as a force for change, more explicitly political and participatory right to food agendas and accountability mechanisms directed at identifying, confronting and remedying inequalities within food systems will need to be implemented.

---

[138]    Sakiko Fakuda-Parr, Terra Lawson-Remer and Susan Randolph, *Fulfilling Social and Economic Rights* (OUP 2015); FAO, IFAD, UNICEF, WFP and WHO, *The State of Food Security and Nutrition in the World 2019: Safeguarding against Economic Slowdowns and Downturns* (FAO 2019); FAO, *FAO's Work on Climate Change: United Nations Climate Change Conference 2018* (FAO 2018).

[139]    Jean Ziegler, Christophe Golay, Claire Mahon and Sally-Anne Way, *The Fight for the Right to Food: Lessons Learned* (Palgrave Macmillan 2011).

[140]    Sandra Moreno Cadena, 'The Declaration and the Struggles of Peasant Women: Gender as an Unachieved Question' cited in Priscilla Claeys and Marc Edelman, 'The United Nations Declaration on the Rights of Peasants and Other People Working in Rural Areas' (2020) 47 The Journal of Peasant Studies 1, 61; Olivier de Schutter, 'Agribusiness and the Right to Food' (22 December 2009) A/ HRC/33.

[141]    Amartya Sen, *Poverty and Famines: An Essay on Entitlement and Deprivation* (OUP 1981).

[142]    Anna Chadwick, *Law and the Political Economy of Hunger* (OUP 2019).

# 9.   The right to health

*Alicia Ely Yamin*

Health rights are in many ways the most complex of rights to theorize and promote through advocacy, as they challenge views of what is natural and normal both in social and in bio-legitimated constructs, as well as demanding that we contest the boundaries of what have been considered the traditional realms of law and politics. Health is deeply and inextricably intertwined with other rights, both civil and political as well as economic, social and cultural; it is also dependent on interpretations of equality and issues such as trade and fiscal policies that relate to economic governance; and, ultimately, the advancement of health-related rights depends upon both the legal and the health systems in a country.

This chapter provides a broad overview of select issues relating to the right to health as it has been elaborated in international law. However, effective theorization and advocacy require an understanding of the interplay and recursive relationship between national and international norms and institutional dynamics. In any specific context, the relation between health and drivers of patterns of health and ill-health that lie beyond the health sector (as well as, often, beyond national borders) implicate distinct regimes of law, institutional frameworks and procedures for advancing health rights, understood as a precondition for social equality and inclusion, as well as part of democracy.

The chapter proceeds as follows. First, it sets out some theoretical starting points for working on the right to health and health-related rights, which are a critical foundation for understanding the nature of the right and making cogent interpretive arguments with respect to the relevant norms under national, regional and international instruments. Second, it highlights selected aspects of normative evolution in the UN treaty-based human rights system, as well as in a variety of different kinds of charter-based law in relation to health rights. Third, the chapter provides a very brief overview of the treatment of health issues and the right to health in regional human rights systems. Fourth, it notes some of the other bodies of international law that are relevant to understand in advancing health rights.

Space precludes any attempt to be exhaustive in this chapter. Rather, I have selected a very few cases, General Comments and other materials to illustrate particular aspects of health-related rights. As suggested throughout, research and advocacy in this area should start from the premise that these norms are open-textured and inherently contested, in terms of both distributional effects and ethical implications, and therefore call for deliberation in legislatures and courts. Thus, the chapter seeks to raise issues for consideration, rather than to dictate what inevitably would be overly facile approaches.

# 1.    OVERVIEW: CRITICAL CONCEPTS

## 1.1    Meaning of Claiming a 'Right to Health'

Health has not historically been conceptualized as a right, nor is it treated as a legally enforceable right today in many countries. Thus, in constructing the normative contours of the right through legal arguments, it is critical to understand the conceptual implications of treating health as a right and not to merely enumerate positive treaty norms or soft law as though they were either self-evident in their interpretation or automatically authoritative.

First, the right to health is not a right to be healthy, which would be absurd. Nor is it a right to all medications and treatments one might need. Asserting that health is a right as a conceptual and philosophical matter implies first that it has special value or moral importance. In a modern rights paradigm, that moral importance stems from the inextricable connection health has to a life of dignity.[1] Because health has both intrinsic and instrumental importance to dignity, inequities in health are arguably normatively more troubling than, for example, inequities in income, as income is purely instrumental to a good life.[2] That is, health is not only itself essential to enable people to carry out their life plans, and in turn to live a life of dignity; it is also difficult to imagine living a flourishing life that includes other rights and aspects of self-government or full participation in one's society without some basic preconditions for the enjoyment of health. In short, in Amartya Sen's capabilities framework, health allows people to enjoy certain essential functions and capabilities; in Norman Daniels' Rawlsian framework, health, including health care, preserves a range of fair equality of opportunity.[3,4]

A second implication – and precondition – of claiming a right to health is that health is subject to societal influence – not just biological accident or individual luck.[5] It does not make sense to speak of a right to anything that is not the result of social and institutional arrangements. Think, for example, of the absurdity of claiming a right to be a talented cook or dancer, or a right to have a good singing voice or physical agility. While these 'gifts' or 'talents' are undoubtedly influenced by wealth, the ability to support training and the like, their contours are not inherently shaped by societal forces. As an empirical matter, not just health *care* but the distribution of health and ill-health has been shown to be deeply affected by power structures – class, gender, race and the like – in society.[6] Further, questions of political economy centrally affect the distribution of health and disease within and across societies.[7] As these asymmetries of power reflect policy choices at multiple levels, they can be changed by concerted human

---

[1]    Norman Daniels, *Just Health: Meeting Health Needs Fairly* (CUP 2008); Amartya Sen, 'Why and How is Health a Human Right' (2008) 372 The Lancet 2010; Alicia Ely Yamin, *Power, Suffering, and the Struggle for Dignity: Human Rights Frameworks for Health and Why They Matter* (U. Penn Press 2016) 73.

[2]    Arthur Kleinman, *Writing at the Margin* (UCP 1997).

[3]    Daniels (n 1).

[4]    Amartya Sen, 'Elements of a Theory of Human Rights' (2004) 32 Philosophy and Public Affairs 315.

[5]    Sen (n 1).

[6]    Yamin (n 1).

[7]    Paul Farmer, *Pathologies of Power: Health, Human Rights, and the New War on the Poor* (UCP 2003) 29–51.

decisions, thereby shifting patterns of health. That is, if health is in large measure socially constructed, it can be socially reconstructed.

It is worth underscoring that, in making claims about changing societal influences on health in order to promote health rights, advocates and scholars are implicitly contesting what is often accepted as *natural*, whether in patterns of health and (ill) health, or categories of normality and deviance. Think, for example, of caste-based disparities in mortality in India, or questions regarding autonomy and entitlement to interventions of non-cisgender persons. Contesting the status quo sometimes requires creative and anti-formalistic interpretations of law, based both on empirical evidence and normative arguments regarding understandings of equality and dignity.

## 1.2    Social and Political Determinants of Health v Medical Care

Both structural factors affecting health outside the health sector and health systems per se are subject to societal influence. Abundant empirical evidence from epidemiology shows that health is a close reflection of patterns of (in)justice in society, based on class, social constructions of race and gender and sexual identity, among other things. Further, 'social determinants' are responsible directly and indirectly for a far greater proportion of health and ill-health than medical care. Social determinants of health are defined as 'the conditions in which people are born, grow, live, work, and age',[8] and include the enjoyment of other rights, such as freedom of movement and information, and rights to education, housing and decent work.

However, health systems are themselves social determinants of health.[9] As with all rights, the right to health requires a just arrangement and functioning of social institutions. The health system – which encompasses both public health goods and health care – is a central social institution in a democratic society. Thus, the financing, priority setting, regulation and normative oversight involved in the health system are crucial to evaluating whether and how a state is protecting and promoting the right to health.[10] This includes labor laws and treatment of health workers, which is often neglected in health rights advocacy despite playing a significant role in the possibilities of realizing the right.

Similarly, political determinants of health, defined by the Lancet-Oslo Commission in 2014 as the 'norms, policies, and practices that arise from transnational interaction', increasingly play an outsized role in global patterns of health, as well as the financing and delivery of health care.[11] Some mechanisms of such political determinants include austerity policies imposed by international financial institutions, the indirect and direct health impacts of climate change disproportionately produced in the economic North and borne by poor populations in the global South, the propagation of harmful gender stereotypes through social and other media and the extractive activities of transnational corporations, including the tobacco, alcohol and sugar industries.

---

[8]    World Health Organization Commission on Social Determinants of Health, *Closing the Gap in a Generation: Health Equity through Action on the Social Determinants of Health* (WHO 2008) 26.

[9]    Sen (n 1).

[10]    Alicia Ely Yamin, *When Misfortune becomes Injustice* (forthcoming SUP 2020).

[11]    Petter Ottersen O et al., 'The Political Origins of Health Inequity: Prospects for Change' (2014) 383 The Lancet 630.

### 1.3    Human Rights-based Approach (HRBA) to Health v Right to Health

For advocacy, it is essential to distinguish between a claim to a legally enforceable right to health and a Human Rights-based Approach (HRBA) to health, which is inherently multi-sectorial and diffuse, precisely because health is affected by so many other factors. The principles underlying an HRBA to health are drawn from the 2003 UN Common Understanding of a Human Rights Approach to Development Assistance and include accountability, transparency, participation, equality/nondiscrimination and the rule of law.[12] Subsequent elaboration of these principles has focused on enabling legal and policy frameworks, multisectoral strategies and plans of action, transparency and equity in budget formulation and execution, effective and fair program implementation, monitoring and evaluation that permits disaggregation and actionable information for social accountability and remedies, which include but go beyond judicial remedies. HRBAs to health also stress the need for international assistance and cooperation, and increasingly the extra-territorial obligations of donor states and other actors.[13]

The line between a right to health and an HRBA to health is a tricky but necessary one to navigate in both strategic advocacy and theorization. Without any distinguishing of what can be carved out as the right to health, that right is inclined to swallow other social determinants and other rights that are essential for a life of dignity. In so doing, the right to health also becomes unenforceable.

On the other hand, it is essential to contemplate in scholarship as well as advocacy the broader drivers of health patterns, which, as discussed, go well beyond the health sector. Without doing so, health matters are likely to be treated as they often are in vertically integrated programs, as isolated modular issues, disconnected from questions of social equality and democracy.

### 1.4    Contested Contours: Evolving Technologies, Epidemiology, Demographics

The parameters of all rights are, by nature, contested, and vary across contexts and time. All rights evolve with technological changes; for example, the right to education as well as freedoms of expression and information have evolved with the growing importance of digital domains. However, perhaps more than any other right, the boundaries of an enforceable right to health, which includes health care as well as public health preconditions (such as water and sanitation) under international law, must be constantly revisited in any given context due to ever evolving technologies as well as economic, epidemiologic and demographic trends. What was once acceptable treatment for tuberculosis, schizophrenia, or any other condition changes, given biomedical advances (as well as other factors, such as drug resistance).

Similarly, in order to adopt *appropriate* or *reasonable* measures under international or domestic law, a country is expected to react to evolving threats to human health, which are affected by aging populations, climate change and immigration patterns as well as disease outbreaks and the rising incidence of non-communicable diseases across the world. Finally, social

---

[12]    United Nations Development Group, 'The Human Rights Based Approach to Development Cooperation Towards a Common Understanding Among UN Agencies' (UN 2003).

[13]    HRC, 'Technical Guidance on the Application of a Human-Rights Based Approach to the Implementation of Policies and Programmes to Reduce Preventable Maternal Morbidity and Mortality' (2 July 2012) A/HRC/21/22.

drivers of health conditions or lack of access to care are subject to evolving social as well as legal norms, such as stigma based on sexual orientation and gender identity.

Moreover, it is not just through directly protecting a constitutional right that health rights are implicated. Theorization through law requires constantly creating narratives and analogies, which then require adaptation. For example, that a person's body is her property has implications for issues such as abortion, but it also has implications for the genetic material obtained from blood and saliva samples, and even skin cells sloughed off without our awareness.

In short, scholarship and advocacy around health rights inherently entails calling for duty-bearers to justify laws, policies and programs in light of a background of constant change. Thus, research and advocacy often call for challenging the boundaries of an existing norm (in constitutional law or other branches of law). In turn, doing so can require enlarging spheres of political deliberation with respect to how health entitlements are financed and distributed. For example, in neoliberal economies that increasingly rely on informal labor, differentiated benefits schemes based on employment status can lead to structural discrimination, including against spousal and child dependents.

## 2. UNITED NATIONS (UN) SYSTEM

Article 25 of the Universal Declaration of Human Rights (UDHR) sets out a right of everyone to

> a standard of living adequate for the health and well-being of himself [sic] and of his [sic] family, including food, clothing, housing and medical care and necessary social services, and the right to security in the event of unemployment, sickness, disability, widowhood, old age or other lack of livelihood in circumstances beyond his [sic] control.[14]

In 1948, the Universal Declaration was promulgated without dissent as a common standard for all humanity; however, it is questionable to assert that every Article in the UDHR has become jus cogens under international law. Nor is the UDHR a treaty that binds states parties in specific ways; it should not be cited as though it were.

### 2.1    UN Human Rights Treaty-based System

#### 2.1.1    International Covenant on Economic, Social and Cultural Rights
The core formulation of the right to health under international law was set out in Article 12 of the International Covenant on Economic, Social and Cultural Rights (ICESCR), promulgated in 1966 (entered into force in 1976). Paragraph 1 establishes that states parties 'recognize the right of everyone to the enjoyment of the highest attainable standard of physical and mental health'. Without defining health, paragraph 2 then sets out that 'the steps to be taken ... to achieve the full realization of this right' include: (a) reduction of the stillbirth rate and of infant mortality, and the healthy development of the child; (b) environmental and industrial hygiene; (c) prevention, treatment and control of epidemic, endemic, occupational and other diseases; and (d) the creation of conditions which would assure to all medical service and medical attention in the event of sickness.

---

[14]    Universal Declaration of Human Rights (adopted 10 December 1948) (UDHR) Article 25.

It is important to note a few elements of this formulation. First, the right to health under international law includes both public health preconditions, such as environmental or sanitary measures, and access to medical care for all. Second, the measures to achieve the right to health necessarily imply *freedoms* (such as bodily autonomy) as well as *entitlements*. Under the ICESCR, unlike the International Covenant on Civil and Political Rights (ICCPR), the right to health was subject to progressive realization in accordance with the maximum extent of a country's available resources. This distinction with the ICCPR is significant in that it has been used to justify treating health as a programmatic aspiration as opposed to an enforceable legal right. Nonetheless, in reality, all rights – civil and political rights and ESCR – are progressively and continually realized; it is counterproductive to think of the achievement of rights as static endpoints. Third, under Article 2 of the ICESCR, states parties are to seek international assistance and cooperation to realize the right, and donors are supposed to provide 'assistance and cooperation, especially economic and technical', to advance the realization of the right, along with other economic and social rights. Note that this language does not commit donor states to any particular level of economic assistance, although political declarations have attempted to set out threshold levels. The Office of the High Commissioner for Human Rights (OHCHR) and the Inter-American Commission on Human Rights (ICHCR), as well as non-governmental organizations such as the Center for Economic and Social Rights, have developed structure (such as laws), process (such as resources and policy efforts) and outcome indicator frameworks to assess whether states are progressively realizing health and other ESCR.[15]

The original formulation of the right to health under the ICESCR is clearly outdated today; for example, it fails to even mention reproductive health. Subsequently, the content of the right to health has been elaborated on significantly under international law, through General Comments and observations of treaty-monitoring bodies (TMBs), as well as through jurisprudence. The CESCR's General Comment No. 14 on the Right to the Highest Attainable Standard of Health was issued by the Committee in 2000, and followed a series of other General Comments that sought to clarify the content of specific rights.[16]

A few points are important to note. First, General Comment No. 14 updated important aspects of the ICESCR, including clarifying that the right to health requires 'measures to improve child and maternal health, sexual and reproductive health services, including access to family planning, pre- and post-natal care, emergency obstetric services and access to information, as well as to resources necessary to act on that information'.[17] Second, the CESCR's inclusion of

---

[15]    Organization of American States, Comisión Interamericana de Derechos Humanos 'Lineamientos Para La Elaboración de Indicadores de Progreso en Materia de Derechos Económicos, Sociales y Culturales' OEA/Ser.L/V/II.132 (19 June 2008); Center for Economic and Social Rights (CESR) 'The OPERA Framework – Assessing Compliance with the Obligation to Fulfill Economic, Social and Cultural Rights' <www.cesr.org/sites/default/files/the.opera.framework.pdf>; Office of the High Commissioner for Human Rights (OHCHR) 'Human Rights Indicators – A Guide to Measurement and Implementation' HR/PUB/12/5 (30 March 2012).

[16]    CESCR, General Comment No. 14: The Right to the Highest Attainable Standard of Health (11 August 2000) E/C.12 /2000/4.

[17]    Ibid para 12.

the underlying determinants of health, such as access to safe and potable water and adequate sanitation, an adequate supply of safe food, nutrition and housing, healthy occupational and environmental conditions, and access to health-related education and information, including on sexual and reproductive health[18]

should be construed, in my view, as underscoring that the right to health is not limited to health care and that health is affected by social factors and power relations, including gender, class, caste and race relations. On the other hand, as noted above, it is important to make clear that the right to health does not swallow all other rights on which it is interdependent, so as to reinforce that the right – as opposed to a broader multi-sectorial HRBA to health – can be clearly circumscribed and judicially enforced.[19]

Third, General Comment No. 14 deployed the structure and various frameworks that had been used in other General Comments by CESCR. One such framework is the so-called AAAQ model of the inter-related elements of the right to health, meaning that health facilities, goods and services (including those relating to public health preconditions of health) be available, accessible, acceptable and of adequate quality.[20] In particular, 'accessibility' included physical and economic accessibility and accessibility on the basis of non-discrimination, and the inclusion of accessible information in order to make health-related decisions.[21] Other TMBs have also adopted this framework and set it out with respect to specific aspects of those treaties.[22] Advocates should consider how these four elements interact for specific populations, and how barriers faced in people's lived realities, such as bureaucratic barriers and delays, constitute failures to achieve AAAQ.

A second framework used in General Comment No. 14 – respect, protect, fulfill (RPF) – sets out that health, like all rights – civil and political rights as well as ESCR – entails obligations by states parties to respect by refraining from direct infringement (such as discrimination), protect against third party interference (such as pollution) and fulfill through positive legislative and other measures (such as extending health coverage).

Fourth, in General Comment No. 14, the CESCR set out an extensive list of core obligations.[23] In 1990, in General Comment No. 3 on the Nature of States Obligations, the CESCR argued that 'a State party in which any significant number of individuals is deprived of ... essential primary health care ... is, prima facie, failing to discharge its obligations under the Covenant'.[24] General Comment No. 14 adopted a very different approach with the lists set out in paras 43 (a–e) and 44 (a–f), which has been justifiably critiqued for failing to 'offer a principled, practical or coherent rationale', as John Tobin has written.[25]

Scholarship and advocacy asserting that these constitute minimum core obligations should recall that CESCR's claim to authoritative interpretation of the ICESCR is defeasible. Notably,

---

[18]   Ibid para 1.
[19]   John Tobin, *The Right to Health in International Law* (OUP 2012) 56.
[20]   CESCR (n 16) para 12.
[21]   Ibid paras 12(c) and 27.
[22]   CEDAW Committee, General Recommendation No. 24: Article 12 of the Convention (Women and Health) (1999) A/54/38/Rev.1 para 22.
[23]   CESCR (n 16) paras 43–45.
[24]   CESCR, General Comment No. 3: The Nature of States Parties' Obligations (14 December 1990) E/1991/23 para 10.
[25]   Tobin (n 19) 240.

the ostensibly 'non-derogable' nature of these obligations has subsequently been walked back even by the CESCR itself. Further, those courts that have adopted minimum core obligations have not used General Comment No. 14 as a starting point, and advocates working in countries with defined packages in health systems would be better placed to begin there. Moreover, other courts have rejected a minimum core approach in favor of a reasonableness review in which General Comment No. 14 remains a factor. Above all, in asserting obligations as part of a minimum core, advocates should take care that they are not undermining progressive realization in practice, which requires advances along all the obligations to respect, protect and fulfill.

CESCR's General Comment No. 22 on the Right to Sexual and Reproductive Health is arguably a more useful starting point for legal and social mobilization regarding the right to health, and updates aspects of General Comment No. 14 in ways that apply beyond sexual and reproductive health. General Comment No. 22 first states clearly that 'The right to sexual and reproductive health is an integral part of the right to health enshrined in Article 12 of the International Covenant on Economic, Social and Cultural Rights', but also that 'It is also reflected in other international human rights instruments'; second, distinguishes between underlying determinants of health (such as water and sanitation) and the far broader range of social determinants, as discussed above; third, provides a far more coherent list of core obligations, including ensuring 'access to effective and transparent remedies and redress, including administrative and judicial ones, for violations of the right to sexual and reproductive health'; and fourth, emphasizes the significance of international obligations, including refraining from actions that interfere with the right, beyond merely providing aid.[26]

As General Comment No. 22 from CESCR makes explicit, General Comments that address health specifically should be read in conjunction with the other relevant General Comments. Those from CESCR include General Comment No. 12 on the Right to Adequate Food,[27] General Comment No. 15 on the Right to Water,[28] General Comment No. 17 on protections for interests in scientific and other production,[29] General Comment No. 19 on the Right to Social Security,[30] General Comment No. 20 on the meaning of equality and non-discrimination,[31] and General Comment No. 24 on human rights and business entities.[32] The meaning of aspects of the right to health should also be interpreted in light of existing soft law guidance from other TMBs, regional treaties and jurisprudence from supra-national tribunals, with an eye to the harmonization of international law.

As described in Chapter 2, the Optional Protocol to the ICESCR, allowing individuals to bring petitions for violations by states parties, entered into force in 2013. In March of 2019, in

---

[26]    CESCR, General Comment No. 22: The Right to the Highest Attainable Standard of Health (4 March 2016) E/C.12/GC/22.

[27]    CESCR, General Comment No. 12: The Right to Adequate Food (12 May 1999) E/C.12/GC/12.

[28]    CESCR, General Comment No. 15: The Right to Water (20 January 2003) E/C.12/GC/15.

[29]    CESCR, General Comment No. 17: The Right of Everyone to Benefit from the Protection of the Moral and Material Interests Resulting from any Scientific, Literary or Artistic Production of which He or She is the Author (25 November 2005) E/C.12/GC/1712.

[30]    CESCR, General Comment No. 19: The Right to Social Security (4 February 2008) E/C.12/GC/19.

[31]    CESCR, General Comment No. 20: Non-Discrimination in Economic, Social and Cultural Rights (2 July 2009) E/C.12/GC/20.

[32]    CESCR, General Comment No. 24: State Obligations Under the International Covenant on Economic, Social and Cultural Rights in the Context of Business Activities (10 August 2017) E/C.12/GC/24.

*SC and GP v Italy*, the CESCR found that (1) the transfer by an in vitro fertilization clinic of an embryo into S.C.'s uterus, against her will (she subsequently miscarried the embryo), and (2) the lack of clarity of the current legal provisions regarding the right of women to waive their consent to the transfer of embryos after fertilization, constitute a violation of the petitioners' right to the highest attainable standard of health. The CESCR highlighted several concepts which are worth reiterating: (1) the right to health contains both freedoms and entitlements and cannot be reduced to any package of services; (2) compliance with the right to health must be interpreted in light of obligations regarding non-discrimination/substantive equality on the basis of gender; and (3) any limitations on the right to health must be compatible with the 'nature of the right', under Article 4 of the ICESCR – the law regarding implantation of fertilized embryos was deemed not to be so as it was, inter alia, opaque in the protections that it afforded and discriminatory as a de facto matter.

### 2.1.2    International Covenant on Civil and Political Rights

The right to health is intimately connected to the right to life, which is defined as a civil right under international law and a fundamental right under national constitutional law. Under the ICCPR, the right to life has evolved from the right to be 'free from acts and omissions that are intended or may be expected to cause [a person's] unnatural or premature death' to a more capacious understanding of the conditions that are necessary for a person to enjoy 'a life with dignity'. General Comment No. 36 updated General Comments Nos. 6 and 14,[33] which had been issued in the 1980s. The extent to which the Human Rights Committee, which supervises compliance with the ICCPR, enlarged its understanding of the right to life is perhaps most evident with respect to abortion rights, where the Committee notes that

> States parties must provide safe, legal and effective access to abortion where the life and health of the pregnant woman or girl is at risk, or where carrying a pregnancy to term would cause the pregnant woman or girl substantial pain or suffering, most notably where the pregnancy is the result of rape or incest or is not viable.

In addition, states parties may not regulate pregnancy or abortion in all other cases 'in a manner that runs contrary to their duty to ensure that women and girls do not have to undertake unsafe abortions, and they should revise their abortion laws accordingly'.[34] Given that the status of abortion has been hotly contested at the national level, as well as in international forums, this determination of the scope of the right to life focusing on the life and suffering of the woman is notable, and a significant shift from earlier Human Rights Committee jurisprudence.

Another significant area for the construction of health rights under the ICCPR – especially given the numbers of forced migrants in the world today – is in relation to those who may not be legal citizens or permanent residents of a given nation, but are nevertheless human beings. In 2018, the Human Rights Committee found in *Toussiant v Canada* that, regardless of legal

---

[33]    HRC, General Comment No. 36: Article 6 (The Right to Life) (2 November 2018) CCPR/C/GC/36; CCPR, General Comment No. 6: Article 6 (Right to Life) (30 April 1982) HRI/GEN/1/Rev.1; CCPR, General Comment No. 14: Article 6 (Right to Life): Nuclear Weapons and Right to Life (9 November 1984) E/C.12/2000/4.

[34]    CCPR (n 33) General Comment No. 36.

status, migrants are entitled to emergency care in situations where their lives could be at risk or their health irreparably damaged.[35]

### 2.1.3   Convention on the Elimination of All Forms of Discrimination against Women

Women's enjoyment of health depends upon non-discrimination across a wide range of other rights. Nonetheless, two Articles in the Convention on the Elimination of All Forms of Discrimination against Women (CEDAW), adopted on 18 December 1979, are of particular relevance for health. Article 12 commits states parties to 'take all appropriate measures to eliminate discrimination against women in the field of health care in order to ensure, on a basis of equality of men and women, access to health care services, including those related to family planning'. However, it also recognizes that women's biological health needs require differential treatment in order for them to enjoy the right to health on an equal footing with men, as a matter of substantive equality in practice.

As women's health is deeply affected by traditional practices and gender norms, it is also important to recognize that in Article 5, CEDAW calls for eradicating harmful traditional practices.[36] Arguably, the CEDAW Committee has interpreted these practices in ways that exotify or condemn non-Western practices, such as female genital cutting, while not paying nearly as much attention to such issues as the high prevalence of cosmetic surgery in certain countries. Thus, this remains a space to reconstruct understandings of diverse manifestations of patriarchy, and their impacts on health, across cultural contexts.

In 1999, the CEDAW Committee issued a General Recommendation on 'Women and Health', which followed other, narrower recommendations on aspects of women's health and took up many of the ideas that had been set out at important UN development and human rights conferences in the 1990s.[37] In that General Recommendation, the CEDAW Committee discussed both discrimination against women and differentiation among women based on class, ethnicity, and similar.[38] Advocacy on health rights in general – not just women's health – should note that intersectional forms of discrimination and disadvantage, which include disability, displacement and age and the like, must be understood not as additive but as a confluence of factors that shape any given person's ability to carry out a life project.[39]

Under the Optional Protocol to CEDAW that allows for individual petitions, the CEDAW Committee has issued a number of ground-breaking decisions on health. One worth highlighting in particular is the *Alyne da Silva Pimentel v Brasil* decision, which related to the maternal death of an Afro-Brazilian woman in a health facility outside of Rio de Janeiro.[40] In that case, the CEDAW Committee: (1) enforced a state's obligations to ensure affirmative entitlements to emergency obstetric care, as a matter of nondiscrimination against women; (2) analyzed intersectional discrimination on the basis of race, gender and class in the instant case; and (3) clarified states' duties to regulate private actors in the health sector, as part of the duty to protect women's rights to health and life.[41] The *Alyne* case is an excellent example of how what

---

[35]   CCPR *Toussaint v Canada* (24 July 2018) CCPR/C123/D/2348/2014.
[36]   CEDAW (adopted 18 December 1979) Article 5.
[37]   CEDAW Committee (n 22) para 3.
[38]   Ibid para 6.
[39]   Ibid.
[40]   CEDAW Committee, *Da Silva Pimental v Brazil* (25 July 2011) CEDAW/C/49/D/2008.
[41]   Ibid.

was once considered a natural if lamentable reality was converted into an issue of political and legal obligation: as Rebecca Cook wrote, 'Maternal deaths can no longer be explained away by fate, by divine purpose or as something that is predetermined to happen and beyond human control ... when governments fail to take the appropriate preventive measures, that failure violates women's human rights.[42] Further, for scholarship and advocacy in this area, it is important to note that the duty to regulate private actors extends the applicability – and in turn the significance – of the decision far beyond the realm of maternal or reproductive health.

### 2.1.4    Convention on the Rights of the Child

The Convention on the Rights of the Child (CRC), adopted on 20 November 1989, both elaborated on the specific obligations of states parties with respect to children's health – children being defined as under 18 years of age, with rights conferred on children even when domestic children's codes only go up to the age of 12 – and set out conceptual frameworks for the implementation of those rights. Article 24 of the CRC takes up some of the language in the World Health Organization (WHO) Constitution's preamble defining the 'right to the enjoyment of the highest attainable standard of health' and goes on to assert that it also includes access 'to facilities for the treatment of illness and rehabilitation of health', to which states parties shall strive to have no child deprived access. The steps states parties should take include measures: (a) to diminish infant and child mortality; (b) to ensure the provision of necessary medical assistance and health care with emphasis on primary health care; (c) to combat disease and malnutrition, including within the framework of primary health care, through, inter alia, the application of readily available technology and through the provision of adequate nutritious foods and clean drinking water, taking into consideration the dangers and risks of environmental pollution; (d) to ensure appropriate pre-natal and post-natal health care for mothers; (e) to ensure that all segments of society, in particular parents and children, are informed, have access to education and are supported in the use of basic knowledge of child health and nutrition, the advantages of breastfeeding, hygiene and environmental sanitation and the prevention of accidents; and (f) to develop preventive health care, guidance for parents and family planning education and services.

The CRC also calls for the abolition of traditional practices prejudicial to the health of children, as CEDAW did with respect to women, and for international cooperation specific to health. The CRC lists a wide array of other relevant rights of children in relation to health, including the right to life. By encompassing survival and development of the child, the CRC opens possibilities for expansive interpretations of civil and political rights to promote child health. Conversely, the CRC includes civil and political rights that are essential to the protection and promotion of health rights, such as the right to official registration of an identity, which, inter alia, provides access to health and social protection benefits. The Committee on the Rights of the Child (CRC Committee) has also issued multiple General Comments that address, directly and indirectly, various dimensions of children's health, and specific Comments in relation to HIV and Adolescent Health in 2003 and the right to health in 2013.[43]

---

[42]    Rebecca J. Cook, 'Human Rights and Maternal Health: Exploring the Effectiveness of the Alyne Decision' (2013) 41 Journal of Law, Medicine and Ethics 109.

[43]    CRC Committee, General Comment No. 15: The Right of the Child to the Enjoyment of the Highest Attainable Standard of Health (17 April 2013), CRC/C/GC/15 Article 24; CRC Committee, General Comment No. 3: HIV/AIDS and the Rights of Children (17 March 2003) CRC/GC/2003/3;

But perhaps the most important contributions made by the CRC and CRC Committee in relation to health rights are the twin concepts of 'evolving capacity' and 'best interests' of the child. The concept of evolving capacity recognizes that a child of five may require far more protection and guidance from parents and other social structures than an adolescent, who also requires freedoms and agency to take decisions such as those involving sexual activity. In turn, the concept of 'best interests of the child' requires that decisions made on behalf of the child can be justified to the child and in light of normative standards. This applies to decisions taken by parents and guardians, such as whether a child should undergo a particular medical treatment, as well as a decision by a state, such as provision of contraception or other care. The best interests standard cannot be capriciously or inconsistently deployed. For example, in *JAB v Spain* (2019) the CRC Committee found that the state had violated the best interests of the child of a Cameroonian migrant child in relation to the right to health in assigning a guardian to the petitioner to ensure he received vaccinations and specific treatments, but providing no representation in a deportation context to determine whether he was a minor or an adult.[44]

### 2.1.5   Convention on the Rights of Persons with Disabilities

The Convention on the Rights of Persons with Disabilities (CRPD), adopted on 13 December 2006, is extraordinarily important to conceptions of health. First, the CRPD defines disability as resulting 'from the interaction between persons with impairments and attitudinal and environmental barriers that hinder their full and effective participation in society on an equal basis with others',[45] thus adopting an understanding of disability that rejects the biology/anatomy-based individualism of the biomedical model. Thus, both the drivers of disability and the penalty of a particular disability, whether physio-motor or psycho-social, are not intrinsically related to the pathology or condition. Rather, they are deeply influenced by social responses. For example, we take for granted that babies cannot walk in the same way as adults and we make social accommodations; we do the same thing for elderly people. It is only for adults in a certain age bracket that we view the accommodations that they require as 'extra'. Similarly, a person born with a disability –whether physical or psycho-social – in a low-income country often faces far greater obstacles to living a life of dignity than a similar person in a high-income context.

In Article 12, the CRPD went further than the 'best interests' standard set out in the CRC, establishing a new standard for equal protection before the law of persons with disabilities. Under Article 12, legal capacity required a 'supported decision-making model', including in crisis situations when the individual might otherwise be judged to have an impaired mental state, and therefore opened the door to 'substitute decision-making' under other treaties, including in accordance with 'best interests' under the CRC.

Advocates and researchers in this area should be aware that this standard is contested. Some see seeking out the 'best interpretation of the individual's will', as opposed to the traditional 'best interests' standard, as having the potential to expose people living with intellectual and psycho-social disabilities to abuse or exploitation. Others have questioned whether it is

CRC Committee, General Comment No. 4: Adolescent Health and Development in the Context of the Convention on the Rights of the Child (21 July 2003) CRC/GC/2003/4.
[44]   CRC Committee, *Convención sobre los Derechos del Niño J.A.B. v España* (31 May 2019) CRC/C/81/D/22/2017.
[45]   CRPD Preamble.

practicable, especially in low-resource settings. Human rights advocacy in the psycho-social disability context has tended to focus on flagrant abuses in facilities;[46] global health and development discussions have in contrast focused on unmet needs for mental health care.[47] In short, there is little academic – or policy-making – discussion that bridges these fields or reconciles the theorization of the right to health with standards of legal capacity in the disability context.

### 2.1.6 International Convention on the Elimination of All Forms of Racial Discrimination

The International Convention on the Elimination of All Forms of Racial Discrimination (ICERD), adopted on 21 December 1965, defines 'racial discrimination' as

> any distinction, exclusion, restriction or preference based on race, colour, descent, or national or ethnic origin which has the purpose or effect of nullifying or impairing the recognition, enjoyment or exercise, on an equal footing, of human rights and fundamental freedoms in the political, economic, social, cultural or any other field of public life.[48]

The relationship between race and health rights is important to understand for both scholarship and advocacy. Under human rights law, it is simultaneously understood that: (1) race is a socially determined construct, not merely grounded in biological or genetic differences; and (2) arbitrary differential treatment based on perceived differences in skin color affect real people's health in complex ways, which manifest through matters such as segregation in housing and other social determinants, as well as discrimination within health systems.

Article 5 of the ICERD sets out a very brief inclusion of states parties' obligations to eliminate discrimination in 'public health, medical care, social security and social services'.[49] In 1996, the UN Committee on the Elimination of All Forms of Racial Discrimination (CERD) issued a General Recommendation expanding on the dimensions of Article 5.[50] Concluding Observations of the Committee have brought into sharp focus the racial discrimination that pervades health systems in much of the world and results in not just abuses but also deprivations of health rights and disparities in both access and outcomes. Further, it is relevant in our current geo-political context, where immigrants are reflexively othered and disparaged, to note that the CERD has explicated how national origin can be used as a proxy for race to impose the same discriminatory stereotypes as well as arbitrary or coercive measures. For example, in *L.G v Republic of Korea*, the Committee found that the state had discriminated against the petitioner and violated her right to health by subjecting foreign teachers to a series of medical tests (including HIV, opiates and, without her consent, a syphilis test).[51]

In short, this section has provided an overview of relevant major treaties in relation to health rights, as well as interpretive guidance by TMBs and jurisprudence. However, there

---

[46]   See Disability Rights International, 'Comments and Suggested Revisions to the UN Committee on the Rights of Persons with Disabilities Draft General Comment No. 5 On the Right of People with Disabilities to Live Independently' (30 June 2017).

[47]   World Bank Group and World Health Organization, *Out of the Shadows: Making Mental Health a Global Development Priority* (World Bank and WHO 2016).

[48]   ICERD Article 1.

[49]   ICERD Article 5.

[50]   CERD, General Recommendation No. 20 on Article 5 (14 March 1996) A/51/18.

[51]   CERD, *L.G. v Republic of Korea* (1 May 2005) CERD/C/86/D/51/2012.

are numerous other international treaties, as well as non-binding UN declarations, that bear on specific populations' health-related rights, including ILO Convention 169 on Indigenous Communities and the UN Convention on Migrant Workers.[52] To be clear: researchers and advocates in this area should always map the terrain of intersecting norms and mechanisms, international as well as regional, that relate to the specific issues that are under study and the needs of populations that are being advocated for.

## 2.2    Charter-based Organs and World Health Organization

### 2.2.1    UN General Assembly

Health rights are inordinately shaped by the parameters of UN development agendas. This has been true historically, from the transformative possibilities created in UN trans-sectorial conferences in the 1990s to the technocratic and vertical approaches of the Millennium Development Goals (2001–15).[53] It is also true today under the Sustainable Development Goals (SDGs), which provide a blueprint for global development from 2016 to 2030.[54] Those 17 SDGs apply to rich and poor countries alike, target inequality as well as poverty, and are intended to be read as inter-dependent. Thus Goal 3 specifically addresses health, and universal health coverage (Target 3.8) has been given extraordinary prominence. Nevertheless, other SDGs, including but not limited to gender equality (Goal 5), reducing inequalities (Goal 10) and access to effective institutions (Goal 16), are also relevant for advancing health rights. The SDGs are 'soft law' but nevertheless are addressed by TMBs, often in concluding observations, and play an important role in shaping policy and funding environments for health – particularly in low-resource, highly aid-dependent countries, but elsewhere as well.

### 2.2.2    Human Rights Council

The Human Rights Council (HRC), a charter-based organ of the United Nations with 53 member states, has adopted multiple resolutions that bear on health-related topics, in addition to playing an important role in suggesting alignments between international obligations and policy in relation to health. Beginning in 2012, the Human Rights Council adopted 'Concise Technical Guidances' on HRBAs to health in the context of maternal mortality and morbidity, child survival, family planning and other matters.[55] However, the Human Rights Council has also adopted resolutions that affect health directly and indirectly and are far from progressive, such as a resolution on the traditional family in 2015.[56] HRC Resolutions should be read as providing complementary interpretive guidance, especially in terms of aligning legal and policy frameworks with programs, which is the principal objective of universal periodic

---

[52]    Convention Concerning Indigenous and Tribal Peoples in Independent Countries (adopted 27 June 1989) International Labor Organization 76th Session; International Convention on the Protection of the Rights of All Migrant Workers and Members of their Families (adopted 18 December 1990).
[53]    United Nations Millennium Declaration (adopted 18 September 2000) UNGA Res 55/2.
[54]    Transforming Our World: The 2030 Agenda for Sustainable Development (adopted 25 September 2015) UNGA Res 70/1.
[55]    HRC (n 13).
[56]    HRC, 'Protection of the family: contribution of the family to the realization of the right to an adequate standard of living for its members, particularly through its role in poverty eradication and achieving sustainable development' (22 July 2015) A/HRC/RES/29/22.

review by the HRC. However, these resolutions and accompanying guidelines should not be seen as conclusory statements as to what the law *is*.

### 2.2.3    World Health Organization

Unlike other specialized agencies of the United Nations, the WHO is both a technical agency and a norm-setting body of the United Nations. The 1946 preamble to the WHO Constitution set out:

> Health is a state of complete physical, mental and social well-being and not merely the absence of disease or infirmity. The enjoyment of the highest attainable standard of health is one of the fundamental rights of every human being without distinction of race, religion, political belief, economic or social condition.[57]

Although featuring in the preamble, this definition has been taken up in many UN documents subsequently, and is critically important in that it challenges the very narrow biomedical paradigm – which understands health as 'the absence of disease or pathology'.

The two most important examples of the WHO's norm-setting role in relation to health rights are: (1) the Framework Convention on Tobacco Control (FCTC);[58] and (2) the International Health Regulations (IHR).[59]

### 2.2.4    Framework Convention on Tobacco Control

The Framework Convention on Tobacco Control (FCTC), which entered into force in 2003, is the first and only treaty negotiated under the auspices of the WHO. In contrast to previous drug control treaties, the FCTC emphasizes 'demand reduction' as in regulation of marketing and claims. Note that the FCTC does not establish a TMB, as in human rights. Disputes are often taken to investment tribunals. For example, in 2010, Philip Morris International launched an arbitration under the 1998 Switzerland–Uruguay bilateral investment treaty against Uruguay's tobacco control measures. In 2016, the International Centre for Settlement of Investment Disputes released its decision in favor of Uruguay with respect to all claims and recognized that regulatory authorities, when making public policy determinations in contexts such as public health, enjoy a 'margin of appreciation'.[60]

### 2.2.5    International Health Regulations

The current 2005 version of the IHR, which entered into force in 2007, was substantially revised in light of SARS and other increasing threats to public health that transcended borders in an ever globalizing world.[61] The IHR binds all members of the WHO but is sometimes argued to be a treaty as opposed to a charter-based instrument, because of the form in which it is written.[62]

---

[57]    Constitution of the World Health Organization (adopted 15 February 1946) UNGA Res 131.
[58]    World Health Organization, Framework Convention on Tobacco Control (adopted 21 May 2003).
[59]    World Health Organization, *International Health Regulations*, 2nd edn (WHO 2005).
[60]    Harold Koh, 'Global Tobacco Control as a Health and Human Rights Imperative' (2016) 57 Harvard ILJ 433.
[61]    WHO (n 59).
[62]    Lawrence O. Gostin et al., 'The Legal Determinants of Health: Harnessing the Power of Law for Global Health and Sustainable Development' (2019) 393 The Lancet Commissions 1857.

The underlying purpose of the IHR is 'to prevent, protect against, control and provide a public health response to the international spread of disease in ways that are commensurate with and restricted to public health risks, and which avoid unnecessary interference with international traffic and trade'. However, the protection of people's rights – from unduly coercive measures to travel restrictions – is an important aim in the IHR as well. The IHR also call on states to strengthen core health capacities and for international assistance and specific efforts at collaboration in supporting resource-poor states in doing so. This intersects with language in human rights law regarding the right to health.[63]

## 3.    REGIONAL HUMAN RIGHTS SYSTEMS

Theorization and advocacy regarding health rights cannot fail to consider the particularities of regional human rights systems. The Inter-American System, the European System and the African System have all developed a significant body of norms relating to health rights and have their own set of institutions and procedures for reviewing state compliance with treaties, setting out broad declarations regarding policy matters and responding to individual petitions. It is beyond the scope of this chapter to review these different systems in any depth. However, the fault lines in conceptual contestation cannot be merely grafted from one to the other, for reasons suggested below, among others.

### 3.1    Inter-American System

The American Convention on Human Rights does not contain a right to health. The right to health was set out in the Additional Protocol to the American Convention on Human Rights on Economic, Social and Cultural Rights (Protocol of San Salvador), which, adopted on 17 November 1988, notably also includes a right to a healthy environment.[64] Until 2018, the right to health was interpreted in individual petitions under the Protocol of San Salvador by the Inter-American Court as part of an overlapping nexus of rights. However, in 2018, in the case of *Poblete Vilches v Chile*,[65] the Court enforced the right to health autonomously, and has subsequently done so in at least one other case as of this writing. The Inter-American Court of Human Rights had long however noted issues such as the conditions of indigenous persons, psychiatric patients and children in prisons as violating standards under relevant law. Further, issues of informed consent, including involuntary sterilizations, had been brought to the Inter-American Commission as early as 1998 (*Mamerita Mestanza v Peru*[66]), and had been decided by the Inter-American Court in *IV v Bolivia* (2016).[67] Similarly, cases of people living with HIV/AIDS had been addressed as a matter of the right to life and non-discrimination.[68]

At least three contextual factors have contributed to shaping the jurisprudence and interpretation of these norms: (1) Latin America is a highly unequal and fragmented region,

---

[63]    WHO (n 59).
[64]    Protocol of San Salvador, A-52 Article 10, 11.
[65]    *Poblete Vilches y Otros v Chile*, IACHR, Case 12.695, Report No. 1/16 (2018).
[66]    *Mestanza Chavez v Peru*, IACHR, Case 12.191, Report No. 66/00 (2000).
[67]    *I.V. v Bolivia*, IACHR, Case 12.644, Report No. 72/14 (2016).
[68]    *Gonzales Lluy et al. v Ecuador*, IACHR, Case N/A, Report No. 89/09 (2015).

along class, gender and ethnic/racial lines – indigenous groups and other minorities face an extreme degree of exclusion that is often reflected in health; (2) the region is dominated by conservative sects of Catholicism and, increasingly, evangelical churches, which limit SRHR being deliberated on at national level and to a certain extent in the Inter-American System (despite enormously robust advocacy in other forums on SRHR); and (3) many constitutions in the region have incorporated international human rights law, including health rights, into domestic law. In turn, the development of jurisprudence relating to health rights, as well as the use of structural mechanisms (such as the amparo and tutela) have been highly developed and have then influenced regional evolution. Finally, many other treaties (such as the Convención Belém do Pará) need to be analyzed when considering rights relevant to a specific subject under regional law.[69]

## 3.2    European System of Human Rights

The European Court jurisprudence has addressed significant health-related issues, often under the right to life and the right to found a family and to self-determination. The European Court uses the standard of 'margin of appreciation' as opposed to reasonableness and has accorded states significant flexibility, especially in relation to areas of health that might be considered 'ethically sensitive', such as SRHR.[70] The European Court has also been far quicker to adopt a procedural approach to contentious issues such as abortion, emphasizing the need to enforce existing laws and provide full and accurate information.[71]

Of note both for advocates and for scholars theorizing how to implement the inherently spider-web-like right to health is that the European Court of Human Rights has begun to utilize what Cali and Koch term as a 'deliberative compliance model', which also affects the kinds of creative remedies that the Court might adopt.[72] That is, the European Court does not so much dictate what actions a state should take to comply with decisions requesting structural remedies, but rather often enters into discussions with the state and maintains continuing supervision. Protocol 16 to the European Convention, called the 'dialogue protocol', will potentially encourage the explication and harmonization of the ECtHR's jurisprudence and holdings and national law.

Under the Social Charter, key right to health cases generally focus on Article 11 (the right to protection of health) and Article 17 (child rights).[73] The Committee has addressed a wide range of topics under these provisions, including: sterilization as a condition of legal gender

---

[69]    Organization of American States, Interamerican Convention on the Prevention, Punishment, and Eradication of Violence Against Women (Convención de Belém do Pará) (adopted 9 June 1994).

[70]    Liiri Oja and Alicia Ely Yamin '"Woman" in the European Human Rights System: How is the Reproductive Rights Jurisprudence of The European Court of Human Rights Constructing Narratives of Women's Citizenship?' (2016) 32 Columbia Journal of Gender and Law 62.

[71]    *A, B and C v Ireland*, No. 25579/05 Eur. Ct. H.R. (2010); *Tysiac v Poland*, Appl. No. 5410/03, Eur. Ct. H.R. (2007).

[72]    Basak Çalı and Anne Koch, 'Explaining Compliance: Lessons Learnt from Civil and Political Rights' in M. Langford, C. Rodríguez-Garavito and J. Rossi (eds), *Social Rights Judgments and the Politics of Compliance: Making it Stick* (CUP 2017).

[73]    European Social Charter (adopted 3 May 1996) Council of Europe Articles 11, 17.

identity;[74] the right to a healthy environment;[75] conscientious objection by healthcare providers;[76] access to abortion services;[77] lack of sexual and reproductive health education.[78] In the *DCI v Belgium* series of cases, the Committee has addressed the exclusion of minor children who are non-nationals.[79]

### 3.3    African System of Human Rights

The African [Banjul] Charter on Human and Peoples' Rights (Banjul Chater), adopted on 27 June 1981, contains both civil and political rights and ESCR, including health. Article 16 states: 'Every individual shall have the right to enjoy the best attainable state of physical and mental health.' In paragraph 2, it continues: 'states parties to the present Charter shall take the necessary measures to protect the health of their people and to ensure that they receive medical attention when they are sick.'[80] As the right to health is sometimes thought to be only applicable in high-income settings, it is important to note that in *Purohit and Moore v The Gambia*, the African Commission found that The Gambia fell short of satisfying the requirements of Articles 16 and 18(4) of the Banjul Charter, noting the connection between the right to health and other fundamental rights and freedoms.[81] The Commission considered the obligation of states parties 'to take concrete and targeted steps, while taking full advantage of their available resources, to ensure that the right to health is fully realized in all its aspects without discrimination of any kind' and urged the government to repeal and replace the discriminatory legislative regime, as well as to provide adequate care for persons suffering from mental health problems.

Advocates of SRHR should be aware of the extraordinarily progressive Protocol to the African Charter on Human and Peoples' Rights on the Rights of Women in Africa (Maputo Protocol), which sets out an expansive right of access to abortion in a regional context in which national laws remain generally restrictive (with some exceptions).[82]

Just as with the United Nations TMBs, regional systems also have both interpretative guidance on the scope of rights and how to evaluate performance, which should be consulted. In the

---

[74]    *Transgender Europe and ILGA-Europe v the Czech Republic*, Complaint No. 117/2015 (2018). European Committee of Social Rights.

[75]    *Marangopoulos Foundation for Human Rights (MFHR) v Greece*, Complaint No. 30/2005, European Committee of Social Rights (2007).

[76]    *Federation of Catholic Families in Europe (FAFCE) v Sweden*, Complaint No. 99/2013, European Committee of Social Rights (2015).

[77]    *International Planned Parenthood Federation – European Network (IPPF EN) v Italy*, Complaint No. 87/2012, European Committee of Social Rights (2014).

[78]    *International Centre for the Legal Protection of Human Rights (INTERIGHTS) v Croatia*, Complaint No. 45/2007, European Committee of Social Rights (2009).

[79]    *Defence for Children International (DCI) v Belgium*, Complaint No. 69/2011, European Committee of Social Rights (2013); Claire Lougarre, 'The Protection of Sexual and Reproductive Health in European Human Rights Law: Perspectives from the Council of Europe' (2018) 14 Contemporary Issues in Law 1; Claire Lougarre, 'Using the Right to Health and to Promote Universal Health Coverage: A Better Tool for Protecting Non-nationals' Access to Affordable Health Care?' (2016) 18 Health and Human Rights 35.

[80]    Banjul Charter Article 16.

[81]    *Purohit and Moore v The Gambia*, Communication No. 241/2001, African Commission on Human and Peoples' Rights (2003).

[82]    Protocol to the African Charter on Human and Peoples' Rights on the Rights of Women in Africa (Maputo Protocol) (adopted 28 March 2003) African Union Article 14.

Inter-American System, indicators for the progressive realization of ESCR, including health, under the Protocol of San Salvador have been developed, as noted above. Often, arguing for a broader policy or structural reform requires not just a narrative of the case but statistical information to assist the decision-making body in offering an assessment of a given problem, and in turn whether it could be considered systemic.

## 4.    OTHER REGIMES IN INTERNATIONAL LAW; TRANSBOUNDARY EFFECTS

Given that health is affected by so many social and political variables, it is not surprising that other legal regimes – not just at national level, but also at international level – should be considered in advocacy and scholarship. Public international law and constitutional law no longer have rigid lines separating them, and it is imperative to connect health to the institutional and legal regimes that affect its realization in both academic scholarship and advocacy.

Space precludes detailed consideration of the many regimes that affect health and intersect with human rights. Nonetheless, it is worth mentioning that, as mentioned above in the context of the Philip Morris decision, investment and trade disputes often affect health. These are often settled at specialized tribunals but Juan Pablo Bohoslavsky, the UN Independent Expert on the Effects of Foreign Debt and other Related International Financial Obligations, has noted the inappropriateness of subjecting sovereign debt disputes to technical tribunals when such issues affect the rights of people, in particular across the global South.

Intellectual property regimes, such as the Trade-Related Aspects of Intellectual Property (TRIPs) Agreement, determine questions of access to medicines as well as control over agricultural practices and inputs (such as genetically modified seeds).[83] The World Trade Organization has a mandate to enforce agreements such as TRIPs against governments. Successful litigation has been carried out in South Africa, India, Kenya and many other countries regarding accessibility of generic medications, parallel importation and compulsory licensing, anti-competitive practices and price gauging.[84] Nonetheless, piecemeal approaches to intellectual property regimes can result in uneven effects within countries (across medications and conditions) and across contexts.

---

[83]    Agreement on Trade-Related Aspects of Intellectual Property Rights (TRIPS Agreement) (adopted 15 April 1994) World Trade Organization Article 27 para 3; The TRIPS Agreement and pharmaceuticals. Report of an ASEAN Workshop on the TRIPS Agreement and its impact on pharmaceuticals. Jakarta, 2–4 May 2000.

[84]    Anand Grover, 'Report of the Special Rapporteur on the Right of Everyone to the Enjoyment of the Highest Attainable Standard of Physical and Mental Health: Access to Medicines' (1 May 2013) A/HRC/23/42; Allan Maleche and Emma Day, 'Right to Health Encompasses Right to Access Essential Generic Medicines: Challenging the 2008 Anti-counterfeit Act in Kenya' (2014) 16 Health and Human Rights 96; Lisa Forman and Jillian Kohler, *Access to Medicines as a Human Rights: Implications for Pharmaceutical Industry Responsibility* (University of Toronto Press 2012).

Additionally, a plethora of environmental treaties are directly and indirectly related to health and often have specific provisions that relate to human health.[85][86][87][88] It is imperative to strategically connect the dots between environmental degradation, planetary health and health rights. Even when we are careful to define the contours of health versus interdependent and related rights, health cannot be isolated from these other issues, because to do so is to revert to a narrow biomedical framework.

Further, environmental damage done by extractive industries illustrates that in considering health rights and the intersecting regimes of trade, environmental law and the like, it is increasingly apparent that advocates need to focus on Extra Territorial Obligations (ETOs). The traditional liberal state and the understanding of state responsibilities have been progressively expanded both by ESCR (including health) and by efforts to bridge the porous public and private spheres, including through SRHR. With ETOs, a wealthy and powerful state would be responsible not just for international assistance and cooperation. It would also be responsible for some transboundary effects of its direct and indirect actions or failure to regulate.[89]

ETOs were defined in the non-binding but influential Maastricht Guidelines on ESC Rights as

> obligations relating to the acts and omissions of a State, within or beyond its territory, that have effects on the enjoyment of human rights outside of that State's territory; and obligations of a global character that are set out in the Charter of the United Nations and human rights instruments.[90]

A state has such ETOs in situations 'over which it exercises authority or effective control'; in which its 'acts or omissions bring about foreseeable effects' on the enjoyment of ESC rights, whether within or outside its territory; and in which 'the State, acting separately or jointly, whether through its executive, legislative or judicial branches, is in a position to exercise decisive influence or to take measures to realize' ESCR. Thus, for example, if a mining company is headquartered in Canada but operates in Peru, where its pollution causes health effects, Canada would be required to exercise oversight over that transnational corporation to provide regulations and effective remedial action in the event of cognizable harms to health. Efforts to expand ETOs in order to promote such accountability are nascent, but are developing rapidly in international as well as national forums.

## 5.    CONCLUSIONS

This chapter has offered a snapshot of important sources and interpretations of international law relating to health rights. The fault lines in advocacy currently vary significantly across

---

[85]    Paris Agreement (adopted 12 December 2015) United Nations Framework Convention on Climate Change.

[86]    Kyoto Protocol (adopted 11 December 1997) United Nations Framework Convention on Climate Change.

[87]    Minamata Convention on Mercury (adopted 10 October 2013).

[88]    Stockholm Convention on Persistent Organic Pollutants (adopted 22 May 2001).

[89]    HRC, 'Legally Binding Instrument to Regulate, in International Human Rights Law, the Activities of Transnational Corporations and other Business Enterprises' (7 July 2018).

[90]    International Commission of Jurists (ICJ), 'Maastricht Guidelines on Violations of Economic, Social and Cultural Rights' (26 January 1997).

contexts and fields, and include: SRHR, mental health, issues around environmental degradation and health effects; the effects of private debt in health (including detention in facilities); and violence. However, this chapter has emphasized that the boundaries of the right to health are in continual flux due to evolving demographic and epidemiological trends, as well as biomedical innovation and cultural understandings of what is required for health.

First, the instability inherent in the norms makes it more readily apparent that arguments regarding the interpretation of any aspect of the right to health must be carefully justified based on normative and empirical grounds. As is evident across these various legal regimes and regions, different premises will produce different interpretations of health-related rights, some of which are contextually dependent, such as in relation to the design of health systems. In making a claim for a right to health, advocates are implicitly arguing that there is some societal responsibility for patterns of (ill)health involved in the specific facts of a case or situation. In the course of that argument, they will need to combat views that construct health: (1) as a matter of individual biology or behavior, isolated from social context; or (2) even if socially determined, as a matter of personal morality or political agendas as opposed to a legal matter.

Second, it is essential to remember that health is closely related to broader social policy; therefore narrow foci on biomedical treatments may produce entitlements for a patient or group of patients but are unlikely to change the underlying drivers of patterns of (ill)health. Third, health systems should be understood as social institutions, governed by fundamental constitutional commitments to equality and dignity. Just as we need to understand a justice system to realize the right to due process, it is not possible to realize the right to health without considering the institutional forms under which it is addressed in a given society. Finally, many of the determinants of health we have discussed, ranging from environmental damage to the marketing of commercial products to pharmaceutical policies, arise in transnational space. Thus, it is increasingly essential to engage and hold accountable the donor states that, through bilateral action and multilateral institutions, make decisions that ultimately affect people's health, including through calling for greater regulation of ETOs by states in the global North.

# 10. The right to adequate housing

*Stuart Wilson*

## 1. INTRODUCTION

There is a basic human interest in being able to 'live somewhere in security, peace and dignity'.[1] The home is 'a zone of personal intimacy and family security'. It will often be 'the only relatively secure space of privacy and tranquillity in what (for poor people in particular) is a turbulent and hostile world'.[2] It is accordingly hard to imagine any complete account of human rights law, in any jurisdiction, that does not recognize, protect and advance the right to a home.

The sanctity of the home is obviously recognized when international law entrenches the right to adequate housing.[3] But respect for the home in international human rights instruments reaches out beyond the explicit right to adequate housing. It is recognized when those instruments entrench privacy rights.[4] It also receives emphasis when addressing the needs of vulnerable groups, such as children, people with disabilities and the elderly.[5]

This ripple effect has an ambiguous impact on property rights. Sometimes the right to adequate housing is reinforced by, and provides additional protection to, the rights of poor and vulnerable people to keep hold of residential property in the face of acts of dispossession. The right to adequate housing often places limits on the rights of financial institutions to extinguish home ownership.[6] It can put a brake on unfair rent increases and on evictions from homes. But the right to property also underpins the very processes of dispossession – gentrification, eviction, foreclosure – that the right to housing seeks to limit. Property rights are often enforced through the extinction of housing rights.

The principal UN instruments reflect this ambiguity. The United Nations Declaration on Human Rights (UDHR) recognizes and entrenches the right to property, but this recognition is not replicated in either the International Covenant on Economic Social and Cultural Rights (ICESCR) or the International Covenant on Civil and Political Rights (ICCPR). The Committee on Economic, Social and Cultural Rights (CESCR) accepts that, where a state has chosen to entrench the right to property, that state has a legitimate interest in ensuring its protection, along with all of the other rights established in the state's legal system, 'so long

---

[1]  CESCR, General Comment No. 4: The Right to Adequate Housing (13 December 1991) E/1992/23 para 7. I would like to thank Fernando Ribeiro Delgado and Joie Chowdhury at ESCR-Net for their help in sourcing some of the regional and domestic jurisprudence dealt with in this chapter. I am also grateful to Julian Brown and the editors of this volume for helpful comments on an earlier draft.

[2]  *Port Elizabeth Municipality v Various Occupiers* 2005 (1) SA 217 (CC) (Port Elizabeth Municipality) para 17.

[3]  See, for example UNDHR Article 25; ICESCR Article 11; ESC Article 31; Charter on Fundamental Rights in the European Union Article 34.

[4]  For example UNDHR Article 12 and AConHR Article 11.

[5]  ICESCR Articles 15 and 23 and CRC Article 27.

[6]  *Jaftha v Schoeman; Van Rooyen v Stoltz* 2005 (2) SA 140 (CC) (Jaftha).

as this does not conflict with the rights contained in the Covenant'.[7] This simply begs the question. Depending on the legal and factual context, housing rights and property rights can either conflict with or reinforce each other. The Covenant entrenches housing rights, but not property rights. It is therefore inevitable that the right to housing will limit and restructure some property rights with which it comes into contact, whatever priority national legal systems give to property rights.

It is this tense relationship between the right to housing and the right to property that renders the right to housing so important, and so contested. At the same time as it places housing at the core of the quest for at least a basic standard of living for everyone, the right can place important limits on the hierarchies of power and processes of dispossession that sustain global capitalism. In this way, the right to housing is often at the center not only of technical debates about how best to deliver housing units of an appropriate standard and location to all those who need them, but also of debates about whose interests come first in decisions about access to land, the exploitation of housing for profit and the practices of major financial institutions in creating and marketing debt instruments secured against residential property.

Given the scale of housing need internationally, and given also that so much economic inequality expresses itself in skewed distributions of land, housing and property, there can be little doubt that meeting the scope and providing the content of the right to adequate housing implies a substantial revision of existing property relationships in a wide variety of contexts. It also implies a substantial redistribution of land, property and, ultimately, wealth. The right to adequate housing is, in many respects, a manifesto for a just and equal society.

If this is correct, then the right to adequate housing presents a powerful challenge to critics of human rights that argue that social rights are 'not enough'[8] to address the substantial economic inequality triggered by late capitalism. Samuel Moyn, in particular, suggests that economic and social rights, at least at the international level, are not geared to tackling inequality so much as ensuring that everyone has access to a basic minimum of goods that keeps them out of poverty. Rights might help tackle poverty effectively, but have historically been ill-suited to the task of curbing excessive wealth. So while rights may help solve the problem of 'insufficiency', they do little to build substantive equality, merely 'nipping at the heels of the neoliberal giant'.[9]

This superficial analysis overlooks the capacity of social rights to disrupt existing property relationships, and the hierarchies of power and stratifications of wealth that underpin them. Insofar as it does this, the right to adequate housing is a potentially powerful tool in challenging inequality. A great deal of capital still depends on land, housing and the financial property rights that are derived from them. Accordingly, the assertion of the right to adequate housing – of the idea of housing as something lived in and used to sustain privacy, dignity and family life, and not just as a means of capital accumulation – must play a critical role in a much broader project to advance struggles for substantive equality, and, perhaps, to challenge or transform capitalism itself.

This chapter considers the right to adequate housing in international law, and in some domestic contexts. I first provide an overview of the right to adequate housing in the principal

---

[7]    CESCR, *Lopez Alban et al. v Spain* (11 October 2019) E/C. 12/66/D/37/2018 para 11.5.
[8]    Samuel Moyn, *Not Enough: Human Rights in an Unequal World* (Belknap Harvard University Press 2018).
[9]    Ibid 8, 216.

United Nations instruments: the UDHR and the ICESCR, and the General Comments, the pronouncements of the Special Rapporteurs, and the limited jurisprudence developed under the Optional Protocol to the ICESCR that elaborate upon the right entrenched in those instruments.

I then turn to the key sites of contestation over the right within international law and some regional and domestic jurisdictions. South Africa, in particular, has been an important site of sustained experimentation and development of the right to adequate housing, and its interactions with existing property rights. I argue that when concrete social struggles have reached international, regional and domestic adjudicative bodies, especially but not exclusively in South Africa, the right to adequate housing has found its greatest traction in challenges to existing property rights. It is in struggles over the upgrading of informal settlements, the eviction of illegal occupiers, the rights of residential tenants in urban areas, the rights of mortgagors and the struggles of women to access housing through, and despite, patriarchal accounts of property law, that the right to adequate housing has sharpened its teeth. I set out how the right has been developed and applied in each of these contexts, and how housing rights struggles in these contexts have the potential to cut to the core of the social property relations that generate and reproduce inequality.

## 2. THE SCOPE AND CONTENT OF THE RIGHT TO ADEQUATE HOUSING IN INTERNATIONAL LAW

The CESCR is empowered, under the Optional Protocol to the Covenant on Economic, Social and Cultural Rights (CESCR-OP), to consider individual complaints of breaches of the ICESCR where a complainant has exhausted his or her domestic remedies. Its communications and recommendations to states party to the ICESCR constitute a growing jurisprudence on that instrument's meaning and application.[10] The CESCR has generated a significant quantity of material on the right to adequate housing.[11]

In addition, the UN Human Rights Council has established a series of 'special procedures' to help it monitor and review the implementation of human rights norms across a wide variety of contexts. These special procedures provide for the appointment of individual experts, often known as 'Special Rapporteurs', to report to the Council on matters affecting their areas of expertise, to conduct individual country visits and to respond to complaints made directly by affected individuals about specific rights violations. These special procedures mandates do not map neatly on to the main UN human rights instruments, because they are not creatures of those treaties. They do, however, generate a substantial quantity of material relevant to the interpretation and enforcement of the provisions of the main UN instruments.

The Special Rapporteur on Adequate Housing's mandate, stated formally as 'adequate housing as a component of the right to an adequate standard of living, and on the right to non-discrimination in this context', speaks directly to the way the right of access to adequate

---

[10]  See, generally, Sandra Liebenberg, 'Between Sovereignty and Accountability: The Emerging Jurisprudence of the United Nationals Committee on Economic, Social and Cultural Rights under the Optional Protocol' [2020] HRQ 48.

[11]  See, for example, CESCR, *IDG v Spain* (19 June 2015) E/C.12/55/D/2/2014.

housing is framed in the ICESCR.[12] The Special Rapporteurs (there have been three, with a fourth expected to be appointed at the expiration of the incumbent's term in mid-2020) produce reports, memoranda, guidelines and other pronouncements on the meaning and impact of the right to adequate housing across a range of themes and circumstances. This material provides a rich source for defining the scope and content of the right to adequate housing.

Beyond the UN, there are a range of regional instruments, such as the African Charter on Human and People's Rights (ACHPR), the American Convention on Human Rights (American Convention), the Arab Charter on Human Rights and the European Social Charter (ESC). These instruments demonstrate a wide variety of approaches to the right of access to adequate housing. The ESC entrenches multiple aspects of the right. The ACHPR does not explicitly provide for a right of access to adequate housing at all, but has found it to be implied in the right to property, which that instrument does entrench. The regional instruments may also have their own enforcement and monitoring bodies, each of which will be a source of 'soft law' on the interpretation and application of the rights they entrench.

At the domestic level, too, some national constitutions provide extensively for the right to adequate housing. They have sometimes developed a significant and binding body of case law on its enforcement. South Africa is perhaps most advanced in its interpretation and entrenchment of the right in its constitutional law. On the other hand, many national constitutions, such as the United States Constitution, fail to provide explicitly for the right to adequate housing, or indeed for any social and economic rights at all. Some states have no constitutionally entrenched human rights framework at all, such as the United Kingdom. Even here, though, ordinary legislation can provide legal recognition of at least some aspects of the right to adequate housing.[13]

It is, of course, impossible to provide an account of the right to adequate housing in all its extensions and contexts in a single book chapter. Instead, I set out below the textual formulation given to the right in the principal UN instruments, and the scope and content of those formulations provided in the 'soft law' sources generated by the CESCR and Special Rapporteur on Adequate Housing.

## 2.1   The Right to Adequate Housing in the UNDHR and the ICESCR

Both the UNDHR and the ICESCR entrench the right to adequate housing as part of a cluster of entitlements that constitute 'an adequate standard of living'.[14] This affirms the obvious, but

---

[12]   ICESCR Article 11 provides for the 'right of everyone to an adequate standard of living for himself and his family, including adequate food, clothing and housing, and to the continuous improvement of living conditions'.

[13]   See, for example, the United Kingdom Homelessness Reduction Act, 2017. The CESCR has made it clear that the international obligation is to ensure effective remedies that give effect to the right to adequate housing, whether or not the right is constitutionally entrenched or given any explicit legal recognition domestically. See CESCR, General Comment No. 9 (7 April 2016) E/C.12/GC/23 paras 5, 7, 14 and 15. See also Chapter 16, on the interdependence of rights, in this volume.

[14]   UNDHR Article 25 (1) states that '[e]veryone has the right to a standard of living adequate for the health and well-being of himself and of his family, including food, clothing, housing and medical care and necessary social services, and the right to security in the event of unemployment, sickness, disability, widowhood, old age or other lack of livelihood in circumstances beyond his control'. Article 11 (1) of the ICESCR is very similar: '[t]he states parties to the present Covenant recognize the right of everyone to an adequate standard of living for himself and his family, including adequate food, clothing and housing,

seldom fully acknowledged, reality that housing is part of a network of mutually dependent and reinforcing human needs. More than mere 'bricks and mortar',[15] a home is the locus of the exercise of a wide range of other human rights. It provides a point of stability in which the family is nurtured, and in which critical aspects of human identity and consciousness are formed. The home is the place to which we retire when we are sick or tired, and from which we strike forth to meet our social needs. Our housing must accordingly not merely be fit for shelter. It must be adequate to allow us to maintain our health, to form loving connections with our families and to mediate and control our social interactions.

The breadth and variety of human interests bound up in the home help to explain why there are two extensive General Comments on the right to adequate housing that elaborate on the ICESCR text.

General Comment 4, adopted at the sixth session of the CESCR in December 1991, aims to give content and meaning to the right to adequate housing, apparently in response to the insufficiency of state party reports submitted to it by that time.[16] At the outset, the Committee makes clear that the right to adequate housing's textual formulation – that housing must be adequate to ensure the well-being of the rights-bearer 'himself' and 'his family' – cannot be taken so literally as to imply that the right only attaches to male-headed households containing nuclear families. The gendered language used in the Covenant notwithstanding, the right extends to households headed by women, and to a wide variety of family types and formations.

The Committee goes on to provide a broad interpretation of the right to adequate housing, and to parse a range of tangible and non-tangible incidents: adequate privacy, security, space, lighting, ventilation, basic infrastructure and location.[17] It then provides a well-known seven-dimension scheme to assess the extent to which the right has been realized in any particular case.

In the first place, housing requires legal security of tenure, which boils down to security against eviction and protection from harassment or from any other threat that might deter access to the home. The form of tenure is secondary to the quality of protection it provides to the occupier. State and private rental, co-operative ownership and even informal settlement occupation may, depending on the circumstances, constitute adequate tenure, provided that a resident is genuinely protected in possession of his or her home.

Second, housing must have access to an appropriate range of services and infrastructure. Facilities 'essential for health, security, comfort and nutrition' must be provided.[18] Depending on the context, these will include safe drinking water; energy for cooking, heating and lighting; sanitation and washing facilities; food storage facilities; refuse disposal; sewers and drains; and access to emergency services.

Third, housing must be affordable. Affordable housing is housing that can be paid for without the sacrifice of any other essential. As soon as a resident is required to sacrifice the purchase of means to meet any other 'basic need',[19] then his or her housing is unaffordable.

---

and to the continuous improvement of living conditions. The states parties will take appropriate steps to ensure the realization of this right, recognizing to this effect the essential importance of international co-operation based on free consent.'

[15]   *Government of the Republic of South Africa v Grootboom* 2001 (1) SA 46 (*Grootboom*) para 5.
[16]   CESCR, General Comment No. 4 (13 December 1991) E/1992/23 para 7.
[17]   Ibid para 7.
[18]   Ibid para 7 (b).
[19]   Ibid para 7 (c).

While this standard has attractive clarity, it is arguably too mean, implying, as it does, that it would be acceptable for a person's financial means to be exhausted simply by meeting his or her 'basic needs'. It would be unfortunate indeed if the international human rights regime were based on such an attenuated vision of life. A better standard might speak to more contextual factors, such as the extent to which the resident lives in a cash economy. It might also seek to make room for an account of human flourishing. However, given that much of the world's population remains without the basic elements of a decent existence, the Committee can be forgiven for its modesty.

Fourth, housing must be habitable. Here, the Committee locates the basic 'bricks and mortar' requirements. Residents must have adequate space, and protection from the cold, from damp, from heat, from rain and from wind. The housing provided must not be prone to health or structural hazards. Nor should it expose a resident to disease.[20]

Fifth, housing must be accessible to the poor and to other vulnerable groups. Those without the resources necessary to access housing must be provided with them. Priority must be given to the needs of HIV-positive people, people with physical disabilities, people who are terminally ill, people who are mentally ill and victims of natural disasters. States must develop plans that include concrete obligations to give these groups priority access to housing.[21]

Sixth, housing must be adequately located. It must permit access to employment opportunities, healthcare services, schools, childcare centers and other social facilities. Housing that requires a resident to pay more in transport to get to work than he or she earns working will not be adequate. Nor will housing that is located in on or immediately proximate to sources of pollution.[22]

Finally, housing must be culturally adequate. The manner of its construction and the materials used must support the expression of cultural identity. The Committee gives no examples of 'cultural adequacy', but it can readily be accepted that housing which makes forms of religious worship or extended family life impossible would not be culturally adequate. Rigidly structured blocks of matchbox flats or houses that provide no space for social exchange, for communal prayer or for play would appear to breach this requirement.

General Comment 4 emphasizes the nested system of rights that are dependent on access to a home. It also acknowledges the rights that residents must be able to access to advance and protect their existing access to adequate housing. Alongside the obvious importance of the home as a locus of dignity, privacy, family life and security, General Comment 4 recognizes the importance of the rights to freedom of expression and association for tenants' groups and other community-based housing movements.[23]

General Comment 4 then addresses the nature and the content of state obligations to give effect to the right to adequate housing in all its dimensions. These obligations include the creation of a policy, legislative and administrative framework within which meaningful state action must then be taken to realize the right. The applicable standard is that these measures must be 'in aggregate … sufficient to realize the right [to adequate housing] for every individual in the shortest possible time in accordance with the maximum available resources'.[24]

---

[20]   Ibid para 8 (d).
[21]   Ibid 8 (e).
[22]   Ibid 8 (f).
[23]   Ibid para 9.
[24]   Ibid para 14.

State measures must also provide individual legal remedies for breaches of the right. Examples of such remedies include the ability to restrain illegal evictions, the ability to obtain compensation for illegal evictions, the ability to make complaints about discrimination in access to and enjoyment of adequate housing and the ability to make complaints about illegal conduct of private sector landlords.[25]

General Comment 4 provides a rich account of the scope and content of the international right of access to adequate housing, and sets meaningful standards against which to assess the conduct of states in giving effect to it.

At the practical level, however, the Committee soon recognized that the principal threat to the right to adequate housing is the prevalence of forced evictions. At its 16th session, in 1997, the Committee adopted General Comment 7 on the ICESCR, which dealt with forced evictions. General Comment 7 also made the right to adequate housing one of only two rights in the Covenant to have two General Comments devoted exclusively to it. The other is the right to education.

General Comment 7 begins by emphasizing security of tenure as a core component of the right to adequate housing. Forced evictions are an interference with the right to secure tenure, and are presumed to be incompatible with the ICESCR as a result. General Comment 7 does not, however, represent an unqualified denunciation of forced evictions in practice. Nor does it prohibit 'evictions carried out by force in accordance with the law and conformity with the provisions of the International Covenants on Human Rights'.[26] What General Comment 7 boils down to is a scheme 'to control strictly the circumstances under which evictions may be carried out'.[27]

General Comment 7 accordingly recognizes that some evictions may be justified, but requires that this justification be made clear in advance, and emphasizes that the range of justifications available for evictions is quite narrow. Failure to pay rent or causing damage to rented property may justify eviction,[28] as might an alternative land use, or the need to use occupied land for a socially beneficial or developmental purpose, such as the installation of infrastructure.[29] The justification must be legally admissible, in the sense that the law warrants an eviction on the basis of the reason given, and the reason itself must be consistent with the Covenant. Accordingly, a justified reason in domestic law may not be recognized as justified under the Covenant. Evictions meant as punitive measures are not permissible, even if authorized by law.[30]

Even where an eviction may be *prima facie* justified, states must ensure that anyone facing eviction has the opportunity the challenge the justification given, and that all 'feasible alternatives' to eviction are explored. Accordingly, even a strong public or private purpose will not justify an eviction if alternative means of achieving that purpose are available. These alternative means must be explored in consultation with those facing eviction.[31]

---

[25]    Ibid para 17.
[26]    CESCR, General Comment No. 7 (20 May 1997) E/1998/22 para 3.
[27]    Ibid para 9.
[28]    Ibid para 11.
[29]    Ibid paras 7 and 17.
[30]    Ibid para 12.
[31]    Ibid para 13.

Where it has been established that there is a compelling and legally authorized purpose to be achieved by an eviction, and that no feasible alternatives to eviction are available, a forced eviction may be carried out. However, General Comment 7 places strict limitations on the manner in which evictions may be implemented. First, there must be 'an opportunity for genuine consultation with those affected'. This is separate and independent from the consultation required in exploring alternatives to eviction. Once it is clear that there is no alternative, a further consultation is required on how an eviction will be carried out. Second, there must be 'adequate and reasonable notice for all affected persons prior to the scheduled date of eviction'. This includes, where applicable, information on the alternative use to which the land or housing is being put. An agent of the state must be present when an eviction is being carried out, and those authorized to carry out the eviction must be clearly identified. Evictions may not be carried out in bad weather, or at night, unless prior consent has been obtained from those facing eviction. Post-eviction legal remedies, for example challenging the legality of the eviction itself or seeking compensation for unlawful conduct during an otherwise lawful eviction, must also be provided.[32]

The most important protection the ICESCR provides is that eviction must not lead to homelessness, or render an evicted person vulnerable to the violation of other human rights, through, for example, the provision of alternative accommodation that is not suitable. Where an evicted person is unable to provide for him- or herself, a state must 'take all appropriate measures, to the maximum of its available resources, to ensure that adequate alternative housing, resettlement or access to productive land, as the case may be, is available'.[33]

The scope and content of the right to adequate housing can be summed up as a right to a home that is an effective holder, protector and facilitator of the locus of human needs associated with it. Where it is necessary to deprive someone of their existing access to such a home, an adequate replacement must be provided. The replacement must be adequate in the sense that it meets all of the requirements for adequate housing that the UNDHR, the ICESCR and the General Comments set out.

## 2.2   Special Rapporteur Reports and Guidelines

That the right to adequate housing has far-reaching implications for economic justice has also been made clear by the work of successive Special Rapporteurs on Adequate Housing. While not formally part of the treaty bodies provided for in the UNDHR and the ICESCR, the Special Rapporteurs play an important role in monitoring and setting standards for the implementation of the right to adequate housing. The UN Special Rapporteur on Adequate Housing monitors the implementation of the right to adequate housing, investigates the state of the realization of the right across the world – including by undertaking country-specific missions – and responds to complaints made about particular violations addressed to her. The Special Rapporteur reports, at least annually, to the Human Rights Council and the United Nations General Assembly.

The work of the three Special Rapporteurs that have so far held the office amply demonstrates the transformative potential of the right to adequate housing. All three Rapporteurs

---

[32]   Ibid para 15.
[33]   Ibid para 16.

have shown a deepening concern with what they call the 'financialization' of housing.[34] Concerns about financialization go beyond the mere use of housing as a tradeable commodity. They address the range of ways in which housing is used for acquisitive purposes. The Special Rapporteur on Adequate Housing's Guidelines for the Implementation of the Right to Adequate Housing (Housing Guidelines) provide a range of examples of financialization.[35] These include the purchase of affordable land and housing for the purposes of gentrification; the use of housing as security for tradeable financial instruments, such as collateralized debt obligations, including packaged residential mortgages; the use of high-value urban land and housing as a secure store of capital, rather than as a dwelling; and the speculative acquisition of large tracts of rural land.[36] These are all, of course, extraneous to the social uses of housing, and to the range of human interests that the right of access to adequate housing is intended to protect. To these features of financialization may be added the use of tenanted housing to profit from rents. While not obviously extraneous to the use of housing as a dwelling, the relationship between landlord and tenant, if left unregulated, creates substantial scope for exploitation.

The Special Rapporteurs have been increasingly critical of these aspects of financialization. The current Rapporteur, Leilani Farha, recommends a number of policy measures to curb them. These include preventing the privatization of public land and housing; maintaining rental regulatory frameworks that preserve security of tenure and affordability for tenants, including rent control and rent freezes; and levying taxes on property speculation and on vacant housing. These are all strongly redistributive measures, which, if implemented, would have a substantial impact on inequality both within and beyond the housing sector.

Other aspects of the Housing Guidelines reinforce this conclusion. They speak to a substantial range of contemporary social struggles that are about more than just a basic minimum of social provision. Sometimes they are, at least indirectly, about creating substantive equality. These include guidelines concerning the upgrading of informal settlements,[37] which are visible manifestations of inequality and inequitable access to land.[38] Even the relatively modest goal of the elimination of homelessness cannot be achieved without powerful implications for social equality.[39] It is perhaps unsurprising that the only country in the world that can plausibly claim to have virtually eliminated homelessness is Finland,[40] which is also one of the most equal.

---

[34]    HRC, Guidelines for the Implementation of the Right to Adequate Housing: Report of the Special Rapporteur on adequate housing as a component of the right to an adequate standard of living, and on the right to non-discrimination in this context (26 December 2019) A/HRC/43/43 paras 64 to 69. See also, Raquel Roinik, *Urban Warfare: Housing under the Empire of Finance*, Verso 2019.

[35]    Guidelines for Implementation, ibid paras 64 to 66.

[36]    Ibid para 65.

[37]    Ibid paras 39 to 42.

[38]    Lauren Royston and Tiffany Ebrahim, Urban Land Reform: Rethinking Informal Settlements <https://landportal.org/blog-post/2020/01/urban-land-reform-rethinking-informal-settlements-pre-apartheid-apartheid-and-post>.

[39]    Ibid 34 paras 29 to 33.

[40]    VonKathrin Glösel, *Finnland hat es geschafft, dass es so gut wie keine Obdachlosen mehr gibt*, 12 November 2019 <https://kontrast.at/housing-first-finnland-obdachlose/>.

## 2.3    Housing Jurisprudence under the Optional Protocol to the ICESCR

The Optional Protocol to the ICESCR permits the CESCR to consider and adjudicate com-plaints of breaches of a state's obligations under the ICESCR, and to make recommendations on remedial action to be taken in the event that a breach is found.[41] The Committee may be approached under the Optional Protocol once a complainant's domestic remedies have been exhausted. States party to the Optional Protocol must consider and respond to the Committee's remedial recommendations within six months of receiving them.[42]

Three of the Committee's decisions under the Optional Protocol have so far concerned the right to adequate housing. The emerging jurisprudence of the Committee is accordingly a source of international housing rights law, which is likely to grow in importance over time, as the Committee receives and considers more complaints.

In *IDG v Spain*,[43] the Committee considered the adequacy of the procedures embedded in Spanish law for giving notice of a bank's intention to foreclose on residential property. After three attempts to serve personally on a distressed customer, a bank in Madrid sought and received the permission of the Spanish courts to publish the foreclosure notice on a public noticeboard. The notice did not come to the complainant's attention, but the bank nevertheless foreclosed on the complainant's mortgaged home shortly thereafter. The complainant only became aware that foreclosure had been authorized when she received the notice that her home was to be auctioned six months later.

The Committee acknowledged that the failure to provide the complainant with pre-foreclosure notice deprived her of the opportunity to advance reasons why her home should not be sold to defray her debt. However, it also acknowledged that the procedure adopted in the Spanish court was not invalid for that reason alone. Where personal service has been attempted, there must come a point at which measures short of actually drawing the attention of the debtor to the impeding act of foreclosure are permissible. The question is when this line is crossed. The Committee held that resort to public notice must be 'a measure of last resort'[44] because of the high degree of likelihood that the foreclosure notice would not come to the attention of the mortgagor. Public notice must accordingly be 'strictly limited to situations in which all means of serving notice in person have been exhausted'.[45] The Committee held that it had not been shown that the Spanish authorities had exhausted all available means to effect personal service. The failure to bring the foreclosure to the attention of the complainant had a significant impact on her right to adequate housing, as it deprived her of the right to defend the foreclosure proceedings. For this reason, the Committee held that the complainant's right to adequate housing had been breached.

The Committee made a series of recommendations, including a recommendation that the complainant's home not be sold unless and until she had been given a reasonable opportunity to defend the foreclosure proceedings. It also recommended that Spain amend its administra-tive and legislative processes to ensure that its foreclosure processes align with the decision of the Committee, and with General Comments 4 and 7 on the ICESCR.

---

[41]    ICESCR-OP Article 9 (1).
[42]    ICESCR-OP Article 9 (2).
[43]    CESCR, *IDG v Spain* (19 June 2015) E/C.12/55/D/2/2014.
[44]    Ibid para 12.3.
[45]    Ibid.

Although purely procedural, the Committee's communication affirmed the practical application of the due process provisions of General Comments 4 and 7 on the ICESCR. Insofar as it required adequate notice of foreclosure – in the form of personal service unless practically impossible – the Committee provided homeowners facing foreclosure with a genuine opportunity to delay, suspend or resist foreclosure proceedings. I have argued elsewhere that even procedural innovations meant to temper administrative process that could lead to a deprivation of adequate housing can have potentially far-reaching redistributive effects,[46] insofar as they force a bank or a landlord to justify the termination of a right of residence, and allow a court to consider the fairness of the termination. The first step in such an inquiry is the resident actually getting notice of the termination.

The potential scope and redistributive impact of an inquiry into the fairness of an impending termination of residence rights is illustrated by the Committee's second communication on the merits of a housing complaint brought before it. In *Djazia and Bellili v Spain*,[47] a couple and their two children faced eviction from their apartment for non-payment of rent. The Committee found that the eviction itself was justifiable, in that it was both procedurally and substantively fair, but that the Spanish government's failure to make suitable alternative accommodation available to the complainants was a breach of the right to adequate housing. The Spanish government recognized that it had obligations to the family but argued that it could not provide them with alternative housing, because its social housing program was oversubscribed, and there was a substantial backlog of people waiting for places on the program. In the absence of a place in social housing, the Spanish government offered Ms Bellili and her children a place in a women's shelter, and Mr Djazia a place in a separate homeless shelter.

The Committee held that the mere existence of a backlog in social housing provision was, in itself, no justification for failing to make an offer of adequate alternative accommodation, especially as the Spanish government had sold off a substantial quantity of social housing stock in the years preceding the complaint. In addition, the offer of shelter accommodation that would have the effect of splitting up the evicted family was inconsistent with the obligation under Article 10 (1) of the ICESCR to 'grant the widest possible protection to the family'. In the result, the Committee recommended that the Spanish government assess the complainants' situation in full consultation with them and 'grant them public housing or any other measure enabling them to enjoy adequate accommodation'.[48]

In *Lopez Alban v Spain*,[49] the Committee dealt with a Spanish housing policy principle that excluded from consideration for social housing those who were currently unlawfully occupying their homes. The complainant lived with her six children in a vacant apartment owned by a bank. She applied to the Spanish government for social housing, but her application was rejected on the basis that she was currently occupying her home without legal title. The complainant was then evicted from the apartment with her children, and passed through a series of emergency shelters that were grossly inadequate to her housing needs. As a consequence of the eviction, the complainant was separated from her eight-year-old twin boys.

---

[46]    Stuart Wilson, *The Law of Dispossession: Property Law, Power and Social Change*, PhD Thesis, University of the Witwatersrand, Johannesburg (2019) 214–15.
[47]    CESCR, *MBD v Spain* (20 June 2017) E/C.12/61/D/5/2015.
[48]    Ibid para 20.
[49]    CESCR, *Lopez Alban v Spain* (11 October 2019) E/C.12/66/D/37/2018.

The Committee found that there were sound justifications for seeking an eviction, in that the Spanish government had a legitimate interest in protecting the property rights of the bank that owned the apartment. That notwithstanding, the Committee found that to comply with Spain's obligations under the ICESCR, the Spanish courts ought to be empowered and required to consider whether eviction in the circumstances of a particular case is a proportionate response to the objective the eviction seeks to achieve. In particular, there ought to be scope for considering whether an eviction could be postponed or suspended pending the implementation of measures to prevent homelessness. There was no such proportionality enquiry mandated in Spanish law, and to that extent Spain was in breach of the ICESCR. The Spanish state's refusal to consider the complainant's application for social housing was, likewise, a disproportionate response to the fact that she was occupying her apartment unlawfully at the time. The exclusion of the complainant from social housing on the facts of this case seems particularly cruel, as the very fact of her unlawful occupation appears to demonstrate the urgency of her need for social housing. It hardly counts as a reason to exclude her from all consideration.

The complainant's eviction, and her consequent homelessness, was accordingly found to be disproportionate. The Committee recommended that the Spanish state establish a legal framework for considering the proportionality of evictions that gives those facing eviction the opportunity to challenge them on proportionality grounds. The Committee also recommended that the Spanish state should establish procedures for genuine consultation with those facing eviction, and a comprehensive plan for the provision of social housing that is free of disproportionately harsh exclusions.

The Committee's decisions illustrate how an inquiry into the fairness of an impending termination of housing rights, or an eviction that has actually taken place, can lead to generation of real and substantive redistributive principles. At the time of the complaint, Spanish law had no domestic rules against homelessness following on eviction, and no requirement for an eviction to be linked to the provision alternative accommodation. The generation of this principle (which had long been established in states of far more modest means, such as South Africa)[50] has clear redistributive potential. As Edwin Cameron, a former Justice of the South African Constitutional Court, has pointed out,[51] the requirement that alternative accommodation be provided by the state in all cases where an eviction would otherwise lead to homelessness implies a substantial and far-reaching redistribution of resources towards poor and vulnerable people facing homelessness. If put into practice, the rule against homelessness on eviction contained in General Comment 7 is far more than a Band-Aid, or a plea for bare sufficiency; it is a strong push towards housing equality, and implies a substantial expansion of housing provision as a component of state welfare provision.

The Committee's jurisprudence is still in its formative phase.[52] However, an examination of regional and domestic jurisdictions that have been engaged in the enforcement of the right to housing demonstrates that the right can be deployed in a variety of contexts to generate

---

[50] See *Grootboom* (n 15), *Port Elizabeth Municipality* (n 2) *City of Johannesburg v Blue Moonlight Properties* 2012 (2) SA 104 (CC) (*Blue Moonlight*).
[51] Edwin Cameron, *What You Can Do With Rights*, Fourth Leslie Scarman Memorial Lecture, Law Commission of England and Wales, Middle Temple Hall, London, 2012 para 37 <www.lawcom.gov.uk/app/uploads/2015/05/Scarman_2012_Justice_Cameron_What_you_can_do_with_rights.pdf>.
[52] See Liebenberg (n 10) for a comprehensive analysis of this early jurisprudence.

substantive principles of general application, and real distributive impact. It is to those juris-dictions that I now turn.

## 3.    THE RIGHT TO ADEQUATE HOUSING IN REGIONAL AND DOMESTIC JURISDICTIONS

Declarations of rights, and expert glosses on their content such as the General Comments provided by the CESCR and the Guidelines and other material produced by the Special Rapporteur, have clear value to the enforcement of the right to adequate housing. But, like all rights, the right to adequate housing is really only given enduring meaning through concrete social struggles.[53] Those struggles can be memorialized in a variety of forms, including litera-ture, art, song, and oral and written history.[54]

The legal meaning of human rights, however, is generally determined by contestation between parties with adverse interests in a specific context: in other words, through litigation. Individual parties (sometimes representative of entire communities and classes of people) submit to adjudication a concrete dispute about what a right means on a given set of facts, and what remedy – what practical resolution of the dispute – flows from that meaning. It is through litigation, through the actual application of law to concrete social struggles, that rights tend to bite hardest – or have their limits thrown into the sharpest relief.

The right to adequate housing in the ICESCR has arguably come alive since the Committee began to adjudicate concrete disputes in specific contexts. Even though the Committee can do no more than 'recommend' individual remedies and programmatic reform to a state party to the ICESCR, its communications in the three housing rights cases set out above provide a powerful account of the meaning of the right to housing as a break on contemporary forms of dispossession, and as a trigger for the re-allocation of resources towards the poor and the vulnerable.

It is, however, in domestic and some regional jurisdictions, where the remedies are stronger and more accessible, that the right to adequate housing has started to come into its own. Its meaning and application have naturally been developed in the context of the struggles in which it has been deployed. These struggles have reflected the priorities that individuals and commu-nities have set for themselves in the realization of the right to adequate housing.

Accordingly, much of the recent history of the right to adequate housing can be related through struggles over the upgrading of informal settlements, the eviction of illegal occupiers, the rights of residential tenants in urban areas, the rights of mortgagors and the struggles of women to access housing through, and despite, patriarchal accounts of property law. It is in these contexts – the failure to recognize informal tenure, the exclusion of poor people and vulnerable communities from metropolitan property regimes, the exploitation of residential tenants and indebted home owners, and gender discrimination – that the right to housing has bitten hardest. In what follows, I provide a summary of the role of the right to housing in each of these struggles. The account given is necessarily incomplete. It is, however, illustrative of

---

[53]    See Richard Wilson (ed), *Human Rights, Culture and Context* (Pluto Press 1997) for powerful arguments in favor of interpreting rights as the outcomes of concrete social struggles from below, rather than as internationally formulated benefits granted from above.

[54]    E.P. Thompson, *The Making of the English Working Class* (Pantheon 1963).

the power of the right to housing as a tool of struggle with potentially far-reaching egalitarian effects.

## 3.1    Informal Settlements

Informal settlements occupy a liminal space in urban life. On the one hand, a substantial portion of the urban labor force lives in informal settlements. In South Africa, for example, 14 per cent of households live in informal settlements, which are concentrated in urban and peri-urban areas. The number of people living in informal housing in South Africa is also on the increase.[55] Notwithstanding the role their residents play in the urban economy, informal settlements are often blind spots in urban policy, including housing policy. They are defined by a series of negatives: they are *without* formality, *without* legality, *without* services and often *without* any recognized social and political structure or representation.

Housing litigation in the context of informal settlements often frames simple claims for inclusion and equality: the claim to the same respect for basic tenure rights enjoyed by those living in formal housing; the claim to the same basic provision of services, such as electricity, water and sanitation; and the claim to the same consideration in urban planning process.

The biggest single disadvantage most informal settlers face is vulnerability to eviction. A wide variety of claims based on the right to adequate housing has sought to establish basic procedural and justificatory requirements for the implementation of an eviction. Legal frameworks that require notice of and a justification for an intended eviction, and the authority of the courts to implement one, tend to attach to formal common law property rights, but seldom to mere occupation itself. This is why the ICESCR and General Comment 7 place such emphasis on the need for reliable legal remedies for those who face eviction. Often, it is precisely the absence of formal tenure rights that both deprive an informal settler of due process protections and render them more vulnerable to actual removal. In *Muhindo James v Attorney General*,[56] the Ugandan High Court found that the Ugandan government's failure to adopt comprehensive legal framework to protect those facing eviction to be a violation of the rights to dignity, life and property entrenched in the Ugandan Constitution, interpreted in light of the right to adequate housing in the ICESCR. The Court directed the government to develop such a framework, and to report back on its progress in doing so within seven months.

Once they have established basic tenure security, in the form of protection against eviction, informal settlers often find themselves without the basic services necessary to sustain an urban home. Water, sanitation and electricity are all vital incidents of the right to housing, at least in an urban setting, where people live in concentrated numbers in a small area. Where services are provided, they are unreliable, or come in forms that show less than the appropriate respect for the residents' dignity. In *Beja v Premier of the Western Cape*,[57] the state had provided toilets to the residents of an informal settlement but had failed to enclose them, with the effect that anyone could be seen using them. In directing that the toilets be enclosed, the South African High Court emphasized the inter-relationship between the rights of access to adequate

---

[55]    Socio-Economic Rights Institute of South Africa (SERI), *Informal Settlement in South Africa: Report 4, Here to Stay: A Synthesis of Findings and Implications* (2019) 5.

[56]    Miscellaneous Cause No 127 of 2016, High Court of Uganda, Civil Division (Judgment dated 25 January 2019).

[57]    [2011] 3 All SA 401 (WCC).

housing, the right to privacy and the right to dignity in the Constitution of the Republic of South Africa, 1996. International law, especially in the form of the UNDHR and the ICESCR, recognizes this inter-relationship too.

The outcome of the *Beja* case could be characterized as a fairly modest application of the right to adequate housing. That informal settlers have the right to go to the toilet in privacy ought not to strike us as a particularly ambitious claim to make. However, that the claim, however small, was made at all, and resulted in a re-allocation of resources to the informal settlement, demonstrates, in principle, that the right to adequate housing has some efficacy in re-allocating resources towards informal settlers, and pressing for more egalitarian outcomes.

A case that illustrates the ability of the right to adequate housing to sustain more ambitious demands is *Melani v City of Johannesburg.*[58] In that matter, a community of 10,000 informal settlers had managed to establish themselves on land to the south of Johannesburg, with some limited access to services, and security of tenure. The state had for many years promised to ultimately upgrade the informal settlement by providing permanent roads; services, including electricity; and formal housing. In 2015 the state abruptly reversed its position, and informed the community that it would be relocated to a large greenfield housing project, called 'Unaville', 11 kilometers further south of the Johannesburg city center. The residents promptly reviewed that decision in the High Court, on the grounds that the right of access to adequate housing, read with the state's informal settlement upgrading policies, required informal settlements to be upgraded *in situ* wherever technically possible. Since an upgrade was technically possible, the state was required to implement one. It followed that the decision to relocate the settlement was unlawful. The High Court agreed, set aside the decision to relocate the settlement and directed the state to formulate a plan to upgrade it *in situ*. This had to be done in genuine consultation with the settlement's residents – a requirement consistent with international law standards embedded in General Comment 4 and the UN Special Rapporteur's Housing Guidelines.

The right to adequate housing accordingly provides a range of tools to informal settlers. These tools can have the rather modest effect of protecting informal settlers against sudden and unforeseen eviction. They can also be deployed to demand much deeper claims on the state's resources. Although the existence of a domestic policy framework is helpful in deploying the right (as it was in both *Beja* and *Melani*), the absence or inadequacy of a domestic policy or legal framework to give effect to the right does not leave informal settlers without remedy. The *Muhindo* case demonstrates that the right can be read to require such a framework to exist, and to compel the state to construct one. Once the framework is legislated, it can be subjected to follow-up critique and litigation. Every step of the process can potentially yield concrete benefits for a claimant community, substantial reform in housing policy and a re-allocation of resources towards the poor.

## 3.2    Evictions of Unlawful Occupiers

The right to adequate housing, and its associated protections against eviction, can be activated to protect the unrecognized interests of unlawful occupiers, such as otherwise 'homeless' occupiers of urban tenements, and itinerant groups, such as the Roma people in Europe.

---

[58]    2016 (5) SA 67 (GJ).

Most legal jurisdictions feature some form of legal pluralism, in which municipal law – law that emanates from a legislature or from common or civil law courts – comes into contact with, and attempts to displace, local mores, customs and use rights. In addition, municipal law can leave completely out of account the social needs of outsider groups, such as travelers, informal settlers, 'squatters' and other people living, temporarily or permanently, on land that they do not formally own. The concept of ownership itself – the concept of exclusive power and domination over land or property to the exclusion of all others[59] – conflicts with older, more socialized systems of communal use rights which it displaces.

Where ownership rights assert themselves over residential uses, the right to adequate housing has the potential to provide a potent shield against displacement of poor and vulnerable people who would otherwise be rendered homeless. In imposing the requirement that evictions, even if they go ahead, ought not to lead to homelessness, the right requires a significant re-allocation of resources to provide alternative accommodation to those who are displaced as a result of legally justifiable eviction. Traditionally, steps taken under domestic law to re-possess property used for residential purposes have seldom been accompanied by justificatory or ameliatory requirements, such as the provision of alternative accommodation on eviction. As we have seen, the CESCR found that no such requirement existed in Spanish law, which was one of the reasons why Spain stood in breach of its Covenant obligations.

However, the new anti-eviction law, based on the right to adequate housing and exemplified in General Comment 7, finds far-reaching application in a range of domestic and regional circumstances. Two sets of cases illustrate the point.

In Europe, the Roma people face arbitrary eviction and inadequate, segregated accommodation in many jurisdictions. In *Centre on Housing Rights and Evictions (COHRE) v Italy*, the European Committee of Social Rights found that the Italian government had permitted numerous evictions to be carried out in breach of 'the dignity of the persons concerned' and had failed to ensure 'that alternative accommodation was made available to them'. The Committee found similar violations in matters relating to the treatment of Roma people in Greece,[60] and also in Portugal.[61]

But it is perhaps in South Africa that the most extensive human rights framework has developed to govern the eviction of unlawful occupiers and to prevent evictions from leading to homelessness. The over-riding principle, now firmly established in South Africa, is that evictions of unlawful occupiers should not lead to homelessness.[62] Where it appears that an eviction might lead to homelessness, a court is required to conduct the necessary enquiries to decide whether and to what extent homelessness would result from an eviction, and to seek input from the state, usually the local authority, on what steps are to be taken to ensure that the unlawful occupiers concerned will have access to alternative accommodation if they are evict-

---

[59]  Carol Rose, *Property and Persuasion: Essays on the History, Theory, and Rhetoric of Ownership* (Westview 1994) 271–72.

[60]  *International Centre for the Legal Protection of Human Rights (INTERIGHTS) v Greece* Complaint No. 49/2008.

[61]  *European Roma Rights Centre v Portugal* Complaint No. 61/2010.

[62]  *Port Elizabeth Municipality* (n 2) para 28; *Occupiers, Shulana Court v Mark Lewis Steele* [2010] 4 All SA 54 (SCA) para 16; *Mathale v Linda* 2016 (1) SA 461 (CC) para 50.

ed.[63] In rare cases, a court will refuse an eviction order outright.[64] More often, though, a court will make a structured eviction order, obliging the local authority to provide accommodation to the unlawful occupiers before the date on which the unlawful occupiers may be evicted, and specifying the nature and location of the alternative accommodation to which the unlawful occupiers are to be relocated.[65]

The state's response to the new duties imposed on it has been sluggish.[66] Eviction applications have, in some cases, taken several years to finalize.[67] Depending on the size of the community involved, and the logistical difficulties with providing alternative accommodation, large communities can establish *de facto* rights of occupation in the years it takes to obtain an eviction order. In *Modderklip*, the unlawful occupiers were simply left where they were, the state bought the land they had occupied, and a low-cost housing development was eventually constructed on it.[68] In the *Ratanang* informal settlement case,[69] the local authority entered into a court-sanctioned 36-month lease with the owner of the property on behalf of the occupiers – effectively, if only temporarily, giving legal recognition to the informal settlers' rights of occupation. In the *Joe Slovo Informal Settlement* case,[70] the conditions placed by the Constitutional Court on the state's right to evict and relocate the occupiers of the informal settlement proved so onerous that the eviction order could not be carried out, and was ultimately discharged.[71] The unlawful occupiers in that case are now negotiating the terms on which the Joe Slovo informal settlement will be upgraded *in situ*.

Even where the unlawful occupiers ultimately have to move, this has had significant knock-on effects for urban planning. A series of eviction cases in the Johannesburg inner city has resulted in the creation of a small, but growing, public housing stock to accommodate unlawful occupiers evicted from buildings in the course of inner city regeneration initiatives.[72] The terms on which that accommodation is provided have opened up a new front in unlawful occupiers' struggles to retain access to the city. The courts have directed local authorities to provide accommodation within a reasonable distance of the land from which unlawful occupiers have been removed.[73] They have also directed that family accommodation be provided,

---

[63]   *City of Johannesburg v Changing Tides* 2012 (6) SA 294 (SCA) para 40.

[64]   *Ekurhuleni Metropolitan Municipality and Another v Various Occupiers*, Eden Park Extension 5 2014 (3) SA 23 (SCA); *All Builders And Cleaning Services CC v Matlaila and Others* (42349/13) [2015] ZAGPJHC 2 (16 January 2015).

[65]   *Hlophe and Others v City of Johannesburg and Others* 2013 (4) SA 212 (GSJ).

[66]   *City of Johannesburg Metropolitan Municipality and others v Hlophe and Others* 2015 (2) All SA 251 (SCA).

[67]   Ibid.

[68]   Kate Tissington, 'Demolishing Development at Gabon Informal Settlement: Public Interest Litigation Beyond Modderklip?' (2011) 27 South African Journal on Human Rights 192.

[69]   *De Clerq and Others v Occupiers of Plot 38 Meringspark, Klerksdorp and Others* case pending at the time of writing. Papers available at <www.seri-sa.org/index.php/19-litigation/case-entries/188-de-clerq-and-others-v-the-occupiers-of-plot-38-meringspark-klerksdorp-and-others-ratanang>.

[70]   *Residents of Joe Slovo Community, Western Cape v Thubelisha Homes and Others* 2010 (3) SA 454 (CC).

[71]   *Residents of Joe Slovo Community, Western Cape v Thubelisha Homes and Others* 2011 (7) BCLR 723 (CC).

[72]   Stuart Wilson, 'Litigating Housing Rights in Johannesburg's Inner City: 2004–2008' (2011) 27 South African Journal on Human Rights 127.

[73]   *Blue Moonlight* (n 50).

and struck down restrictive rules and conditions placed on residence in the housing stock the state provides.[74]

Restrictions have also been placed on the legal steps that private owners and the state can take to prevent the urban poor from moving onto vacant land. The courts have rejected attempts to obtain land occupation interdicts which permit eviction without a court order where unlawful occupiers have moved onto land for a relatively short period – often because they have been evicted from elsewhere.[75] The Constitutional Court, in particular, has disapproved of coercive responses to new land occupations, emphasizing the need to engage with homeless people moving on to land for the first time, and to deal with their needs on a case by case basis.[76]

In practice, this new scheme for the adjudication of eviction cases, the execution of eviction orders and the management of unlawful land occupation has opened up a fairly wide space within which unlawful occupiers can shape the terms of their access to land. South Africa's Apartheid legal regime, in effect immediately before 1994, was buttressed by the overwhelming power that common law eviction proceedings assigned to landowners. This produced a vast number of eviction orders, which were granted and executed irrespective of the social consequences of making large numbers of very poor people suddenly homeless. The post-Apartheid constitutional and statutory scheme for the management of eviction proceedings has instead sought to create a space in which the competing social claims of landowners and unlawful occupiers can be balanced and reconciled, and in which poor people can negotiate the terms of their residence in urban areas. This has led to resettlement of significant tracts of urban land by poor people, and changes in government policy and practice, increasing the availability of public rental housing stock and the frequency with which informal settlement upgrades take place.

## 3.3    The Rights of Residential Tenants

The right to adequate housing often penetrates ostensibly private law relationships concerning the lease of residential property. Given that a large segment of the urban population secures its access to housing through becoming tenants, the right to adequate housing would have significant limitations if its application could not pierce the veil of contractual privity. Instead, the right to housing often supplements and controls the exercise of contractual power by landlord and tenant, by ensuring that restrictive rental practices are prohibited, that rents remain reasonable and affordable, and that tenants have access to remedies where landlords abuse their power. The UN Special Rapporteur's Housing Guidelines emphasize the need to regulate and control the rental sector by '[m]aintaining a rental regulatory framework that preserves security of tenure and affordable housing for tenants, including through rent caps, controls or rent freezes where needed'.[77]

Rent control has long been effective in ensuring affordable rental housing, but its use has receded with the neoliberal turn towards the deregulation of markets and respect for contractual privity, and a renewed focus on regulating the market through the provision of incentives

---

[74]    *Dladla and Others v City of Johannesburg Metropolitan Municipality* 2014 (6) SA 516 (GJ).
[75]    *Zulu and Others v eThekwini Municipality* 2014 (4) SA 590 (CC).
[76]    *Grootboom* (n 15) para 87.
[77]    Ibid 34 para 69 (a) (ii).

rather than the imposition of rules. But, in the context of inherently unequal relationships, that emerge in conditions of oligopoly, such as urban rental housing, 'contractual privity' often boils down the power of the oligopolist to exploit the consumer.

Accordingly, and despite the retreat of rent control as a regulatory instrument, the right to housing has often underwritten more open text, flexibly applied dispute resolution mechanisms that have sought to ensure that the landlord–tenant relationship is fundamentally fair. In South Africa, the role of the right to housing in regulating the landlord–tenant relationship was affirmed and delineated in *Maphango v Aengus Lifestyle Properties.*[78] In that case, a property developer purchased a rundown building in the center of Johannesburg. The tenants in the building at the time were paying rent in terms of leases which guaranteed them significantly lower rents than the property developer could secure on the open market. The property developer therefore offered the tenants a choice – their leases would be terminated and they would have to vacate, or they could elect to pay up to twice their current rent to stay in the property. Not surprisingly, the tenants rejected both options and lodged a complaint with the Rental Housing Tribunal about what they said was an unfair rent. In order to avoid the Tribunal's jurisdiction, the property developer brought an application for eviction in the High Court. The eviction order was granted in the South African High Court, and upheld in the Supreme Court of Appeal.[79] Both courts held that they had no power to interfere with a commercial decision to terminate a lease. The Supreme Court of Appeal also held that, even if it did have such a power, it saw nothing wrong with a property owner terminating a tenant's lease in order to secure a higher rent.[80]

The Constitutional Court disagreed. It held that the Rental Housing Act 'superimposes its unfair practice regime on the contractual arrangement that the individual parties negotiate'.[81] This superimposition means that the Tribunal, and presumably courts as well in appropriate cases, have the power to disallow the termination of a residential lease, and to set rents between the parties.

Because Rental Housing Tribunals are easily accessible, without legal representation, and without any of the fees and formalities imposed on litigants by courts, they constitute a vital space in which tenants can shape the terms of their relationships with landlords. Rental Housing Tribunals have acted as a source of equitable rules for the landlord–tenant relationship, and as an informal dispute resolution space within which landlords and tenants meet on more or less equal terms. One of the most important contributions to the law of landlord and tenant to emanate from the Rental Housing Tribunals is the decision of the Gauteng Rental Housing Tribunal to outlaw the practice of landlords levying service charges on tenants' consumption of electricity and water in residential buildings.[82]

Elsewhere, the right to adequate housing has been used to disallow large programs of gentrification that would significantly reduce the supply of affordable housing. In the *Rechtbank Rotterdam* case,[83] the Dutch courts disallowed the purchase and redevelopment of a Rotterdam

---

[78]   2012 (3) SA 531 (CC).
[79]   *Maphango (Mgidlana) v Aengus Lifestyle Properties (Pty) Ltd* [2011] 3 All SA 535 (SCA).
[80]   Ibid para 34.
[81]   Ibid para 51.
[82]   *Young Ming Shan CC v Chagan NO* 2015 (3) SA 227 (GJ).
[83]   Case No. 7989753 \ CV EXPL 19-36659.

neighborhood on the basis that insufficient community participation had preceded the adoption of a plan that would limit the availability of affordable housing.

### 3.4    Mortgage Bond Foreclosures

In *IDG v Spain*, the CESCR clearly intimated that the right to adequate housing places limits on the steps a financial institution can take to foreclose a loan secured on residential property. In most jurisdictions, the right to adequate housing has a limited impact on the mortgage fore-closure process, largely because it is not generally recognized that homeownership is itself an incident of the right to adequate housing. A loss of ownership of a home does not necessarily imply the deprivation of housing altogether, and defenses against foreclosure tend to focus on non-compliance with the formalities associated with such a process, such as adequate notice of the intention to foreclose. In *IDG v Spain*, those formalities were treated as incidents of the right to adequate housing, in that they were held to be part of the process and remedies to which a mortgagor is entitled under the right to adequate housing.

In South Africa, both the process and substance of the mortgage foreclosure process has been brought under the supervision of the right to adequate housing. In *Jaftha*,[84] the Constitutional Court decided that the execution of a debt against a person's home constitutes an infringement of the right of access to adequate housing in Section 26 (1) of the Constitution of the Republic of South Africa Act, 1996. Although the Constitution might permit an infringement in terms of its limitations clause,[85] the infringement always has to be justified. An infringement of the right of access to adequate housing to recover a debt secured against a home is only justified when it is 'proportional'. In other words, the money lender taking and selling a debtor's house to recover the debt must be a proportionate response to the debtor's default. This principle is generally parsed to mean that alternatives to execution, if they exist, must be explored before the sale of a debtor's home is authorized, and that execution will not be permitted for 'trifling' or relatively small arrears.[86]

The constitutional principle of proportionality opens up important spaces in which debtors can challenge unfair lending practices and even blunt a money lender's rights to execute against their property where – a debtor's failure to repay notwithstanding – it would be dis-proportionate to do so. The proportionality principle differs from other ways of monitoring corporate compliance with the law because, unlike 'watchdog' agencies or media shaming, they link a money lender's right to recover or execute on a debt in every case to the debtor's option to seek alternative dispute resolution, and/or to make good on his arrears, and/or to the overall fairness of executing against a person's home.

Proportionality in debt execution is yet to find itself applied in the context of the interna-tional right to adequate housing, but presents a potentially powerful way of subjecting the excesses of private financial institutions to human rights scrutiny.

---

[84]    *Jaftha* (n 6).
[85]    Section 36 of the Constitution of the Republic of South Africa, 1996.
[86]    *Jaftha* (n 6) para 57.

### 3.5   Gender Discrimination

As the South African Constitutional Court has noted, '[w]omen's access to adequate housing is critical to their enjoyment of other human rights, and a gendered perspective must be adopted in order to give effect to women's right to adequate housing'. The Court also noted that '[t]he right to adequate housing is also integral to women's overall wellbeing. Because women are primarily responsible for taking care of the home, they are particularly vulnerable to gender-based violence outside the home, and adequate housing is necessary for their social empowerment'.[87]

Yet the battleground for women's access to adequate housing has primarily been the exclusion of women from inheritance rights. In *Danamma Suman Surpur & Another v Amar & Others*,[88] the Indian Supreme Court upheld a law that affirmed equal inheritance rights for women. In *Mrs. Lois Chituru Ukeje & Enyinaya Lazarus Ukeje v Mrs. Gladuy Ada Ukeje*,[89] and in *Bhe v Magistrate Khayelitsha*,[90] Nigerian and South African courts, respectively, struck down customary law provisions that excluded women from inheritance rights. The exclusion of women from inheritance was likewise declared to be inconsistent with international non-discrimination laws in the case of *EC and SC*.[91]

Given that household labor and childcare in the home are burdens that fall disproportionately on women, it might have been expected that a stronger, more distinctively housing rights-based jurisprudence would have developed on the issue of gender discrimination. If it is nothing else, the home is a gendered space, and the right to adequate housing ought to start to account for this. The South African Constitutional Court has begun, albeit modestly, to deal with the substantive implications of gender and housing by striking down homeless shelter rules that make childcare practically impossible, by locking shelter residents out during daylight hours.[92] But there is little doubt that a more substantive account of gender and the right to housing remains to be developed in regional and domestic jurisdictions.

## 4.   CONCLUSION

The right to adequate housing sits at the locus of a range of interconnected human interests and power relationships. It is plain from the context in which the right has developed that it is through processes of dispossession, and through challenging the unjust relationships embedded in municipal property law, that the right has found meaning and application. The right is at its most efficacious when used as a tool to resist eviction or foreclosure, and to ensure fairness on contractual regimes.

It is this aspect of the enforcement of housing rights that places limits on the critique of rights as providing no more than basic sufficiency guarantees, and doing little or nothing to

---

[87]   *Dladla* (n 74) para 29.
[88]   Civil Appeal Nos 188–189 of 2018, Indian Supreme Court.
[89]   Supreme Court of Nigeria, Case No. 224/2004.
[90]   2005 (1) SA 580 (CC).
[91]   Views of the Committee on the Elimination of Discrimination against Women under the Optional Protocol to the Convention on the Elimination of All Forms of Discrimination against Women (sixtieth session), Communication No. 48/2013.
[92]   *Dladla* (n 74).

challenge economic inequality. Leaving aside the question of whether more sufficiency for the worst off must necessarily lead to at least some redistribution of resources from the best off, this critique of rights overlooks the ways in which the right to adequate housing challenges and places limits on the property relationships through which economic inequality is asserted. If more housing rights means fewer evictions, no homelessness, fairer rents and limitations on a bank's right to foreclose against homes, such rights must, of necessity, mean a redistribution of resources away from property owners who hold land as a commodity, and in favor of residents who dwell on land as a home. This must also mean more resources to ensure that adequate alternatives exist when people are dispossessed.

These profound economic consequences to the enforcement of the right to adequate housing have yet to be fully explored, either in the theoretical development of the right, or in its practical implementation. Whether or not human rights are 'enough' to tackle inequality, there can be no doubt that the right to adequate housing has a great deal of potential to challenge and reshape the processes of dispossession that reproduce and sustain it.

# 11. The human rights to water and sanitation

*Catarina de Albuquerque and Virginia Roaf*[1]

## 1. THE LEGAL FOUNDATIONS OF THE HUMAN RIGHTS TO WATER AND SANITATION

### 1.1 The Recognition of the Rights to Water and Sanitation as Independent Rights

When the United Nations General Assembly adopted the Universal Declaration of Human Rights (UDHR) in 1948, the human rights to water and sanitation were not explicitly included in the text. This omission can be understood in the context of a time when many countries were not directly represented at the negotiating table: water and sanitation were simply not considered.

The International Covenant on Economic, Social and Cultural Rights (ICESCR) similarly lacks any explicit reference to the rights to water or sanitation. Both the UDHR and the ICESCR provide for the human right of all people to an adequate standard of living, including food, clothing and housing.[2]

As the water and sanitation crisis became more pronounced in the final decades of the twentieth century, bringing negative health and economic consequences with it, the development and human rights community became increasingly aware of the growing importance of water and sanitation. Several of the more recent international human rights treaties refer explicitly to the importance of water and sanitation (separately or together) in realizing human rights, including the Convention on the Elimination of All Forms of Discrimination against Women (CEDAW),[3] the Convention on the Rights of the Child (CRC)[4] and the Convention on the Rights of Persons with Disabilities (CRPD).[5]

In 2002, the Committee for Economic, Social and Cultural Rights (CESCR) adopted General Comment No. 15 on the human right to water.[6] General Comment No. 15 found that the human right to water is implicitly included in the right to an adequate standard of living and the right to health (Articles 11 and 12 of the ICESCR). The use of the term 'including' in Article 11 requires the incorporation of all aspects of an adequate standard of living.

---

[1]  This chapter draws on three previous publications. Sections 1–6 draw on Catarina De Albuquerque and Virginia Roaf, *On the Right Track: Good Practices in Realising the Rights to Water and Sanitation* (2012) and Catarina de Albuquerque, *The Human Rights to Water and Sanitation: A Handbook* (2014). Section 7 draws on Catarina de Albuquerque, 'Report of the Special Rapporteur on the human right to safe drinking water and sanitation: Common violations of the human rights to water and sanitation' (30 June 2014) A/HRC/27/55.

[2]  ICESCR Article 11 (1).

[3]  CEDAW Article 14 (2)(h).

[4]  CRC Article 24 (2).

[5]  CRPD Article 28 (2)(a).

[6]  CESCR, General Comment No. 15: The Right to Water (20 January 2003) E/C.12/2002/11 (General Comment No. 15).

In 2008, the Human Rights Council created the mandate of the Independent Expert on human rights obligations related to drinking water and sanitation.[7] The Independent Expert's first report to the Human Rights Council in 2009 outlined human rights obligations relating to sanitation.[8] Recognition of both water and sanitation as human rights was affirmed by the UN General Assembly in July 2010,[9] and by the Human Rights Council in September 2010.[10] In November 2010 the CESCR adopted a Statement on the right to sanitation, asserting that 'The Committee is of the view that the right to sanitation requires full recognition by states parties in compliance with the human rights principles'.[11] In 2013, the UN General Assembly and the Human Rights Council both reaffirmed recognition of the human rights to water and sanitation in consensus.[12] In 2015, water and sanitation were recognized by the General Assembly as separate human rights.[13]

## 1.2    Interdependence with Other Human Rights

The human rights to water and sanitation are also essential to the realization of many other human rights. Lack of access to water and sanitation can jeopardize the human right to life,[14] as well as the right to health.[15] For instance, unclean water or inappropriate sanitation often leads to diarrhea, which remains the second-largest cause of mortality in children under five.[16] The UN Human Rights Committee has stated that States must ensure access to water and sanitation in order to protect the right to life.[17]

For the realization of the right to adequate housing, access to essential services such as water and sanitation is indispensable.[18] Rights to privacy and physical security are also engaged in situations where women and children have to go to shared latrines or open spaces to defecate.[19] The right to education cannot be guaranteed where water and sanitation services are not available at school. Access to water is essential for agriculture in order to realize the right to adequate food, particularly for marginalized and poor farmers engaged in subsistence and small-scale farming. The right to work can be negatively affected if there is a lack of access to water and

---

[7]    HRC Resolution 7/22 (28 March 2008) A/HRC/RES/7/22.

[8]    Independent Expert on the issue of human rights obligations related to access to safe drinking water and sanitation, Catarina de Albuquerque, Human rights obligations related to sanitation (1 July 2009) A/HRC/12/24 (Human rights obligations related to sanitation, 2009).

[9]    UNGA, Resolution: The human right to water and sanitation (3 August 2010) A/RES/64/292.

[10]    HRC, Resolution: Human rights and access to safe drinking water and sanitation (6 October 2010) A/HRC/RES/15/9.

[11]    CESCR, Statement on the right to sanitation (19 November 2010) E/C.12/2010/1 (CESCR Statement on the right to sanitation).

[12]    UNGA, Resolution: The human right to safe drinking water and sanitation (12 February 2014) A/RES/68/157, and HRC, Resolution: The human right to safe drinking water and sanitation (8 October 2013) A/HRC/RES/24/18.

[13]    UNGA Resolution: The human rights to water and sanitation (22 February 2016) A/RES/70/169.

[14]    UDHR Article 3 and International Covenant on Civil and Political Rights (ICCPR) Article 6 (1).

[15]    UDHR Article 25 and ICESCR Article 12.

[16]    Centers for Disease Control and Prevention, Diarrhea: Common Illness, Global Killer <www.cdc.gov/healthywater/pdf/global/programs/Globaldiarrhea508c.pdf>.

[17]    HRC, General Comment No. 36: Right to Life (3 September 2019) CCPR/C/GC/36 para 26.

[18]    OHCHR, UN-Habitat and WHO, Fact Sheet No. 35: The right to water (2010), pp. 4 and 13: <www.ohchr.org/Documents/Publications/FactSheet35en.pdf>.

[19]    Ibid p. 13.

sanitation at the workplace, particularly for women during menstruation and pregnancy.[20] The right to social security encompasses the right to access and maintain social security or other benefits in order to be able to secure water and sanitation (among other necessary goods).[21]

The lack of access to water and sanitation may lead to inhuman or degrading treatment, particularly in the context of deprivation of liberty. The International Committee of the Red Cross,[22] the Human Rights Committee,[23] the Committee against Torture,[24] and the Special Rapporteur on Torture have expressed concern about poor sanitation and water in detention, out of respect for the dignity of detainees and because many diseases among detainees are transmitted by the fecal–oral route.[25] In these circumstances where people cannot provide their own services, the State must do so. This may also be relevant to homeless people, people living in informal settlements and refugees.[26]

Environmental rights also intersect with the rights to water and sanitation. Finite resources must be protected from overexploitation and pollution, and facilities and services dealing with excreta and wastewater should ensure a clean and healthy living environment.[27]

## 2.    THE CONTENT OF THE RIGHTS TO WATER AND SANITATION

The content of the human right to water was developed in the 2002 General Comment No. 15 of the CESCR on the human right to water.[28] The CESCR subsequently elaborated the norms that apply to the right to sanitation in its 2010 Statement on Sanitation, following on from the 2009 Report of the Independent Expert on human rights obligations related to sanitation.[29]

According to General Comment No. 15, the human right to water entitles everyone to sufficient, safe, acceptable, physically accessible and affordable water for personal and domestic

---

[20]   Human rights obligations related to sanitation, 2009 (n 2) para 38.

[21]   CESCR, General Comment No. 19: The Right to Social Security (4 February 2008) E/C.12/GC/19 para f (18).

[22]   International Committee of the Red Cross, Water, sanitation, hygiene and habitat in prisons (2005), p.58: <www.icrc.org/eng/assets/files/other/icrc_002_0823.pdf>.

[23]   Human Rights Committee, Concluding Observations: Ukraine, 2013, CCPR/C/UKR/CO/6 para 11; Human rights obligations related to access to sanitation, 2009 footnote 61.

[24]   Committee Against Torture, Concluding Observations: United Kingdom, 2004, CAT/C/CR/33/3 para 4 and Concluding Observations: Nepal, 2007, CAT/C/NPL/CO/2 para 31.

[25]   Manfred Nowak, 'Report of the UN Special Rapporteur on torture and other cruel, inhuman or degrading treatment or punishment, Mission to Indonesia' (10 March 2008) A/HRC/7/3/Add.7 para 68; see also: 'Mission to Togo' (6 January 2008) A/HRC/7/3/Add.5 para 42 and Appendix paras 3, 31, 46–47, 70 and 95; and 'Mission to Nigeria' (22 November 2007) A/HRC/7/3/Add.4 para 37 and Appendix paras 41, 95, 101 and 110.

[26]   Catarina de Albuquerque, 'Report of the Special Rapporteur on the Human Rights to Water and Sanitation, Stigma and the Realization of the Human Right to Water and Sanitation' (2 July 2012) A/HRC/21/42 para 53.

[27]   Catarina de Albuquerque, 'Report of the Special Rapporteur on the human rights to water and sanitation, sustainability and non-retrogression in the realisation of the rights to water and sanitation' (11 July 2013) A/HRC/24/44 (Sustainability and non-retrogression) para 21.

[28]   General Comment No. 15 paras 20–29.

[29]   CESCR Statement on the Right to Sanitation (n 11) para 8; Human rights obligations related to sanitation, 2009 (n 8).

use. The human right to sanitation entitles everyone to sanitation services that provide privacy and ensure dignity, and that are physically accessible and affordable, safe, hygienic, secure, socially and culturally acceptable.[30] Sanitation is defined as 'a system for the collection, transport, treatment and disposal or reuse of human excreta, and associated hygiene'.

The content of the human rights to water and sanitation as elaborated by the CESCR encompasses five key aspects: availability, accessibility, quality, affordability and acceptability.[31]

Availability requires that water and sanitation facilities meet people's needs now and in the future. According to General Comment No. 15, 'Water supply must be sufficient and continuous for personal and domestic uses, which ordinarily include drinking, personal sanitation, washing of clothes, food preparation, and personal and household hygiene'.[32] There must be a sufficient number of sanitation facilities to ensure that all of the needs of each person are met. Where facilities are shared, long waiting times should be avoided. In addition, the collection, transport, treatment and disposal (or reuse) of human excreta and associated hygiene must be ensured.[33] Facilities to meet hygiene requirements must be available wherever there are toilets and latrines, where water is stored and where food is being prepared and served, particularly for hand-washing, menstrual hygiene management and the management of children's feces.

Accessibility of water and sanitation requires that infrastructure be located and built in such a way that it is genuinely accessible, with consideration given to people who face specific barriers, such as children, older people, people with disabilities and chronically ill people.[34] For example, the pump fitted to a public well must be easy to use for older people, children and people with disabilities, and the location must be within reach and accessible to all, at all times. Water outlets and sanitation facilities must be placed within, or in the immediate vicinity of, each household, workplace, educational and health institution, as well as any other place where people spend significant amounts of time.[35]

The quality and safety of water and sanitation services must be ensured to protect the health of users and the general public. Water must be free from microorganisms, chemical substances and radiological hazards that constitute a threat to human health.[36] Sanitation facilities must be safe to use and must effectively prevent human, animal and insect contact with human excreta, to ensure safety and to protect the health of users and the community. Toilets must be regularly cleaned and provide hygiene facilities for washing hands with soap and water. Facilities must be available to women and girls for management of their periods, including the disposal of menstrual products. Ensuring safe sanitation further requires hygiene promotion and education, to ensure that people use toilets in a hygienic manner.[37]

Affordability of water and sanitation means that the price paid to meet all water and sanitation needs must not limit people's capacity to buy other basic goods and services, including food, housing, health and education that are guaranteed by other human rights. While interna-

---

[30]   Human rights obligations related to sanitation, 2009 (n 8) para 63; CESCR, Statement on the Right to Sanitation (n 11) para 8.
[31]   General Comment No. 15 paras 12, 53.
[32]   Ibid para 12 (a).
[33]   Human rights obligations related to sanitation, 2009 (n 8) paras 63, 70.
[34]   General Comment No. 15 para 12 (c).
[35]   General Comment No. 15 & CESCR, Statement on the right to sanitation (n 11).
[36]   General Comment No. 15 para 12.
[37]   Human rights obligations related to sanitation, 2009 (n 8) para 74.

tional human rights law does not require services to be provided free of charge, States have an obligation to ensure the affordability of services.[38]

Acceptability is also a critical component of the content of the rights to water and sanitation. Water and sanitation facilities will not be used, if they fail to meet the social or cultural standards of the people they are meant to serve. Acceptability requires respect for dignity and privacy, which are human rights values that permeate international human rights law. Water must be of an acceptable odor, taste and color to meet all personal and domestic uses and water facilities must be acceptable for the intended use, especially for personal hygiene.[39] Sanitation facilities will only be acceptable to users if the design, positioning and conditions of use are sensitive to people's cultures and priorities. Toilets for women and girls must have facilities for menstrual hygiene management, including for the disposal of menstrual materials.[40]

## 3. OBLIGATIONS OF STATES FOR THE REALIZATION OF THE RIGHTS TO WATER AND SANITATION

### 3.1 Obligations to Respect, Protect and Fulfill

The CESCR has elaborated State obligations for the realization of the rights to water and sanitation following its established typology of respect, protect and fulfill.

The obligation to respect the human rights to water and sanitation means that States must refrain from action that will unjustifiably interfere with their enjoyment. As stated in General Comment No. 15:

> The obligation includes, inter alia, refraining from engaging in any practice or activity that denies or limits equal access to adequate water; arbitrarily interfering with customary or traditional arrangements for water allocation; unlawfully diminishing or polluting water, for example through waste from State-owned facilities or through use and testing of weapons; and limiting access to, or destroying, water services and infrastructure as a punitive measure, for example, during armed conflicts in violation of international humanitarian law.[41]

As noted below, States must also refrain from unjustifiable disconnection from services or unaffordable increases in pricing.

The obligation to protect the human rights to water and sanitation requires that States must prevent third parties from interfering in any way with people's enjoyment of these human rights, for example by 'adopting the necessary and effective legislative and other measures to restrain … third parties from denying equal access to adequate water'.[42] As described below, this entails significant obligations on States to regulate service providers in relation to such requirements as non-discrimination and restrictions on disconnections.

---

[38]   General Comment No. 15 para 12 (c).
[39]   Catarina de Albuquerque, 'Report of the UN Special Rapporteur on the human right to safe drinking water and sanitation, Mission to Thailand' (16 July 2013) A/HRC/24/44/Add.3 para 25.
[40]   Human rights obligations related to sanitation, 2009 (n 8) para 80.
[41]   General Comment No. 15 para 21.
[42]   Ibid para 23.

The obligation to fulfill the human rights to water and sanitation requires States to ensure that the conditions are in place for everyone to enjoy the rights to water and sanitation. This requires, for example, the adoption of 'a national water strategy and plan of action …; ensuring that water is affordable for everyone; and facilitating improved and sustainable access to water, particularly in rural and deprived urban areas'.[43] This does not mean that the State has to provide the services directly, unless there are individuals or groups of people who cannot access their rights to water and sanitation through other mechanisms.

Further analysis on the implementation of the obligations to respect, protect, and fulfill can be found later in the chapter.

## 3.2    Progressive Realization and Non-retrogression

States have an obligation to move as quickly and effectively as possible towards full realization of the rights to water and sanitation, using the maximum available resources.[44] The notion of progressive realization recognizes that the full realization of these rights may take time, and faces many technical, economic and political constraints.[45] It is not, however, intended to provide States with an excuse not to act; rather, it acknowledges that full realization is normally achieved bit by bit.[46]

The CESCR recognizes that the resources available to States for the implementation of the rights to water and sanitation will vary with time and economic cycles. Even if resources are very limited, as during financial or economic crises, States are required, as a matter of priority, to ensure that everyone has access to, at the very least, minimum levels of these rights. States should take measures to protect poor, marginalized and disadvantaged individuals and groups by using targeted programs, among other approaches.[47] Deliberate retrogression in the enjoyment of the rights to water and sanitation is not permitted as it frustrates the object and purpose of the treaty. Once services and facilities have been improved, the positive change must be maintained and slippages and retrogression must be avoided.[48]

The obligation to apply the maximum available resources includes the State's duty to raise adequate revenues, through taxation and other mechanisms, and to seek international assistance where necessary.[49] States should raise as much revenue for the rights to water and sanitation as is reasonably possible through taxation.[50]

Although the progressive realization of the rights to water and sanitation may be a gradual and continuous process, there are also immediate obligations. The obligation to ensure minimum essential levels of water and sanitation is considered by the CESCR to constitute an immediate obligation. A State 'must demonstrate that every effort has been made to use all resources that are at its disposition in an effort to satisfy, as a matter of priority, those

---

[43]   Ibid para 26.

[44]   OHCHR, 'Report on austerity measures and economic and social rights' (2012) <http://www.ohchr.org/Documents/Issues/Develpoment/RightsCrisis/E-2013-82_en.pdf>.

[45]   HRC, Resolution: Human rights and access to safe drinking water and sanitation, 2010 A/HRC/RES/15/9 (n 10) paras 2 and 9.

[46]   General Comment No. 15 para 18.

[47]   Ibid para 12.

[48]   Sustainability and non-retrogression (n 27).

[49]   Ibid para 13.

[50]   Ibid paras 33–37.

minimum obligations'.[51] Hence, where minimum essential levels are not ensured, the State is, prima facie, violating human rights, and it bears the burden of proof to demonstrate that it lacks the capacity to do so. The obligation to act to respect, to protect, to provide for essential levels of water and sanitation and to adopt strategies for the fulfillment of the rights to water and sanitation in a participatory, accountable and non-discriminatory way are duties that are immediately binding.[52]

### 3.3    Fragile States

About 1.5 billion people live in fragile environments around the world.[53] Although there is no internationally agreed definition of the term 'fragile States', most development agencies identify a fundamental failure of the State to perform functions necessary to meet individuals' basic needs and expectations because of weak institutions, poor governance, corruption and inefficient decision-making. This could be due to prolonged internal conflict, natural disasters or economic crises, which result in poor or non-existent government.

The ICESCR has no derogation clause, meaning that it is applicable at all times, including in fragile States. Furthermore, 'during armed conflicts, emergency situations and natural disasters, the right[s] to water [and sanitation] embrace[s] those obligations by which states parties are bound under international humanitarian law', which 'includes protection of objects indispensable for survival of the civilian population, including drinking water installations and supplies … ensuring that civilians, internees and prisoners have access to adequate water [and sanitation]'.[54]

In the event of armed conflicts, emergency situations and natural disasters, the human rights to water and sanitation include both human rights and international humanitarian law obligations by which States and other actors are bound. The Sphere Project, initiated by a group of NGOs and the Red Cross and Red Crescent Movement, has developed a set of universal minimum standards in core areas of humanitarian responses to disaster and conflict, including for water and sanitation installations.[55]

## 4.    KEY HUMAN RIGHTS PRINCIPLES FOR THE IMPLEMENTATION OF THE RIGHTS TO WATER AND SANITATION

A number of over-arching human rights and principles are critical to the implementation of the rights to water and sanitation. These include non-discrimination and equality, access to information, participation and accountability.

---

[51]    CESCR, General Comment No. 3: The Nature of States Parties' Obligations (14 December 1990) E/1991/23 (CESCR, General Comment No. 3) para 10.
[52]    Ibid para 10 and General Comment No. 15 para 37.
[53]    World Bank, Helping fragile environments deliver water and sanitation services <http://water.worldbank.org/node/84028>.
[54]    General Comment No. 15 para 2; Geneva Convention Relative to the Protection of Civilian Persons in Time of War Articles 85, 89 and 127; Additional Protocol I (1977) Article 54; Additional Protocol II (1977) Article 14; Rome Statute of the International Criminal Court Article 8.
[55]    Sphere Project <www.spherehandbook.org/en/how-to-use-this-chapter-1/>.

Ensuring non-discrimination and equality requires States to recognize that people face different barriers to access to services and have different needs, whether because of inherent characteristics or as a result of discriminatory practices, and therefore require differentiated support or treatment. As outlined in General Comment No. 15, States must work towards eliminating existing inequalities and discriminatory practices to ensure the equal enjoyment of the rights to water and sanitation.

Socio-economic status is a prevalent form of discrimination in relation to access to water and sanitation. General Comment No. 15 states that 'investments should not disproportionately favour expensive water supply services and facilities that are often accessible only to a small, privileged fraction of the population, rather than investing in services and facilities that benefit a far larger part of the population'.[56]

Disparities in access typically exist not only between and within groups with different incomes, but also between and within other individuals and groups, such as rural and urban populations. Significant disparities based on gender are particularly prevalent, and stigmatization of particular individuals and groups is a deeply entrenched sociocultural phenomenon that often lies at the heart of discrimination in the rights to water and sanitation. For example, there is often stigma attached to menstruating women, due to taboos relating to menstruation. Likewise, the stigma attached to sanitation workers comes from people's misplaced disgust of someone handling (often their own) fecal matter.[57]

The principle of transparency requires that States be transparent and open with respect to all programs, policies and decisions, ensuring the human right to access to information.[58] Individuals and groups must both be aware of their rights to water and sanitation and also know how to claim them. States must therefore ensure that information relating to standards and how to enforce them, as well as progress towards meeting those standards, is available and accessible, and that the mechanisms (including service delivery options) used to ensure that these standards are indeed met are available and accessible to all.[59] As stated by the CESCR, 'Individuals and groups should be given full and equal access to information concerning water, water services and the environment, held by public authorities or third parties'.[60] The provision of information and dialogue with communities tends to reduce conflict and diminish unwarranted criticism while ensuring justified criticism, so as to ensure more constructive dialogue and effective responses to problems.

The right to participation in the realization of the rights to water and sanitation is critical for effective and responsive programs and policies. Participation leads to better-tailored programs that address the needs and expectations of the population that they aim to benefit. It enhances the effectiveness and sustainability of interventions, offering the possibility of social transformation by empowering marginalized communities to effect change. States must obtain the free and informed consent of Indigenous Peoples prior to the approval of any project affecting their lands, territories or water resources and ensure that Indigenous Peoples have the right to

---

[56] General Comment No. 15 para 14.
[57] WASH United, Submission for the UN Special Rapporteur's report on stigma (2012) <www.ohchr .org/Documents/Issues/Water/ContributionsStigma/CSociety/Inputconsultationstigmatization.pdf>.
[58] UDHR Article 19; ICCPR Article 19; CRC Article 17; General Comment No. 15 para 48.
[59] General Comment No. 15 paras 12 c (iv) and 48.
[60] Ibid para 48.

be actively involved in developing water and sanitation programs and administer them through their own institutions.[61]

The principle of accountability covers two important areas. First, it requires monitoring and other control mechanisms of the different actors responsible for ensuring access to water and sanitation services. As further described below, this includes the monitoring of service levels and compliance with standards and targets, as well as monitoring which individuals and groups have access to adequate water and sanitation services and which do not.[62] Second, accountability demands that individuals or groups who consider that their human rights have been violated should have access to courts or other independent review mechanisms, in order that their complaints may be heard and resolved. As described below, access to justice can take many forms, from administrative complaints procedures to judicial processes at local, national, regional and international levels.[63] Building accountability into the realization of the human rights to water and sanitation services also requires the definition of institutional mandates, as described below, clarifying in plans and strategies exactly who is responsible for each obligation and each step of the process.

Finally, the principle of sustainability requires that water and sanitation be provided in a way that respects the environment and ensures a balance of the different dimensions of economic, social and environmental sustainability. Services must be available sustainably for present and for future generations, and the provision of services today should not compromise the ability of future generations to realize their human rights to water and sanitation.[64]

## 5.    REALIZING THE RIGHTS TO WATER AND SANITATION THROUGH RIGHTS-BASED PLANNING, FINANCING AND MONITORING

### 5.1    Rights-based Planning

The incorporation of human rights standards and principles into national and local planning processes is crucial for the realization of the human rights to water and sanitation. Rights-based plans or strategies provide States with tools to improve services and eliminate inequalities in access. Planning must be open and transparent, with opportunities for people to participate actively in decisions relating to their access to water and sanitation. It involves a number of steps: assessment and analysis; setting of targets; allocation of responsibilities; implementation; and monitoring and evaluation.

The first step of a comprehensive planning process is an assessment of the status quo: laws, regulations, policies, financing, accountability mechanisms and barriers to access to services. Both qualitative and quantitative data on access to water and sanitation, with a focus

---

[61]    United Nations Declaration on the Rights of Indigenous Peoples (13 September 2007) UNGA Res 61/295 Articles 23 and 32.

[62]    General Comment No. 15 paras 47–54.

[63]    Léo Heller, 'Report of the Special Rapporteur on the rights to Safe Drinking Water and Sanitation: The Principle of Accountability' (16 July 2018) A/73/162 para 6.

[64]    Catarina de Albuquerque, 'Report of the Independent Expert on the issue of human rights obligations related to access to safe drinking water and sanitation, Progress report on the compilation of good practices' (1 July 2010) A/HRC/15/31/Add.1 para 65.

on disadvantaged areas and individuals, are critical to such assessment, and communities and individuals must be able to participate fully in gathering and assessing information.

Once data and information on significant barriers and inequalities in access have been gathered, specific targets based on a realistic timeframe can be developed to map progress toward the ultimate goal of universal access to water and sanitation services. This will require the development of tailored interventions for specific circumstances and careful monitoring of progress for disadvantaged individuals and groups.[65] When deciding on targets, States must take into account different economic scenarios, and the long-term sustainability of infrastructure, of operation and maintenance systems and, critically, of the institutional and managerial structures.

States should direct their efforts to creating the institutions and structures necessary to ensure an enabling environment so that everyone can exercise their rights, while prioritizing direct assistance for the people and groups who face the greatest barriers to access to water and sanitation services. The assumption that starting by improving services in well-to-do areas thereby increases the amount of money that can be used to later deliver services to disadvantaged individuals or groups has been shown again and again only to work for the non-poor.

In rapidly expanding cities or in countries where significant numbers of people do not have access to water and sanitation services, it may not be possible or desirable to provide the same type of services to all households and settlements. Population densities, the size of settlements, land ownership and tenure security, the scarcity of available water resources, and local capacity to maintain and operate services are all relevant in determining the most appropriate technological options. Whatever technologies are chosen, the national and local standards and targets, including interim standards, must be met, with a view to making the necessary improvements to meet the full standard by a specific date. For example, it may be acceptable in the short term to provide limited services on the edge of a settlement where there are problems with land ownership, tenure or settlement density, as long as medium to longer term planning includes strategies to remove these barriers and provide services that comply fully with national and local standards.

The clear allocation of responsibilities to different ministries and departments (horizontal coordination) and different levels of government (vertical coordination) is crucial to realizing the rights to water and sanitation. Increasingly, States are developing decentralized structures, with one of the intentions being to increase the involvement of users of services in decisions about issues such as service levels and technologies. This requires that more attention be paid to coordinating planning processes between national and local levels, and among local governments to ensure that water and financial resources are shared fairly, both to address disparities in access to water and sanitation across regions and to share common water resources fairly.

The decentralization of functions does not reduce human rights obligations, as local governments are also bound by human rights law. The national government has an obligation to regulate the activities of local governments and to monitor and control their performance to ensure that they comply with international human rights obligations,[66] as well as the relevant national legislation, regulations and policies.[67] Clear lines of responsibility at and between the

---

[65]   General Comment No. 15 para 37(f).
[66]   General Comment No. 15 para 51.
[67]   International Council on Human Rights Policy, *Local Government and Human Rights: Doing Good Service* (2005) pp 20 and 24.

different levels of government are crucial to avoid conflicts of competencies and inefficiency. States must ensure that local authorities have the financial, human and other resources necessary to discharge their duties effectively.

A rights-based realization of the rights to water and sanitation has been particularly challenging in four contexts, which will be discussed in more detail below: informal settlements, rural areas, the provision of services beyond the household and protection of the rights of sanitation workers.

### 5.1.1   Informal settlements

An informal settlement is usually defined by its lack of legal status or irregular tenure of its inhabitants, and by high-density, low-quality housing, without formal streets, electricity, water supply or access to sanitation.[68] The people living in informal settlements often have no documents (such as housing contracts, bank statements or utility bills) that officials would accept as the 'proof of residence' required in order to be connected to formal water and sanitation services. In these settlements water and sanitation services, such as they are, are often provided by informal service providers that are generally unregulated and do not comply with human rights standards.

People living in informal settlements generally have to pay more than those living in formal settlements, to receive unregulated, poor quality services. In cities such as Nairobi, Jakarta and Lima the cost of water is approximately five to ten times higher for households living in informal settlements than for those living in formal settlements in the same city.[69] Equally, people using on-site sanitation, often living in informal settlements, pay more for their sanitation service, including for the emptying of pit latrines and septic tanks, than those who benefit from the sewerage system.[70]

Realizing the human rights to water and sanitation in informal settlements therefore requires the analysis and removal of the barriers created by the legal, physical, social, cultural and institutional status of the settlements.

Where efforts are being made to deliver formal services to an informal settlement, it is crucial that the relevant government agencies and utilities understand the specific context and characteristics of a given settlement, and the efforts that are being made by informal service providers and the residents to improve the situation.

### 5.1.2   Rural areas

People who live in rural areas have consistently worse access to water and sanitation than people living in urban settlements.[71] This discrepancy in access derives from lower budget

---

[68]   Leilani Farha, 'Special Rapporteur on adequate housing as a component of the right to an adequate standard of living and to non-discrimination in this context' (19 September 2018) A/73/310/Rev.1 (2018) para 1.

[69]   UNDP, Human Development Report – Beyond Scarcity: Power Poverty and the Global Water Crisis, (2006) p 52.

[70]   Catarina de Albuquerque, 'Report of the Special Rapporteur on the human rights water and sanitation, Déclaration à la Conclusion de la Visite au Sénégal' (21 November 2011) <https://newsarchive.ohchr.org/FR/NewsEvents/Pages/DisplayNews.asp?NewsID=11625&LangID=F>.

[71]   See WHO/UNICEF Joint Monitoring Programme for Water Supply and Sanitation, Data estimates – tables: <https:washdata.org>.

allocations for rural areas, with more investment devoted to large-scale infrastructure that provides services for formal urban settlements.

Institutional reform and increased financial and human resources are required if the human rights to water and sanitation are to be realized in rural areas.[72] Building communities' capacity through the establishment of community development associations and by providing training and information about their rights and how to enforce them is critical, but this must be supported by external support, whether from local government or service providers.

### 5.1.3   Services beyond the household

Plans must be put in place for access to water and sanitation services outside the household; for example in schools, hospitals, health centers and places of detention, as well as in public places, such as markets.[73] Standards should take into account not only the number of people using these services, but also who the users are likely to be. For example, the particular needs of older persons and pregnant women should be considered for health centers.[74] Refugee camps require service levels that reflect the potential health concerns for people living there.[75]

Water and sanitation services must also be accessible in the workplace, without hindrance, for all employees. This is best clarified in employment codes, requiring businesses to provide accessible and acceptable water and sanitation in the workplace.[76]

### 5.1.4   Protecting the rights of sanitation workers

Sanitation workers play a key role in realizing the human right to sanitation, by emptying pit latrines or septic tanks, cleaning sewers and managing wastewater treatment plants. This involves working with human and animal waste, medical waste, industrial waste, sanitary napkins and other solid wastes. All too often working conditions are unsafe and unhygienic, and have led to injury and death, in violation of international norms and standards concerning safe working conditions, health and dignity.

There is often stigma attached to sanitation work, and people who do these jobs face widespread discrimination. This stigmatization and discrimination is common all over the world but is perhaps most pronounced in South Asia, where people from a particular caste have the job of removing human excrement from dry toilets by hand and carrying it to dumping sites. Most of the people who do this job are women belonging to scheduled castes that have been and continue to be subject to discrimination in all areas of their lives.[77] The practice is a direct violation of the Constitution of India, and of a number of national Acts, as well as a violation of international conventions and covenants to which India is party.[78] Despite existing legis-

---

[72]   See Organisation for Economic Co-operation and Development/Development Co-operation Directorate Secretariat and World Water Council, Donor profiles on aid to water supply (2008).

[73]   General Comment No. 15 para 12(c) i.

[74]   J. Adams, J. Batram and Y. Chartier, Essential environmental health standards in health care (WHO, 2008) <www.who.int/water_sanitation_health/hygiene/settings/ehs_health_care.pdf.pdf>.

[75]   See 'Sphere Project' <www.spherehandbook.org/en/how-to-use-this-chapter-1/>.

[76]   See for example, World Business Council for Sustainable Development, 'The WASH at the Workplace Pledge' <www.wbcsd.org/Programs/Food-Land-Water/Water/WASH-access-to-water-sanitation-and-hygiene/WASH-at-the-workplace-Pledge>.

[77]   B. Singh, *Unseen: The Truth about India's Manual Scavengers* (Penguin Books 2014).

[78]   For example Convention on the Elimination of Racial Discrimination Article 2(1)(C) and Convention on the Elimination of All Forms of Discrimination against Women Article 5(a); the

lation and court cases finding against this practice, there are still hundreds of thousands of manual scavengers in India, including some employed by government agencies.

## 5.2   Financing

States must develop an overall financing strategy to achieve universal access to water and sanitation, incorporating the human rights principles of accountability, participation, access to information and non-discrimination into financing mechanisms. This will ensure that resources are raised fairly and are spent on improving access for those who currently have inadequate access to water and sanitation. In line with the obligation of non-discrimination, revenue should be raised in a way that does not unduly penalize disadvantaged individuals and groups.

Three sources of potential funding for water and sanitation services are generally identified: (i) household and user contributions (for example, self-build, maintenance costs and tariffs); (ii) government-raised financing (for example, taxes paid by residents); and (iii) transfers, which may take the form of grants or loans from international organizations or other States, or as investments from the private sector.

### 5.2.1   Household and user contributions

Households are themselves the major contributors to the realization of the human rights to water and sanitation.[79] Household expenditures may include paying connection charges and tariffs; buying and installing hardware; maintaining the service, including pit-emptying; and paying for soap and hygiene materials. However, 'it is crucial that the tariffs be structured such that those who cannot afford to pay cost price for the delivery of water (and sanitation) services are assisted through supplementary systems that ensure affordability'.[80] The tariff structure for formal service provision must guarantee that people living in poverty have access to adequate services, regardless of ability to pay. This can be achieved either through differential tariffs or by a subsidy or grant system, which is carefully targeted at those who have a low income.[81] There are still challenges to making tariffs affordable. Although households may contribute significantly to water and sanitation services through payments for self-supply or to an informal or community system, there is little information available on these spending patterns.[82] As a result it can be difficult to know the impact on different populations of the costs of water and sanitation services, or whether these services meet affordability standards.

Connection charges can also be a barrier for households if they are set too high or fail to differentiate between low- and high-income households. Some regulatory bodies have reduced or

---

Employment of Manual Scavengers and Construction of Dry Latrines (Prohibition) Act, 1993; Prohibition of Employment as Manual Scavengers and their Rehabilitation Act, 2013; *Safai Karamchari Andolan and Ors. v Union of India (UOI) and Ors* 2014(4) SCALE 165 Supreme Court of India Writ Petition (Civil).

[79]   International Water and Sanitation Centre, Financing WASH services – and turning water into wealth <www.ircwash.org/news/financing-wash-services>.

[80]   Catarina de Albuquerque, 'Report of the Special Rapporteur on the Human Right to Safe Drinking Water and Sanitation to the UNGA on Financing' (3 August 2011) A/66/255 para 20.

[81]   P. Berkowitz, Water Budget Monitoring Education Tool (Centre for Applied Legal Studies and Mvula Trust, 2009), pp 31–41 <www.wits.ac.za/files/res1d6124c660eb4720ae7ff305301c604e.pdf>.

[82]   WHO, UN-Water, GLAAS – The Challenge of Extending and Sustainable Services (2012) p 25.

eliminated connection charges, incorporating the costs into the tariff structure.[83] Pro-poor units within a utility can have a positive impact on ensuring that services are extended to informal settlements, and that the services (including connection charges) are affordable for the poor.[84] However, research also shows that subsidized services are often still more beneficial to the non-poor, and this must be monitored and addressed.[85]

### 5.2.2 State revenue

In many countries, tariffs and other household expenditure can only be expected to cover part of the cost of ensuring access to water and sanitation services, particularly in countries with low rates of access to piped supplies, where significant investment is required,[86] or where there is a significant proportion of the population that is low-income.

Different approaches to revenue-raising affect different population groups differently; for example, value-added taxes (VAT), or consumption taxes, are acknowledged to impact people on low incomes the hardest.[87] Progressive tax regimes that make use of income and wealth taxes are generally a more equitable solution from the perspective of non-discrimination and equality.[88]

Where user contributions and government resources are insufficient, States must request external or international assistance to fill the gap.[89] This may come from donor funding; from bilateral or non-governmental organizations; from loans from banks (national, regional or international) or private sector investments.

These resources are sometimes reflected in the government's budget, but even where they are not, they can have a significant effect on how a State decides to allocate resources to specific sectors, programs and projects.

### 5.2.3 Budgetary allocations

The process for determining budgetary allocations to different regions or areas should take into account existing disparities and inequalities, so that disadvantaged individuals and groups receive higher (and targeted) allocations even when they are living in regions that are otherwise adequately served.[90] It is important to ensure sufficient allocations to informal settlements in urban areas, which often receive smaller per capita allocations than formal settlements.

---

[83] See, for example, Portuguese water regulator, ERSAR <www.ersar.pt/website_en>.

[84] Water and Sanitation Program, Setting up pro-Poor Units to Improve Service Delivery (2009) <www.wsp.org/sites/wsp.org/files/publications/service_delivery_field_note.pdf>.

[85] M. Kariuki et al., Do pro-poor policies increase water coverage? An analysis of service delivery in Kampala's informal settlements (World Bank, 2014) <www.wsp.org/sites/wsp.org/files/publications/Kampala-Service-Delivery-Analysis-Water-PPP.pdf >.

[86] Christelle Pezon, A Water Bank: Securing financing to develop water services to all and for life in low and middle income countries (19 May 2014) <www.ircwash.org/blog/water-bank-securing-financing-develop-water-services-all-and-life-low-and-middle-income>.

[87] Poverty and Social Exclusion, Poorest hit hardest by consumption taxes <http://www.poverty.ac.uk/editorial/poorest-hit-hardest-consumption-taxes>.

[88] R. Balakrishnan et al., Maximum available resources and human rights (Centre for Women's Global Leadership, 2011) pp 11–12 <www.cwgl.rutgers.edu/economic-a-social-rights/380-maximum-available-resources-a-human-rights-analytical-report->.

[89] CESCR, General Comment No. 3 para 13.

[90] Catarina de Albuquerque, 'Report of the Special Rapporteur on the Human Rights to Water and Sanitation, Financing' (3 August 2011) A/66/255 paras 41–44 and 60–71.

Investments and planning must also take into account the long-term costs of water or sanitation provision, in order to avoid retrogression. Too little attention is currently paid to the operation and maintenance costs of providing services, and this has led to loss of access for some communities that had previously received good quality services.[91]

In some countries, recognition of water and sanitation as human rights has been interpreted by States (and others) to mean that access to these human rights should be free or universally subsidized.[92] State subsidies, however, tend to be appropriated by the non-poor, partly because imposed conditions (such as proof of habitation, which people living in informal settlements will not have) are too stringent for those living in poverty to comply with, and partly because the non-poor are better informed and better able to take advantage of subsidies. Where States have decided to provide subsidies to disadvantaged individuals to ensure affordability, these must be carefully designed to reach the intended recipients.[93]

### 5.2.4   Addressing corruption

Widely defined as 'the abuse of entrusted power for personal gain',[94] corruption is both a cause and a result of the State's failure to realize the human rights to water and sanitation and leads to human rights violations. Common examples of corruption in the water sector include falsified meter readings, bribery for new connections, favoritism in public procurement and nepotism in the allocation of public offices. Monopolies in the water and sanitation sectors, large-scale construction projects, limited transparency and accountability systems, high demand for water and resource scarcity all increase the risk of corruption.[95]

Decision-makers often neglect poorer areas when planning new water connections in favor of wealthier districts, due to corrupt practices such as nepotism and favoritism.[96] A lack of transparency in decisions about technology or the contracting of implementing agencies may also lead to more expensive or inappropriate choices. Corruption also affects prices directly when bribes have to be paid for repair work, or for water and sanitation connection or reconnection. All of these corrupt practices disproportionately affect poor and disadvantaged individuals and groups who lack the resources to pay bribes, and the voice to oppose the vested interests of elites. Corruption changes the rules of resource allocation, perpetuates exclusion and distorts accountability, leading to denials of human rights.

Anti-corruption measures and the promotion of human rights are mutually reinforcing. A strong legal structure that encompasses the human rights legal framework can clarify anti-corruption regulations and rules, enhance transparency in procedures, provide systematic

---

[91]   James Skinner, *Where Every Drop Counts: Tackling Rural Africa's Water Crisis* (IIED, 2009).

[92]   Katherine Purvis, 'Water is a human right … but it can have a price' The Guardian (20 October 2016)   <www.theguardian.com/global-development-professionals-network/2016/oct/20/water-human-right-price-united-nations>.

[93]   Luis Andres et al., 'Doing More with Less: Smarter Subsidies for Water Supply and Sanitation' (World Bank 2019) <https://openknowledge.worldbank.org/handle/10986/32277>.

[94]   D. Zinnbauer and R. Dobson, Global Corruption Report 2008: Corruption in the Water Sector (Transparency International 2008) p.6 <www.transparency.org/whatwedo/pub/global_corruption_report_2008_corruption_in_the_water_sector>.

[95]   Water Integrity Network, Policy Brief: Preventing corruption in the water sector (2012) p 1.

[96]   International Council on Human Rights Policy and Transparency International, Integrating human rights in the anti-corruption agenda: Challenges, possibilities and opportunities (2010) pp 7–8: <www.ichrp.org/files/reports/58/131b_report.pdf>.

mechanisms to ensure accountability and render sanctions more effective. The UN Convention Against Corruption underlines the importance of active participation in planning by individuals and groups that are outside the public sector in order to address corruption.[97] Public participation can help limit opportunities for corruption through social monitoring by civil society and independent institutions.[98]

## 5.3 Monitoring

Monitoring is essential to assessing whether States and other actors, including service providers, are complying with the human rights to water and sanitation, and is a prerequisite for holding States and other actors to account for violations or offenses. States have the primary obligation to ensure independent monitoring of all components of the human rights to water and sanitation, as well as to oversee the monitoring undertaken by other national entities or bodies – such as (private or public) service providers.[99] This monitoring should be complemented by the oversight activities of national civil society organizations and of international institutions.

Monitoring of compliance with the human rights to water and sanitation will often be different from the more technical monitoring undertaken by different subnational, national and international bodies, which measure numbers of latrines or the functionality of waterpoints. States must adopt indicators that reflect the legal content of the human rights to water and sanitation. These indicators should be designed not only to measure the outcome in terms of access figures, but also to capture the extent of government efforts and of progress made towards eliminating inequalities.[100] Monitoring must assess compliance with the obligation to progressively realize the rights to water and sanitation applying the maximum of available resources, and States must be held accountable for progress (or lack thereof) in realizing the human rights to water and sanitation. States must develop mechanisms and remedies to hold those accountable to adopted plans and established targets.

It is not acceptable to apply lower human rights standards for poorer or disadvantaged households, and any lower interim targets must not become long-term solutions but must be time-bound. Targets should include all dimensions of the rights to water and sanitation, including participatory rights and access to justice, and assessing progress in overcoming obstacles in access to justice, such as high costs, language requirements, requirements for representation and the geographical location of the courts and other mechanisms.

If not already determined by existing legislation, the monitoring of service provision by regulatory bodies should be an integral part of plans and strategies. There are a number of different mechanisms and institutions at the national and local levels that play a role in monitoring access to water and sanitation. These include State institutions (national statistical offices, line ministries and State-owned service providers), independent State bodies (such as national human rights institutions and independent regulators) and non-State institutions, including

---

[97]  UN Convention Against Corruption Article 13.
[98]  See n 70, p 4.
[99]  CESCR, General Comment No. 15 para 24.
[100]  Ibid para 53.

both service providers themselves and non-governmental and civil society organizations. Public access to relevant information must be ensured for effective monitoring.[101]

The principles of non-discrimination and equality oblige States to look beyond average achievements and to identify disparate impacts or less favorable treatment over time. There is currently a lack of data on many discriminatory practices and this neglect often coincides with a low political profile. The ways in which development, poverty and existing inequalities are measured have a tremendous influence on the direction of policies, the allocation of resources and, ultimately, the effectiveness of responses.

## 6.   OBLIGATIONS OF SERVICE PROVIDERS: THE REGULATORY FRAMEWORK

States rely on a wide range of service providers for the rights to water and sanitation: formal and informal; public, private or public–private partnerships; large and small companies. While the human rights framework does not dictate a particular form of service provision, the State retains its human rights obligations, continuing to bear the duty to ensure access to water and sanitation, regardless of the type of provider chosen.[102] Every service provider, whether formal or informal, publicly or privately owned, must understand what is required of the service in order to comply with the rights to water and sanitation and adapt its procedures, approaches and rules accordingly. States must ensure that the involvement of non-State actors does not result in human rights violations, for example because of disconnections or unaffordable tariffs.[103]

Service provision may be delegated to private companies, to public companies or to State-owned companies that are completely or mostly owned by the State but are legally distinct from the State itself and are therefore governed by commercial law. The State must ensure compliance with the rights to water and sanitation by creating an enabling environment, clarifying who is responsible for service provision and where, and ensuring effective regulation.

An effective regulatory system, based on human rights standards, is vital to ensuring the compliance of both State and non-State actors with the human rights to water and sanitation.[104] States have an obligation to ensure that all instruments for delegating service provision, including contracts, are in line with human rights standards and principles, and contribute to the realization of the human rights to water and sanitation.[105]

When involving non-State actors, States must use regulation as well as service contracts to clarify the service provider's responsibility to ensure affordable services. One of the concerns

---

[101]   K.M. Krchnak, 'Improving Water Governance through Increased Public Access to Information and Participation' (2005) 5 (1) Sustainable Development Law & Policy 34–48, 34–39 <http://digitalcommons.wcl.american.edu/cgi/viewcontent.cgi?article=1408&context=sdlp>.

[102]   HRC, Resolution: Human rights and access to safe drinking water and sanitation (6 October 2010) A/HRC/RES/15/9 paras 6 and 7.

[103]   General Comment No. 15 para 44 (b); Catarina de Albuquerque, 'Report of the Special Rapporteur on the Human Rights to Water and Sanitation on Non-State Service Provision' (17 June 2010) A/HRC/15/31.

[104]   OECD, Private sector participation in water infrastructure (2009) p.25.

[105]   Non-State Service Provision, 2010 (n 103) para 63f.

regarding non-State involvement in the water and sanitation sectors, particularly of transnational companies, is that the private sector often has more economic power than either the State (particularly at the local government level) or a regulatory body. States must ensure that price-setting, along with the setting of other national standards, such as quality, accessibility and service levels, can be managed effectively by the regulatory body.

In most developing countries, formal and informal service provision coexist, with informal provision responding to needs in areas not covered by formal provision. It has been estimated that up to 25 per cent of the urban population of Latin America and almost 50 per cent of the urban population in Africa relies to some extent on small-scale informal providers.[106]

The important role of informal and small-scale providers – both private, for-profit and charitable, non-governmental organizations – cannot therefore be ignored, despite generally operating on their own terms, using technologies and approaches that are unregulated, and compromising on standards such as affordability and quality. To date, far less attention has been paid to the regulation of informal, small-scale providers than to the regulation of utilities and large private companies. States are required to ensure that these operators at the least do not interfere with the enjoyment of the human rights to water and to sanitation, and in the best case that they contribute to the realization of these rights. Legal instruments to regulate the informal water and sanitation sector must be adapted to the decentralized and localized nature of small-scale service provision.[107] It is difficult for a central agency to adequately oversee the activities of small-scale providers, so a different institutional set-up may be required, managed by local governments.[108]

## 6.1 Disconnections and Rationing

A disconnection is the interruption of the delivery of water (and sanitation, in the case of water-borne sanitation systems) and can be temporary or permanent. Disconnections must be restricted to circumstances in which they are justifiable in human rights terms.[109]

Disconnection of services due to inability to pay is unjustified, and constitutes a violation of the human rights to water and sanitation.[110] Disconnection due to non-payment is only permissible if it can be shown that the householder is able to pay but is not paying – in other words, that the tariff is affordable. States must ensure they have effective administrative and judiciary systems that provide the opportunity for individuals to challenge disconnections and receive appropriate remedies. In a case heard at the High Court in Zimbabwe, it was found that because water is a human right, access can only be denied with 'just cause', and service

---

[106] L. Sima and M. Elimelech, 'The Informal Small-scale Water Services in Developing Countries: The Business of Water for Those without Formal Municipal Connections' in J.M.H. Selendy (ed), *Water and Sanitation-related Diseases and the Environment: Challenges, Interventions, and Preventive Measures* (Wiley-Blackwell 2011) p 231.

[107] Catarina de Albuquerque, 'Report of the Independent Expert on human rights obligations related to access to water and sanitation, Non-State Service Provision' (29 June 2010) (A/HRC/15/31).

[108] See, for example, Hydroconseil, Urban Briefing Note. Improving water services in the periurban areas of Maputo, Mozambique: the role of independent providers (2008).

[109] OHCHR, UN-Habitat and WHO, The right to water, Fact Sheet No. 35 (2010) p 34.

[110] General Comment No. 15 para 44a.

providers – in this case the city council – cannot disconnect water supplies without a court order.[111]

When water is scarce or the water service provider is carrying out maintenance or repair work, temporary (but not permanent) disconnections may be justified, but the State has to ensure that its core obligations are fulfilled: it must continue to provide an essential amount of water, and those affected must be informed of the timing and duration of any temporary disconnections.[112] If it becomes necessary to ration water because of scarcity, it is crucial that the most vulnerable or marginalized people are not disproportionately affected.

## 7.    ACCESS TO JUSTICE AND EFFECTIVE REMEDIES FOR THE RIGHTS TO WATER AND SANITATION

The justiciability of economic, social and cultural rights, including the human rights to water and sanitation, has been challenged in the past, but today this debate has become largely irrelevant.[113] At the international level, the question was finally resolved with the adoption of the Optional Protocol to the International Covenant on Economic, Social and Cultural Rights, which entered into force in 2013.[114] The question should no longer be whether the rights to water and sanitation are justiciable or whether courts have a role to play in their enforcement, but rather how courts can best fulfill that role in a meaningful way.

### 7.1    Incorporating the Rights to Water and Sanitation in National Legal Frameworks

While States are free to choose how they realize human rights Article 2 (1) of the ICESCR requires that States employ 'all appropriate by all appropriate means, including particularly the adoption of legislative measures' for the realization of Covenant rights. States must ensure 'sufficient recognition of this right within the national political and legal systems, preferably by way of legislative implementation'.[115] International human rights law does not oblige States to include a guarantee of the human rights to water and sanitation in their constitutions, nor does it prescribe whether such a guarantee should be explicit or implicit, as long as effective remedies are ensured. However, a constitutional guarantee is highly desirable if the rights are to have meaning within the legal framework of a country.

The human right to water, and to a lesser extent the human right to sanitation, have been included in many constitutions adopted in recent years. In 2004, Uruguay became the first State to include an explicit guarantee of the human rights to water and sanitation in its Constitution, stating in Article 47 that 'access to clean water and access to sanitation constitute fundamental human rights'.

---

[111]    *Farai Mushoriwa v City of Harare* (30 April 2014) 1 HH HC 4266/13, High Court Zimbabwe.

[112]    See Drinking Water Inspectorate, Private water supplies – case study (2011/12) <http://dwi.defra.gov.uk/stakeholders/private-water-supplies/case-studies/2011-12.pdf>.

[113]    See Chapter 2.

[114]    Optional Protocol to the International Covenant on Economic, Social and Cultural Rights (OP-ICESCR) (5 March 2009) (A/RES/63/117).

[115]    General Comment No. 15 para 26.

India provides an example of an implicit constitutional guarantee of the rights to water and sanitation. While the rights to water and sanitation are not explicitly mentioned in the 1950 Constitution of India, settled case law from courts at both State and federal level interprets Article 21 of the Constitution – the right to life – as encompassing the right to safe and sufficient water and sanitation.[116]

In addition to constitutional or other recognition of the rights to water and sanitation, access to justice for these rights to water relies on multiple laws, regulations and policies establishing clear, enforceable standards. These may establish, for example, the quantity and continuity of water provision and the maximum time and distance people should have to travel to facilities. States may use international minimum standards as guidance, but should bear in mind that minimum standards may in some cases be greater than international minimum standards, based on the obligations of progressive realization within the maximum available resources), or they may fail to meet an individual's particular needs (as in the cases of people living with chronic diseases or of people with physical disabilities, who often require more water).[117]

## 7.2 Access to Justice for Violations of the Rights to Water and Sanitation

As described in the CESCR's General Comment No. 9, ensuring access to justice and effective remedies is a critical component of State obligations under the ICESCR. Unfortunately, access to justice is often unavailable for violations of the rights to water and sanitation, particularly for marginalized communities. Nevertheless, there is a growing body of jurisprudence from domestic courts, as well as regional and international human rights bodies, showing that all aspects of the rights to water and sanitation, encompassing obligations of respect, protect and fulfill, can be effectively adjudicated and effective remedies provided.

### 7.2.1 Access to justice for violations of the obligation to respect

Courts and human rights bodies have most frequently addressed violations of the obligation to respect the rights to water and sanitation, as these tend to fall most easily within traditional understandings of human rights violations resulting from State action. Some courts have relied on international norms described above to apply domestic law.

The Court of Appeal of Botswana, for example, relied on the right to water as set out in General Comment No. 15, and the General Assembly resolution on the right to water and sanitation, to interpret constitutional provisions.[118] It found that preventing a community of Bushmen from accessing their traditional boreholes amounted to inhuman and degrading treatment. In the context of informal settlements in Argentina, a court found that a discontinuation of water supplied with tanker trucks violated the rights to 'a healthy environment and dignified housing', ordering the resumption of water provision as well as the progressive improvement

---

[116] Anuja Mishra, 'Right to Water as a Human right and Indian Constitution: An analysis of various judgments of Apex Court of India' (April 2018) 23 (4) IOSR Journal of Humanities And Social Science 45–48.

[117] Catarina de Albuquerque, 'Report of the Special Rapporteur on the human rights to water and sanitation, National and local planning for the implementation of the rights to water and sanitation' (4 July 2011) A/HRC/18/33 para 31.

[118] *Mosetlhanyane & Ors v The Attorney General*, 2011, Civil Appeal No. CACLB-074-10, Court of Appeal of the Republic of Botswana paras 19.1, 19.2 and 22.

of the water distribution system.[119] In another case in Argentina, a court considered the situation of impoverished neighborhoods in Córdoba, where wells had been contaminated with fecal and other matter from a water treatment plant overflowing with untreated sewage.[120] The court ordered the municipality to take urgent measures to address the situation, including providing 200 liters of safe water per household per day until a permanent solution was found.

Other cases dealing with violations of the obligation to respect arise from the criminalization of activities linked to access to water or sanitation, such as the prohibition of public defecation or urination when no other options are available. A court in the United States struck down ordinances preventing homeless people from engaging in life-sustaining activities linked to the right to sanitation: 'The harmless conduct for which they are arrested is inseparable from their involuntary condition of being homeless. Consequently, arresting homeless people for harmless acts they are forced to perform in public effectively punishes them for being homeless.'[121]

Courts have also addressed issues of systemic discrimination in access to water and sanitation. In a case in Florida, the court ruled that the municipality could not implement any infrastructure in white majority areas until the African-American majority areas that lacked provision of water were on par with those areas.[122] Similarly, the European Committee of Social Rights ordered remedial action to improve the situation with regard to access to water for Roma.[123]

State action to interfere with access to water has also been found to violate the right to life. The Colombian Constitutional Court found that the disconnection of water services to a woman with chronic kidney failure violated the right to life and ordered the reinstatement of the service.[124] The UN Human Rights Committee found that Bulgaria had violated the right to the protection of home and family, as well as the rights to life and non-discrimination, by allowing the Municipality of Sofia to disconnect the water supply to a Roma community.[125] The Committee requested Bulgaria to issue interim measures requiring the authorities to reconnect the water supply. The Inter-American Court of Human Rights has determined that denying an indigenous community access to ancestral lands denied them access to water and sanitation and violated the right to life.[126]

---

[119]   *Asociación Civil por la Igualdad y la Justicia c/ GCBA s/ Amparo*, Argentina (18 July 2007), Expte. N° 20.898/0 Camara de Apelaciones en lo Contencioso Administrativo y Tributario de la Cdad. de Bs. As., Sala I.

[120]   *Marchisio José Bautista y Otros, Acción de Amparo* (Expte. No 500003/36) (19 October 2004) Ciudad de Córdoba, Primera Instancia y 8a Nominación en lo Civil y Comercial.

[121]   *Pottinger v City of Miami*, 810 F. Supp. 1551 (16 November 1992) District Court, SD Florida, United States.

[122]   *Dowdell and Others v City of Apopka, Florida*, 698 F. 2d 1181 (28 February 1983) United States Court of Appeals, Eleventh Circuit.

[123]   *European Roma Rights Centre v Portugal*, Complaint No. 61/2010 (30 June 2011) European Committee of Social Rights.

[124]   *Flor Enid Jiménez de Correa c/ Empresas Públicas de Medellín* (17 April 2007) T-270/07 Corte Constitucional de Colombia.

[125]   HRC, Communication No. 2073/2011, *Liliana Assenova Naidenova et al. v Bulgaria* (30 October 2012) CCPR/C/106/D/207/2011 paras 9 and 14.2.

[126]   *Yakye Axa Indigenous Community v Paraguay* (17 June 2005), Inter-American Court of Human Rights.

**7.2.2    Access to justice for violations of the obligation to protect**

Courts have also addressed violations of the obligation to protect the rights to water and sanitation, where States have failed to enact and enforce necessary protections from human rights abuses by third parties. The Costa Rican Supreme Court ordered authorities to assess whether a permit should be granted to build a pipeline that would withdraw water from an aquifer, in order to make sure that the pipeline would not deprive the local population of water for personal and domestic use, in violation of the residents' rights, including to a healthy environment.[127] A French court similarly found that a public water company must ensure that the water it provides is not detrimentally impacted by agricultural runoff.[128]

In the well-known case of *SERAC v Nigeria*, discussed in Chapter 3, the African Commission on Human and Peoples' Rights found violations, inter alia, of the rights to life and to health, owing to the failure of the government of Nigeria to monitor the impact of oil operations polluting water in the Niger Delta.[129]

Courts have also required governments to provide protection from stigmatization and discrimination in relation to water and sanitation. The Supreme Court of India observed that 'manual scavengers are considered as untouchables by other mainstream castes and are thrown into a vortex of severe social and economic exploitation', holding that the State must act to prevent the continuation of manual scavenging.[130] In Nepal, the Supreme Court issued an order to eliminate the practice of chaupadi, which forces menstruating women and girls to sleep in isolation from the rest of the family, in a hut or shed, with risks to their health and security. The Court declared that the practice was discriminatory against women and ordered the government to conduct a study on the impact of the practice, to create awareness and to take measures to eliminate it.[131]

Courts have also required governments to ensure adequate participation in the realization of the rights to water and sanitation. In the *Beja* case, a South African court found that a denial of meaningful engagement and effective community participation in decision-making regarding the design and installation of toilets violated constitutional rights.[132]

International organizations may also contribute to the perpetration of violations of the rights to water and sanitation. The United Nations Stabilization Mission in Haiti has come under scrutiny for its role in the cholera epidemic in Haiti in the aftermath of the 2010 earthquake

---

[127]   Sala Constitucional de la Corte Suprema de Justicia, Costa Rica, Sentencia 2009-000262 (14 January 2009).

[128]   *Cour de cassation, Chambre civile 1, France, M. X c. Syndicat d'Adduction d'Eau du Trégor*, 30 May 2006, No de pourvoi: 03-16335.

[129]   *The Social and Economic Rights Action Center and the Center for Economic and Social Rights v Nigeria*, African Commission on Human and Peoples' Rights, App. No. 155/96, 27 October 2001.

[130]   *Safai Karamchari Andolan and Ors. v Union Of India and Ors.* (March 27, 2014) Writ Petition (C) No. 583 of 2003, Supreme Court of India paras 2, 15.

[131]   *Dil Bahadur Bishwakarma v Government of Nepal* (2 May 2006) Writ Petition 3303 of 2004, Supreme Court of Nepal; see also Kabita Pandey, 'Judicial Education on the Convention on Elimination of Discrimination against Women in Nepal' in Anne Hellum and Henriette Sinding Aasen (eds) *Women's Human Rights, CEDAW in International, Regional and National Law* (CUP 2013) p.425; CESCR Concluding Observations, Nepal (16 January 2008) E/C.12/NPL/CO/2 paras 15 and 34.

[132]   *Beja and Others v Premier of the Western Cape and Others* (29 April 2011) 21332/10 High Court of South Africa (Western Cape High Court, Cape Town) para 146 and note 38.

which killed over 8,500 people.[133] In a challenge brought before US courts, however, the US Court of Appeals ruled that the UN is immune from liability under US law.[134]

### 7.2.3   Access to justice for violations of the obligation to fulfill

Violations of the obligation to fulfill may be the most critical category of violations, affecting a large number of victims, yet they have generally received the least attention from courts. Potential claimants face considerable challenges in gaining access to justice for alleged structural or systemic violations. Jurisprudence, including the standards of review developed by courts in recent years, has demonstrated, however, that violations of the obligation to fulfill the rights to water and sanitation can and should be adjudicated and subject to effective remedies.

As discussed in other chapters,[135] a seminal decision on the obligation to progressively realize socio-economic rights was the *Grootboom* case, in which the Constitutional Court of South Africa considered the plight of a community lacking basic shelter, sanitation facilities and access to clean water.[136] To determine whether the State had complied with the obligation of progressive realization, the court held that a reasonable program must: be comprehensive, coherent and coordinated; be capable of facilitating the realization of the right; prioritize the needs of those in the most desperate situations; make appropriate financial and human resources available; be balanced and flexible; make appropriate provision for short-, medium- and long-term needs; be reasonably conceived and implemented; and be transparent. The Court found that the State's programs failed to address as a priority the circumstances of those in the most desperate situations and required the government to take measures to correct this.[137] In the subsequent case of *Mazibuko*,[138] on the right to water, however, the Court failed to apply the more rigorous standard described in the *Grootboom* decision. As described in Chapter 13, the reasonableness standard had been developed in its earlier jurisprudence. The Court dismissed a challenge to the City of Johannesburg's installation of pre-paid water meters in Phiri to charge consumers for use of water in excess of an allowance of 6 kiloliters of water per month, noting however that the litigation itself had ensured that 'continual revision of the policy in the ensuing years has improved the policy in a manner entirely consistent with an obligation of progressive realization'.[139]

Courts have also considered issues of retrogression in rights to water and sanitation. A significant judgment from the Supreme Administrative Court of Greece blocked the planned privatization of the Athens Water Supply and Sewerage Company, on the basis that it could

---

[133] Quoted in Trenton Daniel, 'UN official makes rare case for compensation for Haiti cholera victims', Huffington Post, 10/08/13.

[134] *Georges v United Nations*, 834 F. 3d 88 – Court of Appeals, 2nd Circuit 2016.

[135] See Chapters 10 and 13.

[136] *Government of the Republic of South Africa and Others v Grootboom and Others*, 2000 (11) BCLR 1169 (CC). A/HRC/27/55 12.

[137] Ibid para 96.

[138] *Mazibuko and Others v City of Johannesburg and Others* (2010) (4) SA 1 (CC) (Mazibuko CC); for an in depth analysis of this case, see Jackie Dugard, 'Testing the Transformative Premise of the South African Constitutional Court: A Comparison of High Courts, Supreme Court of Appeal and Constitutional Court Socio-economic Rights Decisions, 1994–2015' (2016) 20 IJHR <http://dx.doi.org/10.1080/13642987.2016.1227324>.

[139] Ibid para 163.

put public health at risk due to the anticipated deterioration of water and sanitation quality.[140] The Portuguese auditing institution found that, by not sharing risks and benefits equally, private–public partnerships largely benefit the private sector, that they are detrimental to the people and that services are often of lower quality, while higher prices are charged.[141]

The Constitutional Court of Colombia, for example, has required authorities to connect housing to water and sewerage and to ensure a sufficient daily amount of water.[142] The Supreme Court of India ordered a municipality to provide basic sanitation to an informal settlement, stating that 'decency and dignity are non-negotiable facets of human rights and are a first charge on local self-governing bodies'.[143]

Courts have also required States to provide services in places of detention, in schools or other public institutions and in times of emergency. The Indian Supreme Court ordered schools to provide adequate toilet facilities in schools.[144] Relying on empirical research showing that 'parents do not send their children (particularly girls) to schools'[145] where sanitation facilities are not provided, the Court found that a lack of toilets violated the right to education. The High Court of Fiji held that prisoners' right to freedom from inhuman and degrading treatment was violated by lack of access to adequate sanitation facilities.[146] The Human Rights Committee, as well as regional human rights bodies, has found human rights violations in a number of cases in which prisoners have been denied access to sanitation.[147]

## 8.  CONCLUSION

The decade which has passed since the rights to water and sanitation were finally recognized as human rights by the United Nations has seen significant progress in understanding their content, principles and obligations, as well as developing laws, policies and practices for the realization of these rights. Dramatic inequalities in access to safe drinking water and sanitation continue, however, and the scale of systemic violations of the rights to water and sanitation remains massive. It is estimated that one in ten people (785 million) still lack basic water

---

[140]  Decision of the Council of State 1906/2014 of 28 May 2014, available from <www.ste.gr/portal/page/portal/StE/ProsfatesApofaseis>.

[141]  Auditoria à Regulação de PPP no Sector das Águas (sistemas em baixa) – Volume I do Relatório Síntese – Fevereiro 2014 <www.tcontas.pt/pt-pt/ProdutosTC/Relatorios/RelatoriosAuditoria/Documents/2014/rel003-2014-2s.pdf>.

[142]  *Hernán Galeano Díaz c/ Empresas Públicas de Medellín ESP y Marco Gómez Otero y Otros c/ Hidropacífico SA ESP y Otros* (5 August 2010) Corte Constitucional, Ninth Chamber of Revision.

[143]  *Municipal Council, Ratlam v Shri Vardhichand & Others*, SCR (1) 97, 29 July 1980.

[144]  *Environment & Consumer Protection Foundation v Delhi Administration* 2012 STPL(Web) 543 SC.

[145]  Ibid para 4.

[146]  *State v Senijieli Boila and Pita Nainoka* (25 October 2004) Fiji HAC032D.04S High Court (Suva).

[147]  See, for example, Human Rights Committee, *M. Robinson v Jamaica*, Communication No. 731/1996, (29 March 2000) in A/55/40 (vol. II), p.128 paras 10.1–10.2; *Institute for Human Rights and Development in Africa v Angola* (22 May 2008) African Commission on Human and Peoples' Rights; *Eugen Gabriel Radu v Romania* (13 October 2009) European Court of Human Rights, Third Section; *Paul Lallion v Grenada*, Case 11.765, Report No. 55/02, Inter-Am. C.H.R., Doc. 5 rev. 1 at 551 (2002).

services, including 144 million who have to drink untreated surface water. In all, two billion people still lack basic sanitation.[148]

These systemic human rights violations can only be effectively addressed through a rights-based framework – the essential features of which have been described in this chapter. More progress and refinement is needed in understanding how best to implement and realize the rights to water and sanitation, but what is most urgently needed is political will on the part of governments, support for meaningful participation of stakeholders and accountability to the human rights norms described above, including through access to justice.

---

[148] Unicef and World Health Organization, Progress on drinking water, sanitation and hygiene 2000–2017: Special focus on inequalities (June 2019) pp.7–8.

# 12. The right to work and rights at work

*Virginia Brás Gomes*

## 1. INTRODUCTION

The right to work and rights at work are enshrined in a number of core human rights treaties that set out obligations for States to respect, promote, protect and realize these rights. All along the period in which the various core human rights treaties were being negotiated, over a span of 50 years, States recognized the relevance of the right to work and rights at work for all those living under their jurisdiction. The formulation of the provisions in the various treaties evolved along the years not only to reflect on-going challenges in general but also to integrate contemporary issues related to the protection of specific groups, such as workers in the informal economy and migrant workers.

The International Covenant on Economic, Social and Cultural Rights (ICESCR or the Covenant)[1] deals more comprehensively than any other human rights treaty with the right to work and rights at work as universal, interdependent and interconnected rights. This chapter draws extensively on the Covenant itself, as well as on its interpretation in the General Comments (GC) of the Committee on Economic, Social and Cultural Rights (the CESCR or Committee), which has often relied on the standard-setting role of the International Labour Organization (ILO) in relation to the general application of employment, protection of wages, labor inspection, occupational safety and health-related Conventions and Recommendations, and specific instruments setting out protection standards for certain groups of workers. Seeking to illustrate trends and obstacles to the realization of labor rights in different regions of the world, the chapter also makes reference to the concluding observations of the Committee to states parties to the Covenant at the end of the reporting cycle.

## 2. LEGAL PROVISIONS AND CROSS-CUTTING PRINCIPLES IN CORE HUMAN RIGHTS TREATIES

The Universal Declaration of Human Rights (UDHR)[2] (Article 23.1–4) refers to the right of everyone to work, to free choice of employment, to just and favorable conditions of work and to protection against unemployment. It also guarantees the right to equal work without any discrimination as well as to form and to join trade unions for the protection of workers' interests.[3] The UDHR recognizes that everyone who works has the right to just and favorable remuneration ensuring for himself and his family an existence worthy of human dignity, and supplemented, if necessary, by other means of social protection. This is indeed a holistic and

---

[1]    Adopted 16 December 1966, entered into force 3 January 1976, 993 UNTS 3.
[2]    Adopted 10 December 1948 A/810 at 71 (1948).
[3]    The right to freedom of association for the protection of interests is reiterated in the International Covenant on Civil and Political Rights (ICCPR), which also prohibits forced or compulsory labor.

far-ranging provision in so far as it highlights the universality of the right – the importance of just remuneration for workers and their families to live in dignity, with recourse, if necessary, to other social protection measures.

In 1990, years after the UDHR's entry into force, the Convention on the Rights of all Migrant Workers and Members of their Families (CMW)[4] established that migrant workers shall enjoy treatment not less favorable than that which applies to nationals of the State of employment in respect of remuneration, other conditions of work and terms of employment. Moreover, it requires states parties to take all appropriate measures to ensure that migrant workers are not deprived of any rights derived from this principle by reason of any irregularity in their stay or employment. In particular, it stipulates that employers shall not be relieved of any legal or contractual obligations; nor shall their obligations be limited in any manner by reason of such irregularity (Article 25). The right to join any trade union and to seek its aid and assistance is also included in this Convention (Article 26).

In turn, the Convention on the Rights of Persons with Disabilities (CRPD)[5] recognizes persons with disabilities' rights to work and employment on an equal basis with others, including the right to the opportunity to gain a living by work freely chosen or accepted in a labor market and a work environment that is open, inclusive and accessible to persons with disabilities. States parties must ensure that persons with disabilities are not held in slavery or in servitude, and are protected, on an equal basis with others, from forced or compulsory labor (Article 27 in its entirety).

Comprehensive anti-discrimination treaties such as the Convention on the Elimination of all Forms of Racial Discrimination (CERD)[6] and the Convention on the Elimination of all Forms of Discrimination against Women (CEDAW)[7] establish the obligation for States to eliminate discrimination in the enjoyment of all human rights, including the right to work and rights at work.

The CERD calls for the elimination of racial discrimination in all its forms, notably in the enjoyment of economic, social and cultural rights (ESCR), in particular the rights to work, to free choice of employment, to just and favorable conditions of work, to protection against unemployment, to equal pay for equal work, to just and favorable remuneration and to form and join trade unions (Article 5(e)(i) and (ii)).

In relation to women, the CEDAW requires the elimination of discrimination in the field of employment in order to ensure, on a basis of equality of men and women, the same rights, in particular, the right to work as an inalienable right of all human beings, including to the same employment opportunities; free choice of profession and employment; promotion, job security and all benefits and conditions of service; vocational training and retraining; equal remuneration; social security; paid leave; and protection of health and safety in working conditions; among others (Article 11(1)(a)).

On a different note, the Convention on the Rights of the Child (CRC) guarantees the right of all children to be protected from economic exploitation and from performing any work that is likely to be hazardous or to interfere with their education, or to be harmful to their health or physical, mental, spiritual, moral or social development (Article 32(1)). However, in stark violation of the Convention, '[a] total of 152 million children – 64 million girls and 88 million

---

[4]   Adopted 18 December 1990, entered into force 1 July 2003, 2220 UNTS 3.
[5]   Adopted 13 December 2006, entered into force 3 May 2008, 2515 UNTS 3.
[6]   Adopted 7 March 1966, entered into force 4 January 1969, 660 UNTS 195.
[7]   Adopted 18 December 1979, entered into force 3 September 1981, 12449 UNTS 13.

boys – are estimated to be in child labour globally, accounting for almost one in ten of all children worldwide'.[8]

The principles of universality, indivisibility, interdependence and interconnectedness, non-discrimination and equality, participation of rights holders, accountability of duty bearers and access to justice are cross-cutting in both the International Covenant on Civil and Political Rights (ICCPR) and the ICESCR,[9] as well in the other treaties.

In spite of some progress in repealing direct discrimination in laws and policies, there are still plenty of examples of indirect discrimination in the access to and enjoyment of labor rights embodied in laws and regulations that are neutral in their formulation but discriminatory in the result. The most important gaps lie in the lack of recognition by States of intersectional or compounded discrimination and the particularly negative and long lasting effects it has on women and persons belonging to vulnerable groups. There is also a lack of recognition of systemic discrimination based on deeply rooted societal prejudices that require a huge change in mindsets. Governments are reluctant to recognize such discrimination because it amounts to a failure of the measures they have taken to combat discrimination without really addressing its root causes. One only needs to look at discrimination against the poor, or minority groups such as the Dalits, or Roma people, or indigenous communities, to know this is true.

Public policies to fulfill women's rights may have eliminated formal discrimination to some extent but there is much to be done in adopting measures for the elimination of de facto discrimination. A good example in the context of labor rights is that progress on the three key interrelated indicators for gender equality is far from satisfactory. The glass ceiling that hinders the access of women to top decision-making posts in public services and private sector companies, the gender pay gap that calls for equal pay for work of equal value, and the sticky floor that perpetuates vertical and horizontal job segregation for women remain practical obstacles to women's substantive equality. Work-related gender-based inequalities are well documented and absolutely need to be corrected, due to the high economic and social costs they entail and the violations of women's labor rights they perpetuate.

Meaningful participation of rights holders and accountability of duty bearers are increasingly relevant for the full enjoyment of all human rights. In fact, they are two sides of the same coin. All rights holders, in particular the most disadvantaged, should be guaranteed the means to participate in decisions that affect the enjoyment of their rights. At the collective level, civil society organizations constituted by citizens who organize themselves formally and informally around common interests of a particular sector or the whole of society (for example, grass-roots organizations, welfare associations, advocacy networks or social movements, platforms, federations and alliances) should also participate in policy making, implementation and evaluation.

The CESCR underlines the importance of consultation in formulating, implementing, reviewing and monitoring laws and policies related to the right to work and rights at work not

---

8    UNICEF, 'Child Labour and Exploitation' <www.unicef.org/rosa/what-we-do/child-protection/child-labour-and-exploitation>.

9    The States Parties to the ICCPR and ICESCR undertake to guarantee that the rights enunciated in the Covenants will be exercised without discrimination of any kind as to race, color, sex, language, religion, political or other opinion, national or social origin, property, birth or other status (ICCPR Article 2(1) and ICESCR Article 2(2)). The States Parties to the Covenants also undertake to ensure the equal right of men and women to the enjoyment of all the rights guaranteed in the Covenants (ICCPR Article 3 and ICESCR Article 3).

only with traditional social partners such as workers and employers and their representative organizations, but also with other relevant organizations, such as those representing persons with disabilities, younger and older persons, women, workers in the informal economy, migrants and lesbian, gay, bisexual, transgender and intersex (LGBTI) persons, as well as representatives of ethnic groups and indigenous communities.[10]

Accountability of duty bearers at all levels needs to be exercised in an accessible, transparent and effective manner. In terms of the enjoyment of ESCR, given that many of the functions of the central government have been decentralized to sub-national and local public and private institutions, there needs to be a clear understanding of what is the responsibility of the different levels as well as human rights training for all those involved in making rights real on the ground without discrimination.

In relation to labor rights, States are accountable for taking measures to ensure that third parties, such as private sector employers and enterprises, do not interfere with the enjoyment of these rights and comply with their obligations. This includes taking steps to prevent, investigate, punish and redress abuse through effective laws and policies and adjudication.

There is now a general agreement that the respect, protection and realization of labor rights involves various extraterritorial dimensions. States must refrain from acts or omissions that interfere, either directly or indirectly, with the realization of these rights in other countries. They should also take measures, including legislative measures, to clarify that their nationals, as well as enterprises domiciled in their territory and/or jurisdiction, are required to respect labor rights throughout their operations extraterritorially. This responsibility is particularly important for States with advanced labor law systems, as home-country enterprises can help to improve standards for working conditions in host countries.[11]

Finally, and perhaps the most important of all the human rights principles, is access to justice, since it enables the rights holder to access an entitlement rather than being a mere receiver of policy benefits depending on political will and resource allocation. All rights holders should have full access to effective remedies in case of violation of their rights, at national, regional and international levels. Effective remedies in case of violations of their rights include reparation, restitution, rehabilitation, satisfaction and guarantees of non-repetition. The right to an effective remedy does not always need to be interpreted as requiring a judicial remedy, since administrative remedies will, in some cases, be adequate. What is important to reiterate is that those living under the jurisdiction of a State have a legitimate expectation, based on the principle of good faith, that all administrative authorities will take account of human rights principles in their decision-making. Any such administrative remedies should be accessible, affordable, timely and effective. Appropriate remedies for the violation of human rights can also become effective by decisions of national human rights institutions, equality commissions and ombudspersons' offices.

Business enterprises, irrespective of size, sector, ownership and structure, should comply with laws that are consistent with the ICESCR, avoiding infringements and addressing any abuse of the right as a consequence of their actions. In situations in which a business enterprise has caused or contributed to adverse impacts, the enterprise should remedy the damage or

---

[10]    CESCR, General Comment No. 23: The Right to Just and Favourable Conditions of Work (27 April 2016) E/C.12/GC/23 para 56.

[11]    See ibid paras 69–73 (on extraterritorial and international obligations in various contexts).

cooperate in its remediation through legitimate processes that meet recognized standards of due process.[12]

## 3.    UNPACKING THE CONTENT OF LABOR RIGHTS UNDER THE ICESCR

The ICESCR proclaims the right to work in a general sense (Article 6). It is not a simple philosophical principle, but it should not be understood as an absolute and unconditional right to obtain employment either. It encompasses all forms of work, whether dependent wage-paid work or independent work. The Covenant explicitly develops the individual dimension of the right to work through the recognition of the right of everyone to the enjoyment of just and favorable conditions of work (Article 7). The collective dimension of the right to work is guaranteed by the right of everyone to form trade unions and join the trade union of his/her choice, as well as the right of trade unions to function freely, the right to collective bargaining and the right to strike (Article 8). Since the right to work cannot be fully realized without taking into account rights at work, Articles 6, 7 and 8 of the Covenant are interdependent and interconnected. Fully aware of these links, the Committee did consider the possibility of a single general comment dealing with the three Articles. It proved to be an impossible mission and the decision was taken to deal with each Article per se.[13]

As is the case for other economic, social and cultural rights, labor rights impose three types or levels of obligations on States: the obligations to respect, protect and fulfill.

## 4.    THE RIGHT TO WORK

Under Article 6 of the Covenant, the obligation to respect requires States to prohibit forced or compulsory labor and refrain from denying or limiting equal access to decent work for all persons, especially disadvantaged and marginalized individuals and groups, including detainees, members of minorities and migrant workers. To comply with the obligation to protect, States have to take measures that prevent third parties from interfering with the enjoyment of the right to work which implies, among other requirements, that increased flexibility of labor markets should not reduce the protection of the worker. The obligation to fulfill requires the adoption of appropriate legislative, administrative, budgetary, judicial and other measures to ensure the full realization of the right to work. It is incumbent upon States to recognize the right to work in national legal systems and to formulate and implement a national employment policy with a view to 'stimulating economic growth and development, raising levels of living, meeting manpower requirements and overcoming unemployment and underemployment'.[14] One of the important means to do so is by establishing specialized public or private employment services at the national and local levels that are able to assist and support individuals in

---

[12]   Ibid paras 74–76 (on obligations of non-state actors).

[13]   See CESCR, General Comment No. 18: The Right to Work (2016) E/C.12/GC/18 and CESCR, General Comment No. 23 (n 10).

[14]   ILO Convention No. 122, concerning employment policy, 1964 Article 1 para 1.

finding adequate employment opportunities.[15] The obligation to fulfill can be further realized through positive measures to enable and assist individuals to enjoy the right to work and to implement technical and vocational training programs to facilitate access to employment as well as through educational and information programs to increase public awareness on the right to work.[16]

For the realization of the right to work as for all other ESCR, States need to comply with core obligations to satisfy, at the very least, minimum essential levels of the rights and with obligations of progressive realization.[17] In order to do so, they need to identify priorities, allocate adequate resources and set targets and benchmarks to monitor implementation. In the context of the right to work, the core obligation of States encompasses the obligation to ensure non-discrimination and equal protection of employment. It is also the right of access to employment, especially for disadvantaged and marginalized individuals and groups, permitting them to live a life of dignity and to avoid all measures that may result in weakening mechanisms for the protection of such individuals and groups. It requires the adoption and implementation of a national employment strategy or plan of action based on a participatory and transparent process that includes employers' and workers' organizations.[18]

An example of the mutually reinforcing role of the CESCR and the ILO is that the call to States by the Committee for the adoption of a national employment strategy or plan of action with clearly identified objectives, targeted measures and an inbuilt monitoring system with indicators and benchmarks to evaluate progress and take corrective measures when needed is reflected in the ILO Employment Policy Convention 122. In its Article 1, the Convention requires that each Member State of the ILO shall declare and pursue, as a major goal, an active policy designed to promote full, productive and freely chosen employment. The corresponding Employment Policy Recommendation and other related instruments provide guidance on a number of elements, such as vocational training and job creation.

The CESCR is often questioned as to why it includes an instrumental obligation (adoption of a national strategy or plan of action) among core obligations that, given their nature and purpose, should be substantive. The reason is that such a strategy or plan of action should be informed by an inclusive discussion with the rights holders and mirror the obligations of the government as a duty bearer, thus reinforcing the universal human rights principles of participation and accountability. In the specific case of the right to work, a national strategy or plan of action is more relevant than ever, given the weakening of employer/employee relations and the increasing recourse to non-standard forms of employment that do not guarantee adequate labor or social protection. (Chapters 13 and 14 address the issues of minimum core, progressive realization and reasonableness.)

---

[15]    A good example is the *Bundesagentur fur Arbeit*, the German federal agency that manages job centers across Germany and administers unemployment benefits: <www.arbeitsagentur.de>.

[16]    CESCR, General Comment No. 18: The Right to Work (6 February 2005) E/C.12/GC/18 paras 27 and 28.

[17]    ICESCR Article 2(1): 'Each State Party to the present Covenant undertakes to take steps, individually and through international assistance and cooperation, especially economical and technical, to the maximum of its available resources, with a view to achieving progressively the full realization of the rights recognized in the present Covenant by all appropriate means, including particularly the adoption of legislative measures.'

[18]    CESCR, General Comment No. 18: The Right to Work (6 February 2005) E/C.12/GC/18 para 31.

Common agreements at regional level have helped to pursue the goals of national employment plans. For example, under the European Employment Strategy, the employment guidelines for European Union (EU) Member States present common priorities and targets for employment policies agreed by national governments, with the main aim of creating more and better jobs throughout the EU. The Strategy now constitutes part of the Europe 2020 growth strategy and has been amended in line with the European Pillar of Social Rights.[19]

All national employment plans in the EU Member States indicate measures to decrease high youth unemployment. Access to a first job constitutes an opportunity for economic independence and, in many cases, a way out of poverty. Vocational training programs, including apprenticeships and on-site skills development and enhancement opportunities offered by companies on their own or through contract with public authorities, are considered high priority. However, the difficulties faced by first time job seekers, some of them overqualified, reveal a continued mismatch between academic qualifications and the needs of the labor market.

National efforts to reduce high youth unemployment are also included in the voluntary national reports on the implementation of the Sustainable Development Goals.[20] The lack of visible results of these efforts remains a major concern for the human rights treaty bodies that very often make specific recommendations related to youth unemployment.

## 5.   RIGHTS AT WORK

Work as specified in Articles 6, 7 and 8 of the ICESCR must be decent work which respects the fundamental rights of the human person as well as the rights of workers and which provides an income to enable workers to earn a living for themselves and their families.

Decent work, as defined by the ILO, is about opportunities for women and men to obtain productive employment in conditions of freedom, equity, security and human dignity. It should be work freely chosen, with adequate social and labor conditions, including protection from work-related hazards. Opportunities for such decent work cannot be limited to certain groups at the expense of others.

At the other end of the line is precarious work that is characterized by uncertainty as to the continuing availability of the work/job; limited control (individually and collectively) over working conditions, the labor process and pace of work; limited access to legal and regu-

---

[19]   See 'The European Pillar of Social Rights as a Revival of Social Europe' <www.euvisions.eu/esu-debate-epsr-a-revival-of-social-europe-garben/>.

[20]   The Sustainable Development Goals (SDGs) include a number of youth employment targets: increase the number of youth and adults who have relevant skills, including technical and vocational skills, for employment, decent jobs and entrepreneurship by 2030 (target 4.4); achieve full and productive employment and decent work for all women and men, including for young people and persons with disabilities, and equal pay for work of equal value by 2030 (target 8.5); substantially reduce the proportion of youth not in employment, education or training by 2020 (target 8.6); develop and operationalize a global strategy for youth employment and implement the Global Jobs Pact of the ILO/modalities of implementation/paragraph 8.b). See United Nations, 'Sustainable Development Knowledge Platform' <https://sustainabledevelopment.un.org>.

latory mechanisms and to social protection; and a high degree of economic vulnerability.[21] Precarious work is not just a labor-market matter, as it has far-reaching consequences beyond the workplace.[22]

The right to work and rights at work enshrined in the Covenant can only be realized through decent work that carries a number of obligations for States: minimum wage; equal pay for equal work or work of equal value; national policy for health and safety at work; work and rest periods; paid annual leave and other leaves; flexible working arrangements; trade union affiliation; collective bargaining; and the right to strike. Based on the experience of the CESCR, some of these are referred to in more detail below.

### 5.1   Minimum Wage

The minimum wage should provide all workers with a decent living for themselves and their families, enabling them to enjoy other rights, such as education, health and an adequate standard of living. States should make consistent efforts towards the adoption of a periodically reviewed minimum wage, indexed to the cost of living, including food, water and sanitation, housing,[23] clothing and additional expenses such as commuting costs, and maintain a regular mechanism to do so, in consultation with employer organizations and trade unions. The elements to be taken into account in fixing the minimum wage are flexible, though they should include the general level of wages in the country, the cost of living, social security contributions and benefits and relative living standards.[24]

In the majority of the states parties to the Covenant, the minimum wage is far from these requirements, even in developed countries.[25] It is seldom of a sufficient amount to enable workers and their families to enjoy a decent living. Minimum wages do not apply equally to all workers and minimum wages by sector and industry are at times lower than the national minimum wage. A permanent structure with the participation of social partners for a regular review of wages, including the minimum wage, is either nonexistent or ineffective. The discussion on the living wage, which has won some international support, can contribute to further eroding the concept of a minimum wage that should ensure decent living.

---

[21]   See generally, International Labour Oraganization, *Meeting the Challenge of Precarious Work: A Worker's Agenda* <www.ilo.org/wcmsp5/groups/public/---ed_dialogue/---actrav/documents/publication/wcms_216282.pdf>.

[22]   A report recently published in Ireland describes how, although such insecurity is prevalent throughout Europe, Ireland differs because of the lack of universal access to state services, such as health care and child care. See Sinead Pembroke, 'Precarious Work Leads to Precarious Lives' *Social Europe* (14 January 2019) <www.socialeurope.eu/precarious-work-precarious-lives>.

[23]   Part II of this book focuses on the contours and development of each of these rights.

[24]   CESCR, General Comment No. 23: The Right to Just and Favourable Conditions of Work (27 April 2016) E/C.12/GC/23 paras 18, 20 and 21.

[25]   Among the shortcomings identified by the European Committee of Social Rights in its Conclusions in 2018, on the Articles of the European Social Charter relating to labor rights in respect of 35 States, is the relatively low rate of compliance with the right to remuneration such as to give workers and their families a decent standard of living. The Committee found that the statutory minimum wage or the lowest paid wage were too low in comparison with the average wage in ten States. See Council of Europe, 'Reporting System of the European Social Charter' <https://www.coe.int/en/web/european-social-charter/national-reports>.

In developing countries, minimum wage legislation and enforcement greatly depend on the government acting as the 'employer of last resort'. Innovative programs can play a role in fostering compliance with a mandatory minimum wage.[26]

## 5.2    Equal Pay for Equal Work or Work of Equal Value

Women workers are often subject to intersectional discrimination that leads to accumulated disadvantages in their professional and personal lives. A comprehensive system of protection to combat gender discrimination and to ensure equal opportunities for women and men to access the job market and enjoy fair working conditions is essential. Employers (whether public or private) should take effective steps and, if necessary, introduce temporary special measures to combat vertical and horizontal segregation by sex and respond to the different requirements of male and female workers.

The provision of equal pay for equal work or work of equal value is covered by international human rights law,[27] proclaimed in the ILO Constitution and enshrined in national constitutions or framework labor legislation.

The formulation in Article 7(a)(ii) of the ICESCR that refers to fair wages and equal remuneration for work of equal value without distinction of any kind, in particular women being guaranteed conditions of work not inferior to those enjoyed by men, with equal pay for equal work, has been interpreted by the CESCR as remuneration for workers that should be equal even when their work is different but nonetheless of the same value when assessed by objective criteria. This requires an on-going evaluation of whether the work is of equal value and whether the remuneration received is equal across a broad selection of functions. In order to assess the value of work, it is important to include skills, responsibilities and effort required by the worker as well as working conditions. Remuneration set through collective agreements should seek equality for work of equal value.

Equal pay for work of equal value is an indispensable element of non-discrimination and substantive equality. However, the principle is still not fully understood and even less put in practice. It is a recurrent theme of discussion between the Committee and states parties to the Covenant during the consideration of national reports with replies from delegations reflecting a varying degree of acceptance and implementation. The violation of the right to equal pay for equal work or work of equal value is one of the documented reasons for the gender pay gap that, together with vertical and horizontal segregation in the labor market, and unequal

---

[26]    The Mahatma Gandhi National Rural Employment Guarantee Act (MNREGA), introduced in India in 200 districts in 2005–6 and extended to the entire country in 2009–10, seeks to provide a guarantee of up to 100 days of employment per household in rural areas. Laborers who cannot find work are to be compensated with a daily unemployment allowance. The link to the minimum wage is clear, though there are a number of writ petitions regarding the non-payment of wages to MNREGA workers on time pending in the Supreme Court. Other questions remain as to whether the NREGA can increase equal access to employment, raise wages and reduce poverty. See Ministry of Rural Development, India, 'The Mahatma Gandhi National Rural Employment Guarantee Act 2005' <https://nrega.nic.in/netnrega/home .aspx>.

[27]    ICESCR Article 7; European Social Charter Article 4 (adopted 18 October 1961, entered into force 26 February 1965) ETS 35, 529 UNTS 89; African Charter on Human and Peoples' Rights Article 15 (adopted 27 June 1981, entered into force 21 October 1986) CAB/LEG/67/3 rev. 5, 1520 UNTS 217.

opportunities for promotions and career advancement, continues to affect women negatively at all stages of their careers.

The 2019 concluding observations of the CESCR to Mauritius provide a good example of concerns and recommendations related to gender-based discrimination.[28] Change will be difficult as long as States continue to take piecemeal measures to deal with a problem that is systemic.[29]

General measures to address negative stereotypes that perpetuate gender inequality should be topped by specific work-related measures, for example, to protect the safety and health of pregnant workers, to ensure equal pay for work of equal value, to set up day-care services in the workplace, to promote flexible working arrangements and to make diversified vocational training and retraining programs accessible and available to women.

### 5.3    Health and Safety at Work

The CESCR has relied on the corpus of ILO instruments as a kind of operational guidance to the normative interpretation of Article 7. The Occupational Safety and Health Convention and its Protocol of 2002 was especially useful in establishing the obligations of States to ensure safe and healthy working conditions. It was also instrumental to identify the technical and operational elements and the appropriate monitoring and enforcement provisions that should

---

[28]    In its concluding observations on the fifth periodic report of Mauritius, the Committee, '[w]hile welcoming the Equal Opportunities Act, the efforts to mainstream gender equality across all ministries and the amendment to the Employment Rights Act in 2013 to establish the principle of equal pay for work of equal value', expressed its concern at 'deep-rooted gender role stereotypes, patriarchal attitudes and persistent discriminatory cultural norms and practices against women' that 'contribute to the low representation of women in decision-making positions in the public sector'. It also highlighted 'the low participation of women in the labor market, the significant gender pay gap and the uneven implementation of the principle of equal pay for work of equal value, particularly in the agricultural sector and the sugar and tea industries, and the persistence of occupational gender segregation'. Recommendations included the 'review and amendment of all existing laws, regulations, norms and practices that are discriminatory against women' and the development of 'policies and programs, including temporary special measures, to achieve substantive gender equality in all areas of economic, social and cultural rights'; the adoption of 'effective measures to end occupational gender segregation and close the gender pay gap, including by providing women with decent work and career development opportunities in non-traditional fields of study and with work on an equal footing with men'; the effective implementation of 'the principle of equal pay for work of equal value, including by establishing methods for an objective appraisal of the work to be performed with a view to providing a classification of jobs that is free of gender bias'; and 'comprehensive measures to eliminate strong gender role stereotypes, including through media campaigns and opinion leaders, and through awareness-raising among the general public on the equal sharing of rights and responsibilities between men and women in the family and society': see CESCR, Concluding Observations Mauritius (8 March 2019) E/C.12/MUS/CO5 paras 23–24.

[29]    In Portugal, the principle of equal pay for equal work is a constitutional provision, reflected in the Labor Code, which establishes the right of workers to equality in working conditions, in particular regarding pay. In reality, very significant differences persist. According to data from 2016, the average salaries of women are inferior to those of men by 15.8 per cent, which means that the disparity in salaries corresponds to a loss of 58 days of paid work for women. Legislation that entered into force in January 2019 is intended to promote three objectives: more and better information for the public, requirements for companies to ensure a transparent remuneration policy and the reinforcement of the role of the Authority for Working Conditions and of the Commission for Equality in Work and Employment.

be incorporated in a national policy for the prevention of accidents and work-related health injury.

A national policy with a human rights-based approach should cover all branches of economic activity including the formal and informal sectors and all categories of workers, including non-standard workers, apprentices and interns, taking into account specific risks to the safety and health of female workers in case of pregnancy. It must also apply to workers with disabilities, without any form of discrimination against them. It should incorporate appropriate monitoring and enforcement provisions and provide adequate penalties in case of violations.

In the context of prevention, further requirements are that it should strive to minimize hazards in the working environment, taking immediate preventative steps to be increased over time in consultation with representatives of workers and employers, addressing workplaces, working environment, work processes, tools, machinery and equipment, as well as chemical, physical and biological substances and agents.[30]

Given that the employer's responsibility for the safety and health of workers is a basic principle of labor law, business enterprises have particular responsibilities in this area. Trade unions and workers' organizations also have the duty to include issues of health and safety at work in collective bargaining and other agreements.

## 5.4    Freedom from Harassment

Freedom from any kind of harassment, including sexual harassment, is a fundamental component of rights at work. Legislation should not only define harassment broadly, but should make explicit reference to sexual and other forms of harassment, including on the basis of sex, disability, race, sexual orientation, gender identity or intersex status. National reports of states parties to the Covenant reflect a variety of shortcomings, such as the lack of a clear definition of sexual harassment in the workplace, the fact that it does not constitute a specific criminal offense – in most cases it is considered sufficient to include it in the anti-discrimination legislation and the penal code – and the insufficiency of prevention mechanisms, procedures for complaints and avenues for redress and reparation.[31] The CESCR has repeatedly called for a definition of sexual harassment in the workplace as well as for specific legislation to criminalize and punish it, in addition to general measures to raise awareness of the prohibition of harassment.[32]

---

[30]    ILO Occupational Safety and Health Convention 1981 (No. 155).

[31]    General Comment No. 23 (n 10) para 48 specifies that 'a national policy to combat all forms of harassment in the workplace to be applied in both the public and private sectors should include the identification of specific duties on employers, managers, supervisors and workers to prevent and, where relevant, resolve and remedy harassment cases'.

[32]    In its concluding observations to Bulgaria, the Committee expressed its concern 'about the prevalence of harassment, including sexual harassment, in the workplace, particularly in the garment sector where the majority of workers are women belonging to marginalized groups'. It was also 'concerned that despite the Law on Protection against Discrimination, of 2004, which includes definitions of harassment and sexual harassment, there is a low level of awareness of sexual and other forms of harassment and a low rate of reporting of harassment'. It recommended raising 'awareness of the prohibition of harassment, including sexual harassment, in the workplace, among employers, employees and the general public'; the existence of 'a harassment-free working environment'; 'effective remedies' for 'victims of harassment'; and sanctions for those responsible. It also recommended 'measures to ensure that women

The growing importance of accepted international standards on harassment and violence in the workplace is at the heart of the ILO's efforts to adopt an international instrument to deal with an issue that is universal in nature and bound to acquire even more complex facets in the changing world of work. Such a binding international instrument, that needs to cover all workplaces, would potentially send out a strong political message and fill in a regulatory gap. Given the tripartite ILO decision-making process, it would enlist the adherence of employer associations and thereby exert influence on the corporate sector, providing more opportunities for practical hands-on guidance. Given its universal nature, the instrument requires a degree of flexibility. Strategies that can help will differ depending on the size of the enterprise, and on whether it is semiformal or informal, among other characteristics.

It is true that this idea has been floating around for more than ten years, but there seems to be a strong intention on the part of the ILO to speed up the process at a time when sexual harassment complaints against the UN – regrettably even in the context of humanitarian and peace-keeping operations – and the #MeToo Movement have brought about a renewed sense of urgency to deal with an old problem that workers, in their great majority women, have long had to face, with huge negative impacts on their careers and personal lives, but above all for their dignity and self-esteem. It would be a major step forward if, at the International Labour Conference, the ILO were to successfully conclude the multi-year process of discussion and negotiation with Member States, employers and worker representatives and proceed to adopt the new international instrument.[33]

### 5.5    Paid Leave and Flexible Working Arrangements

Maternity, paternity and parental leave have a deep bearing on gender equality and the reconciliation of professional, family and personal lives. Whereas maternity leave, with full or partial payment indexed to the salary or with a flat rate benefit, is now fairly included in labor and social security legislations in many countries, paid paternity leave of an adequate duration is still not a common feature. Even less is paid parental leave for various purposes. In countries where it exists, it is still considered to be very much a mother's privilege/obligation. However, one cannot say that there has not been some progress, particularly in the public perception of why the equal sharing of this leave is relevant to enable mothers to continue to perform professionally and fathers to benefit from the private sphere and strengthened family ties. From the author's own national experience, we have come a long way – from the point at which paternity benefit was paid to the father only if the mother was unable to care for the child due to reasons of physical or mental health, to mandatory 100 per cent paid paternity leave of 15 days exclusively for the father in the 30 days following the birth of the child, five of which are to be

---

workers in the garment sector are protected from sexual and other forms of harassment' (see CESCR, Concluding Observations Bulgaria (8 March 2019) E/C.12/BGR/CO/6 paras 23–24).

[33]    In the time between writing this article and its publication, ILO Convention 190 concerning the elimination of violence and harassment in the world of work was adopted.

enjoyed immediately following birth.[34] However, the fact that such leave is part of legislation does not necessarily imply adequate implementation for men and women to enjoy the right.[35]

Together with paid leave for a number of purposes, flexible working arrangements have become increasingly important as a measure to advance gender equality for female and male workers in the professional and private spheres. Such arrangements can involve initiatives in the scheduling of working hours, for example through flex time, compressed working weeks and job sharing, as well as flexibility in the place of work to include work at home, telework or work from a satellite work center. In order not to undermine the right to just and favorable conditions of work, flexibility in working arrangements cannot be understood and implemented in a way that favors only or disproportionately the employer, weakening the entitlements of workers. The increasing complexity of work contracts, such as short-term and zero hour contracts and non-standard forms of employment often catalogued as flexible work arrangements, are no more than a hidden informalization of work, with all the corresponding gaps in labor and social protection. The concluding observations of the Committee to the United Kingdom and Northern Ireland raise these concerns and make recommendations.[36]

---

[34] According to Portuguese social security statistics, fathers who received the paternity benefit in relation to the total number of children born increased from 39.3 per cent in 2005 to 67.3 per cent in 2016. See 'Evolução do gozo de licenças parentais em Portugal – CITE' (Evolution in the Enjoyment of Parental Leaves in Portugal) <http://cite.gov.pt/pt/acite/protecparent006.html>.

[35] In a very recent case, a Portuguese court condemned a cork factory for moral harassment of a worker, maintaining the fine of 31,110 euros for a very serious offense that was previously imposed by the Authority for Working Conditions. The complainant was dismissed in January 2017, allegedly for having exercised her maternity and assistance to family rights. The court considered the dismissal illegal and determined her reintegration. In January 2019 she was dismissed again, accused of defamation, after the company had been fined by the Authority for Working Conditions, which also imposed an additional 6,000 euro fine for irregularities related to the complainant's health and safety at work. Initially, the company said it was going to appeal, but it later decided not to do so and to pay the fine for violation of labor regulations: <www.sabado.pt/portugal/detalhe/corticeira-fernando-couto-multada-em-mais-6000 -euros-pela-act>. In an earlier case, in September 2017, the Lisbon Court of Appeal decided that a male worker subject to unlawful dismissal while enjoying parental leave should be readmitted into the same company, with full recognition of his professional category and compensation for all damages, financial and non-financial, as well as the unpaid salary since his dismissal (Acórdãos do Tribunal da Relação de Lisboa): <www.dgsi.pt/jtrl.nsf/Por+Ano?OpenView26175/15.6T8LSB.L1-4>.

[36] At the end of the dialogue with the State Party over its sixth periodic report, the Committee expressed its concern 'at the high incidence of part-time work, precarious self-employment, temporary employment and the use of "zero hour contracts" … which particularly affect women'; 'about the negative impact that all those forms of employment have on the enjoyment by workers of their right to just and favourable conditions of work'; and 'about the high number of low-paid jobs, which affected in particular certain sectors, such as the cleaning and home-care sectors'. The Committee recommended 'all appropriate measures to progressively reduce the use of temporary employment, precarious self-employment and "zero hour contracts"', including by generating decent work opportunities that offer job security and adequate protection of labor rights; and to '[e]nsure that the labour and social security rights of persons in part-time work, precarious self-employment, temporary employment and "zero-hour contracts" are fully guaranteed in law and in practice' (see CESCR. Concluding Observations United Kingdom of Great Britain and Northern Ireland (2016) E.C.12/GBR/CO/6 paras 31–32.

## 5.6    Labor Rights for Specific Categories of Workers

The full enjoyment of the right to work and rights at work is particularly difficult for certain groups of workers due to the nature and the lack of economic and social recognition of the work they perform. The concepts of informal economy/informal sector/informal employment/ informal activities are used interchangeably and though there are differences in the definition, there is a common reason for their existence: unemployment, underemployment and lack of opportunities in the formal labor market.[37] Men and women live and work in the informal economy because of their need to survive rather than as a matter of choice. Women workers are over-represented in the informal economy as casual workers, home workers or own account workers.[38] Millions are engaged in unpaid work in the home or in family enterprises without income guarantee or social protection. In light of the evolving understanding of the concept of work and workers, informal economy workers are entitled to the protection of their rights to work and at work.

It is by now usual for the human rights treaty bodies to recommend that States make all efforts to transition to the formal economy through concerted measures across several policy areas with the collaborative engagement of involved authorities and institutions. The final triple objective of these efforts would be to facilitate transition of those in the informal economy to more formalized labor, to promote job creation in the formal economy and to prevent further informalization.

It is a long-term endeavor that is not moving as swiftly as one would have envisaged some years ago, when economic growth was more reliable and policies were more conducive to the realization of human rights. On the contrary, the informalization and casualization of what was previously regular employment, seen even in high-income countries, seems to point in the opposite direction. In the meantime, informal economy workers have to be protected from huge decent work deficits, such as ambiguous or disguised employment status, high illiteracy,

---

[37]    In the ILO Resolution concerning decent work and the informal economy (2002), '[t]he term "informal economy" refers to all economic activities by workers and economic units that are – in law or in practice – not covered or insufficiently covered by formal arrangements. Their activities are not included in the law, which means that they are operating outside the formal reach of the law; or they are not covered in practice, which means that although they are operating within the formal reach of the law, the law is not applied or not enforced; or the law discourages compliance because it is inappropriate, burdensome, or imposes excessive costs' (para 3). This Resolution was complemented by the Resolution concerning decent work in global supply chains (2016) that lists the opportunities and challenges for the realization of decent work and inclusive development emerging from global supply chains. Among the challenges, reference is made to 'failures at all levels within global supply chains' that 'have contributed to decent work deficits for working conditions such as in the areas of occupational safety and health, wages, working time, which impact on the employment relationship and the protections it can offer' and 'have also contributed to the undermining of labour rights, particularly freedom of association and collective bargaining' (para 3).

[38]    In its concluding observations on the combined fifth and sixth reports of the Philippines, the Committee expressed its concerns that about 75 per cent of the workforce, for the most part women, were working in the informal economy or in non-standard forms of employment without legal protection, support and safeguards. It also highlighted the precarious working conditions in sweatshops, which are often excluded and hidden from labor inspections, where workers, mostly women, are subjected to exploitation with pay below the minimum wage, long working hours, and unsafe and unhealthy working conditions, and where they are exposed to occupational accidents, abuse and extra demands (see CESCR, Concluding Observation Philippines (7 October 2016) E.C. 12/PHL/CO/5–6 para 27).

low skill levels and lack of training opportunities. They are exposed to inadequate and unsafe working conditions and excluded or not reachable by social security schemes that ensure maternity benefits or pensions. They are also not covered by health, safety and other labor regulations, including freedom of association and collective bargaining.

A major step forward in the protection of informal economy workers is the ILO Social Protection Floor (SPF), which comprises basic social security guarantees to ensure at a minimum that, over the life cycle, all in need have access to a nationally defined set of goods and services, notably essential health care, including maternity care that meets the criteria of availability, accessibility, acceptability and quality. The SPF is also intended to ensure basic income security, at least at a nationally defined minimum level, for persons in active age who are unable to earn sufficient income, in particular in case of sickness, unemployment, maternity and disability, as well as for children and older persons.[39] ILO studies found that it is possible to finance the SPF or some of its components even in low-income countries and therefore States should, in accordance with national circumstances, establish as quickly as possible, and maintain, social protection floors for all residents and children.[40]

The SPF is an important call to attention regarding the inclusion of workers in the informal economy, most of whom are women, as already indicated. Several of the basic guarantees, such as maternal health, childcare and maternity benefits and pensions, contribute towards establishing universal benefits that decrease gender inequalities.[41] The social security guarantees of the SPF reflect the core obligations of States, under Article 9 of the Covenant on the right to social security, to provide, together with access to essential services, a minimum level of benefits to all individuals and families to enable them to acquire at least essential health care, basic shelter and housing, water and sanitation, foodstuffs and the most basic forms of education. Recommendation 202 is instrumental in providing a tool to make the human rights narrative real on the ground by offering States the possibility to put in place SPFs.[42]

Migration is identified as one of the characteristics of globalization that is reshaping the world of work in profound ways.[43] It has led to a rapid increase of migrant workers in search of employment opportunities, whether for permanent settlement or for short-term or seasonal work that will provide an adequate standard of living for themselves and their families, in their reception countries. In spite of national constitutional guarantees of equality, in reality migrant workers, particularly if undocumented, can be subject to discrimination and abusive labor practices that give the employer control over their residence status, which, in turn, exposes them to reprisals.[44]

---

[39]   ILO Social Protection Floors Recommendation, 2012 (No. 202).

[40]   In February 2019, the ILO Committee of Experts on the Applications of Conventions and Recommendations launched a General Survey on Social Protection Floors in Recommendation 202 based on the reports of 114 Governments and the observations of employers' and workers' organizations, documenting the implementation of the Recommendation in law, policies and practice (see ILO, 'General Survey on the Social Protection Floors Recommendation, 2012 (No. 202)' <https://www.ilo.org/global/standards/WCMS_542394/lang--en/index.htm>).

[41]   CESCR, 'Social Protection Floors: An Essential Element of the Right to Social Security and of the Sustainable Development Goals' (2015) E/C.12/2015/1 para 9.

[42]   Ibid 39.

[43]   ILO Declaration on Social Justice for a Fair Globalization (2008) preamble.

[44]   CESCR, 'Duties of States towards Refugees and Migrants under the International Covenant on Economic, Social and Cultural Rights' (2017) E/C.12/2017/1.

At a global level, policy coherence and coordination are crucial to integrate the protection of the rights of migrant workers into the economic and social dimensions of the governance of labor migration flows. At the national level, laws and policies should ensure that migrant status does not lead to discrimination in the enjoyment of labor rights and one way to do so is to introduce in the legislation a specific prohibition of discrimination on grounds of nationality. Female migrant domestic workers are particularly at risk of intersectional discrimination and exploitation due to factors such as dependence on the job and employer due to migration-related debt; legal status; employer practices restricting the ability of these workers to leave the workplace; and the fact that the workplace may be the only shelter available to them.[45]

States should recognize the enjoyment by migrant workers and members of their families of rights at work (Articles 25 and 26 of CMW). They need to strengthen the effective regulation and monitoring of recruitment agencies, labor brokers and other intermediaries, as well as of labor inspectorates.

Access to effective remedies from the competent administrative and judicial authorities is a complex issue for migrant workers, due to lack of specific user-friendly information, particularly when they are not familiar with the language(s) spoken in host countries. States, social partners and local administration authorities should promote campaigns to raise awareness about administrative procedures and available complaints and redress mechanisms among migrant workers.

States should put in place bilateral agreements for the protection of migrant workers and engage in joint monitoring of recruitment practices. This is particularly important to avoid abuse of migrant workers, including domestic workers, and to combat trafficking in persons. Similarly, states parties should seek international cooperation to protect the rights of migrant workers who are employed by enterprises registered in other states parties so as to enable such workers to enjoy just and favorable conditions of work.

Though recognized as the most important tool to monitor working conditions and sanction non-compliant employers, labor inspections remain insufficient and of a restricted scope. Labor inspectors are impacted by a limited mandate, funding deficits, inadequate training and resources and lack of authority.[46] Even in countries where, in accordance with the legislation, no workplace is exempted from labor inspections, in practice informal settings, special economic zones and workplaces of domestic workers are among some of the spaces where labor inspectors are not allowed to fulfill their mandate.

---

[45] See generally, Committee on the Protection of the Rights of All Migrant Workers and Members of their Families (CMW Committee), General Comment No. 1: Migrant Domestic Workers (23 February 2011) CMW/C/GC/1.

[46] In its concluding observations on the fifth periodic report of Germany, the Committee highlighted 'the insufficient number of labour inspections in the agricultural sector, in particular in small workplaces, and the high number of fatal occupational accidents in the sector' (see CESCR, 'Concluding Observations on the Sixth Periodic Report of Germany' E/C.12/DEU/CO/6 (2018) para 40). To South Africa, after its initial report, the Committee recommended an increase in the level of funding allocated to labor inspectorates; the existence of a sufficient number of qualified labor inspectors and the payment of their wages; provision of adequate resources to reduce the high rate of turnover; and the guarantee that compliance orders are duly implemented (see CESCR, Concluding Observations South Africa (29 November 2018) E.C.12/ZAF/CO/1 para 44).

The failure of States regarding the mandate of, and resources made available to, labor inspectorates led the CESCR to raise a number of issues in General Comment No. 23. In order to ensure accountability, states parties are required to establish a functioning system of labor inspectorates, with the involvement of social partners, to monitor all aspects of the right to just and favorable conditions of work for all workers, including workers in the informal economy, domestic workers and agricultural workers. Labor inspectorates should be independent and staffed with trained professionals. Penalties should apply for non-compliance with their recommendations. Labor inspectorates should focus on monitoring the rights of workers and not be used for other purposes, such as checking the migration status of workers.

## 5.7   Trade Union Affiliation, Collective Bargaining and the Right to Strike

ICESCR Article 8 enshrines a number of fundamental rights. Trade union formation and representation rights are clearly spelled out in so far as everyone has the right to form trade unions and join the trade union of his choice, subject only to the rules of the organization concerned, for the promotion and protection of his economic and social interests. A further requirement is that no restrictions may be placed on the exercise of this right other than those prescribed by law and which are necessary in a democratic society, in the interests of national security or public order or for the protection of the rights and freedoms of others.

In its concluding observations, the CESCR has consistently recommended that States ratify ILO Conventions No. 87 on trade union freedom and the protection of trade union rights and Convention No. 98 on the right to collective organization and bargaining.

However, there has been little progress on the part of States, even though these two Conventions are included in the eight ILO 'fundamental' Conventions and associated Recommendations and Protocols that identify core principles and rights in the workplace,[47] and ILO Member States are required to realize the principles included therein even if they have not ratified the Conventions in question. In the future, there could be a joint campaign by the Office of the UN High Commissioner for Human Rights (OHCHR) and the ILO to push for the ratification of the eight fundamental Conventions as part of the core obligations of states parties to the ICESCR to guarantee a minimum essential level of the rights to work and at work, ensure non-discrimination in the enjoyment of these rights and prohibit forced labor and child labor.

A number of States still have reservations in place regarding the content of Article 8. The concluding observations to China (2014) provide a good example.[48]

---

[47]   The ILO Declaration on Fundamental Principles and Rights at Work, adopted in 1998, commits member states to respect and promote principles and rights in four categories (freedom of association and the effective recognition of the right to collective bargaining; the elimination of forced or compulsory labor; the abolition of child labor; and the elimination of discrimination in respect of employment and occupation).

[48]   In its concluding observations on the second periodic report of China, including Hong Kong, China and Macao, China, the Committee expressed concern 'that workers cannot freely exercise their right to form and join trade unions outside the structure of the All China Federation of Trade Unions', as well at the fact 'that the Trade Union Law does not provide for the right of workers to strike'. It reiterated its previous recommendation 'that the Trade Union Act be amended to allow workers to form independent trade unions, both within and outside the structure of the All China Federation of Trade Unions' and also recommended 'that the State party consider the legal recognition of the right to strike'. In addition,

There is plenty of evidence that certain categories of workers, in particular migrant workers, informal sector workers, workers in special economic zones and all those with precarious work contracts, abstain from engaging in trade union activities out of fear of harassment, reprisal, unfair dismissal and even deportation.[49] Given the insufficient labor and social security protection to which they are entitled and the absence of access to justice mechanisms, they prefer to remain invisible, further weakening any possibility of joint action. It is incumbent on States to ensure that all workers enjoy the rights provided for in Article 8 of the Covenant. Trade unions that have, in general, maintained a very traditional approach to workers' protection should strive to enlarge the scope of social dialogue to reflect the concerns of these categories of workers and provide them with a recognized platform to realize their labor rights. There is also some scope for cross-border trade union cooperation.

The right to strike in conformity with the laws of the country is also enshrined in Article 8, which allows for the imposition of lawful restrictions on the exercise of the right by members of the armed forces, of the police and of the administration of the State. However, a number of States continue to consider extensive limitations on the right to strike as lawful and to impose undue administrative restrictions on the exercise of this right in general or by certain groups of workers in particular. In many countries, civil servants often find their right to strike seriously curtailed. One of the reasons is that the legislation regulating the public participation of civil servants in strikes, or other collective pressure actions that interfere with the performance of functions of the recruiting authority or of other authorities, is often rooted in a misguided understanding of public officers as government agents that no longer holds true. There is today a much broader canvas for the duties of civil servants, which has not been matched by legislative and practical advances in the field of participation. The concept of essential services or minimum services remains very broad and at times undefined. It is important for States to establish the list of services, jobs and categories of personnel that are strictly necessary for the performance of a minimum level of service in the event of a strike in public service activities and to clearly lay down the necessary criteria for the establishment of a union.

Law enforcement officers are another group subject to restrictions in their right to unionize and to strike, through overextensive interpretations of the Labor Code and even of the Criminal Code. In some cases, legislative reforms do allow members, for example of the police force, to form and join unions. However, their representatives could face harassment and intimidation.

Though the right to collective bargaining is not expressly referred to in Article 8, it is impossible to think of the right to work and of rights at work without due consideration given to collective bargaining. It is a fundamental right rooted in the ILO Constitution and reaffirmed in the 1998 ILO Declaration on Fundamental Principles and Rights at Work. The ILO defines it as a key means through which employers and their organizations and trade unions can establish fair wages and working conditions. It also provides the basis for sound labor relations. Typical issues on the bargaining agenda include wages, working time, training, occupational health and safety and equal treatment – all essential elements of the normative content of labor rights enshrined in the Covenant. Collective agreements regulate terms and conditions

the Committee strongly urge[d] the State party to consider withdrawing its declaration on Article 8 para 1, of the Covenant' (see CESCR, 'Concluding Observations China, including Hong Kong, China, and Macao, China (13 June 2014) E/C.12/CHN/CO/2 para 23).

[49]   See <www.ilo.org/wcmsp5/groups/public/---ed_dialogue/---actrav/documents/publication/wcms_722482.pdf>.

of employment and they may also address the rights and responsibilities of the parties, thus ensuring harmonious and productive industries and workplaces. Collective bargaining has lost some of its strength given the decrease in trade union affiliation, the exclusion of certain categories of workers from collective contracts, the rise of non-standard forms of employment and the growth of new forms of workers' organizations, but it remains a key means for reducing inequality and extending labor protection.

Restrictions resulting from the decrease in the registration of unions and acts of interference by public authorities in various key sectors in terms of the election of union leaders, collective bargaining rights, access to funding and acts of intimidation – in particular the disproportionate use of fines and the association of the reparation of damages with the exercise of the right to strike – have led to a negative environment. Excessive legal limitations, such as the requirement regarding a trade union's representation of a majority of workers in a given firm or branch of activity, have further weakened their role and the exercise of the rights by their members.

Reports of harassment of trade union leaders and strikers being subjected to discrimination, violence, intimidation and reprisals – at times even in the context of anti-terrorism legislation, imposing serious penalties that could even include the death penalty for acts likely to disrupt the normal operation of public services, or the provision of essential services to the population – are often brought to the attention of treaty bodies by national and international NGOs. The CESCR's decision to include a paragraph in its General Comment No. 23 calling on States to respect, protect and promote the work of human rights defenders and other civil society actors towards the realization of the right to just and favorable conditions of work, including by facilitating access to information and enabling the exercise of their rights to freedom of expression, association, assembly and public participation, was a call to States in response to these concerns.

Effective, speedy and independent investigation into allegations of unfair dismissals related to trade union activities and other violations of trade union rights, as well as enforcement of judicial decisions concerning the reinstatement of dismissed workers and establishment of appropriate compensation for the workers concerned, are important signals of how seriously trade union rights are realized (or not realized).[50] The realization of the rights enshrined in Article 8 is faced with growing constraints due to the reasons already indicated but also due to the ideological divide in our societies, the lack of general accountability on the part of public authorities as duty bearers and the shrinking democratic space for public participation.[51] The

---

[50]    In its concluding observations on the fifth periodic report of Mauritius, the Committee urged 'the State party to ensure that all allegations of harassment and intimidation against trade union activists, particularly in export processing zones, are thoroughly investigated and that those responsible are tried and punished' (see CESCR, Concluding Observations Mauritius (8 March 2019) E/C.12/MUS/CO/5 para 35).

[51]    In its concluding observations on the fourth periodic report of France, the Committee condemned 'the reprisals taken against trade union representatives' and observed 'with concern the shrinking of democratic space for collective bargaining'. It urged 'the State party to adopt effective measures for the protection of persons involved in trade union activities and for the prevention and punishment of all forms of reprisal', 'to ensure that the collective bargaining process is effective and to uphold the right to union representation in accordance with international standards as a means of protecting workers' rights in terms of working conditions and social security' (see CESCR, Concluding Observations France (13 July 2016) E/C.12/FRA/CO/4 paras 27–28).

interpretation of Article 8 would certainly benefit from a long-awaited General Comment by the CESCR.[52]

## 6.    JURISPRUDENCE UNDER THE OPTIONAL PROTOCOL TO THE ICESCR AND THE COLLECTIVE COMPLAINTS PROCEDURE OF THE EUROPEAN COMMITTEE OF SOCIAL RIGHTS

The CESCR has still not received meaningful individual communications under Articles 6, 7 and 8 of the Covenant under its Optional Protocol (OP-ICESCR), in part probably because labor rights are extensively adjudicated at national level. However, some developments have helped to clarify procedural issues and will hopefully pave the way for future substantive views.

Some communications against Spain were brought to the attention of the Committee on a common substantive issue – right to the enjoyment of just and satisfactory conditions of work and right to social security (Articles 7 and 9 of the ICESCR). They were considered inadmissible.[53]

An interesting opportunity to clarify the grounds for inadmissibility was also a case against Portugal, on the right to the enjoyment of just and favorable conditions of work.[54] In this case, though the facts amounting to the alleged violation occurred prior to the date of the entry into force of the OP-ICESCR in Portugal, the Committee was of the view that the communication was not inadmissible because the associated domestic Court cases continued after that date. Nevertheless, the communication was found inadmissible pursuant to Article 3(2)(e) of the OP-ICESCR, on the grounds that the factual allegations made were insufficiently substantiated and did not allow the Committee to assess whether or not there was a violation of the Covenant.

There was also a case regarding the eviction of a migrant couple with two small children from the home they had rented in Madrid, after their lease contract expired,[55] in which the Committee not only identified the failure of the State to allocate alternative housing to the authors, but also called the attention of the Spanish government, as a duty bearer, to institutional policy failures and lack of coordination between government agencies that often lie at the root of several violations. In this particular case, the complainants had not received the support they were entitled to from employment, social security and social service agencies. This case and the views of the Committee are especially significant for reinstating the need to

---

[52]   The CESCR and the Human Rights Committee have adopted a joint statement on freedom of association, including the right to form and join trade unions (E/C/12/66/5) bringing together Article 8 of the ICESCR and Article 22 of the ICCPR. It is a very relevant effort towards a shared interpretation of the right and also a practical example of how harmonization of working methods among the treaty bodies can move beyond purely procedural alignments to strengthening protection.

[53]   CESCR, *F.G.M et al. v Spain* (29 February 2016) E/C.12/57/D/11/2015; CESCR, *J.M.R.H et al. v Spain* (20 June 2016) E/C 12/58/D/12/2016; and CESCR; *E.C.P et al. v Spain* (20 July 2016) E/C.12/58/D/13/2016.

[54]   CESCR, *Coelho v Portugal* (2018) E/C.12/61/D/21/2017.

[55]   CESCR, *Ben Djazia and Bellili v Spain* (20 June 2017) E/C.12/61/D/5/2015.

apply a standard of reasonableness in accessing State policies for the realization of all human rights. (See Chapter 2 for more information on this case.)

A positive example in relation to the right to strike is the case brought to the European Committee of Social Rights by trade union federations and confederations against Belgium.[56] The Committee concluded that there was a violation of Article 6§4 (right to strike) of the European Charter on the ground of restrictions on the right to strike. The government's response in 2017 stated that the Committee's decision had an impact on national case law and that it had been incorporated by certain judges into their interpretation of the right to strike. These arguments were also supported by the Federation of Belgian Enterprises. In its Findings 2018, on the assessment of follow-up to decisions on the merits of collective complaints, the Committee considered that the examples of case law given by the authorities showed, on the one hand, that the Belgian case law on strikes was stable, consistent and predictable and, on the other hand, that the proceedings for unilateral applications guaranteed procedural fairness. Therefore, the Committee held that the situation had been brought into conformity with the Charter and decided to terminate the follow-up to the decision.[57]

## 7.    HUMAN RIGHTS INDICATORS

The assessment of the impact of economic and social policies on the enjoyment of human rights is not possible without indicators and benchmarks that are disaggregated, comparable, accurate, measurable, timely and easy to understand and apply. To assess compliance with core obligations and obligations of progressive realization, States need to have quantitative and qualitative indicators, particularly on the enjoyment of rights by vulnerable and discriminated groups. This information is not always readily available in official statistics, which generally represent mainstream trends of progress or lack of progress but do not provide disaggregation and comparability over a medium time-frame of at least five years.

The OHCHR has developed a framework with a list of illustrative indicators on several CPR and ESCR, including the right to work, encompassing three types of indicators.[58] Structural indicators are those that reflect the ratification of legal instruments, the existence of institutional mechanisms and the adoption of national policies for the promotion and protection of human rights. Process indicators link institutional mandates to results, thereby allowing for measurement of the efforts of governments as main duty bearers, while outcome indicators demonstrate tangible results for the rights holders. The concept is not only to place all human rights on the same footing, putting to rest once and for all the misguided conviction that the realization of ESCR is not measurable, but also to unpack the normative content of each right into characteristic attributes that are clearly subject to a quantitative and qualitative monitoring

---

[56]   *European Trade Union Confederation (ETUC), Centrale Générale des Syndicats Libéraux de Belgique (CGSLB)/Confédération des Syndicats chrétiens de Belgique (CSC), Fédération Générale du Travail de Belgique (FGTB) v Belgium*, Complaint No. 59/2009.

[57]   See European Committee of Social Rights, 'Follow-up to Decisions on the Merits of Collective Complaints: Findings 2018' (2018) 5–6 para 8 <https://rm.coe.int/findings-2018-on-collective -complaints/168091f0c7>.

[58]   OHCHR, *Human Rights Indicators: A Guide to Measurement and Implementation* (HR/PUB/12/5, 2012) 95 (Table 8 on the right to work) <https://www.ohchr.org/EN/Issues/Indicators/Pages/documents .aspx>.

evaluation. In the case of the right to work, the four selected attributes are: access to decent and productive work; just and safe working conditions; training, skills upgrading and professional development; and protection from forced labor and unemployment. The list of indicators are being adapted to the country-specific context and applied by some national governments, national human rights institutions and non-governmental organizations. Other relevant indicators on the right to work are ILO decent work indicators,[59] and indicators to report on the SDGs.[60]

## 8.    CONCLUSION

The concept of work and workers has evolved from the time of drafting the ICESCR, in line with economic and social changes across the world, to include new categories of workers and raise the accountability bar on the part of public authorities and employers regarding working conditions that not only contribute to the well-being of workers and the success of enterprises, but ultimately reinforce the fabric of our societies. The understanding of work will continue to evolve but it will not cease to be an element of our individual and collective identity.

The report of the Global Commission on the Future of Work published as part of the ILO centenary celebration refers to technological advances, such as artificial intelligence, automation and robotics, that will create new jobs, but also to the fact that digital platforms will bring with them new challenges for decent work. They may provide new sources of income to many workers in different parts of the world, but the fragmented nature of the work across international jurisdictions makes it difficult to protect their rights and ensure redress for violations. Millions of jobs will arise from greening the economy but many others will disappear as we transition to clean technologies and scale back from resource-intensive industries. Opportunities in the care sector will continue to grow as life expectancy increases and older people require adequate social and health services.

In its executive summary, the report identifies people's capabilities, institutions of work, and decent and sustainable work as the three areas that deserve increased investment at national and international levels. From the human rights perspective, an essential element is the call in the report for a universal labor guarantee which would include fundamental workers' rights and basic working conditions. Freedom of association and the effective right to collective bargaining are to be guaranteed to all workers – irrespective of their status or contractual arrangements – as well as freedom from forced labor, child labor and discrimination. For all workers, guaranteed working conditions must include an adequate living wage, limits on hours of work and safe and healthy workplaces.

The human rights treaty bodies should remain fully engaged in this discussion and follow the implementation of the report very carefully, not only to hold States to account in how

---

[59]   ILO, 'Decent Work Indicators – Concepts and Definitions' (2013) <www.ilo.org/integration/resources/pubs/WCMS_229374/lang--en/index.htm>.

[60]   Sustainable Development Solutions Network, *Indicators and a Monitoring Framework for the Sustainable Development Goals: Launching a Data Revolution for the SDGs – A Report to the Secretary-General of the United Nations by the Leadership Council of the Sustainable Development Solutions Network* (2015) 160–64 (Goal 8: Promote Sustained, Inclusive and Sustainable Economic Growth, Full and Productive Employment and Decent Work for All) <unsdsn.org/wp-content/uploads/2015/05/FINAL-SDSN-Indicator-Report-WEB.pdf>.

they respect, protect and fulfill the right to work and rights at work, but also because, as in other previous upheavals in the world of work, many will be left behind because they did not have access to, or were not able to benefit from, opportunities that would have enabled them to acquire new skills in a fast changing world and provided a level playing field. Some of the groups identified in this chapter as facing particular difficulties in enjoying their rights may find themselves further disadvantaged, requiring priority attention, and new groups may appear.

There are no doubt complex and crucial links between trade, financial and economic and social policies. But standing above all of them is the goal of equality of rights, conditions and opportunities, which refers broadly to ways in which individuals, families and groups are able to participate fully in society as citizens and to exercise their entitlement to resources, and their ability to contribute to the well-being of themselves, their families and their communities.

# PART III

# CROSS-CUTTING ISSUES

# 13. Unpacking the minimum core and reasonableness standards

*Joie Chowdhury*

## 1. INTRODUCTION

The International Covenant on Economic, Social and Cultural Rights 1966 (ICESCR) recognizes that 'the ideal of free human beings enjoying freedom from fear and want can only be achieved if conditions are created whereby everyone may enjoy his economic, social and cultural rights, as well as his civil and political rights'.[1] As a global community, while we have made concrete advancements in realizing rights, we are very far still from achieving this ideal. This chapter examines how the normative standards of minimum core and reasonableness might contribute to the effective enjoyment of economic, social and cultural rights (ESCR). A discussion on legal standards may seem removed from the real needs of individuals and communities; however, a robust rights framework at the normative level lends itself to key outcomes. Findings of rights violations or strong remedies, for example, can support the translation of textual guarantees into concrete reality.

This chapter is not an in-depth exploration of the concepts of minimum core and reasonableness. The scope is confined to examining where the concepts of minimum core and reasonableness clearly interact as standards of review that courts or international bodies may utilize in adjudicative contexts in evaluating State compliance with their human rights obligations. Following this introduction, the chapter examines the conceptual foundations of the cross-cutting standards, and then turns to a consideration of key related normative developments and practice at the international, regional and domestic levels. Finally, the chapter explores critical fault lines in the context of minimum core and reasonableness, as well as core strategies to sharpen the potential of these standards to realize the transformative power of human rights.

## 2. CONCEPTUAL OVERVIEW

Courts or quasi-judicial bodies utilize a wide range of interpretative approaches or standards of review when adjudicating social rights, including, for example, progressive realization, non-retrogression, proportionality, minimum core and reasonableness. These various standards are not mutually exclusive,[2] and in fact, in ESCR decisions, are adopted in a range of different permutations.

---

[1]   ICESCR Preamble. Adopted 16 December 1966, entered into force 3 January 1976, 993 UNTS 3.
[2]   David Landau, 'Social Rights' in *Max Planck Encyclopedia of Comparative Constitutional Law* (2016) para 19 <http://oxcon.ouplaw.com/view/10.1093/law:mpeccol/law-mpeccol-e172>.

While conceptually the concepts of minimum core and reasonableness are distinct, there are areas of overlap in how these standards have normatively developed over time. In certain contexts, when applying these standards, judicial and quasi-judicial bodies have used one to the exclusion of the other, but in other instances they have been used in combination. Both standards seek to clarify the human rights obligations of States, and anchor judicial review aimed at holding States accountable.

The minimum core standard aims to confer minimum legal content for ESCR. Its main inquiry centers on whether the State is meeting minimum essential levels of a particular right.[3] Reasonableness, on the other hand, guides the review of whether the State is taking reasonable steps to meet its obligations under a particular right.[4]

## 2.1    Minimum Core

The minimum core standard provides specificity and essential normative content to ESCR, which tend to be framed in quite general terms. The concept addresses State obligations, but in doing so deepens the normative content of rights.[5] This helps clarify the parameters of State obligations. The minimum core concept suggests that there are degrees of fulfillment of a right and that a certain minimum level of fulfillment takes priority over a more extensive realization of the right.[6] To provide an example, the core obligations in relation to the right to water include, inter alia, States taking immediate measures 'to ensure access to the minimum essential amount of water, that is sufficient and safe for personal and domestic uses to prevent disease', on a non-discriminatory basis.[7]

A few key elements of minimum core, at least as shaped by the Committee on Economic, Social and Cultural Rights (CESCR),[8] include the obligations to: act in conformity with the principles of non-discrimination and equality; take positive steps to meet obligations; take on a heavy burden of proof and justify non-allocation of resources to meet minimum obligations;

---

[3]    CESCR, General Comment No. 3: The Nature of State Parties' Obligations (14 December 1990) E/1991/23 para 10.

[4]    See, for example, CESCR, 'An Evaluation of the Obligation to Take Steps to the "Maximum of Available Resources" under an Optional Protocol to the Covenant' (10 May 2007) E/C.12/2007/1 paras 8–13; United Nations Economic and Social Council, 'Report of the United Nations High Commissioner for Human Rights on the concept of "progressive realization" of economic, social and cultural rights in international human rights law' (25 June 2007) E/2007/82 para 71.

[5]    See General Comment No. 3 (n 3) where the Committee affirms that states parties have a *core obligation* to ensure the satisfaction of, at the very least, minimum essential levels of each of the rights enunciated in the Covenant. Thus, the primary focus really is on state duties; but in being able to appropriately evaluate state duties, it is important to articulate what constitutes minimum essential levels of a right. For example, the CESCR has interpreted that the right to health includes, *inter alia*, the obligations: '[T]o ensure the right of access to health facilities, goods and services on a non-discriminatory basis, especially for vulnerable or marginalized groups.' See CESCR, General Comment No. 14: The Right to the Highest Attainable Standard of Health (2000) E/C. 12/2000/4 para 43(a).

[6]    David Bilchitz, 'Towards a Reasonable Approach to the Minimum Core: Laying the Foundations for Future Socioeconomic Rights Jurisprudence' (2003) 19 S. Afr. J. Hum. Rts 1, 13.

[7]    CESCR, General Comment No. 15: The Right to Water (20 January 2003) UE/C.12/2002/11 para 37.

[8]    CESCR monitors implementation of ICESCR by its state parties.

formulate a legal and policy framework for the realization of rights; and prioritize the most vulnerable.[9]

'Minimum core' doctrine has been developed by the CESCR in the past decades. However, the concept of a minimum normative content of rights has much deeper roots historically. For example, the German principle of existenceminimum or 'subsistence minimum' derives from the German Basic Law adopted in 1949.[10]

The first formal articulation of minimum core by the CESCR in General Comment No. 3 provides 'that a minimum core obligation to ensure the satisfaction of, at the very least, minimum essential levels of each of the rights is incumbent upon every State party'.[11] The Committee however also notes that 'any assessment as to whether a State has discharged its minimum core obligation must also take account of resource constraints'.[12] Thus, the Committee underlines a sense of the non-negotiable in elaborating on minimum core but then renders it resource contingent. The Committee clarifies, however, that States must demonstrate 'that every effort has been made to use all resources that are at its disposition in an effort to satisfy, as a matter of priority, those minimum obligations'.[13]

Different approaches to understanding minimum core have been advanced. Young, for example, offers three approaches to understanding minimum core. The first approach, the essence approach, locates the minimum content of a right in the protection of liberal values such as human dignity, equality and freedom, and also in the more technical measure of basic needs and survival. The second approach, the consensus approach, situates the minimum core in the minimum consensus surrounding economic and social rights. The third approach, the obligations approach, prescribes minimum content to a right in light of the obligations raised by the right, rather than the right itself. Young recognizes that each of the aforementioned approaches suffers from serious normative difficulties, and that the standard of minimum core may well be indeterminate.[14]

Minimum core, with its absolute nature, is clearly not a simple, consistent, easily applicable legal standard that lends itself easily to evaluation by courts. Other issues also arise in relation to the concept – for example, separation of power-related concerns.[15] Those who support the minimum core standard argue that without identifying tangible content within rights which are often so abstract in their formulation and without explicitly linking such content to the actual satisfaction of material need, ESCR are reduced to meaningless rhetoric.[16]

---

[9]   See, for example, General Comment No. 3 (n 3); CESCR, General Comment No. 13: The Right to Education (8 December 1999) E/C.12/1999/10 para 57; General Comment No. 14 (n 5) para 43; General Comment No. 15 (n 7). See also, Sisay Alemahu Yeshanew, 'Approaches to the Justiciability of Economic, Social and Cultural Rights in the Jurisprudence of the African Commission on Human and Peoples' Rights: Progress and Perspectives' (2001) 11 AHRLJ 317, 321–23.

[10]   Ingrid Leijten, 'The German Right to an *Existenzminimum*, Human Dignity, and the Possibility of Minimum Core Socioeconomic Rights Protection' (2015) 16 Ger. Law J. 23, 29.

[11]   General Comment No. 3 (n 3).

[12]   Ibid.

[13]   Ibid.

[14]   See Katharine G. Young, 'The Minimum Core of Economic and Social Rights: A Concept in Search of Content' (2008) 33 Yale J. Int'l. L. 113, 126–38, 140–48, 151–64.

[15]   Carol Steinberg, 'Can Reasonableness Protect the Poor? A Review of South Africa's Socio-economic Rights Jurisprudence' (2006) 123 SALJ 264, 275–76.

[16]   See for example, Marius Pieterse, 'Eating Socio-economic Rights: The Usefulness of Rights Talk in Alleviating Social Hardship Revisited' (2007) HRQ 796, 799, 804, 820. Pieterse has shifted his

## 2.2    Reasonableness

Judicial and quasi-judicial organs have used the reasonableness standard to review the justi-fiability or reasonableness of States' conduct in the light of their obligations corresponding to ESCR.[17] This standard proposes a 'means–end inquiry', but in a form that is more robust than mere 'rationality review'.[18] To provide an example, to pass muster under the reasona-bleness standard of review in South Africa, in the context of State obligations in relation to the right to have access to adequate housing, the South African Constitutional Court has held that the State must take steps to ensure that its housing program is 'coherent',[19] 'balanced and flexible'[20] and 'comprehensive and workable'.[21] The review process further determined that a 'program that excludes a significant segment of society cannot be said to be reasonable'.[22] The reasonableness standard in the South African context is elaborated in Section 3.3 below.

Reasonableness as a concept has its roots in English administrative law, which was in fact a more forceful iteration of the very deferential legal test set out in the *Wednesbury* case,[23] which enquired only if a decision is so unreasonable that no decision maker could make it. However, the standard has been strengthened over time. While it was replaced in England by the proportionality test,[24] arguably due to England's colonial legacy and thus outsized influ-ence on common law, the 'reasonableness' test persists in several countries.

As a standard of review in ESCR adjudication, the reasonableness approach has been most influentially employed by the South African Constitutional Court. In addition, Article 8(4) of the Optional Protocol to the International Covenant on Economic, Social and Cultural Rights 2008 (OP-ICESCR)[25] provides that when examining complaints under the Protocol, 'the Committee shall consider the reasonableness of the steps taken by the State Party', bearing in mind that States 'may adopt a range of possible policy measures for the implementation of the rights' in the ICESCR. The CESCR has clarified in an earlier statement that in assessing the reasonableness of the measures taken by a state party to meet its human rights obligations under the ICESCR, it may consider:

(a)   the extent to which the measures taken were deliberate, concrete and targeted towards the fulfil-ment of economic, social and cultural rights;
(b)   whether the State party exercised its discretion in a non-discriminatory and non-arbitrary manner;

---

approach to minimum core over the years, as we shall see later in this chapter, but still emphasizes the critical need for concrete rights content.

[17]   Yeshanew (n 9) 325–26; See also, Malcolm Langford, 'The Justiciability of Social Rights: From Practice to Theory' in Malcolm Langford (ed), *Social Rights Jurisprudence: Emerging Trends in International and Comparative Law* (CUP 2008) 3, 43.

[18]   Katharine G. Young, 'Proportionality, Reasonableness, and Economic and Social Rights' in Vicki C. Jackson and Mark Tushnet (eds), *Proportionality: New Frontiers, New Challenges* (CUP 2018) 248, 252.

[19]   *Government of the Republic of South Africa v Grootboom* (2001) 1 SA 46 (CC) para 41.

[20]   Ibid para 43.

[21]   Ibid para 38.

[22]   Ibid para 43.

[23]   *Associated Provincial Picture Houses Ltd. v Wednesbury Corporation* (1948) 1 KB 223 (UK).

[24]   *Young* (n 18) 252–253.

[25]   Adopted 10 December 2008, entered into force 5 May 2013 (28 November 2008) A/63/435.

(c)  whether the State party's decision (not) to allocate available resources is in accordance with international human rights standards;

(d)  where several policy options are available, whether the State party adopts the option that least restricts Covenant rights;

(e)  the time frame in which the steps were taken;

(f)  whether the steps had taken into account the precarious situation of disadvantaged and marginalized individuals or groups and, whether they were non-discriminatory, and whether they prioritized grave situations or situations of risk.[26]

This draws from the criteria that South African jurisprudence has developed in relation to reasonableness.[27]

Reasonableness does not provide defined guarantees. However, it is flexible and nuanced in approach, and adjudicative bodies are clearly striving to create a robust standard that holds States accountable for failures to meet their human rights obligations.

## 3.  MINIMUM CORE AND REASONABLENESS AS CROSS-CUTTING STANDARDS: CONSIDERING NORMS AND PRACTICE

### 3.1  International Context: CESCR

It is within the work of the CESCR that minimum core and reasonableness perhaps find fullest expression as cross-cutting standards in the realm of ESCR. While neither concept is referenced within the ICESCR, both have been developed by the Committee as interpretive tools that support assessment of State compliance with their obligations under the ICESCR.

The CESCR started developing its iteration of the minimum core concept in 1990 in General Comment No. 3.[28] The Committee clarified: 'If the Covenant were to be read in such a way as not to establish such a minimum core obligation, it would be largely deprived of its raison d'être.'[29] The CESCR has gone on to give substance to the ICESCR's enumerated rights, including rights to food,[30] health,[31] education,[32] and water;[33] and national courts have been known to draw on these interpretations when they adopt the minimum core approach.[34] The CESCR has also used the minimum core standard of review when evaluating State compliance under the State reporting process, as well as in adjudicative contexts under the OP-ICESCR.[35]

---

[26]  CESCR (n 4) para 8.

[27]  Yeshanew (n 9) 326.

[28]  Ben T.C. Warwick, The Minimum Core's Place in Social Rights: Fixity vs Dynamism (Workshop Paper IILS Onati, 2017) 1.

[29]  General Comment No. 3 (n 3).

[30]  CESCR General Comment No. 12: The Right to Adequate Food (12 May 1999) E/C.12/1999/5 para 8.

[31]  General Comment No. 14 (n 5).

[32]  General Comment No. 13 (n 9).

[33]  General Comment No. 15 (n 7).

[34]  See, for example, various decisions from the Colombian Constitutional Court (CCC) including *T-859* (CCC, 2003); *T-025* (CCC 2004); CC Decision, *T-585* (CCC 2006).

[35]  CESCR, Views using the standard of minimum core include *Trujillo Calero v Ecuador*, Communication No. 10/2015 (26 March 2018) E/C.12/63/D/10/2015 (*Trujillo*).

The concept is found in 15 of the Committee's 23 General Comments, and up to 2016, more than 100 of its Concluding Observations referenced core obligations.[36] In deepening its commentary on core obligations, the CESCR has aligned the concept with the International Labour Organization's conception of a 'Social Protection Floor' (SPF), emphasizing the content aspect of the concept.[37]

In contrast to minimum core, the CESCR's reference to reasonableness as a standard of review is relatively recent, in direct relation to the adjudicative function of the Committee and first articulated in the Committee's 2007 Statement during the drafting of the OP-ICESCR.[38] Drafting history reveals that the Open Ended Working Group mandated to draft the OP-ICESCR drew on the experience of South Africa's constitutional system,[39] and decided on the reasonableness standard in the context of a highly charged political debate around an appropriate standard of review. The Working Group rejected calls to limit admissible claims to those relating to minimum core obligations rather than to all obligations and refused to accept more deferential evaluative alternatives such as unreasonableness or 'a broad margin of appreciation'.[40] The reasonableness standard is, as we have seen earlier,[41] contained in Article 8(4) of the OP-ICESCR. It is a standard familiar to many common law countries, which may have facilitated its ultimate adoption.[42]

Given the CESCR's authority in the normative landscape of ESCR, it is likely that the reasonableness standard and the robust articulation thereof by the Committee will influence national and regional-level adjudication over time. While UN treaty bodies are different from constitutional courts in role and function, 'there are cross-fertilizations ... in the standards and forms of review'.[43]

An important question, however, is: Which of the two standards of review will the Committee use in its adjudicative function, when assessing the compliance of States with their conventional duties? The OP-ICESCR clearly specifies reasonableness. As previously articulated, in 2007, the CESCR clarified how it intends to interpret the obligations under 2(1) of the Covenant, regarding the obligation of States to take steps to the maximum of their

---

[36]   Warwick (n 28) 2.

[37]   Ibid. See also, CESCR, 'Statement on Social Protection Floors: An Essential Element of the Right to Social Security and of the Sustainable Development Goals' (15 April 2015) E/C12/2015/1.

[38]   See, for example, Lilian Chenwi, 'Unpacking "Progressive Realisation", Its Relation to Resources, Minimum Core and Reasonableness, and Some Methodological Considerations for Assessing Compliance' (2013) 46 De Jure 742, 755.

[39]   Ibid (The wording in OP-ICESCR in relation to reasonableness was derived from the South African case *Government of the Republic of South Africa v Grootboom* (2001) 1 SA 46 (CC).)

[40]   For an overview of the drafting history, see Bruce Porter, 'Reasonableness and Article 8 (4)' in Malcolm Langford and others (eds), *The Optional Protocol to the International Covenant on Economic, Social and Cultural Rights: A Commentary* (PULP 2016) 173, 177–84.

[41]   See n 25 in Section 2.2.

[42]   Catarina de Albuquerque, 'Chronicle of an Announced Birth: The Coming into Life of the Optional Protocol to the International Covenant on Economic, Social and Cultural Rights – The Missing Piece of the International Bill of Human Rights' (2010) 31 HRQ 144, 161. It should be clarified though that the reasonableness standard in OP-ICESCR is linked to the more rigorous standard of review in ESCR adjudication as derived from South African jurisprudence and is to be distinguished from the reasonableness standard that exists in many common law countries, since the legal context can differ greatly. ESCR is not even justiciable in some of these countries. (See Section 2.2 for more context on the history of the reasonableness standard.)

[43]   Young (n 18) 270.

available resources, based on a reasonableness standard.[44] The statement does not reference minimum core while outlining its interpretation of reasonableness. However, while this reading of reasonableness eschews the content aspect of minimum core, it still incorporates key process elements of minimum core as interpreted by the CESCR, including adopting positive steps to meet obligations, complying with the principles of non-discrimination and equality, justifying non-allocation of resources in line with international human rights standards and prioritizing the most vulnerable.[45] The 2007 statement indicates that the CESCR is likely to take an approach that unites essential aspects of the two standards. On the other hand, the only context in which minimum core is explicitly mentioned in the statement is in relation to non-retrogressive measures. However, since then, the Committee has continued to develop and use the minimum core concept in ways beyond just evaluating retrogressive measures.[46]

In the *Trujillo* case determined in 2018,[47] the CESCR utilizes a combination approach, through using the minimum core standard in determining the normative content of the right to social security and then using reasonableness in its evaluation of State compliance with obligations under the ICESCR. The CESCR found that Ecuador had violated Marcia Cecilia Trujillo Calero's rights to social security and gender equality under the ICESCR when it failed to provide her with timely and adequate information on retirement plan eligibility and denied her pension based on disproportionate and discriminatory grounds. In laying out the relevant content aspects of the right to social security, the Committee avers that States are required to, inter alia, 'ensure access to a social security scheme that provides a minimum essential level of benefits'.[48] It references here both the core obligations as laid out in General Comment No. 19, and social protection floors,[49] which provide clarity regarding what is meant by 'minimum essential levels of benefits'.[50] The State draws on the minimum core concept both in terms of minimum content of the right to social security and minimum State obligations pursuant to the right.[51] Determining the scope of the right, including its minimum core content, and corresponding obligations informed the Committee's evaluation of State conduct in this case. In the course of such evaluation, the Committee reasoned that while Ecuador has some scope to adopt measures to regulate its social security scheme, the regulations must be reasonable, among other things, and that the State had not provided sufficient detail in this regard.[52] On this basis as well as other considerations, the CESCR found Ecuador in violation of the right to social security.[53]

Is the Committee then using a combination approach to incorporate 'a reasonableness standard into a core obligations-consistent framework'?[54] It seems this may be the case; however,

---

[44]   CESCR (n 4).
[45]   See n 9.
[46]   For example, in its use of minimum core in the *Trujillo* case discussed below.
[47]   *Trujillo* (n 35).
[48]   Ibid para 11.2.
[49]   CESCR, General Comment No. 19: Right to Social Security (4 February 2008) E/C.12/GC/19 para 59. See also CESCR statement (n 37) paras 7–8.
[50]   *Trujillo* (n 35) para 11.2 and n 17.
[51]   Ibid, read paras 11.2 and 14.2 together.
[52]   Ibid paras 12.1, 19.5.
[53]   Ibid para 21.
[54]   Lisa Forman, 'Can Minimum Core Obligations Survive a Reasonableness Standard of Review Under the Optional Protocol to the International Covenant on Economic, Social and Cultural Rights?' (2016) 47 Ottawa L Rev. 561, 562.

the CESCR's jurisprudence is still nascent. No consistent pattern has clearly emerged yet with respect to its use of standards.[55] How the CESCR plays a role in advancing the effective realization of ESCR will depend on its ability to hold States accountable, and in this context, how it interprets and applies the minimum core standard and reasonableness is significant. The Committee's approach is likely to guide the adjudication of ESCR across jurisdictions.[56]

While detailed examination is beyond the scope of this chapter, it is noteworthy that in addition to the CESCR, other United Nations treaty bodies have adopted or utilized the concept of core obligations as developed by CESCR, including the Committee on the Rights of the Child,[57] as well as the Committee on Persons with Disabilities.[58] As regards reasonableness, for example, the Convention on the Rights of Persons with Disabilities 2006 (CRPD) addresses reasonable accommodations of disability, and the Human Rights Committee has affirmed a number of principles of reasonableness.[59] How these standards interact with each other, both within individual treaty bodies and among them, will further inform international normative developments in relation to the two cross-cutting standards.

### 3.2   Regional Context: African and Inter-American Human Rights Systems

Due to the limited scope of this chapter, this section limits itself to a brief consideration of certain key developments in the African and Inter-American human rights systems.

#### 3.2.1   African system

The African Charter on Human and Peoples' Rights 1981 (African Charter),[60] like the ICESCR, does not contain direct reference to either minimum core or reasonableness. However, the African Commission on Human and Peoples' Rights (the African Commission) has recognized minimum core obligations providing that 'States parties have an obligation to ensure the satisfaction of, at the very least, the minimum essential levels of each of the economic, social and cultural rights contained in the African Charter'.[61] The conception of minimum core therein is a clear reflection of the approach developed by the CESCR. In adju-

---

[55]   In the two other cases in which CESCR has held in favor of the claimants, there is not a clear reference to minimum core, but reasonableness is clearly utilized as a standard of review. See *Mohamed Ben Djazia and Naouel Bellili v Spain*, Communication No. 5/2015 (CESCR, 20 June 2017) E/C.12/61/D/5/2015 (*Djazia*); *IDG v Spain*, Communication No. 2/2014 (CESCR, 1–19 June 2015) E/C.12/55/D/2/2014. Just to note, in *Djazia* para 15.5 and footnote 33, when elaborating on the reasonableness standard, the CESCR cites the 2007 statement which while ostensibly on reasonableness, does include key process elements of minimum core.

[56]   Forman (n 54) 573.

[57]   Warwick (n 28) 2.

[58]   Committee on the Rights of Persons with Disabilities, General Comment No. 4: The Right to Inclusive Education (2 September 2016) CRPD/C/GC/4 para 40.

[59]   Porter (n 40) 200. The CRPD was adopted 13 December 2006, entered into force 3 May 2008, 2515 UNTS 3.

[60]   Adopted 27 June 1981, entered into force 21 October 1986 CAB/LEG/67/3 rev. 5, 1520 UNTS 217.

[61]   African Commission on Human and Peoples' Rights, 'Principles and Guidelines on the Implementation of Economic, Social and Cultural Rights in the African Charter on Human and Peoples' Rights' (2011) para 17. After laying out general minimum core obligations in para 17, the Principles and Guidelines examine the minimum core obligation for each substantive right, including the rights to food, education, health, social security, housing, water and sanitation and work.

dicative contexts, the African Commission has utilized both the minimum core and reasonableness standards in evaluating States' compliance with their human rights obligations. The Commission in its case law has focused, in particular, on the minimum duties of a State rather than the minimum essential levels of a right.[62] As regards reasonableness, the Commission, has for example, urged States to 'take reasonable and other measures',[63] as well as clarified that, where State action is alleged to have interfered with the enjoyment of a human right, 'it is for the Respondent State to prove that such interference is … reasonable'.[64]

Of particular relevance is the *SERAC* case,[65] which addressed allegations against the Nigerian government in relation to a range of ESCR violations attributed to its condoning and facilitating the operations of oil corporations in Ogoniland. The Commission held that:

> The government's treatment of the Ogonis has violated all three minimum duties of the right to food. The government has destroyed food sources through its security forces and state oil company; has allowed private oil companies to destroy food sources; and, through terror, has created significant obstacles to Ogoni communities trying to feed themselves. The Nigerian Government has again fallen short of what is expected of it as under the provisions of the African Charter and international human rights standards, and hence, is in violation of the right to food of the Ogonis.[66]

In its decision, the Commission also specified minimum State obligations in relation to the right to housing.[67] Moreover, the Commission highlighted the obligation of States to 'take reasonable and other measures', but in relation to the right to a generally satisfactory environment.[68] It did not specify what constitutes 'reasonable' steps. In the *SERAC* case, both the reasonableness and minimum core standards are used in reviewing compliance with State obligations, but not in immediately cross-cutting ways and with respect to the same substantive rights – more in parallel with each other, informing the key deliberations of the Commission.

In a later case on the rights of mental health patients in The Gambia,[69] the African Commission, in relation to the right to health, urged the State 'to take concrete and targeted steps' and to realize the right 'without discrimination of any kind'. While this language mirrors, to an extent, the CESCR's reasonableness review, that standard draws key elements from the minimum core doctrine as developed by the CESCR.[70]

---

[62]   Chenwi (n 38) 754.
[63]   *Social and Economic Rights Action Centre and the Centre for Economic and Social Rights v Nigeria* Communication No. 155/96, (2001) AHRLR 60 (ACHPR 2001) para 52 (*SERAC*).
[64]   *Endorois case Centre for Minority Rights Development (Kenya) and Minority Rights Group International on behalf of Endorois Welfare Council v Kenya* Communication No 276/2003, (2009) AHRLR 75 (ACHPR 2009) para 172.
[65]   *SERAC* (n 63).
[66]   *SERAC* (n 63) para 66. The use of the minimum core language in the Ogoni case suggests that the African Commission has been following the jurisprudential debates about the definition of the normative content of ESCR. Another key issue to be noted is that the Commission did not formulate these minimum duties itself but adopted suggestions from the complainants. Fons Coomans, 'The Ogoni Case before the African Commission on Human and Peoples' Rights' (2003) 52 International and Comparative Law Quarterly 749, 755–57.
[67]   *SERAC* (n 63) para 61.
[68]   Ibid para 52.
[69]   *Purohit & Another v The Gambia* Communication No. 241/2001 (ACHPR 2003) para 84.
[70]   Finally, although it has not used clear minimum core language in this case, the Commission 'imported the standards which the ESCR Committee adopted in defining the nature of states' obligations

In the *Ogiek* case,[71] the African Court on Human and Peoples' Rights held that the distinct culture of the Ogiek was centered and dependent on the Mau forest, and that their eviction affects the 'essence'[72] of their right to culture. The Court found that the State had not adequately substantiated its claim that the eviction of the Ogiek population was for the preservation of the natural ecosystem of the Mau Forest and determined that the eviction, as interference with the Ogiek peoples' right to culture, cannot be said to have been warranted by an objective and reasonable justification.[73] While the Court did not apply the minimum core standard directly, or reasonableness test in a substantive way, the cross-cutting standards seem to have been utilized in determining a violation of the right to culture.

The African system's approach is not entirely consistent or coherent yet with regard to minimum core or reasonableness, and in particular their cross-cutting attributes. It remains to be seen how it continues to clarify and deepen these standards and utilize them to hold States accountable.

### 3.2.2   Inter-American system

As regards the Inter-American system of human rights, the American Convention on Human Rights does not explicitly reference either minimum core or reasonableness.[74] However, related standards and jurisprudence within the system recognize at least a variant of the minimum core standard,[75] as well as the reasonableness test.[76]

The *Xákmok Kásek* case,[77] concerning the State's responsibility for the failure to ensure the right of the Xákmok Kásek Indigenous Community to their ancestral territory,[78] is of particular interest. This case on ESCR was one determined through the application of the right to life. It demonstrates the cross-cutting use of the standards of minimum core and reasonableness. As part of the Court's reasonableness assessment, the Court considered State measures taken with respect to 'access to and quality of water', 'diet', 'health' and 'education'.[79] In its analysis, the Court extensively references General Comment Nos. 15, 12 and 13 (on the rights to adequate water, food and education, respectively) of the CESCR, as well as other international standards

---

in the General Comment in which it adopted the minimum core model for the first time. It is probably for this reason that commentators close to the Commission considered its definition of the obligations of states in this case as an indication that it was "leaning towards" or "importing" the minimum core standard of the ESCR Committee.' Yeshanew (n 9) 324.

[71]   *African Commission on Human and Peoples' Rights v Kenya* Application No. 006/2012 (ACtHPR 2017) (*Ogiek*).
[72]   This mirrors the essence approach proposed by Young. See Young (n 14).
[73]   *Ogiek* (n 71) para 145.
[74]   American Convention on Human Rights, Adopted 22 November 1969, entered into force 18 July 1978, OAS Treaty Series No 36.
[75]   See, for example, Annual report of the Inter-American Commission on Human Rights (Annual Report, 1994) 524 ('[T]he obligation of member states to observe and defend the human rights of individuals within their jurisdictions, as set forth in both the American Declaration and the American Convention, obligates them, regardless of the level of economic development, to guarantee a minimum threshold of these rights'). See also, *Case of the Xákmok Kásek Indigenous Community v Paraguay* (Inter-American Court of Human Rights 2010) paras 193–217 (*Xákmok Kásek*).
[76]   *Case of Velásquez-Rodríguez v Honduras* (Inter-American Court of Human Rights 1988) para 174 ('The State has a legal duty to take reasonable steps to prevent human rights violations').
[77]   *Xákmok Kásek* (n 75).
[78]   Ibid para 2.
[79]   Ibid paras 194–217.

articulated for example in the Protocol of San Salvador,[80] and in ILO Convention 169,[81] in particular to determine the minimum essential levels that must be met with respect to these rights – acknowledging for instance that, as per General Comment No. 15 and other key sources, most people need a minimum of 7.5 liters of water a day to meet their basic needs.[82] With respect to the right to food, the Court recognizes that it must determine, inter alia, 'whether the assistance provided satisfied the basic requirements of an adequate diet'.[83] Drawing on General Comment No. 12 on the core content of the right to food, the Court determined that the amount of food provided by the State – approximately 0.29 kilos per person per day – was insufficient to satisfy, even moderately, the basic daily dietary needs of any individual.[84] While referencing the minimum core standard, the Court also reaffirmed, again on the basis of General Comment No. 12, that the right to food goes beyond simple adherence to a minimum baseline, and that '[t]he right to adequate nutrition shall not … be interpreted in a narrow or restrictive sense which equates it with a minimum package of calories, proteins and other specific nutrients'.[85] Arguably, in this specific instance, this sets the bar for the reasonableness test higher than a minimum core standard. Based on its overall analysis, and a combination approach in its use of the reasonableness inquiry and minimum core standard, the Court concluded that the steps undertaken by the State were not sufficient and that consequently it was in breach of the right to a decent life as part of an overarching human right to life of all the members of the Xákmok Kásek Community.[86] In terms of analysis, it is not clear how precisely the Court assessed reasonableness with respect to State conduct.

In a relatively recent development, since 2017, the Court has started adjudicating ESCR cases directly under Article 26 of the American Convention.[87] There are faint indications that the Court may be moving towards a combination approach as relates to minimum core and reasonableness. Consider *Cuscul Pivaral*,[88] a case concerning 49 people diagnosed with HIV, in which the Court ruled that Guatemala had violated the right to health. In establishing the right to health as an autonomous and justiciable right, the Court partially draws on minimum core obligations developed by the CESCR.[89] Moreover, in determining that states have an

---

[80]   Additional Protocol to the American Convention on Human Rights in the Area of Economic, Social and Cultural Rights 'Protocol of San Salvador', adopted 17 November 1988, entered into force 16 November 1999, OAS Treaty Series No 69.

[81]   ILO Indigenous and Tribal Peoples Convention, adopted 27 June 1989, entered into force 5 September 1991, C-169.

[82]   *Xákmok Kásek* (n 75) para 195.

[83]   Ibid para 198.

[84]   Ibid para 200.

[85]   Ibid n 224.

[86]   Ibid paras 214 and 217. See also, on the case in general, Tara Melish, 'The Inter-American Court of Human Rights: Beyond Progressivity' in Malcolm Langford (ed), *Social Rights Jurisprudence: Emerging Trends in Comparative and International Law* (CUP 2008) (updated version of chapter, 2011) 35, 36.

[87]   Cases include, among others, *Acevedo Buendía et al. ('Discharged and Retired Employees of the Comptroller') v Peru* (Inter-American Court of Human Rights 2009); *Lakes of the Field v Peru* (Inter-American Court of Human Rights 2017); *Poblete Vilches and Others v Chile*, (Inter-American Court of Human Rights 2018); *Cuscul Pivaral and others v Guatemala* (Inter-American Court of Human Rights 2018) (*Cuscul*).

[88]   *Cuscul* (n 87).

[89]   The Court highlights an interrelation between the commitment of states to guarantee efficient social security policy and its duty to guarantee health care, and in so doing references para 59 on core obligations under General Comment No. 19 (on the right to social security). *Cuscul* (n 87) footnote 101.

obligation 'to take steps', the Court cited paragraph 8 of the CESCR's 2007 statement which details a standard of reasonableness that also draws on key elements of the minimum core standard.[90] However, in neither instance is the reference to the standard strong enough to establish any intersection between the two standards. As the Inter-American Court takes on more direct ESCR cases, how the system adopts or not, the different standards of review, including minimum core and reasonableness, and to what extent this influences the effective enforcement of rights under the Charter remains to be seen.

### 3.3   Domestic Context: Selected Cases

While in particular judicial systems both minimum core and reasonableness exist as standards of review, courts have often relied on only one or the other. Furthermore, the standards do not necessarily mirror the concepts as developed by the CESCR. They manifest as standards shaped by particular legal histories and political contexts. This section considers some examples of jurisdictions which have embraced a minimum core or reasonableness approach to inform subsequent discussions on how these standards can complement or undermine each other. While the focus is on South Africa, which has led the way in this jurisprudence, other jurisdictions are also briefly considered.

### 3.3.1   A minimum core focus

To date, at the national level, there has not been an extensive use of the minimum core concept as developed by the CESCR. However, domesticated understandings of 'constitutional minimum' or 'the essential minimum of the right' are articulated in different constitutional systems.[91] Colombia provides a clear example of a jurisdiction which explicitly embraces the minimum core standard as shaped by the CESCR, in its ESCR adjudication, deriving the authority to do so from Colombia's monist approach to international law.[92] Several cases have identified the minimum core of ESCR, such as the right to health and the right to housing.[93]

A case in point is T-760/2008,[94] where the Colombian Constitutional Court handed down a decision in which it ordered a dramatic restructuring of the country's health system. It adopted a clear minimum core approach by drawing on the CESCR's right to health framework and giving very specific content to the right to health, including by specifying that the right is immediately enforceable for certain categories of plaintiffs even if they are unable to afford health care. For these categories, the Court has ordered the provision of a wide range of goods and services, including viral load tests for HIV/AIDS as well as anti-retrovirals, costly cancer medications, and even the financing of treatment of patients abroad when appropriate treatment was unavailable in Colombia, all of which are considerably resource intensive measures. Moreover, when pronouncing on the right to health, the Court distinguished an essential minimum core of the right to health based on the POS (mandatory health plan)/POSS

---

[90]   *Cuscul* (n 87) para 142.

[91]   For example, in India, Germany and the State of New York. Some key cases include: *Paschim Banga Khet Mazdoor Samity v State of West Bengal* (1996) AIR SC 2426, 2429; *People's Union for Civil Liberties v Union of India & Ors* (2001) 7 SCALE; *Hartz IV* 1 BVL 1/09 (German Federal Constitutional Court 2010); *Campaign for Fiscal Equity v State of NY* (2003) 100 N.Y. 2d 893.

[92]   Constitution of Colombia 1991 Article 93.

[93]   See n 34.

[94]   CCC decision, *T-760* (2008).

(subsidized mandatory health plan), which was to be immediately enforceable, and other elements that are subject to progressive realization.[95] In another case, T-025,[96] the Colombian Court adopted a minimum core approach. While providing clarity that there were immediate State obligations to be met with respect to internally displaced persons, in practice the Court gave latitude to the State and civil society to shape the more precise content of the core set of entitlements. This provided specificity to the right while avoiding the separation of powers and institutional capacity concerns with respect to minimum core.[97] Variations of the minimum core approach can be said to be adopted by a number of countries, including Germany, the United States (in the context of state constitutions) and India.[98]

The German Federal Constitutional Court has 'explicitly read into the German Basic Law ... well-defined guarantees in the field of socioeconomic policy ... It concerns the constitutionally guaranteed Existenzminimum, or "subsistence minimum," that involves the means for living a life in accordance with human dignity.'[99] Existenzminimum was not inspired by the minimum core standard developed by the CESCR but is a more domesticated conception of the standard. In the *Hartz IV* case,[100] the Court carefully scrutinized the legislature's calculation of welfare benefits and found them unconstitutional in light of the minimum needed to realize the right to human dignity guaranteed by the Basic Law. The judgment even considers that countries can adopt context-specific minimum content for welfare rights. However, while using a minimum core approach to evaluate State obligations, the Court then deferred to the legislature with regard to determining benefits that complied with constitutional guarantees, with an acknowledgment of separation of powers, addressing thus a key critique of minimum core.[101]

Meanwhile, the United States Constitution does not include socio-economic rights, but some state constitutions do. For example, the Constitution of the State of New York has a provision on the right to education. *Campaign for Fiscal Equity (CFE) v State of NY* is an important case under this provision. While the case does not use the precise term 'minimum core' or reference the minimum core interpretations of the CESCR, the case does use terms such as 'constitutional minimum' repeatedly and appears to take a minimum core approach

---

95   CCC decision, *T-760* (2008). For an in-depth review of the case, see Alicia Ely Yamin and Oscar Parra-Vera, 'How Do Courts Set Health Policy? The Case of the Colombian Constitutional Court' (2009) 6 PLoS Med. <10.1371/journal.pmed.1000032>.

96   CCC decision, *T-025* (2004).

97   Landau (n 2).

98   Other jurisdictions that utilize a variation of the minimum core approach include Brazil and Argentina (see Christian Courtis, *Courts and the Legal Enforcement of Economic and Social Rights* (ICJ, 2008) 25), as well as Switzerland and Hungary. (The apex courts of Hungary and Switzerland appear to have adopted a more conservative approach to minimum core where '[t]hey have largely declined to accept any role in examining whether the Government has sufficiently taken steps to realize constitutional social rights – the former merely requiring that such a law or programme exist ... and they instead only look to whether a minimum of the right is met'. See Malcolm Langford, 'Domestic Adjudication and Economic, Social and Cultural Rights: A Socio-legal Review' (2009) 6 (11) Sur. Rev. Int. Direitos Human 91, 103.)

99   Leitjen (n 10) 28.

100   *Hartz IV* (n 91).

101   For a critical in depth look at the case from a minimum core perspective, see generally, Oliver Fuo & Anél Du Plessis, 'In the Face of Judicial Deference: Taking the "Minimum Core" of Socio-economic Rights to the Local Government Sphere' (2015) 19 Law Democr. Dev. 1–28.

in determining government obligations. Here, the Court first allowed the government to act within a specific time frame; when the government did not return with an appropriate policy plan within that time, the Court took it upon itself to frame policy through a panel. So, when it comes to policy-oriented matters, the courts may defer to the State but should also be proactive if the State does not fulfill what is mandated of it.[102]

India adopts a domesticated understanding of the minimum core standard. In Indian case law, there does not appear to be explicit mention per se of minimum core, or acknowledgment of the CESCR's interpretation of the concept. Nevertheless, the standard appears to be used on a regular basis to tease out elements of rights and corresponding State obligations, couched in language such as the essential minimum of the right and what is minimally required.[103]

### 3.3.2    A reasonableness approach

Courts in certain national jurisdictions have adopted reasonableness as a standard of review, including Canada and South Africa. A particularly relevant Canadian case is *Eldridge v British Columbia (Attorney General)*.[104] In this case, involving interpretation for deaf individuals in a health care context, the court held that the right to equality places obligations on governmental actors to allocate resources to ensure that disadvantaged groups have full advantage of public benefits. It found that the government had failed to show a reasonable basis for denying medical interpretation services. The court ordered that the relevant rule in this case be suspended for six months, leaving the government to fashion an appropriate solution, stating that 'there were a myriad of options available to the government'.[105]

Given that the CESCR has adopted its reasonableness standard directly from South Africa, and that the Constitutional Court has engaged in dialogue regarding its choice of reasonableness as its primary standard of review and not minimum core, South African case law is of particular relevance.

The reasonableness standard is directly embedded in the text of the South African Constitution. The country's Constitutional Court, in high profile cases, has outright rejected the minimum core approach. In the case of *Government of Republic of South Africa v Irene Grootboom and Others*,[106] the petitioners, forced by appalling living circumstances to illegally occupy land, were forcibly evicted and, in desperation, settled on a sports field and in

---

[102] See *Campaign for Fiscal Equity v State of NY*, 100 N.Y. 2d 893 (N.Y. 2003) para 3; *Campaign for Fiscal Equity v State of NY*, 8 N.Y. 3d 14, 861 N.E. 2d 50 (N.Y. 2006); *Levittown v Nyquist*, 57 N.Y. 2d 27 (N.Y. 1982).

[103] See for example, *Paschim Banga Khet Mazdoor Samity v State of West Bengal* (1996) AIR SC 2426, 2429; *People's Union for Civil Liberties v Union of India & Ors* (2001) 7 SCALE. See also, Dr S. Muralidhar, 'Economic, Social and Cultural Rights: An Indian Response to the Justiciability Debate' in Yash Ghai and Jim Cottrell (eds), *Economic, Social and Cultural Rights in Practice* (Interrights 2003) 23–32. Indian courts also use a domesticated understanding of reasonableness as a key standard of review. (See generally, Chintan Chandrachud, 'Proportionality, Judicial Reasoning, and the Indian Supreme Court' (2017) 1 Anti-Discrimination Law Review 87; *Olga Tellis v Bombay Municipal Corporation*, AIR 1986 SC 180; *State of Madras v V G Row*, 1952 AIR 196.) However, to the author's knowledge, the Indian Supreme Court has not in any considered way developed its core obligations approach, such as it is, in combination with the reasonableness approach.

[104] *Eldridge v British Columbia (Attorney General)*, (1997) 3 S.C.R. 624.

[105] Ibid. See also, *Eldridge v British Columbia (Attorney General)*, ESCR-Net case summary <www.escr-net.org/caselaw/2006/eldridge-v-british-columbia-attorney-general-1997-3-scr-624>.

[106] *Grootboom* (n 39).

an adjacent community hall. The Constitutional Court found a violation to the right to ade-quate housing under Section 26 of the Constitution (on the right to have access to adequate housing). This decision, which established reasonableness as the standard for evaluating State compliance with constitutionally guaranteed ESCR, held that the State's primary obligation is to act reasonably to provide the basic necessities of life to those who lack them.[107] This rea-sonableness standard as delineated by the Court requires, inter alia, comprehensive programs to meet short, medium and long-term needs, prioritizing the most vulnerable and those in extreme need.[108] Basing its judgment on the reasonableness standard, the Court held that the State housing system in place did not meet the standard of reasonableness, as it unreasonably failed to consider those desperately in need of housing.[109] The Court issued a declaratory order requiring the State to implement progressively, within its available resources, a comprehensive program to realize the right of access to adequate housing with provisions which undertook to provide shelter for those in desperate need of housing either due to intolerable living condi-tions or crisis situations.[110] Another key element of the reasonableness standard that emerged in this case and was developed in subsequent cases is that of 'meaningful engagement', with the Court expressing its expectation that officials of the municipality responsible for housing engage with those occupying land and facing eviction.[111] The Court also emphasized in the case that 'it is fundamental to an evaluation of the reasonableness of state action that account be taken of the inherent dignity of human beings'[112] and that at the very least, evictions be humanely executed.[113] In response to a request from the amicus curiae to delineate an imme-diately enforceable right within the right to housing, the Court noted that the CESCR 'does not specify precisely what the minimum core is',[114] and explicitly rejected the minimum core approach used by the Committee as unavailable to it since it lacks the extensive information resources of the Committee to define the minimum core.[115] While the Court noted that 'there may be cases where it may be possible and appropriate to have regard to the content of a minimum core obligation to determine whether the measures taken by the State are reasona-ble', the Court reiterated that even if it were to be appropriate, the Court would need sufficient information placed before it.[116]

---

[107] Forman (n 54) 569; *Grootboom* (n 39) paras 24 and 44.

[108] *Grootboom* (n 39) para 43.

[109] Ibid para 95.

[110] Ibid para 99.

[111] Ibid para 87. Since *Grootboom*, the principle of engagement has been developed further as 'meaningful engagement' in a range of different cases (see for example, *Port Elizabeth Municipality v Various Occupiers* (2004) 12 BCLR 1268 (CC) paras 39, 41, 43, 12–18; *Occupiers of 51 Olivia Road and Others v City of Johannesburg and Others* (2008) 5 BCLR 475 (CC) paras 14, 17–18, 20, 24–30; *Residents of Joe Slovo Community, Western Cape v Thubelisha Homes and Others* [2009] 9 BCLR 847 (CC) paras 117, 202–02) as 'both a requirement for a reasonable government policy in socio-economic rights cases as well as a remedy where inadequate engagement occurred prior to litigation'. (Shanelle van der Berg, 'Meaningful Engagement: Proceduralising Socioeconomic Rights Further or Infusing Administrative Law with Substance?' (2013) 29 SAJHR 376, abstract.) To read more on meaningful engagement in South African case law, see Lilian Chenwi, 'Implementation of Housing Rights in South Africa: Approaches and Strategies' (2015) 24 Journal of Law and Social Policy 68, 78–80.

[112] *Grootboom* (n 39) para 83.

[113] Ibid para 88.

[114] Ibid para 30.

[115] Ibid paras 32–33.

[116] Ibid para 33.

Another relevant case is *Minister of Health v Treatment Action Campaign* (*TAC* case),[117] in which a constitutional challenge was brought by TAC against the government's policy of limiting the provision of Nevirapine, a drug to prevent mother-to-child transmission of HIV, to select pilot sites. The Constitutional Court, basing its decision yet again on the reasonableness standard, found that the government program in this case failed the reasonableness test and ordered the government to remove without delay the restrictions that prevented Nevirapine from being made available outside the pilot sites. The government was also required, as part of an immediate national program to be created within available resources, to extend testing and counseling facilities related to mother-to-child transmission (MTCT) throughout the public health sector.[118] However, here too, in response to an amicus curiae appeal for a delineation of minimum core, the Court formally rejected the minimum core approach in the case, asserting, among a range of other reasons, that it is impossible to give everyone access to a core service immediately.[119] Yet despite its rejection, the Court again indicated that evidence in a particular case might show that there is a minimum core of a particular service that should be considered in determining whether or not measures adopted by the State are reasonable, and that it may consider minimum core in guiding its assessment of reasonableness.[120]

In another key case, *Mazibuko*,[121] the Constitutional Court not only reiterated its rejection of minimum core but also diluted the reasonableness standard as had been developed in its earlier jurisprudence. In this case, applicants challenged first the City of Johannesburg's Free Basic Water policy, in terms of which 6 kiloliters of water were provided monthly for free to all households in Johannesburg, and second the lawfulness of the installation of pre-paid water meters in Phiri to charge consumers for use of water in excess of their allowance. The imposition of limits left poor households without water for days on a monthly basis.[122] The High Court took a robust rights approach that foregrounded the needs of the most vulnerable. Following a close scrutiny of government action through the reasonableness lens, it found the government in violation of the Constitution, and ordered the City to provide each applicant household and all similarly situated households with 50 liters of water per person per day. On appeal, the Supreme Court also upheld the ruling in favor of the petitioners, holding the City's water supply to be insufficient and therefore unreasonable, and ordering the City to provide 42 liters of water per person per day to the applicants and all similarly situated people.[123] However, the Constitutional Court ruled against the applicants and found that the City's water policy was reasonable because the government had shifted its course during the litigation period, demonstrating flexibility to the Court – a key element of reasonableness.[124] Thus, the

---

[117]    *Minister of Health v Treatment Action Campaign* (2002) 5SA 721 (CC) (*TAC*).

[118]    Ibid para 135.

[119]    Ibid para 32.

[120]    Ibid para 34.

[121]    *Mazibuko and Others v City of Johannesburg and Others* (2010) (4) SA 1 (CC) (Mazibuko); for an indepth analysis of this case, see generally, Jackie Dugard, 'Testing the Transformative Premise of the South African Constitutional Court: A Comparison of High Courts, Supreme Court of Appeal and Constitutional Court Socio-economic Rights Decisions, 1994–2015' (2016) 20 IJHR 1132–60.

[122]    Dugard (n 121) 1132, 1146.

[123]    Constitutional Court of South Africa, 'Lindiwe Mazibuko and Others v City of Johannesburg and Others – Media Summary' (8 October 2009) <www.saflii.org/za/cases/ZACC/2009/28media.pdf>.

[124]    *Mazibuko* (n 121) paras 94–97.

Constitutional Court took a 'highly deferential approach to the policy choices of the City',[125] taking a far more narrow approach to its own interpretation of the reasonableness standard as established in *Grootboom*, despite evidence that more than 100,000 city households did not have enough water.[126] In the case, in rejection of minimum core, the Constitutional Court noted that fixing 'a quantified content might, in a rigid and counter-productive manner, prevent an analysis of context',[127] an important consideration in the reasonableness inquiry. In addition, the Court specified, as a matter of democratic accountability, that it was desirable that the executive and the legislature should determine the content of ESCR because it was their programs and promises that were subjected to democratic choice.[128] While all this may be fine to consider in the abstract, if it results in not meeting fundamental human rights, especially in relation to those most vulnerable and marginalized, then it deprives rights of meaning.

While *Mazibuko* is a significant reminder of how the reasonableness standard, stripped of key substantive elements, can lead to excessive deference to the State to the detriment of human rights, *Grootboom* and *TAC* highlight that depending on how the standard is consti-tuted, 'the reasonableness approach might do similar work to the minimum core to the extent that it forces courts to focus on basic and urgent needs of the most vulnerable, marginalized, and poor people in society'.[129] The cases also demonstrate that the reasonable standard, as adopted in South Africa, belies its perception as a standard without content, with the Court imposing concrete obligations, both procedural and substantive, on the State.[130]

While usage clearly varies across jurisdictions, and although their application by courts and quasi-judicial bodies can at times lack consistency and reasoned analysis, it is evident that minimum core and reasonableness, as standards utilized in the adjudication of economic, social and cultural rights, are developing a more robust character over time, with distinct elements that support the Court's assessment of State compliance with human rights. The following section examines the political faultlines surrounding these standards of review and examines strategies to strengthen their potential to realize the transformative power of human rights.

---

[125] Sandra Liebenberg, *Socio-economic Rights: Adjudication under a Transformative Constitution* (Juta 2010) 469.

[126] Forman (n 54) 570.

[127] *Mazibuko* (n 121) para 60.

[128] Ibid para 61.

[129] Forman (n 54) 570.

[130] This is further reinforced upon analysis of other South African cases relating to ESCR, and recognizing how the reasonableness approach requires States to ensure concrete outcomes, grounded in procedural and substantive obligations, including meaningful engagement with affected communities in eviction proceedings, and housing policy more broadly, as well as very specific minimum require-ments in terms of location and adequacy of alternative accommodations. (See generally *Port Elizabeth Municipality v Various Occupiers* (2004) 12 BCLR 1268 (CC); *Occupiers of 51 Olivia Road and Others v City of Johannesburg and Others* (2008) 5 BCLR 475 (CC)); *Residents of Joe Slovo Community, Western Cape v Thubelisha Homes and Others* [2009] 9 BCLR 847 (CC)). For more on the reasonable approach and what it entails, see generally, Jackie Dugard & Michael Clark, et al., *The Right to Housing in South Africa, in Socio-economic Rights – Progressive Realisation?* (Foundation for Human Rights 2016), <www.fhr.org.za/files/8015/1247/0285/Socio_Economic_Rights.pdf>.

## 4.    EXPLORING THE FAULTLINES

Legal standards such as minimum core and reasonableness are key in adjudicative contexts, and by extension in protecting human rights by creating a strong normative basis to hold States accountable. It is essential that courts, when applying such standards or tests, accompany the application with clear and reasoned analysis, which is critical for 'purposes of both assessing liability and crafting appropriate and responsive remedial measures'.[131] Minimum core and reasonableness have generated a lot of insightful commentary that exposes political faultlines, and simultaneously highlights both the contradictions inherent in these cross-cutting standards and their complementary attributes.

### 4.1    Reasonableness

The reasonableness inquiry has attracted both support and criticism. Liebenberg appreciates how the reasonableness approach provides courts 'with a flexible and context-sensitive basis for evaluating socioeconomic rights claims'[132] while, inter alia, prioritizing in its scrutiny of government measures the requirement of inclusiveness and the needs of the most vulnerable.[133] In support of reasonableness, Porter critiques the absolute nature of minimum core, finding it important that ESCR adjudication be grounded in the individual context of each claim and focus on the underlying interests of the most vulnerable.[134] He demonstrates how the lack of context specificity might render the minimum core approach a counter-productive litigation strategy, permitting respondents to argue that courts must address the universal questions before focusing on the specific case, and then, on this basis, posit that courts are not competent to adjudicate economic, social and cultural rights claims.[135] Porter clarifies that the reasonableness standard must go beyond an entitlement to reasonableness policy, and that the starting point of examination should be the rights and dignity interests of claimants.[136]

The primary critique of the reasonableness standard, often in relation to minimum core which provides normative content to rights, is that the reasonableness standard fails to award meaningful content to ESCR, rendering it excessively subjective in nature.[137] Currie has written that:

---

[131]    Melish (n 86) 37.

[132]    Sandra Liebenberg, 'Socio-economic Right Revisiting the Reasonableness Review/Minimum Core Debate' in Stu Woolman and Michael Bishop (eds), *Constitutional Conversations* (Pretoria University Law Press 2008) 305, 321–22.

[133]    Ibid.

[134]    Bruce Porter, 'Towards a Comprehensive Framework for ESC Rights Practice' (2006) 7 and 10.    <http://socialrightscura.ca/documents/publications/SRAP%20publications/porter_toward_an_esc_rights_practice.pdf>.

[135]    For example, in claims relating to the right to an adequate standard of living in Canada, governments have routinely contended that the lack of expert consensus on a clearly defined poverty line of universal application is proof that courts should not engage with this area of policy. See ibid 9.

[136]    Ibid 12.

[137]    Marius Pieterse, 'Eating Socio-economic Rights: The Usefulness of Rights Talk in Alleviating Social Hardship Revisited' (2007) 29 HRQ 796, 800; Also see David Bilchitz, 'Towards a Reasonable Approach to the Minimum Core: Laying the Foundations for Future Socioeconomic Rights Jurisprudence' (2003) 19 S. Afr. J. Hum. Rts. 1–26; Sandra Liebenberg, 'South Africa's Evolving Jurisprudence on Socio-economic Rights: An Effective Tool in Challenging Poverty?' (2002) 6 Law, Democracy &

reasonableness is no more than a relational standard – ends measured against means. It is not an obligation to provide something specific. Read in this way, the socioeconomic rights are not a right to, say, a roof over your head or anti-retroviral drugs, but only to have evaluated the reasonableness of a decision to provide or not provide these things.[138]

Young asserts that under the reasonableness review, by integrating the analysis of a right's progressive realization, in the same step as defining the right, there is no 'standalone' content. She has commented that:

> this way of defining content is more akin to setting out an institutional guarantee, enclosed in the garb of a justiciable, subjective right. Such an approach has the advantage of keeping the right open to new claims and articulations; nevertheless, it allows the court to obscure its own engagement with the underlying values behind particular rights and the impact of the deprivation on the claimant group. For its critics, this refusal to define content allows reasonableness review to take place in 'a normative vacuum'.[139]

The ruling in *Mazibuko* in favor of the government water policy, despite clear evidence that families did not have sufficient access to drinking water, lays bare the human suffering that may result in adopting a deferential standard of reasonableness.

## 4.2    Minimum Core

Minimum core also has attracted supporters and detractors. Pieterse eloquently elaborates on the emptiness of ESCR jurisprudence which does not embrace the minimum core approach.[140] While his analysis of the core standard seems to have shifted over the years, he continues to emphasize the importance of content development of rights.[141] General pronouncements by the courts do little to advance the broadly formulated rights guaranteed by law. People who are deprived daily of the most basic of amenities need rights to work for them, and minimum core is one way to achieve this. The Colombian and German cases considered earlier provide compelling examples of this approach in practice. If courts wish to meaningfully adjudicate ESCR, then rights must be given content.

Wilson and Dugard have argued that applying the reasonableness test in the abstract, isolated from an understanding of the interests and needs in question,

> [undercuts] the court's ability to engage head on with the claimants' needs and lived experiences of poverty. Instead, the Court tends to prefer a facial examination of State policy, implicitly accepting the conceptions of reasonableness and possibility upon which those policies are drafted and imple-

---

Dev. 159–91; Marius Pieterse, 'Possibilities and Pitfalls in the Domestic Enforcement of Social Rights: Contemplating the South African Experience' (2004) 26 HRQ 882–905. These critiques primarily attach to the reasonableness standard that is used in South Africa; however, the South African version is generally more robust than iterations of the standard elsewhere, and thus the critique would likely apply to most jurisdictions.

138   Iain Currie, 'Bill of Rights Jurisprudence' [2002] Ann. Surv. S. Afr. L. 36, 72.
139   Young (n 18) 262.
140   Pieterse (n 137) 817.
141   Marius Pieterse, 'On "Dialogue", "Translation" and "Voice": A Reply to Sandra Liebenberg' in Stu Woolman and Michael Bishop (eds), *Constitutional Conversations* (PULP 2008) 331.

mented. This tends to reproduce the exclusion from policy formulation and implementation processes which have brought the claimants to court in the first place.[142]

All this considered, Ania has asserted that:

> To reject the minimum core altogether in favour of an approach based solely on examining the reasonableness of state actions in the abstract risks creating the very danger that the CESCR sought to avoid: that the obligation to progressively realize rights will be misconstrued to deprive [ESCR] of meaningful content and legitimize the deprivation of vulnerable and marginalized groups.[143]

Despite its strengths, the perceived absolute nature of minimum core, the lack of contextual consideration in the light of complex realities and its inherent indeterminacy all fuel critique of this standard. Liebenberg has written that 'social needs are in fact interconnected and that no clear-cut distinction exists between core and non-core needs'.[144] Steinberg, on the other hand, has argued that the minimum core approach may have unintended systemic consequences by causing a backlash to perceived judicial activism and thereby '[forestalling] the constitutional conversation between the three branches of government'.[145] Other factors sustaining critique of this standard include: a belief that prioritization of entitlements within rights can lead to distorted allocation of resources;[146] reserving discretion to decide future economic rights cases, an important point especially for countries which have a system of precedents;[147] and concern with lack of capacity and resources of the Court.[148]

### 4.3    Combination Approach

In light of the positive and negative attributes of minimum core and reasonableness, their contradictions are clear. They also converge. For example, the standards, at least as developed by CESCR, clearly share key elements, including urging States to adopt deliberate, concrete and targeted steps to meet obligations, comply with the principles of non-discrimination and equality, prioritize the most vulnerable and meet a high burden of proof in the case of non-allocation of resources.[149]

---

[142]    Stuart Wilson and Jackie Dugard, 'Taking Poverty Seriously: The South African Constitutional Court and Socio-economic Rights' (2011) 22 Stellenbosch L Rev 664, 673.

[143]    Ania Kwadrans, 'Socioeconomic Rights Adjudication in Canada: Can the Minimum Core Help in Adjudicating the Rights to Life and Security of the Person under the Canadian Charter of Rights and Freedoms?' (2016) 25 Journal of Law and Social Policy 78, 90.

[144]    Liebenberg (n 132) 318, 319.

[145]    Steinberg (n 15) 269.

[146]    Murray Wesson, 'Grootboom and Beyond: Reassessing the Socioeconomic Jurisprudence of the South African Constitutional Court' (2004) 20 SAJHR 27, 32; Albie Sachs, 'The Judicial Enforcement of Socio-economic Rights: The Grootboom Case', in Peris Jones and Kristian Stokke (eds), *Democratizing Development – The Politics of Socio-economic Rights in South Africa* (2005) 131, 144.

[147]    Aarthi Belani, 'The South African Constitutional Court's Decision in TAC: A "Reasonable" Choice?' (2004) CHRGJ Working Paper No. 7, 36.

[148]    As was expressed in *Grootboom* (n 39) and *TAC* (n 117).

[149]    Yeshenew (n 9) 329; Adelaide Remiche, *ICESCR Optional Protocol: Reconciling Standards of Review* (Oxford Human Rights Hub 16 July 2013) <ohrh.law.ox.ac.uk/icescr-optional-protocol-reconciling-standards-of-review/>.

Two key perspectives emerge from the aforementioned faultlines that can perhaps be loosely contained under the framing of a combination approach: one advocating for an explicit combination of the two standards, another for an implicit combination, not necessarily of the standards themselves but of essential elements within each standard. These are examined below in turn, focusing more on the implicit combined approach.

### 4.3.1 An explicit combination approach

In the South Africa context, it has been suggested that if the South African court would use the reasonableness test alongside the minimum core approach, then the aforementioned primary critique relating to content would be addressed, and the realization of socio-economic rights would be more effectively achieved.[150] Minimum core review might be utilized to determine specific rights content, and then reasonableness could support evaluation of State compliance with their human rights obligations,[151] hopefully in ways that are mindful of the potential and pitfalls of each standard, and of course in harmonization with other key human rights standards such as proportionality. Through minimum core, a combined approach endows rights with substance and clarity, while maintaining the reasonableness approach allows rights and obligations to be assessed in different contexts, based on meaningful engagement with communities to determine their content and providing the executive the necessary flexibility in executing court orders and attempts to balance individual and community needs against government constraints.

What might this look like in practice? For instance, in the *TAC* case, the court read the rights in question and then, in light of facts and evidence and constitutional values and standards, determined that the government's policies were unreasonable. Bilchitz argues that,[152] in line with the UN Committee's interpretation, the Court could have read into the right to health an obligation to provide services necessary for healthy child development; against this defined content it could then have found that the government's actions in withholding Nevirapine were unreasonable. The Court would also have thus addressed a broader policy question which would have made ESCR something real and meaningful to the masses. In terms of how one version of this approach might look in litigation, in the *Mazibuko* case the COHRE amicus argued that minimum core should be used in determining reasonableness rather than in place of the reasonableness standard.[153]

Such a clear combination is not yet readily apparent in comparative constitutional jurisprudence, although as stated earlier the two standards are used in combination in various case contexts. An explicit combination approach might be the most apparent in interpretative as well as adjudicative contexts in CESCR. However, even with CESCR, the Committee has not yet created a clearly reasoned normative framework of how it will proceed with respect to these cross-cutting standards. CESCR's approach will likely provide States, judges and lawyers with guidance on the use of standards in ESCR litigation.

---

[150] David Bilchitz, *Poverty and Fundamental Rights: The Justification and Enforcement of Socio-economic Rights* (OUP 2007) 139–48; David Bilchitz, 'Giving Socio-economic Rights Teeth: The Minimum Core and its Importance', (2002)119 S. Afr. L. J. 484.

[151] Yeshenew (n 9).

[152] David Bilchitz, 'Towards a Reasonable Approach to the Minimum Core: Laying the Foundations for Future Socioeconomic Rights Jurisprudence' (2003) 19 S. Afr. J. Hum. Rts. 1, 8.

[153] Brief for The Centre on Housing Rights and Evictions (COHRE) as Amicus Curiae supporting Respondents, City of Johannesburg and Others v Mazibuko and Others 2009 (3) SA 592 (SCA) para 15.

### 4.3.2    An implicit combination approach

There can be varied iterations of the implicit combination approach. Diverse constitutional and regional contexts are reflective of this. Consider, for example, the Constitutional Court of South Africa, which rejected the minimum core approach in itself but also referenced it as possibly relevant to its reasonableness analysis. Bilchitz has suggested that the Court in *Grootboom* or *TAC* could not have arrived at the conclusions that it did without giving some content to the right in question,[154] which may indicate an inarticulated and rudimentary implied combination approach. Another implied combination of the cross-cutting standards can be seen in the 2007 CESCR statement, where it clarifies how it will interpret the reasonableness standard and clearly draws on key elements of minimum core.

One compelling standard which implicitly combines key aspects of both minimum core and reasonableness is substantive reasonableness. Commentators who previously supported minimum core have moved away from a rigid formulation of minimum core,[155] while continuing to emphasize the importance of engaging with rights content as a way to make adjudication valuable for those who suffer violations of their rights, especially the most vulnerable.

Liebenberg has proposed the notion of substantive reasonableness to address the main criticisms of reasonableness (inability to provide content) and minimum core (an absolute standard not grounded in context and diverse realities). Substantive reasonableness would preserve the openness and context-sensitivity of reasonableness review that enables greater participation and deliberation in interpreting ESCR. This mode of review would also retain 'the features of the minimum core approach that require heightened scrutiny of acts and omissions which result in a denial of basic needs' and 'include a more principled and systematic interpretation of the content of the various socio-economic rights, the values at stake in particular cases and the impact of the denial of access to these rights on the complainant group'.[156]

Liebenberg emphasizes that courts should first engage with the content of the rights and the context and implications of the alleged violation, and avoid moving swiftly to consider the State's justificatory arguments.[157] Taking this even further, Pieterse adds that it may be important in the context of this approach to separate engagement with the content of a right from the question of whether measures designed to meet corresponding obligations are reasonable in line with that content. He is clear that this does not have to be a minimum core approach per se. In contrast, a 'context-specific, open and flexible deliberation over the content of specific entitlements, their limits and the appropriateness of suggested remedies for their vindication may ultimately enrich deliberative dialogue over the translation of socio-economic rights'.[158]

The substantive reasonableness approach is meant to support a dialogic approach to rights interpretation.[159] The dialogic approach attempts to democratize institutional processes (such as judicial review) through which rights are interpreted.[160] The dialogic approach sits well in

---

[154]    Bilchitz (n 150) 139–45.
[155]    For example, Liebenberg and Pieterse. Contrast between Liebenberg (n 137) 159–91 and Liebenberg (n 132) 303–29; as well as Pieterse (n 137) 796, 800 and Pieterse (n 141) 331–47.
[156]    Liebenberg (n 132) 328, 324–25.
[157]    Ibid.
[158]    Pieterse (n 141) 332, 346.
[159]    Liebenberg (n 132) 303, 328; Pieterse (n 141) 331, 333.
[160]    Liebenberg analyzes both minimum core and reasonableness from the dialogic perspective. She affirms the value of the content-focused approach of minimum core but explains how a comprehensive core standard is ill suited to facilitate dialogue over the content of economic, social and cultural ESCR.

adjudicative contexts both in the litigation and implementation phases as it allows for the participation of multiple contributory perspectives (for example, these may include the views of affected individuals and communities, government actors, jurists, civil society actors, judges and experts) and is a relatively democratic space given the power differentials between, for instance, those facing rights violations and institutional actors. Judges are skilled interpreters of rights and positioned to 'correct for problems occasioned by legislative "blind spots" or "burdens of inertia"'. But judges are not the only key voices in these deliberations, and counter-majoritarian concerns are one among several factors in having judges play an outsized role in rights interpretation and involved policy making.[161] This dialogic approach is evident in *TAC* and *Grootboom*;[162] and, as seen above in the cases in Germany, Colombia and New York, courts have adopted the dialogic approach alongside the minimum core standard. In any case, it is important in this dialogic approach to ensure that it includes the voices of those who have confronted violations of their rights, especially if these are typically marginalized voices.

Finally, with respect to an implicit combination approach, meeting aspirations inherent in each standard can be important and may well support the effective realization of rights. This may involve, for example, as Young proposes, the use of discrete measures which aspire to achieve the same objectivity and concrete guarantees that the minimum core approach is geared towards. There would be a normative difference, of course but the desired effect of the minimum core concept and the discrete measures would be largely similar. Such discrete measures could include, for instance, courts focusing on supervising and enforcing the more positive obligations attached to ESCR by using indicators and benchmarks 'instead of demarcating different rights and obligations as "core" and "non-core"'.[163] This brings a sense of objectivity to rights. Of course, such an approach requires openness and flexibility; otherwise, fixed usage may well damage the substantive promise of human rights. Minimum core sets priorities, and another way to meet that goal is by balancing through proportionality reasoning and costs consideration. Such balancing is not the same as minimum core, which does not focus on efficiency in the same way but is arguably often better suited to ESCR adjudication, given the multitude of competing interests.[164]

While an implicit combination approach in some form seems ideal, and would need to be adopted in harmonization with the many other standards in the area, from an examination of the two standards, minimum core and reasonableness, what clearly emerges is that regardless of how or if these standards are utilized, in all economic, social and cultural rights adjudication, it is essential to engage with the normative development of content, and rigorous scrutiny of State justifications regarding compliance with their rights obligations.

---

She concludes that a reasonableness approach is more aligned with the dialogic approach as it 'avoids closure and creates the on-going possibility of challenging various forms of socio-economic deprivations in the different contexts in which they arise'. Pieterse agrees that a core approach may preclude 'reasonable disagreement over its conceptual foundations, contextual appropriateness, feasibility and logic' but argues that this does not have to be the case. 'It should be possible for courts to engage in a far more gradual, open-ended, context-specific and contingent process of case-by-case elaboration of the essential minimum content of rights, in a manner that invites, rather than forestalls, dialogue.' See Liebenberg (n 132) 303, 320; Pieterse (n 141) 331, 340.

[161] Pieterse (n 141) 331, 337.
[162] And in case law more focused on meaningful engagement. See n 130.
[163] *Young* (n 14) 113, 164–74.
[164] Ibid.

## 5.    A RESPONSIVE APPROACH

In fact, it may not be ideal for courts to adopt a single overarching approach to ESCR adjudication. Colm O'Cinneide makes a strong case for diversity in social rights review, at least in domestic contexts. He writes, with regard to the specific modes of judicial review, that:

> this may be a context where diversity trumps uniformity: it may be better to create tailor made systems of social rights protection for specific jurisdictions than to try and identify a general mode of best practice ... National contexts vary greatly, and it may be the case that home grown modes of social rights review engineered to address specific problem(s) in a given state may be more effective than generic alternatives.[165]

In terms of litigation approaches, it is also important to take a more flexible approach in terms of which standard of review to urge the court to apply, 'using jurisdictionally-appropriate procedural and substantive norms of any hue, as called for by the particular factual circumstances of each concrete case'.[166] Liebenberg has written that courts must 'remain open to new and innovative interpretations of socio-economic rights that better protect the interests and values underpinning these rights', even though '[t]his may entail a measure of sacrifice of the ideals of stability and certainty'.[167]

## 6.    CONCLUSION

It is important to consider that the cross-cutting standards of minimum core and reasonableness simply constitute a small element of what transforms abstract legalese into concrete entitlements. Simply having a strategic approach to standards of review may mean little. Many other factors are essential, including, for example, respect for the rule of law, political will, independence of the judiciary, and the momentum of involved civil society organizations and social movements, for the transformative potential of ESCR to be truly realized.

But whatever approach is adopted in terms of standards, the aim should always be to interpret ESCR in a way that not only addresses individual needs but also systemic concerns, and foregrounds the needs of the most vulnerable. The review process should provide governments with clarity and direction regarding their obligations and enable affected individuals and communities to better hold States accountable. The guiding questions for the human rights community must be how to facilitate a review process that contributes to the effective enforcement of human rights, enables cases to become part of a broader ongoing political dialogue and supports transformative impacts.

---

[165]    Colm O' Cinneide, 'The Problematic of Social Rights − Uniformity and Diversity in the Development of Social Rights Review' in Liora Lazarus, Christopher McCrudden and Nigel Bowles (eds), *Reasoning Rights: Comparative Judicial Engagement* (Hart Publishing 2014) 317.

[166]    Tara J. Melish, 'Rethinking the "Less as More" Thesis: Supranational Litigation of Economic, Social and Cultural Rights in the Americas' (2006) 39 JILP 1, 31.

[167]    Pieterse (n 141) 331, 347.

# 14. Progressive realization using maximum available resources: the accountability challenge

*Allison Corkery and Ignacio Saiz*

## 1. INTRODUCTION

The 'economics' of economic, social and cultural rights (ESCR) has come under the spotlight more and more in recent years. As economic inequality has risen up the political agenda, attention to the ways in which resource distribution 'affects political dynamics and power relations' within which rights are realized has also increased.[1] This chapter argues that, in a time characterized by the regressive accumulation of privilege rather than the progressive realization of rights, the redistributive and egalitarian potential of the concepts of progressive realization and maximum available resources needs to be more fully and effectively tapped.

For many years, the conditionality of the language used in the International Covenant on Economic, Social and Cultural Rights (ICESCR or Covenant) was seen as a weakness – an 'escape hatch' that risked granting governments an excuse to defer their efforts to fulfill ESCR by citing economic constraints.[2] Under Article 2(1) each state party undertakes 'to take steps ... to the *maximum of its available resources*, with a view to *achieving progressively* the *full realisation* of the rights recognised in the present Covenant' (emphasis added).[3] Similar language can be found in other international and regional human rights instruments, as well as in national constitutions.[4] The challenges of assessing compliance with such a vaguely defined and resource-contingent obligation were seen as an indication that these rights were more indeterminate and aspirational than civil and political rights (CPR), and therefore less suited to adjudication and legal enforcement.

---

[1]  Radhika Balakrishnan, James Heintz and Diane Elson, *Rethinking Economic Policy for Social Justice: The Radical Potential of Human Rights* (Routledge 2016).

[2]  Eitan Felner, 'Closing the "Escape Hatch": A Toolkit to Monitor the Progressive Realisation of Economic, Social, and Cultural Rights' (2009) 1 Journal of Human Rights Practice 402.

[3]  Adopted 16 December 1966, entered into force 3 January 1976, 993 UNTS 3.

[4]  See e.g. Convention on the Rights of the Child, adopted 20 November 1989, entered into force 2 September 1990, 1577 UNTS 3 Article 4; Convention on the Rights of Persons with Disabilities, adopted 13 December 2006, entered into force 3 May 2008, 2515 UNTS 3 Article 4.2; American Convention on Human Rights, adopted 22 November 1969, entered into force 18 July 1978, OAS Treaty Series No. 36, 1144 UNTS 123 Article 26. While the African Charter on Human and Peoples Rights does not expressly refer to the principle of progressive realization, the concept is widely accepted and has been implied into the Charter in accordance with Articles 61 and 62, ACHPR, 'Principles and Guidelines on the Implementation of Economic, Social and Cultural Rights in the African Charter on Human and Peoples' Rights' (2010) para 13; Constitution of South Africa (1996) Articles 26–27, 29(1)(b); Constitution of Kenya (2010) Article 43; Constitution of Zimbabwe (2013) Articles 73, 75–77.

Indeed, the Committee on Economic, Social and Cultural Rights (CESCR or Committee) initially appeared to grant states a wider margin of discretion regarding economic policy than in other policy arenas. The Committee's third General Comment, published in 1990, stresses that the ICESCR is 'neutral' as to the economic model a state adopts and 'its principles cannot accurately be described as being predicated exclusively upon the need for, or the desirability of a socialist or a capitalist system, or a mixed, centrally planned, or laissez-faire economy'.[5] As Katherine Young notes, this position should be understood in the context of the ideological backdrop of the Cold War.[6] Nevertheless, it is a position that has enjoyed longevity, at least among some influential actors within the human rights field.

By contrast, in the three decades since General Comment No. 3, economic and political trends have underscored that rights realization is inextricably linked to the particular economic model in place – illustrating the urgency of holding governments to account for how their mobilization and distribution of resources advances or hinders the progressive realization of ESCR. In the decade since the global financial crisis, in particular, the predominant fiscal policy doctrine worldwide has been that of austerity (or 'fiscal consolidation'), characterized by drastic cuts to social spending, decreased investment in public services and reduced social protection programs. Austerity policies, pushed dogmatically by some governments and international financial institutions against growing evidence that they are ineffective as well as inequitable, can be seen as the antithesis of progressive realization, having resulted in a manifestly unjustified backsliding of ESCR enjoyment across all continents.[7]

Recent years have also seen mounting exposure of the ways in which resources that are *potentially* available to the public coffers are pilfered in practice by wealthy individuals and powerful multinational corporations through mass-scale tax evasion and avoidance. These practices are facilitated by states in a myriad of ways, whether by operating as tax havens, promoting a global race to the bottom on corporate tax cuts and incentives, or otherwise undermining international tax reforms in inter-governmental fora. Growing political awareness of the injustice of tax abuse has prompted greater human rights scrutiny of domestic and international tax policy, including how cross-border tax abuse deprives low-income countries of much-needed resources to progressively achieve their human rights and sustainable development commitments.[8]

The adoption of the 2030 Agenda for Sustainable Development in 2015, and the slow progress towards the Millennium Development Goals due to have been met that year, have also provided a further impetus to operationalize the concept of progressive realization. Thanks in large part to civil society advocacy efforts, the 2030 Agenda – with its 17 far-reaching Sustainable Development Goals and 164 targets – is explicitly anchored in human rights stand-

---

[5]    CESCR, General Comment No. 3: The Nature of States Parties' Obligations (14 December 1990) E/1991/23 para 8.

[6]    Katherine G. Young, 'Introduction' in Katherine G Young (ed), *The Future of Economic and Social Rights* (Cambridge University Press 2019) 14.

[7]    Center for Economic and Social Rights (CESR), 'Assessing Austerity: Monitoring the Human Rights Impacts of Fiscal Consolidation' (2018) <www.cesr.org/assessing-austerity-monitoring-human-rights-impacts-fiscal-consolidation>.

[8]    See e.g., International Bar Association Human Rights Institute (IBAHRI), 'Tax Abuses, Poverty and Human Rights' (2013); Philip Alston, 'Report of the Special Rapporteur on Extreme Poverty and Human Rights' (11 August 2014) A/69/297; and CESR, 'Tax Justice and Human Rights: An Overview of CESR Materials' (2019).

ards.[9] It therefore provides a complementary framework of universally agreed, quantitative commitments that can reinforce efforts to hold governments accountable for their progress in fulfilling ESCR. The 2030 Agenda includes an unprecedented commitment to reduce inequality within and between countries – also a hard-won civil society victory, and a recognition that neither human rights nor sustainable development can be progressively realized unless the obscene escalation in economic inequality over the past three decades is halted and reversed.[10]

These and other factors have fostered a growing awareness within the human rights community that questions of unjust resource distribution, and the socio-economic deprivations and disparities it causes, can no longer be veiled from human rights scrutiny. They have prompted renewed efforts to deploy the 'progressive realization' norm and explore new avenues of accountability where it can be invoked and enforced. In directing attention to the links between rights and resources, the language of Article 2(1) of the ICESCR is a strength, not a weakness. How states define and invest in their policy priorities through the budget becomes a human rights issue. As Olivier De Schutter emphasizes, such decisions 'cannot be left to the arbitrary and capricious choices of States', but must be subject to review by courts and other human rights monitoring bodies.[11]

While there has been much progress in clarifying the scope and content of this obligation, there remain significant challenges in holding governments answerable to it in ways that can counter the headwinds outlined above. These challenges are in part conceptual, as the normative contours of Article 2(1) of the ICESCR still remain blurred and imprecise in some respects. But they are also methodological, requiring more effective measures and frameworks for assessing this duty comprehensively. There are strategic challenges as well, given the need to open up new advocacy and accountability pathways through which to give effect to the norm in real-world policy arenas.

This chapter analyzes and addresses these challenges in turn. It begins by unpacking the key normative components of the obligation, highlighting key challenges of interpretation addressed by human rights monitoring bodies. Its primary focus is international human rights monitoring bodies, with selective regional and national examples drawn upon where relevant. It then surveys a range of means and methods which can be used to assess compliance with these norms in practice, stressing the need to go beyond fragmented techniques and to pursue more comprehensive, context-sensitive analytical frameworks that assess progress in rights realization in light of a state's fiscal and other policy efforts. In so doing, it draws on the work of the Center for Economic and Social Rights (CESR), an organization for which the authors both work. It concludes by highlighting some strategic opportunities and entry points for deploying these tools in ways that can advance meaningful accountability and transformative policy change.

---

[9]    United Nations General Assembly, 'Transforming Our World: The 2030 Agenda for Sustainable Development' (21 October 2015) A/RES/70/1. For further discussion of Agenda 2030, see Chapter 18 of this book.

[10]    CESR, 'From Disparity to Dignity: Tackling Economic Inequality through the Sustainable Development Goals' (2017) <www.cesr.org/disparity-dignity-inequality-and-sdgs>.

[11]    Olivier De Schutter, 'Public Budget Analysis for the Realisation of Economic, Social and Cultural Rights: Conceptual Framework and Practical Implementation' in Katherine G. Young (ed), *The Future of Economic and Social Rights* (Cambridge University Press 2019) 527.

## 2.   UNPACKING KEY COMPONENTS OF THE OBLIGATION

The 'progressive realization' provision is one of the key aspects differentiating the ICESCR from the International Covenant on Civil and Political Rights (ICCPR),[12] whose analogous Article does not include any temporal or resource qualification. Nevertheless, the CESCR drew clear parameters around the concept of progressive realization, aimed at preventing it from being 'misinterpreted as depriving the obligation of all meaningful content'.[13] As explained in General Comment No. 3, the concept of progressive realization constitutes a recognition that, for many states, the full realization of all rights will generally not be achievable in a short period of time due to the limits of their available resources.[14] While acknowledging that the progressive realization doctrine is 'a necessary flexibility device, reflecting the realities of the real world', the Committee also stressed that the doctrine 'must be read in the light of the overall objective' of the Covenant, 'which is to establish clear obligations for States' in respect of the full realization of rights.[15]

In this and subsequent general comments on specific rights, the CESCR and other monitoring bodies have helped circumscribe the concept further. Some of the essential features and normative components of 'progressive realization' are analyzed below, together with interpretative questions to which they have given rise. It should be noted that one of the most significant red-line concepts developed by the Committee around the doctrine of 'progressive realization' is with regard to the 'minimum core content' of ESCR, the satisfaction of which is an obligation of immediate priority for all states regardless of levels of resources. Minimum core obligations, which are discussed separately in Chapter 13 of this book, are critically important in defining the boundaries of 'progressive realization' and should be understood as integral to the normative framework of Article 2(1) of the ICESCR.

### 2.1   Achieving Full Realization Progressively and Expeditiously

The term 'progressive realization' is commonly used as shorthand to describe states' commitment, as set out in Article 2(1) of the ICESCR, to take steps to 'achieve progressively the *full* realisation of' the rights recognized in the Covenant (emphasis added). Thus, the formulation of Article 2(1) underscores that the end goal in terms of outcomes is *full* realization, while 'progressively' characterizes the rate of achievement over time. The shorthand term, which replaces 'full' with 'progressive' as the qualifier for 'realization', does not do justice to the maximalist and demanding nature of the obligation, which aims at the fullest possible enjoyment of economic and social rights within the shortest possible timeframe.

While the Committee has not attempted to define what constitutes 'full' realization, there is nothing to indicate that this implies a ceiling of human rights enjoyment. Indeed, the drafters of the ICESCR saw value in the term 'progressively' precisely because it introduced 'a dynamic element', indicating no fixed end goal had been set in relation to the full realization of ESCR,

---

[12]   Adopted 16 December 1966, entered into force 23 March 1976, 999 UNTS 171.
[13]   CESCR, General Comment No. 3 (n 5) para 9.
[14]   Ibid.
[15]   Ibid.

'since the essence of progress was continuity'.[16] Rather, the expectation emerging from the CESCR's review of country reports is that all states should ensure ever-broader enjoyment of rights in practice over time,[17] in terms of both fulfilling the broader dimensions of each right (beyond the minimum core) and moving ever closer to universal rights enjoyment by all those within its jurisdiction.

The CESCR has also sought to make the temporal requirements of 'progressive realization' more stringent. For example, General Comment No. 3 clarifies that it imposes an obligation 'to move as expeditiously and effectively as possible' towards the goal of full realization.[18] This language is repeated in numerous general comments and a handful of concluding observations express concern about the 'slow pace' of progress in various areas.[19] However, what counts as expeditious and effective has not been further elaborated.

## 2.2   The Duty to 'Take Steps'

Another way the CESCR has dealt with the question of progressive realization is by elaborating on the duty to 'take steps' set out in Article 2(1) of the ICESCR. In particular, General Comment No. 3 stresses that:

> [W]hile the full realization of the relevant rights may be achieved progressively, steps towards the goal must be taken within a reasonably short time after the Covenant's entry into force ... Such steps should be *deliberate, concrete and targeted* as clearly as possible towards meeting the obligations recognized in the Covenant (emphasis added).[20]

With regard to specific rights, such as the right to education, the Committee has indicated steps to be taken within a particular timeframe, such as adopting a plan of action on primary education 'within a reasonable number of years'.[21]

Thus, the Committee delineates between the realization of relevant rights, as an obligation of result, and the duty to take steps, as an obligation of conduct. While the former may generally be achieved progressively, the latter is immediate. This distinction between obligations of conduct and of result is not emphasized again in later general comments. Nevertheless, it is implicit in the reasonableness standard used by various monitoring bodies.[22] While categoriz-

---

[16]   Summary record of the 236th meeting of the Commission on Human Rights, 20, quoted in Ahmed Shahid, 'For Want of Resources: Reimagining the State's Obligation to Use "Maximum Available Resources" for the Progressive Realisation of Economic, Social and Cultural Rights' (PhD Thesis, University of Sydney 2016) 62.

[17]   Aoife Nolan, Nicholas Lusiani and Christian Courtis, 'Two Steps Forward, No Steps Back? Evolving Criteria on the Prohibition of Retrogression in Economic, Social and Cultural Rights' in Aoife Nolan (ed), *Economic and Social Rights after the Global Financial Crisis* (Cambridge University Press 2014) 122–23.

[18]   CESCR, General Comment No. 3 (n 5) para 9.

[19]   See e.g. CESCR, 'Concluding Observations: Paraguay' (4 January 2008) E/C.12/PRY/CO/3 para 12(b); CESCR, 'Concluding Observations: Gabon' (27 December 2013) E/C.12/GAB/CO/1 para 27; CESCR, 'Concluding Observations: Sudan' (27 October 2015) E/C.12/SDN/CO/2 para 53.

[20]   CESCR, General Comment No. 3 (n 5) para 9.

[21]   CESCR, General Comment No. 11: Plans of Action for Primary Education (10 May 1999) E/C12/1999/4.

[22]   For a discussion of this standard see Bruce Porter, 'The Reasonableness of Article 8(4) – Adjudicating Claims for the Margins' (2009) Nordisk Tidsskrift for Menneskerettigheter 39.

ing obligations as relating solely to either conduct or result will rarely be exact – many have dimensions of both – putting emphasis on the steps taken by a state appropriately recognizes that states' primary responsibility should relate to their actions, which they directly control. As discussed further in Section 4, conceptualizing obligations in this way can also guide their operationalization in policymaking.

## 2.3    Non-retrogression

The 'natural corollary' of the duty to make progress is a duty not to regress.[23] As the Limburg Principles – widely accepted by human rights monitoring bodies – state, the ICESCR is violated if a state 'deliberately retards or halts the progressive realisation of a right, unless it is acting within a limitation permitted by the Covenant or it does so due to a lack of available resources'.[24] This has come to be known as the doctrine of 'non-retrogression'. Retrogression can be normative (or *de jure*) when entitlements guaranteed by a legal norm are revoked. It can also be empirical (or *de facto*) when there is backsliding in actual rights enjoyment.[25]

As indicated above, the prohibition on retrogression is not absolute. Rather, there is a *prima facie* assumption that regression is a violation. This means the burden of proof shifts to the state to justify its actions. According to the CESCR, a deliberately retrogressive measure requires 'the most careful consideration' and needs to be justified 'by reference to the totality of the rights provided for in the Covenant and in the context of the full use of the maximum available resources'.[26] That said, it has only been in the past ten years or so that human rights monitoring bodies have started to develop criteria to assess the bases on which retrogressive measures might comply with a state's human rights duties.

Permissible limitations on rights are codified and interpreted in different ways by different national,[27] regional,[28] and international bodies.[29] Nevertheless, some criteria for assessing

---

[23]    Nolan et al (n 17) 123.

[24]    United Nations Commission on Human Rights, 'Note Verbale from the Permanent Mission of the Netherlands to the United Nations Office at Geneva addressed to the Centre for Human Rights ("Limburg Principles")' (8 January 1987) E/CN.4/1987/17 para 72.

[25]    Nolan et al (n 17) 123.

[26]    CESCR, General Comment No. 3 (n 5).

[27]    *Kong Yunming v The Director of Social Welfare*, FACV2/2013, Hong Kong Court of Final Appeal (2013); Case No. 2009-43-01, Constitutional Court of the Republic of Latvia (2009); Ruling No. 187/13, Constitutional Tribunal of Portugal (2013).

[28]    *Case of Five Pensioners v Peru*, Inter-American Court of Human Rights (Ser. C) No. 98 (2003) para 103; ACHPR, 'Principles and Guidelines' (n 4) para 20; European Committee of Social Rights, *Panhellenic Federation of Pensioners of the Public Electricity Corporation v Greece*, Complaint No. 79/2012 (2012) paras 64–69.

[29]    CESCR, *Trujillo Calero v Ecuador*, Communication No. 10/2015 (14 November 2015) E/C.12/63/D/10/2015 para 17.1; e.g. CRPD Committee, General Comment No. 4: The Right to Inclusive Education (25 November 2017) CRPD/C/GC/4 para 39; CRPD Committee, General Comment No. 5: Living Independently and Being Included in the Community (27 October 2017) CRPD/C/GC/5 para 43; CESCR, General Comment No. 19: The Right to Social Security (4 February 2008) E/C.12/GC/19; CESCR, General Comment No. 22: The Right to Sexual and Reproductive Health (2 May 2016) E/C.12/GC/19 para 42; CESCR, General Comment No. 23: The Right to Just and Favourable Conditions of Work (7 April 2016) E/C.12/GC/23 para 52; CRC, General Comment No. 19: Public Budgeting for the Realization of Children's Rights (20 July 2016) CRC/C/GC/19 para 31; CESCR, 'Public Debt, Austerity Measures and the International Covenant on Economic, Social and Cultural Rights: Statement' (22 July

retrogressive measures are starting to emerge more consistently from these bodies. These include that a measure be: temporary; legitimate, with the ultimate aim of protecting the totality of human rights; necessary, with all alternative measures comprehensively examined and exhausted; reasonable, with the means chosen the most capable of achieving the legitimate aim; proportionate, in that their human rights benefits outweigh their costs; not directly nor indirectly discriminatory, according priority attention to disadvantaged groups to ensure they are not disproportionately affected; protective of the minimum core content of ESCR; and transparent, based on genuine participation of affected groups in examining the proposed measures and alternatives, subject to meaningful review and accountability procedures.[30]

### 2.4 Non-discrimination

An important question regarding the progressive realization and non-retrogression doctrines is whether progress should be assessed in the aggregate or be disaggregated for specific groups. As noted above, prioritizing disadvantaged groups and ensuring no direct or indirect discrimination is a key factor in determining whether retrogressive measures can be justified. Arguably, it is also a factor in determining whether progress has been satisfactory.[31] For example, in its General Comment No. 5, the Committee on the Rights of the Child (CRC Committee) outlines its expectation that states develop a comprehensive national strategy that prioritizes the most marginalized and disadvantaged children.[32] Similarly, General Comment No. 4 on inclusive education adopted by the Committee on the Rights of Persons with Disabilities focuses on the full and effective participation and achievement of all students, 'especially those who, for different reasons, are excluded or at risk of being marginalised'.[33]

The pledge to 'leave no one behind', which is a core principle of the 2030 Agenda for Sustainable Development, also appears to have influenced a more disaggregated view of progress. In a statement on the 2030 Agenda, for example, the CESCR notes that states must mobilize the maximum of their available resources towards the fulfillment of the Covenant rights, 'particularly for those who are most excluded, disadvantaged and marginalised'. It goes on to note that the Committee has consistently emphasized the importance of 'identifying and prioritizing the needs of those groups that are disadvantaged and vulnerable to systemic and intersectional forms of discrimination'.[34]

---

2016) E/C.12/2016/1 para 4; CESCR, 'Concluding Observations: Sri Lanka' (4 August 2017) E/C.12/LKA/CO/5 para 22; CESCR, 'Concluding Observations: Egypt' (13 December 2013) E/C.12/EGY/CO/2-4 para 18; Magdalena Sepúlveda Carmona, 'Report of the Special Rapporteur on Extreme Poverty on a Human Rights-based Approach to Recovery from the Global Economic and Financial Crises' (17 March 2011) A/HRC/17/34 paras 18–20; Raquel Rolnik, 'Report of the Special Rapporteur on Housing Mission to the United Kingdom of Great Britain and Northern Ireland' (30 December 2013) A/HRC/25/54/Add.2 para 78.

[30]   CESR, 'Assessing Austerity' (n 7) 19–22.

[31]   Lilian Chenwi, 'Unpacking "Progressive Realisation", Its Relation to Resources, Minimum Core and Reasonableness, and Some Methodological Considerations for Assessing Compliance' (2013) 46 De Jure 742, 746.

[32]   CRC, General Comment No. 5: General Measures of Implementation of the Convention on the Rights of the Child (27 November 2003) CRC/GC/2003/5 para 30.

[33]   CRPD Committee, General Comment No. 4 (n 29) para 9.

[34]   CESCR, 'The Pledge to Leave No One Behind: The International Covenant on Economic, Social and Cultural Rights and the 2030 Agenda for Sustainable Development: Statement' (5 April 2019) E/C.12/2019/1 para 7.

## 2.5   Maximum Available Resources

The undertaking to 'take steps' in Article 2(1) is not, in itself, qualified or limited.[35] Nevertheless, there is recognition that resource constraints may constitute a genuine limitation on the number or types of steps taken. While this does not 'alone justify inaction', the 'maximum available resources' doctrine appears as an important proviso on the state's duty to take steps to progressively realize ESCR. This section unpacks the contours of the obligation, as it has been elaborated by international monitoring bodies. It identifies where there have been advances in clarifying what states must do in line with the norm and where the obligations on states remain less clear.

### 2.5.1   Resource allocation

States have the authority to adopt what they consider to be the 'most appropriate policies' to realize rights and 'to allocate resources accordingly'.[36] Thus, states are granted a 'wide measure of discretion' to determine the 'quantum of resources to be set aside to promote the realisation of rights'.[37] The obligation does not require a state to devote all the resources it has at its disposal. Nor, obviously, does it require it 'to devote resources that it does not have'.[38]

Nevertheless, the allocation of resources is not left to the complete discretion of states. As outlined in the Limburg Principles, 'due priority' should be given to the realization of rights in allocating resources. Further, resources should be allocated in a way that is 'equitable and effective'.[39] Equity demands that disadvantaged groups 'be prioritized' in all resource allocation decisions, stresses the African Commission on Human and Peoples' Rights.[40] Another criterion for resource allocation invoked by the CRC Committee, in particular, is 'efficiency' in resource allocation, with cost-effectiveness considerations needing to take into account the obligation to respect, protect and fulfill children's rights.[41]

The CESCR has been consistent in substantiating similar allocation-related obligations across different rights in its general comments. Allocations must ensure that minimum core obligations are met, must account for the needs of vulnerable groups and must combat discrimination, for example. For some rights, general comments have identified more concrete priorities for public financing. For instance, with regard to the right to education, states shall provide free primary education for all.[42] Regarding the right to health, allocations 'should not disproportionately favour expensive curative health services' over 'primary and preventive

---

[35]   CESCR, General Comment No. 3 (n 5) para 2.

[36]   CESCR, 'An Evaluation of the Obligation to Take Steps to the "Maximum of Available Resources" under an Optional Protocol to the Covenant: Statement' (21 September 2007) E/C.12/2007/1.

[37]   Philip Alston and Gerard Quinn, 'The Nature and Scope of States Parties' Obligations under the International Covenant on Economic, Social and Cultural Rights' (1987) 9 Human Rights Quarterly 156, 177.

[38]   Magdalena Sepulveda, *Nature of the Obligations under the International Covenant on Economic, Social and Cultural Rights* (Intersentia 2003) 315.

[39]   Limburg Principles (n 24) paras 27–28.

[40]   ACHPR, 'Principles and Guidelines' (n 4) para 14. See also Constitution of Kenya Article 43(b).

[41]   CRC, General Comment No. 5 (n 32) para 62; CRC, General Comment No. 19 (n 29) para 60.

[42]   CESCR, General Comment No. 13: The Right to Education (8 December 1999) E/C.12/1999/10 para 57.

health care benefiting a far larger part of the population'.[43] With regard to the right to work, resources should be 'allocated to reducing the unemployment rate, in particular among women, the disadvantaged and marginalised'.[44] As regards the right to social security, states should institute non-contributory benefits or other assistance for all persons who find themselves without resources.[45]

How resources are allocated among competing priorities has been a long-standing concern of human rights monitoring bodies in their reviews of states. The CESCR, in particular, has raised concerns in its concluding observations that insufficient resources have been allocated to particular rights and have urged states to: invest limited resources on human rights priorities;[46] increase allocations to particular rights;[47] allocate adequate budgetary resources to reduce regional disparities;[48] achieve a more efficient use of limited resources;[49] and address human rights needs when resources are largely devoted to other purposes (such as debt servicing).[50] However, as the International Bar Association's Human Rights Initiative has pointed out, this has traditionally proven to be an extremely difficult obligation for international monitoring bodies to supervise because of the wide discretionary margin it leaves states.[51] Recently, however, members of the Committee have begun taking stock of past practice and emerging doctrine, in order to identify ways to more effectively assess compliance with the norm.[52]

Arguably, one of the most well-established allocation-related obligations is that states must avoid budgetary cuts that are deliberatively retrogressive. As outlined above, the burden rests on the state to show cuts can be justified.[53] The CESCR has underlined the fact that even in times of severe resource constraints, 'vulnerable members of society can and indeed must be protected by the adoption of relatively low-cost targeted programmes'.[54]

---

[43] CESCR, General Comment No. 14 on the Right to the Highest Attainable Standard of Health (11 August 2000) E/C.12/2000/4 para 19.

[44] CESCR, General Comment No. 18: The Right to Work' (6 February 2006) E/C.12/GC/18 para 26.

[45] CESCR, General Comment No. 19 (n 29) para 50.

[46] See e.g. CESCR, 'Concluding Observations: Georgia' (17 May 2000) E/C.12/1/Add.42 para 26; CESCR, 'Concluding Observations: Bosnia and Herzegovina' (16 December 2013) E/C.12/BIH/CO/2 para 21; CRPD Committee, 'Concluding Observations: Luxemburg' (10 October 2017) CRPD/C/LUX/CO/1 para 21; CMW, 'Concluding Observations: Jamaica' (23 May 2017) CMW/C/JAM/CO/1 para 63.

[47] See e.g. CESCR, 'Concluding Observations: Iraq' (27 October 2015) E/C.12/IRQ/CO/4 para 6; CESCR, 'Concluding Observations: Egypt' (n 29) para 6; CEDAW Committee, 'Concluding Observations: Estonia' (18 November 2016) CEDAW/C/EST/CO/5-6 para 33; CEDAW Committee, 'Concluding Observations: Kenya' (22 November 2017) CEDAW/C/KEN/CO/8 para 39.

[48] See e.g. CRC, 'Concluding Observations: Bangladesh' (30 October 2015) CRC/C/BGD/CO/5 para 55; CRC, 'Concluding Observations: Slovakia' (20 July 2016) CRC/C/SVK/CO/3-5 para 45.

[49] CESCR, 'Concluding Observations: Sudan' (n 19) para 10.

[50] CESCR, 'Concluding Observations: Tajikistan' (25 March 2015) E/C.12/TJK/CO/2-3 para 11; CESCR, 'Concluding Observations: Ecuador' (2004) para 9.

[51] IBAHRI, 'The Obligation to Mobilise Resources: Bridging Human Rights, Sustainable Development Goals, and Economic and Fiscal Policies' (2017) 39.

[52] Rodrigo Uprimny, Sergio Chaparro Hernandez and Andres Castro Araujo, 'Bridging the Gap: The Evolving Doctrine on ESCR and Maximum Available Resources' in Katherine G Young (ed), *The Future of Economic and Social Rights* (Cambridge University Press 2019) 627–38.

[53] CESCR, 'Maximum Available Resources' (n 36) para 9.

[54] CESCR, General Comment No. 3 (n 5) para 12.

### 2.5.2    Resource expenditure

The efficiency and effectiveness of resource allocations also depends on how a state's budget is executed – in other words, how allocated funds are actually spent. The most detailed elaboration of states' obligations regarding resource expenditure comes from General Comment No. 19, published by the CRC Committee. In particular, paragraph 30 stresses that allocated funds 'should not be wasted'. Paragraph 94 calls on states to ensure 'value for money' when goods and services are purchased. Paragraph 95 imposes a duty to 'uncover and remedy the root causes of ineffective and inefficient public spending'. Examples include poor quality goods or services procured; inadequate financial management systems; untimely transfers; unclear roles and responsibilities; poor absorptive capacity; and corruption. Similarly, in General Comment No. 24, the CESCR notes that corruption 'constitutes one of the major obstacles' to realizing human rights. A state violates its obligation to protect when 'insufficient safeguards exist to address corruption of public officials or private-to-private corruption, or where, as a result of corruption of judges, human rights abuses are left unremedied'.[55]

Human rights monitoring bodies have consistently addressed corruption as a concern related to illegal diversion of public money in their country reviews. In recent concluding observations, the CESCR has developed a set of standardized recommendations to states on intensifying efforts to combat corruption.[56] Even though the Committee appears to be addressing this issue on a regular basis, there is scope for more strategic and meaningful recommendations in this regard.

Beyond corruption, inefficient and wasteful expenditure has also been a focus for human rights monitoring bodies. Several bodies have also called on states to ensure that limited resources, public as well as private, are used in the most effective and efficient manner to promote the realization of rights;[57] to fully spend allocations or at least identify reasons for under-spending;[58] ensure allocated funds are not diverted;[59] and strengthen audits to reduce wasteful and irregular expenditure.[60] The Special Rapporteur on Health has stressed that, whether it is public, private or mixed, the system for supplying quality affordable medicines must 'obtain good value for money, minimise waste and avoid corruption'.[61] He has also

---

[55]    CESCR, General Comment No. 24: Obligations in the Context of Business Activities (10 August 2017) E/C.12/GC/24 para 18.

[56]    Among others: (a) Raise awareness among the general public and government officials on the need to combat corruption; (b) Strengthen the enforcement of anti-corruption laws and combat impunity, particularly involving high-level officials; (c) Strengthen the capacity of the judiciary, including to ensure the effective protection of victims of corruption, their lawyers, anti-corruption activists, whistle-blowers and witnesses; (d) Improve public governance and ensure transparency in the conduct of public affairs. See e.g. CESCR, 'Concluding Observations: Republic of Moldova' (19 October 2017) E/C.12/MDA/CO/3 para 17.

[57]    CESCR, 'Concluding Observations: Sudan' (n 19) para 14.

[58]    CESCR, 'Concluding Observations: Kenya' (6 April 2016) E/C.12/KEN/CO/2-5 para 18; CESCR, 'Concluding Observations: Ireland' (8 July 2015) E/C.12/IRL/CO/3 para 27.

[59]    CESCR, 'Concluding Observations: Paraguay' (n 19) para 23. Similarly, it expressed concern about the diversion of allocated funds, e.g. CESCR, 'Concluding Observations: India' (8 August 2008) E/C.12/IND/CO/5 para 32.

[60]    CRC, 'Concluding Observations: Saudi Arabia' (25 October 2016) CRC/C/SAU/CO/3-4 para 9; CRC, Concluding Observations: Democratic Republic of the Congo (28 February 2017) CRC/C/COD/CO/3-5 para 10.

[61]    Paul Hunt, 'Report of the Special Rapporteur on the Right to Health on Maternal Mortality and Access to Medicines' (13 September 2006) A/61/338 para 68.

criticized trade policies that compel states to establish forums governing preferred medicine lists as 'a waste of crucial administrative resources that could be spent delivering health goods and services'.[62] The Special Rapporteur on Extreme Poverty has argued that imposing prison sentences for non-payment of fines on those unable to pay is 'a considerable waste' of resources.[63] The Special Rapporteur on Water and Sanitation has urged states 'to avoid duplication of efforts and waste of resources'.[64]

Another important question is whether privatization and public private partnerships (PPPs) are an effective use of resources. Several human rights monitoring bodies have expressed concerns about the negative impact of privatization and PPPs on the accessibility of quality goods and services – focusing mainly on education and, to a lesser extent, health care.[65] Looking at this issue through the maximum available resources doctrine could strengthen this analysis further.

### 2.5.3   Resource mobilization

Revenue-generating powers give a state a degree of control over the financial resources that are 'available' to it. Thus, the maximum available resources doctrine includes an obligation to mobilize resources – from different sources – in line with human rights standards and principles. The mobilization of resources domestically, through taxation, and the mobilization of resources internationally, through overseas development assistance and government borrowing, have received particular attention by human rights monitoring bodies.

There is emerging consensus about the critical importance of taxation as a sustainable source of public revenue; a powerful redistributive tool; and a critical area to enhance democratic process principles, accountable governance and active citizenship. As the Special Rapporteur on Extreme Poverty highlights, low levels of revenue collection constitute 'a major obstacle to the capacity of the state to finance public services and social programmes', on which the people living in poverty are 'particularly dependent'.[66] Taxation has also received attention from the Human Rights Council. In Resolution 34/11, for example, the Council calls on states 'to seek to reduce opportunities for tax avoidance, to consider inserting anti-abuse clauses in all tax treaties and to enhance disclosure practices and transparency in both source and destination countries, including by seeking to ensure transparency in all financial transactions between Governments and companies to relevant tax authorities'.[67]

As with allocation decisions, states have discretion in formulating taxation policies most appropriate to their circumstances. However, this discretion is not without limits. The

---

[62]   Anand Grover, 'Report of the Special Rapporteur on the Right to Health on Access to Medicines' (1 May 2013) A/HRC/23/42 para 29.

[63]   Magdalena Sepúlveda Carmona, 'Report of the Special Rapporteur on Extreme Poverty' (n 29) para 43.

[64]   Catarina de Albuquerque, 'Report of the Special Rapporteur on the Human Right to Safe Drinking Water and Sanitation' (11 July 2013) A/HRC/24/44 para 27.

[65]   See e.g. the 'Abidjan Principles on the Right to Education', which focus on the need to regulate private involvement in education and have been recognized by UN and regional human rights experts: <www.abidjanprinciples.org>.

[66]   Magdalena Sepúlveda Carmona, 'Report of the Special Rapporteur on Extreme Poverty' (22 May 2014) A/HRC/26/28 para 44.

[67]   HRC, 'Resolution 34/11: The Negative Impact of the Non-repatriation of Funds of Illicit Origin to the Countries of Origin on the Enjoyment of Human Rights, and the Importance of Improving International Cooperation' (10 April 2017) A/HRC/RES/34/11 para 7.

Concluding Observations of the CESCR increasingly voice concerns about the sufficiency of revenue raised (including the need to tackle tax evasion and avoidance and to review tax exemptions);[68] the distribution and progressivity of the tax burden;[69] efficiency and incentives that the tax system creates to promote rights enjoyment;[70] and the sustainability of domestic tax systems.[71] From this, it emerges that taxation should ensure that 'adequate' or 'sufficient' revenue is generated and be 'fair', 'progressive' or 'socially equitable'.[72] The African Commission on Human and Peoples' Rights uses similar language, affirming that states have an obligation to institute an 'effective and fair' taxation system.[73] The CRC Committee has also emphasized the importance of ensuring that resource mobilization is 'sustainable', both 'for current and future generations'.[74]

General Comment No. 24, issued by the CESCR in June 2017, identifies concrete situations in which a state would fail to meet its obligations regarding resource mobilization. Focusing specifically on corporate tax, it states:

> Lowering the rates of corporate tax solely with a view to attracting investors encourages a race to the bottom that ultimately undermines the ability of all States to mobilise resources domestically to realise Covenant rights. As such, this practice is inconsistent with the duties of the states parties to the Covenant.[75]

### 2.5.4   Non-financial resources and sustainable development

Somewhat surprisingly, human rights monitoring bodies have not offered an authoritative definition of resources. In particular, whether or not non-financial resources should be considered in assessing compliance with the norm and, if so, how, remains unclear. As the discussion above illustrates, most have focused primarily, if not almost exclusively, on financial resources. Nevertheless, a number of scholars have argued that there is legitimate scope to interpret resources more expansively – to include human, technical, scientific, cultural and natural resources, for example.[76]

---

[68]   CESCR, 'Concluding Observations: Paraguay' (20 March 2015) E/C.12/PRY/CO/4 para 10; CESCR, 'Concluding Observations: Burundi' (16 October 2015) E/C.12/BDI/CO/1 para 14.

[69]   CESCR, 'Concluding Observations: Namibia' (23 March 2016) E/C.12/NAM/CO/1 para 24; CESCR, 'Concluding Observations: Republic of Macedonia' (15 July 2016) E/C.12/MKD/CO/2-4 para 42.

[70]   CESCR, 'Concluding Observations: Mongolia' (7 July 2015) E/C.12/MNG/CO/4 para 16; CESCR, 'Concluding Observations: Uganda' (8 July 2015) E/C.12/UGA/CO/1 para 19.

[71]   CESCR, 'Concluding Observations: Venezuela' (7 July 2015) E/C.12/VEN/CO/3 para 6.

[72]   See, e.g., CESCR, 'Concluding Observations: Canada' (23 March 2016) E/C.12/CAN/CO/6 para 10; CESCR, 'Concluding Observations: Paraguay' (n 68) para 10; CESCR, 'Concluding Observations: United Kingdom (14 July 2016) E/C.12/GBR/CO/6 para 17; CESCR, 'Concluding Observations: Burundi' (n 68) para 14; CESCR, 'Concluding Observations: Costa Rica' (21 October 2016) E/C.12/CRI/CO/5 para 15.

[73]   ACHPR, 'Principles and Guidelines' (n 4) para 15.

[74]   CRC, General Comment No. 19 (n 29) para 63.

[75]   CESCR, General Comment No. 24 (n 55) para 37.

[76]   See e.g. Sigrun Skogly, 'The Requirement of Using the "Maximum of Available Resources" for Human Rights Realisation: A Question of Quality as Well as Quantity?' (2012) 12(3) Human Rights Law 393; Robert E. Robertson, 'Measuring State Compliance with the Obligation to Devote the "Maximum Available Resources" to Realizing Economic, Social, and Cultural Rights' (1994) 16(4) Human Rights Quarterly 693.

The need to clarify obligations regarding natural resources is growing more urgent as the risk of irreversible climate breakdown and ecological crisis looms ever closer. As the Special Rapporteur on Extreme Poverty highlights, 'the vast majority of economic growth, development, and poverty reduction since the industrial revolution has depended on exploitation of natural resources, despite the social and environmental costs'.[77] Advancing the sorts of transformational policies needed to address the climate crisis will demand much more 'systematic engagement' with ESCR, he continues.[78]

In particular, 'much more needs to be done to fill in significant gaps and uncertainties about the obligations of States'.[79] Human rights monitoring bodies have addressed the more immediate adverse impacts of natural resource exploitation, in particular on Indigenous Peoples and other communities who rely directly on natural resources.[80] Concerns about the broader distributional effects of natural resource exploitation, in particular failure to use revenue generated to advance ESCR, have also been raised.[81] But overall this appears to have been less of a focus to date. Drawing on, and continuing to develop and systematize, the norms that unpack obligations related to non-financial resources, particularly regarding sustainability, could be one way to clarify obligations regarding natural resources.

## 2.6 Extraterritorial Obligations Regarding Resources

In an increasingly globalized economy, the extraterritorial dimension of the maximum available resources doctrine is of growing significance. The aspect that has received the most attention by the CESCR and other international human rights monitoring bodies is with regard to obligations of international cooperation and assistance. General Comment No. 3 'notes that the phrase "to the maximum of its available resources" was intended by the drafters of the Covenant to refer to both the resources existing within a State and those available from the international community through international cooperation and assistance'.[82] This means when states do not have sufficient resources to honor their minimum core obligations or to take progressive steps towards broader ESCR realization, they must seek international assistance.

Nevertheless, the duty of states to seek international support 'loses much of its significance in the absence of clear duties of other states, or of international agencies, to provide such support as may be requested'.[83] As De Schutter argues, the correlative duty to respond to any request for support remains ill-defined. In particular, 'both the duty-bearers and the content remain vague and contested', making this obligation difficult to enforce until further

---

[77] Philip Alston, 'Climate Change and Poverty: Report of the Special Rapporteur on Extreme Poverty and Human Rights' (17 July 2019) A/HRC/41/39 para 39.

[78] Ibid para 68.

[79] Ibid para 71.

[80] See e.g. CESCR, General Comment No. 24 (n 55) para 18; CESCR, 'Concluding Observations: Democratic Republic of the Congo' (16 December 2009) E/C.12/COD/CO/4 para 13; CESCR, 'Concluding Observations: Honduras' (11 July 2016) E/C.12/HND/CO/2 para 46(a); *African Commission on Human and Peoples' Rights v Kenya*, Application No. 006/2012.

[81] See e.g. ACHPR, 'Pretoria Declaration on Economic, Social and Cultural Rights in Africa' (17 September 2004) ACHPR /Res.73(XXXVI)04 para 3; CESCR, 'Concluding Observations: Chad' (16 December 2009) E/C.12/TCD/CO/3 para 23; CESCR, 'Concluding Observations: Sudan' (n 19) para 15.

[82] CESCR, General Comment No. 3 (n 5) para 13.

[83] De Schutter (n 11) 584.

clarified.[84] The Committee has highlighted that international cooperation for the realization of ESCR is an obligation of all states, and is particularly incumbent upon those states that are in a position to assist others.[85] This is reinforced in the Maastricht Principles on Extraterritorial Obligations on Economic, Social and Cultural Rights, adopted in 2011. The CESCR and CRC Committee have consistently stressed that states with capacity to assist are expected to do so – regularly recommending developed countries meet their commitment to dedicate 0.7 per cent of GNI or GDP to development assistance.[86] But their analysis has not gone beyond the quantity of assistance, to look at quality.

A second dimension that human rights monitoring bodies have elaborated relates to the extraterritorial impacts of a state's international economic policies, for example when a state (acting bilaterally or as a member of an international organization) provides loans to other states. This is an important normative development given the potential for conditions attached to a loan to undermine a state's ability to mobilize resources, for example through progressive taxation or counter-cyclical monetary policies. The Guiding Principles on Foreign Debt and Human Rights, endorsed by the Human Rights Council in June 2012,[87] set out actions that lending states should take, including: satisfying themselves that a borrower state has made an informed decision to borrow and that the loan is to be used for a public purpose; conducting due diligence or obtaining assurances from the borrower state that the loan funds will not be wasted through official corruption, economic mismanagement or other unproductive uses; satisfying themselves that the borrower state is capable of servicing its external debt without compromising its human rights obligations; and not financing activities or projects that violate, or would foreseeably violate, human rights in the borrower state.[88] In a statement issued in 2016, the CESCR affirms the obligation on lending states not to 'impose obligations on borrowing States that would lead them to adopt retrogressive measures in violation of their obligations under the Covenant'.[89]

A related issue is the spill-over effects of a state's domestic economic policies. The most definitive statement on this by the CESCR is General Comment No. 24 on human rights obligations in the context of business activities. In it, the Committee states that providing excessive protection for bank secrecy and permissive rules on corporate tax may affect the ability of states where economic activities are taking place to meet their obligation to mobilize the maximum available resources.[90] A number of the Committee's concluding observations

---

[84]    Ibid.

[85]    CESCR, General Comment No. 3 (n 5) para 14.

[86]    See e.g. CRC, General Comment No. 5 (n 32) para 61; CESCR, 'Concluding Observations: Belgium' (4 January 2008) E/C.12/BEL/CO/3 para 27; CESCR, 'Concluding Observations: Germany' (12 July 2011) E/C.12/DEU/CO/5 para 33; CESCR, 'Concluding Observations: Japan (10 June 2013) E/C.12/JPN/CO/3 para 32; CESCR, 'Concluding Observations: Portugal' (8 December 2014) E/C.12/PRT/CO/4 para 19.

[87]    HRC, 'Resolution 20/10: The Effects of Foreign Debt and Other Related International Financial Obligations of States on the Full Enjoyment of all Human Rights, Particularly Economic, Social and Cultural Rights' (18 July 2012) A/HRC/RES/20/10.

[88]    Ibid paras 38–40.

[89]    CESCR, 'Statement on Public Debt' (n 29) para 10.

[90]    CESCR, General Comment No. 24 (n 55) para 37. To combat abusive tax practices by transnational corporations, States should combat transfer pricing practices and deepen international tax cooperation, and explore the possibility to tax multinational groups of companies as single firms, with developed countries imposing a minimum corporate income tax rate during a period of transition.

also express concerns with cross-border tax evasion, financial secrecy, illicit financial flows and global corruption.[91]

The Committee on the Elimination of all forms of Discrimination against Women set out the steps that a state should take in line with its extraterritorial obligations in this area in its concluding observations on Switzerland in 2016. In particular, it recommended undertaking independent, participatory and periodic impact assessments of the extraterritorial effects of its financial secrecy and corporate tax policies on women's rights. It also called on Switzerland to ensure that trade and investment agreements negotiated recognize the primacy of its obligations under the Convention and explicitly consider their impact on women's rights, as well as to strengthen its legislation governing the conduct of its corporations in relation to their activities abroad.[92] These recommendations respond to evidence presented by CESR and its partners about the negative impact of Switzerland's policies on the ability of other states to mobilize resources for the fulfillment of women's rights.[93]

Another important question is how the maximum available resources doctrine intersects with norms related to the human rights obligations of corporations. Foreign direct investment (FDI) is a critical channel through which states mobilize resources, for example. Nevertheless, it remains relatively underexplored by human rights monitoring bodies. One of the few normative statements about state obligations in this area comes from the Working Group on the Right to Development, which notes that FDI

> should contribute to local and national development in a responsible manner, that is, in ways that are conducive to social development, protect the environment, and respect the rule of law and fiscal obligations in the host countries. The principles underlying the right to development … further imply that all parties involved, i.e. investors and recipient countries, have responsibilities to ensure that profit considerations do not result in crowding out human rights protection.[94]

## 2.7 Transparency, Participation and Accountability Regarding Resources

Finally, there have been important normative developments related to process principles as they apply to the maximum available resources doctrine. Arguably, focusing on strengthening these principles – particularly on making budgetary decisions more democratic – can help to overcome the difficulty in determining an appropriate margin of discretion states should have regarding resource decisions.[95] In its General Comment No. 19 on the right to social security, the CESCR adds procedural criteria to assess whether retrogressive measures are justified, including whether there was genuine participation of affected groups and whether there was an

---

[91] CESCR, 'Concluding Observations: Uganda (n 70) para 10; CESCR, 'Concluding Observations: Honduras' (11 July 2016) E/C.12/HND/CO/2 para 20; CESCR, 'Concluding Observations: United Kingdom' (14 July 2016) E/C.12/GBR/CO/6 para 16; CESCR, 'Concluding Observations: Lichtenstein' (3 July 2017) E/C.12/LIE/CO/2-3 para 9; CESCR, 'Concluding Observations: Russia' (16 October 2017) E/C.12/RUS/CO/6 para 19.

[92] CEDAW Committee, 'Concluding Observations: Switzerland' (25 November 2016) CEDAW/C/CHE/CO/4-5 paras 40-41.

[93] CESR et al, 'Swiss Responsibility for the Extraterritorial Impacts of Tax Abuse on Women's Rights: Submission to the Committee on the Elimination of Discrimination against Women' (2016).

[94] Working Group on the Right to Development, 'Report of the Working Group on the Right to Development on its Seventh Session' (22 February 2006) E/CN.4/2006/26 para 59.

[95] De Schutter (n 11) 616.

independent review of the measures.[96] In concluding observations, the Committee has focused on transparency in resources decisions. For example, it has found it regrettable that states do not provide disaggregated data on social spending.[97] It has also encouraged states to implement the Extractive Industries Transparency Initiative (EITI), in particular regular disclosure of revenues received from extractive industries.[98] However, one procedural issue that is less clear is the roles and responsibilities of different branches of government (executive, legislative and judicial) and different levels of government (national, regional, local) in relation to resources.

## 3.   ASSESSING COMPLIANCE WITH THE OBLIGATION IN PRACTICE

Determining whether a state is progressively achieving the full realization of ESCR, by taking steps to the maximum of its available resources, presents significant empirical challenges. Much has been written about how the progressive realization of rights can be measured, drawing on quantitative social science methods in particular.[99] Nevertheless, linking such measures to an evaluation of whether steps have been taken to the maximum of available resources has proven more challenging.

As outlined in this section, there is growing interest in adopting and adapting budget analysis techniques to evaluate whether states are generating, allocating and spending their resources in line with their obligation to progressively realize rights. However, establishing that a state has failed to meet this obligation requires an 'evidential link' between particular conduct (for example a tax measure, budget appropriation or regulatory omission) and the 'factual outcome' for rights realization.[100] For this reason, budget analysis needs to be used *in conjunction with* other measurement techniques appropriate for assessing other components of the obligation, such as analysis of outcome data over time, and of the policy interventions that resource allocations have enabled. This section outlines efforts to systematize the use of different measurement techniques, as well as to incorporate them into a holistic framework for assessing progressive realization.

### 3.1   Rights-based Budget Analysis

A growing number of human rights monitoring bodies, international agencies and non-government organizations are starting to do more rigorous and regular 'budget work', which encompasses a range of different activities related to government budgets.[101] These

---

[96]   CESCR, General Comment No. 19 (n 29) para 42.

[97]   CESCR, 'Concluding Observations: Dominican Republic' (21 October 2016) E/C.12/DOM/CO/4 para 17; CESCR, 'Concluding Observations: Costa Rica' (n 72) para 17.

[98]   CESCR, 'Concluding Observations: Democratic Republic of the Congo' (n 80) para 13.

[99]   Chenwi (n 31); Allison Corkery and Sally-Anne Way, 'Integrating Quantitative and Qualitative Tools to Monitor the Obligation to Fulfill Economic, Social and Cultural Rights: The OPERA Framework' (2012) 30 Nordic Journal of Human Rights 324.

[100]   Nolan et al (n 17) 127–28.

[101]   Ann Blyberg, 'Government Budgets and Rights Implementation' in Jody Heymann (ed), *Making Equal Rights Real: Taking Effective Action to Overcome Global Challenges* (Cambridge University Press 2012) 198–201.

activities vary in terms of who is involved, when in the budget cycle they take place and what tools they use.[102] A common feature of much of this work is the use of simple descriptive statistics to analyze a government's budget, in order to reveal insights into whether resources are being mobilized, allocated and spent in line with the duty to progressively achieve the full realization of ESCR, as well as with other relevant human rights norms. Nevertheless, there is still wide variation in the indicators and benchmarks used.

Analyzing a government's budget within a human rights framework necessitates a process of 'translating' human rights standards into budgetary 'concepts, terms, and line items'.[103] This is because the figures in a budget are always relative. Analyzing whether budgetary figures are high or low, for example, involves asking high or low *relative to what?* Taking a hypothetical example, say the social housing budget goes from 100 million in 2015 to 200 million in 2020. Doubling the social housing budget may seem quite significant. However, what if the government's overall budget tripled in that same period? As a percentage share, the social housing budget actually shrinks. What if, due to inflation, the cost of constructing social housing increases 150 per cent over the same period? In this scenario, the government's purchasing power decreases, so the budget does not stretch as far.

Because of this relativity, to analyze the budget it is often necessary to convert budgetary figures into comparable indicators. Some examples of comparable indicators include government revenue as per cent of GDP; tax revenue as per cent of government revenue; allocation ratios for different sectors and sub-sectors; and per capita or per unit allocations for different sectors and sub-sectors.[104] To date, there has not been a great deal of systematization in the indicators used by human rights monitoring bodies to analyze government budgets. However, emerging practice of the CESCR illustrates that it is starting to ask for more consistent budgetary information from states in its lists of issues.

Nevertheless, the limited availability of data and statistics presents a very real practical challenge in undertaking comprehensive human rights budget analysis. In 2016, for example, the International Budget Partnership (IBP) conducted a global survey of civil society groups undertaking budget work, receiving 176 responses from 70 countries. Less than a third of respondents gave positive ratings (8–10 out of 10) for accuracy, timeliness and consistency of budget information. Only one in five were satisfied with the comprehensiveness and accessibility of available information. A lack of granularity and difficulty in cross-referencing, or comparing, data was cited as the largest constraint on greater uptake of budget information. Government capacity and willingness to respond to these demands for more detailed and better organized budget data depends 'on a range of political and technical factors' that inevitably vary across countries, IBP concludes.

Another challenge is how to interpret statistics, including against relevant baselines and benchmarks. The Covenant itself is 'devoid of any specific allocational benchmarks', as Philip

---

[102] For example, some activities are led by government, others by parliamentarians, others by civil society; some take place when the budget is formulated by the Treasury, others when parliament approves it, others when ministries track their expenditures, others span across these phases of the budget process; some are focused on analysing the content of the budget, others on making the process more transparent and participatory. For a summary of methodologies for analyzing budgets, see OHCHR and IBP, 'Realizing Human Rights Through Government Budgets' (2017) 145–53.

[103] Blyberg (n 101) 211.

[104] See e.g. OAS, 'Progress Indicators for Measuring Rights under the Protocol of San Salvador' (2015).

Alston and Gerard Quinn emphasize.[105] Thus it has been necessary to look to other sources. CESR draws on a range of sources in its work. These include targets to which a state has committed in international or regional agreements, or in national policies, programs or plans; recommendations from United Nations agencies and other organizations or experts; targets advocated by civil society groups, grassroots organizations, affected communities and other rights holders; and comparisons of data between similarly situated countries, within a country or for different population groups.

Again, there has been limited systematization in the benchmarks used by human rights monitoring bodies in interpreting budgetary data. Human rights monitoring bodies have reiterated the importance of states setting 'appropriate' benchmarks, in general, in order to monitor progress and inform policymaking – as numerous general comments, concluding observations and special procedures reports attest. However, little guidance is given on what constitutes an appropriate benchmark. Some bodies have advocated for the use of country comparisons.[106] Others have emphasized that the process of setting benchmarks must be democratic and actively involve civil society organizations.[107] Others refer to political commitments. As noted above, the CESCR and CRC Committee have taken the agreement that high income countries should dedicate 0.7 per cent of GNI or GDP to official development assistance as a benchmark to define the obligation of international assistance, for example.[108] A number of general comments of the CESCR envisage a process of 'scoping' through which states and the Committee jointly consider national benchmarks, which then provide the targets to be achieved during the next reporting period.[109] However, there is little evidence in the concluding observations that this practice has been systematized in the Committee's periodic reviews.

### 3.2    Efforts to Link Resources and Rights Realization

It is perhaps unsurprising that benchmarks specifically related to the use of resources remain so ad hoc because benchmarks cannot 'substitute for a deeper analysis'.[110] Ultimately, looking at budget figures alone is not enough to determine compliance with the duty to progressively realize ESCR; the task is to interrogate the reasonableness of resource decisions in light of their impact on the fuller realization of human rights over time. This is the 'evidential link' that it is necessary to establish.

---

[105]    Philip Alston and Gerard Quinn, 'The Nature and Scope of States Parties' Obligations under the International Covenant on Economic, Social and Cultural Rights' (1987) 9 Human Rights Quarterly, 177 and 181.

[106]    See e.g. Catarina de Albuquerque, 'Report of the Special Rapporteur on Water' (n 64) para 61; Anand Grover, 'Report of the Special Rapporteur on Health' (n 62) para 23.

[107]    See e.g. CESCR, General Comment No. 12: The Right to Adequate Food (12 May 1999) E/C.12/1999/5 para 29.

[108]    De Schutter (n 11) 585.

[109]    CESCR, General Comment No. 14 (n 43) para 58; CESCR, General Comment No. 15: The Right to Water (20 January 2003) E/C.12/2002/11 para 54; CESCR, General Comment No. 17: The Right of Everyone to Benefit from the Protection of the Moral and Material Interests Resulting from any Scientific, Literary or Artistic Production of Which He or She is the Author (12 January 2006) E/C.12/GC/17 para 50; CESCR, General Comment No. 18 (n 44) para 47; CESCR, General Comment No. 19 (n 29) para 76.

[110]    De Schutter (n 11) 595.

A number of initiatives have sought to provide a quantitative metric linking resources and ESCR realization. One example, proposed by Sakiko Fukuda-Parr, Terra Lawson-Remer and Susan Randolph, calculates a composite score known as the Social and Economic Rights Fulfilment Index (SERF Index) based on several outcome indicators incorporating the rights to food, education, health, adequate housing and decent work. The index assesses countries' overall ESCR performance, taking into account their respective level of development, using data for GDP per capita as a proxy for 'available resources'. Specifically, an 'achievement possibilities frontier' is calculated for each indicator, representing the highest level of enjoyment of a right historically achieved by other states at that level of GDP. This innovative approach, since elaborated in the Human Rights Measurement Initiative (HRMI),[111] provides a way to compare countries' ESCR performance in quantitative terms, taking into account their different income levels. However, using the achievement possibility frontier to set the bar in terms of the performance expected of states is somewhat arbitrary, in that it does not, so far, account for factors other than GDP that may explain differences in rights outcomes. As with all indices, care must be taken in terms of the conclusions drawn from the scores, as these should serve as a starting point for further qualitative assessment of the state's rights-related policy efforts, rather than as a conclusive measure of ESCR compliance.

The need for a more nuanced assessment that links available resources to human rights outcomes through policy expenditures is addressed by De Schutter, who proposes a broader conceptual framework with three dimensions: resources–spending–outcomes. This framework considers resource mobilization and spending jointly, relating these complementary dimensions to outcomes, that is, to the effective levels of enjoyment of ESCR. Unsatisfactory outcomes, such as widespread homelessness or inequitable access to health care, will only be an infringement of the ICESCR 'if such outcomes reflect not simply an inability of the State to improve the situation, but an unwillingness to do'. This means showing 'that resource mobilisation could have been improved, or that spending priorities could have been defined differently, or both, in order to achieve better outcomes'.[112] Such judgments would likely involve more qualitative and contextualized assessments of a country's policy priorities.

### 3.3  OPERA: A Comprehensive Framework for Assessing Progressive Realization in Light of Fiscal and Other Policy Efforts

Crude correlations directly linking resource allocations to levels of rights realization have obvious limitations. As De Schutter emphasizes, the same levels of investment 'may have more or less impact' on rights, depending on how efficiently resources are used and, in particular, whether they meet the priority needs of the population, particularly those of low-income groups.[113] For this reason, linking resources to the norms of progressive realization and non-retrogression needs to be part of a broader assessment that unpacks the effects of resourcing decisions on the implementation of relevant policies, and the effect of these policy efforts on increased or decreased enjoyment of rights. The policy decision-making process is also important to analyze. This triangulation of the three areas of analysis of relevance to progressive realization – the resources that are available, the policy interventions and processes

---

[111]  Human Rights Measurement Initiative, 'Portal' <www.humanrightsmeasurement.org>.
[112]  De Schutter (n 11) 560.
[113]  De Schutter (n 11) 600.

they enable, and the human rights outcomes resulting from these – can involve 'a complex computation of a wide range of sophisticated statistical and other information'.[114] Thus, a more comprehensive investigation demands a combination of research methods to ensure better corroboration between a broad selection of evidence.

To do this methodically, CESR has developed an analytical framework that combines quantitative and qualitative research methods in a four-step framework known as OPERA. OPERA stands for Outcomes; Policy Efforts; Resources; and Assessment. Each step aims to assess a core aspect of the obligation to fulfill ESCR and provides a 'checklist' of the relevant standards and principles against which a state's conduct should be assessed. By assessing a state's conduct against each of these core dimensions, the framework aims to systematically link evidence about a state's performance in terms of its obligations of result with its performance in terms of its obligations of conduct. This enables a more rigorous assessment as to whether or not a particular deprivation constitutes a human rights violation.[115]

The OPERA framework is distinctive in that it explicitly links the human rights standards and principles that underpin the obligation to fulfill ESCR (including progressive realization, non-retrogression and minimum core obligations) with suggested methods for how they might be measured. It eclectically draws from a range of tools and techniques – including the use of quantitative indicators, benchmarks and budget analysis, but also qualitative analysis, perception surveys and individual case narratives – structuring them around a step-by-step framework to evaluate whether or not a state is meeting its obligations to fulfill ESCR. As the framework was originally developed to support NGO advocacy, to date it has primarily focused on techniques that use simple quantitative data, which human rights advocates will be able to apply relatively easily. CESR has drawn on OPERA in dozens of projects carried out with partners in different countries to make the case that states are failing to meet their obligation to take steps to progressively realize rights to the maximum of available resources.[116]

For example, OPERA underpins the Egypt Social Progress Indicators (ESPI), developed by a coalition of Egyptian researchers, independent experts and civil society groups, with strategic and methodological support from CESR. Macroeconomic reforms implemented after the 'Arab Spring' in 2011 have led to severely deteriorated living conditions for average Egyptians. However, the experience of those being left behind is not captured by the indicators used by international financial institutions and other economic actors. As outlined below, the OPERA-based Egypt Social Progress Indicators systematically link retrogression in rights realization with failures to generate, allocate and spend resources in line with human rights obligations.

In terms of outcomes, analysis of data on key indicators related to a range of ESCR showed widespread and sometimes increasing deprivation in a context of extreme inequality. For example, the national poverty rate was 27.8 per cent in 2015, meaning more than 26 million people were living in economically precarious situations and struggling to meet basic needs;

---

[114]    Nolan et al (n 17) 127–28.

[115]    CESR, 'The OPERA Framework: Assessing Compliance with the Obligation to Fulfill Economic and Social Rights' (2012).

[116]    Case studies outlining how CESR has used OPERA in Angola, Egypt, Guatemala, Ireland, Kenya and South Africa can be found at <http://cesr.org/opera-practice-case-studies-applying-cesrs-monitoring-framework>.

this had increased from 26.3 per cent in 2012–13.[117] Meanwhile, Egypt's wealth Gini coefficient was a staggering 91.7 per cent in 2017, making it the third most unequal country in the world by this measurement.[118]

Quantitative and qualitative analysis of policies and programs related to economic and social rights revealed that the goods and services they provide were limited in terms of where they were available, their quality and who is able to access them. For example, Egypt's three cash transfer programs only covered approximately 49 per cent of the total population considered poor in 2015.[119] Community assessments carried out in 2017 to assess the quality of services in 209 hospitals showed that less than half of the criteria for quality were met on average.[120] Only a quarter of the units originally planned under Egypt's Social Housing Project had been delivered by July 2018.[121]

Budget analysis uncovered low social investment – a trend which began before 2011 and continued afterwards – combined with taxes that placed an inequitable burden on the poor. For example, in the 2017/18 financial year, the government allocated 1.34 per cent of GDP to health, lower than the constitutional commitment of 3 per cent. Education was allocated 2.6 per cent of GDP, while the constitutional commitment is 6 per cent. Low spending in turn results from low tax revenue, which was 13 per cent of GDP at the end of 2016/17. Egypt's revenue from corporate income taxes had decreased over the past decade, from 1.9 per cent of GDP in 2006/07 to 1.3 per cent of GDP in 2016/17, due to tax avoidance, weak administration and extensive incentives. At the same time, Egypt introduced a regressive Value Added Tax, which shifts the burden of revenue mobilization to lower-income citizens.[122]

Broader analysis of the Egyptian political economy contextualized these trends showing how successive administrations had prioritized austerity, which international financial institutions and other creditors promote without regard for their human rights consequences, while critical voices from NGOs and civil society groups, unions and opposition parties were frequently repressed – at times violently. Crackdowns against trade unions were widespread, for example. In the 'Workers' Rights Index' of 2018, Egypt was ranked the fifth worst country in the world with regard to the legal protection of workers' rights.[123]

As this example shows, a nuanced and comprehensive assessment of progressive realization requires marshaling a range of evidence and structuring it under a triangulated analysis of ESCR outcomes over time, the policy efforts shaping these and the resources enabling or constraining these efforts, assessed in light of all relevant contextual factors (including the broader human rights situation in the country and the role of international actors). In several

---

[117] ESPI, 'Percentage of the Population below the National Poverty Line' (2018) <www.progressegypt.org/en/indicator.html#percentage-poverty>.

[118] ESPI, 'Egypt's Wealth Gap' (2018) <www.progressegypt.org/en/indicator.html#wealth-gap>.

[119] ESPI, 'Estimated Percentage of Poor Covered by Cash Transfer Programs' (2018) <www.progressegypt.org/en/indicator.html#cash-transfer>.

[120] ESPI, 'Average Score of the Community Assessment Portal for Egyptian Hospitals' (2018) <www.progressegypt.org/en/indicator.html#hospitals>.

[121] ESPI, 'Action to Improve Affordability in Social Housing Projects' (2018) <www.progressegypt.org/en/indicator.html#mortgage-access>.

[122] ESPI, 'Tax Revenue as a Percentage of GDP' (2018) <www.progressegypt.org/en/indicator.html#tax-gdp>.

[123] ESPI, 'Obstacles to Exercising Labour Rights in Practice (2018) <www.progressegypt.org/en/indicator.html#labour-rights>.

instances where CESR and its partners have brought well-substantiated evidence structured along these lines to international human rights bodies, they have been able to raise specific concerns and recommendations regarding apparent retrogression,[124] discrimination,[125] and breach of extraterritorial obligations not to deprive other states of their maximum available resources to progressively fulfill ESCR.[126]

## 4.    OPERATIONALIZING THE OBLIGATION IN POLICYMAKING

Ultimately, giving effect to these norms means going beyond analysis of human rights compliance and ensuring that a state's obligation to dedicate the maximum of its available resources to the progressive realization of ESCR is *embedded* in the way that economic policy is conceptualized and developed. Nevertheless, advancing a human rights-based approach means grappling with deeply entrenched power imbalances in economic policymaking.[127] There are a number of promising initiatives that have sought to do this by improving transparency, facilitating public participation in decision-making, seeking to align policy priorities with human rights commitments and broadening the criteria for assessing policy impact. This emerging area of praxis is a promising development in terms of embedding analytical tools such as the OPERA framework into policymaking, in order to operationalize the normative standards and principles outlined in this chapter. This section highlights a select number of developments which present strategic opportunities in this regard. These illustrative examples come from the international human rights system or are human rights initiatives at the national level, which are potentially replicable elsewhere; others are processes within the spheres of economic and development policy.

### 4.1    Initiatives within the Human Rights Arena

In March 2019, the Human Rights Council adopted Guiding Principles on Human Rights Impact Assessments of Economic Reforms,[128] developed through a consultative process led by the Independent Expert on the effects of foreign debt on human rights. The Independent Expert has argued that the state's responsibility to ensure its economic policies do not violate human

---

[124]    CESR, Médicos del Mundo, Oxfam et al, 'Statement: UN Urges Spain to End Detrimental Austerity Measures' (2018) <www.cesr.org/united-nations-urges-spain-end-detrimental-austerity-measures-0>.

[125]    CESR, IEJ and Section 27, 'Statement: South Africa Urged to End Austerity Measures amid "Unacceptably High Levels of Inequality"' (2018) <www.cesr.org/south-africa%C2%A0urged-end-austerity-measures-amid-unacceptably-high-levels-inequality>.

[126]    CESR, 'Switzerland Held to Account for Cost of Tax Abuse on Women's Rights' (2016) <www.cesr.org/switzerland-held-account-cost-tax-abuse-womens-rights>.

[127]    See e.g. Dena Freeman, 'De-Democratisation and Rising Inequality: The Underlying Cause of a Worrying Trend' (2017) International Inequalities Institute Working Paper 12.

[128]    HRC, 'Resolution 40/8: The Effects of Foreign Debt and Other Related International Financial Obligations of States on the Enjoyment of Human Rights' (5 April 2019) A/HRC/RES/40/8.

rights 'implies a duty to carry out human rights impact assessments to evaluate and address any foreseeable effects'.[129]

Human rights impact assessments can provide empirical evidence 'to properly assess the proportionality and legitimacy of economic measures' from a human rights perspective, the Guiding Principles stress. Accordingly, they should be carried out both *ex ante* – to assess the foreseeable impacts of proposed policy changes – and *ex post* – that is, looking back to assess the actual impacts of policy change and implementation. To ensure that impact assessments are 'independent, robust, credible and gender responsive', the Guiding Principles recommend using a variety of quantitative and qualitative tools and methods, including participatory ones, and carefully comparing the human rights impact of different scenarios. States' decisions on economic policies should be consistent with the outcome of human rights impact assessments.

Initiatives that seek to incorporate human rights into the government's policymaking process are also important opportunities to advance commitments to and monitoring of progressive realization. Scotland's National Performance Framework is a promising example. The Framework lists priority National Outcomes that 'describe the kind of Scotland it aims to create'. These outcomes reflect the values and aspirations of the people of Scotland, are aligned with the United Nations Sustainable Development Goals and help to track progress in reducing inequality. Respecting, protecting and fulfilling human rights is an explicit outcome. There are currently 81 economic, social and environmental indicators that track progress on the outcomes and give a measure of national wellbeing.[130] To date, there is not a well-developed process for ensuring that the National Outcomes are reflected in economic policy. However, there is a growing body of work on human rights budgeting in Scotland, to which CESR has contributed. Notably, a key recommendation of the government-established Budget Process Review Group was that it should be possible to track budget allocation and expenditure against impact and progress within the National Outcomes.[131]

The CRC Committee has also advocated for this kind of approach to rights-based policymaking and public financing. In recent years, its concluding observations have consistently included recommendations to this end.[132] In particular, it has advocated for comprehensive assessment of the budget needs of all children; results-based budgeting that includes a child rights perspective; defining budgetary lines for children; and a tracking system with specific indicators to monitor and evaluate the adequacy, efficacy and equitability of the distribution of

---

[129]   Juan Pablo Bohoslavsky, 'Guiding Principles on Human Rights Impact Assessments of Economic Reforms: Report of the Independent Expert on the Effects of Foreign Debt' (19 December 2018) A/HRC/40/57.

[130]   Scottish Government, 'National Performance Framework', see <https://nationalperformance.gov.scot/>.

[131]   Scotland Budget Process Review Group, 'Final Report' (June 2017) <www.parliament.scot/S5_Finance/Reports/BPRG_-_Final_Report_30.06.17.pdf>.

[132]   CRC, 'Concluding Observations: Romania' (30 June 2009) CRC/C/ROM/CO/4 para 12; CRC, 'Concluding Observations: Saudi Arabia' (n 60) para 9; CRC, 'Concluding Observations: New Zealand' (21 October 2016) CRC/C/NZL/CO/5 para 7; CRC, 'Concluding Observations: United Kingdom' (12 July 2016) CRC/C/GBR/CO/5 para 13; CRC, 'Concluding Observations: Mongolia' (12 July 2017) CRC/C/MNG/CO/5 para 9; CRC, 'Concluding Observations: Panama' (28 February 2017) CRC/C/PAN/CO/5-6 para 9.

resources. Similarly, the Committee on the Elimination of all forms of Discrimination against Women has called for states to implement gender-responsive budgeting.[133]

This focus on results-based budgeting echoes a broader trend towards increasing prescriptiveness in the 'dialogic' remedies and recommendations made by human rights monitoring bodies. In particular, these bodies are sketching out more detail about the shape that policies and plans for the progressive realization of ESCR should take. For example, policies and plans should be action oriented; set reasonable timeframes for 'achievable' benchmarks; establish 'strong and focused' bodies to ensure implementation; be evaluated through 'measurable' indicators; and, significantly, facilitate meaningful citizen engagement.[134] Such requirements can deepen democratic policymaking. Nevertheless, as Sandra Liebenberg cautions, due attention should be paid to mitigating the risks of 'co-optation, manipulation and dissipation of organisational energy and solidarity'.[135]

### 4.2    Initiatives within the Economic Policy Arena

In terms of increasing transparency and scrutiny over budgetary decisions, the Open Budget Index is an initiative that has had a notable influence. First published in 2006, the Index scores countries on public availability of budget information, opportunities for the public to participate in the budget process and the role and effectiveness of formal oversight institutions, including the legislature and the national audit office. The Index has prompted concrete shifts in practice in a number of countries. In South Africa, for example, the National Treasury is partnering with a coalition of civil society organizations promoting budget transparency and public participation to co-develop an online budget portal. Launched in February 2018, the portal – named Vulekamali – publishes easily accessible data in a user-friendly format. While the Treasury was already publishing extensive budgetary information on its website, there was recognition that use of this data was not as extensive as it could be, hampering public participation. The portal aims to strengthen civil society involvement in the budget process by facilitating more effective information sharing, analyses and research that enables citizens to have informed discussions on different government policies.[136] What makes this an interesting example is the iterative process through which the portal is being developed; active 'user' involvement is encouraged throughout its development to ensure the data provided is responsive to user needs.

---

[133]    CEDAW Committee, 'Concluding Observations: Guatemala' (22 November 2017) CEDAW/C/GTM/CO/8-9 para 15.

[134]    CESCR, *Djazia and Bellili v Spain*, Communication No. 5/2015 (21 July 2017) E/C.12/61/D/5/2015 para 29(d); ECSR, *Mental Disability Advocacy Center v Bulgaria*, Complaint No. 41/2007 (2008) para 47; CEDAW Committee, *Pimentel v Brazil*, Communication No. 17/2008 (27 September 2011) CEDAW/C/49/D/17/2008 para 7.6; Constitutional Tribunal of Peru, *Azanca Alheli Meza García v Ministry of Health*, Case No. 2945-2003-AA/TC (2004) paras 37–38; ACHPR, 'Principles and Guidelines' (n 4) paras 26–30.

[135]    Sandra Liebenberg, 'The Participatory Democratic Turn in South Africa's Social Rights Jurisprudence' in Katherine G Young (ed), *The Future of Economic and Social Rights* (Cambridge University Press 2019) 209; see also Cesar Rodriguez-Garavito, 'Empowered Participatory Jurisprudence: Experimentation, Deliberation and Norms in Socioeconomic Rights Adjudication' in the same volume.

[136]    South Africa National Treasury and IMALI YETHU, 'South Africa Online Budget Data' <https://vulekamali.gov.za/>.

Participatory budgeting initiatives also have the potential to advance rights-based economic policymaking. Initiatives vary greatly in their scope and scale, but all are based on the premise that community members should have genuine authority to deliberate and decide how resources are allocated.[137] The best known example of participatory budgeting comes from Porto Alegre, in Brazil. Initiated in 1989, community participation in determining the municipal budget has been an 'enormous success' overall over the past few decades, both in terms of deepening direct democracy and in ensuring the effectiveness of budgetary decisions; it also resulted in a 'massive shift' towards spending that benefited the poor.[138] These advances are now under threat following the clearly retrogressive fiscal austerity measures put in place in late 2016, including a 20-year public expenditure freeze condemned by international and regional human rights bodies as well as national and international NGOs.[139]

Broader initiatives to 'rethink' economy policymaking, while not explicitly framed as human rights-based, also offer important lessons. For example, in May 2019 the New Zealand government attracted global attention when it unveiled its first 'wellbeing' budget. There are five priorities in the budget, which were selected using a collaborative and evidence-based approach; a number of features of the approach are worth highlighting. First, data from the Treasury's Living Standards Framework Dashboard was combined with expert advice to identify outcomes where New Zealand could and should be doing better, taking a long-term intergenerational view. Second, to break down agency silos, ministers had to work together to develop packages of initiatives to achieve these outcomes. Third, the impact of the budget will be measured broadly, to include not just the country's financial health, but also the health of its natural resources, people and communities. The government intends to amend the Public Finance Act to ensure that wellbeing objectives, together with fiscal objectives, continue to guide budgets and fiscal policy going forward.[140]

### 4.3    Initiatives within the Development Arena

The international process with perhaps the most far-reaching implications for advancing accountability for the progressive realization of ESCR is the 2030 Agenda for Sustainable Development. Although progressive realization is not explicitly referenced in the Agenda, the full range of human rights obligations which should underpin sustainable development are referenced prominently. As a set of goals and targets to be achieved by all countries by 2030, relating to key aspects of ESCR fulfillment, Agenda 2030 is in many respects a potential vehicle for monitoring progressive realization. Moreover, the SDGs and the Addis Ababa Agreement on Financing for Development include commitments to mobilize resources to fulfill the right to health, to reduce inequality and to increase international cooperation and assistance. Nevertheless, as Chapter 18 of this book highlights, ensuring that these commit-

---

[137]   Paul O'Connell, 'Let Them Eat Cake: Socio-Economic Rights in an Age of Austerity' in Aoife Nolan, Rory O'Connell and Colin Harvey (eds), *Human Rights and Public Finance: Budgets and the Promotion of Economic and Social Rights* (UK edn, Hart Publishing 2013) 71. See also World Bank, 'Participatory Budgeting' (2007).

[138]   Ibid.

[139]   CESR, 'Factsheet: Brazil's Human Rights Advances Imperiled by Austerity Measures' (2017) <http://www.cesr.org/factsheet-brazils-human-rights-advances-imperiled-austerity-measures>.

[140]   New Zealand Minister of Finance, 'Budget Policy Statement' (December 2018) <https://treasury.govt.nz/sites/default/files/2018-12/bps-2019.pdf>.

ments are used to hold governments and international institutions accountable to their duties of progressive realization will require vigilance and sustained advocacy from human rights and other civil society actors.

## 5.    CONCLUSION

There is no doubt that the unjust distribution of resources within and between countries fuels poverty and inequality, having a profound impact on the realization of ESCR. Traditionally, human rights monitoring bodies have been hesitant to tackle the 'economics' of rights. This has left states with a wide margin of discretion to determine the quantum of resources they set aside and, as a result, the pace at which ESCR are progressively realized.

Narrowing this discretion presents a number of significant challenges: conceptual, methodological and strategic. As outlined in this chapter, the scope and content of the obligation to progressively realize ESCR using maximum available resources has been elaborated by human rights monitoring bodies. Nevertheless, the normative contours of Article 2(1) still rely on imprecise concepts such as 'fair' and 'effective' and remain blurry in some respects, in particular regarding its extraterritorial dimensions. Further, there is a need for more comprehensive, context-sensitive, analytical frameworks to establish the 'evidential link' between resource decisions and their impact on the realization of human rights over time – necessary to assess compliance with these norms in practice.

In a time that is characterized by the regressive accumulation of privilege, rather than the progressive realization of rights, the redistributive and egalitarian potential of the concept of progressive realization needs to be more fully and effectively tapped. New advocacy and accountability pathways through which to give effect to the norm in the real-world policy arena are opening up. These strategic opportunities provide entry points for deploying these tools in ways that grapple with deeply entrenched power imbalances in economic policymaking to advance meaningful accountability and transformative policy change.

# 15. Interdependence of human rights

*Bruce Porter*

## 1. INTRODUCTION

The primary source and authority for the modern principle of interdependence of human rights is the oft-cited statement in the Vienna Declaration and Programme of Action (Vienna Declaration) adopted by consensus on 25 June 1993 at the Second World Conference on Human Rights: 'All human rights are universal, indivisible and interdependent and inter-related. The international community must treat human rights globally in a fair and equal manner, on the same footing, and with the same emphasis.'[1]

The same statement, with an important improvement, was adopted by the UN General Assembly in its resolution creating the new UN Human Rights Council in 2006, adding to the previous four qualities a fifth: 'mutually reinforcing'.[2] The five attributes are distinct, but the combination of all four or five of the listed attributes is usually referred to either as 'indivisibility', 'interdependence', or both. In this chapter, the principle of 'interdependence' is used to refer to the combination of the five attributes.

The affirmation of interdependence in the Vienna Declaration so as to place economic, social and cultural (ESC) rights 'on the same footing and with the same emphasis' as civil and political rights marks the beginning of a human rights restoration project aimed at reconstructing the original holistic architecture of rights embodied in the Universal Declaration of Human Rights (UDHR).[3] The principle of interdependence is central to this project not simply as a statement about how the two categories of rights are to be regarded as conceptually related, but also as a dynamic principle of interpretation and application of human rights through which the norms and contents of different rights inform, reinforce, nurture and grow together in response to human rights claims emerging from human experience. Interdependence thus refers to the unity of purpose of human rights protections, so that they are interpreted and applied not as separate or reified entities, but as parts of an integrated and coherent commitment to recognizing the 'inherent dignity' and the 'equal and inalienable rights of all members of the human family'.[4]

---

[1] Vienna Declaration and Programme of Action, adopted by the World Conference on Human Rights in Vienna on 25 June 1993 para 5.

[2] UN General Assembly, Human Rights Council Resolution (3 April 2006) A/RES/60/251, Preamble para 3.

[3] Universal Declaration of Human Rights (adopted 10 December 1948) UNGA Res 217 A (III) (UDHR), Preface.

[4] For elaborations of this understanding of interdependence, see Craig Scott, 'The Interdependence and Permeability of Human Rights Norms: Towards a Partial Fusion of International Covenants on Human Rights' (1989) 27 Osgoode Hall LJ 769; Craig Scott, 'Reaching Beyond (without Abandoning) the Category of Economic, Social and Cultural Rights' (1999) 21 Human Rights Quarterly 633; Alicia Yamin, 'The Future in the Mirror: Incorporating Strategies for the Defense and Promotion of Economic, Social, and Cultural Rights into the Mainstream Human Rights Agenda' [2005] Human Rights Quarterly

In accordance with the Vienna Convention on the Laws of Treaties (VCLT),[5] interdependence demands that human rights be interpreted in context, and in light of the object and purpose of human rights treaties – not in relation to distinctions between categories of rights based on the nature of the obligations placed on governments. Those broader objects and purposes are described in the UDHR as recognizing 'the inherent dignity and the equal and inalienable rights of all members of the human family' and recognizing economic, social and cultural rights (ESCR) 'as indispensable for dignity and the free development of personality'[personhood].[6]

This chapter describes the inclusion of ESC rights claimants as equal in dignity and rights through the principle of interdependence as a 'work in progress' with a lot at stake. It traces the evolution of the idea of interdependence from an earlier notion premised on the unequal status of ESCR to the modern conception premised on equal access to justice and 'human rights made whole'. It describes, with reference to developments described in greater detail in other chapters, the development of interdependence in the jurisprudence of the Committee on Economic Social and Cultural Rights (CESCR) and the Human Rights Committee and within regional systems. Important applications of interdependence within the other seven UN treaty bodies outlined in Chapter 1 are unfortunately beyond the scope of this chapter.

The chapter argues that both civil and political rights and ESC rights have been damaged by their separation and that a failure to adequately engage with the principle of interdependence is continuing to allow many of the most egregious systemic violations of human rights, lying in the interstices between categories of rights, to go unchallenged. It calls for a more inclusive and transformational paradigm of human rights based on a modernized understanding of the interdependence of human rights and the full inclusion of those whose claims to equal dignity and rights have been marginalized or silenced.

## 2.   HISTORICAL DEVELOPMENT

### 2.1   Interdependence in Response to the Separation of Rights

As described in Chapters 1 and 2, ESCR were included in the UDHR as fundamental human rights indispensable for dignity and personhood[7] and equally subject to 'the right to an effective remedy by the competent national tribunals'.[8] With the subsequent division of the rights in the UDHR into two covenants in the early 1950s, however, in the era of the Cold War and US dominance in international human rights discourse, ESCR came to be viewed as poor

---

1200; Ioana Cismas, 'The Intersection of Economic, Social, and Cultural Rights and Civil and Political Rights' in Eibe Riedel, Gilles Giacca and Christophe Golay (eds), *Economic, Social, and Cultural Rights in International Law: Contemporary Issues and Challenges* (OUP 2014); Lilian Chenwi, 'Permeability of Human Rights in the African Charter' (2014) 39 Suppl SAYIL 93; Sandra Ratjen and Manav Satija, 'Realizing Economic, Social, and Cultural Rights for All' in Riedel, Giacca and Golay (eds), *Economic, Social, and Cultural Rights in International Law*.

5    Vienna Convention on the Law of Treaties (adopted 23 May 1969, entered into force 27 January 1980) 1155 UNTS 331.

6    UDHR Article 22.

7    UDHR Article 22, male pronoun omitted.

8    UDHR Article 8.

cousins to CPR, characterized as 'second generation' rights, aspirational objectives of State socio-economic policy and development, rather than as rights to be claimed and adjudicated and requiring effective remedy.

The principle of interdependence first became prominent during the debates in the early 1950s about whether to draft a unitary human rights covenant or two separate covenants. Proposals advanced for dividing human rights in the UDHR into two covenants were initially rejected on the basis that all human rights are 'interdependent and interconnected' and that 'the spirit of the Universal Declaration' is tied to the unity of rights.[9] Proponents of separation, however, argued that the rights could be separated into two covenants at the same time as affirming their interdependence.[10] States proposing separate covenants, led by the USA and the United Kingdom in 1952 succeeded in securing the adoption of a resolution calling for the drafting of two distinct covenants, while affirming the principle of interdependence in the same manner as in the previous resolution and noting the 'unitary aim' of the two covenants.[11]

The distinction between the two categories of rights with respect to access to justice was suggested, but in no way explicitly stated, in the different provisions of the International Covenant on Civil and Political Rights (ICCPR) and the International Covenant on Economic, Social and Cultural Rights (ICESCR). The ICCPR commits States, in Article 2(3), to ensuring access to 'competent judicial, administrative, legislative or other authorities' within the legal system to determine their rights and provide 'effective remedies'.[12] The ICESCR, on the other hand, is silent on the requirement of effective remedies, committing States to the progressive realization of ESCR 'by all appropriate means, including legislation' and 'to the maximum of available resources'.[13] And most significantly, unlike the ICCPR, the ICESCR was adopted without an accompanying optional complaints procedure to provide access to justice when domestic remedies have been exhausted or are unavailable.

Each covenant, however, affirms interdependence in its preface. The ICESCR recognizes 'that, in accordance with the Universal Declaration of Human Rights, the ideal of free human beings enjoying freedom from fear and want can only be achieved if conditions are created whereby everyone may enjoy [their] economic, social and cultural rights, as well as [their] civil and political rights'. The ICCPR includes the same paragraph with some additional wording, referring to 'the ideal of free human beings enjoying civil and political freedom and freedom from fear and want'. These paragraphs, according to the annotations, 'were intended to underline the unity of the two covenants while at the same time maintaining the distinctive character of each'.[14] As Craig Scott has observed, the tension between unity and distinctiveness 'can only be mediated by means of an elaboration of the principle of interdependence'.[15]

---

[9]   Scott, 'The Interdependence and Permeability of Human Rights Norms' (n 4) 799–801, footnotes 107 and 113.

[10]   UNGA Res. 421 (V), Part E (4 December 1950).

[11]   UNGA Res 543 (VI) (5 February 1951). See Scott, 'The Interdependence and Permeability of Human Rights Norms' (n 4) 799, footnote 106.

[12]   ICCPR Article 2(3).

[13]   ICESCR Article 2(1).

[14]   General Assembly, Annotations on the Text of the Draft International Covenants on Human Rights, 10 UN GAOR Annexes (Agenda Item 28, Pt.II), AN2929 (1955) Ch. III at para 8, cited in Scott, 'The Interdependence and Permeability of Human Rights Norms' (n 4) 811, footnote 140.

[15]   Scott, 'The Interdependence and Permeability of Human Rights Norms' (n 4) 811, footnote 140.

Prior to the Vienna World Conference on Human Rights, the concept of interdependence was not generally articulated as a challenge to the unequal status accorded ESCR, and in fact may have reinforced it. Rather than being understood as interdependence between two equally important categories of fundamental human rights – recognizing ESCR as human rights because they are 'indispensable for dignity and the free development of personality', as in the UDHR – interdependence was understood as a dependence of civil and political rights on a commitment by States to social and economic development. The Tehran Proclamation, issued in 1968 at the first World Conference on Human Rights, described interdependence in these terms:

> Since human rights and fundamental freedoms are indivisible, the full realization of civil and political rights without the enjoyment of economic, social and cultural rights is impossible. The achievement of lasting progress in the implementation of human rights is dependent upon sound and effective national and international policies of economic and social development.[16]

The Final Act of the Tehran World Conference of 1968, adopting the report of the Second Committee, did suggest room for further progress. It recognized 'the close relationship between public administration, the participation of citizens in the decision making, planning, or programming process and the fulfilment of economic and social rights', and noted a 'trend towards incorporating these rights in national constitutions and providing means of defence against violations of these rights'.[17] It called upon States to 'focus their attention on developing the material means of protecting, promoting and realizing economic, social and cultural rights, as well as on developing and perfecting legal procedures for prevention of violations and defence of these rights'.[18]

## 2.2    The Emergence of the Committee on Economic, Social and Cultural Rights in the 1990s: Interdependence and Domestic Implementation

The hierarchical view of interdependence that predominated prior to the Vienna Declaration was reflected in and reinforced by the supervisory systems that were initially put in place for the respective categories of rights. As described in Chapter 1, civil and political rights compliance was assessed by independent human rights experts appointed to the UN Human Rights Committee. The Human Rights Committee considered both State reports and individual communications, generating a significant body of jurisprudence. ESCR, on the other hand, were originally assessed by a sessional working group of 'governmental experts' of the Economic and Social Council, on the basis of periodic reports by State parties which provided general data on economic development.[19]

As noted in Chapter 2, the CESCR as an independent body of 'experts with recognized competence in the field of human rights' was not established until 1985. Even with the creation of the Committee, the review of compliance with ESCR continued at first to consist primarily of

---

[16]    Proclamation of Teheran, Final Act of the International Conference on Human Rights, Teheran (22 April to 13 May 1968), A/CONF 32/41 (Proclamation of Teheran) 3 para 13.

[17]    Final Act of the International Conference on Human Rights, Tehran (22 April to 13 May 1968) A/Conf.32/41, Part XX1 (Tehran Final Act) 17.

[18]    Ibid para 6.

[19]    E/RES/1985/17 (28 May 1985).

dialogue with State delegates regarding social policy and economic development. The absence of a petition procedure or any role for rights-holders meant that the circumstances and concerns of rights-holders was rendered invisible, and the link between social programs, legislation and socio-economic data being reviewed with core human rights values of human dignity and the free development of personhood, as affirmed in the UDHR, was difficult to engage. It was only in the early 1990s – under the leadership of a new chairperson, Philip Alston – that the CESCR really began to engage with ESCR as fundamental rights. In 1993, the Committee adopted a new procedure for civil society engagement, including oral submissions from civil society organizations from the State under review.[20]

In the years following the Vienna World Conference, and in the face of resistance from some State delegates who continued to expect more of a social policy dialogue than a review of human rights compliance, the CESCR began to focus more intently on measures taken by State parties to ensure access to effective remedies for ESCR and asked States to provide information about relevant jurisprudence. In most States under review, ESCR were not directly justiciable, so the reports on jurisprudence and dialogue regarding access to remedies focused on the application of interdependence to rights considered justiciable.[21] After a number of States contested the Committee's view that the implementation of the Covenant required the provision of effective remedies or that courts had any obligation to provide remedies by way of interpretations of domestic law, the Committee adopted General Comment No. 9 (1998) on the domestic implementation of the Covenant.[22]

General Comment No. 9 represented a significant turning point in the understanding of interdependence. It clarified for the first time that the principle of interdependence, properly understood, and in accordance with the Vienna Declaration, means that the textual differences between the ICESCR and the ICCPR, with only the ICCPR referring to the requirement of effective remedies before judicial or other competent authority, does not alter the requirement of access to effective remedies for all human rights as affirmed in the UDHR.[23] The Committee observed that while the ICESCR provides some flexibility about how effective remedies will be ensured, and remedies need not always rely on courts rather than administrative tribunals or other adjudicative procedures, any rigid distinction between the two categories of rights is unacceptable both because it is contrary to the principle of interdependence and because it has unacceptable discriminatory consequences for disadvantaged groups:

> The adoption of a rigid classification of economic, social and cultural rights which puts them, by definition, beyond the reach of the courts would thus be arbitrary and incompatible with the principle that the two sets of human rights are indivisible and interdependent. It would also drastically curtail the capacity of the courts to protect the rights of the most vulnerable and disadvantaged groups in society.[24]

General Comment No. 9 also establishes a critical link between interdependence and the rule of law. The CESCR noted that many courts had acknowledged in principle that ESCR should

---

[20]   Bruce Porter, 'Socio-economic Rights Advocacy: Notes from Canada' (1999) 2(1) ESR Review 1.
[21]   See, for example CESCR, Concluding Observations: Canada (10 June 1993) E/C.12/1993/5.
[22]   CESCR, General Comment No. 9: The Domestic Application of the Covenant (3 December 1998) E/C.12/1998/249.
[23]   Ibid para 3.
[24]   Ibid para 10.

inform the interpretation of all law, but in practice, courts either failed to apply this principle effectively or refused to apply it at all.[25] Interpreting domestic law in conformity with international human rights law, according to the Committee, is not optional: 'Neglect by the courts of this responsibility is incompatible with the principle of the rule of law, which must always be taken to include respect for international human rights obligations.'[26] Importantly, the obligation to interpret domestic law in conformity with ESCR also applies to the interpretation of CPR, most noticeably the right to equality and non-discrimination:

> It is generally accepted that domestic law should be interpreted as far as possible in a way which conforms to a State's international legal obligations. Thus, when a domestic decision maker is faced with a choice between an interpretation of domestic law that would place the State in breach of the Covenant and one that would enable the State to comply with the Covenant, international law requires the choice of the latter. Guarantees of equality and non-discrimination should be interpreted, to the greatest extent possible, in ways which facilitate the full protection of economic, social and cultural rights.[27]

The obligation to ensure access to effective remedies for ESCR, therefore, does not necessarily require the direct incorporation of ESCR into domestic law. ESCR may be protected by various combinations of legislation, programmatic entitlements and interdependence with CPR. Direct incorporation is the CESCR's preferred option, but in the context of periodic reviews, the CESCR was learning that it was important to engage constructively with the particularities of different legal systems around a more flexible concept of effective remedies. Most States provided constitutional guarantees linked to the rights guaranteed in the first three Articles of the UDHR. These are the right to be treated as 'equal in dignity and rights'; the right to the equal enjoyment of fundamental rights without discrimination; and the right to 'life, liberty and security of person'. Though these foundational rights had been categorized as civil and political rights when rights were separated, they actually bridge the two categories within the unified architecture and purpose of the UDHR.[28]

The CESCR therefore paid particular attention to the interpretation of rights to life, to the dignity or security of the person and to equality, noting as a positive development court decisions interpreting these rights as interdependent with ESCR and expressing concern when courts adopted, or when governments urged courts to adopt, interpretations that would deny protection of ESCR.[29] The CESCR recommended that, where necessary, judges be provided with training on ESCR rights and how they should be applied in the interpretation of domestic law.[30] As described in Chapter 16, the CESCR followed up General Comment No. 9 with a short General Comment on national human rights institutions, noting that they too 'have a potentially crucial role to play in promoting and ensuring the indivisibility and interdependence of all human rights'.[31]

---

[25]   Ibid para 13.
[26]   Ibid para 14.
[27]   Ibid para 15.
[28]   UDHR Articles 1, 2 and 3.
[29]   CESCR, Concluding Observations: Canada (1998) E/C.12/1/Add.31.
[30]   CESCR, Concluding Observations: Canada (1993) E/C.12/1993/5 para 19.
[31]   CESCR, General Comment No. 10: The Role of National Human Rights Institutions in the Protection of Economic, Social and Cultural Rights (10 December 1998), E/C.12/1998/25.

## 2.3 Interdependence under the OP-ICESCR

The affirmation of interdependence on 'an equal footing' in the Vienna Declaration included a somewhat tentatively worded commitment (the issue remained contentious) to address the longstanding differential treatment of ESCR by developing an Optional Protocol to the ICESCR (OP-ICESCR).[32] As detailed in Chapter 2, 15 years later, the OP-ICESCR was adopted.[33] It was described by the then High Commissioner on Human Rights, Louise Arbour, as 'human rights made whole'.[34]

### 2.3.1 Textual support for interdependence in the OP-ICESCR

The text of the OP-ICESCR provides significant support for the principle of interdependence around which human rights are to be 'made whole'. The Preface reaffirms 'the universality, indivisibility, interdependence and interrelatedness of all human rights and fundamental freedoms'. The OP-ICESCR includes the description of interdependence from the prefaces of the two covenants but, as a gesture of renunciation of any categorical divide, lists the categories of rights alphabetically, affirming that 'free human beings enjoying freedom from fear and want can only be achieved if conditions are created whereby everyone may enjoy civil, cultural, economic, political and social rights'.[35]

Article 8(4) of the OP-ICESCR adopts the standard of reasonableness for the review of measures taken by States to progressively realize ESCR, drawing on the description of that standard in the South African Constitutional Court's decision in *Grootboom*.[36] As noted in Chapter 2, the CESCR had adopted, for the Open Ended Working Group, a statement regarding the criteria it might apply in assessing the reasonableness of measures taken for compliance with progressive realization under Article 2(1). These included a number of requirements linked to interdependence with CPR, including: whether there have been 'transparent and participative decision-making processes'; whether discretion has been exercised in a non-discriminatory and non-arbitrary manner; whether resources have been allocated 'in accordance with international human rights standards'; whether the precarious situation of disadvantaged and marginalized individuals or groups has been addressed; whether the measures adopted are non-discriminatory; and whether 'grave situations or situations of risk' have been prioritized.[37]

---

[32] Vienna Declaration (n 1) para 75: 'The World Conference on Human Rights encourages the Commission on Human Rights, in cooperation with the Committee on Economic, Social and Cultural Rights, to continue the examination of optional protocols to the International Covenant on Economic, Social and Cultural Rights.'

[33] UN General Assembly, Optional Protocol to the International Covenant on Economic, Social and Cultural Rights: resolution/adopted by the General Assembly (5 March 2009) A/RES/63/117 (OP-ICESCR).

[34] See discussion in Chapter 2; Louise Arbour, 'Human Rights Made Whole' Project Syndicate [June 26, 2008]

[35] OP-ICESCR Preface.

[36] Bruce Porter, 'Reasonableness and Article 8(4)' in M Langford and others (eds), *The Optional Protocol to the International Covenant on Economic, Social and Cultural Rights: A Commentary* (Pretoria University Law Press 2016) 173–202, 186.

[37] CESCR, 'An Evaluation of the Obligation to Take Steps to the "Maximum of Available Resources" under an Optional Protocol to the Covenant' E/C.12/2007/1 (10 May 2007) para 8. See Chapter 14.

### 2.3.2   Interdependence in the OP-ICESCR jurisprudence

UN treaty bodies frequently draw on the jurisprudence of other treaty bodies, but they only have authority under their respective optional protocols to admit and consider the merits of allegations of violations of rights that are contained within their own treaty. The CESCR cannot formally consider an allegation, for example – or make a finding – that a violation of the right to health under the ICESCR also constitutes a violation of the right to life or cruel and inhuman treatment under the ICCPR. This presents some challenges in the application of international jurisprudence to the interpretation of interdependent rights under domestic law. A finding by the CESCR that a certain policy constitutes a violation of the right to health without reference to the right to life may inadvertently discourage domestic courts from recognizing the interdependence of these two rights. In jurisdictions where only the right to life is considered justiciable, a failure to recognize interdependence may deny access to justice for those whose right to life is violated by a denial of access to health care.

The CESCR, however, has been able to rely on the affirmation of interdependence in the Preamble to both the ICESCR and the OP-ICESCR, the inclusive understanding of reasonableness and the inclusion in the ICESCR itself of rights to non-discrimination and equality (Article 2(2)), gender equality (Article 3) and protection of the family, mothers and children (Article 10), as a basis for a rigorous application of the principle of interdependence. Without actually making findings of violations of civil and political rights under the ICCPR, the CESCR has made it clear that violations of ESCR frequently also constitute violations of CPR.

In its emerging jurisprudence under the OP-ICESCR, the CESCR has adopted the phrase 'read together' to describe the application of interdependence between rights in the Covenant. In assessing State obligations in the context of an eviction of a family with children at the termination of a lease, considered in the case of *Ben Djazia et al. v Spain*,[38] the CESCR stated that 'obligations with regard to the right to housing should be interpreted together with all other human rights obligations and, in particular, in the context of eviction, with the obligation to provide the family with the widest possible protection (Article 10 (1) of the Covenant)'.[39] It noted that effects of evictions on women, children, older persons, persons with disabilities or other vulnerable individuals or groups who are subjected to systemic discrimination must receive particular attention and that alternative accommodation must be negotiated in a manner that respects all human rights, prevents stigmatization and complies with the right of access to information, 'communicated in a transparent, timely and complete manner'.[40] Noting that the alternative housing offered to the petitioner would have split up the family, the Committee found a violation of Article 11(1), 'read separately and in conjunction with Articles 2 (1) and 10 (1) of the Covenant'.[41]

The CESCR's consideration of the right to sexual and reproductive health in the case of *SC and GP v Italy* demonstrates a serious commitment to interpreting and applying ESCR in light of their interdependence with civil and political rights.[42] As noted in Chapter 9, the CESCR found in this case that an embryo had been transferred into S.C.'s uterus without her consent

---

[38]   *Ben Djazia et al. v Spain* (20 June 2017) CESCR E/C.12/61/D/5/2015 paras 20–21.
[39]   Ibid para 15.4.
[40]   Ibid paras 15.2 and 17.2.
[41]   Ibid para 19.
[42]   CESCR, *SC and GP v Italy* (7 March 2019) E/C.12/65/D/22/2017. See the discussion of this case in Chapter 9.

by an in vitro fertilization clinic. The CESCR held that this violated the petitioner's right to health under Article 12 of the ICESCR, read in conjunction with Article 3, women's right to equality. While the finding was restricted to the two Articles of the ICESCR, the Committee supported its reasoning by recalling, from General Comment No. 22, that the right to sexual and reproductive health is interdependent with other human rights and 'intimately linked to civil and political rights underpinning the physical and mental integrity of individuals and their autonomy, such as the rights to life; liberty and security of person; freedom from torture and other cruel, inhuman or degrading treatment'.[43] The Committee also noted that the right to sexual and reproductive health entails both freedoms and entitlements. The freedoms include 'the right to make free and responsible decisions and choices, free of violence, coercion and discrimination, regarding matters concerning one's body and sexual and reproductive health'.[44]

The CESCR has also applied interdependence to recognize the intersection of gender equality with the right to social security. As noted in Chapter 5, the CESCR found in *Trujillo Calero v Ecuador* that the disqualification of a woman from a pension scheme because she was unable to pay six consecutive monthly contributions constituted a violation of the right to social security in Article 9 'read together' with the right to non-discrimination in Article 2(2) and the right to equality of women and men in Article 3.[45]

Sandra Liebenberg has pointed out that in its emerging jurisprudence under the OP-ICESCR the CESCR has also emphasized procedural and participatory elements of ESC rights that are interdependent with procedural guarantees applied to civil and political rights and with the idea of 'participatory justice' and 'deliberative democracy'.[46] In its first case, *IDG v Spain*, the CESCR stated that 'appropriate procedural protection and due process are essential aspects of all human rights but are especially pertinent in relation to a matter such as forced evictions'.[47] Required protections include adequate and reasonable notice for all affected persons prior to any eviction or mortgage foreclosure and access to legal aid. Consultation must be informed by equality rights in order to assess the impacts on groups subject to systemic discrimination or with unique needs.[48]

As noted in Chapter 2, the CESCR has also adopted a participatory model for the consideration of and follow-up to communications, encouraging third party amicus submissions from human rights organizations and engaging civil society and rights claimants in the implementation of remedial measures.[49] As Liebenberg points out, this emphasis on participation is consistent with modern understandings of 'deliberative democracy'.[50] Incorporating these

---

[43]   Ibid para 8.1. See CESCR, General Comment No. 22: The Right to the Highest Attainable Standard of Health (4 March 2016) E/C.12/GC/22. In the General Comment, the CESCR states quite explicitly at para 10 that 'lack of emergency obstetric care services or denial of abortion often leads to maternal mortality and morbidity, which in turn constitutes a violation of the right to life or security, and in certain circumstances can amount to torture or cruel, inhuman or degrading treatment'.

[44]   Ibid.

[45]   CESCR, *Trujillo Calero v Ecuador* (26 March 2018) E/C.12/63/D/10/2015. See Chapter 5.

[46]   Sandra Liebenberg, 'Participatory Justice in Social Rights Adjudication' (2018) 18(4) Human Rights Law Review 623.

[47]   CESCR, *I.D.G. v Spain*, (17 June 2015) E/C.12/55/D/2/2014 para 15.2.

[48]   Ibid.

[49]   See Chapter 2.

[50]   Liebenberg, 'Participatory Justice' (n 46). See also Lilian Chenwi, 'Democratizing the Socio-economic Rights-enforcement Process' in Helena Alviar García, Karl Klare and Lucy A. Williams (eds), *Social and Economic Rights in Theory and Practice: Critical Inquiries* (Routledge 2014) 178.

concepts into ESCR adjudication addresses concerns about tensions between justiciable ESCR and democracy and opens the door to reconceiving remedies so as to be more responsive and effective in the context of ESC rights.[51]

## 3.   INTERDEPENDENCE IN REGIONAL SYSTEMS

As described in Chapters 3, 4 and 5, regional systems have developed protections of ESCR independently of the international human rights system and in some respects have led the way. The understanding of interdependence has evolved in similar fashion at the regional level, often in reference to the Vienna Declaration, and there has been a significant degree of cross-pollination between the international (UN) and the regional systems. A review of complex developments in regional systems regarding the interdependence of ESCR and civil and political rights is beyond the scope of this chapter but it is important to note some significant advances in the application and understanding of interdependence that have emerged at the regional level, and that are now playing an important role internationally.

### 3.1   Interdependence in the African System

As noted by Lilian Chenwi, interdependence has been seen as one of the unique features of the African Charter on Human and Peoples' Rights (the African Charter).[52] Adopted 12 years before the Vienna World Conference, the African Charter affirms interdependence in the following terms:

> [I]t is henceforth essential to pay a particular attention to the right to development and that civil and political rights cannot be dissociated from economic, social and cultural rights in their conception as well as universality and that the satisfaction of economic, social and cultural rights is a guarantee for the enjoyment of civil and political rights.[53]

While the emphasis on the satisfaction of ESC rights as a prerequisite for the enjoyment of civil and political rights is somewhat reminiscent of earlier formulations in the Tehran Proclamation, the central statement that civil and political rights cannot be dissociated from ESC rights 'in their conception as well as universality' has provided a solid basis on which to develop a substantive conception of interdependence, applied by the African Commission on Human and Peoples' Rights (African Commission) in both the consideration of individual cases and in authoritative commentary.

As described in Chapter 3, the African Commission has applied interdependence to derive protection in the African Charter of a number of ESCR that were not explicitly enumerated

---

[51]   Gustav Muller, 'Conceptualizing Meaningful Engagement as a Deliberative Democratic Partnership' (2011) 22 Stellenbosch L. Rev 742; Lilian Chenwi, '"Meaningful Engagement" in the Realisation of Socio-economic Rights: The South African Experience' (2011) 26(1) Southern African Public Law 128.

[52]   African Charter on Human and Peoples' Rights (adopted 27 June 1981, entered into force 21 October 1986) CAB/LEG/67/3 rev 5, 1520 UNTS 217 (African Charter); Chenwi, 'Permeability' (n 4) 94.

[53]   African Charter, Preface.

in its text. The Charter identifies only a limited number of ESCR for protection: rights to work, health, education, protection of the family and the right to economic, social and cultural development, along with the rights to life and to property.[54] By reading these rights together, as interdependent with guaranteed rights, and with reference to unifying human rights values, the African Commission has concluded that rights to housing, water, sanitation, food and social security are guaranteed as implicit or derived rights in the Charter.[55]

The African Commission first applied this approach to interdependence in response to individual communications. In *SERAC v Nigeria* the Commission found that environmental degradation had 'made living in Ogoniland a nightmare' and concluded that 'the most fundamental of all human rights, the right to life, has been violated'.[56] It also found that the right to housing and protection from forced evictions, guaranteed by a joint and interdependent reading of the rights to property, health and protection of the family had been violated.[57] In *Free Legal Assistance Group v Zaire*, the Commission found that mismanagement of finances and failure to provide water and other services violated the right to health.[58] In *Sudan Human Rights Organisation and Centre on Housing Rights and Evictions v Sudan*, the Commission found that in addition to the rights identified in *SERAC v Nigeria*, forced evictions in that case also violated the right to freedom from cruel and inhuman treatment, for which the Commission relied on jurisprudence from the UN Committee against Torture.[59]

Building on its unique jurisprudence on interdependence, the African Commission adopted the 'Pretoria Declaration on Economic, Social and Cultural Rights' in 2004.[60] The Declaration noted that despite the consensus on the indivisibility of human rights, ESCR 'remain marginalised in their implementation' and that resistance to ESCR 'excludes the majority of Africans from the enjoyment of human rights'.[61] The Declaration recognized 'the urgent need for human rights, judicial and administrative institutions in Africa to promote human dignity based on equality and to tackle the core human rights issues facing Africans including, food security, sustainable livelihoods, human survival and the prevention of violence'.[62] The Declaration affirmed that ESCR explicitly provided for under the African Charter, read together with other rights in the Charter, such as the right to life and respect for inherent human dignity, imply the recognition of ESCR not explicitly guaranteed in the Charter.[63] The resolution also called for the preparation of Guidelines on the Implementation of ESCR.[64]

---

[54] Chapter 3.

[55] Chapter 3.

[56] *Social and Economic Rights Action Centre and the Centre for Economic and Social Rights v Nigeria* Communication 155/96 (ACHPR 2001) (*SERAC v Nigeria*) para 67.

[57] Ibid para 63.

[58] *Free Legal Assistance Group v Zaire*, Communications 25/89, 47/90, 56/91 and 100/93 (joined) (ACHPR 1995) para 47.

[59] *Sudan Human Rights Organisation & Centre on Housing Rights and Evictions (COHRE) v Sudan*, 279/03-296/05, (ACHR 2009) para 159, citing *Hajrizi Dzemajl et al. v Yugoslavia*, Communication No. 161/2000 CAT/C/29/D/161/2000 (2002).

[60] 'Pretoria Declaration on Economic, Social and Cultural Rights' ACHPR /Res.73 (XXXVI) 04.

[61] Ibid Preface.

[62] Ibid.

[63] Ibid para 10.

[64] ACHPR /Res.73 (XXXVI) 04 para 4.

The African Commission's 2011 'Principles and Guidelines on the Implementation of Economic, Social and Cultural Rights'[65] (Principles and Guidelines) draw from the CESCR's General Comment No. 9 to affirm that the principle of interdependence demands the rejection of any rigid categorization of rights and that ESCR 'entitle affected individuals and peoples to effective remedies and redress under domestic law'.[66] The Principles and Guidelines adopt a holistic interpretive approach emphasizing that rights must be read together, informed by evolving international human rights norms and tied to unifying human rights values of dignity and equality in rights. Most significantly, they state that the same interpretive approach should be followed by courts and administrative tribunals under domestic law. Domestic law 'must be interpreted as far as possible in a way which conforms to State parties' obligations under the African Charter':[67]

> [W]here economic, social and cultural rights are not expressly included in the constitution of a State party, the courts and administrative tribunals should strive to protect the interests and values underlying these rights through an expansive interpretation of other rights, for example, the rights to life, human dignity, security of the person, equality and just administrative action.[68]

While the Principles and Guidelines derive ESCR from the particular rights guaranteed in the African Charter, they define their meaning and content with reference to broader human rights values linked to human dignity, drawing on international human rights jurisprudence. They define the right to housing as 'the right to gain and sustain a safe and secure home and community in which to live in peace and dignity'.[69] They note that the right to food is inherent in the rights to life and health and the right to economic, social and cultural development, 'is indivisibly linked to the inherent dignity of the human person and is indispensable for the fulfilment of other human rights that are also enshrined in the African Charter'.[70] The right to social security 'can be derived from a joint reading of a number of rights guaranteed under the Charter including (but not limited to) the rights to life, dignity, liberty, work, health, food, protection of the family and the right to the protection of the aged and the disabled'.[71]

As described in Chapter 3, this approach to interdependence has now been applied in the emerging jurisprudence of the African Court. In the *Ogiek* case, for instance, the Court found that the eviction of the Ogiek community from ancestral lands in the Mau Forest of Kenya violated the right to land as well as rights to culture, free disposal of wealth and natural resources and economic, social and cultural development.[72] The Court drew on the UN Declaration on the Rights of Indigenous Peoples to recognize the obligations of the State to take positive

---

[65]   'Principles and Guidelines on the Implementation of Economic, Social and Cultural Rights in the African Charter on Human and Peoples' Rights' (ACHPR October 2001) (Principles and Guidelines). See Chapter 3.

[66]   Ibid para 21.

[67]   Ibid para 25.

[68]   Ibid para 24.

[69]   Principles and Guidelines (n 65) para 78. See CESCR, General Comment No. 4: The Right to Adequate Housing (13 December 1991) E/1992/23.

[70]   Ibid para 84.

[71]   Ibid paras 80–82.

[72]   *African Commission on Human and Peoples' Rights v Kenya* Application No. 006/2012, Judgment (ACtHPR 2017) (*Ogiek*).

measures to support the rights of Indigenous Peoples to development.[73] Unfortunately, the Court departed from the African Commission's interdependent interpretation of the right to life, stating that 'it is necessary to make a distinction between the classical meaning of the right to life and the right to decent existence of a group. Article 4 of the Charter relates to the physical rather than the existential understanding of the right to life.'[74]

## 3.2  The Inter-American System

As described in Chapter 5, ESCR in the Inter-American System of Human Rights, as in the international system, were first treated as equal rights integrated within a unified framework but were subsequently relegated to separate status based on distinctions related to justiciability. The American Declaration of the Rights and Duties of Man, adopted in 1948, contemporaneous with the UDHR, recognizes ESCR on an equal footing with civil and political rights, including the rights to health (which includes social measures respecting food, housing, clothing), education, work, social security, culture and property (as meets the essential needs of decent living and helps to maintain the dignity of the individual).[75] The American Convention on Human Rights (ACHR) on the other hand, adopted in 1969, includes a wide range of civil and political rights but references ESCR only as a commitment, in Article 26, to the progressive realization of 'the rights implicit in the economic, social, educational, scientific, and cultural standards set forth in the Charter of the Organization of American States'.[76]

The Protocol of San Salvador,[77] adopted in 1988, provides for a limited number of ESCR, subject to periodic reports on progress submitted to a Working Group. The Protocol includes a strong statement of interdependence, noting

> the close relationship that exists between economic, social and cultural rights, and civil and political rights, in that the different categories of rights constitute an indivisible whole based on the recognition of the dignity of the human person, for which reason both require permanent protection and promotion if they are to be fully realized.[78]

The jurisdiction of the Inter-American Commission on Human Rights (IACHR) and the Inter-American Court on Human Rights (IACtHR) to consider petitions alleging violations of rights under the Protocol is restricted to trade union and education rights, though interde-

---

[73]  UN General Assembly, United Nations Declaration on the Rights of Indigenous Peoples (2 October 2007) A/RES/61/295 2 (UNDRIP).

[74]  *Ogiek* (n 72) 154.

[75]  American Declaration of the Rights and Duties of Man, OAS Res XXX adopted by the Ninth International Conference of American States (1948) OEA/Ser L V/II.82 Doc 6 Rev 1 at 17 (1992) Articles XI, XII, XIV, XVI, XIII, XXIII.

[76]  American Convention on Human Rights (adopted 22 November 1969, entered into force 18 July 1978) 1144 UNTS 123, (ACHR) Article 26.

[77]  Additional Protocol to the American Convention on Human Rights in the Area of Economic, Social and Cultural Rights. Adopted at the Eighteenth Regular Session of the General Assembly of the Organization of American States, San Salvador, El Salvador, 17 November 1988.

[78]  Ibid Preface.

pendence with other rights in the Protocol may be referenced to interpret the provisions of the ACHR.[79]

In light of this history, the adjudication of ESCR under the ACHR has relied significantly on their interdependence with guaranteed CPR, and most significantly on interdependence with the right to life. The IACtHR has developed the concept of the right to life as the right to a dignified life (*vida digna*), which, as will be discussed below, has now been incorporated into the interpretation of the right to life under the ICCPR. The concept was first described in the *Villagrán Morales et al. ('Street Children') v Guatemala* case, in which the IACtHR stated that the right to life 'is not only the right of every human being not to be deprived of life arbitrarily, but also the right not to be prevented from having access to the conditions that guarantee a dignified existence'.[80]

The IACtHR has since applied the *vida digna* principle in a number of other cases, including several related to Indigenous Peoples' claims to rights to food, housing and culture on their ancestral lands. In *Sawhoyamaxa v Paraguay*, an Indigenous community was displaced from their lands and left to live on the side of a road without housing, potable water, sanitation or access to health care.[81] The Court found that these conditions constituted a violation of the right to a dignified life and took the occasion to explain the important transformation that had been instituted in the Court's jurisprudence on the right to life, previously viewed as a negative right:

> Some remarkable decisions by the Court have shifted the focus towards the other side of the right to life which, seen from yet another perspective, constitutes the other face of State duties: beyond the mere omission curbing arbitrariness or mitigating punishment, action is required to create conditions to guarantee a decent existence. In this view, the right to life is restored to its original status as an opportunity to choose our destiny and develop our potential. It is more than just a right to subsist, but is rather a right to self-development, which requires appropriate conditions.[82]

The other right in the IACHR through which the IACtHR has leveraged significant protection of ESC rights through interdependence is the right to property. As with the right to life, this has been achieved by interpreting the right not only within a negative rights framework, as protection from State interference, but also as a substantive right to land, housing, water, food and other ESCR.[83] The interpretation of the right to property by the IACtHR has also drawn significantly on the UN Declaration on the Rights of Indigenous Peoples.[84] Beginning with its decision in *Mayagna (Sumo) Awas Tingni Community v Nicaragua*, the IACtHR has emphasized the close ties of Indigenous Peoples with their traditional territories and held that

---

[79]    Ibid Article 19. *Jorge Odir Miranda Cortez et al. v El Salvador* [2000] Case 12.249, Report No. 29/01, OEA/Ser. L/V/II.111 Doc. 20 rev 284 para 36.

[80]    *Villagrán Morales et al. v Guatemala* (19 November 1999) IACtHR, Series C No 77 para 188 [male pronoun deleted].

[81]    *Sawhoyamaxa Indigenous Community v Paraguay* (29 March 2006) IACtHR Series C No 146.

[82]    Ibid para 18.

[83]    For a summary of this jurisprudence, see *Kaliña and Lokono Peoples v Suriname* (25 November 2015) IACtHR (*Kaliña v Suriname*) paras 129–32.

[84]    UNDRIP (n 73). Article 25 states: 'Indigenous Peoples have the right to maintain and strengthen their distinctive spiritual relationship with their traditionally owned or otherwise occupied and used lands, territories, waters and coastal seas and other resources and to uphold their responsibilities to future generations in this regard.'

their right to property must respect their traditions of collective ownership and ensure that their culture is safeguarded. In *Kaliña and Lokono Peoples v Suriname*, the Court found that the laws of Suriname violated the right to property by failing to ensure the collective rights of the Kaliña and Lokono peoples of access to a river that was essential to both their cultural life and their survival.[85]

Despite the relatively weak protections of ESCR in the IACHR, the jurisprudence now establishes, on the basis of interdependence of ESCR with the right to life and the right to property, an interpretive foundation on which ESCR claims can be adjudicated in reference to a unifying framework of core human rights values linked to equal dignity, drawing on international human rights law, including the ICESCR and the UN Declaration on the Rights of Indigenous Peoples.

### 3.3 The European System

As described in Chapter 4, the European Social Charter (ESC) represents a unique advance internationally, engaging with systemic violations of ESC rights through a collective complaints system. At the same time, it is marginalized by distinctions with respect to enforceability and domestic implementation. Civil and political rights guaranteed by the European Convention on Human Rights (ECHR) are enforceable by the European Court of Human Rights (ECtHR) and in national courts, while the decisions of the European Social Rights Committee are not considered binding by state parties. Moreover, the rights in the ECHR are framed and interpreted within a predominantly negative rights paradigm, while the ESC is viewed as guaranteeing more positive rights. It is important, therefore, that the different status and understandings of the two categories of rights be mediated by a recognition of their interdependence.

The European Committee on Social Rights (ECSR), as stated in Chapter 4, has promoted interdependence by emphasizing interpretation based on common human rights values and norms, through which it gives 'life and meaning to fundamental social rights'.[86] It has focused on human dignity as 'the fundamental value and indeed the core of positive European human rights law – whether under the ESC or under the European Convention of Human Rights':[87]

> [T]he rights guaranteed are not ends in themselves but they complete the rights enshrined in the European Convention of Human Rights. Indeed, according to the Vienna Declaration of 1993, all human rights are 'universal, indivisible and interdependent and interrelated' (para 5). The Committee is therefore mindful of the complex interaction between both sets of rights.[88]

The ECSR has emphasized that under the Vienna Convention, a treaty shall be interpreted 'in the light of its object and purpose' and that the object and purpose of the ESC is linked to the unifying purposes of human rights.[89] In *FIDH v France*, considering the issue of access to

---

[85]   *Kaliña v Suriname* (n 83) paras 152–60.
[86]   *Complaint No 14/2003: International Federation of Human Rights Leagues (FIDH) v France* (ESRC) para 29.
[87]   *FIDH v France* para 31.
[88]   Ibid para 28.
[89]   Ibid para 28; Vienna Convention on the Law of Treaties Article 31.

health care for migrants without legal status, the ECSR noted that the complaint 'is connected to the right to life itself and goes to the very dignity of the human being'.[90]

The ECSR has also adopted and promoted the idea of substantive equality as a bridge between social rights and the right to equality in the ECHR.[91] In *Complaint No. 27/2004: European Roma Rights Centre v Italy*, the ECSR held that measures to ensure the right to housing of Roma under the ESC are also required by the right to equal treatment, because indirect discrimination can arise 'by failing to take due and positive account of all relevant differences or by failing to take adequate steps to ensure that the rights and collective advantages that are open to all are genuinely accessible by and to all'.[92] In *Complaint No. 15/2003: European Roma Rights Centre v Greece*, the ECSR made a similar finding and referenced the decision of the European Court in *Connors*, in which the Court found that Article 8 of the ECHR requires positive measures to protect the Roma's way of life.[93]

The ECtHR has been less inclined towards substantive interdependence. Much has been made of its decisions in *Airey v Ireland*, finding that 'there is no water-tight division separating that sphere from the field covered by the Convention'.[94] It should be remembered, however, that the issue at stake in the *Airey* case was access to legal aid for a judicial hearing relating to separation from an abusive husband. The idea that the case overlapped with ESCR seemed to be largely premised on the fact that it involved a positive obligation and the allocation of resources to ensure access to legal representation in a civil rights issue.

As further outlined in Chapter 4, there have been numerous cases in which the ECtHR has applied rights to freedom from inhuman and degrading treatment (Article 3), the right to private and family life (Article 8), the right to non-discrimination (Article 14) and the right to property (Article 1 of the First Protocol) that engaged issues that relate to ESCR. Failure to provide basic social and medical support to vulnerable individuals, to ensure decent conditions in reception centers for asylum seekers or to exempt victims of domestic violence accommodated in special housing from cuts to housing benefit have been found to violate rights under the ECHR.[95] As noted by Colm O'Cinneide in Chapter 5, however, all of these decisions have been made within the confines of a presumption that the justiciable human rights in the ECHR are 'essentially directed at the protection of civil and political rights' and which provide a 'wide margin of discretion' when making decisions about the allocation of resources.[96]

---

[90]   *FIDH v France* para 30.

[91]   H. Cullen, 'The Collective Complaints System of the European Social Charter: Interpretative Methods of the European Committee on Social Rights' (2009) 9 Human Rights Law Review 61; C. O'Cinneide, 'Equality and Non-Discrimination Rights within the Framework of the European Social Charter' [2015] European Discrimination Law Review 1.

[92]   *Complaint No. 27/2004: European Roma Rights Centre v Italy* (ECSR Decision on the Merits, 7 December 2005); *Complaint No. 13/2002: Autism-Europe v France* (ECSR Decision on the Merits, 4 November 2003) para 52.

[93]   *Complaint No. 15/2003: European Roma Rights Center v Greece* (ECSR Decision on the merits adopted 8 December 2004) para 20 citing *Connors v the United Kingdom* (ECtHR Judgment, 27 May 2004) Application No. 66746/01 para 84.

[94]   *Airey v Ireland* (9 October 1979) ECtHR 1980 2 EHRR 305 para 26.

[95]   *J.D. and A v The United Kingdom* (ECtHR Judgment of 24 October 2019) Application nos 32949/17 and 34614/17. See Chapter 4.

[96]   See Chapter 4, *N v the United Kingdom* (ECtHR Judgment of 27 May 2005) Application no. 26565/05.

The progress that has been made by the ECtHR's recognition of interdependence has not overcome the discriminatory consequences of the dominant negative rights paradigm that still prevails. This has been particularly evident in the ECtHR's application of the right to life in Article 2 of the ECHR. There is no reason why the obligation to protect the right to life by law under the ECHR should not be interpreted, as within the African and Inter-American systems, as imposing obligations on States to address systemic socio-economic conditions that deprive people of a dignified life and, in fact, lead to premature death – particularly in a region with abundant resources to ensure a dignified life for all.

States' positive obligations to protect the right to life under the ECHR have been largely restricted to the context of the administration of health care or to persons in the care of the State, or to particularly vulnerable individuals who should have been provided care.[97] The right to life has not been applied, for example, to require measures to address the growing problem of homelessness in Europe and the right to equality has not been applied to address its disproportionate effects on persons with disabilities and other protected groups. The Office for National Statistics for England and Wales estimated that in 2018 726 homeless people died in England and Wales – a 22 per cent rise from 2017.[98] Similar increases occurred throughout Europe. A full recognition of interdependence, based on the equal dignity and rights of all members of the human family, would cross the boundary between civil and political rights and ESCR to require urgent action in response to this crisis.

While the application of interdependence within the European system has certainly challenged any rigid categorical division between ESCR and CPR, the prevailing negative rights framework under the ECHR also creates what Scott has referred to as a 'ceiling' that restricts the full application of interdependence.[99] The separate treatment of rights that are equally essential to life and equality within the ESC has meant that the ECtHR and national courts have denied access to justice for many of the most egregious violations of these rights. This ceiling effect has immense discriminatory consequences for those whose lives are at risk because of inaction and policies of governments with abundant resources to both create and leave unaddressed systemic conditions in society that are grossly incompatible with the objects and purposes of human rights.

## 4.    INTERDEPENDENCE AT THE UN HUMAN RIGHTS COMMITTEE

With 116 state parties to the Optional Protocol to the ICCPR (OP-ICCPR) and only 24 states parties to the OP-ICESCR, rights claimants advancing claims based on the interdependence of rights are significantly more likely to seek remedies under the OP-ICCPR than under the OP-ICESCR. Until recently, the Human Rights Committee seemed unlikely to venture very

---

[97]    See ECtHR, 'Guide on Article 2 of the European Convention on Human Rights Right to Life' (updated on 31 August 2019) <https://www.echr.coe.int/Documents/Guide_art_2_ENG.pdf>.

[98]    Office of National Statistics, Deaths of homeless people in England and Wales: 2018. <www.ons.gov.uk/peoplepopulationandcommunity/birthsdeathsandmarriages/deaths/bulletins/deathsofhomelesspeopleinenglandandwales/2018>.

[99]    Scott, 'Reaching Beyond' (n 4) 638.

far in the direction of any interdependence of ICCPR with ESCR, but new developments give grounds for hope.

## 4.1    The Right to Equality and Non-discrimination (ICCPR Article 26)

The issue of interdependence has most frequently been addressed by the Human Rights Committee in applying the right to non-discrimination under Articles 2 and 26 of the ICCPR to existing social benefit schemes. In such cases, remedies have extended benefits to previously excluded groups so as to enhance the protection of ESCR, with resource consequences. Such claims, even when based on a formal equality model of prohibiting differential treatment, are at least superficially interdependent with ESC rights claims. State parties have argued, in fact, that they are beyond the scope of the ICCPR because they fall in the domain of the ICESCR.

The two historic cases in which the Human Rights Committee first dealt with this issue were first *Broeks v The Netherlands*,[100] and then *Zwaan-de Vries v The Netherlands*,[101] in which the petitioners challenged their disqualification from social security benefits and unemployment benefits on the basis that they were married when men would not have been similarly disqualified. The Netherlands argued that both petitions addressed obligations with respect to the right to social security under Article 9 of the ICESCR, subject to progressive realization, and were beyond the scope of Article 26 of the ICCPR. The petitioners countered that the rights in the two covenants are 'highly interdependent', citing the wording of the Separation Resolution at the General Assembly and the preambles of the two covenants.[102] The Human Rights Committee examined the travaux préparatoires of the ICCPR and found no conclusive commentary that would limit the scope of Article 26 of the ICCPR applied to the enjoyment of rights contained in the ICESCR.[103] It held that discrimination in relation to access to social security programs is within the scope of Article 26.

The Human Rights Committee's position was not, however, based on a principle of substantive equality in which the particular needs of women for social security would be considered through an equality lens, and the right to social security would be seen as a component of the right to equality. Rather, interdependence was regarded as a one-way street. The right to non-discrimination could inform obligations with respect to social security but the right to social security does not, according to the Committee, inform women's right to equality. The Human Rights Committee did not entertain the possibility that women's right to equality and non-discrimination could oblige States to adopt social security legislation that addresses women's socio-economic disadvantage:

> Although Article 26 requires that legislation should prohibit discrimination, it does not of itself contain any obligation with respect to the matters that may be provided for by legislation. Thus it does not, for example, require any State to enact legislation to provide for social security. However, when such legislation is adopted in the exercise of a State's sovereign power, then such legislation must comply with Article 26 of the Covenant.[104]

---

[100]    *Broeks v The Netherlands*, Communication 172/1984, CCPR/C/29/D/172/1984.
[101]    *Zwaan-de Vries v The Netherlands*, Communication 182/1984, CCPR/29/D/182/1984.
[102]    Ibid para 5.9.
[103]    Ibid para 12.2.
[104]    Ibid para 12.4.

The idea that a State could ensure equality for women by equally depriving men and women of social security is what has been referred to as 'equality with a vengeance'.[105] In its General Comment No. 18 on the right to non-discrimination, the Human Rights Committee defines discrimination as any distinction, exclusion, restriction or preference based on prohibited grounds 'which has the purpose or effect of nullifying or impairing the recognition, enjoyment or exercise by all persons, on an equal footing, of all rights and freedoms'.[106] The reference to all rights and freedoms would seem to provide a basis on which to develop a more substantive understanding of the right to equality and non-discrimination in which inaction or failures to take appropriate measures to address systemic socio-economic inequality, linked to ESCR obligations, would be requirements equally emanating from the guarantee of equality. In its General Comment No. 28 on the equal rights of men and women guaranteed in Article 3 of the ICCPR, the Human Rights Committee explains that States must take steps to remove obstacles to the equal enjoyment of rights in the ICCPR, including the right to life. 'The State party must not only adopt measures of protection, but also positive measures in all areas so as to achieve the effective and equal empowerment of women.'[107] In general, however, the Human Rights Committee has been hesitant to apply a substantive equality approach that would be interdependent with ESCR.

The CESCR has developed a more robust understanding of interdependence of women's equality and ESCR which could just as easily be applied by the Human Rights Committee. In its General Comment on the right to social security, the CESCR has outlined a number of requirements linked to gender equality, including equalization of the compulsory retirement age; equal benefits in both public and private pension schemes; adequate maternity leave and eliminating the factors that prevent women from making equal contributions to contributory benefit schemes, such as lower wages, intermittent participation in the workforce or bearing sole responsibility for the care of children.[108]

In the context of State reports and concluding observations, the Human Rights Committee has invoked a more substantive understanding of the right to equality similar to the CESCR's, referencing disproportionate poverty, unemployment and inadequate housing or homelessness as potential violations of Articles 2 and 26, and requiring positive measures.[109] Applying this approach in reviewing State reports but not in examining petitions, however, has entrenched the idea that substantive equality and the enjoyment of ESCR are more in the realm of social policy than of human rights.

---

[105] *Schachter v Canada* [1992] 2 S.C.R. 679 para 30.

[106] UN Human Rights Committee, General Comment No. 18: Non-discrimination (10 November 1989), HRI/GEN/1/Rev.1 at 26 (1994) para 7.

[107] HRC, General Comment No. 28: Article 3 (The Equality of Rights between Men and Women) (29 March 2000), HRI/GEN/1/Rev.9 (Vol. I) para 3.

[108] CESCR, General Comment No. 19: The Right to Social Security (4 February 2008) E/C.12/GC/19 paras 19 and 32.

[109] See, for example, HRC, Concluding Observations: Lithuania (31 August 2012) CCPR/C/LTU/CO/3 para 8.

## 4.2      The Right to Life (ICCR Article 6)

### 4.2.1     General Comment No. 36

In its first General Comment on the right to life, General Comment No. 6 (1982), the Human Rights Committee emphasized that the right to life should not be interpreted narrowly or understood in a restrictive manner. It stated that the protection of the right to life requires that States adopt positive measures such as measures to address malnutrition, infant mortality and epidemics.[110] In concluding observations following consideration of State reports, the Committee has at times referred to the need for positive measures to address systemic violations of the right to life, including measures to address homeless and food security.[111] In the consideration of petitions, however, the Human Rights Committee has, until recently, engaged with interdependence of the right to life with ESCR in only the most limited fashion, and primarily in the context of conditions of detention.[112]

The issue of interdependence of the right to life with ESCR, however, was prominently open for review during the consultations and drafting of a new General Comment on the right to life, leading up to its adoption in October 2018.[113] The new General Comment moves decisively in the direction of recognizing the interdependence of the right to life with ESCR. Significantly, Latin American members of the Committee were able to secure support for the critical inclusion of a reference to 'the right to a dignified life', thereby opening Article 6 to the interpretive possibilities developed by the IACtHR.

General Comment No. 36 also states that the duty to protect life requires measures 'to address the general conditions in society that may give rise to direct threats to life or prevent individuals from enjoying their right to life with dignity'. Such conditions may include 'deprivation of Indigenous peoples' land, territories and resources' and 'widespread hunger and malnutrition and extreme poverty and homelessness', and measures called for may include 'access without delay by individuals to essential goods and services such as food, water, shelter, health care, electricity and sanitation' as well as measures 'designed to promote and facilitate adequate general conditions … such as social housing programmes'. The General Comment also recognizes the interdependence of the right to life and environmental rights, stating that the obligation to respect and ensure the right to life, and in particular life with dignity, depends, inter alia, 'on measures taken by states parties to preserve the environment and protect it against harm, pollution and climate change caused by public and private actors'.[114]

Given the history of the Human Rights Committee's differentiation between general obligations raised in the context of periodic reviews and obligations to be considered in the context of petitions, a critical question relating to the drafting of General Comment 36 was whether States' failures to address general conditions in society that deprive people of the right to a dignified life must be subject to effective remedy. An earlier draft of the General Comment

---

[110]   HRC, General Comment No. 6: Right to Life (30 April 1982), HRI/GEN/1/Rev 1 at 6.

[111]   See, for example, HRC, Concluding Observations: Peoples' Republic of Korea (27 August 2001) CCPR/CO/72/PRK para 12; UN Human Rights Committee, Concluding Observations: Canada (7 April 1999) CCPR/C/79/Add.105.

[112]   See *Ms. Yekaterina Pavlovna Lantsova v The Russian Federation*, Communication No. 763/1997 (26 March 2002) CCPR/C/74/D/763/1997; *Barkovsky v Belarus* (13 August 2018) CCPR/C/123/D/2247/2013.

[113]   HRC, General Comment No. 36 (3 September 2019), CCPR/C/GC/36.

[114]   Ibid paras 26, 62.

contained a paragraph that referred to the 'wide-ranging obligations' imposed on States by Article 6 but proposed to limit admissible claims to victims whose rights have been 'directly violated by acts or omissions attributable to the States Parties [to the Optional Protocol], or are under a real and personalized risk of being violated'.[115] Significantly, after concerns were raised about limiting access to justice for critical systemic issues, the paragraph was deleted from the final text.

### 4.2.2   *Toussaint v Canada*

The question left open in General Comment No. 36 about access to justice has been at least partially answered in the Human Rights Committee's ground-breaking decision in the case of *Nell Toussaint v Canada*, adopted at the time that General Comment No. 36 was being finalized.[116] Nell Toussaint had lived and worked in Canada as an undocumented migrant for almost a decade and was denied access to health care (other than emergency hospital care) because of her immigration status. She challenged this in domestic courts as a violation of the right to life and to non-discrimination under the Canadian Charter of Rights and Freedoms (Canadian Charter). The domestic courts agreed that Toussaint's life had been put at risk, with long-term health consequences, but found this violation of the right to life was justified as a means to promote compliance with immigration law. Toussaint filed a petition alleging, inter alia, violations of Articles 6 and 26 of the ICCPR. Canada responded by citing previous Human Rights Committee jurisprudence stating that the right to health is not contained in the ICCPR, and that the right to life 'cannot be interpreted to include a positive obligation to provide comprehensive health insurance coverage to foreign nationals unlawfully present in the territory'.[117] The Human Rights Committee answered this argument by stating that 'the author has explained that she does not claim a violation of the right to health, but of her right to life, arguing that the State party failed to fulfil its positive obligation to protect her right to life which, in her particular circumstances, required provision of emergency and essential health care'.[118] Accordingly, the Committee found the claims under Article 6 admissible.[119]

In its consideration of the merits, the Committee referred to the requirement of positive measures to protect the right to life, including 'the right to enjoy a life with dignity' and found that Toussaint's rights to life and non-discrimination had been violated. The Committee held that 'as a minimum, States parties have the obligation to provide access to existing health-care services that are reasonably available and accessible when lack of access to health care would expose a person to a reasonably foreseeable risk that can result in loss of life.'[120] In considering

---

[115] Draft General Comment 36 on Article 6 of the International Covenant on Civil and Political Rights: Revised Draft Prepared by the Rapporteur. Adopted on First Reading at the 120th Session. Para 15. Text in square brackets shows proposed additions on which consensus had not been reached on First Reading.

[116] *Nell Toussaint v Canada*, Communication 2348/2014 (24 July 2018) CCPR/C/123/D/2348/2014. It should be noted that I acted as a co-representative for Toussaint.

[117] 'Submission of The Government of Canada on the Admissibility and Merits of the Communication to the Human Rights Committee of Nell Toussaint Communication No. 2348/2014' (2 April 2015) paras 21, 95. <www.socialrightscura.ca/documents/legal/tousaint%20IFBH/Canada%20-%20Submissions%20on%20Merits.pdf>

[118] Ibid para 10.9.

[119] Ibid para 10.9.

[120] Ibid para 11.3.

whether the distinction between regular and irregular migrants was based on a reasonable and objective criteria, the Committee emphasized that the interest at stake in this case was the right to life. 'States therefore cannot make a distinction, for the purposes of respecting and protecting the right to life, between regular and irregular migrants.'[121] The implications of the decision, however, will hopefully be that discriminatory denials of the equal enjoyment of the right to a dignified life linked to violations of a wide range of ESCR will now be considered to ground justiciable claims and access to effective remedies.

## 5.    RECLAIMING EQUALITY IN RIGHTS THROUGH INTERDEPENDENCE: THE WAY FORWARD

### 5.1    Inequality in Rights and the 'Negative Inference'

Prior to Toussaint's claim being heard by lower courts in Canada, the Supreme Court of Canada considered a similar claim to access to health care to protect the right to life advanced by patients with considerably more financial means than Toussaint. The claimants in *Chaoulli v Quebec* challenged legislation that prevented wealthier health care consumers from creating private health care plans to avoid waiting times for certain essential services in the public health care system.[122] In upholding the wealthier care consumers' claim, the Chief Justice explained, in terms reminiscent of the Human Rights Committee's rationale in *Broeks*, that 'the [Canadian] *Charter* does not confer a freestanding constitutional right to health care. However, where the government puts in place a scheme to provide health care, that scheme must comply with the *Charter*'.[123] The Chief Justice's statement did not, in fact, address the question of whether a failure to provide essential health care may violate the right to life, but it was relied upon by the Federal Court of Appeal to dismiss Toussaint's claim, characterizing it as a claim to a self-standing right to health care, and it has been relied upon in subsequent cases to affirm that 'the current state of the law in Canada is that Section 7 of the Charter's guarantees of life, liberty and security of the person do not include the positive right to state funding for health care'.[124] In other words, the state of the law in Canada is that wealthy people's right to life protects them from being denied access to health care but poor people's right to life does not.

The reasoning applied by Canadian courts, at the encouragement of the Canadian government, is what Craig Scott and Philip Alston have called 'negative inference'.[125] Rather than interpreting the right to life as interdependent with ESCR, which Canada has recognized under international law, some courts have drawn a negative inference from the absence of ESCR in the Charter. Those whose right to life or equality is violated by government interference or action enjoy the protection of the right to life. However, when the same rights and interests

---

[121]   Ibid para 11.7.
[122]   *Chaoulli v Quebec (Attorney General)* (2005) 1 S.C.R. 791.
[123]   Ibid para 104.
[124]   *Canadian Doctors for Refugee Care v Canada (Attorney General)* 2014 FC 651.
[125]   Craig Scott and Philip Alston, 'Adjudicating Constitutional Priorities in a Transnational Context: A Comment on Soobramoney's Legacy and Grootboom's Promise' (2000) 16(2) South African Journal on Human Rights 206, 227–28.

require government action or positive measures, the right to life or equality is not protected. This is the legacy of the divorce of ESCR from CPR. Rather than focusing on the interest meant to be protected and the broader purposes of human rights, the focus has been redirected to categories of obligations of governments, on the basis of which unequal categories of rights and unequal categories of claimants are divided. The issue at stake is not just about how the right to life is or is not protected by courts. It is about which lives matter within the dominant human rights paradigm and which do not.

## 5.2   Interdependence and the Current Human Rights Crisis

Many of the most critical systemic violations of human rights now lie in the interstices of the two categories of rights, constituting overlapping violations of ESCR and CPR. Violations of ESCR linked to unprecedented socio-economic inequality; erosion of universality of social programs; corporate capture of housing, land and services; and the climate emergency are interwoven with new attacks on democracy and freedom of expression, criminalization of those whose social and economic rights are violated by homelessness and poverty and increased racism and xenophobia.

Not just ESCR but also civil and political rights have been damaged by the separation of the categories. An estimated one-third of deaths worldwide are linked to poverty, clearly engaging the rights to life and equality for the groups that are disproportionately affected.[126] However, States' failures to take appropriate measures to protect and value these lives have not been effectively challenged as violations of the rights to life and equality. The right to non-discrimination for racial and ethnic minorities has not been effectively applied in conjunction with the right to housing to remedy systemic racial and ethnic inequalities linked to disproportionate homelessness or marginalization in cities. Equality guarantees for persons with disabilities have not challenged unacceptable levels of unemployment or the growing numbers of persons with intellectual, mental health and physical impairments living in homelessness.[127] Protections for refugees and asylum seekers have failed to provide meaningful protection for growing numbers of migrants driven from their homes by poverty or loss of livelihood. These violations of human rights tend to escape human rights-based responses, both in the administration of justice and in the political priorities of governments, because they lie in the largely neglected and uncharted territory between the two categories of rights.

## 5.3   Retrieving the Human Dimension of Human Rights

Until the adoption of the OP-ICESCR, ESCR at the international level were rights without claimants. The rights tended to be described and understood in reference to States' obligations rather than to the circumstances, perspectives or dignity interests of claimants.

The lives of rights-holders are not divided into categories of rights, nor are the often multiple violations they face. For a single mother left unable to provide necessary nutrition to a child to sustain life, there is no categorical divide between the right to life and the right to food, and

---

[126]   Anne-Emanuelle Birn, 'Addressing the Societal Determinants of Health: The Key Global Health Ethics Imperative of Our Times' in Solomon Benatar and Gillian Brock (eds), *Global Health and Global Health Ethics* (CUP 2011) para 43.

[127]   UNGA Report of the Special Rapporteur on the Right to Housing (12 July 2017) A/72/128.

no distinction between first or second generation rights. The struggle for access to food, with many dimensions, is often linked to systemic discrimination based on gender, race, ethnicity or disability as well as to socio-economic deprivation and is experienced through these and many other intersectionalities. In this sense, the affirmation of interdependence of rights on an equal footing in the Vienna Declaration was a call to reground human rights in the integrity, complexity and multidimensional struggles that characterize the lives of rights-holders. As Scott has suggested:

> The term interdependence attempts to capture the idea that values seen as directly related to the full development of personhood cannot be protected and nurtured in isolation. It is not meant to create the impression of relationships between rights as entities with some kind of objective existence that goes beyond intersubjective understandings.... It is important to remember that the idea of interdependence has been developed not for the sake of rights but for the sake of persons.[128]

The development of the principle of interdependence focused on the inherent dignity and worth of persons that began in the 1990s was also a result of courts and human rights bodies beginning to actually hear claims and engage with the circumstances in which people were living. Advances in access to justice for ESC rights meant that the voice and lived experience of claimants could become central to the process of elaborating the content of ESCR and the obligations that flow from them. Rather than assessing the reasonableness of programs and policies primarily in relation to the concerns and rationale of governments in a two-way dialogue, rights claimants provide a contextual foundation for assessing what constitutes a reasonable response to the circumstances in which they live.[129] When claimants are actually heard, interdependence, or what is referred to from the claimants' perspective as 'intersectionality', emerges as a lived reality.

The Constitutional Court of South Africa in the *Grootboom* case, which established the normative framework for reasonableness review subsequently incorporated into the OP-ICESCR, rejected an earlier deferential standard of review in response to the 'intolerable circumstances' in which Irene Grootboom and her community, and millions of others, were living.[130] These circumstances were seen not only to violate the specific right to housing in Article 26 of the South African Constitution, but to constitute an assault on the core values affirmed in its preamble: '[h]uman dignity, the achievement of equality and the advancement of human rights and freedoms.' The decision begins by noting that the case 'brings home the harsh reality that the Constitution's promise of dignity and equality for all remains for many a distant dream'.[131]

Similarly, the Colombian Constitutional Court's ground-breaking decision in T-025, granting a wide-ranging, progressively implemented and participatory remedy for violations of

---

[128]   Craig Scott, 'Interdependence and Permeability of Human Rights Norms' (n 4).

[129]   Stuart Wilson and Jackie Dugard describe a tendency of South African courts adjudicating ESC rights to prefer 'a facial examination of state policy, implicitly accepting the conceptions of reasonableness and possibility upon which those policies are drafted and implemented. This tends to reproduce the exclusion from policy formulation and implementation processes which have brought the claimants to court in the first place.' Stuart Wilson and Jackie Dugard, 'Taking Poverty Seriously: The South African Constitutional Court and Socio-Economic Rights' (2011) 22 Stellenbosch Rev 664, 673.

[130]   Bruce Porter, 'Reasonableness and Article 8(4)' in M Langford and others (eds), *The Optional Protocol to the International Covenant on Economic, Social and Cultural Rights: A Commentary* (Pretoria University Law Press 2016) 173, 186.

[131]   *South Africa and Others v Grootboom and Others*, 2001 (1) SA 46, 2000 (11) BCLR 1169 1.

the rights of internally displaced persons to health, housing, education and social assistance, was premised on an initial finding of interdependence of these rights with CPR, including the rights to life, to choose one's place of residence, to freely develop personality, to freedom of expression and association, and to the protection and reunification of the family.[132]

Some of the most significant advances in interdependence of ESCR with the right to life have emerged from India – one of the States that pushed for the separation of the two covenants in the 1950s. The Indian Constitution, which came into force in 1950, recognized civil and political rights as fundamental rights subject to access to justice but accorded ESCR the status of non-justiciable 'directive principles'. The right to life, therefore, was justiciable, but the right to food and housing were not. Some of the early judges of the Indian Supreme Court, however, displayed a willingness to engage in a human and empathetic way with the circumstances of claimants. This eventually compelled the Court to reject the false separation between directives for State policy and the rights of citizens. As early as 1981, the Indian Supreme Court had recognized that

> the right to life includes the right to live with human dignity and all that goes along with it, namely, the bare necessaries of life such as adequate nutrition, clothing and shelter and facilities for reading, writing and expressing oneself in diverse forms, freely moving about and mixing and commingling with fellow human beings.[133]

As described in Chapter 8, in the case of *People's Union for Civil Liberties v Union of India and Others*,[134] the Court was driven by its outrage at the prospect of widespread starvation when surplus grain was rotting in storage to issue a series of interim orders that saved thousands of lives and resulted in legislative implementation of the right to food.

Remedying the unequal status of ESCR is not, therefore, as simple as including these rights in constitutions as justiciable rights, as desirable as that is. Those who have been excluded from the human rights movement must be accorded substantive equality, not just formal equality. The dominant paradigms related to the content of rights, the obligations of governments, the role of courts and the types of remedies that are required must be transformed by the inclusion of ESCR claimants as equal participants in the human rights movement.

There is much to be gained on both sides of the human rights divide from a reconciliation of a 70-year separation. The negative rights paradigm that dominates CPR, and human rights practice generally, must be transformed by a constructive engagement with ESCR. This will allow civil and political rights to transcend the discriminatory denial of protection to claimants whose civil and political rights are denied by socio-economic deprivation. At the same time, ESC rights advocacy and adjudication must be transformed by engaging with civil and political claims so as to overcome the tendency to marginalize the claimant in a two-way conversation between courts and legislatures, focused on the nature of government obligations rather than on claimants' circumstances and entitlements.

There is a lot at stake in a successful outcome of the reconciliation. As noted above, a more inclusive paradigm of human rights is critical to address current human rights challenges, which tend to fall in territory between the two covenants. Moreover, many of the current

---

[132] *Decision T-025* (2004) Colombian Constitutional Court.
[133] *Francis Mullins v The Administrator Union* (13 January 1981) Supreme Court of India.
[134] In the Supreme Court of India, Civil Original Jurisdiction, Writ Petition (Civil) No. 196 of 2001.

challenges are themselves products of the separation of rights. Governments' inaction on poverty, inadequate housing and hunger is often linked to the idea that these are social policy challenges, not fundamental human rights violations. As was affirmed at the Vienna World Conference in 1993, recognizing everyone as equal in dignity and rights requires States to place ESC rights on an equal footing with civil and political rights, based on the principle of interdependence. This is a critical work in progress.

# 16. Advancing economic and social rights through national human rights institutions

*Mario Gomez[1]*

## 1. INTRODUCTION

The past 25 years has seen a huge growth in independent institutions across many parts of the world. These institutions have included national human rights institutions (NHRIs), gender and women's commissions, ombudspersons, public defenders, children's commissions, commissions to combat bribery and corruption, right to information commissions and temporary bodies such as truth commissions and reparations commissions. Many of these commissions emerged against a backdrop of political transitions in different parts of the world, whether from dictatorship to democracy, or from war to peace. They were promoted by liberal cosmopolitan ideologies that placed faith in new institutions to preserve and promote the democratic gains that were the result of these political transitions. Many of these institutions have implications for the advancement of ESCR in their respective jurisdictions.

Twenty years ago, the Committee on Economic, Social and Cultural Rights (CESCR) adopted two General Comments, No. 9 and No. 10, that recognized the role that NHRIs could play in promoting and ensuring the interdependence and indivisibility of all human rights and identified several possible roles that NHRIs could play in relation to ESCR. The views of the Committee could be applied with equal relevance to other independent institutions such as gender commissions, children's commissions and reparations commissions.

Since these two General Comments, many NHRIs and other independent institutions have begun to work on advancing ESR in their respective countries.[2] Some NHRIs have begun to work on vulnerable and disadvantaged groups and explored issues of intersectionality, indivisibility and interdependence.[3] Other NHRIs, however, have not pursued ESR with the same

---

[1] My thanks to the Centre for Asian Legal Studies (CALS) and the National University of Singapore, where much of the writing took place, and to Panuga Pulenthiran for some of the early research.

[2] The Scottish Human Rights Commission has initiated several activities on ESR: see Katie Boyle, *Models of Incorporation and Justiciability for Economic, Social and Cultural Rights* (Scottish Human Rights Commission 2018). The Jordanian NHRI has engaged in budget monitoring and the South African Human Rights Commission engages in activities around ESR every year. In the Asia-Pacific region, several NHRIs have held public inquiries on ESR. These are more fully discussed later in this chapter. See also Global Alliance of National Human Rights Institutions (GANHRI), 'Mérida Declaration – The Role of National Human Rights Institutions in implementing the 2030 Agenda for Sustainable Development' (10 October 2015) <https://nhri.ohchr.org/EN/ICC/InternationalConference/12IC/Background%20Information/Merida%20Declaration%20FINAL.pdf> at 3; and GANHRI, 'Amman Declaration and Programme of Action' (7 November 2012) <https://nhri.ohchr.org/EN/ICC/InternationalConference/11IC/Background%20Information/Amman%20PoA%20FINAL%20 -%20EN.pdf>.

[3] The Sri Lankan Human Rights Commission previously worked on internally displaced persons: see Mario Gomez, 'National Human Rights Commissions and Internally Displaced Persons: Illustrated

vigor – either because they believe that they lack an explicit mandate to work on ESR, because they believe that the political context requires them to focus on other areas of intervention, or because they believe that ESR are not a priority for their work.

Given the potential that NHRIs and other independent commissions have to advance ESR, one would have expected greater institutional momentum on ESR.[4] Given that poverty and inequality is a feature of both the global north and the global south, one would have thought that NHRIs would have prioritized ESR irrespective of the political context and their institutional constraints. Tangible outcomes could provide added impetus to the work of independent institutions. More creative use of their mandates and better use of the strategies available at their disposal could have resulted in more important work on advancing ESR globally. While there has been some progress, it has been less than one would have imagined given the broad range of strategies that NHRIs can potentially employ in their work.

This chapter asks if NHRIs and independent institutions can play a transformative role in advancing ESR in those societies in which they operate. What roles may these institutions play? How can they best engage with state and other actors? In which areas should they prioritize resources and where may they achieve tangible outcomes? While the focus of this chapter is on NHRIs, some of the arguments may apply with equal force to other independent institutions.[5]

## 2.   NATIONAL HUMAN RIGHTS INSTITUTIONS (NHRIS)

An NHRI is an entity set up under the constitution or by way of statute with a mandate to protect and promote human rights. In doing this it may perform a variety of functions, which include investigating complaints; promoting human rights education; litigating; conducting public inquiries; documentation; conducting research; and advice to government institutions. It may also address systemic and structural human rights issues and respond to individual and group complaints. Many NHRIs focus on vulnerable groups and individuals and the 'worst off'. Several NHRIs engage with parliaments, the executive, the courts and civil society organizations.

NHRIs, and other independent institutions, have grown in recent decades as governments, donors, the United Nations and global civil society have placed faith in institutions to consolidate gains in democracy and promote human rights. The creation of NHRIs in a country

---

by the Sri Lankan Experience' (Brookings Institution 2002). The Commission has more recently set up a separate unit to address the rights of persons living with disabilities.

[4]   See Eva Brems, Gauthier de Beco and Wouter Vandenhole (eds), *National Human Rights Institutions and Economic, Social and Cultural Rights* (Intersentia 2013) and the examples from Bolivia, India, Ethiopia, Ghana and the Netherlands discussed in that book. See also the several examples discussed in Allison Cockery and Duncan Wilson, 'Building Bridges: National Human Rights Institutions and Economic, Social and Cultural Rights' in Eibe Riedel, Gilles Giacca and Christophe Golay (eds), *Economic, Social, and Cultural Rights in International Law* (Oxford University Press 2014) 473–97.

[5]   For some early thinking on the subject see Mario Gomez, 'Social Economic Rights and Human Rights Commissions' (1995) 17 *Human Rights Quarterly* 155 and Mario Gomez, 'The Role of Human Rights Commissions in the Realization of Economic, Social and Cultural Rights' in 'Circle of Rights: Economic, Social and Cultural Rights Activism, A Training Resource', International Human Rights Internship Program and Asian Forum for Human Rights and Development (2000).

has sometimes accompanied a political transition and has been viewed as one way of trying to ensure that the transition stays on track and does not get derailed.[6] In some other parts of the world the institution of the Ombudsman and the Public Defender has been vested with a human rights jurisdiction. NHRIs have also been established at the state, provincial or other regional level.

NHRIs are now strongly embedded as part of the domestic and international human rights architecture and have played an important role in the development of both domestic and international standards on human rights.[7] For example, NHRIs participated in the development of the standards contained in the Convention on the Rights of Persons on Disabilities, and more recently in the generation of the Global Compact on Migration.[8] NHRIs have a designated role in the Universal Periodic Review Process of the Human Rights Council and have increasingly participated in reviews of state parties by the CESCR.[9] The Convention on the Rights of Persons with Disabilities has an innovative monitoring mechanism that is discussed below.

The growth of NHRIs has occurred in two phases. While NHRIs have been in existence from the 1940s, the first being set up in Saskatchewan, Canada in 1947,[10] the 'modern' NHRI is different from many of the older institutions set up in Canada, the UK and New Zealand. Many of the older institutions were 'complaints oriented' and tended to focus on equality and other civil and political rights. For example, the Saskatchewan Human Rights Commission focuses on receiving and investigating complaints and attempting to mediate complaints; where mediation fails, it refers the matter for adjudication to the Court of Queen's Bench.[11]

---

[6]   One of the earliest 'modern' NHRIs was the Philippines Human Rights Commission established in 1987, soon after the political transition and the fall of former President Marcos.

[7]   See the views of the other treaty bodies on the role of NHRIs: the Human Rights Committee (Paper on the relationship of the Human Rights Committee with National Human Rights Institutions, adopted by the Committee at its 106th session, 15 October–2 November 2012, CCPR/C/106/3); the Committee on the Rights of the Child ('The role of independent national human rights institutions in the promotion and protection of the rights of the child', 15 November 2002, CRC/GC/2002/2); the Committee on Enforced Disappearances ('The relationship of the Committee on Enforced Disappearances with national human rights institutions', adopted at the Committee's seventh session, 15–26 September 2014, CRD/C/6) and the Committee on the Elimination of Racial Discrimination, General Recommendation No. 17: The Establishment of National Institutions to Facilitate the Implementation of the Convention (Forty-second session, 1993), A/48/18 at 116 (1994).

[8]   See for example the Guidelines adopted by the UN Committee on Disabilities at its 16th Session on Independent Monitoring Mechanisms and NHRIs: <https://nhri.ohchr.org/EN/IHRS/TreatyBodies/PersonsDisabilities/Pages/Guidelines.aspx> and the conclusions of the meeting between the UN Committee on Disabilities, NHRIs, independent monitoring mechanisms designated under Article 33.2 (IMMS) of the Convention on the Rights of Persons with Disabilities, and organisations of persons with disabilities (DPOs) to exchange views in September 2014: <https://nhri.ohchr.org/EN/IHRS/TreatyBodies/PersonsDisabilities/Pages/default.aspx>. See also the conclusions of the meeting organized by the National Human Rights Council of Morocco (CNDH) and the Network of African National Human Rights Institutions (NANHRI), 'The Role of African NHRIs in the Process of Negotiations leading to the adoption of the Global Compact for Safe, Orderly and Regular Migration' in May 2017 in Niamey, Niger: <www.cndh.org.ma/an/press-releases/global-compact-migration-special-event-role-african-nhris>.

[9]   See for example the procedures for the participation of other stakeholders in the Universal Periodic Process: <www.ohchr.org/en/hrbodies/upr/pages/NgosNhris.aspx> and <https://nhri.ohchr.org/EN/IHRS/UPR/Documents/FINAL%20ICC%20paper%20on%20NHRIs%20UPR%20follow%20up.pdf>.

[10]   Saskatchewan Human Rights Commission <http://saskatchewanhumanrights.ca/>.

[11]   Ibid.

The second wave of NHRIs started in the late 1980s and saw the establishment of NHRIs with broad mandates and a capacity, at least in theory, to engage in a variety of activities. The modern NHRI tends to have a broad mandate combining a complaints resolution function, an educational function, an advisory function and a law reform function. They also tend to interact more closely with civil society than the older commissions.[12]

The Second World Conference on Human Rights, held in Vienna, Austria in 1993, provided impetus to the establishment of NHRIs. The Vienna Declaration and Programme of Action, adopted unanimously by the Conference, declared:

> The World Conference on Human Rights reaffirms the important and constructive role played by national institutions for the promotion and protection of human rights, in particular in their advisory capacity to the competent authorities, their role in remedying human rights violations, in the dissemination of human rights information, and education in human rights. The World Conference on Human Rights encourages the establishment and strengthening of national institutions, having regard to the 'Principles relating to the status of national institutions' and recognizing that it is the right of each State to choose the framework which is best suited to its particular needs at the national level.[13]

In 1995, added momentum was provided when the United Nations appointed a Special Adviser on National Institutions to work with the High Commissioner for Human Rights. As of May 2019, there were 123 NHRIs who were members of the Global Alliance of National Human Rights Institutions (GANHRI).[14] Of those institutions, 79 were in full compliance with the Paris Principles, 34 were 'not fully in compliance' with the Paris Principles and 10 were assessed as not being in compliance with the Paris Principles.[15]

## 3.    THE 'PARIS PRINCIPLES'

NHRIs received prominence after the United Nations began to actively promote the concept. In 1991 the Centre for Human Rights in Geneva organized a consultation on NHRIs. One of the results of this meeting was a statement of principles titled 'Principles relating to the Status and Functioning of National Institutions for the Protection and Promotion of Human Rights ('Paris Principles')'.[16] These principles were subsequently endorsed by the Commission on Human Rights in 1992 and the General Assembly and Vienna World Conference in 1993.

---

[12]    See also Bruce Ackerman, 'The New Separation of Powers' (2000) 113(3) Harvard Law Review 642–729; Mark Tushnet, 'Fifth-Branch Institutions: South Africa' in David S. Law (ed.), *Constitutionalism in Context* (Cambridge University Press 2019); Mark Tushnet, 'Institutions Protecting Constitutional Democracy: Some Conceptual and Methodological Preliminaries' (2020) 70 University of Toronto Law Journal 95; Mark Tushnet, 'Institutions Protecting Democracy: A Preliminary Inquiry' (2018) 12(2) Law & Ethics of Human Rights 181–202, available at <https://doi.org/10.1515/lehr-2018-0010>.

[13]    Vienna Declaration and Programme of Action; part 1 para 36.

[14]    Global Alliance of National Human Rights Institutions (GANHRI) <www.nhri.ohchr.org>.

[15]    Ibid.

[16]    'Principles relating to the Status and Functioning of National Institutions', E/CN.4/1992/54, Annex (1992).

Since then the UN and the Human Rights Council have adopted several resolutions urging states to set up and strengthen NHRIs in accordance with the Paris Principles.[17]

The Paris Principles emphasize that these institutions should operate independently of government and have the necessary resources and infrastructure to function effectively. They also draw attention to the flexibility of these institutions and state that the members of these commissions should be drawn from different sections of society. Some NGOs, among them Amnesty International, have also issued guidelines on human rights commissions.[18] The Amnesty standards emphasize that while human rights commissions can be an important mechanism for the protection of human rights, they can never replace and should not in any way diminish the legal structures enforced by an independent and impartial judiciary.

While the Paris Principles may have been overtaken by subsequent developments, they still remain the global benchmark for assessing the work of NHRIs and provide the overarching framework to the Office of the United Nations High Commissioner for Human Rights (OHCHR) and GANHRI for its accreditation process.[19]

The Paris Principles also find recognition in the Sustainable Development Goals (SDGs). Goal 16 of the SDGs seek to 'promote peaceful and inclusive societies for sustainable development, provide access to justice for all and build effective, accountable and inclusive institutions at all levels'.[20] Target 16.A.1 of Goal 16 refers to the 'existence of independent national human rights institutions in compliance with the Paris Principles'.

## 4.   THE GLOBAL ALLIANCE OF NATIONAL HUMAN RIGHTS INSTITUTIONS (GANHRI)

At a conference held in Tunis in 1993, NHRIs established the International Coordinating Committee of NHRIs to help coordinate the activities of the NHRIs globally. In 2016, the International Coordinating Committee changed its name to the Global Alliance of National Human Rights Institutions (GANHRI). GANHRI is incorporated as a legal entity under the Swiss law and has a Bureau that consists of 16 'A-status' NHRIs representing the four regions of GANHRI: Africa, the Americas, Asia-Pacific and Europe.

GANHRI, in partnership with OHCHR, accredits NHRIs according to the Paris Principles as either fully compliant (A-status) or partially compliant (B-status). The Sub-Committee on Accreditation (SCA) of GANHRI reviews and analyzes accreditation applications received by OHCHR and makes recommendations to the GANHRI Bureau on the compliance of NHRIs with the Paris Principles. The SCA is composed of one 'A-status' NHRI from each of the four regional groupings. Members of the SCA are appointed by the regional groupings for

---

[17]   'National institutions for the promotion and protection of human rights', UN General Assembly, 48th Session, A/RES/48/134 (4 March 1994); 'National institutions for the promotion and protection of human rights', UN General Assembly, 72nd Session, A/RES/72/181 (2017), 'National human rights institutions', UN Human Rights Council, A/ HRC/RES/39/17 (2018), 'The role of the Ombudsman, mediator and other national human rights institutions in the promotion and protection of human rights', UN General Assembly, 72nd Session (Dec 2017) A/RES/72/186.

[18]   Amnesty International, 'Proposed Standards for National Human Rights Institutions', IOR 40/01/93 (January 1993).

[19]   Global Alliance of National Human Rights Institutions (GANHRI) <www.nhri.ochr.org>.

[20]   Goal 16 of the Sustainable Development Goals <sustainabledevelopment.un.org/sdg16>.

a renewable term of three years. As of May 2019, there were 123 NHRIs who were members of the GANHRI, out of which 79 NHRIs were fully compliant with the Paris Principles.[21] In assessing compliance GANHRI *does not* take into account if the mandate of the NHRI has express reference to ESCR, or if in practice the NHRI is dealing with a broad spectrum of human rights issues including ESCR.

'A-status' NHRIs have the right to participate in UN human rights mechanisms such as the Human Rights Council and the UN Working Groups, as well as in regional human rights mechanisms. They provide additional information to these UN bodies, provide information on good practices in implementing human rights norms, highlight challenges for realizing human rights and help international bodies develop relevant recommendations for human rights enforcement and advancement.

## 5.  NHRIS AND THE INTERNATOINAL COVENANT ON ECONOMIC, SOCIAL AND CULTURAL RIGHTS (ICESCR)

In its General Comment on the Domestic Application of the Covenant, the CESCR made some key observations that are worth restating.[22] The Committee drew attention to the basic principle that states should use all the means at their disposal to give effect to the rights recognized in the Covenant.[23] The Committee also observed that the norms in the ICESCR must be recognized in appropriate ways within the domestic legal order; appropriate means of redress, or remedies, must be available to any aggrieved individual or group; and appropriate means of ensuring governmental accountability must be put in place.[24] While highlighting the relevance of legal remedies and observing that it would be difficult for a state to justify excluding judicial remedies from the requirement of realizing Covenant rights 'by appropriate means',[25] the Committee also drew attention to the relevance of administrative remedies. The Committee observed that those living within a state's jurisdiction would have a legitimate expectation that administrative authorities will take account of the Covenant in their decision-making and that such administrative remedies would be accessible, affordable, timely and effective.[26]

That same year the CESCR adopted a second General Comment that dealt specifically with the role of NHRIs in the advancement of ESCR.[27] The Committee observed that Article 2(1) of the ICESCR required each state party to take steps with a view to achieving progressively the full realization of the Covenant rights by all appropriate means. It identified one way through

---

[21]  Global Alliance of National Human Rights Institutions (GANHRI) <www.nhri.ohchr.org>.

[22]  CESCR, General Comment No. 9: The Domestic Application of the Covenant (3 December 1998) E/C.12/1998/24.

[23]  Para 2.

[24]  Para 2.

[25]  Para 3.

[26]  Para 9.

[27]  CESCR, General Comment No. 10: The Role of National Human Rights Institutions in the Protection of Economic, Social and Cultural Rights (10 December 1998), E/C.12/1998/25 (General Comment No. 10).

which important steps could be taken, as being the work of national institutions for the promotion and protection of human rights.[28]

The Committee noted that NHRIs have a potentially crucial role to play in promoting and ensuring the indivisibility and interdependence of all human rights but that unfortunately, this role has too often either not been accorded to these institutions or been neglected or given a low priority by them. It was therefore essential that full attention be given to economic, social and cultural rights in all of the relevant activities of these institutions. The Committee listed the range of activities that NHRIs could perform in relation to economic and social rights:

1. Promoting educational information programs designed to enhance awareness and understanding of ESCR, both within the population at large and among particular groups such as the public service, the judiciary, the private sector and the labor movement.
2. Scrutinizing existing laws and administrative acts, as well as draft bills and other proposals, to ensure that they are consistent with the requirements of the International Covenant on Economic, Social and Cultural Rights.
3. Providing technical advice, or undertaking surveys in relation to ESCR, including at the request of public authorities and or other appropriate agencies.
4. Identifying national level benchmarks and indicators against which the realization of Covenant rights can be measured.
5. Conducting research and inquiries designed to ascertain the extent to which particular ESCR are being realized, either within the state as a whole or in areas or in relation to communities of particular vulnerability.
6. Monitoring compliance with specific rights recognized under the covenant and providing reports thereon to the public authorities and civil society.
7. Examining complaints alleging infringements of applicable ESCR standards within the state.

To this list provided by the Committee may be added the following tasks:

8. Conducting public inquiries or national inquiries in cases where there is evidence to suggest a violation of ESCR or in cases of systemic violations of ESCR.
9. Monitoring government policy and budgets and suggesting changes so that they advance ESCR.
10. Advising government departments and institutions, and the private sector, on how best to integrate practices, into policy, budgets, and legislation that best advances ESCR.
11. Inquiring into violations and abuses on its own initiative.
12. Acting as an independent *amicus curiae* in litigation before courts, and in other interventions before administrative tribunals or other independent commissions.

---

[28]   The Committee continues to highlight the role of NHRIs in the realization of ESC; see for example the Committee's comments on the periodic reports submitted by Cape Verde and Niger, in the Global Initiative for Economic, Social and Cultural Rights, 'The Committee of Economic, Social and Cultural Rights – 2018 Yearbook', available at <https://static1.squarespace.com/static/5a6e0958f6576ebde0e78c18/t/5d1e4828eaad05000174a4ac/1562265823952/CESCR-Yearbook-2018-Final.pdf>.

13. Issuing 'public comments' (as the treaty bodies do) on ESCR that will help develop a fuller and richer understanding of these rights, especially in the particular local context in which the NHRI or the independent institution operates.
14. Submission of reports where the state is a party to the ICESCR or other international treaty, and the state report is being considered by the relevant Committee.[29]
15. Conducting joint campaigns with NHRIs and independent commissions from other countries on themes of common interest.
16. Developing national action plans or Bills of Rights for the advancement of ESR and other human rights.[30]
17. Monitoring the implementation of judicial decisions.
18. Functioning as a 'court-appointed' monitor of judicial decisions.
19. Documentation and research.
20. Establishing regional or provincial sub-commissions to facilitate public access and help it conduct the above activities.
21. Preparing an Annual Report to be submitted to Parliament and be placed before the public.
22. Writing to ministries and other government institutions to request information on how they have advanced or implemented ESR and integrated ESR into their policies, programs and budgets, or requiring regular reporting of such measures.
23. Conducting periodic consultations with the public and private sectors on the progress achieved in advancing ESR.
24. Interacting regularly with the media to see that ESR figure in media reports and analysis.
25. Monitoring the recommendations of the international human rights treaty bodies and special procedures.
26. Contributing to the development of global standards on human rights.
27. Contributing to the universal periodic review process at the Human Rights Council.[31]

## 6. NHRIS AND THE CONVENTION ON THE RIGHTS OF PERSONS WITH DISABILITIES

The Convention on the Rights of Persons with Disabilities (CRPD) was one of the first human rights treaties to recognize civil and political rights and economic, social and cultural rights as part of a single treaty. The CRPD also contains an innovative monitoring mechanism, unique among human rights treaties.[32] According to Article 33(2) and (3) of the Convention:

---

[29] In 2018 the CESCR received 11 parallel reports from NHRIs: see the Global Initiative for Economic, Social and Cultural Rights, 'The Committee of Economic, Social and Cultural Rights – 2018 Yearbook' at p.7, available at <https://static1.squarespace.com/static/5a6e0958f6576ebde0e78c18/t/5d1e4828eaad05000174a4ac/1562265823952/CESCR-Yearbook-2018-Final.pdf>.

[30] The Northern Ireland Commission for Human Rights made recommendations for the development of a Bill of Rights for Northern Ireland: <www.nihrc.org/>.

[31] See also Mario Gomez, 'From Rhetoric to Realization: Delivering Socio-Economic Rights through Courts and Commissions' in C. Raj Kumar and D.K. Srivastava (eds) *Human Rights and Development: Law, Policy and Governance* (LexisNexis 2006) 65–94.

[32] The Optional Protocol to the Convention against Torture and Other Cruel, Inhumane or Degrading Treatment or Punishment, also provides for the designation of one or more focal points within the government for matters relating to the implementation of the Convention and the establishment of a frame-

2.  States Parties shall, in accordance with their legal and administrative systems, maintain, strengthen, designate or establish within the State Party, a framework, including one or more independent mechanisms, as appropriate, to promote, protect and monitor implementation of the present Convention. When designating or establishing such a mechanism, States Parties *shall take into account the principles relating to the status and functioning of national institutions for protection and promotion of human rights.* (emphasis added)
3.  Civil society, in particular persons with disabilities and their representative organizations, shall be involved and participate fully in the monitoring process.

The CRPD is unique in that in designating or establishing a monitoring mechanism, the state is required to take into account the Paris Principles.[33] The Committee on the Rights of Persons with Disabilities subsequently adopted 'Guidelines on Independent Monitoring Frameworks and their participation in the work of the Committee'.[34] These Guidelines emphasize the variety of roles that NHRIs could potentially play in implementing the standards contained in the CRPD.[35]

## 7.   INSTITUTIONAL FLEXIBILITY

One of the biggest advantages of NHRIs is the institutional flexibility they bring to their work. In theory, NHRIs and similar institutions can perform a broad range of functions and activities, even if not all NHRIs have explored the full gamut of their potential powers. In some cases, NHRIs may be curtailed by their legal foundation and mandates. In most cases, though, NHRIs engage in a range of strategies that includes litigation, monitoring, budget analysis, public inquiries and public education. Unlike most courts, they can engage in initiatives of their own volition, which may include helping victims advance human rights claims and access courts and administrative remedies. For example, in South Africa, the Promotion of Equality and Prevention of Unfair Discrimination Act allows the South African Human Rights Commission to institute proceedings under the Act and allows the Commission to assist complainants to institute proceedings in the equality courts set up under the legislation.[36]

The institutional flexibility of NHRIs offers a particular advantage in advancing ESR. ESR require multiple strategies for their realization, ranging from litigation to budget monitoring to advocacy and awareness-raising. NHRIs by their very nature are capable of multiple activities that straddle all of these options, and in that sense provide an exciting vehicle for the delivery of ESR in those societies in which they operate.

The other advantage that NHRIs carry is their position between state and civil society and within the larger framework of institutional governance. Provided with either a constitutional

---

work for the monitoring of its provisions at the national level. However, unlike the CRPD it does not make express reference to the 'Paris Principles'.

[33]   Article 33(2) of the Convention on the Rights of Persons Living with Disabilities.

[34]   'Guidelines on independent monitoring frameworks and their participation in the work of the Committee on the Rights of Persons with Disabilities', see the annex to the CRPD Rules of Procedure, CRPD,/C/1/Rev.1, 10 October 2016 <www.un.org/en/ga/search/view_doc.asp?symbol=CRPD/C/1/Rev .1>.

[35]   See for example paras 3, 4 and 5.

[36]   Sections 20(1)(f) and 25(3)(a) of the Promotion of Equality and Prevention of Unfair Discrimination Act (Act No 4 of 2000) (PEPUDA) of South Africa.

or a statutory mandate, they are endowed with the credibility and legitimacy that constitutional and legal recognition brings. This enables NHRIs to have access to state institutions, public officials and other officials, and to proactively engage with them to shape policy and practice. It also enables them to confront these institutions in cases where there is evidence of a violation or systemic violation, and to help victims claim access to administrative or legal remedies.

Being located in this ambiguous space between state and civil society allows NHRIs to access information and documents that civil society would not generally be able to access. This position also allows NHRIs to engage with government officials and private actors more closely than civil society would be able to do, and to demand standards of accountability that civil society would be unable to demand. In many situations they have the capacity and reach to help victims access courts and administrative remedies. Their reports and recommendations are also likely to have a stronger impact within government than civil society findings and reports. Their location within this ambiguous space helps NHRIs to interact with other independent institutions and organizations such as gender commissions, ombuds offices, employers' organizations and chambers of commerce, and to coordinate their activities with the work of these institutions and organizations and engage in collaborative endeavors. There is an additional factor which makes NHRIs potentially significant actors. Failure to protect human rights is sometimes related to the lack of political will on the part of state structures. NHRIs have the potential to catalyze this political will on the part of political actors and institutions because of their legal status, their public profile, their access to resources and their location within the overall governance framework.

The institutional flexibility available to NHRIs is illustrated by a recent survey of 41 NHRIs on the strategies they have employed to prevent and combat gender-based violence.[37] In seeking to prevent gender-based violence, in the home, in public spaces and in other contexts such as conflict situations, NHRIs from different parts of the world have used a variety of interventions. These interventions straddled public education, awareness-raising and media campaigns, including specific training and capacity building exercises for those working in specific sectors, such as health care professionals, lawyers, police officers, educators, local government officials and social workers. It included the submission of shadow reports to international treaty bodies and workshops and seminars that explored how concluding observations and recommendations could be implemented and taken forward domestically.[38]

It extended to studies on the 'war against drugs and extra-judicial killings' conducted in partnership with civil society, universities and church-based groups; other data collection initiatives; public inquiries; work on intersectionality and vulnerability; and advocacy around law and policy reform. It also included the monitoring of budgets and government austerity measures, and understanding their impact on women's rights, how changes in tax and welfare policies were affecting women and other vulnerable groups, studies on women heads of household (especially those with young children), working with the private sector to implement the

---

[37]   'Preventing and Eliminating All Forms of Violence Against Women and Girls: The Role of National Human Rights Institutions', GANHRI and German Institute of Human Rights (2019) <www.nhri.ochr.org>.

[38]   Between 2016 and 2018, 32 NHRIs (A and B-status) submitted parallel reports to the CEDAW Committee during the reporting procedure of their own state: 'Preventing and Eliminating All Forms of Violence Against Women and Girls: The Role of National Human Rights Institutions' (GANHRI and German Institute of Human Rights 2019) p.14, <www.nhri.ochr.org>.

SDGs and how small and medium enterprises could empower women. Several NHRIs worked with internally displaced persons and refugees and looked at the impact of armed conflict on women. Supporting victims to claim remedies and assisting victims with litigation also formed part of the interventions that NHRIs made with regard to gender-based violence.

The potential that NHRIs have exists, in theory, yet many NHRIs around the world have not made maximum use of it. While NHRIs may perform a broad range of functions, their interventions have been restricted by human and financial resources and the socio-political context in which they operate. Even in cases where there exists a will within the NHRIs to exercise the full range of interventions, they may be forced to prioritize their interventions. State control over financial resources, and volatile political contexts, may force NHRIs to prioritize some rights and certain types of interventions over others. Attention to context would then be important in shaping interventions related to ESR, as would pressures from domestic civil society and other stakeholders, including other independent institutions.

## 8.     INCLUSION OF ESR IN THE MANDATE OF NHRIS?

NHRIs' broad mandates to promote and ensure the protection of human rights in general should be interpreted and applied so as to give equal attention to ESR. When enabling legislation for NHRIs is drafted or revised, ESRs should be explicitly included and NHRIs given a full mandate and responsibility to promote them and to ensure access to effective remedies.

In analyzing the work of three African NHRIs and the impact their work has had on ESC, Beredugo and Viljoen conclude that an explicit mandate is important in helping NHRIs advance ESR. They note:

> Against this background, we conclude that the confluence of the following factors would see the greatest improvement in the role of NHRCs in advancing the domestic implementation of socio-economic rights: the constitutionalisation of socio-economic rights; giving an explicit legal mandate on socio-economic rights to NHRCs; the strengthening (of) the institutional independence and capability of these institutions, especially in terms of providing adequate institutional, operational and financial independence and autonomy; and support of NHRCs by other public accountability institutions, such as the judiciary and parliament.[39]

Of those NHRIs with an explicit mandate to enforce ESR, South Africa's Human Rights Commission (SAHRC) is the most widely known. The SAHRC has been given a specific mandate to monitor the realization of all human rights as well as a special mandate in relation to socio-economic rights.[40]

Section 184(3) of the South African Constitution obliges the Commission to collect information from relevant organs of the state on the measures they have taken to realize the socio-economic rights of housing, health care, food, water, social security, education and the environment.

---

[39]   Ayebaesin Jacob Beredugo and Frans Viljoen, 'Towards a Greater Role and Enhanced Effectiveness of National Human Rights Commissions in Advancing the Domestic Implementation of Socioeconomic Rights: Nigeria, South Africa and Uganda as Case Studies' (2015) 48(3) The Comparative and International Law Journal of Southern Africa 430.

[40]   Section 184(3) of the Constitution of South Africa and Human Rights Commission Act 54 of 1994.

Each year the Human Rights Commission must require relevant organs of state to provide the Commission with information on the measures that they have taken towards the realization of the rights in the Bill of Rights, concerning housing, health care, food, water, social security, education and the environment.[41]

There is no obligation on the state entities to proactively disclose information. They are requested instead to respond to a request of the SAHRC.[42]

In compiling Section 184(3) reports the SAHRC sends open-ended questionnaires to government departments seeking information on the realization of a particular ESR. The questionnaires seek information on policy, legislative, budgetary and other measures adopted by the relevant government department. It also includes questions on vulnerable groups, and problems encountered by the departments, the measures taken to address these problems and indicators of progress. As of 2019, the SAHRC had produced nine Section 184(3) reports.[43] In its most recent report for 2012–13, the Commission noted the difficulties it has encountered in obtaining information from government departments. The Commission sought information from seven government departments for that report. None of the departments met the deadline and two had to be threatened with legal action before they submitted the required information.[44]

While the SAHRC has been challenged on some occasions, it has also done important work, especially with regard to the right to access sufficient water and decent sanitation and the right to access adequate housing, illustrating the impact that NHRIs can have on the progressive realization of ESR.[45]

## 8.1    The South African Human Rights Commission and the Right to Water and Sanitation

The Constitution of South Africa, in Section 27(1)(b), guarantees everyone the right of access to sufficient water and requires the state to adopt reasonable legislative and other measures to progressively realize this right within its available resources. However, the Constitution does not explicitly provide for the right to sanitation. The right to sanitation has been derived from other sections in the Constitution, including the right to a clean environment, health and dignity.

---

[41]    Section 184(3). See also D. Horsten, 'The Role Played by the South African Human Rights Commission's Economic and Social Rights Reports in Good Governance in South Africa' (2006) 9 Potchefstroom Elec. L.J. 1 and Ayebaesin Jacob Beredugo and Frans Viljoen, 'Towards a Greater Role and Enhanced Effectiveness of National Human Rights Commissions in Advancing the Domestic Implementation of Socioeconomic Rights: Nigeria, South Africa and Uganda as Case Studies' (2015) 48(3) The Comparative and International Law Journal of Southern Africa 401–30.

[42]    Section 184(3).

[43]    South African Human Rights Commission <www.sahrc.org.za>.

[44]    South African Human Rights Commission <www.sahrc.org.za>, '9th Section 184(3) Report on Economic and Social Rights, SAHRC (2012–2013)' 10.

[45]    See South African Human Rights Commission, 'Report on the Right to Access Sufficient Water and Decent Sanitation in South Africa: 2014, <www.sahrc.org.za/home/21/files/FINAL%204th %20Proof%204%20March%20-%20Water%20%20Sanitation%20low%20res%20(2).pdf> and South African Human Rights Commission, 'Water and Sanitation Research Brief' (March 2018) <www .sahrc.org.za/home/21/files/The%20Right%20to%20Water%20&%20Sanitation%20-%20Monitoring %20the%20Implementation%20of%20the%20SAHRCs%202014%20Recommendations%2020117 -2018.pdf>.

The SAHRC's 2014 report on water and sanitation was triggered by two complaints it received alleging that two municipalities had built unenclosed toilets. The SAHRC inquired into these complaints and held that there was a violation of the rights to dignity, privacy and a clean environment. This was followed by national and provincial hearings by the SAHRC between August and December 2012 on the right to access water and sanitation, and consultations with key government stakeholders in 2013. After further consultations in the nine regions that hosted the public hearings, the SAHRC issued its 2014 report with recommendations for ensuring access to water and sanitation. The recommendations included capacity building for local authorities and regular engagement with vulnerable communities to ensure adequate access to water and sanitation.

In 2018, the SAHRC issued another report that assessed progress on its recommendations in the interim three-year period.[46] Information provided by departments of the state and key stakeholders, coupled with the SAHRC's independent research, formed the basis for the subsequent report. In its 2018 assessment, the SAHRC once again flagged the reluctance of key government agencies, including the departments of Water and Sanitation, the Department of Cooperative Governance and Traditional Affairs and the Department of Mineral Resources, to provide relevant information.[47]

## 8.2    The South African Human Rights Commission and the Right to Housing

The SAHRC has also made important interventions with regard to the realization of the right to adequate housing.[48] In a recent research policy brief the SAHRC looked at the policy and implementation of access to housing for those with special needs, including persons with physical, intellectual and psychiatric disabilities; the elderly; victims of domestic abuse; orphans; homeless people; persons under substance rehabilitation; and parolees, ex-offenders and juvenile offenders.

Using qualitative research techniques, the policy brief highlighted the plight of persons with special needs regarding their specific housing needs and recommended the formulation of a special policy that provides for funding to build facilities for persons with special needs. The policy brief provided recommendations to government, to ensure that persons with special needs are able to exercise their right to adequate housing.

In its recent annual Trends Analysis Report, the SAHRC notes the increase in the number of ESR-related complaints.[49] The SAHRC comments:

---

[46]   South African Human Rights Commission, 'Water and Sanitation Research Brief' (March 2018), article available at <www.sahrc.org.za/home/21/files/The%20Right%20to%20Water%20&%20Sanitation%20-%20Monitoring%20the%20Implementation%20of%20the%20SAHRCs%202014%20Recommendations%2020117-2018.pdf>.

[47]   Ibid.

[48]   See for example, South African Human Rights Commission, 'Creating an Enabling Environment for the Realisation of the Right to Adequate Housing for Persons with Special Needs: Expediting the Special Needs Housing Policy and Programme', Economic and Social Rights Research Policy Brief 2016/2017 (2017) <www.sahrc.org.za/home/21/files/SAHRC%20Research%20Policy%20brief%202016-2017%20–The%20Right%20to%20Adequate%20Housing%2031%20March%202017%20-v3.pdf>.

[49]   South African Human Rights Commission, 'Annual Trends Analysis Report 2016/17', available at <www.sahrc.org.za/home/21/files/SAHRC%20Trend%20Analysis%202016%20-%202017.pdf>.

The 2016/17 figures illustrate a complete shift in the hierarchy of complaints. ESR related complaints far exceed three of the four remaining complaints categories, namely, administrative action, labour relations; and arrested, detained and accused persons. ESR complaints (631) are second on the hierarchy of complaints, with equality (705) the highest. More significantly, when ESR complaints (631) are taken together with other socio-economic rights complaints relating to housing (297) and education (289), the total number of socioeconomic rights complaints (1,217) exceeds equality complaints (705) by 512 in the 2016/17 year.[50]

## 9.    PUBLIC INQUIRIES

The 'public inquiry' or 'national inquiry', among its many variations, has been one of the most frequent strategies used by NHRIs to gather data on systemic violations of ESR. The term public inquiry is used here in preference to national inquiry because the public hearing forms an intrinsic part of this process.

The public inquiry has several advantages, among them the ability to gather data on systemic violations through public testimony and the testimony of experts; the capacity to detect individual violations and take steps to redress those; the capacity to raise public awareness both in the locations in which the hearings are conducted and also at the broader country-wide level; and the capacity to influence policy and practice through the subsequent engagement with state and other actors. In some cases, it may provide a 'baseline survey' for subsequent inquiries held at a later stage. It also provides an opportunity to engage with the media on important human rights issues.[51] In many cases ESR involves complex scenarios and the inter-relationship among a range of different actors. The public inquiry is a potent strategy to address this complexity and identify the patterns and the actors resulting in systemic violations of ESR.[52] In some cases the public inquiry may be a consequence of a high number of complaints with regard to a particular issue, as in the case of the Malaysian inquiry into the land rights of Indigenous peoples, or the case of the South African Human Rights Commission's inquiry on land rights.[53]

A public inquiry is an inquiry into a human rights issue that affects a group of persons or a large population group. It is generally initiated after prior research or surveys by the NHRI, or complaints received by the NHRI, establish that there is a case that warrants a more detailed inquiry. Most public inquiries are conducted in a transparent manner with prior notice. They entail testimony from members of the public and from experts. The report or reports will contain recommendations for policy and practice addressed to a variety of state and non-state actors. They may also form the basis for subsequent public education and public awareness initiatives. They may also result in court action and action before administrative tribunals.

---

[50]    Ibid 21.

[51]    See generally 'Manual on Conducting a National Inquiry into Systemic Patterns of Human Rights Violation', Asia Pacific Forum of National Human Rights Institutions and Raoul Wallenberg Institute of Human Rights and Humanitarian Law (September 2012).

[52]    Most of the examples listed in the Manual above in n 22 consist of violations of ESR.

[53]    The SUHAKAM Inquiry is available at <www.suhakam.org.my> and the report of the South Africa Human Rights Commission is available at <www.sahrc.org.za/home/21/files/Access%20to%20Housing%202015.pdf>.

In their manual on national inquiries, the Asia-Pacific Forum of National Human Rights Institutions and Raoul Wallenberg Institute of Human Rights and Humanitarian Law, listed fourteen steps in the conduct of a public inquiry:

> 1. Choose the issue; 2. Prepare a background or scoping paper; 3. Identify, consult and engage stakeholders; 4. Draft objectives and terms of reference; 5. Appoint Inquiry Commissioners and staff; 6. Gather other resources; 7. Finalize an inquiry plan; 8. Obtain information: research and evidence; 9. Conduct public hearings; 10. Develop recommendations; 11. Prepare the report; 12. Release the report; 13. Follow up; 14. Evaluate.[54]

### 9.1    Suhakam's Inquiry into Land Rights of Indigenous Peoples in Malaysia

Suhakam's inquiry into the land rights of Indigenous people was triggered by a large number of complaints to the Commission. The inquiry established a tension between the model of development pursued by the state, and the land rights of Indigenous peoples and the disruption of their way of life. Among its recommendations, the Commission established that the state should follow a human rights-based approach to development to ensure that communities have rights to participate in decision-making and access to prior and informed consent when land is being expropriated for development purposes.

The Commission invited public submissions before starting the hearings and engaged a wide range of stakeholders, including government departments and agencies, non-governmental organizations, Indigenous communities, private companies, the media and other groups and individuals.

One of the objectives of the inquiry was also to build public awareness on the rights of Indigenous peoples and their way of life. In this respect, Suhakam made a special effort to involve and engage the media to play an educational role. The inquiry also presented an opportunity for the Indigenous people to submit historical evidence in support of their oral evidence before the Commission.

### 9.2    The Inquiry on the Right to Health in India

The Indian National Human Rights Commission initiated a series of public hearings on the rights to health in partnership with Jan Swasthya Abhiyan (JSA) or People's Health Movement – India, a network of several hundred health and civil society organizations.[55] The

---

[54] 'Manual on Conducting a National Inquiry into Systemic Patterns of Human Rights Violation', Asia Pacific Forum of National Human Rights Institutions and Raoul Wallenberg Institute of Human Rights and Humanitarian Law (September 2012).

[55] See 'Manual on Conducting a National Inquiry into Systemic Patterns of Human Rights Violation', Asia Pacific Forum of National Human Rights Institutions and Raoul Wallenberg Institute of Human Rights and Humanitarian Law (September 2012) 102. The Manual lists the following among the inquiries conducted by NHRIs in the Asia-Pacific Region: Australian Human Rights and Equal Opportunity Commission (now the Australian Human Rights Commission) National Inquiry into Homeless Children, 1989 <www.humanrights.gov.au/human_rights/housing/index.html#youth _1989>; National Inquiry into Human Rights and Mental Illness, 1993 <www.humanrights.gov .au/disability_rights/inquiries/mental.htm>; National Inquiry into the Separation of Aboriginal and Torres Strait Islander Children from Their Families, 1997 <www.humanrights.gov.au/social_justice/ bth_report/index.html>; National Inquiry into Rural and Remote Education, 2000 <www.humanrights

process included public inquiries in different parts of the country and participatory surveys to understand the facilities in primary health care centers and rural hospitals. The regional public hearings culminated in a national public hearing with the participation of health officials from the central government and the several states in December 2004. Policy recommendations were presented and a National Action Plan on the 'Right to Health' was developed. The reports documented individual violations as well as structural violations. The Indian commission continued this work with several subsequent inquiries into the right to health. This also generated orders from the commission to compensate individuals and groups. The process attracted the participation of civil society and several organizations working in the health sector in India.[56]

### 9.3    The South African Inquiry into the Right to Adequate Housing

The right to access to adequate housing is found in Section 26 of the South African Constitution, and in terms of this Section, the state is obliged to take reasonable legislative and other measures within its available resources to achieve the progressive realization of this right. In addition, Section 26 provides for security of tenure by protecting persons against eviction or the demolition of one's home without an order of court made after considering all relevant circumstances. There have been some important cases, interpreting these Sections, decided by the Constitutional Court on these rights.[57]

In 2015, following its report on access to water and sanitation (discussed above), the South African Human Rights Commission initiated an 'investigative hearing' into the right to adequate housing.[58] One of the conclusions of the report on water and sanitation related to the failure of local government to provide adequate service delivery. The February 2015 Investigative Hearing of the SAHRC on adequate housing focused on a number of issues,

---

.gov.au/human_rights/rural_education/>; National Inquiry into Children in Immigration Detention, 2004 <www.humanrights.gov.au/human_rights/children_detention_report/index.html>; National Inquiry into Discrimination against People in Same-Sex Relationships: Financial and Work-Related Entitlements and Benefits, 2007 <www.humanrights.gov.au/human_rights/samesex/report/index.html>; Human Rights Commission of Malaysia National Inquiry into the Land Rights of Indigenous Peoples in Malaysia, 2012 <www.suhakam.org.my/web/682315/1>; Independent Commission on Human Rights in Palestine National Inquiry into Employment of Persons with Disabilities (commenced 2011); National Human Rights Commission of India National Inquiry on the Right to Food, 2004; National Inquiry on the Right to Health Care, 2004; National Human Rights Commission of Mongolia National Inquiry on Freedom from Torture, 2006 <www.asiapacificforum.net/members/full-members/mongolia/downloads/annual -reports/ Annual_Report_2006.pdf>; New Zealand Human Rights Commission National Inquiry into Accessible Public Land Transport, 2005 <www.hrc.co.nz/disabled-people/inquiry-into-accessible-public -land-transport-for-people-withdisabilities/>; Inquiry into Discrimination and Human Rights Issues for Transgender People, 2008 <www.hrc.co.nz/human-rights-environment/action-on-the-transgender -inquiry/resources>.

[56]   See also Justice B.C. Patel, 'The Role of NHRC in Protecting and Promoting the Economic and Social Rights of Vulnerable Groups in India' in Eva Brems, Gauthier de Beco and Wouter Vandenhole (eds) *National Human Rights institutions and Economic, Social and Cultural Rights* (Intersentia 2013) 79–148.

[57]   See for example *Government of the Republic of South Africa and Others v Grootboom and Others* 2001 (1) SA 46 (CC).

[58]   See South African Human Rights Commission Investigative Hearing Report: Access to Housing, Local Governance and Service Delivery (2015) <www.sahrc.org.za/home/21/files/Access%20to %20Housing%202015.pdf>.

including urbanization, town planning, the upgrading of informal settlements, the role of the private sector, the manner in which evictions are carried out and the role of third parties in these processes. One of the key factors underpinning the approach of the SAHRC was that the right to adequate housing is intrinsically linked to other rights, such as the right to water and sanitation and the rights to public participation, equality, human dignity and access to information.

The report made several far-reaching recommendations for the realization of the right to adequate housing. One of the conclusions was that the needs of the 'worst off' had not been prioritized so far, with the focus on the 'world class' city narrative resulting in a focus on private sector investment over the needs of vulnerable communities. These policies had failed to reverse the legacy of 'apartheid era' special planning. Low capacity at local government level, varying interpretations of law and policy, poor housing products provided by third party contractors and poor monitoring mechanisms were also reasons why many sections of the South African population did not have access to adequate housing. Lack of access to information, low levels of security of tenure and poor coordination among the different tiers of government were also identified as being problematic.[59]

## 10.    MONITORING POLICY AND BUDGETS

Monitoring policy and budgets is another intervention that NHRIs are particularly well placed to undertake. This requires competent and well-equipped staff within the NHRI or access to a pool of external experts to assist with analyzing information and drawing conclusions on the impact that policy and budgets are having on the ESR of individuals and groups, especially the most vulnerable groups. Monitoring can help establish if policy and public spending are privileging certain groups over a period of time, if there has been public participation across a broad spectrum in the development of policy and budgets, if the conditions of disadvantaged groups are being exacerbated and what alternatives may be pursued to ensure that ESR is advanced across the entire population spectrum.[60]

Monitoring would entail analyzing public budgets, public spending and public policies and making the connection with the impact that these policies are having on ESR. One of the objectives would be to demonstrate that even by 'staying within existing resources' an adjustment to public policy and spending could help advance ESR for identified groups, especially those who are most disadvantaged.

One of the more difficult challenges is to monitor 'progressive realization' against acceptable and credible indicators. While this may challenge most NHRIs, one way to proceed would be to develop partnerships with universities and think tanks and develop a long-term plan to monitor progressive realization of ESR. NHRIs may want to consider the development

---

[59]   See also the inquiry launched by the Kenya National Commission on Human Rights (KNCHR), *Living Large: Counting the Cost of Official Extravagance in Kenya* (2005), that documented evidence of the misuse of public resources by the government: <www.khrc.or.ke/>.

[60]   See for example Kofi Quashigah, 'The Monitoring Role of the Ghana Commission on Human Rights and Administrative Justice (CHRAJ) in the Protection of Economic, Social and Cultural Rights' in Eva Brems, Gauthier de Beco and Wouter Vandenhole (eds) 'National Human Rights Institutions and Economic, Social and Cultural Rights' (Intersentia 2013), 107–27.

of a 'vulnerability spectrum' or 'vulnerability index' that will enable it to identify vulnerable groups or those groups on the edge of vulnerability and make specific recommendations for the guarantee of ESR for those who are 'worst off'.

Britain's Equality and Human Rights Commission (EHRC) has developed a Methodology Framework for assessing the state of human rights and equality in Britain. It provides one possible model for NHRIs to monitor and comment on the state of a wide range of human rights in a society.

In its latest report, 'Is Britain Fairer? The State of Equality and Human Rights 2018', the EHRC presents a comprehensive picture on the state of equality and human rights in Britain.[61] The Methodology Framework developed by the EHRC consists of six major areas of life, each of which contains three 'core' indicators. The six areas are education, work, living standards, health, justice and personal security and participation. In some, there are supplementary indicators.

Within each indicator, the Measurement Framework identifies the 'structure', the 'process' and the 'outcomes'. The 'structure' relates to the laws affecting equality and human rights across Britain. The EHRC makes observations about the overall efficacy of this legal framework and considers where changes may be needed to ensure greater equality and better protection of human rights. The 'process' relates to the efforts that are being made by governments to effectively implement the obligations contained in human rights and equality standards, including the implementation and evaluation of public policies. In 'outcomes', the EHRC presents an analysis of the experiences and end results for individuals and groups in relation to the various indicators. This includes the outcomes for people with differently protected characteristics, people with certain combinations of protected characteristics and those 'at-risk' groups specified in the Measurement Framework.[62]

## 11.    NHRIS AND THE 'WORST OFF'

The Committee on Economic, Social and Cultural Rights has noted that a state where significant numbers are deprived of essential foodstuffs, of essential primary health care, of basic shelter and housing or of the most basic forms of education would prima facie be failing to discharge its obligations under the Covenant.[63]

Jurisprudence from some of the global courts, notably the Brazilian, Colombian, Indian, German and South African courts, has established that states cannot evade their 'basic' or 'minimum' obligations by pleading a lack of resources. Where groups are in a state of 'crisis' or 'vulnerability' then states are obliged to respond immediately. Although ESR entail the expenditure of resources, they also entail a threshold level below which state conduct cannot sink. Global jurisprudence also observes that the concept of progressive achievement encapsulated in these rights enables courts to monitor their realization over a period of time.[64]

---

[61]    'Is Britain Fairer? The State of Equality and Human Rights 2018' (June 2019) <www.equalityhumanrights.com/sites/default/files/is-britain-fairer-accessible.pdf>.

[62]    Ibid 272–76.

[63]    General Comment No 3, 1990.

[64]    See Mario Gomez, Conor Hartnett and Dinesha Samararatne, 'Constitutionalizing Economic and Social Rights in Sri Lanka', Centre for Policy Alternatives, Working Paper No 7 on Constitutional

These state obligations are discussed in Chapters 14 and 15. For example, the recent report by the British EHRC identifies certain vulnerable groups, including persons with disabilities, children in poverty, certain ethnic minorities and those in detention, where there has been a regression and the picture remains 'bleak'.[65]

These conceptual frameworks developed by domestic courts provide a strong impetus for NHRIs to demand similar standards of accountability from the state in their monitoring activities on policy and budgets. Where there is data and analysis from monitoring activities to support the conclusion that pockets of the population are being deprived of essential goods and services, which is in conflict with the idea of human dignity, the NHRI concerned should then be able to demand that the state in question act immediately to ameliorate this state of affairs. Given that poverty in its many variations is a feature of both the global north and global south, NHRIs may want to consider prioritizing the 'worst off' irrespective of the political context in which they work.

## 12.  NHRIS AND LITIGATION

In her recent report to the Human Rights Council, the Special Rapporteur on the Right to Housing makes the following observation:

> National human rights institutions should provide public legal education and assistance to rights claimants to access justice for the right to housing through all available mechanisms. They may assist rights holders to bring cases to courts or tribunals by initiating claims jointly with rights holders, by participating as third parties or amicus, by providing necessary evidence on systemic issues or by supervising the implementation of remedies. The Defensoría del Pueblo in Colombia has conducted site visits in order to hear directly from communities, forwarded information about systemic violations of the right to housing to municipal or national authorities and followed up with strategic litigation on the right to housing when necessary. The Scottish Human Rights Commission is playing a leading role in developing models for ensuring effective remedies for the right to housing and other socioeconomic rights.[66]

---

Reform, September 2016 <www.cpalanka.org> and Katie Boyle, *Models of Incorporation and Justiciability for Economic, Social and Cultural Rights* (Scottish Human Rights Commission 2018), Chief Justice Alejandro Linares, 'Colombian Constitutionalism: Judicial Review, Rights and Rule of Law', presented at the conference on 'Constitutional Review in Asia: Promoting Equality, Integrity and the Rule of Law', October 2018, International Centre for Ethnic Studies, Sri Lanka, on file with the author; Katharine G. Young, 'Constituting Economic and Social Rights' (Oxford University Press 2012); Magdalena Sepulveda, 'The Constitutional Court's Role in Addressing Social Injustice' in Malcolm Langford (ed.), *Social Rights Jurisprudence: Emerging Trends in International Law* (Cambridge University Press, 2008) 144.

[65]  Is Britain Fairer? The State of Equality and Human Rights 2018' (June 2019) <www .equalityhumanrights.com/sites/default/files/is-britain-fairer-accessible.pdf> at 8. See also Laurien J.L. Koster, 'Equal Treatment, an Effective Mechanism to Protect Human Rights in the Netherlands?' in Eva Brems, Gauthier de Beco and Wouter Vandenhole (eds) *National Human Rights Institutions and Economic, Social and Cultural Rights* (Intersentia 2013), 149–66.

[66]  'Access to justice for the right to housing', Report of the Special Rapporteur on adequate housing as a component of the right to an adequate standard of living, and on the right to non-discrimination in this context, A/HRC/40/61 at p.16.

Litigation provides the 'cutting edge' to human rights. Without legal remedies the notion of human rights would lose much of its potency. Litigation is one of the most effective ways of locating responsibility and accountability and then mobilizing for the realization of remedies. Litigation and interventions before administrative tribunals often provide the best way of delivering concrete outcomes for individuals and groups that are subject to violations of ESR. Litigation can also help develop an understanding of some difficult concepts. This is especially true when the litigation is participatory in nature and the court allows *amici curiae* to intervene. The willingness to resort to international and comparative material can help in clarifying issues and provide relevant analogies. Litigation can also help in raising awareness, provide a useful educational tool and prod policy reform.[67] One way of looking at litigation in the case of ESR is to think of adjudication as an institutional dialogue, where the court can order the legislature or executive to 'rethink' a flawed policy without necessarily declaring it void.[68]

An NHRI can support litigation for victims in several ways. First, it can provide legal advice and help a victim access legal or administrative remedies. This it could do by helping the victim petition in an appropriate court or administrative tribunal. Second, it can intervene strategically in significant cases as an *amicus curiae*. Third, it can initiate legal action on behalf of a victimized or vulnerable group on its own. This court action could emerge as a result of complaints the NHRI has received, as a result of surveys or research it has conducted or as a result of the public inquiries it has launched. Fourth, it may, in appropriate cases, initiate litigation to compel a public official to act in accordance with its recommendations. Fifth, the NHRI may monitor court orders, and in some cases the court may specifically request the NHRI to monitor a court decision.[69]

## 13.    TRANSNATIONAL DIALOGUE ACROSS NHRIS

One of the consequences of the growth of NHRIs has been the global and regional alliances that have emerged. Both the regional and global alliances, through the accreditation and other processes, have provided support to NHRIs in a variety of different ways. What has emerged is a transnational dialogue of NHRIs, speaking to each other and learning from each other,

---

[67]    See Mario Gomez, 'From Rhetoric to Realization: Delivering Socio-Economic Rights through Courts and Commissions' in C. Raj Kumar and D.K. Srivastava (eds) *Human Rights and Development: Law, Policy and Governance* (LexisNexis 2006) 65–94 and Open Society Foundations, 'Strategic Litigation Impacts: Insights from Global Experience' (2018), available at <www.opensocietyfoundations.org>.

[68]    As the Colombian, Indian and South African courts have done on several occasions. See *Aguero, Aurelio E v GCBA*, Buenos Aires Administrative Court of Appeals, December 2003 and *Occupiers of 51 Olivia Road, Berea Township and 197 Main Street, Johannesburg v City of Johannesburg and others*, CCT 24/07 and Gomez, Hartnett and Samararatne, 'Constitutionalizing Economic and Social Rights in Sri Lanka', Centre for Policy Alternatives, Working Paper No 7 on Constitutional Reform, September 2016 <www.cpalanka.org>.

[69]    See also the work of the Colombian *Defensoria del Pueblo*, and the *Argentinean Defensoria*, discussed in Allison Cockery and Duncan Wilson, 'Building Bridges: National Human Rights Institutions and Economic, Social and Cultural Rights' in Eibe Riedel, Gilles Giacca and Christophe Golay (eds) *Economic, Social, and Cultural Rights in International Law* (Oxford University Press 2014) 473, 480 and 484.

regionally and also globally. This dialogue, as it expands, has the potential to strengthen the work of NHRIs in implementing and advancing ESR.

## 14.   INSTITUTIONAL AND TRANSFORMATIVE IMPACTS

NHRIs rely on a number of factors to drive their impact.[70] Among them are the personality, the commitment and the dynamism of those at leadership level. All institutions, whether public, private or independent, rely on imaginative and creative leadership to drive transformative potential. Leaders of NHRIs will need not only to be dynamic in their thinking and independent in their approach, but also to show the capacity to engage astutely with political actors, the media and public opinion. The dynamism and skills of those at other tiers of the NHRI will also affect their performance. Societies that have undergone political transitions benefit from new appointments at the leadership level. Yet, transforming the culture at mid and lower levels can be a challenge, and internal organizational cultures and processes can display resistance to change, even if there is will at the leadership level.

The availability of adequate financial and human resources would also affect the impact that NHRIs can have. Control of financial resources is a way through which the legislature and executive can control the NHRIs, including the quality of human resources. The obligation of funding a NHRI should ideally lie with the state. In some cases, NHRIs have the capacity to access additional financial resources from international donors and private foundations.

The political culture and the democratic space that exists for NHRIs to operate will also drive impact. Clearly, a more tolerant political culture and open space for NHRIs to function will significantly enhance their impact. At moments of oppression, NHRIs will need to re-strategize and ensure that they prioritize those human rights issues that are under most threat.

Public benefit can drive the resilience, creativity and sustainability of NHRIs and independent commissions. Should NHRIs and other independent commissions begin to have a public impact and create tangible public benefit, this will add momentum to the work of these commissions, whether it be with regard to ESR or in other areas.[71] Public support for an NHRI can be crucial when the democratic space closes and in ensuring that these institutions stay resilient at times of political crisis.

An NHRI's relationship and engagement with civil society, and the space that civil society correspondingly has for influencing the work of NHRIs, will have an impact on the realization of ESR. Strong partnerships with civil society will ensure that NHRIs stay briefed on individual violations and systemic issues. Civil society partnerships will also help monitor and add pressure for implementation of NHRI recommendations to state entities. Partnerships will also drive innovative and bold interventions. Strong partnerships with civil society and public support for NHRIs would be important should democratic backsliding occur, helping them

---

[70]   See also Mario Gomez, 'The Right to Information and Transformative Development Outcomes' [2019] Law and Development Review 837 <https://doi.org/10.1515/ldr-2019-0046>.

[71]   See for example the work of the Sri Lankan Right to Information Commission and Mario Gomez, 'The Right to Information and Transformative Development Outcomes' [2019] Law and Development Review 837 <https://doi.org/10.1515/ldr-2019-0046>.

stay resilient. At these times of crisis and oppression, NHRIs benefit from support from civil society and the public to ensure that they remain robust and independent.

The connections and engagements NHRIs have with similar institutions from other parts of the world, whether it be NHRIs or other independent institutions, and with regional and global alliances will also help shape their work and practice, and provide support at moments of crisis.

Sri Lanka's brief experience with a right to information (RTI) legal regime illustrates two points that have relevance for NHRIs and independent institutions working on ESC in other parts of the world.[72] The RTI Commission established under the Sri Lankan legislation has endeavored to provide a fair hearing and to scrupulously observe the rules of natural justice in the appeals it has heard, which arise after the initial request for disclosure of information is refused by the public officer concerned. Second, it has balanced an adversarial and an engaging approach and in many orders has 'persuaded' state officials to disclose information that should be in the public domain.[73] An order from the Commission has provided cover for public officers who may have feared reprisals should they disclose information.[74]

## 15.    A LARGER INSTITUTIONAL DIALOGUE

This chapter has sought to ask if NHRIs and independent institutions can be transformative in their approach to ESR. The answer to this depends on whether NHRIs are willing to see themselves as one part of a larger institutional landscape that seeks transformation of social structures and inequalities through different methods and at different levels. The answer also depends on whether NHRIs are able to make optimum use of the broad range of strategies available to them, even if their legal mandate is ambiguous. An explicit statutory or constitutional mandate, as we have noted above, will no doubt assist these institutions.

The enforcement and realization of ESR call for a broad range of actions and interventions involving a number of different of state and non-state actors. NHRIs, because of the capacity they have to engage in a broad range of interventions, their location between state and civil society, their capacity to engage with both state and civil society organizations and their constitutional or statutory mandate, are uniquely placed to intervene to advance ESR. The effectiveness of NHRIs will be constrained by limits to financial and human resources, the political context and priorities of the state in which they operate, and by persons in positions of leadership within the institutions. Yet, within those parameters, NHRIs possess an ability to unleash a momentum that can generate tangible outcomes around ESR, including for those in particularly vulnerable situations.

---

[72]    See the Right to Information Act, No 12 of 2016 and Article 14A of the Sri Lankan Constitution, introduced by the Nineteenth Amendment to the Constitution in 2015. See also RTI Commission of Sri Lanka, 'Selected Orders of the Right to Information Commission of Sri Lanka 2017–2018' (February 2019) <www.rticommission.lk/ web/images/pdf/books/selected-orders-of-the-rtic-06032019.pdf> and Kishali Pinto-Jayawardena (ed), *Reflections on Sri Lanka's RTI Act & RTI Regime* (Right to Information Commission of Sri Lanka 2019).

[73]    Mario Gomez, 'The Right to Information and Transformative Development Outcomes' [2019] Law and Development Review 837 <https://doi.org/10.1515/ldr-2019-0046>.

[74]    Ibid.

The work of NHRIs should be viewed as one part of a wider legal and political strategy for the realization of ESR. It is one part of a larger process of rights implementation. This strategy encompasses the courts, other independent institutions, the legislature, the executive, international and domestic civil society and international human rights processes. This strategy may require NHRIs to be confrontational at moments and engaging at other moments. It may require NHRIs to suspend remedies and allow the executive and legislature time to modify policies and practice. At other times it may require the NHRI to hold that there have been violations of ESR or help victims access remedies before courts or administrative tribunals. A larger institutional dialogue will also help maintain institutional resilience at times of political crisis and democratic push-back. For NHRIs, being transformative will require a vision and a plan of action that encompasses strategic engagement, principled decision-making and creative interventions.

# 17. Economic policy and human rights
*Radhika Balakrishnan and James Heintz*

## 1.    INTRODUCTION

Economics and human rights are intimately connected. The policy choices made by a government affect both directly and indirectly the enjoyment of rights within that country's borders and, increasingly, in other countries. Yet economic policies are routinely formulated and implemented without any concern for their impact on human rights. Moreover, human rights experts and advocates often focus primarily on the more readily defined legal dimensions of rights and do not adequately consider human rights obligations in the context of economics. This is particularly true for macroeconomic policies – areas such as government spending, tax systems, debt management, monetary policy, and financial regulation.

This chapter examines how a human rights framework giving due regard to economic, social and cultural rights (ESCR) can be applied to assess and evaluate economic policies. The chapter begins with a consideration of the ethical basis of the dominant approach to economic thinking and contrasts this with what human rights has to offer. It then shows how various human rights obligations and principles could be applied to economic policy. To make the discussion more concrete, a number of macroeconomic policy areas are considered: government spending, taxation, deficit spending and debt, and monetary policy. Globalization presents challenges to both economic policy formulation and the human rights framework. Therefore, the chapter concludes with a discussion of extraterritorial obligations (ETOs) and their implications for economic policy.

## 2.    A NORMATIVE FRAMEWORK FOR ECONOMICS

The human rights approach provides a normative framework for evaluating economic policies and assessing their outcomes. It represents an alternative to the ethical foundation of the dominant theoretical framework in economics, neoclassical economics, which is based on the ability of individuals to make choices that maximize their own individual happiness or satisfaction, termed 'utility'. Because neoclassical economics typically assumes that utility cannot be compared across individuals, the ethical consequences of distributive outcomes receive scant attention. Unless it is assumed that everyone has identical preferences, the utility of the rich cannot be directly compared to the utility of the poor. All that concerns neoclassical economics is that individuals are able to make the best choices for themselves. Because of this, competitive markets are often considered the best institutional arrangements for producing desired social outcomes. They are assumed to support individual choice and free exchange, allowing individuals to optimize their utility without worrying about the utility of others. Other institutions that interfere with the operation of markets are then viewed as compromising these ideal outcomes. For instance, within the neoclassical framework, government actions are frequently seen to 'distort' the operation of markets.[1]

However, markets frequently fail to produce idealized outcomes. The 2008 global financial crisis represents an example of the limits of relying on deregulated markets. Markets play a potentially important role in coordinating economic activity to produce the goods and services one needs and wants. But they do not do so equitably. Left on their own, markets may generate undesirable outcomes with no tendency to correct these problems – widespread unemployment, insufficient income to meet basic needs for a sizable share of the population, environmental degradation, economic crises, and growing inequality, to name a few. The ethical framework of neoclassical economics is often insufficient to reflect these enormously important social concerns.[2]

Furthermore, the dominant economic theories neglect many aspects of our economies that affect people's lives. Because of its narrow focus on markets, economics relies on variables that capture this single dimension, and assign values based on prices and the process of market exchange. One of the most widely used indicators for judging economic performance is gross domestic product (GDP) – the sum of the market value of all newly produced goods and services within an economy over a specified period of time. But GDP excludes many activities essential for the sustained functioning of our economies – such as the unpaid work parents perform in raising the next generation. Pollution that harms the environment and people's health is rarely counted. This can produce perverse outcomes in which productive activities that harm the environment actually raise GDP. Some things which people value highly, such as their friendships and meaningful relationships, do not have market prices. If they were exchanged on markets, the nature of these relationships would be transformed and corrupted.

For these reasons, a different normative and ethical framework is needed. The human rights framework represents such an alternative. It goes beyond market transactions and stresses a broader range of objectives and outcomes that have the potential to increase the substantive freedoms and choices people enjoy in their lives. The goals of social justice are expressed in terms of the realization of rights – both civil and political rights and economic, social and cultural rights (ESCR). These rights include the right to food, the right to work, the right to an adequate standard of living, the right to housing, and the right to education, among others. Instead of focusing narrowly on self-regarding measurements of welfare, the human rights approach allows for a complex interaction between individual rights, collective rights, and collective action. It sees policy as a social and political process that should conform to human rights standards, not a purely technocratic exercise. Instead of prioritizing a single institutional approach (for example, free markets), the human rights approach allows for institutional pluralism. It incorporates an understanding of the paradoxical character of governments, recognizing that states can both enable and deny social justice, and that individuals need protection against misuse of state power, as well as requiring the power of the state to be harnessed to realize their rights.[3]

---

[1]   Radhika Balakrishnan and Diane Elson, 'Introduction: Economic Policies and Human Rights Obligations' in Radhika Balakrishnan and Diane Elson (eds), *Economic Policy and Human Rights: Holding Governments to Account* (Zed Books 2011) 128.

[2]   Radhika Balakrishnan, James Heintz and Diane Elson, *Rethinking Economic Policy for Social Justice: The Radical Potential of Human Rights* (Routledge 2016) 32–39.

[3]   Ibid 5–6.

## 3.   THE RELATIONSHIP BETWEEN ECONOMIC POLICIES AND HUMAN RIGHTS

Economic policies have significant impacts on the realization of human rights. However, human rights activists, experts, and practitioners usually fail to grapple with how the development and implementation of economic policies impact on the achievement of those rights. For instance, macroeconomic policies shape the environment within which rights are realized. They affect the resources available to governments for fulfilling and protecting rights. They influence the availability of paid employment and people's living standards. They mediate the enjoyment of rights such as the right to housing. The relationship between human rights and economic policy runs in both directions. Human rights provide an ethical framework for evaluating economic policies. But an understanding of economic policies is also essential for the realization of rights.[4] For the purposes of this discussion, this section of the chapter focuses on those obligations which have the most direct relevance for economic policy. Human rights obligations entail three specific duties with respect to economic and social rights (ESR), as elaborated by the United Nations (UN) Committee on Economic, Social, and Cultural Rights (CESCR), based on the Maastricht Guidelines on Violations of Economic, Social, and Cultural Rights of 1997 (Maastricht Guidelines). These are: the obligation to respect rights; the obligation to protect rights; and the obligation to fulfill rights.[5] *The obligation to respect rights* requires states to refrain from interfering with the enjoyment of ESR. For example, the state will have failed to comply with its obligation to respect the right to housing if it engages in arbitrary forced evictions. *The obligation to protect rights* requires states to prevent violations of such rights by third parties. Therefore, a state's failure to ensure that private employers comply with basic labor standards may amount to a failure to meet its obligations to protect the right to work or the right to just and favorable conditions of work. *The obligation to fulfill rights* is understood by the CESCR as being composed of three elements – to facilitate, provide, and promote rights. It requires states to take appropriate legislative, administrative, budgetary, judicial, and other measures toward the full realization of such rights. Thus, the failure of states to provide essential primary health care to those in need may amount to a violation.

With regard to economic policy, the obligations to fulfill and protect are of particular importance. The obligation to fulfill implies that governments should formulate economic policies so that their policy choices support the realization of rights over time. For instance, budget cuts to key government programs could undermine the obligation to fulfill. The obligation to protect implies a duty to regulate the economy in such a way as to prevent individuals, corporations, and institutions from taking actions that threaten people's rights.[6]

Furthermore, each of these three core obligations has two dimensions as discussed in the Maastricht Guidelines: the obligation of conduct, which requires that states make efforts to comply with the human rights standard in question, and the obligation of result, which requires

---

[4]   See generally, Balakrishnan and Elson (n 1).

[5]   Maastricht Guidelines on Violations of Economic, Social, and Cultural Rights (Maastricht, Netherlands, 22–26 January 1997) part II para 6.

[6]   Radhika Balakrishnan and James Heintz, 'Human Rights Dimensions of Fiscal and Monetary Policies: United States' in Radhika Balakrishnan and Diane Elson (eds), *Economic Policy and Human Rights: Holding Governments to Account* (Zed Books 2011) 52–73.

that states show progress in meeting the standard in terms of actual realized outcomes. The Guidelines explain these obligations in the following terms:

> The obligation of *conduct* requires action reasonably calculated to realize the enjoyment of a particular right. In the case of the right to health, for example, the obligation of conduct could involve the adoption and implementation of a plan of action to reduce maternal mortality. The obligation of *result* requires states to achieve specific targets to satisfy a detailed substantive standard. With respect to the right to health, for example, the obligation of result requires the reduction of maternal mortality to levels agreed at the 1994 Cairo International Conference on Population and Development and the 1995 Beijing Fourth World Conference on Women.[7]

With regard to economic policy, an assessment of the obligation of conduct would look at the policy choices made and whether these decisions are consistent with the realization of rights. For instance, adopting financial regulations to minimize the risk of a crisis that would lead to widespread unemployment represents conduct on the part of the state aimed at protecting rights. However, the adoption of policies does not guarantee that the desired outcomes are always forthcoming. Therefore, it is also important to examine results. Does increased spending on reproductive health services for women (conduct) actually lead to lower maternal mortality rates (result)?[8]

A number of key principles underscore the duties of governments to take actions consistent with the realization of ESR. These principles also apply to economic policies. They include: progressive realization and non-retrogression; the use of maximum of available resources; non-discrimination and equality; minimum core obligations; and accountability, transparency, and participation.[9]

The International Covenant on Economic Social and Cultural Rights (ICESCR),[10] Article 2, specifies that states parties have the obligation of 'achieving progressively the full realization of the rights recognized in the present Covenant to the maximum of available resources'. This obligation recognizes that the resources at the disposition of a government are limited, and that fulfilling ESR takes time. Despite these constraints, this principle establishes that the realization of human rights is an unavoidable obligation and governments must take steps towards the full realization of rights. Policy-makers cannot defer human rights responsibilities to a later, imaginary date, when conditions may be more favorable.[11]

---

[7]  Maastricht Guidelines (n 5) para 7.

[8]  Radhika Balakrishnan and Diane Elson, 'Auditing Economic Policy in the Light of Obligations on Economic and Social Rights' (2008) 5(1) Essex Human Rights Review 1, 3–4.

[9]  Ibid 5–9.

[10]  Adopted 16 December 1966, entered into force 3 January 1976, 993 UNTS 3.

[11]  International Covenant on Economic, Social and Cultural Rights (ICESCR) (1966). Office of the High Commissioner for Human Rights <www.ohchr.org/EN/ProfessionalInterest/Pages/CESCR.aspx>. Progressive realization imposes a 'specific and continuing' (CESCR, General Comment No. 12: The Right to Adequate Food (12 May 1999) E/C.12/1999/5 para 44) or 'constant and continuing' (CESCR, General Comment No. 15: The Right to Water (20 January 2003) E/C.12/2002/11 para 18) duty to move as 'expeditiously and effectively as possible' (CESCR, General Comment No. 3 para 9; CESCR, General Comment No. 12 para 44; CESCR, General Comment No. 15 para 18) towards full realization of rights for men and women. These steps toward full realization of rights must be 'taken within a reasonable short time after the Covenant's entry into force for the States concerned' and such steps should be 'deliberate, concrete and targeted as clearly as possible' in order to meet the obligations of States (CESCR, General Comment No. 3: The Nature of State Parties' Obligations (14 December 1990) E/1991/23 para 2;

Related to the principle of progressive realization is that of non-retrogression. The principle of non-retrogression implies that once a certain level of enjoyment of a right is achieved, that right should not be taken away or the level of realization reduced. There may be extraordinary situations, outside of a government's control, when retrogression is unavoidable. But any action that leads to retrogression must be subject to scrutiny. The CESCR has stated in its General Comment No. 3 that there is a strong presumption that actions by the government that lead to a deterioration in the enjoyment of ESR are not permitted: 'Moreover, any deliberately retrogressive measures in that regard would require the most careful consideration and would need to be fully justified by reference to the totality of the rights provided for in the Covenant and in the context of the full use of the maximum available resources.'[12]

Following from this, Article 2(1) of the ICESCR also includes the idea of 'the maximum of available resources'. The principle of maximum available resources mandates that governments must fully use the resources at their disposal in the pursuit of human rights goals. This does not mean governments must abandon the everyday tasks of governing to focus exclusively on human rights. But it does mean that policies intended to preserve and enhance human rights must be a fully developed and well-integrated part of every government's larger governing agenda and be supported by the allocation of necessary resources as a matter of priority. The principle of maximum available resources applies to all resources available to the government, including financial and economic resources.

The definition of maximum available resources has not yet been fully elaborated by the CESCR.[13] The Committee has clarified that 'the phrase "to the maximum of its available resources" was intended ... to refer to both the resources existing within a State and those available from the international community'.[14] Since it is impossible to take steps toward the progressive realization of human rights without resources, the maximum available resources obligation is both a protect- and fulfill-bound obligation.[15] The concept of maximum available resources requires further development in order to demonstrate that governments must mobilize resources, not simply administer existing resources, in order to meet human rights obligations. In other words, the resources available to governments for the realization of rights are not fixed or arbitrary. They are themselves the outcome of deliberate policy choices, institutional arrangement, and power dynamics within national and global economies.

Budget decisions and taxation are the policy areas that are most obviously relevant to claims based on the principle of maximum available resources. But there are other areas, in addition to government spending and taxation, which affect the resources available to government to support the realization of rights. These include development assistance, debt and deficit financing, and monetary policies. For these reasons, maximum available resources should be examined in terms of five types of policy: (i) government expenditure; (ii) government

---

CESCR, General Comment No. 12 para 43; CESCR, General Comment No. 14: The Right to the Highest Attainable Standard of Health (11 August 2000) 12/2000/4 para 30; CESCR, General Comment No. 15 para 17). See Chapters 13 and 14 of this book.

[12]   CESCR, General Comment No. 3 (n 11) para 9.

[13]   See Chapter 14 of this book for a description of the Committee's commentary and jurisprudence on this issue.

[14]   See CESCR, General Comment No. 3 (n 11) para 13.

[15]   Radhika Balakrishnan, Diane Elson, and Raj Patel, 'Rethinking Macroeconomic Strategies from a Human Rights Perspective' (2010) 53(1) Development 27–36.

revenue; (iii) development assistance; (iv) debt and deficit financing; and (v) monetary policy and financial regulation.[16]

The principle of non-discrimination and equality further informs how a government's duties with respect to human rights must be carried out. The Universal Declaration of Human Rights (UDHR),[17] Article 2, duplicated in the ICESCR and other human rights treaties, states: 'Everyone is entitled to all the rights and freedoms set forth in this Declaration without distinction of any kind, such as race, colour, sex, language, religion, political or other opinion, national or social origin, property, birth or other status.' The principle of non-discrimination and equality, applied to the rights outlined in the ICESCR, requires more than just legal recognition. It demands that resources be channeled to support the equal enjoyment of rights for marginalized or particularly oppressed groups.[18]

In addition to non-discrimination across socially constructed groups, the human rights framework prioritizes vulnerable individuals, those whose enjoyment of rights falls below a basic standard of decency, for special attention. Governments that are parties to the ICESCR are under a 'minimum core' obligation to ensure the satisfaction of, at the very least, 'minimum essential levels of each of the rights' in the ICESCR. This means that it is the duty of the state to prioritize the rights of the poorest and most vulnerable. The CESCR has clarified the meaning of minimum core levels:

> A minimum core obligations to ensure the satisfaction of, at the very least, minimum essential levels of each rights is incumbent on each State party. Thus, for example, a state party in which any significant number of individuals is deprived of essential foodstuffs, of essential primary health care, of basic housing and shelter or of the most basic forms of education is, prima facie, failing to discharge its obligation under the Covenant.[19]

Finally, the principle of accountability, participation, and transparency means that governments are obliged to provide mechanisms through which people can hold the state accountable, can participate in policy making, and can access the information required to do so. This requires that all economic policy measures be transparent, involve participation of the public, and be accountable in terms of fulfilling economic social and cultural rights. The focus on accountability, participation and transparency implies well-informed democratic processes, grounded in human rights law, to evaluate policy options. Policies that are set, for example, with no consultation or participation, or which only benefit a few rich people, violate this principle.[20]

---

[16]    Radhika Balakrishnan, Diane Elson, James Heintz and Nicholas Lusiani, 'Maximum Available Resources & Human Rights: Analytical Report' (Center for Women's Global Leadership, Rutgers University 2011) 5.

[17]    Adopted 10 December 1948, A/810 at 71.

[18]    CESCR, General Comment No. 20: Non-Discrimination in Economic, Social and Cultural Rights (2 July 2009) E/C.12/GC/20 paras 13 and 34.

[19]    CESCR, General Comment No. 3 (n 11) para 10. The Committee has clarified that this is a continuing obligation, requiring states with inadequate resources to strive to insure enjoyment of rights (at para 11). However, even in times of severe resource constraints, states must insure that rights are fulfilled for vulnerable members of society through the adoption of relatively low-cost targeted programs (at para 12; see also General Comment No. 12 (n 11) para 28, General Comment No. 14 (n 11) paras 18 and 48, and General Comment No. 15 (n 11) para 40).

[20]    Balakrishnan and Elson (n 1).

# 4. APPLYING HUMAN RIGHTS TO SPECIFIC MACROECONOMIC POLICIES

These aspects of the human rights framework – the obligations to respect, fulfill, and protect; the obligations of conduct and result; and the principles of progressive realization, non-retrogression, maximum of available resources, non-discrimination and equality, minimum core obligations, and accountability, participation, and transparency – can be used to evaluate and assess economic policies and their outcomes. To demonstrate how the human rights approach can be applied to economic policies, this section of the chapter considers a number of areas of macroeconomic policy, including government spending, taxation, debt management, and monetary policies.

## 4.1 Government Spending

The obligation to fulfill human rights specifically requires governments to take appropriate budgetary measures to support the progressive realization of rights. How governments spend the financial resources at their disposal represents a critical dimension of budget policies. At the most basic level, governments should not spend money in ways that violate the obligation to ensure human rights. Beyond this, budget allocations should be made in such a way as to promote the enjoyment of human rights.

There are three central aspects of government expenditures relevant for the realization of rights: first, the overall size of government spending; second, the allocation of expenditures to specific areas within the budget; and third, the effective use of those resources to support desired outcomes, such as ensuring access to better education, health, and housing. Governments get the resources available to finance expenditures from government revenues, in most cases through taxation, and from public borrowing. Taxation and public debt will be discussed later. This section focuses on the allocation of those financial resources and whether budget allocations translate into meaningful outcomes with respect to the realization of rights.[21]

A human rights audit of government spending decisions should consider both the obligation of conduct and that of result. With regard to the obligation of conduct, the audit should examine the budgetary allocation of spending to areas that support the realization of specific rights, given the total amount of resources available. Do budget allocations adequately support health, education, income transfers to low income households, housing policy, to give a few examples? Have these allocations been rising or falling over time? Are these allocations similar to other countries that possess comparable public resources? In addition, expenditures in areas that do not support rights, such as military spending or supporting benefits for special interest groups, need to be analyzed when determining whether governments are using the maximum of available resources. Furthermore, when considering the resources available to realize rights, it is important not to limit the analysis of public expenditures to social spending, since the realization of some ESR, such as the right to work, requires an examination of other areas of spending: for example, is financing available for needed public investments?[22]

---

[21]  Balakrishnan and Elson (n 8) 11–14.
[22]  Ibid 11–14.

With regard to the obligation of result, analysis of government spending should identify indicators that demonstrate whether changes in spending actually translate into realized outcomes. Examples of such indicators could include the share of the population with access to healthcare, child mortality rates, educational attainment or school enrollment rates, and actual delivery of physical infrastructure. In some cases, it may be difficult to attribute a particular change in spending to an identified outcome. For example, numerous factors determine the overall unemployment rate, not simply budget policy. However, a comparison of conduct and result can reveal potential areas of concern. If maternal mortality rates increase despite more spending on health services, it suggests a potential problem.[23]

Government spending can be evaluated with respect to other human rights principles, such as non-discrimination and equality. Take the human right to education as an example. The distribution of education spending should not allocate more funds per student or child to more privileged groups than to disadvantaged groups. In addition, spending allocations can be cross-checked with the educational attainment of different social groups. If it is found that educational outcomes of the group with the lowest share of expenditure are worse than those groups with higher shares of expenditure, this suggests that the government may be in violation of its obligation of result.[24]

To satisfy the principle of accountability, transparency, and participation with respect to government spending, states must make relevant data available to the public at large and must be held accountable through a process of popular participation and control. Identifying conduct violations is straightforward in this instance: are relevant data (such as rates of government expenditure, detailed demographic data, and so on) freely available? Are there routines and procedures in place to ensure an appropriate level of accountability through participation?[25]

## 4.2   Taxation[26]

Governments obtain revenue from numerous sources, but taxation is usually the most important. Since these resources are essential for governments to fulfill and protect rights, taxation is a critical aspect of the principle of using the maximum of available resources. Governments have an obligation of conduct to introduce and implement tax laws and systems of tax administration that are capable of generating sufficient revenue for realization of human rights. These tax policies must comply with other human rights obligations, such as non-discrimination, transparency, accountability, and participation. Poor administration of the tax system, that allows significant evasion and avoidance from wealthy persons, businesses, and organizations, should be understood as a failure to comply with human rights obligations.

The obligation of conduct is particularly important for the evaluation of tax policies. For example, if tax revenue as a share of GDP is low compared to other similar countries with comparable economic structures and tax administration is poor, with significant leakages due

---

[23]   Ibid 3–4.

[24]   Ibid 11–12.

[25]   Balakrishnan and Elson (n 1) 1-28.

[26]   For examples of a thorough explanation of tax policy in the US and Mexico, see Lourdes Colinas and Roberto Constantino, 'Taxation and Economic and Social Rights in Mexico' in Balakrishnan and Elson (eds) (n 1) 131–53, and Radhika Balakrishnan, 'Taxation and Economic and Social Rights in USA' in Balakrishnan and Elson (eds) (n 1) 153–75.

to tax evasion and avoidance, this indicates that governments may not be taking adequate steps to mobilize domestic resources to support the realization of ESR. With improvements in tax policy and administration, governments could increase the resources at their disposal and move closer to achieving the maximum of available resources.

Raising the amount of revenue collected may require a combination of increasing tax rates, introducing new taxes, and improving tax collection. Tax avoidance and evasion lead to substantial loss of revenue for governments. Bribery and corruption of tax officials are also common problems in many countries, leading to significant leakages and an inability to mobilize the maximum resources possible.

The obligation of result is also pertinent for the evaluation of tax policy. For example, tax systems can impact the distribution of income, with implications for the realization of rights. Some types of taxes, such as income tax, are designed to be progressive, with the higher income groups paying a larger share of the income in income tax than the lower income groups. However, recently in many countries, there has been greater reliance on indirect taxes, and these tend to be more regressive (that is, less progressive). Specifically, the importance of value added taxes (VAT) has increased. While VAT may represent an effective way for government to mobilize revenue, these and similar taxes tend to be regressive, since low income households and individuals spend a much larger share of their income on consumption and therefore pay a larger share of their income in VAT than those with higher incomes. If a regressive tax system impairs the actual enjoyment of rights, it represents a problem with regard to the obligation of result. Similarly, there is a need to ask if the share of revenue coming from corporate profits has fallen and that coming from individuals has risen, and if tax on the incomes of the wealthy has fallen, relative to the tax burden of low- and middle-income people and households. These shifts in tax burdens may have implications for the realization of rights.

The principle of non-discrimination is relevant for evaluating tax policy from a human rights perspective. Consider gender inequality. The system of personal income tax may create a disincentive for married women to participate in the labor market because the tax is levied on married couples through a joint-filing system, on their joint income. Insofar as married women tend to be the secondary earners in the household, this means that they face a higher effective tax rate on the first dollar they earn than they would face as an individual, because their earnings are added to those of their spouse.

To satisfy the principle of accountability, participation, and transparency, tax policy must be determined through a democratic process that is accountable to the needs of everyone, including the poorest and most vulnerable members of society. This process must include mechanisms for democratic majorities both to remove onerous tax burdens on some income and wealth groups, and to levy taxes on others. Decisions about tax law at every level – and significantly at the municipal level, in the case of preferential tax policies that are offered to entice large investors —must be made in a transparent manner, and must be subject to popular review and redress of grievances.[27]

---

[27]    Balakrishnan and Elson (n 1) 1–28.

**4.3   Deficit Spending and Debt**

Total government spending is not limited to the revenues available in a particular budgetary period. When government spending exceeds total government revenue within a particular budget, governments borrow to make up the difference. The amount governments borrow to finance current budget expenditures is the budget deficit. A common way that governments borrow is by selling bonds to investors. The buyers of bonds effectively lend money to the government. The terms of repayment depend on the type of bonds issued. However, governments may also borrow by taking loans from other governments, commercial banks, and international financial institutions such as the International Monetary Fund and the World Bank. To adequately assess fiscal policy using a human rights lens, debts and deficits must be taken into account.

It is important to recognize the difference between budget deficits and the accumulated public debt. Deficits represent how much is borrowed to cover the gap between revenues and expenditures in a particular budget. The total outstanding amount owed to bondholders and other creditors, is the public debt. The public debt represents a claim on future budgets as the interest and principal of the debt has to be paid. These payments, based on the nature of the underlying debt, are called debt servicing costs.

On the one hand, borrowing increases the resources available to government. But since deficit spending incurs debt servicing costs, large debt burdens may compromise future spending. Therefore, the principle of maximum of available resource must be considered over time, not restricted to a single snapshot at a given moment.

Creditors typically represent the short-side of the market, since they control access to scarce financial resources and demand for loans frequently exceeds supply. The threat of withholding access to financial resources, and the ability to demand repayment on specified terms, gives lenders power over borrowers. Debt becomes a disciplinary device that can be used to shape government policy, reinforce global dependencies, and restructure economies. To give a concrete example, the sovereign debt crisis that enveloped a number of European countries, including Greece, Ireland, and Portugal, led to a series of bailouts to stabilize the afflicted economies. However, these bailout packages included conditionalities that supported the adoption of austerity policies. National economic policies were, to varying degrees, dictated by the bond holders.

For these reasons, debt may either facilitate or, ultimately, undermine the realization of rights. Two key questions arise when considering whether borrowing might positively or negatively affect human rights. First, to what extent are the expenditures financed through borrowing actually contributing to the better enjoyment of rights? If the financial resources are directed towards other uses, the need for borrowing should be questioned. Second, will those expenditures raise the productive capacity of an economy in such a way as to generate future income that can be used to repay the debt? Borrowing can have a positive impact on the aggregate income in an economy if it is invested in ways that increase productive capacity, through investment in physical and human resources, such as transportation infrastructure, education and sustaining a productive work force.[28]

---

[28]   Balakrishnan, Heintz and Elson (n 2) 69–73.

Government spending may also be necessary to prop up an economy during recessions or crises. When private incomes and spending collapse, the performance of the market economy is undermined. During hard times, governments can borrow to pay unemployment insurance benefits, increase direct spending on social services and infrastructure, and maintain public employment. In this way, deficit spending helps to prevent retrogression with regard to human rights. Applying human rights principles to deficit spending suggests that fiscal policy should be counter-cyclical rather than pro-cyclical, expanding aggregate demand in a downturn and contracting it in an upturn.

To assess whether a state is satisfying the obligation of conduct with regard to the principle of equality and non-discrimination, one should ask if a government's willingness to borrow is disproportionately helping or harming particular income or identity groups. For example, if the state refuses to borrow funds for the purpose of rebuilding infrastructure and assisting in population recovery after a traumatic weather event, one might ask whether a particular demographic is disproportionately harmed by that weather event, and so disproportionately suffers from the government's unwillingness to borrow. If one determines that the government previously borrowed to assist in the recovery from similar events, one must then ask which demographic group, if any, benefited from that former willingness to borrow, and whether the different response to a more recent event may be linked to the disadvantaged or marginalized status of those affected.[29]

## 4.4   Monetary Policy

Monetary policy refers to decisions taken by the monetary authority, most often a central bank, that influence the money supply, credit, interest rates, and exchange rates in an economy. By impacting on the supply of money and credit, monetary policy has the potential to affect purchasing power, the overall level of demand, and the available monetary resources. Monetary policy also influences key prices that affect the distribution of income and resources. Interest rates represent a transfer of money from borrowers to lenders. Exchange rates influence the degree to which tradable sectors (such as exporters and business that compete with imports) are favored relative to non-tradable sectors (such as sectors that are relatively unaffected by global competition).

There is a division within economics concerning the impact of monetary policy. Some economists subscribe to the idea of the 'neutrality of money'. According to this viewpoint, changes in the money supply only affect the average price level and inflation. They do not affect the real economy with regard to output, real income (that is, income adjusted by the average price level), and employment. Basing monetary policy on this view, many central banks focus primarily, or even exclusively, on maintaining very low rates of inflation.

However, others argue that monetary policy affects both the real and the money economies. Lower interest rates may encourage private sector investment and expand the economy's capacity to produce goods and services and create jobs. A large supply of credit encourages consumers to spend more, helping to stimulate production of goods and services. A more competitive exchange rate allows exports to expand their markets and grow. Moreover, lower

---

[29]   Balakrishnan and Elson (n 8) 14–16.

interest rates can reduce the debt servicing costs on the public debt and make fiscal policies more sustainable.

When monetary policy has real economic impacts, it will also affect the environment in which ESR are realized. This suggests that the actions of central banks in the conduct of monetary policy constitute a potentially important aspect of the obligation to fulfill. It also implies that central banks, within a human rights framework, need to consider trade-offs that could lead to retrogression. For instance, overly aggressive anti-inflation policies that drive up unemployment rates could represent retrogression with regard to the right to work.

In a globalized economy, in which international financial markets have been liberalized, many governments face constraints in using monetary policy to affect real economic outcomes. A government that expands the money supply and lowers interest rates may experience financial outflows, as investors seek higher returns in other financial markets. This could have unintended consequences for domestic financial markets. In contrast, countries that raise interest rates to achieve low inflation may attract inflows of short-term financial investment. These inflows can lead to an overvalued exchange rate, hurting businesses and workers in exporting or import-competing sectors. These cross-border financial flows increase the complexity of monetary policy decisions and may constrain the choices available to central banks.[30]

The principle of non-discrimination is rarely applied to monetary policies. However, monetary policies that operate with disinflationary bias may have negative consequences for employment and an adequate standard of living and may adversely affect particular groups. It would be a mistake to think that unfavorable consequences are neutral to race, ethnicity, or gender. Studies have shown that disinflationary policies in industrial and developing countries result in women and racial or ethnic minorities paying disproportionately for monetary policies that adversely affect employment.[31]

The obligation to protect also must be considered. Compliance with human rights obligations and principles suggests a need to adequately regulate financial markets and adopt more measured responses to financial crises. For instance, deregulation of financial markets allowed global investors to take decisions that led to the 2008 global financial crisis. The outcome of the crisis in many countries has been a retrogression of ESR. The lack of any systematic mortgage regulation in the US markets, which allowed predatory lending to flourish, also represents a failure with regard to the obligation to protect and, given the demographics of those caught up in the subprime mortgage crisis – mostly people of color and women – a violation of the principle of nondiscrimination and equality. Similarly, the use of resources by governments and central banks to bail out financial institutions, and the subsequent imposition of austerity budgets without demanding greater accountability of the rescued banks and investment firms, could be said to violate the principle of maximum available resources, along with a number of other human rights principles.

The principle of maximum available resources could be used to justify reform that requires financial institutions to support the progressive realization of economic rights, since the

---

[30] Radhika Balakrishnan and James Heintz, 'Human Rights Dimensions of Fiscal and Monetary Policies: United States' in Balakrishnan and Elson (eds) (n 1) 52–73.

[31] See generally: Elissa Braunstein and James Heintz, 'Gender Bias and Central Bank Policy: Employment and Inflation Reduction' (2008) 22(2) International Journal of Applied Economics 173–86; Stephanie Seguino and James Heintz, 'Monetary Tightening and the Dynamics of U.S. Race and Gender Stratification' (2012) 71(3) American Journal of Economics and Sociology 603–38.

'available resources' include the credit and monetary systems. This could be achieved, for example, by requiring banks to provide credit to populations shut out of financial services on favorable terms or by regulating the extension of credit so that a portion of loans supports affordable housing, health care facilities, or investments that generate jobs in areas of high unemployment. Recognition of ESR as entitlements that the state must defend would alter, at least to some extent, the power dynamics in credit markets. For these reasons, the human rights framework suggests a fundamentally different approach to monetary policy and financial governance.[32]

## 5.    ECONOMIC POLICY AND HUMAN RIGHTS IN A GLOBALIZED WORLD[33]

This chapter has argued that applying a human rights approach to economic policy provides a framework for evaluating and assessing policy choices that differs markedly from the way in which standard economic theory judges the desirability of the decisions taken and their associated realized outcomes. However, there are important challenges that must be addressed when applying human rights to the analysis of economic policies. In recent decades, the economies of the world have become increasingly interconnected. What happens in one economy has spill-over effects on other countries. As already noted, financial flows across borders may limit policy options and affect the outcomes of choices made. Today's corporations operate in many countries simultaneously and move operations and activities between their affiliates. Production processes are fragmented, with different stages of production scattered across a variety of countries.

The growing integration of the world's economies means that actions taken by one government affect the economic environment elsewhere, with important implications for the realization of rights. These new realities create significant challenges for governments with regard to fulfilling their obligations to support the realization of human rights. But they also present challenges to the human rights framework. Within the human rights approach, the state is the primary duty bearer and consideration of obligations and principles centers on the national level – the duties governments have for respecting, protecting, and fulfilling rights within their borders. This leaves open the question of how to deal with the interrelationships between national economies and the actions of transnational actors.

The idea of ETOs is one approach for addressing these challenges. Within the human rights approach, ETOs refer to acts and omissions of a government that affect the enjoyment of rights outside of the state's own territory.[34] Given the current interdependencies that characterize the process of globalization, the question of ETOs is central to understanding the barriers to realizing human rights and suggests ways of expanding the human rights framework to take on these

---

[32]    See generally, James Heintz and Radhika Balakrishnan, 'Debt, Power, and Crisis: Social Stratification and the Inequitable Governance of Financial Markets' (2012) 64(3) American Quarterly 387–409.

[33]    See Balakrishnan, Heintz and Elson (n 2) chapter 7 for further elaboration on this.

[34]    Maastricht Principles on Extraterritorial Obligations of States in the Area of Economic, Social, and Cultural Rights (2012) <www.etoconsortium.org/nc/en/main-navigation/library/maastricht-principles/?tx_drblob_pi1%5BdownloadUid%5D=23> (Maastricht ETO Principles).

international dynamics. This idea is not new and the need for international coordination and cooperation, now discussed under the moniker of ETOs, was recognized under the ICESCR.[35] The ICESCR recognizes that countries have obligations with regard to the realization of ESR beyond their borders. Article 2(1) of the ICESCR states that governments should 'take steps, individually and through international assistance and cooperation, especially economic and technical, to the maximum of its available resources, with a view to achieving progressively the full realization of the rights recognized in the present Covenant by all appropriate means'.

Various human rights treaty bodies have elaborated this idea of ETOs. For instance, General Comment No. 12 of the CESCR focuses on the right to food and explicitly recognizes the importance of international cooperation to address issues of food security, hunger, famine, and lack of basic nutrition.[36] Similarly, in General Comment No. 14 on the right to health, the Committee recognizes a collective responsibility to address the risks associated with diseases that can be transmitted across international borders.[37] Although the General Comment is about global public health challenges, there are important parallels to economic governance, such as the need to prevent the spread of financial crises from one country to another.

Given the need to elaborate the nature of ETOs within the human rights framework, a group of experts on international law and human rights met in Maastricht, in the Netherlands, in 2011 to develop a set of principles on ETOs in the area of ESCR. The outcome of this conference was the Maastricht Principles on Extraterritorial Obligations of States in the Area of Economic, Social and Cultural Rights (Maastricht ETO Principles). The Principles explicitly recognize that the policies adopted by governments at the national level have the potential to impact on the realization of rights beyond their own borders:

> The human rights of individuals, groups, and peoples are affected by and dependent on the extraterritorial acts and omissions of States. The advent of economic globalization in particular, has meant that States and other global actors exert considerable influence on the realization of economic, social, and cultural rights across the world.[38]

One of the goals of the Maastricht ETO Principles was to clarify the legal parameters in which obligations with respect to social and economic rights are met.[39] The Principles have been further supported by expert commentary that identifies the existing treaties, agreements, and covenants which provide a legal foundation for the Principles.[40] Despite the drafting of the

---

[35]   Balakrishnan, Heintz and Elson (n 2) 103–22.

[36]   CESCR, General Comment No. 12 (n 11) paras 36–37. See also, generally, Rolf Künnemann, 'Extraterritorial Application of the International Covenant on Economic, Social, and Cultural Rights' in Fons Coomans and Menno T. Kamminga (eds), *Extraterritorial Application of Human Rights Treaties* (Intersentia 2004) 201–31.

[37]   CESCR, General Comment No. 14 (n 11) para 40. See also, generally, Fons Coomans, 'The Extraterritorial Scope of the International Covenant on Economic, Social, and Cultural Rights in the Work of the United Nations Committee on Economic, Social, and Cultural Rights' (2011) 11(1) *Human Rights Law Review* 1–35.

[38]   Maastricht ETO Principles (n 34) Preamble.

[39]   Margot E. Salomon and Ian Seiderman, 'Human Rights Norms for a Globalized World: The Maastricht Principles on Extraterritorial Obligations of States in the Area of Economic, Social and Cultural Rights' (2012) 3(4) Global Policy 458–62.

[40]   See Olivier de Schutter, Asbjørn Eide, Ashfaq Kalfan, Marcos Orellana, Margot Salomon and Ian Seiderman, 'Commentary to the Maastricht Principles on Extraterritorial Obligations of States in the Area of Economic, Social and Cultural Rights' (2012) 34(4) Human Rights Quarterly 1084–1169.

Principles and their justification within existing international law and treaties, the Maastricht ETO Principles are simply a framework proposed by a group of experts. They are not themselves legally binding on governments, but represent an authoritative interpretation of the ETOs of states under binding international human rights treaties.

One of the central issues associated with ETOs is the question of jurisdiction: whether human rights agreements extend to situations outside of the state's territory.[41] An essential contribution of the Maastricht ETO Principles is to clarify when jurisdiction for human rights obligations applies beyond territorial borders. The Principles also recognize that questions of sovereignty come into play. To the extent that globalization limits independent policy choices by governments, this represents a loss of sovereignty. Since the state is the prime duty bearer within the human rights framework, a loss of sovereignty raises questions of whether states have the full set of tools at their disposal to meet their human rights obligations. For these reasons, the question of international coordination and cooperation is central to the Maastricht ETO Principles.

The Principles use the obligations already discussed – to respect, protect, and fulfill – and extend these to globalized economies. For instance, the extraterritorial dimensions of the obligation to fulfill rights include the requirement that states should create an environment conducive to realizing rights through international cooperation in a range of different areas: international trade, investment, finance, taxation, environmental protection, and development cooperation.[42] This includes actions within international organizations – such as the UN, UN agencies, the World Bank, the International Monetary Fund, and the World Trade Organization, among others – that contribute to the realization of rights within and beyond a country's own territory.[43]

The extraterritorial aspects of the obligation to protect also have significant implications for economic governance, specifically regulating the actions of businesses operating across national boundaries.[44] A critical aspect of the obligation to protect is the obligation to establish a regulatory framework that prevents international organizations and transnational corporations from taking actions that undermine the realization of rights beyond a country's borders.[45] Importantly, the obligation to protect recognizes that omissions by governments, such as one state's failure to adequately regulate the actions of third parties in ways that have negative consequences for rights elsewhere, may constitute a violation of human rights.[46] The failure to adequately regulate US financial markets prior to the 2008 financial crisis that resulted in the retrogression of rights beyond the US border could be interpreted as a failure of the extraterritorial obligation to protect. As Mary Dowell-Jones points out, '[p]roblems that emerge in esoteric financial markets like credit derivatives can rapidly contaminate broader financial markets and the global economy, causing huge human costs'.[47]

---

[41]   See generally: Salomon and Seiderman (n 39); De Schutter et al (n 40); Sigrun Skogly and Mark Gibney, 'Introduction' in Mark Gibney and S. Skogly (eds), *Universal Human Rights and Extraterritorial Obligations* (University of Pennsylvania Press 2010) 1–9.

[42]   Maastricht ETO Principles (n 34) Principle 29.

[43]   Ibid.

[44]   Ibid Principles 23–27.

[45]   See generally, de Schutter et al (n 40).

[46]   Maastricht ETO Principles (n 34) Principle 24.

[47]   Mary Dowell-Jones, 'International Finance and Human Rights: Scope for a Mutually Beneficial Relationship' (2012) 3 *Global Policy* 467–70, 467.

The extraterritorial obligations of states with regard to economic governance are not limited to the regulation of corporate behavior, but also include the policy choices governments make.[48] Actions by one country in the conduct of economic policy, particularly a large influential economy, can affect the economic environment of other countries with potential important consequences for the enjoyment of rights.

Exchange rate policies provide a concrete example of how states' policy choices are interdependent. If one economy devalues its exchange rate (that is, reduces the value of its currency relative to other currencies), the goods and services it exports will become relatively cheaper, while imports will become more expensive. As a result, other countries may experience a decline in the volume of goods and services they are able to sell – the actions of one country affect economic outcomes elsewhere. In order to counteract the devaluation, central banks may respond by lowering their own exchange rates. But if the exchange rate policy of these other countries is being dictated by a larger, more influential economy (that is, the country that first devalued its currency), this represents a loss of sovereignty and raises questions about a government's ability to autonomously fulfill and protect rights.[49]

Because of these, and numerous other, interrelationships, the Maastricht ETO Principles emphasize the need to create an 'enabling environment' for the realization of rights.[50] Applied to monetary policy, for example, this would imply that those conducting interest rate and exchange rate policy in one country should consider the effects that it has on the macroeconomic outcomes in other countries. Pushed further, the ICESCR's language on international cooperation and the Maastricht Principles discussion of obligations with respect to economic policies imply that there is a need to coordinate economic policies across countries in ways that facilitate the enjoyment of ESR.

## 6.   CONCLUSION

The human rights approach provides an alternative normative framework for assessing economic policies firmly rooted in an impressive number of national and international laws, agreements, and declarations. It not only represents an ethical system, distinct from that associated with neoclassical economics, but it also has an established institutional foundation, reflected in legal systems, organizations, and modern principles of justice. It requires that policies be formulated and resources allocated in ways that support the realization of rights, using instruments such as public spending, taxation, government borrowing, and monetary policy, with the objective of improving people's lives, not simply promoting faster growth.

Governments need to be held to account for violations of human rights that may result from how they conduct their economic policies and in whose interests those policies operate. This requires fostering a vibrant and participatory democracy where the government can discipline the actions of finance and transnational corporations and correct power imbalances in the economy. As Article 28 of the UDHR suggests, economic policy represents an aspect of a national and international order that must support the realization of rights over time for all the world's people.

---

[48]   Maastricht ETO Principles (n 34), Principles 23–7.
[49]   Balakrishnan, Heinz and Elson (n 2) 103–22.
[50]   Maastricht ETO Principles (n 34) Principle 20.

# 18. The 2030 Agenda for Sustainable Development: opportunity or threat for economic, social and cultural rights?

*Kate Donald[1]*

## 1. INTRODUCTION

The 2030 Agenda – which comprises the 17 Sustainable Development Goals (SDGs) and their targets – is something that all economic, social and cultural rights (ESCR) advocates will have to contend with, to some extent, over the years to 2030. Even beyond then, the legacy of the 2030 Agenda may endure, in much the same way as the Millennium Development Goals altered and conditioned the development landscape – not least in terms of funding flows and data availability. But why should ESCR advocates pay attention to a non-binding, temporally constrained political agreement when there is a complex, comprehensive and legally binding system of human rights obligations to draw from and grapple with?

The simple answer is that ESCR advocates may not have much choice. Sadly, the 2030 Agenda currently seems to have far more political salience – among governments, and even among many UN agencies – than the normative regime of human rights, for reasons that will be explored later in this chapter. The SDGs may prove to be an unavoidable reference point in discussions with governments, policy-makers, international institutions and donors – even with human rights mechanisms themselves. But beyond these instrumental reasons, the SDGs do have something – perhaps even a surprising amount – to offer to the ESCR community. But in order to use them more effectively as a lever for improved ESCR enjoyment, we need to have a nuanced understanding of their content, strengths and weaknesses. This chapter outlines these with regard to ESCR, in terms of the content on paper of the SDGs, and in terms of their implementation at the time of writing.

The 2030 Agenda and the SDGs have to be understood in relation to their precursor, the Millennium Development Goals (MDGs). The MDGs, which had mixed success in terms of achievement, were broadly criticized (including by many in the human rights community) as being too narrow, too technocratic and top-down and too outcome-focused, and for overlooking externalities and inequalities.[2] The SDGs were in many ways – from process to content – a response to these perceived limitations. While the MDGs were drafted in a very non-participatory fashion by a small group in the proverbial basement of the United Nations

---

[1] The views expressed in this chapter do not necessarily reflect the views of the Center for Economic and Social Rights (CESR), where I am Director of Program.

[2] For two excellent and comprehensive critiques of the MDGs from a rights perspective, see Sakiko Fukuda-Parr and Alicia Ely Yamin (eds), *The MDGs, Capabilities and Human Rights: The Power of Numbers to Shape Agendas* (Routledge 2015); and Malcolm Langford, Andy Sumner and Alicia Ely Yamin (eds), *The Millennium Development Goals and Human Rights: Past, Present and Future* (CUP 2013).

(UN) headquarters in New York, the SDGs were formulated over a number of years, through a number of broad consultations and negotiations, ranging from Member States within the UN, to the 'My World Survey' (which claims to have been the biggest survey in history), to the Secretary-General's 'High Level Panel of Eminent Persons'. Whereas the MDGs were largely goals for so-called developing countries, with only the targets on financial assistance really meant to apply to richer countries, the SDGs are in fact universal – goals and targets for every country to achieve, no matter how poor or wealthy, large or small. The SDGs are also far more broad and more detailed than their predecessors. There are 17 goals and 169 targets, as opposed to the 8 goals and 21 targets of the MDGs. Moreover, the goals themselves cover a much more comprehensive range of issues, including climate change, consumption and production patterns, peace and justice and ocean life. One need only look at the respective gender equality goals to see the difference. MDG 3 only had one target, on gender parity in primary and secondary education (there was a separate goal on maternal health), whereas SDG 5 includes issues ranging from violence against women to unpaid care work, child marriage and equal land rights. The inclusion of a goal (SDG 10) and targets which commit to tackling inequalities and discrimination (as well as an overarching pledge to 'Leave No One Behind') was a particularly significant departure from the MDGs, which were widely acknowledged to be myopically focused on aggregate outcomes, and were stretched over a time period (2000–15) during which inequality actually increased in much of the world.

In this initial assessment, then, it seems clear that the SDGs are much more 'rights-friendly' than the MDGs. This is certainly true. Human rights obligations apply to all countries, like the universal SDGs; all countries face immense challenges to full human rights enjoyment and truly *sustainable* development. No country is off the hook. Participation and broad consultation is a cornerstone of the human rights approach. Human rights standards cover an extremely broad gamut of issues, and indeed their breadth is still expanding, as can be seen by the increased acceptance of environmental rights. The idea that human needs or development priorities can be boiled down to a set of politically convenient, technocratic outcomes is anathema to the very foundation of the human rights regime. So, from this starting point, one can confidently say that the SDGs are a major advancement in terms of their compatibility with human rights compared to the MDGs. Of course, it is possible to make a very legitimate criticism of the whole idea of global development targets, and excellent scholars have done so.[3]

It is also important to note that the 2030 Agenda is also *formally* anchored in human rights, a fact which gets explicit acknowledgment in the Agenda's official text, 'Transforming Our World: The 2030 Agenda for Sustainable Development'. The SDGs 'seek to realize the human rights of all' and 'envisage a world of universal respect for human rights and human dignity'; they are 'grounded in the Universal Declaration of Human Rights, international human rights treaties … [and] informed by other instruments such as the Declaration on the Right to Development'.[4] The following section examines whether this grounding is indeed evident in the goals and targets themselves, specifically the goals which are most closely related to ESCR.

---

[3]   See e.g. Sakiko Fukuda-Parr, 'Global Goals as a Policy Tool: Intended and Unintended Consequences' (2014) 15(2–3) Journal of Human Development and Capabilities 118–31.

[4]   UN General Assembly Resolution 70/1, 'Transforming our World: The 2030 Agenda for Sustainable Development' (21 October 2015) A/RES/71, preamble and paras 8 and 10.

## 2.    APPLES TO ORANGES? COMPARING THE SDGS' CONTENT TO CORRESPONDING ESCR STANDARDS

At first glance, it is easy to see resonance between the SDGs and ESCR, with goals corresponding very closely in their major themes to ESCR standards: there are goals on education (4), health (3), water and sanitation (6), food (2) and decent work (8). Goal 11, to 'Make cities and human settlements inclusive, safe, resilient and sustainable', overlaps to some extent with the right to adequate housing.[5] There are also multiple targets which reference the need for social protection/security (for example, in Goals 1 and 10). Moreover, there are also goals on cross-cutting ESCR issues, such as poverty (1), gender equality (5), inequalities (10) and the environment (multiple goals). This resonance led the UN Secretary-General to declare the SDGs and ESCR 'a convergent agenda'.[6]

What is also clear on initial examination is that explicit rights language is mostly absent in the goals and targets. Goal 3 is titled 'ensure healthy lives' rather than 'realize the right to health'; Goal 4 commits to '[e]nsure inclusive and equitable education' rather than the right to education for all; and so on. As Chapman states: 'None of the SDGS are framed as a human rights entitlement guaranteeing that all people having a right to the services and benefits with governments accountable for its availability and for equal access.'[7] This was a deliberate omission rather than an oversight, with many UN Member States resistant to incorporation of clear human rights language in the goals and targets.[8]

The Danish Institute for Human Rights has claimed that more than 90 per cent of the goals and targets are linked to international human rights and labor standards.[9] This is overly simplistic, however; of course almost all of the goals and targets *can* be linked to human rights standards, but as always, the devil is in the detail, the interpretation and the implementation. Moreover, in many of these cases an explicit reference to the most relevant rights was deliberately resisted. In most cases, it is more accurate to characterize the goals and targets as having human rights 'parallels', to borrow Audrey Chapman's term.[10]

As Winkler and Williams observe, the targets 'implicitly reflect human rights language',[11] certainly far more so than the MDGs ever did. Many of them include concerns such as access, affordability, universality and equity; they are (reasonably) sensitive to the potential of direct

---

[5]    Although for a critique, see UN Human Rights Council, 'Report of the UN Special Rapporteur on Adequate Housing as a Component of the Right to an Adequate Standard of Living, and on the Right to Non-discrimination in this context' (4 August 2015) A/70/270, especially para 33.

[6]    UN Secretary-General, 'Report of the UN Secretary-General on the Question of the Realization in all Countries of Economic, Social and Cultural Rights' (14 December 2016) A/HRC/34/25.

[7]    Audrey R. Chapman, 'Evaluating the Health-related Targets in the Sustainable Development Goals from a Human Rights Perspective' (2017) 21(8) International Journal of Human Rights 1098, 1099.

[8]    For an explanation of this resistance, see Claire E. Brolan, Peter S. Hill and Gorik Ooms, '"Everywhere But Not Specifically Somewhere": A Qualitative Study on Why the Right to Health is Not Explicit in the Post-2015 Negotiations' (2015) 15(22) *BMC Int Health Hum Rights* <www.ncbi.nlm.nih.gov/pmc/articles/PMC4546170/>.

[9]    Danish Institute for Human Rights, *Human Rights and the 2030 Agenda for Sustainable Development* (Danish Institute for Human Rights 2018).

[10]    Chapman (n 7).

[11]    Inga T. Winkler and Carmel Williams, 'The Sustainable Development Goals and Human Rights: A Critical Early Review' (2018) 21(8) International Journal of Human Rights 1023, 1027.

and indirect discrimination to erect barriers to access; and they include crucial determinants of human rights enjoyment. Unlike the MDGs, which tended to focus on reducing, inter alia, poverty and maternal mortality by a certain percentage, the SDGs set certain 'zero targets' in an acknowledgment that *any* prevalence of certain things (for example, extreme poverty or violence against women) is simply unacceptable. This could be seen as a parallel to the minimum core of ESCR, although certainly if this had been applied strictly one would see more of these types of targets.

Rather than exhaustively analyze each relevant goal and target for its human rights alignment, this chapter builds on the general assessments offered above with a closer analysis of SDG 3 on health, and how it corresponds to the right to health as reflected in the International Covenant on Economic, Social and Cultural Rights (ICESCR) and corresponding General Comments (in particular General Comment Nos. 14 and 22).[12]

## 2.1   Right to Health and SDG 3

Christophe Golay claims that the content of SDG 3 and its related targets cover the 'main elements' of the right to health, as it has been defined in international human rights law.[13] However, none of the targets are framed in rights language.[14] The absence of human rights framing is significant beyond mere semantics, because rights imply a set of corresponding obligations from a designated duty-bearer, and intrinsically encompass the possibility for claims of accountability against that duty-bearer. However, even if the framing of the SDG 3 targets is overlooked, is it accurate to say that the core components of the right to health are covered? By looking through the lens of two SDG 3 targets, on universal health coverage and on sexual and reproductive health, it can be determined that unfortunately this is not the case.

Certainly, the inclusion of a target (3.8) on universal health coverage in the SDGs is a hugely positive step: the World Health Organization (WHO) has claimed that universal health coverage is 'a practical expression of ... the right to health'.[15] Target 3.8 also covers important elements of the right to health, as it specifies the necessity of financial risk protection, access to quality essential healthcare services and access to safe, effective, quality and affordable essential medicines and vaccines for all. However, as Chapman notes, 'paths to UHC [universal health coverage] and the way the goal is conceptualized are not necessarily consistent with international human rights principles, and target 3.8 falls short of human rights requirements in key ways'.[16] For example, the target does not convey the need to prioritize the most disadvantaged people in the process of expanding coverage, or that basic health services should be provided free of cost (or at least heavily subsidized) to them. As the UN Special

---

[12] For more detailed analysis of how the SDGs overlap with ESC rights, see generally, Christophe Golay, *No One Will Be Left Behind: The Role of the United Nations Human Rights Mechanisms in Monitoring the Sustainable Development Goals that Seek to Realize Economic, Social and Cultural Rights* (Geneva Academy 2018); UN Secretary-General (n 6).

[13] See Golay (n 12).

[14] WHO, 'Health in the Post-2015 Development Agenda', World Health Assembly, A66/47 (1 May 2013).

[15] WHO, 'Positioning Health in the Post-2015 Development Agenda', WHO Discussion Paper (October 2012).

[16] Chapman (n 7).

Rapporteur on the right to health has noted: 'Without those clear commitments, there is a risk that universal health coverage efforts will entrench inequality.'[17]

Another important element of Goal 3 is the target (3.6) to 'ensure universal access to sexual and reproductive health-care services' by 2030.[18] This target is a particularly clear illustration that SDG 3 indeed does not cover the 'main elements' of the right to health, at least if one defines the full gamut of reproductive rights as being among these main elements, which in a feminist approach is essential. Indeed, in the first line of its General Comment, the UN Committee on Economic, Social and Cultural Rights (CESCR) states that the 'right to sexual and reproductive health is an integral part of the right to health'.[19] Women simply cannot enjoy their right to health if they are denied access to the full range of reproductive health services, including abortion. CESCR's General Comment No. 22 also makes clear that abortion is a necessary component of reproductive health services, while it is conspicuously (albeit unsurprisingly) missing in SDG 3.[20] As Chapman says, 'the reproductive health targets in the SDGs refrain from taking a rights-based approach, focus on a technical approach, and do not address underlying structural issues impeding women's right to equality and their ability to control their own lives'.[21]

These omissions have led other scholars to the conclusion that SDG 3 incorporates the right to health only from a 'minimalist perspective'.[22] Also worth noting is the critique of the UN Special Rapporteur on the right to health, who has faulted SDG 3 for (among other things) not featuring mental health more prominently.[23] Of course, it is perhaps unrealistic to expect that SDG 3 would be a complete recounting of every element of the right to health, but this is exactly why an explicit reference to health as a human right would have been useful, because it would then have acknowledged the crucial relevance of human rights norms, principles and standards relating to health, without having to restate every single element. It would also have helped by providing a fuller guide to implementation.

Limited space precludes a deeper analysis of each one of the SDGs and their overlaps/gaps with regard to corresponding ESCR obligations, but the findings would be largely similar. The goals and targets with parallels among ESCR standards have the strength of being far more rights-aligned than those in the MDGs, in particular in their relative comprehensiveness, and inclusion of concerns around universality, access, non-discrimination and equity. However,

---

[17]    UN Human Rights Council, 'Report of the UN Special Rapporteur on the Right to Health' (2 April 2015) A/HRC/29/33.

[18]    There is a corresponding (and somewhat stronger) target in Goal 5 on gender equality. Target 5.6 commits to: 'Ensure universal access to sexual and reproductive health and reproductive rights as agreed in accordance with the Programme of Action of the International Conference on Population and Development and the Beijing Platform for Action and the outcome documents of their review conferences.' Women's rights advocates pushed for the more rights-aligned language of 'sexual and reproductive health and rights', but too many Member States were opposed to recognizing the concept of sexual rights, hence the bifurcated phrasing. See International Women's Health Coalition, 'Power Lessons: Women's Advocacy and the 2030 Agenda' (2017) <https://iwhc.org/wp-content/uploads/2017/03/Power-Lessons-Report-4.pdf>.

[19]    CESCR, General Comment No. 22 on the Right to Sexual and Reproductive Health (2 May 2016) E/C.12/GC/22.

[20]    Ibid.

[21]    Chapman (n 7) 1103.

[22]    Brolan et al (n 8).

[23]    UN Special Rapporteur on the Right to Health (n 17).

there are still important gaps and omissions which make it a stretch too far to say that these goals and targets are in any way an adequate proxy or alternative for ESCR standards. And given the prominence and political salience of the 2030 Agenda, there is a risk that the SDGs *will* be seen as an alternative, and may be considered in policy-making processes *in place of* the corresponding human rights standards.

However, a less zero-sum interpretation may be more persuasive. Rather than displacing human rights, the two frameworks can be used in complementary fashion, with ESCR standards helping to fill in the gaps in (and implementation plans for) the SDGs. As the UN Special Rapporteur on the right to health has said, '[w]ith careful attention to human rights, global and national efforts towards the Goals can support the realization of the right to health'.[24] This will, however, require some political will to do so, likely spurred by encouragement from actors such as civil society organizations, international or regional human rights mechanisms, and national human rights institutions. It is also important to remember that the SDGs must be viewed in the context of the 2030 Agenda Declaration, which does clearly state: 'The new Agenda is guided by the purposes and principles of the Charter of the United Nations, including full respect for international law. It is grounded in the Universal Declaration of Human Rights, international human rights treaties.' This gives advocates a solid basis to claim that implementation of the goals and targets (whatever their textual omissions or vagaries) should be guided by corresponding human rights standards.

## 3.   ARE ESCR PRINCIPLES REFLECTED IN THE SDGS?

Beyond whether specific rights (and their content) are reflected in the 2030 Agenda, an equally important question is whether core ESCR principles have permeated the commitments. This section briefly examines to what extent several ESCR principles – non-discrimination and equality; maximum available resources, progressive realization and non-retrogression; minimum core; international cooperation and extraterritorial obligations; accountability – can be found in the Agenda.

At the outset, it is worth stating clearly that none of these principles can be found verbatim in the Agenda – a fact which should not be surprising to the reader at this point. However, there are important ways in which several of these principles can be excavated from the Agenda's commitments, some more so than others.

### 3.1   Equality and Non-discrimination

Of the ESCR principles examined here, equality and non-discrimination are in many ways the most evident in the Agenda and the goals and targets. Indeed, this was one of the great victories of civil society activism and lobbying during the negotiation of the SDGs, with the inclusion of strong commitments to tackle inequality – and not just poverty – being a steadfast demand of almost every major civil society contingent throughout the process.[25] In the end, as well as Goal 5 on gender equality, the final Agenda included Goal 10 promising to reduce

---

[24]   UN Special Rapporteur on the Right to Health (n 17).

[25]   See Sakiko Fukuda-Parr, 'Keeping out Extreme Inequality from the SDG Agenda – The Politics of Indicators' (2019) 10(Suppl 1) Global Policy 61.

inequalities within and among countries, several discrimination and equality-sensitive targets in other goals, and an overarching pledge (in many ways the centerpiece of the Agenda) to 'Leave No One Behind' in implementation. Leaving no one behind is also elaborated to mean 'endeavor[ing] to put the furthest behind first',[26] which is very much in harmony with how human rights instruments articulate progress towards true equality and non-discrimination (in other words, equality does not necessarily mean equal treatment and may mean giving priority to disadvantaged groups). In addition, the need for greater disaggregated data to monitor implementation of the agenda across different population sectors and groups has been a major focus in the discussion around monitoring and indicators.[27]

As noted previously, the goals and targets show much greater sensitivity to equity and equality concerns than the MDGs did. For example, the first two targets of Goal 6 commit to 'achieve universal and equitable access to safe and affordable drinking water for all' and 'achieve adequate and equitable sanitation and hygiene for all' by 2030. The education goal even has 'inclusive and equitable' in its title. Of course, the concept of equity has important differences with that of equality,[28] but the extensive commitment to equity in service provision in the ESC rights-related goals across the agenda is nevertheless a major leap in aligning them with human rights principles.

Moreover, discrimination gets several explicit mentions, and at several points in the Declaration and targets, the need to reach disadvantaged and discriminated-against groups is stressed. For example, the Declaration states that:

> We emphasize the responsibilities of all States, in conformity with the Charter of the United Nations, to respect, protect and promote human rights and fundamental freedoms for all, without distinction of any kind as to race, colour, sex, language, religion, political or other opinion, national or social origin, property, birth, disability or other status.[29]

The inclusion of 'other' status became a point of contention in the final stages of the Agenda's negotiation, due to the desire of several Member States that these protections not be seen as covering lesbian, gay, bisexual, transgender and queer (LGBTQ) individuals, but deletion of this clause was thankfully averted.[30] In addition, target 10.3 commits to eliminating discriminatory laws, policies and practices, and target 16.b to '[p]romote and enforce non-discriminatory laws for sustainable development'.

---

[26]   UNGA, 'Transforming Our World' (n 4) Declaration.

[27]   See for example UN Secretary-General's Independent Expert Advisory Group on a Data Revolution for Sustainable Development, 'A World That Counts: Mobilizing the Data Revolution for Sustainable Development' (2014).

[28]   With 'equality' being a more expansive and human rights-aligned formulation, encompassing the notion of 'substantive equality', and the need for differentiated treatment – prioritizing the most disadvantaged – to achieve greater equality of results. See Alda Facio and Martha I. Morgan, 'Equity or Equality for Women? Understanding CEDAW's Equality Principles' (IWRAW Asia Pacific 2009). For a good explanation of substantive equality, see UN Women, *Progress of the World Women 2015–16: Transforming Economies, Realizing Rights* (UN Women 2015) 35–37.

[29]   This list of enumerated groups is very similar to that in the ICESCR, with the welcome addition of 'disability'.

[30]   See Kate Donald, 'Strong Commitments in Final SDG Text, Despite Sordid Final Compromises' (CESR blog, August 2015) <www.cesr.org/strong-commitments-final-sdg-text-despite-sordid-final -compromises>.

In many ways, the really groundbreaking element of the 2030 Agenda with regard to equality and discrimination is Goal 10.[31] This goal commits to reducing inequality both within and between countries, with associated targets on income inequality; social and political empowerment and inclusion; equality-promoting fiscal, wage and social protection policies; financial regulation; migration; and more democratic governance of the global economy. It includes both horizontal (group-based) and vertical inequalities. One particularly striking element is target 10.3, which commits to '[e]nsure equal opportunity *and reduce inequalities of outcome*' (emphasis added). This acknowledgment that extreme inequalities of outcome are unacceptable is unprecedented in a global development agreement, and very much in line with the emphasis that human rights gives to substantive, *de facto* equality. The same target also recognizes the need to eliminate 'discriminatory law, policies and practices' and target 10.2 commits to 'empower and promote the social, economic, and political inclusion of all, irrespective of age, sex, disability, race, ethnicity, origin, religion or economic or other status'.

Tackling economic inequality is also an important component of this goal, explicit in targets 10.1 and 10.2 and implicit in target 10.4. Economic inequality is increasingly recognized as an urgent threat by human rights advocates,[32] and firmly at the top of political agendas worldwide (although, it has to be said, still more at the level of discourse than action). Economic inequality has been shown to have a number of detrimental human rights effects, perpetuating poverty, social exclusion and creating stark disparities in access to health, education, housing and other services essential to the enjoyment of economic and social rights.[33] It is also, as the UN Secretary-General has noted, 'strongly correlated with social inequalities and discrimination, interacting with them in a vicious circle to create and deepen marginalization and disadvantage'.[34] Tackling current levels of extreme economic inequality is also crucial to achieving many of the goals across the Agenda.[35] For example, eradicating extreme poverty by 2030 will be impossible without also tackling economic inequality.[36]

Goal 10, then, is a great strength of the agenda from the perspective of ESCR. However, some of the rights-realizing potential of this goal and its targets are somewhat undercut by the vagueness of the targets,[37] and – as will be discussed later – that of the associated indicators.

---

[31] This goal was one of the most difficult to reach agreement on. See Sakiko Fukuda-Parr (n 25) 64–65.

[32] See for example, Philip Alston, 'Extreme Inequality as the Antithesis of Human Rights' (OpenGlobalRights, 27 August 2015) <www.openglobalrights.org/extreme-inequality-as-the-antithesis-of-human-rights/>.

[33] CESR, *From Disparity to Dignity: Tackling Economic Inequality through the Sustainable Development Goals* (CESR 2016). See also Gillian MacNaughton, 'Vertical Inequalities: Are the SDGs and Human Rights Up to the Challenges?' (2017) 21(8) International Journal of Human Rights 1052–56, for an excellent summary of the scope and impacts of economic inequality.

[34] UN Secretary-General (n 6).

[35] See Kate Donald and Jens Martens, 'The Increasing Concentration of Wealth and Economic Power as an Obstacle to Sustainable Development – and What to Do About It' in Civil Society Reflection Group on the 2030 Agenda for Sustainable Development (ed), *Spotlight Report on Sustainable Development 2018* (Global Policy Forum and others 2018) <www.2030spotlight.org/en/book/1730/chapter/1-increasing-concentration-wealth-and-economic-power-obstacle-sustainable>.

[36] See e.g. Ilmi Granoff and others, *Zero Poverty, Zero Emissions: Eradicating Extreme Poverty in the Climate Crisis* (ODI 2015).

[37] See Gillian MacNaughton (n 33) 1057–61.

Gender equality is evidently a core part of the principle of equality and non-discrimination, and it is both mainstreamed and given a stand-alone goal in the 2030 Agenda. In ways that parallel the discussion of Goal 3 above, Goal 5 on gender equality is imperfect from a human rights perspective, but does manifest several important strengths.[38] The very first target of Goal 5 makes the lofty promise to '[e]nd all forms of discrimination against all women and girls everywhere' by 2030. It includes targets across a range of highly relevant rights issues, including sexual and reproductive health and unpaid care work, which is a major barrier to women's equal enjoyment of ESCR.[39] It also includes a commitment (target 5A) to 'undertake reforms to give women equal rights to economic resources, as well as access to ownership and control over land and other forms of property, financial services, inheritance and natural resources', reforms which have repeatedly been emphasized as necessary by the CESCR,[40] as well as by the UN Committee on the Elimination of Discrimination against Women (CEDAW Committee).[41] However, this target is sadly undermined with the addition of the clause 'in accordance with national laws', which allows States to avoid any real action on this issue.

### 3.2   Progressive Realization, Non-retrogression and Maximum Available Resources

Neither of the (inter-linked) principles of progressive realization and non-retrogression are explicitly contained in the Agenda, although one could argue that, given that it sets goals and targets to be achieved by 2030, they are somewhat 'baked in' to the concept. The question of resources, on the other hand, is a major plank in the Agenda.[42] Just as human rights experts, scholars and advocates have begun to interrogate more seriously the 'maximum available resources' (MAR) clause of ICESCR Article 2, the question of how to pay for sustainable development is taken much more seriously in the SDGs as compared to the MDGs, going far beyond aid. Article 2 of the Covenant implies that States should prioritize the realization of ESCR in their choices about how to raise and use resources, and the CESCR has increasingly urged States to raise more revenues more fairly, and to allocate them more proactively towards social spending and public service provision, in order to comply with their Covenant rights.[43] The SDGs include a number of goals and targets which seem aligned with this. For example, target 3.c commits to '[s]ubstantially increase health financing'. Unfortunately, the goals for education and water and sanitation do not include equivalent (equally necessary) commitments. Target 10.4 recognizes the importance of fiscal policy in moving countries 'progres-

---

[38]   See Shahra Razavi, 'The 2030 Agenda: Challenges of Implementation to Attain Gender Equality and Women's Rights' (2016) 24(1) Gender & Development 25–41, for an excellent analysis of the strengths and weaknesses of the Agenda from a women's rights perspective.

[39]   See UN Human Rights Council, 'Report of the UN Special Rapporteur on Extreme Poverty and Human Rights' (9 August 2013) A/68/293.

[40]   For example, in CESCR, General Comment No. 16: The Equal Right of Men and Women to the Enjoyment of All Economic, Social and Cultural Rights (11 August 2005) E/C.12/2005/4.

[41]   For example, in CEDAW Committee, General Recommendation No. 34: The Rights of Rural Women (7 March 2016) CEDAW/C/GC/34.

[42]   Another set of global commitments agreed in 2015, the Addis Ababa Action Agenda on Financing for Development, includes far greater detail on how sustainable development should be financed, but space precludes a human rights analysis of this document here.

[43]   See for example CESCR, 'Concluding Observations on the Initial Report of South Africa' (29 November 2018) E/C.12/ZAF/CO/1 and 'Concluding Observations on the Fourth Periodic Report of Argentina' (1 November 2018) E/C.12/ARG/CO/4.

sively' towards greater equality, which is symbiotic with the recent efforts of the CESCR to make fiscal policy more central to its analysis of whether States are meeting their obligations with regard to Article 2.[44] Goal 17 also incorporates a number of targets related to resources, including on tax, official development assistance (ODA), trade, debt and investment.

So, the 2030 Agenda does include various commitments regarding different ways that States should raise revenue; but it does not, unfortunately, ever make explicit that rights realization (or even sustainable development) should be the focus of States' resource decisions. Indeed, overall, the Agenda is somewhat contradictory in this regard. As well as being home to important (and rights-aligned) commitments on decent work, Goal 8 enshrines continued economic growth as a priority, when in reality, as Diane Frey says, both the SDGs and human rights 'are "growth neutral"' – that is, they should be achieved whether there is economic growth or not.[45] As Shahra Razavi writes, 'the 2030 Agenda seems to take for granted some key elements of the currently dominant economic agenda, centred on continued growth, trade liberalization, and 'partnerships' with the private sector'.[46] This 'business-as-usual' tendency of the SDGs is in constant tension with its commitment to 'transformation'; and, as will be explored later in this chapter, as implementation of the Agenda gets under way it is the former that is sadly winning out, especially with regard to financing. So, while the SDG commitments to achieving ESCR-related goals within a certain timeframe, and some of the associated targets, can be seen as aligned with Article 2 of the ICESCR, the absence of any explicit commitment or accountability to the maximum available resources principle and other components of progressive realization as a firm human rights obligation means that in practice, the goals and targets do not give States much incentive to reorient their fiscal and budgetary priorities towards ESCR.

### 3.3    Minimum Core

It would take a full article to analyze how far the 2030 Agenda's goals and targets are compatible with the minimum core obligations States hold in relation to economic and social rights. For here, it will have to suffice to say that the SDGs do mark an important advancement on the MDGs in this regard. This is particularly so with the inclusion of 'zero targets' – a plethora of targets which commit to 'eliminate', 'end' or 'eradicate' certain grave threats to human rights, such as extreme poverty, violence and discrimination against women, hunger and malnutrition, preventable deaths of newborns and children under five and practices such as child marriage and female genital mutilation. Similarly, there are a range of targets which aim to ensure universal access to a certain public good or service crucial to rights realization (often overlapping with a recognized element of States' minimum core obligations); such as free primary and secondary education for all boys and girls, and safe and affordable drinking water for all. Although critics have written off such targets as unrealistic (which at the current pace of implementation, they may well be), in human rights terms they are a vast improvement on the MDGs which generally settled for proportional reductions in scourges such as extreme

---

[44]   Ibid; see also CESCR, General Comment No. 24: State Obligations under the International Covenant on Economic, Social and Cultural Rights in the Context of Business Activities (10 August 2017) E./C.12/GC/24, which includes content on progressive tax policy e.g. paras 23 and 29.

[45]   Diane F. Frey, 'Economic Growth, Full Employment and Decent Work: The Means and Ends in SDG 8' (2017) 21(8) International Journal of Human Rights 1164, 1165.

[46]   Shahra Razavi (n 38) 27.

poverty or hunger, which are unequivocally human rights violations and therefore should not be acceptable at any level. The education MDG was also inconsistent with the minimum core of the right to education, in that it did not specify that primary education should be provided free; SDG 4 does make this clear.

### 3.4    Extraterritorial Obligations and International Cooperation

The principle that human rights obligations do not stop at national borders is a key part of the normative framework of international human rights. The SDGs, in many ways, do rest on the idea of international cooperation between countries. For instance, the Declaration acknowledges that 'national development efforts need to be supported by an enabling international economic environment, including coherent and mutually supporting world trade, monetary and financial systems, and strengthened and enhanced global economic governance' and that the 'global nature of climate change calls for the widest possible international cooperation'. The SDGs do still envisage official development assistance (ODA) as playing a central role in development cooperation, recommitting 'developed' countries to the 0.7 per cent GNI target. But they also emphasize South–South cooperation, and international cooperation on issues such as debt, trade, water and technology. Goal 10, discussed above, also includes targets to tackle inequality *between* countries. As MacNaughton says: 'While human rights generally address intra-state issues, inequalities between countries may have substantial impact on the realisation of human rights as well as the achievement of sustainable development. Therefore, these inequalities must also be considered "human rights issues".'[47]

However, perhaps unsurprisingly, the SDGs do not go nearly as far as they should or could on this issue, with the negotiations often getting stuck on the inclusion of the 'common but differentiated responsibilities' (CBDR) principle. Global South countries were insistent that this key principle from the Rio Declaration be incorporated and expanded to apply to issues beyond climate change – that is, an acknowledgment that all countries have a role to play in fostering global sustainable development, but industrialized, rich countries may have special responsibilities in this regard, given the history of colonialism, their far greater climate footprint and economic power. This principle is linked to extraterritorial human right obligations (ETOs),[48] which the UN treaty bodies (including CESCR) have increasingly begun to emphasize with regard to the policies and actions of 'developed' countries such as Switzerland, the UK and Norway on sustainable development globally.[49]

However, in the end, Global South countries had to settle for a rather wan reiteration of CBDR in the context of the Rio Declaration.[50] The efforts that Global North countries should make to address problems which are largely of their own making, and far more in their power

---

[47]    Gillian MacNaughton (n 33) 1051.

[48]    See CESR and Third World Network, 'Universal Rights, Differentiated Responsibilities: Safeguarding Human Rights Beyond Borders to Achieve the SDGs' (2015) <http://cesr.org/sites/default/files/CESR_TWN_ETOs_briefing.pdf>.

[49]    For some examples, see Kate Donald, 'SDG 10: Invoking Extraterritorial Human Rights Obligations to Confront Inequalities Between Countries' in Civil Society Reflection Group on the 2030 Agenda for Sustainable Development (ed), *Spotlight on Sustainable Development 2018* (2018) <www.2030spotlight.org/en/book/1730/chapter/sdg-10-invoking-extraterritorial-human-rights-obligations-confront-extreme>.

[50]    See UNGA, 'Transforming Our World' (n 4) Declaration para 12.

to tackle, are generally stated in terms of voluntary 'cooperation' rather than anything more binding. Moreover, in many cases certain problems which unequivocally require targeted action from rich countries (such as illicit financial flows, which are facilitated by the financial secrecy policies of Global North jurisdictions) are treated as a neutral apolitical problem which it is equally incumbent upon all States to tackle (see target 16.4). This creates inevitable difficulties with pinpointing responsibility for implementation, and with seeking accountability if these targets are not met.

### 3.5    Accountability

This leads us to an unavoidable problem of the 2030 Agenda when viewed through a rights lens: the lack of any real accountability system or mechanisms to monitor progress or lack thereof. A lot has been written elsewhere, including by this author, about the many deficits of the 2030 Agenda in this regard.[51] There is no space to rehearse all these arguments again here. However, these deficits have to be a major factor in an assessment of whether the Agenda is rights-aligned or not.

Despite the persistent efforts of advocates, not least the Post-2015 Human Rights Caucus,[52] even the words 'monitoring' and 'accountability' were resisted in the negotiations, in favor of the much more anodyne 'follow-up and review'. (Although Goal 16 does commit to building 'accountable and inclusive institutions' at all levels, this does not seem to apply to the Agenda itself.) Proposals for robust accountability processes,[53] universal peer review or mandatory reporting were consistently watered down.[54] Instead, the Agenda has a wholly voluntary system of reporting and review, at the complete discretion of States themselves (some of whom may choose to never report at all). The 'Follow-up and Review' section of the Agenda does include 'principles' for these processes, which include that they will be 'open' and 'participatory' and 'respect human rights',[55] but there is no mechanism for ensuring these principles are followed, or penalty for not doing so. Indeed, the 'Voluntary National Reviews' (VNRs) presented so far at the annual High-Level Political Forum on Sustainable Development, where SDG progress is officially reviewed, have been very mixed in terms of quality, with most of them quite superficial and focused on giving a positive vision of progress,[56] and with national civil society groups often reporting that they are marginalized from the national process or only included tokenistically.[57]

---

[51]    See e.g. Kate Donald and Sally-Anne Way, 'Accountability for the Sustainable Development Goals: A Lost Opportunity?' (2016) 30(2) Ethics and International Affairs 201.

[52]    See Post-2015 Human Rights Caucus, 'The Post-2015 Agenda Won't Deliver Without Human Rights at the Core' (CESR website, 2014) <http://archive.cesr.org/article.php?id=1648>.

[53]    See for example CESR and Office of the UN High Commissioner for Human Rights (OHCHR), *Who Will Be Accountable? Human Rights and the Post-2015 Development Agenda* (United Nations 2013).

[54]    See e.g. CESR, 'Evading Accountability Post-2015 Will Eviscerate the Agenda's Ambition' (CESR blog 2015) <www.cesr.org/evading-accountability-post-2015-will-eviscerate-agendas-ambition>.

[55]    UNGA 'Transforming our World' (n 4) para 74.

[56]    See Kate Donald and Mahlatse Ramoroka, 'Five Key Take-aways from the 2018 High Level Political Forum', (CESR blog 30 July 2018) <www.cesr.org/five-key-takeaways-2018-high-level -political-forum>.

[57]    See for example Civil Society Working Group for the 2030 Agenda, Spotlight Synthesis Report: The 2030 Sustainable Development Agenda in Brazil (2017) <https://brasilnaagenda2030

It is also important to note that corporate accountability appears nowhere. Indeed, this is one of the most worrying aspects of the Agenda's final outcome, given that the private sector is granted a privileged role in the Agenda as written, and in implementation so far.[58] Goal 17, for example, promises to '[e]ncourage and promote effective public, public-private and civil society partnerships', where all the emphasis so far has concentrated on public–private partnerships (PPPs). Paragraph 67 of the Agenda does include a reference to the Guiding Principles on Business and Human Rights, as demanded by advocates,[59] but proposals for example for *ex ante* human rights impact assessments for private sector partnerships were rejected out of hand. In general, in the official documents and unofficial rhetoric of the 2030 Agenda, the private sector is seen as an uncomplicated positive actor, with none of the nuance or safeguards that would be necessary from the human rights perspective, for example as shown in the CESCR's General Comment No. 24 on state obligations in the context of business activities.[60] So, for example, massive privatization of public services would, on paper, be compatible with the 2030 Agenda, despite the fact that it would likely have very detrimental consequences for human rights enjoyment (and ultimately, the achievement of many goals and targets related to equality and inclusion).[61]

However, while the official accountability 'infrastructure' of the 2030 Agenda remains extremely weak, many human rights monitoring mechanisms are seizing opportunities to consider SDG implementation and progress in their work. For example, UN treaty bodies are increasingly asking States questions related to their SDG implementation during the periodic reporting process, and incorporating recommendations related to the 2030 Agenda into their concluding observations. Both the CESCR and the CEDAW Committee, for instance, have now incorporated a standard clause/recommendation related to the 2030 Agenda into their concluding observations. For example, CESCR consistently recommends that:

> the State party take fully into account its obligations under the Covenant and ensure the full enjoyment of the rights enshrined therein in the implementation of the 2030 Agenda for Sustainable Development at the national level, with international assistance and cooperation when needed. Achievement of the Sustainable Development Goals would be significantly facilitated by the State party establishing independent mechanisms to monitor progress and treating beneficiaries of public programmes as rights holders who can claim entitlements. Implementing the Goals on the basis of the principles of participation, accountability and non-discrimination would ensure that no one is left behind.[62]

---

.files.wordpress.com/2017/07/spotlight-report-cswg-brazil-hlpf2017.pdf>; Arab NGO Network for Development and others, 'Response to Voluntary National Review Report of Lebanon' <www.annd.org/data/file/files/VNR%20LEBANON%20REPORT%20english.pdf>.

[58]    See Civil Society Reflection Group on the 2030 Agenda for Sustainable Development, *Spotlight on Sustainable Development 2017: Reclaiming Policies for the Public* (2017); and Global Policy Forum, 'Highjacking the SDGs? The Private Sector and the Sustainable Development Goals' (Global Policy Forum 2018).

[59]    See e.g. Post-2015 Human Rights Caucus, 'Rights Before Profit: Recommendations on Corporate Accountability' (2015) <http://archive.cesr.org/downloads/post2015_corp_accountability.pdf>.

[60]    See CESCR, General Comment No. 24 (n 44).

[61]    See UN Human Rights Council, 'Report of the Special Rapporteur on Extreme Poverty and Human Rights' (26 September 2018) A/73/396 (2018).

[62]    See for example CESCR, 'Concluding Observations on the Sixth Periodic Report of Bulgaria' (29 March 2019) E/C.12/BGR/CO/6.

The CEDAW Committee's equivalent language emphasizes the importance of realization of substantive equality for women through the implementation of the Agenda.[63] The CESCR has also incorporated other recommendations to state parties relevant to the SDGs, for example urging South Africa to consider General Comment No. 19 on the right to social security when implementing the SDGs.[64]

The CESCR has also released an official statement, outlining how the Covenant can help guide implementation of the SDGs, and highlighting how 'the Committee is increasingly integrating the Sustainable Development Goals in its work, including under the periodic reporting process, so as to enhance the synergies between measures adopted in the context of the 2030 Agenda and the realization of Covenant rights'.[65] Various other treaty bodies have also provided input into the annual High-Level Political Forum, outlining progress, challenges and gaps as they see them, based for instance on State reports.[66] The CEDAW Committee has also explicitly mentioned the 2030 Agenda and specific targets in recent General Recommendations related to women's ESCR, such as General Recommendation No. 36 on the right of girls and women to education,[67] and General Recommendation No. 37 on gender-related dimensions of disaster-risk reduction in the context of climate change.[68] Many national human rights institutions are also incorporating monitoring SDG progress into their work.[69] So, although the 2030 Agenda 'follow-up and review' system does not grant the human rights monitoring ecosystem an official role in SDG monitoring, these mechanisms are carving out a niche for themselves nonetheless. Although it is unclear so far what effect (if any) these interventions are having on State implementation in practice, such efforts are potentially important steps in – at the very least – consistently highlighting to States that their human rights obligations have relevance and should be considered when implementing the SDGs or monitoring progress in this regard.

---

[63] See e.g. in CEDAW Committee, 'Concluding Observations on the Fourth Periodic Report of Botswana' (14 March 2019) CEDAW/C/BWA/CO/4: 'The Committee welcomes the international support for the Sustainable Development Goals and calls for the realization of de jure (legal) and de facto (substantive) gender equality, in accordance with the provisions of the Convention, throughout the process of implementing the 2030 Agenda for Sustainable Development. The Committee recalls the importance of Goal 5 and of the mainstreaming of the principles of equality and non-discrimination throughout all 17 Goals. It urges the State party to recognize women as the driving force of the sustainable development of the State party and to adopt relevant policies and strategies to that effect.'

[64] CESCR, 'Concluding Observations on the Initial Report of South Africa' (29 November 2018) E/C.12/ZAF/CO/1.

[65] CESCR, 'The Pledge to Leave No One Behind: The ICESCR and the 2030 Agenda for Sustainable Development' (5 April 2019) E/C.12/2019/1.

[66] See e.g. Committee on the Right of the Child, 'Contribution to the 2030 Agenda for Sustainable Development in Response to a Call for Inputs by the High-Level Political Forum on Sustainable Development'(2019) <https://sustainabledevelopment.un.org/content/documents/21804CRC_HLPF _2019_Contribution_14.03.19.pdf>.

[67] CEDAW Committee, General Recommendation No. 36: The Right of Women and Girls to Education (27 November 2017) CEDAW/C/GC/36.

[68] CEDAW Committee, General Recommendation No. 37: Gender-related Dimensions of Disaster Risk Reduction in the Context of Climate Change (13 March 2018) CEDAW/C/GC/37.

[69] See for example the work of the Mexico Comisión Nacional de Derechos Humanos to align their work with the SDGs, at <http://informe.cndh.org.mx/menu.aspx?id=40117>. See also the 'Mérida Declaration: The Role of National Human Rights Institutions in Implementing the 2030 Agenda for Sustainable Development, adopted at the Twelfth International Conference of the International Coordinating Committee of National Institutions for the Promotion and Protection of Human Rights' (2015).

### 3.5.1    The SDG indicators: Undermining accountability and rights alignment?

A core part of accountability is being able to monitor effectively the extent to which targets are or are not being met. Identifying or designing the correct indicators is thus a crucial part of accountability efforts, as progress is ultimately judged through the lens of the indicators selected. As the Center for Economic and Social Rights (CESR) wrote in 2015, when calling for indicators that are aligned with human rights principles and standards, 'the choice of indicators could cement or undercut the ambition of the entire post-2015 sustainable development agenda'.[70] Unfortunately, as it has played out so far, the choices have mainly fallen on the 'undercut' side. Sakiko Fukuda-Parr has written persuasively about how the indicators selected for Goal 10 have fatally weakened the radical potential of the goal, embracing instead a neoliberal 'framing', for example in the political choice to include the World Bank's 'shared prosperity' indicator rather than the Gini or the Palma, which would actually measure the gap between the rich and the poor.[71]

Another stark example of how the indicators undermine even the more human rights-aligned aspects of the agenda relates to target 10.2. The target, also described above, commits to 'empower and promote the social, economic and political inclusion of all, irrespective of age, sex, disability, race, ethnicity, origin, religion or economic or other status' by 2030. The sole indicator selected to measure progress towards this target is: 'Proportion of people living below 50 per cent of median income, by age, sex and persons with disabilities.'[72] Admittedly, the use of the words 'empower' and 'promote' in the target make appropriate measurement choices somewhat challenging, but the choice of indicator is still absurdly inadequate. Not only does it conflate inequality with poverty, but it equates social, economic and political inclusion with where on the income distribution one may sit. Even as a measure of poverty, this is very far from reflecting a multi-dimensional human rights perspective, such as that of the CESCR, that poverty is 'a human condition characterized by the sustained or chronic deprivation of the resources, capabilities, choices, security and power necessary for the enjoyment of an adequate standard of living and other civil, cultural, economic, political and social rights'.[73] In addition, where the target, admirably, disaggregated by many of the prohibited grounds of discrimination under international human rights law, the indicator limits itself to only age, sex and disability. Many more examples could be given, including the prolonged struggle (unresolved at the time of writing) to redefine 'illicit financial flows' for the indicator for target 16.4 to exclude corporate tax evasion[74] – but 10.2 is a distressing example of how the indicators selected so far have tended to unravel potentially promising commitments related to human rights.

Of course, the process of setting indicators is a complicated one, necessitating technical, political and ethical judgments. Difficult choices do have to be made. But currently it

---

[70]    CESR, *The Measure of Progress: How Human Rights Should Inform the Sustainable Development Goal Indicators* (CESR 2015).

[71]    See Sakiko Fukuda-Parr (n 25).

[72]    See United Nations, 'Sustainable Development Goal 10: Targets & Indicators' <https://sustainabledevelopment.un.org/sdg10>.

[73]    CESCR, 'Statement adopted by the Committee on Economic, Social and Cultural Rights on 4 May 2001' (10 May 2001) E/C.12/2001/10 para 8.

[74]    See Alex Cobham, 'Target 2030: Illicit Financial Flows' (Real Institute Elcano 2018) <www.realinstitutoelcano.org/wps/portal/rielcano_en/contenido?WCM_GLOBAL_CONTEXT=/elcano/elcano_in/zonas_in/ari81-2018-cobham-target-2030-illicit-financial-flows>.

seems that progress towards the SDGs will be judged through the lens of a set of indicators which do not come close to capturing the full ambition of the Agenda, with the most human rights-sensitive targets often the most distorted or neglected.[75] Not only the accountability but also the implementation of the agenda will suffer, as accurate monitoring is essential for signposting what is going wrong and where. As Roberto Bissio has argued: 'The SDGs were rightly celebrated as a paradigm shift in how the international community understands sustainable development, by expanding the definition of poverty, including a concern about inequalities, being universally applicable and transformative. This is not the picture that will emerge from the current set of ... indicators.'[76]

## 4.   IN PRACTICE: IS IMPLEMENTATION SO FAR LIVING UP TO THE (LIMITED) PROMISE OF THE AGENDA WITH REGARD TO ESCR?

So far, this chapter has mostly concentrated on how well the 2030 Agenda aligns with ESCR and principles in theory (on paper). However, at the time of writing, there are already three years of implementation to analyze. Therefore, this section asks to what extent implementation so far is living up to the promises in the Agenda, particularly those elements that are most important for ESCR realization. Of course, this analysis is very general and based on the author's own research and perspective; obviously, national experiences and processes differ. However, this section also draws on several trends observed from country VNRs presented at the High Level Political Forum (HLPF) over the last few years, as well as analysis from civil society actors in several different national contexts.

So far, it seems clear that implementation of the SDGs is not going far and fast enough, as acknowledged by the UN Secretary-General and other high-level officials.[77] For example, in May 2019, UN Deputy Secretary-General Amina Mohammed warned that the 'clear message' of the two most recent UN reports on SDG progress were that 'we are off track when it comes to achieving the Sustainable Development Goals and that a deeper, more ambitious, more transformative and more integrated response is urgently needed to get back on track'.[78] The Organisation for Economic Co-operation and Development (OECD) has found that OECD countries (among the richest countries in the world) need to accelerate implementation, and on certain aspects, including Goal 2 on hunger, Goal 5 on gender equality, Goal 10 on inequalities

---

[75]   See Kate Donald, 'The Politics of "Progress": UN Report Paints a Highly Partial Picture of SDG Implementation' (CESR blog, June 2017) <www.cesr.org/politics-%E2%80%98progress%E2%80%99 -un-report-paints-highly-partial-picture-sdg-implementation>.

[76]   Roberto Bissio, 'SDG Indicators: The Forest is Missing' (Global Policy Watch April 2018) <www .globalpolicywatch.org/blog/2018/04/25/sdg-indicators/>.

[77]   UN Secretary-General, 'Special Edition: Progress Towards the Sustainable Development Goals: Report of the Secretary-General (Advance Unedited Version)' (UN Economic and Social Council 2019).

[78]   United Nations, 'Sustainable Development Reports Underscore Need for Robust Action on Means of Implementation, Deputy Secretary-General Stresses at Briefing' (22 May 2019) DSG/SM/1284-ENV/ DEV/1955 <www.un.org/press/en/2019/dsgsm1284.doc.htm>.

and Goal 16 on peace justice and strong institutions, many countries are 'moving in the wrong direction'.[79]

Moreover, the majority of States are 'cherry-picking' which parts of the agenda they want to prioritize,[80] mostly based on their existing developmental or political priorities (despite the fact that the Agenda is meant to be, like human rights, integrated and indivisible).[81] Hence, certain parts of the Agenda are getting short shrift in implementation so far; not surprisingly, these are mostly those elements which are most potentially 'transformative' or would require most profound structural change or changes in power distribution.[82] These are the elements that are, arguably, most important for human rights realization. On the whole, despite all the rhetorical commitment to transformation, it is 'business-as-usual' that is prevailing, despite the fact that all available evidence shows that the possibility of reaching the Goals by 2030 is merely a mirage if the current status quo continues.[83] Goal 10 – whose importance from an ESCR perspective is discussed above – is proving particularly vulnerable to 'strategic neglect',[84] with very few countries pursuing the kinds of robust redistributive policies that would be necessary to tackle extreme inequality and wealth concentration. As the Global Inequality Report found in its 2018 edition: 'In a future in which 'business-as-usual' continues, global inequality will further increase.'[85]

This business-as-usual approach is most visible in policy areas related to corporate regulation, environmental policy, financing and fiscal policy. Certain policy trends – some of which predate the SDGs – are evident, and continue to sweep the globe, despite being almost certainly incompatible with achieving the goals and targets. One of these is austerity – now apparent in hundreds of low-, middle- and high-income countries[86] – which, with its combination of social spending cuts, labor flexibilization and regressive taxation, is clearly antithetical to huge numbers of the SDG targets (especially those related to increasing access to quality public services, and reducing inequalities) and to realization of ESCR.[87] Indeed, many countries that

---

[79]    OECD, *Measuring Distance to the SDG Targets 2019: An Assessment of Where OECD Countries Stand* (OECD 2019).

[80]    See e.g. Office of the UN High Commissioner for Human Rights, 'Warning against 'Cherry-picking' amongst Global Goals, UN Experts Say Human Rights Cannot Be Ignored', UN News (12 July 2016) <https://news.un.org/en/story/2016/07/534232-warning-against-cherry-picking-among-global-goals-un-experts-say-human-rights>.

[81]    For the example of Ecuador, see Philipp Horn and Jean Grugel, 'The SDGs in Middle-income Countries: Setting or Serving Domestic Development Agendas? Evidence from Ecuador' (2018) 109:c World Development 73.

[82]    For an overview, see Jens Martens, 'Redefining Policies for Sustainable Development' in Civil Society Reflection Group on the 2030 Agenda for Sustainable Development (ed), *Spotlight on Sustainable Development 2018* (July 2018).

[83]    Susan Nicolai and others, *Projecting Progress: Reaching the SDGs by 2030* (ODI 2015).

[84]    CESR (n 33).

[85]    World Inequality Lab, World Inequality Report 2018 (2018), online executive summary at <https://wir2018.wid.world/>.

[86]    Isabel Ortiz and others, 'The Decade of Adjustment: A Review of Austerity Trends 2010–2010 in 187 Countries, 2015', ESS Working Paper No. 53 (International Labour Organization, Columbia University and The South Centre, 2015).

[87]    For analysis of the impacts of austerity on economic, social and cultural rights, see Aoife Nolan (ed), *Economic and Social Rights after the Global Financial Crisis* (CUP 2014). For further analysis on specific countries, see CESR, 'Spain Factsheet' (CESR 2018) <www.cesr.org/sites/default/files/FACTSHEET-Spain(EN)-June2018-FINAL.pdf>; UN Human Rights Council, 'Report of the Special

are vocally trumpeting their commitment to the SDGs – for example, Egypt,[88] Colombia,[89] South Africa[90] – are at the same time adopting or persisting with regressive economic policies, including cutbacks to public spending. In its VNR report to the HLPF in 2017, the Brazilian government even tried to characterize its recent extreme measures to freeze real public spending for 20 years as 'fiscal discipline' aligned with its Agenda commitments, a contradiction decried by civil society actors in the country.[91]

Meanwhile, very little, if any, action is being taken to reduce inequalities between countries (or to take ETOs seriously), especially with the recent pushback against multilateralism, led in particular by the United States. ODA commitments continue to go largely unmet, with many donor countries instead pushing for changing the parameters to include private investments in ODA accounting.[92] Any real action to rebalance global economic governance (as demanded by target 10.6) is being fiercely resisted by Global North countries, aided in some cases by the international financial institutions.[93] For instance, the calls from the G77 and large coalitions of civil society for an intergovernmental tax body where countries could discuss tax policy and systems on the basis of equals under the auspices of the UN have been consistently squashed by EU Member States, the US and other wealthy countries.[94] Relatedly, action to combat illicit financial flows (IFFs) – target 16.4, and also an indispensable element for redistributing wealth and raising the 'maximum available resources' to realize ESCR as enshrined in Article 2 of the ICESCR – has been largely non-existent so far. Indeed, attempts are being made by certain actors to redefine the indicator for target 16.4, to ensure that the indicator would *not* include cross-border corporate tax abuse in its definition of IFFs.[95] This further removes the policy incentives for governments and inter-governmental actors to seriously crack down on practices

Rapporteur on Extreme Poverty and Human Rights: Visit to the United Kingdom of Great Britain and Northern Ireland' (23 April 2019) A/HRC/41/39/Add.1.

[88]  See e.g. Egypt Social Progress Indicators, *ESPI Annual Report 2018* (2018) <www.progressegypt.org/files/espi_annual_report_2018.pdf>.

[89]  CESR, 'Colombia UPR Factsheet' (CESR 2018) <www.cesr.org/sites/default/files/Colombia-Factsheet-English.pdf>.

[90]  CESR, 'South Africa Factsheet' (CESR 2018) <www.cesr.org/sites/default/files/FACTSHEET-Artwork-Online-Nov%206%20FINAL.pdf>.

[91]  See e.g. Civil Society Working Group for the 2030 Agenda, 'Spotlight Synthesis Report: The 2030 Sustainable Development Agenda in Brazil' (2017) <https://brasilnaagenda2030.files.wordpress.com/2017/07/spotlight-report-cswg-brazil-hlpf2017.pdf>; Grazielle David, 'The Unreality of Promoting the SDGs without a Sufficient Budget', National Report for Spotlight Report on Sustainable Development 2018 (Social Watch 2018) <www.socialwatch.org/node/18072>.

[92]  Jesse Griffiths, 'Aid for the Private Sector: Continued Controversy on ODA Rules' (ODI blog, 17 October 2018) <www.odi.org/blogs/10699-aid-private-sector-continued-controversy-oda-rules>.

[93]  See Grazielle David, Kate Donald and Mahinour El-Badrawi, 'The IMF's Role in Economic Governance: Conducive to Reducing Inequalities Within and Among Countries?' in Civil Society Reflection Group on the 2030 Agenda for Sustainable Development, *Spotlight Report on Sustainable Development 2019* (Global Policy Forum and others July 2019).

[94]  See e.g. Phillip Inman, 'Rich Countries Accused of Foiling Effort to Give Poorer Nations a Voice on Tax' *The Guardian* (London, 14 July 2015) <www.theguardian.com/global-development/2015/jul/14/financing-for-development-conference-addis-ababa-rich-countries-accused-poorer-nations-voice-tax>; Sophie Edwards, 'The G77 will Push for 'Tax Justice' through a UN Tax Body, Says Ecuador's Foreign Affairs Minister' (*Devex* 13 January 2017) <www.devex.com/news/the-g77-will-push-for-tax-justice-through-a-un-tax-body-says-ecuador-s-foreign-affairs-minister-89442>.

[95]  Alex Cobham (n 74).

such as transfer pricing and profit shifting, which significantly limit the resources available to advance towards sustainable development, substantive equality and rights realization.[96]

Overall, a partial overview of trends in implementation so far does not indicate a lot of promise for anyone hoping that the more positive and rights-aligned aspects of the Agenda would shine through in practice.[97] States will need to take the exhortations to 'transformation' in the Agenda a lot more seriously over the years to 2030 if there is any hope of reaching the goals in full – in particular, they will need to prioritize aspects that are particularly crucial to ESCR, including tackling inequalities and socio-economic exclusion and discrimination, rebalancing power asymmetries and putting in place truly redistributive public financing measures.

## 5.    CONCLUSION

This assessment has shown that while the 2030 Agenda has many promising aspects, and is an immeasurable improvement on the very reductive Millennium Development Goals in terms of its degree of alignment with ESCR and human rights in general, it does exhibit many gaps and weaknesses that should give rights advocates pause before offering a fulsome embrace. However, will the SDGs ultimately help or hinder ESCR realization? It is this author's opinion that, if rights advocates are able to leverage and use the SDGs strategically, with a nuanced understanding of their flaws and strengths, then the 2030 Agenda does provide opportunity to drive forward advancements in ESCR. Of course, one could argue that the 2030 Agenda 'crowds out' attention to human rights obligations, and provides a distraction rather than a boost. This is certainly a real risk that has to be guarded against. But the very fact that a holistic achievement of the SDGs looks to be impossible without also respecting, protecting and fulfilling ESCR should give us hope (whereas many of the MDGs could in theory have been reached without also realizing human rights). Can governments really meet the target on social protection floors and 'leave no one behind' in doing so while ignoring human rights? Are the goals on water and sanitation, education and health likely to be reached without real attention to direct and indirect discrimination, especially given their targets' explicit emphasis on universal access and equity? Can the various goals and targets related to public service provision, or Goal 10 on tackling inequalities, realistically be implemented without raising and devoting the 'maximum available resources' to ESCR? Frankly, this seems highly unlikely, if not impossible. The SDGs may be infuriatingly vague at times, but their breadth and their rejection of a purely technocratic style do make them less susceptible to the rights-blind bureaucratic box-ticking that sometimes characterizes development initiatives (even if, as described above, the indicator selection may be reintroducing some of these risks).

---

[96]   For one analysis of the impact of financial secrecy and IFFs on human rights, see CESR and others, 'Swiss Responsibility for the Extraterritorial Impacts of Tax Abuse on Women's Rights, Submission to CEDAW Committee 2016' (2016) <www.cesr.org/sites/default/files/switzerland_cedaw_submission _2nov2016.pdf>.

[97]   For independent, annual overviews of global progress in implementation and structural obstacles to such progress, see Civil Society Reflection Group on the 2030 Agenda for Sustainable Development, *Spotlight Report on Sustainable Development*, editions in 2016, 2017, 2018 and 2019 (Global Policy Forum and others).

The fact that, to an untrained observer, or even to a development policy-maker, the SDGs may in fact be more accessible, detailed and progressive than human rights standards should also not be overlooked. For instance, while the deficiencies of the SDG target on universal health coverage have been discussed above, the text of the ICESCR does not in fact mention UHC once – one has to dive into the General Comments and other interpretive documentation to find that. So the SDGs do give some more-or-less progressive and rights-aligned guidance to policy-makers, who – whether we like it or not – may in reality be unlikely to engage with the details of human rights jurisprudence and standards.

The breadth and scope of the 2030 Agenda, and its incorporation of truly core human rights issues such as equality, non-discrimination, social protection, universal access to public services, participation and access to justice, mean that there is unquestionably more than enough in there for ESCR advocates to work with. Of course, this 'something for everyone' characteristic of the SDGs is also why the Agenda is vulnerable to co-option by profit-driven multinational corporations (increasingly engaging in so-called 'SDG washing'[98]) and authoritarian or repressive governments. So, the battle for definition and ownership of the Agenda is very much still ongoing, which is why it is especially crucial that human rights advocates engage and stake their claim. As the Chairpersons of the UN treaty bodies have said, the implementation of the SDGs should be seen as 'an important step on the longer, and continuous, road towards the full and effective realization of all human rights for all'.[99]

Ultimately, the most transformative potential likely lies in using rights and the 2030 Agenda in conjunction: leveraging the political salience and rhetoric of the SDGs, while insisting on the robust detail of human rights standards as a guide for implementation and a benchmark for monitoring. Human rights advocates and practitioners can use the helpful elements of the 2030 Agenda as a political entry point for their ESCR work, while also monitoring and critiquing SDG implementation from a human rights perspective. Indeed, many are already doing so. With persistence, in many contexts, human rights practitioners and monitoring bodies can influence implementation and monitoring, including through using existing human rights tools, methodologies and mechanisms.

---

[98]   Adam Fishman, 'Responsible Business Report Finds High Risk of "SDG Washing"' (*IISD SDG Knowledge Hub*, 29 May 2018) <http://sdg.iisd.org/news/responsible-business-report-finds-high-risk-of-sdg-washing/>.

[99]   Office of the UN High Commissioner for Human Rights, 'Joint Statement of the Chairpersons of the UN Human Rights Treaty Bodies on the Post-2015 Development Agenda' (May 2013).

# 19. The climate crisis: litigation and economic, social and cultural rights

*Siri Gloppen and Catalina Vallejo[1]*

## 1. INTRODUCTION

This chapter explores the significance of climate litigation for economic, social and cultural rights (ESCR), and vice versa. Litigation has become increasingly important as a strategy to force action to address the climate crisis. Court cases have been lodged before domestic and international courts and tribunals across the globe. They have been brought to force climate mitigation policies and regulations, to reduce the emission of greenhouse gases into the atmosphere, to demand compliance with existing rules, and to push for more equitable and adequate policies, both for mitigation and for climate adaptation. In this growing body of litigation, ESCR are at stake in multiple ways.

Climate change poses severe threats to ecosystems and the ESCR of future generations, as well as to vulnerable groups already living whose lives and livelihoods are threatened by sea-level rise, unseasonal droughts or other climate-linked disasters and diseases. When governments build new coal plants, grant concessions for oil drilling, invest in new airport runways or fail to regulate and prevent harmful actions by the fossil fuel industry and others, this mitigation failure can be seen to constitute a risk or violation of the ESCR of current and future humans. Similarly, adaptation failure – lack of action to protect those already at risk from changes in the climate and related disasters – is a breach of their ESCR.

Climate mitigation and adaptation measures may themselves also threaten ESCR. Closing of power plants and high carbon emission industries may cause loss of jobs and livelihoods, and threaten energy supplies and economic growth, which in turn makes ESCR realization more difficult; less carbon-intensive energy sources such as hydroelectric dams, windmills and soybean farms cause displacement; and deforestation-prevention programs may disrupt traditional ways of life.

Against this backdrop, it is not surprising that ESCR feature, in different forms and ways, in climate litigation. Climate change litigation includes lawsuits to increase coherence between states' international commitments and declarations on climate risks and their domestic actions, as well as cases where people – not only citizens but also residents and people (at risk of being) internationally displaced due to climate change – challenge governments and fossil fuel corporations for the realization of their duties of care and protection, which are increasingly framed as human rights claims in the context of climate change.[2] In a broad sense, ESCR are at stake in all climate litigation. However, it is only the cases where ESCR are used explicitly

---

[1]    The work on this publication was supported by a grant from the University of Bergen Centre for Climate and Energy Transformation.
[2]    Jacqueline Peel and Hari M Osofsky, 'A Rights Turn in Climate Change Litigation?' (2018) 7 Transnational Environmental Law 37.

in the argumentation, or where ESCR form part of the legal basis, that fall within the scope of ESCR-related climate litigation in this chapter.

Section 2 of the chapter introduces the emergence of climate litigation and the role of ESCR within it. In Section 3 we explore climate litigation in different areas of the law, and show how ESCR arguments feature within the litigation in different ways. Section 4 discusses advances and challenges within the different types of ESCR-based climate litigation, while Section 5 discusses the potential of ESCR-based climate litigation and points to what we could expect in the near future.

## 2.   THE EMERGENCE OF CLIMATE LITIGATION AND THE ROLE OF ECONOMIC, SOCIAL AND CULTURAL RIGHTS

### 2.1   Climate Change and Human Rights

The connection of climate claims to human rights is becoming clearer,[3] thanks in part to human rights bodies' recent work on states' human rights obligations in relation to climate change.[4] This interpretative work has shown that state obligations associated with ESCR – such as the right to adequate housing, food, water or health – are of high relevance in relation to climate change, particularly requiring states to take preventive measures to reduce the impacts of climate change on the enjoyment of these rights and to provide remedies if harms have occurred.[5] In this chapter we approach human rights – civil and political, along with economic, social and cultural – as an integral set of interconnected norms that seek to protect the dignity of the human person without discriminations of any kind. Thus in this chapter we use 'human rights-based climate litigation' and 'ESCR litigation' indistinctively.

According to the Office of the United Nations High Commissioner for Human Rights (OHCHR), at the national level states have an obligation to protect people from the harmful effects of climate change. This includes an obligation to adopt a legal and institutional framework that assists those within their jurisdiction to adapt to the effects of climate change. While states have some discretion to decide on the adaptation measures they adopt, they should ensure that they result from a process that provides for informed public participation; take into account national and international standards; are neither retrogressive nor discriminatory; and are implemented once adopted.[6] With respect to mitigation, since the dangerous accumulation

---

[3]   While climate change creates conditions of socio-environmental risk, including threats to life and property, its nature as a super-wicked problem with economic, ecological and social aspects in its causation makes it especially critical for the enjoyment of ESCR, such as the right to self-determination of peoples, the right to work and social security including social insurance, the right to an adequate standard of living for individuals and families, to adequate food, clothing and housing, to the continuous improvement of living conditions, to the enjoyment of the highest attainable standard of physical and mental health and to education.

[4]   OHCHR, 'Mapping Human Rights Obligations Relating to the Enjoyment of a Safe, Clean, Healthy and Sustainable Environment' (2014); OHCHR, 'Report of the Special Rapporteur on the Issue of Human Rights Obligations Relating to the Enjoyment of a Safe, Clean, Healthy and Sustainable Environment' (1 February 2016) A/HRC/31/52.

[5]   Annalisa Savaresi and Juan Auz, 'Climate Change Litigation and Human Rights: Pushing the Boundaries' (2019) 9 Climate Law 244.

[6]   OHCHR, 2016 (n 4) para 68.

of greenhouse gases in the atmosphere – which threatens ESCR – responds to cumulative processes over a long period, the reduction cannot occur by the mitigation efforts of a single state. States, therefore, have obligations under human rights law to mitigate their own emissions,[7] within the frame of the duty of international cooperation.[8]

The UN Framework Convention on Climate Change (UNFCCC) Conference of the Parties (COP) has officially recognized that the adverse effects of climate change affect the enjoyment of human rights and that the effects of climate change will most strongly affect those who are already vulnerable due to geography, gender, age, indigenous or minority status and disability.[9] For example, environmental injustice puts current and future vulnerable populations at higher risk of climate change-related health burdens such as waterborne disease and potentially new diseases arising out of a warmer climate and changing living conditions.[10] And people living in poverty in disaster-prone areas, or who are forced to migrate for climate-related reasons, are even more vulnerable to harm from more intense and more frequent storms, hurricanes and droughts, as well as from pandemics like the outbreak of the SARS-CoV-2 virus (whether these are climate-related or not).[11]

## 2.2    The Emergence of Climate Litigation

Reducing greenhouse gas emissions into the atmosphere may be one of the greatest collective action challenges faced by humanity, and courts are playing an increasingly important role in tackling it, as individuals and groups are increasingly turning to litigation as part of a manifold set of mobilization strategies to advance governance transformations in the face of the climate crisis.

Litigation has been particularly salient in political circumstances where the political establishment has been ideologically averse to climate action, as has frequently been the case in the United States of America (US), where the first cases emerged in the 1990s. From 2009 onwards the development of climate case law accelerated and took on a more global profile,[12] and since 2013 a new wave of constitutional and administrative law climate cases has emerged in different parts of the world. Perhaps the best known of these is the *Urgenda* case, challeng-

---

[7]    As stated in the cases *Leghari v Federation of Pakistan* (Lahore High Court Green Bench, 2015); *Massachusetts v Environmental Protection Agency* (US Supreme Court, 2007); *Urgenda Foundation v State of the Netherlands* (District Court of The Hague, 2015), and *Future Generations v Government of Colombia* (Supreme Court of Justice of Colombia, 2018). We explain these cases later in this chapter (the cases were all won – at least in significant parts – by the litigants).

[8]    OHCHR, 'Report of the Special Rapporteur on the Issue of Human Rights Obligations Relating to the Enjoyment of a Safe, Clean, Healthy and Sustainable Environment, A/HRC/31/52' (n 4) para 71.

[9]    Sébastien Jodoin and Katherine Lofts, 'Economic, Social and Cultural Rights and Climate Change: A Legal Reference Guide' http://academicsstand.org/.

[10]    Major killer diseases such as malaria are spreading to new areas with a warming climate. Some have also speculated that the COVID-19 virus disrupting the world in 2020 could be linked to climate-related changes which, jointly with economic development strategies, bring high density human settlements and livestock into closer proximity to wild animals. See Michael Roberts, 'It Was the Virus That Did It' (2020) <https://thenextrecession.wordpress.com/2020/03/15/it-was-the-virus-that-did-it/>.

[11]    Ibid.

[12]    Jacqueline Peel and Hari M Osofsky, 'Litigation's Regulatory Pathways and the Administrative State: Lessons from U.S. and Australian Climate Change Governance' (2013) 25 Georgetown Int'l Envtl. Law Review 207.

ing the Dutch government's climate mitigation policies. This case, which is discussed in depth below, sparked a wave of similar cases on climate and human rights against governments after it brought a lower-court victory for the plaintiffs in 2015.[13]

The first *Urgenda* case victory came at a time when developments in the global climate governance regime made litigation even more important as a climate governance strategy. When the UNFCCC COP 21 in Paris in 2015 failed to reach agreement on emissions, it adopted a bottom-up approach based on nationally determined contributions (NDC). The decentralized nature of the Paris Agreement, with NDCs that are insufficient to reach the aim of limiting global warming to two degrees and multiple blockages in the fair distribution of responsibilities for climate mitigation and adaptation among states at the international level, means that it is now mostly left to social mobilization at the national and subnational levels to secure state self-restraint, responsibility and coherent climate action.[14]

Climate governance in the post-Paris era has thus increased the relevance of domestic accountability mechanisms, including climate litigation against both governments and corporations. To meet the agreed temperature goal it is necessary that states not only implement their intended contributions and report transparently on the process, but also strengthen their commitments periodically. These international obligations can easily be ignored or poorly accomplished by states due to the high political costs of implementing climate policies under the dominant (unsustainable) development models. This is why climate litigation has been key in holding governments accountable for their climate governance performance.

Some litigation directly uses climate change norms and science, treating it as an exceptional legal issue,[15] but there is also litigation that does not make specific mention of it and still is relevant in the context of climate change.[16] Climate change is a complex issue resulting from the interconnection of different environmental and social phenomena. For example, cases on oil spills, gas flaring or energy efficiency are relevant to a cumulative transformation of the climate crisis, even though such cases may not be framed by litigants as climate litigation. Here we use the term climate litigation mainly for cases using climate change explicitly as an argument by the parties or the court, but also include cases that, while not directly argued on

---

[13]   The case, *Urgenda Foundation v The Netherlands* [2015] HAZA C/09/00456689 (24 June 2015), was lodged in 2013 and finally decided by the Supreme Court on 19 December 2019). On the arguments and legal implications of the case brought by the Urgenda Foundation against the Dutch government, see, for example, Jolene Lin, 'The First Successful Climate Negligence Case: A Comment on Urgenda Foundation v. The State of the Netherlands (Ministry of Infrastructure and the Environment)' (2015) 5 Climate Law 65; Suryapratim Roy and Edwin Woerdman, 'Situating Urgenda v the Netherlands within Comparative Climate Change Litigation' (2016) 34 Journal of Energy & Natural Resources Law 165; Josephine van Zeben, 'Establishing a Governmental Duty of Care for Climate Change Mitigation: Will Urgenda Turn the Tide?' (2015) 4 Transnational Environmental Law 339; Roger Cox, 'A Climate Change Litigation Precedent: Urgenda Foundation v the State of the Netherlands' (2015) 79 <www.cigionline.org/sites/default/files/cigi_paper_79.pdf>.

[14]   Benoit Mayer, 'State Responsibility and Climate Change Governance: A Light through the Storm' (2014) 13 Chinese Journal of International Law 539; Christina Voigt, 'State Responsibility for Climate Change Damages' (2008) 77 Nordic Journal of International Law 1; Roger Cox, *Revolution Justified* (Planet Prosperity Foundation 2012).

[15]   John Copeland Nagle, 'Climate Exceptionalism' (2010) 40 Environmental Law 53.

[16]   Kim Bouwer, 'Climate Consciousness in Daily Legal Practice' (*Oxford University Press's blog*, 2015) <https://blog.oup.com/2015/05/climate-consciousness-daily-legal-practice/>.

the basis of climate impacts, clearly aim to impact climate mitigation or adaptation, by relying on other relevant environmental concerns.

The adjudication of climate change responsibilities by the courts faces some critical barriers. Among them are the idea of uncertainty over climate science and the understanding of single actors' emissions being only a 'drop in the ocean'. The latter means that a single particular contribution is minimal when compared to the sheer size of a global problem. The consequence of this argument is that no single actor could be fairly declared liable, or that a change in their actions would not be a meaningful contribution. Thus, judicial orders of this type would lack basic causality and redressability conditions. Another barrier to adjudication is the anthropocentric paradigm of development inherent to many societies. Greenhouse gas emissions from activities such as driving, farming and electricity generation still appear to be 'minor, common, and beneficial, which are precisely the characteristics that make them immune from liability or regulation under the dominant interpretations of the harm principle'.[17] As Kysar and Ewing put it, 'the macroscale demands of climate change governance are thus obscured by microscale focus on disaggregated activities and harms, rather than on the systems in which they are embedded'.[18] In the next sections we analyze how these barriers have played out in climate litigation and how they might influence changes in ESCR perspectives in the near future.

### 2.3    The Role of ESCR in Climate Litigation

As noted above, climate change puts at risk the ESCR of all humans, but most particularly those of already marginalized communities, who often have the least access to public support and state protection. Consequently, equality and the progressive realization of ESCR should play a key role in the design and implementation of climate mitigation and adaptation policies in all countries. Although specific references to international human rights law are not included in the UNFCCC,[19] or in the Kyoto Protocol,[20] during international negotiations a number of states, particularly the groups of Small Island Developing States (SIDS) and Least Developed Countries (LDC), have called attention to the human rights aspects of climate change. The Paris Agreement, in its preamble, acknowledges that climate change is a common concern of humankind, and that consequently

> Parties should, when taking action to address climate change, respect, promote and consider their respective obligations on human rights, the right to health, the rights of indigenous peoples, local communities, migrants, children, persons with disabilities and people in vulnerable situations and

---

[17]    Douglas A Kysar and Benjamin Ewing, 'Prods and Pleas: Limited Government in an Era of Unlimited Harm' 360 <http://digitalcommons.law.yale.edu/fss_papers>.

[18]    Ibid.

[19]    UN General Assembly, United Nations Framework Convention on Climate Change: resolution A/RES/48/189 1992. Opened for signature 4 June 1992, entered into force 21 March 1994 (United Nations Framework Convention on Climate Change).

[20]    UNFCCC, Kyoto Protocol to the United Nations Framework Convention on Climate Change (10 December 1997) FCCC/CP/1997/L.7/Add 1. The final version of the Protocol was issued as part of the Third Conference of the Parties (COP 3) report: FCCC/CP/1997/Add.2.

the right to development, as well as gender equality, empowerment of women and intergenerational equity.[21]

The protection of ESCR in the creation and execution of climate policies has also been played out in climate litigation, sometimes as secondary or supportive arguments in civil and administrative law cases, and at other times as the central claim of constitutional cases. In Sections 3 and 4 below we present this typology and explain in more detail how ESCR arguments have been used.

Most human rights-based climate litigation is directed against governments, given that under human rights law the main duty-holder is the state, including when fossil fuel companies are state owned. However, even if the UNFCCC and the 2015 Paris Agreement attribute to states the duty to curb emissions, it is mostly private corporations who cause them and profit from them. Recent developments in attribution science have thus stimulated a surge in climate litigation against corporate actors, and recent studies suggest that several multinational corporations are responsible historically for the largest share of global greenhouse gas emissions.[22] As a result, the responsibility of corporations for human rights breaches associated with climate change has also increasingly come under the spotlight.[23]

## 3. VARIATIONS WITHIN ESCR-RELATED CLIMATE LITIGATION

The climate-related court cases that have most powerfully captured the popular imagination are arguably those invoking the rights of future generations to life, health, a healthy environment, food and water, as argued in *Future Generations v Colombia*, about halting deforestation in the Colombian Amazon; and the rights to private and family life of present and future generations, as argued in *Urgenda v The Netherlands*, about increasing ambition in national emission cuts. These constitutional cases invoke the protection of ESC rights directly as arguments for more stringent climate mitigation action. But the use of ESCR arguments in climate litigation can be found also in other areas of the law and in less exceptional cases. In this section, we first look more systematically at the climate court cases that use ESCR arguments in five different areas of the law (Section 3.1). Then, we contemplate some of the claims, actors and norms more deeply to bring out the most salient dimensions within ESCR-related climate litigation (Section 3.2), which we organize towards a typology.

### 3.1 Areas of Climate Litigation

The range of court cases across the world pressing for better climate mitigation and adaptation displays diverse framings and creative approaches. Within the broader corpus of climate liti-

---

[21]   UNFCCC, Paris Agreement to the United Nations Framework Convention on Climate Change (13 November 2015) FCCC/CP/2015/10/Add.1, issued as part of COP 21, entered into force on 4 November 2016.

[22]   Richard Heede, 'Tracing Anthropogenic Carbon Dioxide and Methane Emissions to Fossil Fuel and Cement Producers, 1854–2010' (2014) 122 Climatic Change 229 <http://link.springer.com/10.1007/s10584-013-0986-y>.

[23]   Savaresi and Auz (n 5).

*Table 19.1      Areas of climate litigation with exemplary ESCR cases*

| | 1. Civil Law (tort) | 2. Administrative Law | 3. Constitutional Law | 4. International Law | 5. Criminal Law |
|---|---|---|---|---|---|
| **a. Mitigation** | *Comer v Murphy Oil (USA 2009) Ramirez v Exxon Mobil Corp. (USA 2019)* (P) | *Greenpeace Australia Ltd v Redbank Power (1994) EarthLife v South Africa (2018)\* Plan B Earth v the UK (2018)(P)\* Massachusetts v EPA (the USA 2007)\** | *Urgenda v Netherlands (2015)\* Juliana v the USA (2015) Greenpeace et al. v Norway (2017) Future Generations v Colombia (2018)\** | *Inuit Peoples v the USA (2005)* | *Mapuche Confederation of Neuquén v YPF (Argentina 2018)* (P) |
| **b. Adaptation** | *Kivalina v Exxon et al. (USA 2008)* | *Ironstone Community v NSW Minister for Planning et al. (Australia 2011)* | *Leghari v Pakistan (2015)\* Decision C-035/16, Constitutional Court of Colombia (2016)\** | *Inuit Peoples v the USA (2005) Petition of The Maldives to the OHCHR under Res. 7/23 (2008)* | |

*Notes:*
\* Case decided in favor of plaintiffs/in favor of climate protection.
(P) Decision pending at the time of writing.

gation, we can, as indicated in Table 19.1, distinguish five main areas, categorized according to the body of law they use as the basis for adjudication: (1) civil law (tort), (2) administrative law, (3) constitutional law, (4) international law and (5) criminal law prosecutions. Each of these areas has cases related to (a) climate mitigation and (b) climate adaptation. And within each of the ten subsets we find cases that involve ESCR. In the table, exemplary cases are given for each subset. For a comprehensive overview of the rapidly expanding universe of climate litigation cases, see the Sabin Centre climate litigation database.[24] Table 19.1 reflects what we currently see happening in terms of areas of law by which climate change is litigated in ways that involve ESCR. In the future we could potentially also see ESCR-related climate litigation in other areas of law.

### 3.1.1   Civil law (tort) cases
Climate-related civil law cases typically seek compensation from fossil fuel corporations for climate-related damages. The damages may include adaptation measures, but the overarching motivation is to force mitigation, including by raising public awareness. These are cases against private actors, who (save provisions for horizontal application of rights) are not the guarantors of constitutional rights or human rights under international law, yet violations of

---

[24]   The information on all court cases we present in this paper was retrieved from the litigation database of the Sabin Center for Climate Change Law, Columbia Law School, unless otherwise indicated. See Sabin Center for Climate Change Law, 'Climate Change Litigation Databases' (2020) <http://climatecasechart.com/>.

ESC rights to life, health and a healthy environment and livelihood are often central in the description of harms.

Litigation examples within this category, where ESCR arguments figure centrally, are *Kivalina v Exxon* [12-1072 (2008) USA], where native Alaskans sought damages from oil and power companies for impacts of climate change on their village including climate displacement and relocation costs; and *Comer v Murphy Oil* [12-60291 (2009) USA], an action seeking housing damages related to Hurricane Katrina under tort law. More recently, in *Ramirez v Exxon Mobil* [3:16-cv-3111 (2016) USA], plaintiffs used a securities fraud class action to allege that Exxon failed to disclose climate risks to investors and had therefore infringed financial regulations in place since 1933 in the US. The result of this petition is pending at the time of writing.

### 3.1.2   Administrative law

Administrative law cases constitute the bulk of climate litigation so far.[25] As we have argued elsewhere, administrative law cases are perhaps the part of the climate litigation corpus with the highest impact and the most potential.[26] They vary widely in their subject matter, seeking, for example, more stringent emission standards; enforcement of existing rules; more climate-inclusive environmental impact assessments for new projects; and court declarations of state responsibility for climate change mitigation or adaptation, for example, related to subsidies for investments or climate-related disaster preparedness. The right to access information is often central in these cases, but the extent to which ESCR feature explicitly as part of the legal basis in administrative law climate litigation depends on the nature of the legal system.

While often far-reaching in their effects, administrative law cases are for the most part 'unspectacular', in the sense of not being high profile in terms of publicity or innovative landmark decisions in legal terms, but rather being decided by the courts using routine legal doctrines rather than exceptional, precedent breaking ones. An illustrative case in this sense is *Massachusetts v EPA* (549 U.S. 497), decided by the US Supreme Court in 2007. The court ruled that greenhouse gases are pollutants within the meaning of the US federal statute for regulation of pollution, the Clean Air Act. The court, in this case, acknowledged that there were increasing levels of $CO_2$ in the global atmosphere, which – along with methane, nitrous oxide and other greenhouse gases – trapped heat on earth and produced global warming, changing the earth's climate and threatening Massachusetts citizens' public health and welfare.[27] This was an extremely consequential case, not least since, on the basis of climate science, it offi-

---

[25]   Michal Nachmany and Joana Setzer, 'Global Trends in Climate Change Legislation and Litigation: 2018 Snapshot' (2018) <www.lse.ac.uk/Grantham>; Meredith Wilensky, 'Climate Change in the Courts: An Assessment of Non-U.S. Climate Litigation' (2015) 6 Duke Environmental Law & Policy Forum 131; David Markell and JB Ruhl, 'An Empirical Assessment of Climate Change in the Courts: A New Jurisprudence or Business as Usual?' (2012) 64 Florida Law Review 15; Jacqueline Peel and Hari M Osofsky, *Climate Change Litigation: Regulatory Pathways to Cleaner Energy* (Cambridge University Press 2015).

[26]   See Catalina Vallejo and Siri Gloppen, 'Red-Green Lawfare? Climate Change Narratives in Courtrooms' in Jackie Dugard, Asuncion Lera St. Clair and Siri Gloppen (eds), *Climate Talk: Rights, Poverty and Justice* (Juta Law 2013). Catalina Vallejo, 'Suing the State for Climate Change' PhD thesis (Universidad de Los Andes, Bogota 2018). Catalina Vallejo and Siri Gloppen, 'The Quest for Butterfly Climate Adjudication' (Paper Prepared for the Workshop on 'Climate Litigation' at New York University 9–11 March 2020) (2020).

[27]   See further Nagle (n 15).

cially established $CO_2$ as a pollutant to be regulated – in a political context where climate science was highly controversial. But from a legal point of view it was routine in that the court, as in other cases, merely applied the Clean Air Act on the basis of scientific evidence.

One of the first cases using administrative law to push for climate action, with the arguments in part touching upon ESCR concerns, was *Greenpeace Australia Ltd v Redbank Power Co.* ([1994] 86 LGERA 143 Australia). Using the language of 'global warming', it challenged a state council decision to grant permission for a coal power station that would harm the atmosphere and have a major impact on health, agriculture, ecosystems, rainfall and snow cover. The case was dismissed because climate harms were considered speculative and economic development was prioritized. Still, the court did impose a scheme of emissions offset through forestation. Jurisprudence is rapidly changing in this area, at least in some jurisdictions. Courts have started to accept the need to include the projected greenhouse gas emissions of proposed power plants in environmental impact assessments before licensing.

An example from South Africa is *EarthLife Africa Johannesburg v Minister of Environmental Affairs and Others* [Case no. 65662/16 (2018)], where an environmental organization successfully applied to the High Court to challenge the Department of Environmental Affairs' approval to develop a 1200 MW coal-fired power plant that would operate until at least 2060, with large $CO_2$ equivalent emissions per year. Australia has several successful cases in this area, and in early 2020 an appellate court in the UK ruled that the government acted unlawfully by approving an expansion of Heathrow International Airport without considering the country's commitment to meeting the Paris Agreement goals (*Plan B Earth and Others v Secretary of State for Transport*, [2020] EWCA Civ 214, 2018). ESRC arguments or concerns featured in all these cases.

Notwithstanding these developments, we find, as will be discussed in more detail below, that when environmental concerns compete with major economic considerations, the jurisprudence tends to favor economic considerations without a rigorous examination of the principles of sustainable development; norms that are part of the global regulatory regime on climate change; or relevant soft law as expressed in the 2015 Oslo Principles on Global Climate Change Obligations.[28]

### 3.1.3   Constitutional law

Climate-related claims brought before domestic courts on the basis of breaches of constitutional rights typically demand protection from the state for communities most vulnerable to climate-related harms, for future generations, and increasingly also for the ecosystems themselves, including through the granting of legal personhood and rights protection to rivers and ecosystems such as the Amazon. This is the type of case where ESCR commonly features most explicitly as a central legal basis.

For example, in the *Urgenda Foundation v State of the Netherlands* case mentioned earlier, litigants challenged the Dutch state's duty of care to protect the rights of its citizens to life and welfare in the context of climate change, and succeeded. In *Leghari v Federation of Pakistan* [(2015) W.P. No. 25501/201], the Lahore High Court Green Bench derived a duty of protection which is comparable to the one created in the Dutch case. In this case, a Pakistani farmer sued the national government for failing to execute the National Climate Change Policy of

---

[28]   See 'Oslo Principles on Global Climate Change Obligations | Global Justice Program' <https://globaljustice.yale.edu/oslo-principles-global-climate-change-obligations>.

2012 and the Framework for Implementation of Climate Change Policy (2014–30). The court, citing domestic and international legal principles, determined that 'the delay and lethargy of the state in implementing the Framework offend the fundamental rights of the citizens' and imposed remedies related to the creation of a governmental body to carry out the policy. We might be seeing much more of this area of litigation in the coming years.

In Colombia, in *Future Generations v Ministry of the Environment and Others (2018)*, 25 youth plaintiffs sued several bodies within the Colombian government and several corporations, in the plaintiffs' name and that of future generations, to enforce their claimed rights to a healthy environment, life, health, food and water. The plaintiffs successfully alleged that their rights were threatened by climate change, along with the government's failure to reduce deforestation and ensure compliance with a target for zero-net deforestation in the Colombian Amazon by the year 2020 (as agreed under the Paris Agreement). A surprising outcome of this case was the recognition by the Supreme Court of Justice of Colombia, of legal personhood to the Colombian Amazon as a subject of rights. This legal development resonates with the recent recognition of legal personality to animals and rivers as a means to grant them special legal protection.[29]

The former cases discuss climate change impacts as the main cause of ESCR violations, but climate change can also be used as a secondary or supportive argument in rights violations argued on the base of other environmental harms. For example, in the 2005 ruling of *Gbemre (and Iwherekan community) v Shell Petroleum Development Company of Nigeria Ltd et al.* (FHC/B/CS/53/05), a Nigerian federal court ruled that oil companies must stop flaring gas in the Niger Delta. Jonah Gbemre – a representative of the Iwherekan community in the Niger Delta – sued the Nigerian government and Shell Petroleum. The court argued that the practice of gas flaring was unconstitutional because it violated the fundamental rights to life and dignity of humans provided in the Constitution of Nigeria and the African Charter on Human and People's Rights. The case very briefly mentions how gas flaring generates large $CO_2$ emissions and thus contributes to climate change. Although the decision did not deliberate upon the effects of gas flaring on climate change, it helps raise awareness about the direct and indirect rights violations caused by gas flaring: direct harms to life and health through local air pollution, and indirect ESCR violations through pollution of the global atmosphere.

### 3.1.4   Public international law

Some climate cases rely on international human rights law as a legal basis. Petitions under this category are filed before international courts or human rights commissions regarding the adverse effects of climate change on indigenous peoples; communities with deprived adaptation capacity, such as inhabitants of small island states; and other communities who are especially vulnerable to the effects of climate change due to poverty or a particularly dangerous geographical location. There are also cases regarding places considered world heritage sites. The dominant argument in this type of case is that the governments and cor-

---

[29]   See Paola Villavicencio Calzadilla, 'A Paradigm Shift in Courts' View on Nature: The Atrato River and Amazon Basin Cases in Colombia' (2019) 15 Law Environment and Development Journal 49; Cass R Sunstein, 'The Rights of Animals' (2003) 70 The University of Chicago Law Review 387; Erin O'Donnell and Elizabeth Macpherson, 'Voice, Power and Legitimacy: The Role of the Legal Person in River Management in New Zealand, Chile and Australia' (2019) 23 Australian Journal of Water Resources 35.

porations most responsible for global emissions have an obligation to transform their energy policies and to assist communities in other countries who (despite low emissions) are suffering climate-related harms and lacking means of their own to adapt.

The cases in this category are few and have generally been unsuccessful. The 2005 petition by the Inuit peoples to the Inter-American Commission on Human Rights (IACHR) argued that climate policy failures in the US were contributing to the harmful effects of climate change damage in the Arctic. The petition had both mitigation and adaptation claims but was rejected and does not appear to have changed the formal US position. However, it probably increased the public profile of Arctic climate change impacts. Similarly, there is the 2008 Maldives petition to the High Commissioner for Human Rights (OHCHR), presented under Human Rights Council Resolution 7/23 'Human rights and climate change'. The Maldives, as a small island state in the Indian Ocean, is prone to land loss and even disappearing due to sea-level rise. The petition argued the state's risk is a result of 'social processes beyond its sovereign control'.

So far, public international law petitions have not resulted in orders or recommendations to states to curb their greenhouse gas emissions; neither have they resulted in any declarations on human rights violations or protection for communities claiming special vulnerability. Hence, in terms of direct effects, not much has been achieved. The use of international law to adjudicate state responsibilities over climate-related risks and harms thus continues to be challenging.[30]

Scholars have called for the applicability of the law of state responsibility *between states* to claim greenhouse gas emissions as an internationally wrongful act.[31] But while it is generally possible to invoke international state responsibility for climate change damages, there are – as explained by Christina Voigt – conceptual uncertainties.[32] First, international state responsibility has not played a practical role in the environmental context. Most transboundary environmental concerns are solved through diplomatic means (even the most critical ones, such as Chernobyl). The case law is thus scarce and provides little guidance on complex environmental claims such as climate change damage. Second, obligations based on treaties demand interpretation, and while an obligation to prevent climate harm could be read into the UNFCCC, there is a tendency to choose the interpretation least restrictive on state responsibility. Third, while there is a customary principle of the prohibition of transboundary harm, it is based on the breach of an obligation of due diligence in the regulation and control of harmful activities, which places a heavy burden of proof on the injured state. Fourth, the multiplicity of polluters and victims poses evidentiary difficulties, and there is no clear rule in international law on how to apportion damage between multiple wrongdoers or causes of climate change. Finally, there is little guidance on how ecological harm could be compensated.

Given the consensual nature of international litigation – states must ratify agreements and accept the jurisdiction of an international court – it is also difficult to force compliance, or even to find a forum with jurisdiction to hear an international claim against another state. Thus, in practice, very few cases claiming responsibility for environmental damages have been handled

---

[30]   Norma A Polizzi, 'Can International Law Adapt to Climate Change?' [2020] Environmental Claims Journal 1; Voigt (n 14); Mayer (n 14).

[31]   Mayer (n 14); Voigt (n 14).

[32]   Voigt (n 14).

in this way.[33] And due to their geopolitical location, the most affected states have the least diplomatic power in international negotiations. This all contributes to the fragmentation of responsibility for dangerous greenhouse gas accumulation in the atmosphere.[34]

For now, the use of accountability mechanisms in domestic law promises better results as citizens seek coherence between a state's external climate discourse and its internal practices.[35] Examples of such internal practices include: licensing of new carbon-intensive projects; investing public funds in carbon-intensive projects domestically or abroad; not providing information to the public about these investments when required; ignoring adaptation needs or not implementing existing adaptation policies; violating the principles of non-discrimination and non-retrogration in the realization of ESCR; having deficient policy targets for greenhouse gas reduction; not including the effects of climate change in urban planning and new development projects; or investing in renewable energy businesses that violate human rights, among others.

### 3.1.5   Criminal law

Criminal prosecutions have so far not been extensively used for the protection of forests specifically acting as carbon sinks, or to prevent private actors from undertaking carbon-intensive industrial activity in violation of greenhouse gas emissions regulations. The reason is that under existing law such activities are not even considered illegal. However, criminal codes in many countries include different acts causing environmental harm as crimes. As we mentioned in Section 2 of this chapter, many of those crimes and prosecutions, even if not framed as climate-oriented, can be relevant in the context of climate change,[36] and there could be a good number of such criminal investigations in many countries.

What we know for sure is that criminal law has been used by private actors to prosecute climate protestors for trespassing or vandalism, in cases of boycotts or disturbances in the normal operation of fossil fuel industries.[37] A recent example is the UK trial of Angela Ditchfield, an Extinction Rebellion (XR) activist arrested for spray-painting two XR symbols onto the headquarters of a county council during a protest in 2018. She argued a legal excuse to commit vandalism because she believed that climate disaster posed an imminent threat to land and homes. She was found not guilty at Cambridge Magistrates' Court. The use of criminal prosecutions and the overall use of strategic lawsuits against public participation (SLAPP suits),[38] or the so-called green backlash, is likely to gain much more importance in the near future, as social mobilization around the climate crisis increases.

Domestic courts have started to hear charges of climate-related corruption, misinformation and harms against companies (often supplementary to tort claims). An example, at the domestic level, of criminal law cases invoking climate change is *Mapuche Confederation of Neuquén v YPF* (2008), in which the Mapuche Confederation of Neuquén, Argentina, brought

---

[33]   Ibid.

[34]   Mayer (n 14).

[35]   Ibid.

[36]   Bouwer (n 16).

[37]   See Sabin Center for Climate Change Law, 'Protesters Archives' (2020) <http://climatecasechart .com/non-us-case-category/protesters/>.

[38]   SLAPPs are typically regarded as a threat, designed to close down democratic free speech and protest. See Christopher J Hilson, 'Environmental SLAPPs in the UK: Threat or Opportunity?' (2016) 25 Environmental Politics 248.

a criminal complaint asserting that mishandling of toxic waste has resulted in contamination that threatens the environment and public health. The complaint discusses a United Nations report that called on the Argentine government to reconsider the decision to allow fracking in the Vacca Muerta valley because of the greenhouse gas emissions associated with shale gas development. The complaint seeks a criminal investigation into the waste sites, and names the Argentine energy company YPF, Total, Exxon, Pan American Energy, Pampa Energía, the Secretary of Territorial and Environmental Development, the Subsecretary of the Environment, the Provision Director of Environmental Situations and Special Residuals Management and the Provincial Budget Director.

At the international criminal law level, there is a push by civil society organizations to develop an international crime of ecocide as an amendment to the Rome Statute. The idea of ecocide as an international crime to stand alongside genocide as the fifth crime against peace was at the forefront of various discussions in international law fora between 1972 and 1996, and was originally included in the Rome Statute but was dropped from the 1996 draft. It has since been taken forward by Polly Higgins,[39] and by organizations such as Extinction Rebellion.[40]

To sum up so far, climate litigation is a rapidly growing field and we see ESCR arguments playing a role in cases traversing different areas of the law. In what follows we identify some dimensions within ESCR climate litigation, aiming at a better understanding of their variations in terms of perspectives, actors, temporality, rights claimed and climate policy orientation. This analysis assists in thinking about how the climate crisis might influence future developments in ESCR, which we address in the final section of the chapter.

### 3.2    Analyzing ESCR-related Climate Litigation

As the discussion above indicates, ESCR can – and do – enter into most areas of climate litigation either as central or secondary arguments, but are particularly central to cases within the constitutional and international law categories, where rights violations and the allocation of state responsibility are directly at stake. In Section 4 we analyze more deeply some of the cases introduced earlier, and included in Table 19.1, and we explain how ESCR were argued in these cases. But first we outline a framework for analyzing ESCR-related climate litigation. This is presented in Table 19.2, where we isolate the central dimensions within this body of litigation to help us better understand the different approaches, and think about what these might mean for the future of ESCR in the context of the climate crisis.

Considering the body of climate cases that resort to ESCR arguments, the first distinction to be made regards the *rights bearers*. Some of the cases concern what we normally think about as ESC rights bearers, namely *people living today*. But since the most catastrophic harms are likely to affect *future generations*, these also feature as subjects to which ESCR protection is owed. There are also cases focusing on nature, with *ecosystems as rights bearers*. These are not

---

[39]    Polly Higgins, Damien Short and Nigel South, 'Protecting the Planet: A Proposal for a Law of Ecocide' (2013) 59 Crime, Law and Social Change; Jonathan Watts, 'Polly Higgins, Lawyer Who Fought for Recognition of "Ecocide", Dies Aged 50' *The Guardian* (2019) <www.theguardian.com/commentisfree/2019/mar/28/destruction-earth-crime-polly-higgins-ecocide-george-monbiot>;    Stop Ecocide, 'Polly Higgins' <www.stopecocide.earth/polly-higgins>.

[40]    Ecocide 'Extinction Rebellion' <https://rebellion.earth/tag/ecocide/>.

*Table 19.2    Analytical framework for ESCR-related climate litigation*

| | Rights bearers | | |
| --- | --- | --- | --- |
| | Currently alive | Future generations | Nature |
| **Temporality of ESC violations** | Current<br>Near future (risks) | Future | Current<br>Future |
| **ESCR claims** | Family life, health, water, housing, culture, work | Family life, health, housing, water, food | Biocultural rights and rights of nature |
| **Climate orientations** | Mitigation, adaptation, resistance to climate action | Mitigation | Mitigation |

ESCR cases strictly speaking, and in some ways can be seen to question the very basis of the anthropocentric worldview providing the basis for human rights. However, claims for the protection of ecosystems as living entities that need protection in their own right are inextricably interconnected to the rights to land, water and a sustainable environment for peoples living in these ecosystems, often indigenous communities. As ESCR-like cases, they are included here.

The second distinction, related to the first, regards the *temporality of the ESCR violations.* In some cases, these are manifest harms violating people's ESCR at present, and where the main focus of the claim is on adaptation; more often, these are *(potential) future ESCR violations*, more or less preventable. The focus here is typically on mitigation efforts (to cut greenhouse gas emissions) but also on adaptation measures, such as plans and resources for those who have to move due to sea-level rise.

The third dimension is the *ESC rights that are used in the litigation* as (part of) the basis for making the claim. These include, among others, the rights to work, housing, health, food, water, family life and culture. Arguments for the protection of the right to a healthy environment have been particularly significant and versatile. They feature in a range of cases: to claim for mitigation measures to protect against future harms; to stop activities such as gas flaring and fracking, which are both contributing to greenhouse gas emissions and polluting in ways that pose immediate threats to air and water supplies; and to claim for adaptation measures, such as clean-up of rivers and removal of vulnerable populations groups from the worst-affected areas.

The last dimension is the *orientation of the claim* vis-à-vis efforts to meet the climate crisis. Some ESCR claims (such as those on behalf of future generations) are making claims for *mitigation efforts*; others (such as inhabitants of low-lying areas experiencing flooding and at risk of being submerged) make claims for *adaptation measures*; yet others are *resisting* or claiming protection against climate actions (such as windmills, deforestation projects or hydroelectric dams) that have violated or that threaten their ESCR. The latter category also includes cases where developers have been allowed to take advantage of climate-related disasters or concerns. Examples of this are where developers, often aided by new zoning requirements, are permitted to build hotels and other businesses on lucrative shoreline properties, with the (usually poor) people who originally inhabited and made their livelihood on this land being moved or prevented from returning, allegedly as climate-precautionary measures.

## 4.    ADVANCES AND CHALLENGES IN ESCR CLIMATE LITIGATION

As we have seen, climate change litigation using human rights arguments has seen some positive outcomes in both mitigation and adaptation efforts. Regarding mitigation, we have seen the protection of the rights to life, health and a healthy environment as a legitimate basis for holding governments to account for climate change, as in *Leghari v Pakistan* and *Urgenda v The Netherlands*. We also see the recognition of legal personhood of ecosystems as subjects of rights, as in *Future Generations v Colombia*. These are cases that set important precedents and promise innovative future outcomes, which are most likely to occur in jurisdictions where litigants are overcoming procedural requirements for access to environmental justice, and where there are favorable legal opportunity structures to address climate change.[41]

Mitigation court cases have hosted interesting debates that show tensions between ESCR rights and climate policy, particularly about the right to work in an era of energy transition. Adaptation cases include important debates about the protection of water sources and water rights in the context of climate change. In what follows, we highlight challenges around the rights to work, sustainable livelihoods, housing and family life, as they play out in court cases discussing airport expansions, developments affecting water sources and carbon sinks and housing projects foreseeably prone to climate impacts.

### 4.1    Right to Work – The Case of Airport Expansions

The right to work raises practical and symbolic concerns in the context of climate litigation, in a predominantly carbon-based economy transitioning to a low-carbon one. Protecting the right to work has been key in debates on proposed airport expansions. Below we discuss how three licensed airport expansion projects have been challenged by communities on climate protection grounds, with climate concerns pitted against economic considerations and the right to work. The cases, two in the UK and the other in Austria, question the need and legality of a city's increased air traffic and air connection capacity.

In *Barbone and Ross (on behalf of Stop Stansted Expansion) v Secretary of State for Transport* ([2009] EWHC 463), a UK court dismissed an application by the Stop Stansted Expansion group which challenged the granting of permission for an increase in capacity of London's Stansted Airport, under the Town and Country Planning Act 1990. The plaintiffs claimed that the government had failed to consider the project's greenhouse gas emissions when granting the planning permission. The court stated that the government had considered

---

[41]    Joana Setzer and Lisa Benjamin, 'Climate Litigation in the Global South: Constraints and Innovations' (2019) 9 *Transnational Environmental Law* 77. Legal opportunity structures refers to arenas where individuals and social movements can readily access and harness the power of receptive courts to pursue previously unrealized rights claims through litigation of justiciable rights, and where court decisions are complied with. They are now frequently used by social movements and individuals to enhance or replace existing political strategies to affect policies. See Chris Hilson, 'New Social Movements: The Role of Legal Opportunity' (2002) 9 *Journal of European Public Policy* 238; Bruce M Wilson and Camila Gianella-Malca, 'Overcoming the Limits of Legal Opportunity Structures: LGBT Rights' Divergent Paths in Costa Rica and Colombia' (2019) 61 *Latin American Politics and Society* 138; Lisa Vanhala, 'Legal Opportunity Structures and the Paradox of Legal Mobilization by the Environmental Movement in the UK' (2012) 46 *Law and Society Review* 523.

the impacts of the project on climate change, but that its commitment to tackling the problem of climate change and reducing emissions across the economy did not mean that every sector of the economy was expected to follow the same path. This case shows how the climate problem defies coherence between a state's international acknowledgment of the urgent need of all states to mitigate climate change, and identifying actual carbon-intensive projects that add to the accumulation of greenhouse gases in the atmosphere. In this case both the executive and the judicial branch prioritized economic growth and the resistance-oriented right to work over sustainable development arguments, including the right to work and other ESCR of future generations.

In the 2017 Austrian case *In re Vienna-Schwechat Airport Expansion* (case W109 2000179-1/291E), plans for a third runway at the Vienna Schwechat airport were submitted for review by the government of the state of Lower Austria. In February 2017, Austria's Federal Administrative Court decided the case in favor of the plaintiffs, arguing that authorizing the runway would do more harm than good to the public interest, primarily because it would run counter to Austria's national and international obligations to mitigate the causes of climate change. The appellate Federal Administrative Court examined expected changes in future air traffic, the emissions impacts of those changes, and the extent to which it would be possible for the airport to control or limit various sources of emissions. It also considered the economic benefits of the additional runway, the adverse impacts of climate change on Austria, and the state of Austria and Europe's efforts to reduce emissions generally, and those from air traffic particularly. The court concluded that a third runway would increase Austria's annual $CO_2$ emissions by between 1.79 and 2.02 per cent by 2025. This did not align with Austria's 2020 transport sector emissions reduction target of 2.25 per cent. The Court also observed that short-term gains in the form of commerce or creation of jobs were outweighed by the likely economic consequences of a destabilized climate.

In June 2017 the Austrian Constitutional Court overturned the Federal Administrative Court's decision. The Constitutional Court cited several errors that led the lower court to improperly give weight to climate change and land use considerations in the balancing test it used to consider the public's interest in a third runway. The errors identified by the Constitutional Court included: misconstruing the Air Traffic Law's instruction to consider environmental protection over-broadly by factoring in environmental impacts beyond those directly attributable to air traffic; wrongly including in emissions projections aircraft emissions attributable to flight segments other than landing and take-off; improperly superimposing regional greenhouse gas emissions reduction targets on an analysis of legal rights and obligations under the federal Air Traffic Law; and misapplication of the Kyoto Protocol and Paris Agreement, which the Constitutional Court explained are the source of international obligations for Austria but are not generally applicable in the domestic legal context.

As noted earlier, the recent UK case *Plan B Earth and Others v Secretary of State for Transport* ([2020] EWCA Civ 214), filed in 2018, had a different outcome. A UK appellate court overturned a first instance decision and ruled that the government acted unlawfully by approving an expansion of Heathrow Airport without considering the country's commitment to meeting the Paris Agreement goals. The claimants argued that the national policy supporting the airport expansion violated the Planning Act 2008 and the Human Rights Act of 1998. On 27 February 2020, the Court of Appeal held that by failing to consider the Paris Agreement, the Secretary violated the Planning Act and the requirement to undertake a strategic environmental assessment pursuant to EC Council Directive 2001/42/EC. The court therefore concluded that the ANPS is invalid and must be redone. The court further ruled that in completing a new ANPS, the Secretary should consider the non-carbon dioxide climate impacts of aviation and the effects of emissions beyond 2050, both of which had been omitted from the original analysis. In February 2020 two private parties with an interest in the expansion appealed to the Supreme Court. The Supreme Court agreed to hear the appeal and the decision is pending at the time of writing.

In all of these cases, the right to work is a concern – specifically in relation to the jobs potentially lost in the transition to a low-carbon economy, which has been played as an argument against adopting mitigation measures. However, the right to work might also be negatively affected by a lack of proper mitigation of climate causes, as changes in ocean acidity and temperature may impact fisheries and increase rainfall variability and water salinization, affecting the agricultural sector and impacting employment.[42] Extreme weather events might affect the right to work due to changes in infrastructure, transportation and the disruption of business activities. Some businesses might decide to relocate from vulnerable areas, resulting in job losses and related displacement.[43] Climate-related pandemics may cause major economic disruptions and job loss. State mitigation measures such as projects under the Clean Development Mechanism (CDM) or Reducing Emissions from Deforestation and Forest Degradation (REDD+) in developing countries also have the potential to affect the livelihoods of agriculture or forestry workers.[44] Central to these cases, viewed through the lens of Table 19.2, is the conflict between the present, resistance-oriented right to work of currently living rights bearers, and the mitigation-dependent future ESCR rights of vulnerable groups and future generations.

Clearly, a range of livelihoods will be impacted by climate change, and states need to work with workers of impacted sectors to provide them the skills and resources needed to adapt to changing circumstances or transition to alternative livelihoods in a way that respects the right to work as conceived in Article 6 of the International Covenant on Economic, Social and Cultural Rights (ICESCR).[45] As the inevitable energy transition picks up speed, we expect more climate litigation to focus on states' duties to realize the right to work in conditions of equality, protecting the most vulnerable and without retrogression. Access to resources and sustainable livelihoods are linked to the right to an adequate standard of living under Article 11 of the ICESCR. The ICESCR understands the family as a primary unit for the care and education of children, which requires support to carry out this role. Specifically, families need access to housing, clean water, food and sustainable livelihoods. In this sense, climate change poses a threat to the wellbeing of families, especially to those already vulnerable due to geography and marginalization, as it may restrict access to the resources that allow the family unit to function.[46] In the next sections, we present climate litigation tapping into issues of sustainable livelihoods and adequate standards of living.

---

[42]   Marek Harsdorff, Maikel Lieuw-Kie-Song and Mito Tsukamoto, 'Employment Working Paper No. 104: Towards an ILO Approach to Climate Change Adaptation' (2011) 130 <http://apgreenjobs .ilo.org/resources/employment-working-paper-no.-104-towards-an-ilo-approach-to-climate-change -adaptatio>. As cited in Jodoin and Lofts (n 9).

[43]   Jodoin and Lofts (n 9).

[44]   Ibid.

[45]   Ibid.

[46]   Ibid.

## 4.2    Right to Water – Cases of Water Resilience and Carbon Sinks

A significant outcome of climate adaptation litigation has been the use of the notion of climate resilience to protect water sources and carbon sinks.[47] In *Alanvale Pty Ltd v Southern Rural Water Authority* ([2010] VCAT 480), the Australian company challenged a water authority's decision to deny licenses for groundwater extraction. The Tribunal held that the water authority's claim that there was a risk of over-allocating the groundwater supply was substantiated by the possibility of rainfall being scarce as a result of climate change. Similarly, in *David Kettle Consulting v Gosford City Council* ([2008] NSWLEC 1385 Australia), Coca-Cola Amatil appealed the conditions placed on a permit for water extraction at a water bottling plant, which restricted the rate of extraction and total extraction levels. The court granted the permit without the conditions through 2011. But, considering the impacts of climate change on rainfall, the court suggested that the extraction rates and levels should be re-evaluated using more timely data.

Carbon sinks (capturing and storing $CO_2$) have also played a significant role. In the 2013 Indian case *In re Court on its own motion v State of Himachal Pradesh and others* (Ap 237 (THC)/2013 – CWPIL No. 15 of 2010) and in the Colombian constitutional *Decision C-035/16* (2016), the courts used the norms of the global regulatory framework for climate change to prohibit deforestation practices and degradation of ecosystems resulting from mining and other extractive activity in ecosystems serving as carbon sinks. These cases focus simultaneously on both mitigation and adaptation and refer to the protection of water resources threatened by extractive or polluting activities. The water resources gain a new level of importance in the face of climate change, since they are both vital to protect human rights and serve to remove $CO_2$ from the atmosphere. Both climate adaptation and mitigation are considered when planning land use in these areas. So far, these are the only two cases addressing deforestation in the context of climate litigation, but this might become a widely explored avenue for litigation in the future.

The Colombian case refers to the nature of paramo ecosystems as both carbon sinks and water reservoirs, and their importance for climate resilience. There are two Australian cases that refer to the special need to protect water resources in the context of climate change. *Paul v Goulburn Murray Water Corporation & Ors* ([2010] VCAT 1755) challenges a decision by a local water authority, the Goulburn Murray Water Corporation, in Victoria, Australia, to issue two licenses allowing the extraction of groundwater for use in irrigation on farms. The plaintiff challenged the licenses because the use of water would be unsustainable, particularly in light of the projected impacts of climate change and associated water shortages. While the Tribunal noted that there was some uncertainty about the impacts of climate change and that uncertainty may lead to the application of the precautionary principle,[48] it found on the

---

[47]    A sink is defined as 'any process, activity or mechanism which removes a greenhouse gas, an aerosol or a precursor of a greenhouse gas from the atmosphere. Forests and other vegetation are considered sinks because they remove carbon dioxide through photosynthesis.' See United Nations Climate Change, 'Glossary of Climate Change Acronyms and Terms' (2020) <https://unfccc.int/process-and -meetings/the-convention/glossary-of-climate-change-acronyms-and-terms>.

[48]    The precautionary principle is one of the most important guiding norms of environmental law. Its purpose is to allow authorities to take (often costly) protective measures, even when the risks of not taking them are uncertain. Article 3 of the UNFCCC states that 'the Parties should take precautionary measures to anticipate, prevent or minimize the causes of climate change and mitigate its adverse effects. Where there are threats of serious or irreversible damage, lack of full scientific certainty should not be

technical evidence before it that the water use would be sustainable considering the range of estimates for the impact of climate change on water levels in the region.

Using the lens of Table 19.2, we see that these cases are able to draw strength from integrating different concerns across each of the four dimensions – aligning the adaptation-related concerns regarding the right to water of people living today, currently and in the near future, with the climate mitigation-related rights of future generations, biocultural rights and the rights of nature.[49]

### 4.3    Rights to Housing and Health – Cases Foreseeing the Impacts of Climate Change

Australia is the country with the most climate litigation after the US, which is remarkable given their differences in size, population, economic context and legal culture. Australia not only has an economy that relies heavily on fossil fuel extraction – which makes mitigation litigation both relevant and challenging – but is also an island state where climate change impacts such as sea-level rise, ocean acidification and human displacement in nearby Pacific islands are already very present. For these reasons, Australian activists have built up important experience with climate adaptation court cases, and ESCR discussions are central to many of them.

Many of the Australian cases are about coal mine licenses with a mitigation orientation. Others assess the impacts of climate change in proposed mining, housing and other planning developments, which is also known as *reversed impact assessment.*[50] In such assessments, an environmental impact assessment is conducted before administrative authorities license new projects, in order to know what climate risks the projects are prone to. When studying the cases we saw a difference in the courts' handling of climate change cases seeking declarations of liability and compensation, compared to cases with a preventive purpose. For example, courts seem more prone to accept the scientific consensus on climate change and its potential harms in reverse impact assessment cases than in cases when a declaration of liability is implied.

Courts (outside, but also many inside, the US) have generally accepted the scientific consensus on climate change and used it to order certain ESCR preventive measures,[51] as in the Australian adaptation coal case *Ironstone Community Action Group Inc. v NSW Minister for Planning and Duralie Coal Pty Ltd.* ([2011] NSWLEC 195), where a plaintiff challenged the extension of an existing coal mine due to its negative effects on biodiversity, water quality, threatened species and public health. Specifically, it was argued that the Giant Barred Frog, a threatened species, would be negatively affected through habitat destruction and the coal

---

used as a reason for postponing such measures, taking into account that policies and measures to deal with climate change should be cost-effective so as to ensure global benefits at the lowest possible cost. To achieve this, such policies and measures should take into account different socio-economic contexts, be comprehensive, cover all relevant sources, sinks and reservoirs of greenhouse gases and adaptation, and comprise all economic sectors. Efforts to address climate change may be carried out cooperatively by interested Parties.' United Nations Framework Convention on Climate Change (n 19).

[49]    Macpherson E., Torres Ventura J. and Clavijo Ospina F., 'Constitutional Law, Ecosystems, and Indigenous Peoples in Colombia: Biocultural Rights and Legal Subjects' [2020] *Transnational Environmental Law* 1; Abate, R.S., *Climate Change and the Voiceless: Protecting Future Generations, Wildlife, and Natural Resources* (Cambridge University Press 2019).

[50]    Peel and Osofsky (n 12).

[51]    Wilensky (n 25). Many US courts also accept the evidence.

mine's direct contribution to climate change. The court re-approved the extension, but under the condition that the defendant prepare and implement a biodiversity management plan for the project.

Another example is *Northcape Properties v District Council of Yorke Peninsula* ([2008] SASC 57 Australia). In this case, the South Australian Supreme Court upheld a local council decision to refuse development consent for the division of a large piece of coastal land into smaller portions, roads and reserves, on the basis of unacceptable climate change risks of the proposed development. The court found the proposed development in violation of the council's development plan, and considered that hazardous sea-level rise over the next 100 years due to climate change was a sufficient basis to support the refusal of the coastal development application.

In similar cases, developers of new residential building projects in coastal cities of Australia have seen their licenses reversed by the courts on grounds of flooding risk after hazardous sea-level rise over the next 100 years due to climate change. In *Charles & Howard Pty Ltd v Redland Shire Council* ([2007] QCA 200 Australia), the owner of a property located on the northwest coast sought to build a residence close to the water but was refused by the local council due to risk of flooding. After an appeal, the Supreme Court of Queensland upheld the decision and noted that climate change was increasing the flood risks of concern to the council.

As noted earlier, we see a tendency for judges to accept scientific consensus, especially in adaptation cases. In climate change adaptation cases in Australia, courts have adjudicated the obligation of local councils to consider sea-level rise connected to climate change, when deciding on requested licenses for new construction projects – that is, to include climate change in their risk assessment through coastal hazard vulnerability assessment that accounts for sea-level rise predictions. According to Peel and Osofsky, in cases like these the courts have operated as flexible, deliberative and participatory sites for the creation of regulations, which is one of the ways in which litigation influences climate regulation and allows for a more complete understanding of governance in the context of complex problems.[52]

Some cases defy this trend, though, such as *Nucifora v Valuer-General* ([2013] QLC 19 Australia), concerning the valuation of a property in the context of climate change. Two property owners appealed a land valuation in court, arguing that the land was overvalued because it did not consider permanent changes in weather patterns due to climate change. The judge dismissed the appeal, finding that the plaintiffs had failed to show that the farm was permanently devalued because of climate change. In its reasoning, the court noted that climate change was 'still a subject of considerable public debate'.

Judges seem more conservative in their consideration of climate science to attribute liability for harms, but precedents in adaptation cases and notably in some mitigation cases are promising for the future of ESCR-based climate mitigation litigation. As noted previously, in the 2007 US mitigation case *Massachusetts v EPA* (05-1120), the Supreme Court held that greenhouse gases are 'pollutants' within the meaning of the US federal statute for regulation of pollution, known as the Clean Air Act. The court acknowledged that there were increasing levels of $CO_2$ in the global atmosphere, which, along with methane, nitrous oxide, and other greenhouse gases, trapped heat on earth and produced global warming, changing the earth's climate and threatening Massachusetts citizens' public health and welfare.

---

[52] Peel and Osofsky (n 12).

Against the backdrop of legally blocking climate denial in the executive branches of many countries, a foundational achievement of the judiciary and litigants has been to settle the scientific consensus on the risks that climate change poses to ESCR for current as well as future rights bearers, flowing from the acknowledgment of the reports produced by the Intergovernmental Panel on Climate Change (IPCC). By doing so, judges here and there are balancing the political branches by tackling the temporality challenge: understanding climate change and its effects on future generations and ecosystems as a present and concrete problem for which small incremental solutions can and must be implemented.[53]

### 4.4 Climate-related Displacement

The United Nations High Commissioner for Refugees (UNHCR) has raised awareness about climate change as a driver of displacement and the need to protect people displaced in the context of disasters. Extreme weather events such as severe drought, tropical cyclones, hurricanes and flooding are becoming more frequent and difficult to predict. While most disaster displacement is internal, displacement across national borders is also a reality and will increase, particularly among inhabitants of small state islands affected by sea-level rise. Climate-related displacement can be interrelated with violent conflicts, creating a complex reality unforeseen by the international law instruments on refugee protection and leaving many people unprotected.[54] Litigation has emerged to address climate-related displacement, but so far courts have been reluctant to declare any responsibility of states to protect persons who seek refugee status due to climate-related risk.

In *Ioane Teitiota v The Chief Executive of the Ministry of Business, Innovation and Employment* ([2015] NZSC 107), a Kiribati citizen appealed the denial of refugee status in the New Zealand High Court, arguing that the effects of climate change on Kiribati (rising sea levels and environmental degradation) are forcing citizens off the island. The Court found that these impacts did not qualify the appellant for refugee status because the applicant was not subjected to persecution as required by the 1951 United Nations Convention Relating to the Status of Refugees. In the ruling, the court expressed concern about expanding the scope of the Refugee Convention and opening the door to millions of people affected by climate change-related harms.

The applicant appealed the decision, and the Court of Appeals noted the gravity of climate change but said that the Refugee Convention did not appropriately address the issue. The applicant appealed again, but the Supreme Court of New Zealand affirmed the lower courts' conclusions. It was noted, however, that its decision did not rule out the possibility that climate change-related environmental degradation or other natural disasters could create a pathway into the Refugee Convention or protected person jurisdiction.

A communication about the case was then filed with the UN Human Rights Committee, which dismissed it on the merits in January 2020, in a split decision (United Nations CCPR/C/127/D/2728/2016). While recognizing that environmental degradation and climate change constitute serious threats to the ability of present and future generations to enjoy the right to

---

[53] Brian Preston, 'The Influence of Climate Change Litigation on Governments and the Private Sector' (2011) 2 Climate Law 485.

[54] Office of the High Commissioner for Refugees, 'Climate Change, Natural Disasters and Human Displacement: A UNHCR Perspective' (2009) <ww.unhcr.org/climate>.

life, the Committee upheld New Zealand's decision 'that Teitiota had not provided evidence that he faced any real chance of being harmed in a land dispute, would be unable to grow food or access potable water, or otherwise faced life-threatening conditions'.[55] Accepting the claim that sea-level rise is likely to render Kiribati uninhabitable, the Committee found that 'given the 10–15 year timeframe, there was sufficient time for intervening acts by the government of Kiribati to protect its citizens'.[56] The dissenting members argued, among others, that the Committee placed an unreasonable burden of proof on Teitiota to establish a real risk of danger of arbitrary deprivation of life.

In a very similar case, *In re: AD Tuvalu* ([2014] Cases 501370-371), a family from Tuvalu appealed after being denied resident visas in New Zealand. The family argued the risk of suffering the adverse impacts of climate change if they were deported to Tuvalu. The Tribunal acknowledged that climate change impacts may affect the enjoyment of human rights, but refused to elaborate on whether they provided a basis for granting resident visas. The New Zealand Immigration and Protection Tribunal granted the requested visas based on other factors, including the presence of the husband's extended family in New Zealand, the family's integration into the New Zealand community and the best interests of the children.

The lack of success in cases concerning the ESCR and refugee status of people who are forcibly displaced for climate-related reasons can in part be ascribed to the gradual onset and resilience-related nature of most climate-related displacement (making it difficult to determine when someone was forced to flee for climate-related reasons),[57] and to the highly politicized nature of refugee and migration policy. But it also shows the statist bias inherent in human rights protection, where, despite the universality of rights, states, as the main duty-bearer, see their obligations primarily towards their own citizens.

Displacement also evidences the great vulnerability of cultural rights and the rights of indigenous peoples in the context of climate change. The above mentioned petition by the Inuit Circumpolar Conference to the IACHR seeking relief from ESCR violations by the US requested the adoption of mandatory measures to limit its greenhouse gas emissions, to consider their impacts on the Arctic, to establish and implement a plan to protect Inuit culture and resources and to provide assistance necessary for Inuit peoples to adapt to the impacts of climate change that cannot be avoided. Earlier we mentioned how climate change faced several barriers for legal adjudication. One of the reasons for this is the difficulty of proving harms in accordance with traditional legal frameworks of individual causality, due to scientific uncertainty and the 'drop in the ocean' arguments. Precisely, in this early climate litigation case (2005), the IACHR rejected the petition arguing lack of proof of actual rights violation and damages suffered by the Inuit peoples, and sadly no precautionary measures were issued.

While this line of litigation has so far not been successful, litigation on the right to family, culture and livelihood specific to migration is likely to gain momentum with more widespread human displacement related to the effects of climate change.

---

[55]   See the summary of the case at <http://climatecasechart.com/non-us-case/un-human-rights-committee-views-adopted-on-teitiota-communication/?cn-reloaded=1&cn-reloaded=1>.

[56]   Ibid.

[57]   See Vikram Kolmannskog, 'Climate Change, Environmental Displacement and International Law' (2012) 24 Journal of International Development 1071.

5.    CONCLUDING REFLECTIONS: THE POTENTIAL OF ESCR
      IN CLIMATE LITIGATION AND PERSPECTIVES FOR THE
      FUTURE

The climate crisis has sparked a wave of litigation that uses ESCR claims in different ways. Climate litigation exposes a fundamental challenge inherent in ESCR and associated litigation, which is to respect planetary limits. To satisfy the rights to health, education, housing, food, water and everything that life with dignity demands in societies across the world requires resources, and the easiest path towards progressive realization is through resource-extractive economic growth. The anthropocentric and predominantly individual focus of economic and social – and, to a lesser extent, cultural – rights makes it difficult to consider the planetary limits. At the same time, when the planetary perspective is incorporated, ESCR litigation is a powerful tool in the struggle for climate justice – between generations and contemporary populations.

Climate change mitigation and adaptation policies and all legal measures adopted by governments during the energy transition need to involve an understanding of the right to equality, non-discrimination and non-retrogression in the terms of the ICESCR. States must observe the protection of ESCR in the design, implementation and monitoring of mitigation and adaptation measures.

Due to multiple blockages in the fair distribution of responsibilities for climate mitigation and adaptation among states at the international level, developing states' responsibility for self-restraint and coherent climate action is now left to social mobilization, including with domestic courts. Courts perform important democratic functions in addressing collective action problems. It is in their mandate to adjudicate and enforce legal responsibilities when actors lack incentives to undertake them. Domestic courts thus play a potentially fundamental role in the national and subnational governance of the climate problem.

Climate litigation faces three important barriers: scientific uncertainty in the attribution of causality; the generalized idea that individual mitigation efforts constitute only a 'drop in the ocean' and thus are not cost-effective; and finally the predominant anthropocentric view on economic development, which underestimates human embeddedness in ecological systems and under which most polluting activities are considered legal. ESCR arguments have played out in climate litigation in different areas of the law, and in the jurisprudence we see how the first and second barriers are being successfully overcome. State obligations to protect current citizens' and future generations' rights to private and family life, health, water and housing have been key to the adjudication of climate responsibilities.

Our analysis of climate litigation, however, led us to conclude that sustainable development and the application of the precautionary principle still need much attention from the courts. In most cases of major economic importance – regarding licenses for airport expansions and fossil fuel extraction – economic concerns have been favored over the pressing need to take precautionary measures to mitigate climate change. The creation of jobs and boosting local economies feature as central reasons for this prioritization, while climate change as a threat to the right to work is not sufficiently discussed. The pollution of the global atmosphere, for the most part, continues to be considered as an externality of the fossil fuels industry, fixable through management techniques. The protection of the ESCR of indigenous peoples and other communities and individuals at risk of climate displacement has also not been analyzed by the courts with a precautionary lens.

The hegemonic idea of development based on continuous economic growth – in which the law is embedded – remains untouched in most jurisdictions, but there are important exceptions in the jurisprudence. Over the coming decades, climate change is perhaps the issue with the biggest potential to destabilize the status quo due to its complex and overarching nature, crossing socio-economic and environmental issues. Based on the evolution of ESCR-related climate jurisprudence, we think that unconventional rights bearers such as future generations and ecosystems will increasingly be present, influencing a shift in ESCR perspectives towards biocultural rights.

ESCR-based climate litigation could, and to some extent does, play an important role in monitoring and checking the evolving energy transition. Civil society and the judiciary are key to preventing the green economy from reproducing the inequalities brought about by the carbon-intensive economy, where both the profits and benefits from fossil fuels are dispropor-tionately enjoyed by a privileged minority while the externalities are shouldered by communi-ties who also lack access to energy and welfare. The concentration of greenhouse gases in the atmosphere goes hand in hand with the accumulation of privilege and excess in consumption beyond socio-economic and cultural wellbeing. The climate crisis inevitably challenges an understanding of ESCR that are progressively realized only for a few, currently living, and with disregard for planetary boundaries. In sum, the transition we are undergoing is likely to bring new ecological perspectives on economic, social and cultural rights and ESCR litigation.

# Index